The Interpretation of
St. John's Revelation

BY

R. C. H. LENSKI

THE WARTBURG PRESS
Columbus, Ohio

PRINTED 1951

MADE IN U. S. A.

Lowell Guebert

Πᾶσι τοῖς ἠγαπηκόσι τὴν ἐπιφάνειαν αὐτοῦ

II Tim. 4:8

NOTE: The translation of the text is an effort in some measure to indicate the Greek wording and the Greek constructions for readers to whom this may be helpful. The following abbreviations are used:

R. = A. T. Robertson, A Grammar of the Greek New Testament in the Light of Historical Research. 4th edition.

B.-D. = Friedrich Blass' Grammatik des neutestamentlichen Griechisch, vierte, voellig neugearbeitete Auflage, besorgt von Albert Debrunner.

C.-K. = Biblisch-theologisches Woerterbuch der Neutestamentlichen Graezitaet von D. Dr. Hermann Cremer, zehnte, etc., Auflage, herausgegeben von D. Dr. Julius Koegel.

B.-P. = Griechisch-Deutsches Woerterbuch zu den Schriften des Neuen Testaments, etc., von D. Walter Bauer, zweite, voellig neugearbeitete Auflage zu Erwin Preuschens Vollstaendigem Griechisch-Deutschen Handwoerterbuch, etc.

M.-M. = The Vocabulary of the Greek Testament Illustrated from the Papyri and other non-Literary Sources, by James Hope Moulton and George Milligan.

G. K. = Kittel, Theologisches Woerterbuch zu dem Neuen Testament.

C. Tr. = *Concordia Triglotta, Libri symbolici Ecclesiae Lutheranae.* German-Latin-English. St. Louis, Mo. Concordia Publishing House.

INTRODUCTION

In Revelation the Apostle John presents the prophetic visions that were given him to see and to hear on a certain Sunday in the year 95 while he was in exile on the small island Patmos opposite the southern coast of the Roman province Asia, toward the end of the reign of the great persecutor of the church, the Emperor Domitian. The apostle wrote Revelation by the Lord's own order (1:19); divine Inspiration guided his pen.

This is a summary of what we should know about the last book of the New Testament.

* * *

John had lived and labored in and out of Ephesus since the days of the Jewish War which destroyed the Jewish nation. Domitian died September 18, 96. This date makes it necessary to place the visions of Revelation in the year 95. John was not exiled by the emperor himself; he was condemned to exile by the proconsul of the province of Asia, "who would not have been able upon his own authority to punish in this way a preacher of the gospel and an adherent of the Christian faith if he had not felt himself authorized so to act by some decree issuing from the Imperial Government, or some regulation tolerated by it, by which the propagation of the Christian religion was to be checked by the courts or the police," Zahn, *Introduction* III, 409. How long the exile continued we do not know. There is nothing to prevent us from dating Revelation in the year 96, the actual year of Domitian's death. Nerva ruled until

98, then followed Trajan. John was released after Domitian's death and died during Trajan's reign.

From Revelation itself we learn that the visions and John's writing the record of them were simultaneous. While the repeated commands: "Write!" Γράψον! in 1:19; 14:13; 19:9 might leave the question open as to just when John was to do this writing, John's own statement in 10:4, "When the seven thunders spoke, *I was about to be writing,*" and then a voice from heaven forbade him, "Seal the things the seven thunders said, and *do not write them!*" informs us that he was continuing to write, and that the other commands "Write!" have reference to immediate writing.

John is to write "into a book" (1:11); in 22:6-19 we see "this book" completed save for the last few sentences. The angel (22:7-15) and Jesus (22:18, 19) speak of "this book" as one that has already been written, see 22:19: τῶν γεγραμμένων ἐν τῷ βιβλίῳ τούτῳ. It is, therefore, incorrect to think that John wrote in Patmos some time after he saw the visions or waited even until he returned to Ephesus. To say that this presents John as writing in "excitement" because he was "in spirit," and that thus oddities crept into his language, is to misconceive what the phrase "in spirit" means. John's mental faculties were in no way disturbed; on the contrary, they were stimulated, exalted, and functioned with perfection. A disturbed mind is not a good instrument for properly receiving anything; the disturbance would interfere with the reception as well as with the subsequent reproduction in writing.

Is Revelation the last of John's writings? John's Epistles were written near the time of the composition of his Gospel, shortly before or shortly after. This is a point of minor interest. See the introductions to the Epistles of John. "Not one of the church fathers (Irenæus, Clement, Origen, Eusebius) says that John wrote the Gospel after his return from Patmos and therefore after the completion of Revelation." Zahn, *Introduction* III, 198 — see the entire note of Zahn. The testimony of Irenæus is of especial value since he was born about 120 and was a pupil of Polycarp, who in turn was a pupil of John. Irenæus was also acquainted with Papias, "a hearer of John" and a friend and companion of Polycarp.

It is Irenæus (*Heresies* III, 4, 4) who states that John lived until the time of Trajan (98-117). Eusebius (*Church History* 5, 8) quotes Irenæus to the effect that Revelation was seen almost in the memory of men then living, namely "toward the end of the reign of Domitian" (who died in 96). All this evidence warrants the conclusion that Revelation is the last of John's writings. When at this late date some discredit Irenæus and the ancient tradition that supports his testimony, they are able to offer as a substitute nothing that is in any way comparable to this patristic evidence for truthworthiness. Why in his *Offenbarung*, p. 34, Zahn reverses himself and dates Revelation in 95 and the Fourth Gospel in 98-100, he fails to indicate even in a note. The fact that this dating which places the Gospel so late rests on tradition, the tradition itself does not show.

The question as to which of John's writings is last is really immaterial; the main thing is that we possess these writings. Yet we are all interested in all that can still be safely established in regard to them.

Was it the Apostle John who saw these visions and wrote Revelation?

We need not discuss the surmise that the "John" who names himself in Revelation was John Mark, the writer of the Second Gospel. Even Dionysius dismissed this supposition. Entirely to be excluded is the view that Cerinthus wrote Revelation. Cerinthus was the antichristian opponent of John who denied the deity of Jesus, the efficacy of his blood, etc. See the introduction to I John.

The assumption that the writer of Revelation was "the presbyter John," a certain John who also lived in Ephesus and was contemporaneous with the Apostle John — two graves in Ephesus, each containing a John, at a later date caused confusion regarding which of the two was that of the apostle — calls for more attention because in modern times this "presbyter John" is made the author also of the Fourth Gospel and of the Johannean Epistles, for both II John and III John begin, "The presbyter," etc.

This view regarding a "presbyter John" being the writer of Revelation begins with Dionysius of Alexandria, a pupil of Origen, who was active from 231-264 and was called "the great" by the Greek fathers, "the teacher of the Church Catholic" by Athanasius. Dionysius was a strong opponent of the chiliasm of his day which sought to justify itself, as this error still does, by a reference to Revelation. In order to deal a telling blow to the chiliasts Dionysius made "the presbyter John" and not the Apostle John the author of Revelation, yet he regarded Revelation as an inspired writing. Just how Dionysius hoped to strike a mortal blow at chiliasm by this theory concerning the writer of Revelation is not apparent.

Our modern critics at times hail Dionysius as the first scientific New Testament critic. Dionysius, however, acted from a true motive. The critics call his motive "dogmatic," which to them means unscientific. As far as critical acumen is concerned, Dionysius is a warning and not an example.

Dionysius misread a statement made by Papias. The latter tells us how eager he was to hear what "the *presbyters*" Andrew, Peter, Philip, Thomas, James, John, Matthew "*said*" (εἶπεν) and what both Aristion and the *presbyter* John *"are saying* (λέγουσιν)." We at once see that Papias does not call Aristion a presbyter; only the others are presbyters to him. That, too, is why he places Aristion before "the presbyter John"; if he had written, "What both the presbyter John and Aristion are saying," we might think that Aristion, too, is regarded as a presbyter.

At the second mention of John, Papias carefully repeats the term, *"the presbyter* John," to show beyond question that he has in mind the John listed among the seven whom he has just called "the presbyters"; for if in this second instance he had written only "John," the reader might take this to be a different John from the one mentioned in the list of seven termed "the presbyters." Papias makes certain that we think of the same man when "the presbyter John" is mentioned, one of the seven presbyters he has just named.

Papias speaks first of the seven, of what they *"said"* (aorist), because this refers to the past. To this he adds "what both Aristion and the presbyter John *are saying* (present tense)," because these two are still present — Papias can still hear what these two say. The others have departed, Papias still has Aristion and John — the latter living until the time of Trajan, probably until after the year 100. Why Papias should call the apostles "presbyters" ("elders") in an eminent sense we see from John's own letters, II John and III John, where he so designates himself.

Despite the careful clarity of Papias, Dionysius insisted that Papias spoke of two Johns, one the apostle, the other "the presbyter." Eusebius (about 270 to 340) adopted the view of Dionysius and, for the same reason, dislike of the chiliasm that sought its support in Revelation (*Church History* III, 39). Thus was launched this view about a "presbyter John."

It was adopted by speculative modern critics and has run this course as regards the Fourth Gospel: at first this "presbyter John" is still thought of as an eyewitness of the gospel events and the writer of the Fourth Gospel; next he is only in a modified sense an eyewitness although still the writer of the Gospel; finally he is neither an eyewitness nor the writer but only a kind of prototype of both. At first he still has the name "John"; then this fades out, and we hear only of "the presbyter," "the Elder." During the next step he gets a second name and is now titled "Elder Theologus." He also has a biography: He is an Alexandrine Jew, conversant with Hellenic philosophy, of the type of Apollos, carrying forward distinctive Pauline teachings although these are strangely made to center in the Logos, a term that was never used by Paul.

Yet, until the time of Origen and including him († 254) the whole church knew of only *one* John, i. e., the apostle. The Alogi rejected his writings but were not acquainted with a second John. When Cerinthus was made the author of Revelation he is thought to have impersonated the Apostle John. It is thought that Papias speaks of a second John, but no one knew him to be a second until about 250 when Dionysius made the discovery. Despite Eusebius this discovery remained dormant until it was revived at our present late date.

One step farther, and we are through. The Apostle John is said to have died as a martyr, either together with his brother James in 44 (Acts 12:2) or together with the other James (the Just) in 62 or 66. Thus it is thought that the Apostle John did not live in Ephesus, was not exiled to Patmos, etc. Then, of course, the apostle did not write what the church has ever accepted as coming from his pen. The field is left to some second John. In fact, we must change our dates for all these writings, and not only the dates but also the background for these writings, and must cancel the ancient testimony. On this supposed early death of the apostle see Zahn, *Introduction*, III, 205, etc.; *Offenbarung*, 94.

* * *

For the reader's convenience we list the succession of Roman rulers.

Tiberius, d. March 16, 37.

Caligula (Cajus Cæsar) March 16, 37 to January 24, 41.

Claudius, January 24, 41 to October 13, 54.

Nero, October 13, 54 to June 9, 68.

Galba, d. January 15, 69.

Otho, d. April 16, 69.

Vitellius, d. December 21, 69.

Vespasian proclaimed emperor in Alexandria, July 1, 69.

Titus, June 23, 79 to September 13, 81.

Domitian, September 13, 81 to September 18, 96.

Nerva, September 18, 96 to January 25, 98.

Trajan, January 25, 98 to August 117.

Every effort to date Revelation during the reign of Claudius is unsatisfactory. John was not slain by Herod in 44 together with his brother James nor together with James the Just in 62 or 66.

More effort is made to date Revelation either during the reign of Nero or immediately after. This is done for internal reasons. It is thought that the Temple is still standing (11:1); it is assumed that Revelation operates with the myth regarding Nero. Instead of having died, he was supposed to have fled to the Parthians so as at some future time to return to Rome with a mighty host. When time went on without his return, the myth was expanded: Nero would arise from the dead for this grand return to Rome. If Revelation operates with this fiction, we must lay it aside as a cheap, uninspired book that is worthy of no serious study.

It is the so-called *zeitgeschichtliche* interpretation of Revelation which refers to Nero and this fiction regarding Nero, namely that the events of Nero's reign and those occurring shortly after, including the Jewish War, comprise the contents of Revelation. This dating of Revelation at or near the time of Nero involves more than Nero and this fiction about him; it regards Revelation as "a tract for the times," namely the times when this "tract" was written. When we are told that Revelation, nevertheless, has great ethical value, this is but the usual plea which dissolves all the historical New Testament writings into mere ethical values. Whether Jesus actually lived or not, whether he said and did what the Gospels record or not, makes little difference, we have the ethical "lessons" which these stories teach although the stories themselves are not true. So also this ancient timely tract, Revelation, which was written to encourage the Christians of a faraway day, still has its ethical "lessons" for us at this late date although the predictions contained in the "tract" were religious fancies.

* * *

Tregelles (*New Testament Historical Evidences*) observes: "There is no book of the New Testament for which we have so clear, ample, and numerous testimonies in the second century as we have for the Apocalypse. The nearer the connection of the witnesses with the Apostle John, the more explicit their testimony." Revelation came into the hands of the seven prominent churches in the province of Asia immediately after it was written, which already means a great deal as regards its writer, the Apostle John, its date, and its promulgation in the churches. Other churches in the territory over which John presided must have soon secured copies.

Nevertheless, Revelation was not universally accepted. The Peshito (= *simplex*, sc. *versio*), the oldest Syriac version of the New Testament, dated in the second century, contained neither Revelation nor II Peter, II John, III John, and Jude. The history of the Peshito still needs clearing up. Whether the reason for omitting these writings was the same in each case we do not know. We note further that there is no reference to Revelation in some of the early writers in whose writings we should rather expect to find such references. It cannot be stated that they did not as yet possess Revelation. Those of a later time who pass by Revelation seem to have had their special reasons. The nature of Revelation and the difficulty of its interpretation were evidently deciding factors. Many writers of this time make very little use of Revelation for this reason alone.

The early chiliasts, Papias himself being one of them, did not further the acceptance of Revelation by their chiliastic misuse of it. We have seen how this reacted on Dionysius and on Eusebius. The latter classed Revelation among the antilegomena. The simple fact is that Revelation was not universally accepted. Yet the Council of Laodicea (some time between 343 and 381) placed Revelation into the canon if we may consider its 60th canon genuine. So did the Council of Carthage in 397. Ever since that time Revelation has maintained its place in the canon. Yet because of the historical fact that it was not universally accepted during the first centuries many place Revelation among the deuterocanonical books which are indeed canonical but form a separate class for the reason indicated.

Luther applied his subjective criterion not only to James but also to Revelation and wrote in 1522, "My spirit cannot adjust itself to the book." He thought the apostles should write in plain language and not in symbolical terms or in visions. He retained Revelation and the other antilegomena in the canon but did not number the pages on which these were printed. In 1545 (Erlangen edition, vol. 63, 158-169) he corrected himself, which we should not fail to note. Zwingli was radical and declared outright, "Not a Biblical book." Though in his commentary he does not expound Revelation, Calvin maintains the apostolic authority of Revelation, and his judgment is recorded in some of the Reformed confessions.

In arriving at our estimate of the canonicity of Revelation we must not let the pronouncements of individual church writers and church leaders weigh unduly. This applies not only to the men we have already named but also to the large number of commentators of all the past centuries to the present day. Their interpretations present a bewildering and an unsettling tangle. It would require libraries and years of labor to compile a firsthand inventory. Most of the popular expositions are reverent enough but are rather light, make an effort to be timely and to bring applications, and thus carry only slight conviction. The factor that placed Revelation into the canon and has made its canonical position impregnable is inherent in the book itself. What scholars have done with these visions or may yet do, is of little importance in this respect. The rank and file of Christendom has been content not to penetrate behind every veil; it has ever felt the presence of God and the majesty of Christ although the details of the visions remain enigmatic. The fanatics, who make a specialty of Revelation and of its most mysterious parts, have not disturbed the host of sober minds in the church; rationalistic critics have been entirely passed by.

Here is the place to confess anew: "I believe in the Holy Ghost, the holy Christian Church, the Communion of Saints!" This church has ever recognized the voice of God in Holy Writ.

* * *

The difference in language between Revelation and John's other writings is more marked in the original than in our English translations. When, for instance, a preposition is followed by a nominative, this is lost in English where no case ending marks the nominative. So also when a nominative is placed in apposition with an accusative. The grammars speak of "solecisms." Some commentators are still more derogatory. To say that John did not know his Greek as he should is not true, for Revelation has much excellent Greek. The anomalies are not those of a bungler, they are altogether *intentional and significant.* In fact, the difference in style from John's other writings extends far beyond the language and the wording; it is a difference that reaches into the very conception and the contents and thus to the divine Revelator himself.

An easy explanation is that the same author did not write Revelation and the other Johannine writings; or, when John is regarded as the author of Revelation, to say that he wrote Revelation early, *before* he knew Greek properly; or that John had somebody polish the language of his Gospel and his Epistles before they were sent out.

The Lord intended the language of Revelation to be different from that of John's other writings. The Lord intended the difference to be so great that even the dullest reader should at once be struck by this fact. The Lord's purpose in this is entirely obvious. Every reader is at once to see and to understand that Revelation is not at all a composition by John, not even as far as the language of Revelation is concerned, for even the language is not that which is native to John. This book is *"the Revelation of Jesus Christ, which God gave to him, to signify to his slaves what things must occur shortly*" (1:1). In other words, this book is in the highest sense *Jesus Christ's book*, and the very language proclaims that great fact. John does the writing, but the very language is *different* from his own. This is our answer to the question regarding the linguistic differences.

More should be said on this important subject.

Zahn (*Introduction*, III, 387) states: "From the name ἀποκάλυψις, a title never borne by any writing before the time of Revelation, has been derived the idea of an 'apocalyptic literature.'" Revelation is thus placed into the general category of Jewish apocalypses; it is ranked in the same class with the *Book of Enoch*, the *Book of the Twelve Patriarchs*, the *Book of Jubilees*, *IV Ezra, the Apocalypse of Baruch, the Sibylline Oracles*, the *Ascension of Moses*, and the *Ascension of Isaiah*. If the visions of Daniel, of Ezekiel, and of Zechariah are added, they, like Revelation, are not differentiated from the pseudo-apocalypses of the Jews but are classed as "apocalyptic literature." Spurious and genuine writings are considered together, and what is regarded as being common to all these writings is designated as characteristic of all this literature.

The procedure is the same as that followed in regard to the so-called *Religionswissenschaft*, "Science of Religion." All religions are studied together, and then abstractions and generalizations are made on the basis of such study. This method is labeled scientific, the results are regarded as scientifically assured. Does not the botanist, the zoologist thus take a group of specimens that form a genus or a species and scientifically arrive at the distinctive marks which all in any one class bear? Why, to be sure! But in a study of this "apocalyptic literature" one mark is overlooked; it happens to be the main one, namely, truth, genuineness, reality.

God and the idols should not be considered together, for God alone is God, and the idols and all gods are non-existent. Daniel, Ezekiel, Zechariah, John received their visions from God; the other Jewish writers composed their own or drew from false sources.

How does John's Revelation fare when it is considered as a specimen of "apocalyptic literature"? We are told: "John uses the common devices of the apocalyptic writers, little tricks to startle, to draw attention, to impress with deep, mysterious meaning. John uses also the common apocalyptic sources and materials and uses them in his own way." But John goes much farther. Moffatt, *The Expositor's Greek New Testament,* finds "a large haggadic element" in such writings; a reflection of the religious syncretism which prevailed especially in Phrygia and in the surrounding districts; conceptions that have a Babylonian background; analogous conceptions in the Egyptian religion are fairly common; Hellenic traits, though fewer and fainter, are not inconspicuous, although Orphic features are scarcely recognizable; the Zoroastrian influence is strongly marked; the Nero-redivivus myth is there. Mithraism is indistinct: Titan, the number of the Beast = Mithra as sun-god; Buddhistic or Indian parallels are scanty and as a rule remote.

In order to understand Revelation we are told to reach back into paganism, far beyond the historic age. The commentary that proceeds on this principle then consists of notes that find many references to pagan customs and ideas in John's writing. We are told that the Asiatic Christians were well acquainted with these. Did they not see in Ephesus Ἄρτεμις πολύμαστος, on whose statue winged bulls and rams appeared? Moreover, we are told that one must understand the psychology of "John."

Yet John, Daniel, Ezekiel, and Zechariah cannot be classed with the pseudo-writers of apocalypses. The latter "transported themselves hundreds and thousands of years into the past, clothed themselves with the illustrious names of hoary antiquity, and then addressed themselves to the credulous public of their own day," Zahn, *Introduction,* III, 387. John and the Old Testament prophets *saw* the visions they report and report them by divine inspiration. When John's report recalls anything that is recorded in Matt. 24, the great eschatological discourse of Jesus, in Daniel, or in any other New Testament revelation, this is not due to John but to God who gave this ἀποκάλυψις to Jesus Christ to show to his slaves.

As to style and wording we have an analogy in Luke, but only an analogy. When Luke writes apart from his sources he uses his literary Greek, but when he reproduces his sources he is so true to them that his Greek reads like a literal translation of the Old Testament and like the LXX. Luke used and reproduced material he had himself gathered from the original witnesses; not so John. In Revelation substance and language were equally given him by God through Jesus Christ and the Spirit. This applies also to the entire structure of Revelation. The arrangement of the visions is *not* that of John or of any artistry due to his skill. The details of each vision are *not* John's invention. The symbolical terms, expressions, images are *not* products of John's mind; they are as far beyond his mind as they still are beyond ours. John is as much the recipient as we are today; he was made the immediate recipient, we receive mediately through him.

John wrote divine prophecy not divination — *Weissagung* not *Wahrsagung.* To John apply both II Pet. 1:21 and I Pet. 1:11, the latter pertaining to the meaning of the visions. John penetrated more truly and more deeply than we, but only because his soul was more fully given to God and to the cause of Jesus Christ.

* * *

We shall not call John an "apocalyptist." Many do this with no ulterior thought; but others do it in order to put John into the general class who have produced the so-called "apocalyptic literature." God alone is the apocalyptist (1:1). We shall not speak of *"John's* Apocalypse"; it is *God's,* John himself says so. "Apocalypse" is the Greek work, "Revelation" the Latin word.

Revelation is prophecy. There is some confusion in regard to the meaning of prophecy (1:2). Immediate prophecy is given directly by God and reveals not only the future but together with it also the divine realities of the present and of the past. Prophets in this supreme sense were those of the Old Testament, the Baptist, Jesus himself, and his apostles. Revelation is a book of prophecy in this sense. Agabus (Acts 21:10) was a prophet of an entirely minor type to whom only this or that minor future event was directly revealed. The view is untenable that the first church had many such prophets and that prophets and prophecy of this immediate kind are referred to in I Cor. 14:1, etc.; 29, etc. Paul speaks about the gift of mediate prophecy, a gift to be desired, cultivated, and used by *all* Christians. This gift appropriated, repeated, restated, set forth the meaning of the prophetic Word which God had revealed immediately to those who were prophets in the supreme sense. We can all prophesy mediately by means of the Word.

Revelation refers to mystery. It is both the act of unveiling a mystery and the result of such an act. The mystery and the mysteries here referred to pertain to the kingdom, to the rule and the triumph of our Lord Jesus Christ. The human mind is unable to penetrate into this mystery; yet we are to know this mystery, hence God himself comes and withdraws the veil. By means of his gracious revelation we are able to know. We believe God's revelation and thus know. Unbelief scoffs at the revelation and thus, despite the unveiling, knows nothing. The whole mystery is really unfathomable. Rom. 11:33-36. The aim of revelation is to unveil the mystery so that what is revealed may redound to our salvation. This applies to all the parts of the mystery and to its revelation. All is soteriological whether the veil is withdrawn from the past, the present, or the future of the kingdom. Morbid minds seek for more.

Revelation does not completely withdraw the veil. We know only in part, we prophesy only in part; we see through a glass darkly, I Cor. 13:9, 12. In due time, when sight follows faith, we shall know more. This applies to the future of the kingdom. The ultimate future, the consummation, is beyond comprehension; revelation can show us the final glory of the Holy City only in figures and in symbols. Paul alone saw Paradise and then could not tell what his spirit had seen (II Cor. 12:1, etc.). The future until the Parousia and the last judgment is likewise revealed only in part. The times and the seasons are left in the ἐξουσία of God, Acts 1:7. Revelation leaves them there. Revelation does let us see "what things *must* be shortly," ἃ δεῖ γενέσθαι ἐν τάχει. This is the "must" of inner necessity. With regard to what Christ is in grace and in power with his kingdom and rule, with regard to what Satan is, the things Revelation unveils *must* necessarily occur, and the end simply *must* be as it is here foretold and portrayed.

Like Matt. 24 and II Thess. 2, Revelation unveils some of the details of the war against the Son of man. We are able to recognize the main human allies of Satan, their devilish character, their terrible judgment. Ever the Lamb is enthroned, worthy to receive all glory, and receiving it. This is the Lamb that has been slain. "I am the First and the Last, and the One living: and I was dead, and lo, living am I for the eons of the eons, and I have the keys of the death and of the hades." With him are all who have fellowship in his kingdom, sealed forever as his own. The satanic power must work itself out, but its defeat and its doom are absolutely certain. As the Living One triumphed in his death, so he and his own ever triumph amid the raging of the dragon until the final judgment ends the conflict forever. This is the burden of Revelation. Amid all the details it presents this grand main fact stands supreme.

Revelation is a book of Promise and of Judgment. The Promise is intended for those who are sealed; the Judgment is intended for Satan and for all who are allied with him. While both Promise and Judgment attain their consummation at the last day, this climax is assured at every preceding step. The final outcome is inevitable. All the advance judgments come from Christ; they are all answers of Christ to the foe. But amid all the war and the devastating judgments on the foe the Promise keeps and crowns his own. This cannot be otherwise. This is more of the burden of the book.

The unveiling of this ἀποκάλυψις reveals still more. The films that tend to becloud our vision of the realities are removed. We know, indeed, from the Old Testament prophecies and from all the rest of the New Testament that Jesus is the Son of God and is now infinitely exalted on the throne of God in his human nature. Revelation unveils him fully; it shows us the *Tremendous Christ* as he really is. The first vision, 1:9-20, presents Christ alone. It is overwhelming. John, who once reclined on Jesus' bosom, lay before Christ as one dead. This is the Christ with whom the universe and the church have to deal. Revelation unveils him. If we could always carry this picture of Christ in our hearts, how much of our insipid discussion about Christ would utterly disappear! How much of our cheap treatment of his Word, of our littleness of faith, of our compromises with the world would vanish!

The same is true with regard to Satan and his allies. The film that tends to becloud our eyes is removed. The whole satanic horror is here exposed. Our last illusions about Satan and his kingdom of darkness are dissipated.

God's apocalypse had to do this unveiling in figurative, symbolical language. This is on our account. It is the adequate means for the effect to be attained, a true and decisive realization of the realities which confront us. We are the stake in the battle. Our eyes must be opened truly to see. The figures and the symbols exceed all literal language in attaining this divine effect. We minimize and even lose this effect when we seek to translate this symbolical language into literal equivalents and then grow discouraged when we find it cannot be done. Some of the symbols are monstrous, utterly unearthly, combinations of figures never made before, or, if made elsewhere in Scripture, just as fearful. Consider the grasshoppers mentioned in 9:7-11. Translation into literalness is not the divine intent, for the intent is *the effect upon our hearts and our minds*, for which literal language would be too weak. Symbolism unveils while it still leaves veiled. By what it unveils and by the means used for this the reality still left veiled is made to leave a powerful impression. What is put into human words suggests what cannot be put into human words, suggests it as being beyond words, beyond all common human conception. The veiled is there, a reality, and we know it is there. This, the designed effect, is secured.

* * *

Revelation is not a parable or a series of parables. Nevertheless, the aim of Revelation is much the same as that stated by Jesus in Matt. 13:11-15. The slaves of Jesus Christ are to know (1:1). Theirs is to be divine certainty, divine assurance, unshaken confidence, the most effective comfort, and thus the ὑπομονή, the brave perseverance (13:10; 14:12; 1:9; 2:2, 3, 19) that makes victors (ὁ νικῶν, "the one conquering," 2:7, 17:26; 3:5, 12:21). "The one who did persevere (ὁ ὑπομείνας) to the end, he shall be saved," Matt. 24:13. Revelation has never failed of its purpose. For the slaves of Satan it is a sealed book.

Revelation is soteriological but at the same time eschatological and telic. From its beginning to its end it is focused upon the end. This end is the eternal triumph of the kingdom, the foe being eliminated forever. Revelation is the book of hope and stimulates the longing of hope. It is the answer to the cry: "How long, O Lord!"

Revelation is not a drama. Revelation was not composed by John in the capacity of a dramatist. Its structure is not that of a tragedy. Revelation is the prophecy of continuous triumph — triumph absolute is its end.

* * *

Views regarding the structure of Revelation are connected with its interpretation. Some divide it into two main parts, others into seven or more. Often this division depends on the amount of history Revelation is thought to include. For some Revelation covers only the general period of John, in particular the fall of Jerusalem and the fall of the Roman Empire with Nero and the Nero-redivivus myth as the center. Others find in it all of history since Christ's first advent plus the history of the church — all this in chronological sequence. Some speak of cycles, some of recapitulation. Many attempt to locate our own times at some point in the prophecies. Some regard only the seven letters to the seven churches as pertaining to the present and place all the rest into the future to be realized shortly before the end; sometimes even these seven churches are made prophetic of the end. Some seek to interpret in a purely historical way, while others idealize or allegorize. It is bewildering and discouraging. But one sees how thus the book has come to be divided in a variety of ways. Seven parts seem attractive because seven plays a great role throughout the book.

Are there really ordinary divisions in Revelation? To be sure, each vision stands out distinctly, and we can mark off fairly well one after another. Yet when one seeks for something more, others are able to point out his inadequate combinations or something still more serious in his conception of the book. Ordinary books have blocks of thought; we see through their structure and note how one block is built upon another. Yet in I John we find a totally different structure: a basic fact and then an upward and ever-widening spiralling until the end is reached. It is not claimed that Revelation has such a plan, but I John teaches us that building with blocks is not the only structural plan found in Scripture.

In seven different places Revelation reaches the end of the world: 6:12-17; 7:9-17; 11:18; 14:4-20; 16:17-21; 19:11-21; 20:7-15. The note of the end is struck already in two of the letters, "Till I come" (2:25); "Behold I am coming quickly!" (3:11). Again, Revelation presents a number of scenes in heaven with great doxologies. To these scenes we may add the first revelation of Christ in 1:9-20. Yet we are unable to use these features for making divisions in a convincing way, although it has been attempted: a heavenly scene introducing each part and then earthly scenes following it. We frankly give up the attempt to divide this book in an ordinary way. At most one could detach 1:9-3:22, and again chapters 21 and 22, but what about all that lies between?

As far as the writer is able to see, the visions, from first to last, present lines or vistas. These start at various points, but like radii or rays all focus upon the final judgment and the eternal triumph. The final visions (chapters 21 and 22) present the triumph at length. All history is covered, but not as we read history but only as God sees it. The veiling clouds open now and again and allow us to see vision after vision until at last our eyes behold the vision of the Holy City itself. Times and seasons are not for us to know (Acts 1:7), but the sure triumph, glorious over and amid them all, is. I am able to offer no more regarding the structure.

CHAPTER I

The Caption

1) The book begins with an independent nominative:

REVELATION OF JESUS CHRIST

This is intended as the title, hence is anarthrous and unconstrued. The genitive is subjective: Jesus Christ made this Revelation; not merely possessive. In the introduction we quote Zahn as proof for the fact that prior to John no book was entitled Ἀποκάλυψις. We there describe what "Revelation" means: unveiling mystery which, except for proper unveiling, no one can know. In v. 3 John defines: "the words of the prophecy." In 22:17: "the words of the prophecy of this book." This Revelation consists of prophecy and records "the things that must occur shortly." It reveals future events which Jesus Christ unveiled.

Prophecy does not deal exclusively with the future; often it reveals the true inwardness of the past and of the present; this Revelation deals almost entirely with the future. It thus constitutes a part of all Scripture prophecy, in particular of all prophecy concerning the future. We think especially of the revelation Jesus made in Matt. 24, of all that he and the apostles said regarding his Parousia, in particular also of II Thess. 2. All this, of course, connects with similar revelations in the Old Testament. The book before us presents the fullest revelation of the future which, therefore, also Jesus Christ himself made. Like all such prophecy, this, too, is not a complete history written in advance.

While revelation foretells, it does this for soteriological ends, to prepare, to fortify God's people, not to satisfy curiosity. The prophecy reveals as much as serves this wholesome end and in the way that best secures this end.

This book contains "Jesus Christ's Revelation" but as now defined: **which God gave to him for him to show to his slaves the things that must occur shortly; and he signified** (them), **having granted a commission through his angel to his slave John who** (here in this book) **has testified to the Word of God and to the testimony of Jesus Christ,** (namely) **to all things, as many as he saw.**

Already the genitive "of Jesus Christ" makes the ἀποκάλυψις definite; the relative clause does this still more, for this is the particular revelation "which God gave to him," namely to Christ, "for him to show to his slaves," which Christ then did show by using John, one of his slaves. The ultimate source of this revelation is God himself. The line of transmission is: from God — to Jesus Christ — to Christ's slave John — to all the other slaves of Christ. This is emphasized in v. 2. John has here made testimony to the Word of *God* who gave this revelation to Christ and to *Christ's* testimony which revealed all these things to John. In every revelation a knowledge of the source is essential. The contents of this revelation are tremendous; the greater is the need of certainty regarding the source. False prophets have ever operated with fabricated communications from God; John himself warns against them in I John 4:1: Test out every spirit whether he is from God!

When God gave Jesus Christ this revelation is not said, as little as the time is stated in Matt. 28:18: "There was given to me all authority in heaven and on earth." Compare John 13:3. Many passages attest that, when God *gives* to Jesus Christ, this means to

Christ's human nature. We may note John 5:19-23, 26, 27; 8:28, 38; 12:49, 50; 17:8, 22; hence also we confess accordingly, *C. Tr.* 1033, 55, etc. The claim that here "God gave to Jesus Christ" means to the Son in his divine nature stands challenged already by the name "Jesus Christ" which always designates him according to his earthly life and to his office that was accomplished by means of his human nature.

The infinitive denotes purpose, and its subject is Jesus Christ: "for Christ to show to his (Christ's) slaves." The verbs agree in meaning with ἀποκάλυψις, — δεῖξαι and ἐσήμανεν, and then εἶδε: this revelation Jesus showed; signified its meaning; all that comprised it John saw. Since Christ is to show (aorist, in one great showing), the three pronouns αὐτοῦ refer to Christ: Christ's slaves — Christ's angel — Christ's slave John. "Slaves" and "slave" contain no reference to office. We belong to Christ who bought us with a price (I Cor. 6:20; 7:23); he is our Lord. We are precious to him; we obey him alone in a delightful service. See the beautiful passage John 10:4, 5. We hear his voice alone, not the coaxing of a stranger. The main connotation in δοῦλος is that Christ's will is wholly our will. This is what Paul means when he calls himself "slave of Jesus Christ" as in Rom. 1:1. John here does the same. Christ used one of his slaves to show this revelation to all of his slaves.

"His slaves" and "his slave John" are not to be understood in different senses. Of course, John was an apostle; he does not call himself an apostle in this connection because that term refers to the entire office of testifying to the gospel, while here Christ uses him only for showing this revelation to those who are already slaves of Christ like John himself. Yet it is an exaggeration to say that in apostolic times hundreds of Christians received direct revelations from Christ. See the introduction on this subject of immediate and mediate prophecy in regard to which so much confusion is found.

This revelation covers "the things which must occur shortly," again defined as "all the things as many as (ὅσα) John saw." Δεῖ may express any type of necessity, and the aorist γενέσθαι is constative. Some conceive this "must" as expressing an absolute divine decree. We fear that this says too much. God does not decree the action of the devil and of his instruments. God decrees the office, work, and triumph of his Son, as the eternal King. Note Ps. 2, especially v. 6, 7; Ps. 110 to the same effect. With this decreed, all who set themselves in opposition "must" be crushed, but their opposition has not been decreed. When God made Christ the Savior and the King, this brought not peace but a sword upon earth. This was inevitable. The kingdom of hell is bound to rage against the kingdom of Christ. Christ invades the evil kingdom and destroys the works of the devil. Hence the things that John saw "must occur." This is the meaning of δεῖ.

For ἐν τάχει the Germans have the phrase *in Baelde*, we must use the adverb "shortly," as we also do for the Greek adverb ταχύ (22:7, 12, 20). Neither phrase nor adverb means "swiftly," both mean "shortly," "soon," — "the period is near" (v. 3). Even when John received the visions, the times and the seasons remained veiled. The things he saw would occur shortly, the time for them was "near." How much time would be required before the end would be reached is not intimated here. This question will be discussed in 22:7.

What it was intended that Christ should do, he did: "and he signified (them) to his slave John." The Greek needs no object. Whether we supply a plural or a singular object makes no material difference because "the things that must occur" constitute the "revelation" which God gave to Christ. Formally we prefer "them" because "the things which" (ἅ) immediately precedes.

Signified "it" in our versions is a little ambiguous, since it might mean that showing these things to the slaves was indicated (by God or by Christ) to John. The verbs "to show" and "to signify" match the form of the "revelation," namely the visions which John "saw" (v. 2).

The modifier, ἀποστείλας διὰ τοῦ ἀγγέλου αὐτοῦ, "having granted a commission through his angel," is to be construed with "he signified." While we construe: Christ "signified . . . to his slave John," the one whom he commissioned is also John (certainly not the angel). We note that in ἀποστείλας there lies the idea of ἀπόστολος; but by using the participle the noun "apostle" is avoided. The noun would refer to John's entire apostolic function (would include too much), the participle refers to this particular commission, the writing of this revelation for the slaves of Christ. We see how exact this wording is, and how this participle adds to the *slave* John this particular and certainly high apostolic commission. John was not to preach this revelation; his commission was to write it so that it would be read and heard in the churches (v. 3). Note 22:16, "in the *churches*" (not in the whole world); in 22:18, "the words of the prophecy of *this book*"; in 1:3, "the things that have been *written*." "*Write* into a book and *send* to the seven churches!" (1:11).

The text says that Christ commissioned John "through his angel." Many authorities regard this angel as an *angelus interpres*, as though the text read that Christ commissioned his angel as an interpreter for John. No angel is commissioned; the commission was made by Christ διὰ τοῦ ἀγγέλου αὐτοῦ. Here we have an example of modernistic exegesis. This *genre* of literature, we are told, loves the cumbrous category of an intermediate agent; rabbinic and apocalyptic tradition always functions with such an angel. It was not confined to Judaism; the Hellenic religions have their dæmons as intermediaries. Milton's Uriel is also noted. Why not also the dæmon who always told Socrates what to do? John is thought to use the common apocalyptic manner of writing. Yet we are told that this angel interpreter has little interpreting to do in these visions, he is evident in only 17:1 and 21:9, and it is a question whether he was always the same angel, so that John must have written this caption after finishing the book when he had only these last angel-interpretations in mind. These modernistic explanations are highly unsatisfactory.

Our task is to look for John's commission. We have not far to seek. Throughout Revelation angels are employed in dealing with John. We note especially 22:6: God "commissioned his angel to show to his slaves what things must occur shortly." When Christ commissions, God commissions. "His angel" does not necessarily mean only one and the same angel. Such singulars are at times generic. Any angel, now one, now another, would be "his (Christ's and God's) angel." Here the statement is made that the angel conferred the commission on John; in 22:6, God commissioned his angel to show to his (God's) slaves what he desired to reveal. There is no *angelus interpres,* no apocalyptic mechanics.

2) The relative clause states that John carried out this commission, wrote what he saw, sent the book, — the seven churches have it now: "who (here in this book) testified to the Word of God and to the testimony of Jesus Christ, (namely) to all the things as many as he saw." In ἐμαρτύρησε we have an epistolary aorist. John places himself at the moment when his book is read in the churches as the written record of him who "testified." We should use the perfect, "has testified"

(R. 844). John's commission was "to testify" in writing. This matches "what all he saw." One can testify to what one saw.

John does not express it in so bare a way; he says that he testified to "the Word of God and to the testimony of Jesus Christ" and then in apposition, "to the things as many (ὅσα) as he saw." He thus reverts to v. 1, to *God* who gave this revelation, to *Christ* who showed and signified it to his slave. What John has written in testimony is no less than "the Word of God," no less than "the testimony of Jesus Christ." There is no need to say that in the visions he both saw and heard; the one verb suffices.

Some interpreters think that John refers to his apostolic work in which "he testified to the Word of God and to the testimony of Jesus Christ"; but the apposition, "what all he (John) saw" prevents this idea. The point is here not the general gospel testimony of John as it is in v. 9; but the testimony laid down in this book, embracing "what all John saw" (our English, "had seen"). In this caption John properly uses his name and the third person. That he is none other than the Apostle John we have shown in the introduction. He alone saw this revelation, received this commission, and must thus name himself and not omit his name as he does in his other writings. He is the one mouthpiece for two other witnesses, God and Christ (see 22:6-19). His name "John" is sufficient for the seven churches who know no other "John" with whom this John could be confused. In v. 9 he speaks of his exile, but not in order to identify himself, but only to inform the churches why he was in Patmos and that there he saw.

3) John writes more than a bare caption; he adds a beatitude or benediction: **Blessed the one reading and the ones hearing the words of the prophecy and keeping the things that therein have**

been written! For the period is near (cf., 22:7, 14). On μακάριος (singular because it is followed by a singular), *'ashre* in Ps. 1:1, see the notes on Matt. 5:3. We have an exclamatory judgment or verdict. The epistolary aorist in v. 2 shows that John thinks of the hour when his book will be read by the lector in each of the churches, the assembled congregation hearing "the words of the (i. e., this) prophecy." The plural article is to be construed with both participles: "the ones hearing and keeping." To keep means to preserve in the heart by faith, to let no one tamper with the treasure (add to, subtract from "the words of the prophecy of this book," 22:18, 19), to let what is kept mold and shape our lives. These keepers are blessed indeed. God's favor rests upon them for time and for eternity.

One hears "the words" as they are read, the λόγοι with their meaning. We may also say that one keeps the *logoi* (John 14:23), i. e., does the *logoi* (Matt. 7:24). John specifies by changing the object: "keeping the things that have been written" (and thus are on permanent record) in this prophecy." The blessing is for those who keep and live up to the things recorded in this book of prophecy. All these things are to preserve us true, in faith, assurance, comfort, perseverance, victory.

The manner in which ancient manuscripts were written made it difficult to read them, especially at first. Study was required. Only one copy of Revelation was sent to each of the seven churches; the congregations thus at first only heard Revelation read by the appointed skilled lector. Even when later on many copies were made, these were costly, few could possess one. But in those days men's memories were trained so that they retained to a high degree what they could receive only by hearing it read. On "prophecy" see the introduction. Revelation is throughout immediate prophecy. John employs the right word. Prophecy = revelation (v. 1). John has here written as a prophet in the supreme sense of the word; we know how he received "this prophecy" and wrote "the words of the prophecy of this book" (22:18, 19).

"For the period is near," the καιρός during which these things shall occur. The word always denotes a season or a period, longer or shorter, that is marked by what it contains; χρόνος, "time," has no such connotation, it merely extends. The period for the occurrence of what Revelation records was clearly near in the year 95. Although the end has not yet come, and the καιρός is still in progress, so much of what was to occur (γενέσθαι, v. 1) has already occurred, that now, surely, we may look the more eagerly for the end.

In this caption we certainly hear the familiar voice of John. Outstanding are the words μαρτυρία, μαρτυρέω, and τηρέω, the use of the first two in the same sentence, and the use of the third with its object "the words," etc. This caption was added to Revelation by John after the visions and the recording of them were completed; there is nothing here that differs from John's style and its familiar sound.

The Address, the Opening Doxology and Assurance, and the Great Signature, v. 4-8

4) Like the caption (v. 1-3), this address, etc., were also added after all the rest had been written. In the introduction we have indicated how and when the visions were written. John is told to write to the seven churches; these are not left to his selection, they are named for him (v. 11). John thus writes this formal address. **John, to the seven churches in Asia: grace to you and peace from the One who Is and the One who Was and the One who is Coming, and from the seven spirits who** (are) **before his throne, and from**

Jesus Christ, the Witness, the Faithful One, the Firstborn from the dead, the Ruler of the kings of the earth!

This reads like the usual greetings which introduce the ancient Christian letters. But the three ἀπό phrases are wholly distinctive and reflect the contents of the book. In reading this letter-like greeting we must note that it follows v. 1-3: John greets the churches while sending them the "revelation of Jesus Christ," "the words of this prophecy."

Thus this greeting conveys far more than the greeting of a letter conceived and composed by John himself in his usual apostolic capacity.

The name "John" is all that is needed after v. 1-3. So also the simple dative, "to the seven churches in Asia." They were designated for him, hence there is no reason for a discussion regarding the article: *"the* seven," etc., and to tell us that there were other, even other important churches in the proconsular province of Asia, of which Ephesus was the capital.

The greeting, "grace to you and peace," is entirely regular. The dative "to you" (second person) makes the greeting personal. "Grace" is the unmerited favor of God in Christ Jesus together with all the blessings this favor bestows upon us as unworthy sinners. "Peace," *shalom,* the German *Heil,* is the gift of peace, the objective condition when all is well with us in our relation to God through Christ. See this peace in John 20:19, 21; and in 14:27. Placed in the condition of peace, our hearts are to feel and enjoy this peace and, whenever they become disturbed, are to recover the serenity, the feeling of safety that belongs to those who have received objective peace from God. "Let us have (so as to enjoy) peace with God through our Lord Jesus Christ," Rom. 5:1 — ἔχωμεν, hortative subjunctive.

The threefold use of ἀπό conceives the gifts of grace and peace as coming "from" the Triune God as supreme blessings to these churches. God sends these gifts, his unmerited favor and its resultant *Heil*, to rest upon and to be received and enjoyed by these churches. This greeting calls upon them so to receive and to possess what God sends them.

All this that is so much like the greetings found in Paul's letters needs little comment. It is a different matter with regard to the objects of the threefold ἀπό; for these are not simple designations such as "from God the Father and from our Lord Jesus Christ," although "the Father" appears in v. 6. Here is the Trinity, and each Person is designated in accordance with the revelation made in the visions of this book. Nothing similar to this appears elsewhere in Scripture. This greeting with these designations belongs to Revelation, could not belong to any other document. As Revelation reaches out beyond what the other Scripture contains, so these designations of the Persons go beyond what we usually meet. They are a part of the ἀποκάλυψις, the unveiling, made in these visions. Here is what the ancient prophets saw of God in the visions granted to them, but here is more, no less than the last and final revelation of God in the visions granted to the last prophet of all.

Let us consider the anomalous wording. The first ἀπό is followed by a triple nominative. This should not be called crude grammar, nor should it be said that John was ἀγράμματος and imitated Jewish "apocalyptics." In this very connection John has used two ἀπό with their regular genitives. So the fact is that here ὁ ὤν is not a nominative but a genitive. The whole designation is indeclinable and thus stands for any case. Naturally so. No man could decline ὁ ἦν. To find an undeclined expression in Greek is not a novelty; look at πλήρης (declinable, yet undeclined in John 1:14, and R's own judicious remarks, 1204): "The papyri have taught us to be chary about charging John with being ungrammatical in πλήρης χάριτος. These matters simply show that the New Testament writers used a living language and were not automata." To say that the same pen did not indite both the Fourth Gospel and Revelation; or that John knew little Greek when he wrote Revelation and better Greek when he wrote the Gospel; or that somebody polished the Gospel for him; or that "excitement" is the reason for the language used in Revelation — is to do John an injustice.

On the idea of excitement see the introduction. There was none during the visions but the very opposite, highest clarity of mind — Jesus could use no disturbed, upset mind to record his revelation. Moreover, this piece (v. 1-8) was written after the visions had ceased. Add to this the fact that ὁ ὢν καὶ ὁ ἦν καὶ ὁ ἐρχόμενος is not John's own wording but is taken from heavenly lips by John, v. 8; 4:8; 11:17; 16:5. Did these lips speak faulty grammar? Or did John compose this whole book on the basis of his own imagination?

It will not do to follow the suggestion of R. 135 regarding ὁ ἦν, that in Homer ὁ is used as a relative. The three ὁ are *alike*, are three articles, one of them is not a relative equal to ὅς. Yet ἦν is not a participle as ὢν and ἐρχόμενος are. The point may be seen in English: "the Being One and the Was One and the Coming One." "Just as τό can be placed before any part of speech whatever when the reference is to objects, so ὁ can be used (cf., ὁ ἀμήν, 3:14) when the reference is to persons," Zahn, *Introduction,* III, 435. Like all other verbs, εἶναι has no imperfect participle; lacking an aorist indicative, it often uses its imperfect indicative instead. So here the finite imperfect ἦν is drafted to serve in place of an imperfect participle, a non-existent form. In v. 8 this entire designation comes from the lips of

Jesus. Object if you wish, but do not find fault with John, go to the proper Person.

No one claims or can claim that this is ordinary grammar. It is also obvious that it is not intended to be. We have similar phenomena in all human languages as translators especially know — a word is forced to do what it does not otherwise do. We force it because of the thought to be expressed. This is not ignorance, it is intelligence working with a medium of language that lags in its forms and has gaps. Our English has many such gaps. Even the richer Greek falls short. Why did it not form an imperfect participle? It failed to do so — that is all. Yet when we force some word to fill such a gap and do it intelligently, then, as in this case, everybody at once and without effort understands. So here nobody fails to understand. And no one can suggest what to put in place of ἦν without ruining the whole designation. Trench and others offer the explanation that this designation is left indeclinable to indicate the immutability of God; but this does not commend itself. It would be an odd device.

In v. 5, after the genitive ἀπὸ Ἰησοῦ Χριστοῦ, the three appositions are nominatives. Revelation has this construction in other places, while often there is agreement in case in appositions. So these nominatives are intentional. Turn them into genitives and see what you lose, especially in the second and the third appositions both of which have dependent genitives — in the third you would then have three genitives. Altogether you would have nine genitives in succession. At this price you would have appositional case agreement, and if John had written thus, every grammarian would object to this volume of genitives. These remarks apply only here; we shall look at similar instances as they appear. In general let us say, such nominatives stand out; they are arresting and thus more effective — we may call them deictic.

"The One who Is and the One who Was and the One who is Coming" is found only in Revelation. Applied here to the First Person, this designation is employed by Jesus in v. 8 also with reference to himself as the Second Person who is co-equal with the First; thus also in the doxologies in 4:8; 11:17; 16:5. This divine name does not reproduce the Hebrew *Yahweh*, "I am that I am," in the Greek of Exod. 3:14: ἐγώ εἰμι ὁ ὤν, Isa. 41:4; nor the Targum on Exod. 3:14: *qui fuit, est, et erit*, or on Deut. 32:39: *ego ille, qui est et qui fuit et qui erit*. Ὁ ἐρχόμενος is not "The One who Shall Be." Christians cannot accept the suggestion that to John's readers this sacred designation, coming from heaven itself, "would be quite familiar" since they knew the song of the doves at Dodona: "Zeus was, Zeus is, Zeus shall be," and also in the titles of Asclepius and Athēnē; Minerva (= Isis) at Sais: "I am all that hath been and is and shall be: my veil no mortal yet hath raised."

Ὁ ὤν, "the One who Is," means, "Who Is timelessly from eternity to eternity." Καὶ ὁ ἦν, "and the One who Was," means, "Who Was before time and the world began." See ἦν in John 1:1, "In the beginning *was* the Logos" — then already he *was*. Corresponding with this second is the third: ὁ ἐρχόμενος, "and the One who is Coming" when time shall be no more, when he shall come for the final judgment. This last is not a substitute for "the One who Shall Be," either linguistically or otherwise. "The Coming One" is highly Messianic.

In Old Testament prophecy the double Coming was seen as a unit. See our exposition of Matt. 11:3. The fact that here the First Person is termed "the One Coming," and in v. 8 the Second Person is thus designated causes no difficulty for those who believe John

10:30; 14:9, 10. In I John 5:20 both the Father and Jesus Christ, his Son, are called ὁ ἀληθινὸς Θεός. The Father comes to judgment in his Son. Is — was — is coming are not expressions merely of eternal being like: is — was — shall be. The terms are soteriological and end eschatologically. The Father (and Christ) is coming to bring the kingdom to its glorious consummation. A thousand signs proclaim that presently he will be here to fulfill his last promise. Our whole hope is in "the One who is Coming."

The phrase, "and from the seven spirits before his throne," causes no language difficulties. In 3:1, Christ is "the One who has the seven spirits" and with them the seven stars. In 4:5 seven lamps of fire burning before the throne are called "the seven spirits of God." In 5:6 the Lamb has seven horns and seven eyes, "which are the seven spirits of God, having been commissioned into all the earth." All the Scriptures testify that grace and peace come to us sinners from *God* alone. These seven spirits before the throne are *God.* No created source for grace and peace can be named besides the Father and Jesus Christ. In Paul's greetings and in II John two Persons are named as the source, God the Father and the Lord Jesus Christ. The interpreters do not note the absence of the Third Person. Here the three ἀπό phrases introduce the Trinity. The seven spirits denote the Third Person, the Holy Spirit.

This designation, as well as the one for the Father, John adopts from the visions. The way in which he here uses it when naming the Trinity interprets the passages of the vision. In 3:1, Christ *has* the Holy Spirit and as such addresses the church at Sardis. In 4:5, in the first vision of heaven which forms the advance assurance for the triumph of Christ's rule, seven *lamps of fire* burning before the throne symbolize the Holy Spirit through whom God and Christ rule. In

5:6, when the Lamb that has been slain and is standing in the midst of the throne about to open the seals of the book is pictured with seven *horns* and seven *eyes*, the powers of the Holy Spirit, sent forth into the whole earth to execute the rule of the Lamb, are referred to. In connection with these three passages we recall John 16:8-11, the Holy Spirit convicting the world concerning sin, concerning righteousness, and concerning judgment. Here in John's greeting the Father and Jesus Christ and also the Spirit are the fount of grace and peace for the church. Yet he is sent forth also into all the earth (5:6) to convict the world, even as the One Coming will come for the whole earth, and as Jesus Christ is the Ruler of the kings of the earth.

"The throne of God" and of the Lamb symbolizes their majesty, power, glory, and rule. When the Holy Spirit is said to be *"before"* the throne we understand this preposition as symbolizing the Spirit's going forth (5:6) on his mission to effect the triumph of the kingdom. "Before the throne" should not be understood as denoting a local place. "The throne" itself is not a chair but the symbol of God's infinite majesty, power, and dominion. It thus has no local space in front of it. "Before" expresses the relation of the Spirit to God's majesty, power, and dominion, the relation which reaches out into all the world. See the prepositions and the adverbs in 4:3, etc., none of which signify space or location, all of which denote relation to the throne.

When in Revelation the Spirit is named as "the seven spirits of God," this is the same symbolic seven that is found in the seven churches; seven = three, the number of God, plus four, the number of the earth, the world, and men — God, through the Spirit, dealing with men. In the case of the churches seven indicates the union of God through the Spirit with the church which is filled with the Spirit while the rest of men who close their hearts against God and his Spirit are left to the conviction of judgment (John 16:8-11).

In our opinion this "seven," then, does not refer to Isa. 11:2: the spirit of wisdom, understanding, counsel, might, knowledge, fear of the Lord — which also are only six designations and not seven. Since the "seven" of the Spirit and the "seven" of the church agree, i. e., since the Spirit fills the church and bestows God's grace and peace, we go back to Zech. 4:2, to the golden candelabrum with seven lamps that were fed with olive oil. Hence also we have the golden seven-branched candelabrum in the Temple of God's people Israel. "As many as are led by the Spirit of God, they are the sons of God," Rom. 8:14. Since seven = three united with four, we do not see that "the seven spirits who are before God's throne" refers to seven powers, virtues, gifts, or effects of the Holy Spirit. I Cor. 12:4, etc., also shows no less than eight different gifts of the selfsame Spirit.

The seven spirits are not seven "throne angels"; aside from all else, Revelation never uses πνεύματα with reference to good angels (in 16:14, they are evil). This is not Jewish apocryphal fiction borrowed from Tobit 12:15: "I am Raphael, one of the seven angels who stand before the Lord"; or from the *Book of Enoch*: "the seven first white ones," the angelic retinue of the Lord. Some find here an early Babylonian conception: the seven spirits of the sky, sun, moon, and five planets; or the Persian Amshaspands.

We should look not only at "the *seven* spirits," but at this "*seven*" combined with the clause "who (are) *before* his throne." "Seven" must be understood in connection with this significant relation. This ἐνώπιον, "before," appears again in 4:5, and is explained in 5:6 by ἀπεσταλμένοι, "having been *commissioned* into all the earth." So he is ever called "the *Holy* Spirit," whose *work* is to make holy — his very name referring to his work. Thus we must combine all these expressions; this "seven" points to the Spirit's commission to proceed from the throne and to make God and men one. Compare further the exposition of 3:1; 4:5; 5:6. To think of seven gifts, seven powers, and the like, or to divide the Spirit into seven parts, is unscriptural. Here he imparts only these two, "grace and peace," and this he does as being *before* the throne, when executing the commission of the throne as the Son, too, executed and executes his commission.

5) The third giver of grace and peace to the churches who is equal to the Father and the Spirit is "Jesus Christ," this plain name including his human nature (as it does in v. 1, 2), because by means of this nature he became our Lord and Savior and opened the fount of grace and peace for us. He is here named last because of the following doxology and all the rest that deals with him. As three terms are used as a designation for the First Person, so three appositions describe the Second.

Ὁ μάρτυς ὁ πιστός, adds the adjective with a second article, thus emphasizing it as much as the noun (R. 776). Note 3:14: "the Witness, the Faithful and Genuine"; 22:20: "Saith the One witnessing these things"; also 1:2, 9: "the witness (or testimony) of Jesus Christ (of Jesus)." It is debated whether in our verse "the Faithful Witness" refers to Christ's testimony in this book (on the strength of v. 2 and 22:20, "these things") or to Christ's witness in his earthly mission as in John 18:37 (Rev. 1:9). We decide for the latter; as we also do in 3:14, from which John takes this title. The very adjective "faithful" makes us think of all the testimony recorded in the four Gospels; the very next designation also referring to his death and his resurrection.

"The First-born of the dead" is not, like the other, taken from Jesus' own lips but is like Paul's "the Firstborn from the dead" in Col. 1:18, companion to "Firstborn of all creation" in v. 15 (see the author's exegesis of these passages). Christ died and rose again. By this act he broke the power of death for us. Heb. 2:14, 15. Thus he is the Firstborn of the dead, we, joined to him by the Spirit in grace and in truth, are the later born whom he will raise from the dead to share his glory. Phil. 3:21. Ps. 88:27 goes with the following designation: "I will make him my Firstborn, higher than the kings of the earth."

First, all of Christ's testimony here on earth; next, his death and his resurrection; finally, his eternal enthronement: "The Ruler of the kings of the earth." This is not the same title as the one found in 17:14 and 19:19, for in these two passages the lords and kings are we ourselves whom our King has made to sit with him in his throne. These others are all "the kings of the earth," the mightiest among men, and symbolically the powers they represent, not merely in the political field, but in all the earthly domains of life. Revelation has much more to say about these kings, especially about all their wickedness. In Ps. 2:1-3 we see them conspiring against the Lord. "Yet have I set (anointed) my *King* upon my holy hill of Zion (upon Zion, the hill of my holiness)." All nations to the uttermost parts of the earth are his inheritance and his possession. When they rebel, he shall break them with a rod of iron, dash them in pieces like a potter's useless vessel. "Blessed are all they that put their trust in him!" Neither this nor any other term that is here applied to Christ has its source in rabbinical speculation. The exalted rule of Christ is exhibited in the following ἀποκάλυψις Ἰησοῦ Χριστοῦ. The three appositions are a complete description.

Revelation rings with doxologies. Here, after this description of Jesus, John offers his own which is drawn from the one found in 5:9, 10. **To the One**

loving us and loosing us from our sins in connection with his blood — and he made us a kingdom, priests to his God and Father: to him the glory and the might for the eons of the eons!

John begins with two participial datives and then follows with a finite verb. This is regarded as faulty grammar by some interpreters. Yet αὐτῷ refers to him whose acts are here listed; and by making the third statement finite instead of participial John elevates this third statement above the participial ones. The main fact is that Christ made us a kingdom, etc.; the subsidiary facts are that he loves us and did loose us from our sins and that *by these acts* he made us a kingdom. Three participles would say less.

Τῷ ἀγαπῶντι ἡμᾶς is durative. This Witness, Firstborn, King, loves us with his love of comprehension and corresponding purpose and in this love, King that he is, loosed us from our sins. One article is used with both participles, "loosed" an aorist to express the one act of ridding, freeing, setting us loose from all our sins. The A. V. follows the inferior reading λούσαντι, "washed us," which does not harmonize with Christ as King or with us as a kingdom. A King frees by a royal verdict. Here John confesses all his own as well as his readers' sins; here he glorifies Christ for his own and his readers' pardon from their sins. "In connection with his blood" names the sacrifice which expiated our sin and our guilt (I John 1:7; 2:2 and 4:10, "expiation for our sins"). "His blood" is more than "his death," for one may die without pouring out his blood; blood is shed in sacrifice for expiation. Here belong all the other "blood" passages. Such a price Christ paid in his love to make us his own who are freed from all sin.

6) And thus "he made us a kingdom, priests to his God and Father." In 5:9, 10 it is stated: "Thou wast slain and didst purchase unto God with thy blood

from every tribe and tongue and people and nation, and didst make them to God a kingdom and priests, and they reign upon the earth." "Kingdom, priests," and in 5:10, "Kingdom *and* priests," refers back to Exod. 19:6, which is used also in I Pet. 2:9. What Israel was to be Christ made us to be.

This King establishes his own kingdom. "The kings of the earth" (v. 5) and their kingdoms (political and in other domains) are mere shadows of what we see in Christ's kingdom; so that it is a mistake to think of the latter in terms of the former. Christ cannot be dethroned. Where he is and rules with his power and his grace there he produces his kingdom, and this is not merely a mass of subjects (δοῦλοι, v. 1) but recipients of his kingdom, partakers of it, children, sons, heirs of God, joint heirs of their King, royal like himself, all kings, who reign with their King on the earth and shall reign with him in glory forever. We, slaves of sin and Satan, exalted to be such a kingdom! Earth has no parallel.

But do we reign on earth, here where the worldly lord it? Some would say that we do so spiritually; but that is inadequate. The Word of our King reigns; that Word is ours, by it we reign with our King. See the author's little volume *Kings and Priests*. Think what it means to give up the Word or any part of it, to injure our connection with the King and the means by which we reign with him.

To say "he made us a kingdom" is more exact than to say, "he made us kings," for we are not so many separate little kings like the kings of the earth, each in his separate, selfish kingdom or domain, often in conflict with each other. "Kingdom" equals unity, the *Una Sancta,* one body and only one. It is better to let the dative modify both "kingdom" and "priests," as 5:10 indicates. John does not follow I Pet. 2:9 and use the abstract "priesthood," but Rev. 5:10 where "priests," a concrete plural, is used. He individualizes: every one of us is a priest. This is a holy kingdom, all who are in it are priests.

In Israel no king performed priestly functions; these were reserved for a special class, and that class did priestly duty for the people. Here there is "a royal priesthood" (I Pet. 2:9). As Christ is King and Priest in one, so we are "a kingdom," all are "priests." Ours is no longer the work of offering bloody sacrifice, for the blood of Christ is all-sufficient for expiation. Our priestly function is "to offer the sacrifice of praise unto God continually, that is fruit of lips confessing his name," Heb. 13:15. The thought is not that we Christians do this priestly work for the world as Israel's priests served for the people of Israel. The world is the kingdom of darkness. This is not a missionary thought. "Priests to his God and Father" speaks only of our own relation to God.

Αὐτοῦ is to be construed with both nouns: God is Christ's "God and Father." The basic passage is John 20:17; also, "my God, my God" in Matt. 27:46. He is Christ's God according to his human nature, Christ's Father according to his divine nature. Add Rev. 20:6: "They shall be priests of God and of Christ and shall reign with him a thousand years." God and Christ receive our priestly sacrifice of confession equally in glorification of his name.

"The glory and the might for the eons of the eons" John derives from 5:13. "The glory" is often ascribed to God as it is here ascribed to Christ. His glory cannot be increased, for it consists of all his divine attributes. John's doxology ascribes all the glory to Christ, glorifies Christ on his part, and demands that this be done. The same is true with regard to "the might," the κράτος, which is not strength merely as it is possessed but as it is put forth in full action. "Dominion" in our versions is not exact.

The strongest expression for our "forever" is εἰς τοὺς αἰῶνας τῶν αἰώνων, "for the eons of the eons"; many eons, each of vast duration, are multiplied by many more, which we imitate by "forever and ever." Human language is able to use only temporal terms to express what is altogether beyond time and is timelessness. The Greek takes its greatest term for time, the eon, pluralizes this, and then multiplies it by its own plural, even using articles which make these eons the definite ones.

Eternity must not be conceived as a succession of time to which our mentality is bound, not even as "endless time" which is really a meaningless expression, for time cannot be time unless it both begins and ends. Yet we cannot think except in terms of time. Genesis begins with "in the beginning"; Rev. 10:6 declares "that time, χρόνος, shall no longer be." Time with its ceaseless flow, never faster, never slower, is one of the most wonderful creations of God on which we may well ponder more. All times and periods are in God's ἐξουσία, Acts 1:7. John derives also "Amen" from the doxologies found in chapter 5, which is the transliterated Hebrew word "truth," "verity," that is set at the end of a doxology as a seal of confession and solemn assurance. C.-K. 143. "Amen," thus employed, voices faith and confession.

7) At this point John might at once have proceeded with v. 9, the account of the first and fundamental vision. He does better. In dramatic form he states *the summary theme* of the whole book, of all the revelations he has seen (v. 7), and in v. 8 appends *Christ's own signature.*

Lo, he is coming in company with the clouds! And there shall see him every eye and such as pierced him. And there shall beat themselves in mourning over him all the tribes of the earth. Yea, amen! Acts 1:11: "He shall come in the manner you beheld him going into the heaven." Dan. 7:13: "One like the Son of man *came* with the clouds of heaven." Rev. 14:14: "And I looked and, lo, a white cloud, and upon the cloud One sat like unto the Son of man," etc. Matt. 24:30: "Then there shall *appear* the sign of the Son of man in the heaven." "The Coming One" was his great name in Old Testament prophecy: "He that *cometh* after me is mightier than I," Matt. 3:11. Like the Baptist, the prophets generally saw the two comings combined into one; but Mal. 3:2 saw the second separately: "Who may abide the day of his *coming?*" This is the coming which is the hope of Christ's kingdom and priests, their cry: "Amen! *Come,* Lord Jesus!" (22:20). This is the coming that shall bring consternation to all his foes.

It is the coming for the purpose of judgment at the last day. I Thess. 4:15, 16 describe briefly "the coming of the Lord": "He shall descend from heaven with a shout, with the voice of the archangel, and with the trump of God." Here, too, "the clouds" are mentioned. They are not figurative but real. Yet as actual clouds they symbolize Christ's majesty and power whether the preposition used is μετά as here, or ἐπί as in Matt. 24:30, or ἐν as in Luke 21:27. The clouds are the chariot on which he comes.

"And there shall see him every eye." Matt. 25:32: "all nations." That includes both of your eyes, both of mine. "And such as did pierce him," οἵτινες is both qualitative and causal. This is taken from the prophecy in Zech. 12:10. Under the cross on Calvary John himself witnessed this piercing, the thrust of the lance into the side of Jesus, and in John 19:34-37 he quotes Zechariah, neither there nor here following the LXX with its verb κατορχεῖσθαι, "to insult," but the Hebrew *dagar,* ἐκκεντεῖν, "to pierce." See the exposition of John 19:37. The piercing was fulfilled on Calvary; "shall see" will be fulfilled at the last day. Zech. 12:10

is not used differently in John 19:37 than it is used here. There John quotes Zechariah with reference to the fulfillment of the piercing, for it was an astounding act that a soldier should transfix Jesus, who was already dead, with a lance, yet this was actually done. Here John refers to the rest of the fulfillment, that all those who were such as pierced him and because they were such (οἵτινες) shall actually *see* him whom they pierced on Calvary even as Zechariah said. There are two steps in the fulfillment, that is the only difference.

That John intends to say that all the unbelieving Jews "shall see" Jesus whom they pierced, shall at the last day see that it was the very Son of God whom they pierced and rejected, is beyond question. What the hardened Jews (Rom. 11:7 ἐπωρώθησαν) now refuse to see, they "shall see" at that day. Some include all other unbelievers, whose unbelief consents to the act of the Jews and thus makes that act its own. The extension seems justified. The old view that at his coming Christ will appear anew hanging on the cross is extravagant and unscriptural. Whether at the judgment he will have the marks of the five wounds in his glorified body as he did at the time of his appearance in John 20:20, 27, who can say? See these passages.

"And there shall beat themselves in mourning all the tribes of the earth." The same words occur in Matt. 24:30; they are a repetition of Zech. 12:10, "And they shall mourn for him (κόψεται ἐπ' αὐτὸν κοπετόν, LXX) as one mourneth for his only son, and shall be in bitterness for him, as one that is in bitterness for his firstborn." The verb means to beat the breast in grief as the ancients did. Zechariah pictures the hopeless bitterness of this grief, he compares it to that for an only, a firstborn son, who is dead and gone beyond recall. Let us say at once that this beating in Zechariah, in Matthew, and in Revelation is *not* that of repentance. At Christ's Parousia "all the tribes of the earth" will not repent — it will be too late. Nor can this beating be separated into that of repentance on the part of some and that of despair on the part of the others. Only chiliasts add that the Jews will be the repentant tribe.

Some interpret as though only the eyes of those living at the time of the Parousia shall see Christ; all men shall see him. This announcement must be read together with v. 4. The blessed ones of v. 4 will look up and lift up their heads, for their redemption draws nigh (Luke 21:28), the manifestation of the sons of God (Rom. 8:19), what we shall be when we shall see him as he is (I John 3:2). All the rest shall call to the mountains and the rocky cliffs: "Fall on us, and hide us from the countenance of the One Sitting on the throne and from the wrath of the Lamb!"

Ναί, ἀμήν, "Yea, amen!" seals the prophetic announcement. Yes, so it will be in truth. "Yea" is Greek, "amen" is the Hebrew of v. 6.

8) This statement is sealed with Christ's own signature. **I am the Alpha and the Omega, saith the Lord God, the One who Is and the One who Was and the One who is Coming, the Almighty!** This signature is even threefold. Some suppose that it is the Father who here speaks and thus say that in only two places in Revelation God speaks, here and in 21:6-8. But the latter passage is certainly spoken by Christ, so also is 22:13.

It is fruitless to search Jewish and pagan literature for the source of something that resembles this name Alpha and Omega. Nowhere is a person, to say nothing of a divine Person, called "Alpha and Omega," or in Hebrew "Aleph and Tau." G. K. 2, etc., has collected the little material that is to be found on the use of letters of the alphabet; but this material nets very little to show that letters of the alphabet were used as names for persons. "To keep the Torah from aleph to tau" (rabbinical) is only our common "from a to z."

To speak of *John's* inventing this name for Christ is unwarranted; John does not in any statement of his own appropriate this name for Jesus; in the three passages in Revelation in which it occurs John lets Christ himself utter this name.

"The Alpha and the Omega" uses the first and the last letter of the Greek alphabet, from which fact it is proper to conclude that the language used in the visions was Greek, even as John wrote the record of them in Greek; he did not translate from the Aramaic. The seven churches in Asia (ἡ Ἀσία, always with the article) spoke Greek. In 21:6 and 22:13 the appositions occur: "the Beginning and the End," "the First and the Last," and some think that "the Alpha and the Omega" is only a variant of these and means the same thing. Yet these are letters of the alphabet and not only sounds (because in the Greek they happen to be vowels — in the Hebrew tau and in the English z are consonants) but *written* letters. Ἐγώ is emphatic: "*I* am the Alpha and the Omega" (A. V. in better English: "Alpha and Omega") = None other than I alone am *God's revelation for men* and that in *written* form.

The Scriptures are "they that testify of *me*" (John 5:39). "No man cometh to the Father but by *me*" (John 14:6), by me as testified to and revealed in the Scriptures. That is why Jesus bears the name Logos, Word, in 19:13, "the Logos of God." I am the one, the only and the complete revelation; besides me there is no other. All the visions of this book come from *him*, are the Ἀποκάλυψις Ἰησοῦ Χριστοῦ (v. 1). Read 22:18, 19, in the light of this Α and Ω, and you will understand.

Κύριος ὁ Θεός (see also 4:8) is John's own designation of the Speaker who here says "I." It cannot be questioned that this is the Old Testament designation of God, so that we see why some think that here, too, the

Father, *Yahweh 'Elohim,* is referred to; they can point also to the next two names: "the One who Is," etc., which is used with reference to the Father in v. 4, and to "the Almighty." But here "the Lord God" and the other names designate the Second Person as is clear from "Alpha and Omega," here, in 21:6, and in 22:13. This is Christ's signature, the signature of his deity. The book is signed in advance by Christ as the One who is no less than "Lord God," co-equal with the Father. That is why the first name which he here signs is the name "Alpha and Omega." These two great letters have passed into universal use in the church; we place them on our altars and elsewhere in the churches. Our people regard them as a reference to Christ, and they are right.

"The One who Is," etc., explained in v. 4, is now used by Christ to designate himself. The third member of this name, "the One who is Coming," had to be explained in v. 4, where it helps to name the Father and his coming in and through his Son Jesus Christ, so that now fittingly Christ uses this whole name also as a designation for himself. We once more note that it is eschatologically soteriological.

Ὁ Παντοκράτωρ, found often in the LXX (for *Shadai* and *Zᵉba'oth*) but only once in the other New Testament writings (II Cor. 6:18), appears nine times in Revelation. The word means *der Allgewaltige,* "He who has all might" (note τὸ κράτος, "the might," in v. 6, in a doxology to *Christ*). The view that here the Father is referred to because "the Almighty" is regularly employed as a designation for him also in Revelation, cannot be based on the use of this term alone. Here it is appositional to "the Alpha and the Omega," and this is a designation *of Christ used by Christ,* it is never used by the Father as a designation for himself. As here, so in 21:6 and 22:13 Christ says: "I am the Alpha and the Omega." This name is always construed with ἐγώ or with ἐγώ εἰμι. It is this fact regarding "the Alpha and the Omega" that decides both who the One so called is and who is referred to by all the appositions, including "the Almighty." Even κράτος in v. 6 prepares us to regard ὁ Παντοκράτωρ as a reference to Christ, to say nothing of the context, preceding and following, that speaks of Christ.

John's Vision of Christ, 1:9-20

9) We shall consider the visions one by one as John saw them without attempting any other form of division for the book. This first vision is basic in every way: John sees *Christ.* It naturally includes chapters 2 and 3, the special letters to the churches. The next vision (chapter 4) reveals the throne in heaven. How basic this is, we shall also see.

I, John, your brother and fellowshipper with (you) **in the tribulation and kingdom and endurance in connection with Jesus, was in the island, the one called Patmos, because of the Word of God and the testimony of Jesus.** "I, John," with its pronoun, is like Dan. 7:15; 8:1; 9:2 (Rev. 22:8). This is not "the apocalyptic manner," nor is it an appeal to "authority." The authority is that of a personal witness and nothing more. In the Fourth Gospel John could omit the use of his name, for the events there recorded had also been witnessed by others, and three other records of them had already been made. John alone saw these visions. Twice John has named himself in the third person, now he properly and naturally uses the first.

"Your brother," etc., places John among all his readers as being one of them — note "slave" and "slaves" in v. 1. The latter stresses the relation to the Lord, "brother" the resultant relation of Christians to one another. One article is used with "brother" and "fellowshipper with (you)," συγκοινωνός containing the idea of fellowship — "companion" (A. V.), "partaker" (R. V.) are less apt. The word means that something is κοινός or common to someone with (σύν, associative) others. What this is the ἐν phrase indicates. "Your brother" might lead us to think only of oneness in faith and in love; the second word suggests much more.

Again one article makes a unity of the nouns. Each, of course, is distinct, yet what they contain is always found together: tribulation — kingdom — endurance. Θλῖψις is pressure brought on by the hostility of the world and in this sense "affliction" or "tribulation." Hence the third term is ὑπομονή which means more than "patience," namely, "remaining under" in the sense of bravely enduring and persevering to the end, no matter how severe the pressure becomes. In Matt. 24:13 ὁ ὑπομείνας is "he that did endure to the end," he who bravely persevered.

Between "affliction" and "endurance" John places "kingdom." Strange combination! Yet not strange. When the affliction sets in, the kingdom produces the endurance. Even the order of the three words is illuminating. Were it not for the kingdom, which the world opposes, there would be no affliction for the partakers of the kingdom; were it not for the powers of the kingdom, its partakers could not endure. In v. 6 we hear that Christ "made us a kingdom," hence we should not think that the kingdom lies entirely in the future. Here the thought is our common lot in the kingdom, the rule of Christ's grace and power. Our very affliction shows that his grace has been active in us, our endurance also shows this. We are the kingdom, in it, partakers of it, lifted to royalty in it — these are only variant expressions for our connection with the King and his rule of grace.

Revelation speaks of the kingdom as it is found in this world and as it must come to its triumphant consummation. Revelation is the final call to us to endure the tribulation connected with the kingdom and to share in that triumph; in fact, the triumph has already begun. The last phrase "in connection with Jesus" modifies all three nouns. The simple name "Jesus" (used twice in this verse) recalls him who is now on his eternal throne in heaven but who once walked amid affliction here on earth where John still walked and followed him.

John says: "I was in the island, the one called Patmos," and with the διά phrase he indicates why he was there, "because of the Word of God and the testimony of Jesus." The aorist simply states the fact. These visions were not seen in Ephesus but on this islet. Some think that John should have said, "I was banished to Patmos" if the old tradition regarding his banishment is true. They thus question its truth and think that John went to Patmos to preach there or even to receive these visions there. But there were too few people on this tiny island to necessitate preaching save by some ordinary missionary, and why the giving of these visions should call for such an island has never been made plausible. There is no evidence that the banishment is a late invention to glorify John and to make a sort of martyr of him.

Some think that John should say more, but John is not the one to thrust his personal affairs forward where such a procedure can well be avoided. "I was in the island called Patmos for the sake of the Word of God and the testimony of Jesus." This is ample. The island, we know, (Pliny, *Hist. Nat.*, IV, 12-13) was used as a place of exile for the better class of offenders and suspects, especially under the black regime of Domitian and again under Diocletian. There were mines in Patmos, but whether the aged John was compelled to do some heavy work in these mines, no one knows. Exile such as this was a most miserable existence.

There is debate as to whether "the Word of God and the testimony of Jesus" is to be taken in the same sense as in v. 2, i. e., whether in v. 2 John refers to his apostolic preaching in general as he evidently does here in v. 9. In my former study (*Saint John,* 139, etc.) I thought so and hereby correct myself (see v. 2). The same wording found in v. 2 and in v. 9 might, indeed, justify my former conclusion, but the difference in context refutes that view. I take it that in v. 2 John refers to the contents of Revelation to which he testified in this book which, like the whole gospel for which he was exiled, is equally "the Word of God and the testimony of Jesus Christ" and is thus called no less in v. 2. In v. 4 Jesus is called "the Faithful Witness."

10) **I was in spirit on the Lord's day and heard behind me a voice great as a trumpet speaking: What thou seest write into a book and send it to the seven churches, to Ephesus, and to Smyrna, and to Pergamum, and to Thyatira, and to Sardis, and to Philadelphia, and to Laodicea!**

John relates the facts in a clear and simple way. On a Sunday during his exile on Patmos he was ἐν πνεύματι, "in spirit." Since the earliest apostolic times Sunday was the Christians' day for assembly and public worship. Here, for the first time, we meet the designation "the Lord's day," ἡ ἡμέρα Κυριακή. The Greek has an adjective whereas we must employ a genitive. Christ made the first day of the week peculiarly his own by rising from the dead on this day and by sending his Holy Spirit on this day of the week. Both Easter and Pentecost made Sunday "the Lord's day." And after the day had been thus distinguished, the apostolic church chose it as its day of public, congregational worship. Every Sunday during his exile John must have longed for the hours of public worship in Ephesus, his lonely heart seeking such satisfaction as it could find in private worship.

On this particular Sunday ἐγενόμην ἐν πνεύματι. The aorist is not ingressive, it merely states the fact, "I was." The phrase means "in spirit," and we should not capitalize the word as though the Holy Spirit were referred to. This is John's own *pneuma*. Some misunderstand the phrase when they speak of John's "excitement" and the like. In Acts 10:10, the word ἔκστασις, "ecstasy," is used, but we cannot go to our English dictionaries for a description of this state, since they take their definition from modern psychologists who describe pathological states they have observed.

Our natural senses, mind, and spirit are ordinarily operative and responsive in regard to the natural world about us. But God is able to inhibit this common response and to bring man's spirit into direct contact with the invisible, spiritual world and with the things that are in God's own mind and yet do this in ways that accommodate themselves to finite human perception for God's own specific and gracious purposes. There is nothing morbid or pathological in this divine act. It is beyond the means and the methods of psychologists because it is miraculous, a state that is wrought directly by God himself. When, with Luke, we call it "ecstasy," this is due to the fact that the spirit is taken out of the ordinary range of contact and for the time being is placed into one that is wholly new and superior. God has given revelations by means of dreams, but neither Peter in Acts 10:10 nor John on this Sunday slept and dreamed. Their spirit was wide awake, its powers were exercised with exalted clarity. This state is never self-induced and is not dependent on some preparation to bring it on.

It must be clearly distinguished from all self-induced states such as the trance of a spiritualistic medium, the visions of a clairvoyant, so-called second sight, the mental states which mystics seek to achieve, the East Indian practice of Yogism, the visions of false prophets in Old Testament times. These are morbid, highly pathological, and, with few exceptions, an abuse of the spirit. Any supposed visions and revelations from God in such self-induced states are deceptions. To abuse one's spirit in this manner is highly dangerous. Delitzsch, *Biblische Psychologie,* 284, etc., treats this subject briefly.

John's first sensation "in spirit" was that of a mighty voice addressing him. The aorist, "I heard a voice," states the simple fact and nothing more, and the accusative means that John heard what the voice said. Two things deserve notice: the ordinary sensations and actions are used: John hears, sees, feels, tastes (10:9), turns, falls prostrate, etc.; yet wonderful things are revealed to him, are made to pass before him in a condescension of the great Revelator to John as a human instrument. The voice was "behind" John. Why not before or above him? All we venture to say is that the mighy sound of that voice and the command it utters are, first of all, to impress John, then the other sensations are to follow. It is the order the Revelator chose.

The voice is "great," and the quality of greatness is pictured to the reader, "as of a trumpet," loud, reverberating, with great volume and penetration. "*As* of a trumpet" shows that nothing but a human simile is intended. Some hesitate to identify the speaker in this case, though why they do so is hard to say since only one person is mentioned in the sequel, and since the word of command he utters fits his lips in every way. It is Jesus. The ringing penetration of his voice is in harmony with his divine majesty. In the Greek participle "saying" the case is attracted to the genitive of the immediately preceding noun, "of a trumpet," and thus is not irregular in any way.

We are unable to assume that the voice here heard by John was that of an angel. Jesus himself "commissioned" John (v. 1) to write. Jesus himself says in v. 18, "Write them," etc. When we are told in v. 1 that Jesus commissioned John "through his angel," this refers to the employment of angel after angel in the visions in which an angel could serve the Lord's purpose in revealing this and that to John. So also at times such an angel repeats the Lord's command that John is to write. The original command, we see, comes from the lips of Jesus himself.

11) "What thou seest write into a book" refers to all the visions John is about to receive, which will, indeed, fill "a book," βιβλίον, the one we now have. The two imperatives "write" and "send" are peremptory, authoritative aorists. In the introduction we explain why we think that John wrote at the time he received the visions and not after they had been completed; in *Saint John* we made a mistake regarding this point.

Not for John himself are these visions intended but for the seven churches. John is to write a permanent record. This is not John's revelation but Christ's; John is only the human instrument. To speak of John's authorship is misleading. To say that John copied the methods of Jewish apocalyptics by letting the voice speak *behind* him and by receiving the command to *write* is to make Revelation a piece of literature which John (usually it is an impersonator of John or a forger) conceived and wrote at leisure, a piece of fiction, "a tract for the bad times" cast in apocalyptic mold. Why, then, study the book?

The seven churches are now named; John addresses them already in v. 4. They are listed geographically from the standpoint of Patmos. This order is retained in chapters 2 and 3. Take a map and draw a line from city to city. With Pergamum the north is reached; with Laodicea the south. Thyatira and Sardis are Greek plurals. On the history of these cities and the churches in them see the Bible Dictionaries.

Jesus selects these seven churches not John. There were many others in the region, some of them of great prominence. The number seven is surely symbolical as it was in v. 4, "the seven spirits," and in the rest of Revelation the number seven is symbolical by divine intent. What we have said regarding seven in v. 4 may be repeated here, in v. 13 in connection with the seven golden lamp pedestals, and in v. 16 regarding the seven stars. Seven = three plus four, the number of the Trinity and the number of the world. We still speak of north, south, east, west, the four directions of the wind (the compass), the four corners of the earth. The addition three plus four denotes union. When God is united with men on earth, we have the church. This union is produced by the Spirit who is thus presented as "the seven spirits," and these are "before the throne" because of the spirit's mission. "The seven churches" point to the basic idea of the whole *Una Sancta,* God's union with us sinners here on earth through the Holy Spirit in this mission "before the throne." This is as far as we are able to explain the number used in "the seven churches."

This symbolic number (note the article) makes "the seven churches" representative of the church as such. This is the impression we gain especially from the letters addressed individually to the seven churches. The conditions existing in these seven churches at the time when John was granted this "*apocalypsis* of Jesus Christ" have repeated themselves in various ways during all subsequent ages. Thus this writing was to be directed to "the seven churches," but not to them exclusively but representatively. Your church, my church, is to compare itself with these seven churches. Are the true, high, holy things in this and in that one of the seven; are the false, base, and wicked things in this or in that one of the seven found in your church, in mine? That is why Revelation is found in the canon. These prophecies are intended for the churches of all the ages.

These seven churches and their varied spiritual conditions existed *together* in the year 95. Churches that manifested similar conditions existed all around them. So it has been ever since, so it is now. We cannot join in the opinion that the seven *contemporary* churches represent the *successive course* of the church through all the ages. We consider it fanciful to say that Ephesus pictures the apostolic church; Smyrna, the postapostolic martyr church; Pergamum, the Oriental Greek church; Thyatira, the Occidental papal church; Sardis, the Protestant, dead orthodox church; Philadelphia, the faithful Lutheran Church; Laodicea, the church just prior to the millennium — or any variation of this scheme of succession, whether it is with or without a final millennium as the climax. Even the history of the past nineteen centuries does not fit such a succession.

12) John continues his simple narration without even an exclamation or a dramatic expression to indicate what he felt. **And I turned to see the voice which** (thus) **was speaking to me. And having turned, I saw seven golden pedestal lamps and in the midst of the pedestal lamps One like** (the) **Son of man, clothed to the foot and girdled at the paps with a golden girdle.**

Following a natural impulse, John turned "to see the voice," i. e., the speaker behind him. The ἥτις is qualitative, "which thus," which was of such a kind, strong as a trumpet; and the imperfect ἐλάλει = was in the act of speaking. John turned before the speaking had been completed. As here, so throughout, John acts in a natural manner, although all that he sees, hears, etc., is a superearthly vision.

The moment he turned about he saw what he now describes. There were seven λυχνίαι, not "candlesticks" (our versions) but grand pedestals, each bearing an ancient vessel for oil, each vessel having a nozzle in which lay a wick burning with a clear, brilliant flame. These grand holders were, it seems, placed in a circle, their lamps were elevated, so that the Lord stood (and walked, 2:1) in their midst. They were made of gold, the most precious metal, and thus shone with great splendor. The lamp pedestals and their lighted lamps are plainly symbols and represent the seven churches, yet not as some of these churches were but as all of them ought to be.

We may, of course, think of the seven-branched candelabrum that stood in the Tabernacle, Exod. 25:31, etc., or of the one mentioned in the vision of Zech. 4:2; but there the seven were joined to one base, here the seven stand in a circle, and the Lord is in their midst. "The churches of the Lord are lampstands as bearers of his light which is to benefit their entire surrounding and ultimately the whole world. They are not themselves the light, just as little as a lampstand by itself is able to shine, but their light is that of Christ's Spirit who works by means of Word and sacrament and not only illumines them but also makes them instruments for illuminating others." Kemmler. John, however, saw no symbol for the world; for the condition of the churches themselves is the main feature of this first vision. Jesus calls his disciples the light of the world (Matt. 5:14). They are this collectively. Here each church appears as burning with the light of the Word that is maintained by public preaching and teaching.

"Golden" symbolizes the preciousness of each church. No base metal belongs in the church. In all the world there is nothing so valuable as the churches which hold aloft the shining Word of the gospel. The world may not prize this kind of gold, the Lord himself bestows it (3:18). We may say that as many real churches as exist at any time, so many pedestal lamps lift aloft their precious light. In 2:5, in the epistle addressed especially to Ephesus, the warning is issued that, unless this church repents, the Lord will move its lampstand from its place so that it will no more stand for his glory with the others.

13) "And in the midst of the pedestal lamps One like (the) Son of man," etc. From him came the voice; no one else is mentioned. Here we think of him as standing although in 2:1, he speaks also of walking. It is Jesus. "One like the Son of man" names him as is done in Dan. 7:13, which is the basis of the briefer designation so constantly used by Jesus himself while he was here on earth: "the Son of man." He is man and yet more than man. Here he appears with his human nature glorified. That glory John had seen on the Mount of Transfiguration long years before; now he beholds it anew, more fully, more significantly revealed. It may be that the correct reading is the accusative υἱόν, as it is in 14:14, and not the dative υἱῷ which is so regular with ὅμοιος. R. 530 registers only the occurrence of these accusatives, while B.-D. 182, 4 and B.-P. 898 call them "a solecism." John uses the dative rather frequently; might it be possible that ὅμοιον is here used, not as a substantive, but only as an ordinary modifying (not governing) adjective, so that "Son of man" is intended to be the object of "I saw"?

His appearance is described in detail. First two perfect participles with their present force, "clothed — girdled." The color of the robe is not mentioned, so we cannot designate it. But its length is given by ποδήρη, the accusative being common after passives (just like the following "golden girdle"): "reaching to the feet" (third declension, but the accusative with the inflection of the first, R. 258). This word is used either as an independent noun or with an appropriate noun understood: *bekleidet mit einem Talar.* This flowing vestment was bound with a girdle at the paps and not at the waist or the hips because Jesus stands at rest and is not in action. The girdle belongs to the vestment; it is also made of gold like the royal pedestal lamps. The imagery is that of majesty. Some think of Jesus as Priest because the Jewish high priest officiated in a long, white robe that was girdled at his breast although the girdle was only ornamented with gold (Exod. 28:8; 39:5). We are unable to find priestliness in the figure here described.

14) John describes the head and the hair, the eyes, the feet, the voice. **Moreover (δέ), his head and his hair white as wool, as snow; and his eyes as flame of fire, and his feet like gold-bronze as in a fired furnace; and his voice as a voice of many waters.** Δέ adds all of the following to v. 13. "His head and his hair," with αὐτοῦ placed forward, means that the head, as far as the hair is concerned, had this wonderful whiteness. Dan. 7:9, "the hair of his head like the pure wool." We find the whiteness of both snow and wool mentioned in Isa. 1:18, and there they describe the sinner as cleansed of his scarlet and crimson-red sin. We think that this passage with the symbol of the hair that is white as snow and wool intends to represent Jesus as being crowned with holiness. We thus discard the idea that the crown of white hair signifies age (even the weakness of age has been added), age then symbolizing eternity. This view is supported by a reference to "the Ancient of days" in

Dan. 7:9, but this expression is *not* used in our passage. Some speak of heavenly purity, which, however, is equal to holiness.

We note that we here have more than the mere color of whiteness. Angels appear in white robes; Revelation uses the white color in many connections. Here it is the snowy whiteness of the hair crowning the head of Jesus, the holiness of his very person as he appears in the midst of his church which is gold and shining with the light of his holy truth and Word. He is the Lord in his holy Temple, the church, the Holy One of God, so named in Mark 1:24; Luke 4:34; Acts 2:27; 3:14; 13:35 (Ps. 16:10); Heb. 7:26.

"His eyes as flame of fire" describes their all-penetrating power before which absolutely nothing is hidden; Dan. 10:6, "as lamps of fire." These flamelike eyes are again mentioned in 2:18 and are there also combined with the gold-bronze feet; fitly so when we think of "the woman Jesebel" and her fornication.

15) "His feet like gold-bronze as in a fired furnace." The etymology of χαλκολίβανος has not yet been cleared up. Does it mean "fine brass," "gold bronze," "brass of Lebanon"? Cancel the "burnished" of the R. V. The readings of the participle vary; if it is a dative singular or a nominative plural, all is simple, but if the true reading is a feminine genitive singular, πεπυρωμένης, we probably have a genitive absolute with the feminine genitive noun understood: "as in a furnace, (a furnace) having been fired up." The sense is that the feet of Jesus resembled "gold-bronze," not as this is when it is cold, but as it appears when it is glowing in the intense fire of a furnace. Where such feet tread they utterly blast and instantly turn to ashes everything they touch or even approach.

Jesus is the One Coming in judgment. The feet come. We connect his feet with this act. Here they symbolize the consuming wrath that will come and consume all the enemies of Jesus and of his church. We thus have symbolized holiness — omniscience — omnipotence of wrath.

To this description of the figure is added that of his voice. In v. 10 John heard it "as of a trumpet," powerful, penetrating. It is now described "as a voice (sound) of many waters," i. e., full of elemental, resistless, overwhelming power like the sound of a roaring cataract or the crashing ocean breakers. The voice "speaks" in v. 10; it utters the Speaker's will. None will ever be able to challenge and to stand against the elemental force of Jesus' voice and his will.

16) **And having in his right hand seven stars.** Beginning with v. 14 there are no verbs. None are needed for the dramatic strokes with which the Lord is pictured. So now in v. 16 two nominative participles suffice. The ἔχων is not an error in case, nor is it an independent sentence or a parenthesis (R. 414). The Greek participle has case, number, and gender, and these make it flexible beyond anything we have in English; we have pointed this out in other pertinent connections in the New Testament. Here even the English is perfectly plain. It is the One here described of whom it is now said, "and having in his right hand," etc. The participle conveys more exactly what is meant than would a finite verb, namely that this is an additional feature of the One whom John saw.

The Lord's "right hand" is his majestic power. He holds the stars of the firmament in his right hand; his hand spans the heavens. Jesus himself interprets: "The seven stars are angels of the seven churches." We recall Dan. 12:3: "They that be wise shall shine as the brightness of the firmament; and they that turn many to righteousness as the stars forever and ever." To think of actual angels, guardian angels of the churches, will not do; for how would letters penned by John be sent to such angels? These cannot be messengers that were sent to John on Patmos by the seven churches; none such are mentioned in the account. To allegorize and to make personifications of the spirit of the churches is unwarranted. These "seven stars" are the pastors of the seven churches. They are distinguished from the churches as such (lampstands) and yet belong to them and in the seven letters are held responsible for the condition of their churches. The word ἄγγελος means "messenger"; so the prophet mentioned in Hag. 1:13, and the priests in Mal. 2:7 are called angels (messengers) of the Lord. While the seven stars match the seven pedestal lamps, and the singular "angel" is used in chapters 2 and 3, we need not think of only one pastor for each church; each may have had several "elders," who are collectively called a star and a messenger (angel), or one of the elders may have been the chief or the president. Although some regard this as an argument for the date of Revelation, the time being the turn of the first century, we are willing to let this pass. When each church began to have but one pastor is a question.

"In his right hand" matches the Lord's standing in the midst of the seven lampstands and yet brings out a difference. Both the lampstands and the stars belong to the Lord, both shine with the light of faith and of confession kindled by the Word, both have a beauty and a glory from above. But the preachers of the church, as the Lord's messengers to the church, are in a peculiar way "in his right hand" to act as his agents and ministers in the churches, there to carry out his will and his alone. The right hand symbolizes majestic authority, the Lord's will, purpose, intent, and the power back of them. He is their authority; his purpose they serve; his will they execute; his Word they speak; his power is back of all that they rightly do in his name.

The stars are far above the earth; they move majestically in their courses. The movements and the agitations that are abroad on earth do not affect them. Their light and the place they hold are ever the same. It is light reflected from the sun, the galaxy of heaven moving in heavenly harmony. Here is a vision of the office of the holy ministry which every church and every pastor should note. Stars — not human gaslights, or will-o'-the-wisps. Stars — not doormats on which men wipe their feet. Unchanging stars — not men who are always out of breath in an effort to catch up with the changing times of the earth.

And out of his mouth a great sword, two-edged, sharp, going forth. This, too, is not ordinary language. The deictic nominative stands alone and needs no verb; the participle is only a descriptive modifier like the two adjectives. Μάχαιρα is the short sword in a scabbard attached to the belt; but ῥομφαία is a great, long, heavy sword, almost as tall as a man, that is wielded with both hands, a weapon of the Thracians. This word is sometimes translated "spear" (Ps. 35:3). In 19:15, 21 we also have this *romphaia* going out of the Lord's mouth. The same word appears in 2:12, 16; 6:8; Luke 2:35; I Sam. 17:45, LXX, when David cuts off Goliath's head. Because of its size the great sword was attached to a shoulder sling. For our "two-edged" the Greek says "two-mouthed," the two edges biting, devouring like two mouths. "Sharp" is added. It was whetted to a keen edge so as to bite deeply. Ἐκπορευομένη, "going forth," describes the mighty sword in its mission of destruction and judgment. The durative participle is qualitative.

No hand swings this sword. The Word of this Almighty One (v. 8) is itself living and energetic (Heb. 4:12) and does whereunto it is sent. Compare Isa. 11:4: "He shall smite the earth with the rod of his mouth." The short sword of the Spirit is our offensive weapon against Satan, Eph. 6:17. No enemies are mentioned here, but see 19:15, 21. Here the churches and their ministers shall realize who it is that is in their midst as in Ps. 2:11, 12.

Another verbless deictic nominative: **And his appearance as the sun shines in its power.** This closes the description, hence we regard ὄψις as *Ansehen* (as in John 7:24) and not as "countenance" (our versions). After the details of garment, girdle, head and hair, eyes, feet, etc., one does not expect a description of the face but of the whole "appearance," the sum total of the vision. This is "as the sun shines in its power." In his transfiguration the face of Jesus shone as the sun (Matt. 17:2), but the word used there is πρόσωπον, which is found in Rev. 4:7; 9:7; 10:1; etc. Here the glory of the Lord is unveiled in all its majesty and splendor, it is as the sun at noon, too intense for mortal eyes to behold save "in spirit" (v. 10). Yet this is the Lord, so glorious in might, whom we so often forget, challenge with our disobedience, contradict with our wisdom, offend with our mistrust. Read the whole passage, v. 12-16, in lines as follows:

And I turned to see the voice which was speaking to me.
And having turned, I saw seven golden pedestal lamps,
And in the midst of the pedestal lamps One like (the) *Son of man,*
Clothed to the foot and girdled at the paps with a golden girdle.
Moreover, his head and his hair white as wool, as snow.
And his eyes as flame of fire,
And his feet like gold-bronze as in a fired furnace.
And his voice as a voice of many waters;
And having in his right hand seven stars.

And out of his mouth a great sword, two-edged, sharp, going forth.
And his appearance as the sun shines in his power.

17) The effect produced on John was overwhelming. **And when I saw him I fell at his feet as dead.** John records the simple fact and nothing more. We do not think that those passages should be referred to which state that no man may look upon God and live, for here Jesus intended to reveal himself to John, and John saw him and yet did not die. He fell "as dead," he became unconscious, he swooned. See the effect of the Tranfiguration in Matt. 17:6. The view that John sank down in love, was thus active as well as passive, is untenable. He was overwhelmed. This was not fear in the sense of fright or terror but fear in the sense of overmastering awe. John was still alive, his soul still in his body, he was "in spirit" and his powers of perception were opened to the other world; yet even under these conditions this was the effect produced upon him. Let this effect upon John together with the description he gives us of Jesus help us to realize who deals with us in the church.

John lay "as dead." Then the Lord stooped **and he laid his right** (hand) **upon me.** This was an action kind and gracious that bestowed blessing and help. We are offered no further information in regard to John, we are not told that the Lord raised him up, or that he arose of his own accord. The author effaces himself in the divine presence. Not what he did is of importance to his readers but what the Lord said unto him — words of utmost importance for all: **saying: Be not fearing! I am the First and the Last, and the Living One and I was dead, and lo, living am I for the eons of the eons; and I have the keys of the death and the hades. Write, then, the things thou**

didst see, and the things that are, and the things about to occur after these, the mystery of the seven stars which thou didst see on my right (hand) **and the seven pedestal lamps, the golden. The seven stars are angels of the seven churches; and the pedestal lamps, the seven, are seven churches.**

The present imperative forbids a continuation of fearing. This is the word that is almost regularly spoken to poor mortals when heavenly beings come into contact with them. Our sinful, mortal state is bound to succumb in fear before such presences from above. Because of the grace that is contained in these revelations the recipients of them are bidden not to fear.

18) Before the Lord repeats the command to write which was given already in v. 11, he names himself. He is the center of the entire revelation that is now being vouchsafed to John. The Lord's designation of himself is like a signature and a seal that is here placed at the head of the whole revelation. This is one of those mighty "I Am" from the lips of Jesus which is a revelation of himself that expresses his absolute authority to reveal all that follows and voices the power of him who speaks and reveals. "Blessed the one reading and the ones hearing the words of this prophecy and keeping the things written therein!" (v. 3).

"I am the First and the Last" undoubtedly designates Jesus as *God.* "I am the Alpha and the Omega" in v. 8 is a close parallel to which 21:6; 22:13 add another: "the Beginning and the End." There is no doubt regarding the similarity. A question may be raised in regard to possible differences. We have already said that Alpha and Omega are letters, the first and the last of the Greek alphabet, and thus refer to *language,* to the divine spoken or written *Word.* "I am the First and the Last" takes up the idea of *time* and thus refers to the whole course of human *history* from the first day to the last. "I am the Beginning and the End" refers to a great, extended *work or plan* which has an inception and a consummation. We venture to combine the three: 1) in all revelation, 2) in all human history, 3) in all the work and plan of the kingdom — Jesus, the glorious, mighty Jesus whom John here sees, stands at both ends, embracing, governing, controlling the whole. This is his stupendous greatness, absolute supremacy, infinite glory.

Luthardt has the application: "If he stands at the end as at the beginning, who will dare to vaunt himself in the middle?" and Steffann: "Who would not cling to him to the end, to whom the end belongs?" This is what Paul expresses in Eph. 1:10: the administration of all the periods of time is in Christ's hands, and in him are summed up all the things in heaven and on earth. He, the Head of the church, fills all things in all ways, Eph. 1:22, 23. He is the Firstborn of all creation; all the things have been created through him and for him, Col. 1:15, 16.

We find two designations: 1) "the First and the Last"; 2) "the Living One — and I was dead, and lo, living am I for the eons of the eons" — see the temporal phrase in v. 6. Ὁ ζῶν should not be rendered by a relative clause: "he that liveth"; it is a substantive: "the Living One," the participle is qualitative: the One whose mark it is that he lives forever. How this is to be understood is stated coordinately with καί: "and I was dead, and lo, living am I for the eons of the eons."

The aorist records the past fact that Jesus was at one time dead. He died on the cross and lay in the tomb. Although no interjection is used with this expression, the fact that he whom John here sees (v. 13, etc.) should ever have been dead is astounding. The interjection "lo" marks as being equally astounding this fact that he who was dead is "living" and that for evermore. Both his having been dead and his eternal living refer to his human nature — he is the incarnate Son of God.

The fact that he died for our sins and rose for our justification is not stated here, but it underlies this designation as it does in v. 5: "the First-born of the dead." Here the result is made prominent, which does not stop with time but extends into the other world: "and I have the keys of the death and of the hades." As being "the Living One" who was dead and yet is living forever these keys are in his possession. In Matt. 16:19 Jesus calls them "the keys of the kingdom of the heavens," and as the one who owns these keys he bestows them on Peter, namely the power to bind and to loose, to open the door of Christ's rule of grace to the repentant sinner and to lock that door against the impenitent sinner. This is the same as opening death and hell to the impenitent and closing them for the penitent.

We may admit that in 6:8 and in 20:14 "the death and the hades" are personified. This is not the case here where Jesus says he has *"the keys* of the death and of the hades." "The death" cannot be a place like "the hades" so that the keys unlock and lock both alike. "The keys" is plural as it is in Matt. 18:19, in order to convey the idea that the double power is referred to, namely to keep from hell and to consign to hell, in Matthew to bind and to loose (John 20:23); yet in Rev. 3:7 we have only one key, "the key of David," for opening so that no one shuts and for shutting so that no one opens. We thus say that Christ has the double power ("the keys") to save from and to consign to "the death (this state) and the hades" (this place). It is worth noting that "the death" and "the hades" are articulated like "the sin" and "the death" in Rom. 4:12. Throughout Romans Paul distinguishes between "sin" (in general, whatever is of this nature) and "the sin," this deadly, damning power.

Yet, when considering Revelation, more must be said about hades, especially in view of 6:8 and 20:14. The word means "the unseen place." It is used as a general designation for hell. It should not be capitalized as is done in the R. V., for we do not capitalize heaven. In 6:8, "the death" slays men in judgment, and "the hades" keeps following in order to gather the souls of those slain in judgment. "The hades" is the unseen place that swallows up the human souls of the damned until the judgment day. Thus in 20:13 "the death and the hades" give up "the dead, those that are in them," and in 20:14, both the death and the hades are thrown into the lake of the fire. The fact to be noted well is that in 1:18; 6:8; 20:13, 14, "the death and the hades" appear *in conjunction.* In other words, Revelation uses ὁ ᾅδης as a name for the place into which "the death" delivers *the souls* of the human beings who are damned. Until judgment day hell functions only for the souls of the damned and is thus termed "hades," the unseen place. When hell is mentioned as receiving both the souls and the bodies of the damned, Jesus calls hell "the Gehenna" and "the Gehenna of the fire," and in Rev. 20:14, 15, "the lake of the fire," in 21:8, "the lake, the one burning with fire and brimstone, which is the death, the second." How "the death and the hades" are at last thrown into "the lake of the fire" we shall see in 20:14.

Nothing is gained by citing the rabbinical notion of "four keys, of life, of the graves, of food, of rain," and by pointing to the fact that Elijah requested the two that were used for rain and for the resurrection but was told that three were not given, those of birth, of resurrection, of rain. Equally valueless are the claims that we here have the Christian adaptation of Babylonian-Gnostic myths about the conqueror of the underworld who broke open its doors, stole its keys, and came back. The descent to the underworld of Isthar, of the Mandæan Hibil-Ziwa, plus the idea of various Gnostic sects are sometimes added. But these views do not help us to understand the designation of himself which the Lord uses.

The word ᾅδης is used ten times in the New Testament: four times by Jesus in Matthew and in Luke, four times in Revelation, twice in Acts as a translation of the Hebrew *sheol.* The LXX had no other Greek word for *sheol.* Yet *sheol* is used in two senses in the Old Testament: "a place into which one descends, comparable to a belly," *mit einem Bauche vergleichbar,* Ed. Koenig, *Woerterbuch.* In the first place, a study of all the Old Testament passages reveals the fact that *sheol* is used with reference to all the dead, they all pass into *sheol* at death. The context in which these passages occur shows that all the dead leave the earthly life, home, friends, possessions, pleasures, etc., and pass over into a state where these no longer exist. In the second place, in the Old Testament *sheol* is used with the reference to the damned; in these passages the context and the descriptions are terrible accordingly; they now picture hell. It is thus not the simple word *sheol* that is decisive but the description that goes with the use to which the word is put.

Neither the Greek nor the English has a word that corresponds to the Hebrew *sheol.* Hence the translations given in the A. V. are of necessity interpretative. When *sheol* refers to the dead in general, the A. V. uses "grave." When *sheol* refers to men who are damned, the A. V. uses "hell." In the New Testament matters are far simpler, for the New Testament writers wrote Greek and used "hades," and this only in the sense of the place for the damned, even in Acts 2:27, 31 where the Hebrew *sheol* is rendered "hades" ("hell"). This summarizes the linguistic data although more may be added.

Modern learning has proposed a new view. It is offered in G. K. 146, etc., but is found in many modern commentaries and dictionaries. They tell us of a third place that is neither heaven nor hell. This intermediate third place is *"die Unterwelt,"* "the underworld," but it is commonly termed the *Totenreich.* We are told that the conception is pagan, and the pagan sources are offered. We are also told that it became the ancient Jewish idea of the hereafter: all the dead go to this "realm of the dead" and there lead a shadowy existence. According to G. K. and others, after the Exile this *Totenreich* was thought of as containing two compartments, one for the damned, the other for the saints, and Luke 16:19, etc., is referred to as a survival of this conception. Others introduce Christ's descent into hell, i. e., this descent into this realm of the dead where he released the Old Testament saints.

Many go farther. Since this *Totenreich* is not yet hell, probation after death is added. At the time of his descent Christ is said to have preached the gospel in this realm (on this and other similar views see I Pet. 3:19). Mission work is thus carried on in *sheol* (hades), for it is assumed that, if Christ preached the gospel there, he would make provision for the continuance of such preaching. Just who is now doing this preaching is not said.

We are told that Jewish views in regard to *sheol* changed as time went on. At first the resurrection was not known. The idea of a resurrection was introduced from Persia after Solomon's time and was then developed after the Exile. So at first both godly and ungodly remained in *sheol* forever; then the godly remained there only temporarily; finally the godly did not go to *sheol* at all. In the New Testament the latter views were still in conflict; for in Luke 16:19, etc., we are told, Jesus speaks of Dives, Abraham, and Lazarus as being in *sheol.*

It is not necessary for us to show that these views are not the teaching of the Bible.

19) The command to write is reiterated from v. 11. But now οὖν bases the renewed command on the great designation Jesus has just given himself in v. 17, 18. In their discussion of Inspiration our dogmaticians distinguish between the *impulsus sive mandatum ad scribendum,* and the *suggestio rerum.* We have that mandate in v. 11, and elsewhere, in 14:13; 19:9; 19:5, we have the things to be written in the visions. The fact that John was to write at once we see from 10:4: "I was about to be writing," ἔμελλον γράφειν, which Zahn treats rather superficially (*Introduction,* III, 405).

In v. 11 the singular ὃ βλέπεις, "what thou seest," summarizes all before John had seen anything. Then in v. 13 and in v. 17 he "saw." When he is now told to write, the plural is employed, "the things thou didst see, and the things that are, and the things about to occur after these." "The things that thou didst see" must be those referred to by the same aorist verb (εἶδον, in v. 13 and v. 17), namely the vision of v. 10 to 20. We cannot understand how this clause with its aorist after these other aorists can refer to all the visions. This first vision of Jesus himself is the basis and in a manner also the key for all the visions that are to follow. For the majesty and the power of the glorified Lord dominate Revelation from beginning to end. This first vision had to be recorded for us so that we may read all the other visions in its light.

We cannot translate καί . . . καί, "both . . . and," for what John had already seen is not "both the things that are and the things that are about to occur." These are additional things. Nor can we understand ἅ εἰσι as "what they mean" (i. e., what the things John saw *mean*). This is advocated because εἰσί is plural while μέλλει is singular, and because two more εἰσί follow in v. 20, all three are then to be understood as "mean": the seven stars *mean* angels of the seven churches, the pedestal lamps *mean* seven churches. But this view is refuted by the temporal clause, "the things about to occur *after these*," i. e., after the ones that are. "After these" cannot be referred back to mean, "after the things thou didst see." "After these" joins "are" and "about to occur." The present things and the future things are connected. This appears already in the seven epistles where the *present* condition of the seven churches is described from the viewpoint of the Lord, and where promises and warning threats regarding *the future* are added. In the same way we find present things and resultant future things in the rest of Revelation.

In true prophetic fashion the great visions now to be granted John present all that is to follow from the present onward. They are given in single portraits in which the actual stretches of time covered in each are only symbolized or foreshortened or disregarded. So the old prophets and the Baptist painted the two comings of Christ and his kingdom of grace and of glory as one grand portrait. The times and the periods (Acts 1:7) are committed to the Father's authority. The same is true in Revelation regarding the things that will occur after them. "After them" is all that we know in regard to their time of occurrence.

So we do not accept the idea that the Lord here presents the program of Revelation, the division of the book into three parts: first part, "the things thou didst see" (1:9-20); second part, "the things that are" (chapters 2 and 3); third part, "the things about to occur" (the rest of the book). Nor are there just two parts: chapter 1, introduction; chapters 2 and 3, part one; chapters 4-22, part two. These divisions are not balanced. In this very first vision of Christ the symbols as well as the names used for Christ cover the future; the same is true with regard to the seven letters, while in the rest of the visions the present is interwoven with the future. What Jesus tells John to write *summarizes* and does not present a division.

As for ἅ εἰσι with its plural, this views the things that are as being a number of such things, and they are various and different. The conditions obtaining in the churches are not alike, for which reason also seven and not merely one are chosen. Then also the things that are in heaven are included. "Are" is correct, for these are timeless. The singular verb in ἃ μέλλει γίνεσθαι views these things which are about to occur in their unity or, we may say, in their climax and consummation which is one, the constant and final triumph of Christ and his kingdom. The uneven grammatical forms do not of necessity indicate a disregard of common grammar. Neuter plurals may have the verb in the singular or in the plural in the Greek. Nor is it John who here employs the verbs; the change of verbs is made by Jesus and is not due to John.

20) The fact that Jesus here tells John the sum of the visions is plain from the apposition: "the mystery of the seven stars which thou didst see on my right (hand), and the seven pedestal lamps, the golden ones." This mystery is to be revealed; this is the ἀποκάλυψις Ἰησοῦ Χριστοῦ (v. 1). It deals with the seven stars and the seven pedestal lamps that have already been seen by John. "The mystery" is by no means merely the interpretation of what these stars and these pedestal lamps signify, namely ministers and churches (v. 10); "the mystery" includes all that pertains to these stars and these pedestal lamps as here shown to John. "The mystery" = "the words of this prophecy," "the things written in it" (v. 3).

Thus Jesus at once says: "The seven stars are angels of the seven churches; and the pedestal lamps, the seven, are seven churches." Their relation to Christ, the First and the Last and the Living One (v. 17), the Alpha and the Omega, the One who Is and the One who Was and the One Coming, the Almighty (v. 8), has already been set forth in the exposition of v. 13 and 16, also the significance of the number seven as it appears repeatedly in this chapter beginning with v. 4. Jesus says outright who is referred to because he now dictates a separate message to each of these seven churches. This vision simply continues.

CHAPTER II

The Seven Letters, chapters 2 and 3

The Letter to Ephesus, 2:1-7

1) **To the angel, the one of the church in Ephesus, write.** The order in which the letters are dictated is that found in 1:11; it is geographical and has nothing to do with a prophetic, chronological succession of churches and church conditions to the end of time. The seven churches and their varying conditions existed *simultaneously* when Jesus dictated these letters in the year 95. They are typical of the conditions obtaining in the churches of all time irrespective of the number that at any time may belong to the one type or to another.

We have already explained ἄγγελος (v. 16, "stars"). Ephesus lies nearest to Patmos and is thus made the first in the series. The church in Ephesus may include more than one congregation of this large city. So the *angelos* may include the entire eldership although many think of only one pastor, the head pastor or bishop. This is true with regard to each of the seven churches: Jesus dictates the letters; John takes the dictation and writes as the dictation proceeds. The reason for this view is explained in the introduction and in 1:19.

The Acts tell us how Paul founded the church at Ephesus, how long he labored there, and how from this center he spread the gospel in the great province, note Acts 19:26. That his Epistle to the Ephesians was intended for Ephesus and was not an encyclical we have endeavored to show in the introduction to Ephesians. That Rom. 16 belongs to Romans and not to

Ephesians we have shown in the proper place. Paul had appointed Timothy supervisor of the entire church work in the Asian field — see the introduction to the letters to Timothy. Ephesus had been the headquarters of John since the Jewish War, for the past twenty-five years. The Ephesian church was founded in 55 and was thus forty years old. Its location in the capital of the province gave it high standing almost from the start. These are the important data.

The seven letters are alike in having a form of their own. The same command to John to write precedes each one. They do not have the common epistolary form; there is no greeting in the nominative, followed by a dative, etc. All the letters begin: Τάδε λέγει and a name for him who "declares these things." This is stated in the third person. But at once there is an *οἶδα*, "I know," in the first person, followed by a statement of the condition of the church, after which come promises, threatening warnings, etc. At or near the end appears the refrain: "The one having an ear, let him hear," etc., and the promise to "the one conquering," ὁ νικῶν. These are true letters dictated by the Lord.

We do not think that each was to be sent as a separate letter, but they form a part of the entire *βιβλίον* (v. 11), the whole of which was to be sent. In this "book" these seven churches are personally addressed in turn; yet all are to read all these personal letters together with the rest of the book.

These things declares the One holding the seven stars in his right (hand), **the One walking in the midst of the seven pedestal lamps, the golden ones: I know, etc.** In the case of each letter the Lord designates himself in terms that are taken from chapter 1, and each of the designations is different. Each designation has its individual bearing on the individual church addressed. The reference to the seven stars (1:16) appears also in 3:1. The substitution of ὁ κρατῶν in place of the ἔχων found in 1:16, is more than a mere verbal change; likewise, the change to περιπατῶν ἐν μέσῳ involves more than the ἐν μέσῳ used in 1:13. These changes register an advance. We note τὸ κράτος in 1:6; and ὁ παντοκράτωρ in 1:8, both denoting "might" as put forth in mighty action. The Lord "has" the seven stars but he has them as "the One holding" them, using them in his might and almightiness, even as they are "in his right hand," which signifies his majesty and omnipotence. So the participle "walking in the midst" adds the idea of majestic activity in the midst of the churches. On the pedestal lamps and on the stars see 1:13, 16.

Now the first great: "I know": **I know thy works and thy toil and endurance and that thou canst not bear base ones and didst try those calling themselves apostles and are not and didst find them liars and hast endurance and didst bear because of my Name and hast not wearied.** Οἶδα speaks of intellectual knowledge and does not, like γινώσκω, add an affect and effect on him who knows. The three nouns: "thy works and thy toil and endurance" are divided into two by the two σου, one modifying "the works," the other "the toil and the endurance" (ὑπομονή is explained in 1:9). The Lord knows all the works, whatever can be termed "works"; in particular "the toil" connected with some of them, for some were hard, of which one might easily grow weary, hence "the endurance," the perseverance, keeping on despite the toil. These first nouns are general.

Specifications follow in the form of clauses: "and that thou canst not bear base ones," δύνῃ as in Luke 16:2; R. 312. Κακοί are base people, "bad ones," in the moral sense, from the standpoint of Christianity. He is *kakos* who is good-for-nothing in regard to the thing in which he ought to be good: a cowardly soldier is *kakos,* likewise a lazy student, and thus a disgraceful church member. The word is not πονηροί, viciously wicked; "evil" is not exact. The eldership of the Ephesian church cannot bear good-for-nothing members, those we call dead timber, who care little or nothing for Christ, the gospel, and the church, nominal members.

A second specification points in a different direction: "and didst try those calling themselves apostles and are not and didst find them liars." This is couched in two aorists and refers to false teachers, men who claimed to be apostles, who appeared in Ephesus with this claim but who, when tested by the eldership, were exposed as liars. The aorists do not say whether such men appeared only once or several times. The word "apostles" cannot mean apostles in the narrow sense, for the Twelve and Paul were too well known. Their claim was that they were apostles in the wider sense, men who had a commission from Christ, teachers of the true gospel. The idea that they claimed to have seen Jesus himself is not contained in the word. Some identify them with the Nicolaitans mentioned in v. 6, but we think that the latter were only one group and not the whole class of liars that were exposed in Ephesus. "And are not" is parenthetical just as we still insert such a remark, which also explains the tense. I John 4:1 had been followed in Ephesus; the pseudo-teachers had been unmasked as liars.

3) The triple statement: "and hast endurance and didst bear because of my name and hast not wearied," with its three tenses, present, aorist, perfect, does not sound like a third specification but like a summary. This, then, is the same endurance and the same tirelessness mentioned in v. 2. Note "endurance" in 1:9, remaining under a load, persevering and not giving up. "Thou hast" means thou hast now.

"And didst bear because of my name" means on definite occasions, once or oftener in the past. There is a play on the verb "thou *canst not bear* base ones" and "thou *didst bear* because of my name," namely a lot of burdens and hardships for my sake. At one time bearing is intolerable, again bearing is done with a smile. The important thing is not to bear base ones in the church and yet to bear any number of burdens for the sake of Christ's name. Βαστάζειν = to pick up and to lift, to bear or carry. "Name" as here used = the gospel revelation of Christ by which alone he makes himself known to us, by which alone we apprehend and know him. Διά = because of, for the sake of, on account of. The phrase signifies that thou didst bear because thou art true to me and to the gospel by which thou didst know me.

The perfect κεκοπίακας = all along in the past to the very present "thou hast not wearied," grown tired, fainted, in toil; the corresponding noun is κόπος which is found in v. 2. All that the Lord states in v. 2, 3 is high praise which we regard as a reference not only to the ἄγγελος as the pastor or pastors of the Ephesian church but also to the church, whether this consisted of one or of several congregations in this city.

4) **Nevertheless, I have against thee that thou hast left thy first love.** This is strong reproach. Love has not died altogether, but its first ardent vigor has declined and is still in this low condition (on the personal endings in the perfects cf., R. 337). The love here mentioned is not only love to the brethren, for this love and the love to Christ are never separate, the former is the evidence for the latter (I John 4:20). The applicatory remarks, based on the idea of brotherly love, that dissension was rife in Ephesus, that contention naturally appears where orthodoxy is maintained, etc., etc., are beside the mark. Only the pure Word produces a pure faith, and this in turn produces pure love. To call brotherly love the *articulus stantis aut cadentis ecclesiae* is to think that apples can grow where there

is no tree. Ἀγάπη is the love of true comprehension and understanding coupled with corresponding purpose. Thus its decline is lack of this understanding with which diminution of the energy of its proper purpose goes hand in hand. As for the understanding and purpose of love, note how Jesus makes it plain: "If a man love me, he will keep my words" (John 14:15, 23; 15:10-14). Love itself is misconceived when it is supposed that it can be great and strong without faithfulness to the Word. No plant is strong without good, rich soil.

The condition in Ephesus, the decline of the first love as manifested by the lessening of "the first works" (v. 5), was the evidence of a decline in faith and in faithfulness to the Word. This decline had not proceeded to the extent of accepting those who called themselves apostles while they were nothing of the kind, among them the Nicolaitans (v. 6). Love was not absent, but the first love had been left. This was an alarming sign. For love ought to grow the longer we know Christ, the more we make his Word our own. Love is comprehension and corresponding purpose. When decline sets in, in place of robust, healthy development we should be alarmed. For the next step is still greater darkening of knowledge of the Word, inroads of error, loud claims of love while no longer knowing what genuine love for Christ and for true believers is. Only the first decline had occurred in Ephesus. It had to be checked and changed into augmentation before it proceeded any farther.

5) **Keep remembering, therefore, whence thou hast fallen and repent and do the first works!** This is the cure to be applied. First the present, durative imperative: constant remembering is to be the constant impulse toward recovery. Οὖν bases this admonition on the reproach just uttered, a reproach that is to be removed. Recalling the noble past and the subse-

quent decline which still continues (perfect: "whence thou hast fallen") is to stimulate the whole life of faith in the Word so that it will again fruit in full love and in all the evidence of such love. Remember, ever remember! A noble past ought not to have an ignoble present with a still more ignoble future in prospect. A noble past condemns an ignoble present but by that very condemnation ought to restore the present and to assure the future. Many are ready to boast of their past as an excuse for their sloth in the present but thus only condemn themselves.

The next two imperatives are ringing, peremptory aorists: "and repent (completely) and do (decisively) the first works!" as was done in the first love during the days gone by. This is the same call we find in Matt. 3:2, which also has μετανοεῖν, the Hebrew *nicham*, "repent by changing the mind," and *schub*, "to turn." Originally the verb meant "to perceive afterward" (μετά), i. e., when it is too late; the Scriptures deepen this into a religious change of the heart, sorrow for sin, and turning to the Lord. It is the call of grace to the unconverted which is filled with power to produce repentance; it is the same call of grace, with the same power, to the converted when decline in their spiritual life sets in. In fact, as Luther says, our whole life is to be a constant or ceaseless repentance, *dass das ganze Leben seiner Glaeubigen auf Erden eine stete oder unaufhoerliche Busse sein soll.* I John 1:8-10.

The evidence of true repentance is: "do the first works." "Do, therefore, fruits worthy of the repentance," Luke 3:8. Here these fruits are "the first works" which once graced the Ephesians so richly. Repentance without amendment is pretense and not genuine. Both peremptory aorists are, of course, also constative.

But if not, I am coming for thee and I shall move thy pedestal lamp out of its place if thou dost not re-

pent. This is the Lord's warning threat. It is sent now while there is still time to repent. Εἰ δὲ μή = "else," "otherwise." It is a condensed protasis also in English. "I am coming," a futuristic present, recalls "the Coming One" mentioned in 1:8. The *dativus commodi* "for thee" = as far as thou art concerned and is not an illiterate "to thee," as some regard it on the basis of a study of the papyri. The Coming One comes not only in judgment at the last day but also in many preliminary judgments as also the following visions show.

The nature of the verb "to come" permits the future sense of the present tense while the verb "to move" does not; hence we have the future tense: "and I will move thy pedestal lamp out of its place," which reverts to the symbolic expression used in 1:13. Poignantly, significantly the protasis is repeated: "if thou dost not repent," the aorist to express actuality: "if thou dost not actually repent."

If it remains impenitent, Ephesus shall be rejected by the Lord as no longer being one of his churches. Its glorious place shall know it no more. This will be the act of the Lord's judgment when the day of grace which was unused shall come to its end. There is now no Christian church of any denomination in Ephesus which lies in total ruin. Yet this fate is not what is here foretold but rather that whatever organization may be left in Ephesus, the light of Ephesus as a church shall go out entirely; whatever it may call itself, it will no longer be accepted by the Lord as being his church. Many a church of today that is located in still flourishing cities is removed from its place in the kingdom. First the lamp grows dim, finally it goes out. *Hin ist hin, jetzt haben sie den Tuerken.* Luther.

6) **But this thou hast, that thou dost hate the works of the Nicolaitans, which also I on my part hate.** This is registered as a hopeful sign. Ephesus

still *loves* the Lord and the true church to such an extent that it *hates* this sect which the Lord also *hates*. It loves the Lord by keeping true to his Word over against this sect. Note John 14:23, which is quoted above. Where such love for him, his truth, and his church shows itself by such hate of those who are out to oppose these, there is great hope that this love may be revived to its pristine strength and original energy. This is the real substance of the statement. We take "the works" of the Nicolaitans to include their whole activity and not merely the immoralities they practiced but equally their work of promulgating their doctrines.

The most one can say in regard to the minor question as to who the Nicolaitans were, is that they were an early Gnostic sect. All else is uncertain. See the survey in Smith, *Bible Dictionary*. The attempt to find a symbolic meaning in Νικόλαος, which is based on the etymological meaning of the word ("conqueror of people"), and thus to regard "Nicolaitans" as another term for "Balaam" used in v. 14 with its etymological meaning *Bala' 'am*, "devourer of people," we consider fanciful.

The main debate centers around the question as to whether the Nicolaus mentioned in Acts 6:5 was the founder of the Nicolaitans, either designedly or inadvertently by the use of certain unguarded utterances of his which were afterward caught up and misused by the Nicolaitans who of their own accord named themselves after him. The contention regarding this point arose early. It scarcely merits serious consideration. Jesus did have a Judas in his following, but for this fact we have the fullest historical attestation. We have nothing of the kind in regard to any one of the first seven deacons in Jerusalem. It is a moral law not to make a noble Christian man a Judas without full evidence that he turned out to be a Judas. The Eighth

Commandment binds exegetes and Bible scholars as well as ordinary Christians.

Here even the interval of time is an important factor. The incidents recorded in Acts 6 occurred in the year 31, Revelation was written in the year 95. The early Gnosticism has Cerinthus as its chief and did not originate in Jerusalem but in another locality and at a later date. The one plausible assumption is that one of the Cerinthian pupils by the name of Nicolaus became prominent in Ephesus about the year 95 and with his following merited the hate of the Ephesian eldership and church. In Pergamum (v. 14) these heretics were more successful.

7) **The one having an ear, let him hear what the Spirit is saying to the churches!** Who does not recall this command which was given repeatedly by Jesus when he was here on earth (Matt. 11:15; 13:9, 43; Mark 4:24)? The view of some commentators that John is here posing as a prophet and is really ordering that his writing be read and heard in the churches is unfair to John. It is Jesus who speaks here and not John; this is the same order that is found in Matt. 11:15; etc. When Jesus orders, "Write!" in 1:11, 19; 2:1, etc., what purpose has the writing but to be read (1:3: "the one reading — those hearing — the things written") and thus to be heard in the churches? The idea that John composes these seven letters should not be entertained.

Everyone has an ear, in fact, two. God gave everyone an ear so that he may hear. Hence the guilt when one who has an ear does not hear. You who have an ear have no excuse. If you do something to your ear so that, hearing, you do not hear when the Lord speaks (Matt. 13:15) you stand self-condemned. This does not have a double sense, it is not a play on physical and spiritual ears and hearing. However, the aorist signifies: "let him actually, effectively hear!" The Lord always speaks so that he shall be heard effectively.

Jesus does not say, "What *I* am saying to the churches," but, "What the Spirit is saying." Some commentators have stated that "the Trinitarian formula had not yet been adopted." But John the Baptist knew about the Trinity, and all the Jews were Trinitarians. Nor does Jesus here identify himself with the Spirit. He and the Spirit are and remain two Persons here and throughout the Scriptures. Yet what is true in regard to the First and the Second Person according to John 10:30; 14:9-11, is also true in regard to the Second and the Third; in the one you have the other. Here the Spirit is named because it is his especial work to operate through the means of grace and to effect faith by hearing (Rom. 10:17) and all its fruits, love, endurance, etc.

Although it is addressed to the ἄγγελος of the Ephesian church, this letter is not intended only for the Ephesian church but for "the churches," for all seven, yea for all churches of all places and all times. Is the clause, "what the Spirit is saying," equally broad, including the whole gospel, all that constitutes the Scriptures? We understand "is saying" as equal to "is now saying by the mouth of the Lord."

Despite those who taboo this word, the Lord here *dictated* these seven letters to John and did that in the literal sense of the word. So the ancient prophets received verbatim messages: "Thus saith the Lord!" Not a few portions of Scripture are quite literally dictation or its equivalent. The Ten Commandments were *written* by God himself. Throughout Revelation, John reports exactly the words he heard spoken; thus in 1:17-20; in 4:1, 8, 11; etc. If the words of Satan and of men, good and bad, are reproduced exactly, shall not also the words of God and of Christ be equally reproduced?

When our dogmaticians speak about dictation, they have something else in mind. They use three *illustrations* of Inspiration: 1) an amanuensis, 2) the plectrum striking the strings of the lyre, 3) the flute played by the musician. These are to illustrate the *causa efficiens* and the *causae instrumentales,* the inspiring Spirit and the human writers. To charge the dogmaticians with "a dictation theory" because of one of these illustrations is to go only a third of the way, one must then add the lyre and the flute theory as well, and then the absurdity becomes plain, for no illustration is a "theory." All good writers and teachers use illustrations, and no one says them nay. An illustration may be apt or may be faulty. This applies also to these three older ones. If one does not think an illustration apt, he may offer a better one and see how it will be received.

The command to hear is followed by the promise: **To the one conquering, I will give to him to eat from the wood of the life which is in the Paradise of God.** While the command to hear appears unchanged in these letters, the promise to "the one conquering," ὁ νικῶν, varies in formulation. Moreover, the first three letters place the command to hear before the promise, the last four after the command. All these things are significant and at the same time beautiful.

The qualifying present participle is always used, "the one conquering," but it is quite timeless and almost like the noun "the conqueror." The participle has no object, and we should not add one or dispute about what is to be added, just as we should add nothing to the noun "the victor." We also decline to give the word a forensic meaning as though a coming off victorious with acquittal after a trial before the heavenly Judge is indicated; none of the statements regarding the victor contain such a forensic thought. The connotation of these seven participles is victory over hostile forces. Only once, in v. 26, a second elucidating participle is added, "the one keeping to the end my works." The thought does not refer to victory finally achieved at the end of life (to express such a thought the aorist participle would be used) but to the believer who stands as "the victor" from beginning to end. This is a point worth noting.

Δώσω αὐτῷ appears only four times in the letters. The dative pronoun emphasizes "the victor" in the sense of "to him alone," this substantivized participle being twice retained in the nominative (v. 26; 3:21). The victor, only the victor, shall receive a reward. We may say that this reward is won by him yet not as the spoils of victory from the enemy but as a gift from the Lord, a gift of the Lord's abounding grace. "I shall give" means when the victor appears before his Lord. Here the gift is expressed by an infinitive, "to eat from the wood of the life," i. e., from its fruit. In Gen. 2:9 the LXX translates the Hebrew *'etz* by the Greek ξύλον, "wood," not by δένδρον, "tree," and we have τὸ ξύλον τῆς ζωῆς, "the wood of the life" in Gen. 2:9, here in Revelation, and three times more in 22:2, 14, 19. It is at least remarkable that this same word ξύλον, "wood," is employed in Acts 5:30; 10:39; 13:29; Gal. 3:13; I Pet. 2:24 regarding the cross on which Jesus died, and that these passages go back to this word found in the LXX of Deut. 21:22, 23 which makes "wood" and suspension on wood (tree or post) the mark of being accursed of God, Gal. 3:13, quoting Deut. 21:23 to this effect.

A connection is indicated, one that extends from Gen. 2:9 to these four passages in Revelation. We regard the genitive as qualitative, "the wood or tree whose quality is the life," the eternal life which God wanted us to have, which Jesus obtained anew for man after his fall, which shall be ours in all its fulness after we enter Paradise. "The wood of the life" has been referred to the gospel, the fruit of which is the life or salvation; or to the Holy Spirit who bestows the life; or to Christ himself who bestows all spiritual gifts and gives us his body to eat in the Holy Supper. Yet the four passages in Revelation take us to Paradise and thus back to Gen. 2:9, 24. The promise given in Rev. 2:7 is that the victor shall eat from the wood of the life, which (wood) is in the Paradise of God; he shall taste and enjoy all the blessedness of eternal life in the Paradise of heaven by means of his soul at death and by means of his body and his soul after the resurrection.

Παράδεισος is a beautiful park, here "the Paradise of God," which takes us back to Gen. 2:8, etc. Paul was caught up into the heavenly Paradise, II Cor. 12:4, the only person in regard to whom such an experience is recorded. When we are told that this is *not* the Paradise mentioned in Luke 23:43, into which the angels carried the soul of Lazarus, we again meet the Romanizing view which speaks of a third place between heaven and hell, the so-called "realm of the dead," in the upper story ("Paradise") of which the souls of the blessed rested until at the time of his descent into hell Christ carried them into heaven, or, as some claim, where the blessed dead will remain until the resurrection. See the exposition of Luke 23:43. The Paradise concerning which Jesus speaks to the malefactor is the Paradise concerning which Jesus speaks to the angel of the church in Ephesus but now as signifying heaven and earth made one in the consummation (Rev. 21:1, etc.). Neither of our versions adopts the reading, Paradise "of *my God.*" This does not imply that God is not the God of the glorified Lord (as this is said in 1:6), but that the pronoun is not textually attested.

Ephesus was the church where John himself had had his headquarters, yet John is not brought into any special relation to this church because he had made it his headquarters for years. Throughout these seven letters the Lord uses John only as his instrument for communicating his messages. John's relation to all the churches is thus the same. The accident of his residence in one of them is of no importance. He is the apostle of the Lord for all of them. His faithfulness as such an apostle is unquestioned; not so the faithfulness of the eldership or ministry in some of these churches.

Ephesus is a sample of the congregations and the bodies whose *love has begun to decline.* Perhaps its pastorate and its membership were not yet aware of this fact; the Lord, however, was. It is manifestly wrong to call Ephesus a dead orthodox church. When this is done by those who have pietistic conceptions of love and cast aspersions on orthodoxy, it is doubly condemned by the Lord himself, first in v. 2, in the commendation for exposing the pretended apostles as liars, and secondly in v. 6, in the commendation for hating the heretics whom also the Lord hates.

The Letter to Smyrna, 8-11

8) **To the angel, the one of the church in Smyrna, write:** See v. 1, which includes also the notes on the opening words: Τάδε λέγει and οἶδα.

These things declares the First and the Last who was dead and became alive. The Lord varies the designation of himself. "The First and the Last" (see 1:17) = the One at the beginning and at the end of *history,* from whom and for whom all history exists, who controls all of it for the sake of his church. "Who was dead and became alive" restates 1:18 and uses two historical aorists, both stating only the past facts, the death that occurred on Calvary, the resurrection that occurred in the tomb in Joseph's garden. This designation applies perfectly to the contents of this letter, in particular also to the martyrdom awaiting some of the believers in Smyrna. This is a letter from the Lord who himself was put to death by his enemies and yet rose again in glory.

9) **I know thy tribulation and thy poverty — but thou art rich! — and the blasphemy from those claiming themselves to be Jews and are not but** (are) **a synagogue of Satan.** The Lord "knows." That alone is comfort for those who are facing martyrdom. On θλῖψις, "pressure," "affliction," see 1:9; here there is a reference to all the tribulation which the members were enduring for the sake of their faith. "And thy poverty" is placed between "tribulation" and Jewish "blasphemy" and thus does not imply that all the members belonged to the poorer class, but that their poverty in earthly possessions was due to persecution. Work and patronage in business may have been withheld from the Christians; again, mobs may have looted their homes, shops, and bazaars. We take it that all this does not apply to the ἄγγελος alone, either as the main elder or as the eldership, but to the entire church, the elders being in the forefront.

"But thou art rich" is inserted parenthetically; spiritual riches are referred to (cf., 3:18; Matt. 6:20; Luke 12:21; I Cor. 1:5; II Cor. 6:10).

The cause of the suffering is "the blasphemy from (ἐκ, source) those claiming themselves to be Jews and are not but (are) a synagogue of Satan." These are, indeed, Jews; ἑαυτούς means that they on their own part claimed to be Jews over against Gentiles and pagans. "And are not" is the Lord's verdict. It is like the other, "but thou art rich." By birth and by religion they were outwardly Jews but not inwardly. In Rom. 2:29 Paul makes this same distinction. We need not try to reproduce their "blasphemy." This strong term means vicious vilification of the Messiah and of the Christians who worshipped him, all manner of denunciations, slanders, etc. The Acts furnish us examples of how the Jews incited Gentile mobs and lodged accusations against the Christians with the Gentile magistrates.

The Lord calls these Jews "a synagogue of Satan." "Synagogue" is the right word. This does not refer to a building but to those who assembled and concocted their blasphemies and planned their assaults there. They were doing Satan's work; "a synagogue of Satan" is the Lord's verdict upon them. The word *ἐκκλησία* (really an "assembly" called together) had been used as a designation for the "church" (v. 1 and 8) and is never used in a base sense as "synagogue" is here used. Satan stirs up persecution; the Jews of Smyrna were his willing tools; the pagan authorities were incited and worked up by them.

It may well be possible that Polycarp was at the head of the church in Smyrna at this time. He suffered martyrdom February 23, 155, but at that time had been a Christian already for eighty-six years, probably having been baptized in the year 69. Like his friend Papias, he was a pupil of John's. See what is known of his life in Meusel, *Kirchliches Handlexikon.* His tomb is shown on the acropolis back of Smyrna.

10) The Lord has no word of censure for the church at Smyrna. This is one of the churches with which the Lord is entirely pleased; that at Philadelphia is another but of a different kind. **Be not fearing the things thou art about to suffer! Lo, the devil is about to throw some of you** (partitive *ἐκ*) **into prison in order that you may be tried. And you shall have tribulation during ten days. Keep on being faithful until death, and I will give to thee the crown of the life!** Perhaps we should read *μηδέν* instead of just *μή*: "Nothing be fearing in regard to the things thou

art about to suffer!" Then the relative clause would be in apposition to "nothing" or merely adverbial.

The Lord is fortifying the church for what is yet to come. Everything is in the hands of "the First and the Last" who therefore says, "Never be afraid!" He was dead and became alive; he can carry us through death to life and promises to do so. It is easy to write this in my study, it is a different matter when prison and death are at the door.

The Lord states what the near future will bring. "Lo, the devil will throw some of you into prison!" The Jews will succeed in stirring up the pagan authorities to arrest some of the Christians for alleged crimes. This was easily accomplished. Criminal practices were frequently charged against Christians during all the periods of persecution. Some historical novels try to reproduce such accusations. The poor victims were not only imprisoned in dungeons but were often examined under frightful scourgings and torture.

"In order that you may be tried" does not mean to be tried in the pagan court; for this thought lies in the imprisonment: every prisoner had to face trial. This refers to trial of faith. Although the devil is the real instigator of the arrest as he is of the blasphemy in the accusations, it is the Lord's purpose that those who are arrested be tried by suffering for his name's sake. The verb here means "to try" and not "to tempt." The agent in the passive is the Lord; the aorist is effective: be completely tried. Moreover, now we have the plural and "some of you" whereas a moment ago we had "thou art about to suffer." We thus see that these letters are intended for the "angel" and his entire church just as each letter is also intended for all the churches.

"And thou shalt have tribulation (the same word that was used in v. 9) during ten days," genitive of the time within; the accusative would mean extent of time: all along for ten days. Severe tribulations shall flare up now and again *during* these ten days. In what sense is "ten" used? Some have thought of ten actual days; more, of ten as denoting a short, determined, fixed, limited time. Some let ten days = ten years under Domitian and Decius. The argument that this is not a vision and that therefore ten must be taken literally would apply also to "days" over against years. Yet in these letters the Lord himself uses symbolical expressions; the seven stars and the seven pedestal lamps in which also the number seven is symbolical. So we take "during ten days" to mean "during a complete period," one that is long enough for the complete trial according to the Lord's purpose. "Ten" is here not multiplied by itself, and for this reason this period is not one of great duration. The actual duration is *not* revealed by this "ten." Polycarp suffered martyrdom in 155, which was sixty years after 95, the date of Revelation. The ten days, we think, included also his martyrdom. Whether we prefer the reading with the future indicative ἕξετε or the one with the present subjunctive ἔχητε (which is also governed by ἵνα) makes little difference since the subjunctive, too, has a future meaning.

The call to keep on being faithful unto death is fortified by the great promise that the Lord, who himself was dead and lived, will give to the faithful one the crown of the life. Δώσω has the same force it had in v. 7, as does also ἡ ζωή. We cannot restrict this call and this promise to the angel of the church just because they are worded in the singular. We do not even restrict them to the future martyrs who will be put to death by the magistrates. A martyr's bloody death is not the only evidence of "being faithful to death." John himself did not die as a martyr. The Lord wants only a limited number of martyrs, but he wants all of us to be faithful unto death in whatever measure of tribulation he allots to us in order to try us. Matt. 24:13.

Trench makes a pronounced distinction between στέφανος, the German *Kranz,* and διάδημα, *Krone* (12:3; 13:1; 19:12), the former being the Latin *corona,* the latter *diadema.* The former was the wreath bestowed in civic games, for civic worth, for military valor, for nuptial joy, and for festal gladness; it was plaited of oak, ivy, parsley, myrtle, or olive, or an imitation of these or other leaves in gold, sometimes of flowers, violets or roses. Trench claims that στέφανος is never the emblem of royalty, that this was exclusively the "diadem." But the diadem was not a crown made of metal and jewels such as we now attribute to kings but only a narrow fillet that was bound about the brow, so that a number of them could be worn at the same time. Orientals wore a blue ribbon, ornamented in white, in their turban. Trench's view is substantially correct, but in Matt. 27:29 and the parallels the *stephanos* is used as a mark of royalty ("*King* of the Jews"), to which Trench scarcely does justice. This is true also regarding II Sam. 12:30; I Chron. 20:2; Ps. 21:3; Ezek. 21:26. In the New Testament the Christians are pictured not only as victors but also as reigning with Christ. While thus στέφανος often means "chaplet," as Trench has it, the word may also mean a "crown" that is worn by a king. This is the more the case in the New Testament where the King and the Victor is one. Note Thayer.

In our passage we need not insist on royalty, victory is enough. "The crown of the life" has the epexegetical or appositional genitive: the life = the crown. This is the life of glory in heaven which is symbolized by a glorious crown.

11) **The one having an ear, etc.** See v. 7. **The one conquering** (see v. 7) **shall in no way receive damage from the second death.** The passive is to

be taken in the sense of "to be hurt," and ἐκ states from what source the hurt cannot come. The second death (20:6, 14; 21:8) is defined in 21:8; it is eternal damnation in the lake that burns with fire and brimstone. The crown of the life and the hurt caused by the second death are opposites. To shrink from physical death under persecution is to plunge into the second death. To save the physical life under persecution is to forfeit the eternal crown of the life.

Smyrna is a sample of *the church that is passing through actual martyrdom.* Smyrna was not the first to have this experience. The church in Jerusalem had its first martyr Stephen (Acts 7) and its other notable martyr, John's own brother James (Acts 12:2) and also the other James who was not an apostle, in the year 66 (probable date.) The first congregation at Rome had many martyrs when, in the year 64, these Christians were accused by Nero of burning Rome, the crime of which he was being accused by the populace, which he, therefore, shifted to these Christians. During the ten great persecutions of post-Apostolic days the number of the martyr churches was greatly increased; this has continued down to our own day.

The Letter to Pergamum, verses 12-17

12) **And to the angel, etc.** See v. 1.

13) **These things declares the One having the great sword, the two-edged, the sharp one: I know where thou art dwelling,** (even) **where the throne of Satan is. And thou art holding fast my name and didst not deny my faith even in the days of Antipas, he my witness who was killed at your side where Satan is dwelling.** "These things declares" introduces also this third letter. Here the Lord designates himself as "the One having the great sword," etc., that was seen by John in 1:16, but now the two adjectives

are added by means of articles which makes these adjectives appositions (R. 776) and most emphatic. This "great sword" (see 1:16) with its two edges (mouths) and its sharpness is the symbol of omnipotent power which will (in the imagery of the Greek "two-mouthed") devour the Lord's enemies when it descends in judgment.

Here is the "Stronger One" of Luke 11:22, against whom "the strong one" (Satan) cannot prevail. This great sword is, of course, ready to smite the archfiend and his cohorts but it will make war also against the unfaithful (v. 16). This sword is to inspire courage in the hearts of the faithful confessors and to dispel all fear while at the same time it is to inspire fear and bring to repentance all who are unfaithful and have begun to deny when they should confess. So many see only the loving, compassionate Christ and forget that he is also the Christ "having the great sword, the double-edged, the sharp one."

Once more, "I know" (see v. 2). Here the Lord knows "where thou art dwelling," namely, "where the throne of Satan is," and in the last clause, "where Satan is dwelling." Both statements refer to the pagan city Pergamum as being a citadel of Satan himself where he had established himself as a king on his throne in supposedly permanent residence. What this means for the church in Pergamum the Lord knows and takes into account.

This city was a legal center for the district and at the same time an old stronghold of emperor worship, where already in 29 B. C. a temple had been built to the divine Augustus and the goddess Roma, which was served by a powerful priesthood. Especially abhorrent to the Christians was the local cult of Aesculapius whose symbol was the serpent, which was called "the god of Pergamum" but to Christians was the symbol of the serpent of Eden. In addition to these pagan cults there towered on the Acropolis a throne-like altar of Zeus Soter (Savior) which commemorated the defeat of the barbarian Gauls by Attalus about 240 B. C., which was decorated with a famous frieze of the gods warring against the giants whose human bodies had serpentine tails. Built under Eumenes II about 180 B. C. and dedicated to Zeus and Athena Nicephoror, and rediscovered in 1878, this great altar was more an imposing monument than a place of worship. See Zahn, *Introduction,* III, 420, etc.

Commentators debate as to which of these features is referred to by "the throne of Satan." Zahn takes it to refer to the cult of Aesculapius. He points out that under Diocletian Christian stonecutters from Rome carved out in the quarries of Pannonia not only pillars, capitals, and baths, but also victories, cupids, and even the sun-god in his chariot but refused to carve an image of Aesculapius, for which refusal they were put to death as being followers of Antipas of Pergamum. So much at least is certain that the Lord himself (not John as some say) regarded Pergamum as the one city among the seven where Satan even had his throne and thus ruled as king. All seven were thoroughly pagan, this one was the worst.

Καί adds only the further fact which the Lord knows although we might translate "and yet." In this capital of Satan "thou art holding fast my name," my ὄνομα. A study of the word shows that "my name" = my revelation by which I made myself known to you, by which you have apprehended me and now confess me. Various unsatisfactory explanations of ὄνομα are found in the commentaries. One great evidence of this holding fast is added: "and didst not deny my faith even in the days of Antipas, he my witness who was killed at your side (παρ' ὑμῖν, plural), etc." The aorist is historical. No information about these days and about this notable martyr of Pergamum has come down to us. That he was the bishop of the church and was burned alive in a heated metal image of a bull during the days of Domitian is a legend that appeared in the tenth century. The views that he was really Timothy or the confessor Athanasius of Alexandria disregard the name "Antipas." There is no reason to assume that this name is symbolical, for "Antipas" is only the shorter form of "Antipatros"; here the name is regarded as indeclinable, and the form is not an error for Ἀντίπα (R. 255).

"My faith," with the enclitic μου, can scarcely mean "the faith in me," "my" being the objective genitive. C.-K. 890 fails in explaining this genitive because Koegel regards πίστις as subjective in every New Testament passage, *fides qua creditur*. Here and in many other instances "faith" is objective, *fides quae creditur*. The church did not deny the doctrine of Christ. The ὄνομα and the πίστις are in substance the same, even as we say to deny the name and to deny the faith. The days of Antipas which reached their climax when he was killed must have tried the entire church; all stood firm, none denied the gospel of Christ. The Lord acknowledges this glorious fact.

The grammars point out the fact that ὁ μάρτυς is irregular, a nominative apposition which should be a genitive after the genitive "of Antipas." "My witness" is a nominative that is attracted to the nominative ὅς: "he my witness who was killed." Παρ' ὑμῖν is not "among you" (R. 614) but "at your side." Note that, as in v. 10, we now have the plural, which shows that these letters were intended for each church in its entirety and not merely for the ἄγγελος or bishop. That martyrdom is the result "where Satan is dwelling" is to be expected.

14) Now the censure as in v. 4: **Nevertheless, I have against thee a few things, that thou hast there such as are holding fast the teaching of Balaam who**

taught to Balak to throw a trap before the sons of Israel, to eat things sacrificed to idols and to commit fornication. Thus hast thou also such as are holding fast the teaching of Nicolaitans in a similar manner. "A few things" does not say that these were not of a grave nature but that they were few, namely a few cases of church members who held to the teaching of Balaam and thus to that of the Nicolaitans. Ὅτι is not causal but epexegetical with ὀλίγα. The two κρατοῦντας are without articles: "such as hold fast."

We find the story of Balaam in Num. 22 to 24, his death in 31:8 and Josh. 13:22. The Lord refers to what Balaam did according to Num. 31:16: he gave cunning counsel to Balak to entice Israel after all attempts to put a curse on Israel had failed. The διδαχή of Balaam refers to his "doctrine," his evil principle, namely to secure personal advancement and money by ungodly means, a "doctrine" that finally brought him a violent death. This word is emphasized; we have it repeated in "the doctrine" of the Nicolaitans and in the verb "he taught" Balak. The dative "to Balak" is exceptional, for otherwise, as also in v. 20, "to teach" is construed with the accusative of the person (R. 482).

A σκάνδαλον is the crooked stick to which the bait is affixed in a trap and by which the trap is sprung. "Stumblingblock" in our versions is unsatisfactory; the Greek has a different word to express this idea; in Rom. 9:33 both words occur. The difference is material. One may stumble even to the extent of falling without being killed, but when one is caught in a deathtrap one is always killed.

Balaam induced Balak to set a deathtrap for the sons of Israel. The epexegetical infinitive explains this: "to eat things sacrificed to idols (εἰδωλόθυτα) and to commit fornication." Balaam's counsel (Num. 31:16) to Balak was to induce Israel to commit these sins, which Balak did (Num. 25:1-5) with frightful success. Now, the Lord says, the church in Pergamum has some members that are holding to the same teaching and are running to the idol feasts and the fornication practiced in the pagan temples in order to gain immunity and pagan favor for themselves.

The two aorist infinitives express actuality. This eating and this fornicating also go together. It was so in the case of the sons of Israel; it is so in the case of these members in Pergamum who were repeating Israel's folly. We see no reason for taking "to commit fornication" in a figurative sense. In these idolatrous centers it was always a great temptation to yield to the old ways, to listen to pagan neighbors and friends, and with them to go to the great idol feasts and celebrations, there to eat in honor of the idol and to embrace the temple prostitutes and thus to obtain pagan approval. Paul fought against these temptations during his time. These indulgences were, however, also supported by apologists who argued that they were perfectly allowable to Christians, yea were evidence of their maturity and their strength. It was claimed that what the flesh and the body did was immaterial and did not effect the spirit, or that giving rein to the flesh was the way in which to master the flesh. The old heresies were thus full of immoralities. As far as Balaam is concerned, it is important to note that the present reference to him is only the last of a long series in Scripture, which shows why his story is told at such length in Numbers; see how he appears in Deut. 23:4; Josh. 13:22; 24:9, 10; Micah 6:4; II Pet. 2:15; Jude 11; and here. In various ways Balaam is a strong Scriptural warning.

15) "Thus hast thou also such as hold fast the doctrine of Nicolaitans in a similar way." Both "thus" and the adverb "in a similar way" or "similarly" state that the members in Pergamum who "hold fast the doctrine of the Nicolaitans" are those referred to in v. 14

by "such as hold fast the doctrines of Balaam." The opinion that in v. 14, 15 we have *two* sets of evil members in Pergamum overlooks these adverbs. In v. 6 we have "the works of the Nicolaitans," now "the doctrine of Nicolaitans." There is no article, hence this means such as belonged to this sect. By their doctrine they sought to justify their works. What is to be said in regard to "Nicolaitans" is offered in connection with v. 6.

16) **Repent, therefore!** See the same command in v. 5. Who is to repent? While the command is in the singular, the whole church is involved. Rightly so, for the guilt of tolerating errorists attaches not merely to the elder or the elders, but in varying degrees to the entire membership. This applies also to a larger church body. This does not in any way relieve the leadership; its guilt will always remain in its full intensity.

But if not, I am coming for thee quickly — the same warning threat as in v. 5 — **and will do battle with them with the great sword of my mouth,** the same ῥομφαία that was mentioned in v. 13 and in 1:16. Μετά refers to those who are enemies, ἐν to the terrible sword that shall strike them; we render both "with." I am coming "for thee" (not "to thee") means that judgment shall strike the leadership and the entire congregation; "will battle with them" means that the mighty One of 1:13-16 will smite these adherents of the Nicolaitans with the devastating power of the Word. "Quickly" is added because the Lord will not wait long. "I am coming" (v. 5) recalls "the One Coming" of 1:8. As in v. 5, this refers to a preliminary judgment and not merely to the final one. Remarks to the effect that by tolerating heretical members a church only helps to bring them into greater judgment fail to state that the Lord will also judge a church that is guilty of such weak tolerance: "I am coming *for thee*" and not only to do battle *with them.*

17) **The one having an ear, etc.,** = v. 7. **To the one conquering, I will give to him of the manna, the one that has been hidden, and I will give to him a white pebble, and upon the pebble a new name written which no one knows save the one receiving it.** This is the promise. In regard to τῷ νικῶντι δώσω αὐτῷ, see v. 7; also v. 11, Ὁ νικῶν, κτλ. "I will give" is the voice of the Lord's heavenly grace. "Of the manna" is plainly a partitive genitive; "a stone" is the accusative after the same verb δώσω. The difference in the cases is perfectly correct (R. 441).

We agree with Trench, *Epistles to the Seven Churches*: "There can, I think, be no doubt that allusion is here made to the manna which, at God's express command, Moses caused to be laid up before the Lord in the Sanctuary, Exod. 16:32-34; cf., Heb. 9:4. This manna, as being thus laid up, obtained the name 'hidden.' . . . This 'hidden manna' . . . represents a benefit pertaining to the future kingdom of glory." It is the counterpart of "the wood of the life" in v. 7, which bears its wonderful fruit (22:2). All the statements regarding the heavenly joys are given in figurative language, and one of them is our eating and drinking there — note the feast in Matt. 8:11. The symbolism of the hidden manna is most appropriate here after the eating of things offered to idols in v. 14. In John 6:30, etc., Jesus calls himself (his flesh and blood, i. e., himself as sacrificed for us) the manna, "bread from heaven," to be eaten by faith. The fact that in John 6:49, etc., Jesus is "the living bread," while in Revelation "the hidden manna" indicates the heavenly bliss, causes no difficulty. Trench rightly says, "the best commentary is to be found in I Cor. 2:9; I John 3:2."

Many inadequate interpretations are offered. A curious one is that this is a reference to the Lord's

Supper. Another is that "having been hidden" refers to the disappearance of the Ark of the Covenant since the destruction of the Temple, the manna thus being now hidden. In such passages as II Macc. 2:4, etc., the Apocalypse of Baruch 6:5-10; 29:8, it is stated that before the destruction of Jerusalem the Prophet Jeremiah took the Ark of the Covenant with its sacred contents and also the altar of sacrifice and hid them in a cave and closed the cave, so that when some who went along hurried back to mark the place they could not find it. "The hidden manna" is not a reference to II Macc. or to the Apocalypse of Baruch with its remark, "The treasury of manna will again descend from on high."

By repeating "I will give," the grace of the giving is emphasized and the second gift is made to stand out as being distinct from the first. Ψῆφος = pebble; the adjective "white" may well imply that a diamond is referred to. "A new name having been written" on this stone, ὄνομα καινόν, means a name "new" as replacing one that is old, the perfect participle indicating that, once written, this name remains. The remarkable thing is that no one knows this name save the person who receives the pebble. We think that those are correct who take this name to be the name for the person who receives the pebble and not a secret name of God or of Christ.

The most varied interpretations are offered. Reference is made to the Talmud which states that together with the manna precious stones and pearls fell from heaven and were picked up by the Israelites in the desert. But the Lord says that each person receives only one pebble, and that this one is inscribed with a name that is known only to him. Some think of this stone as being a ticket of admission to the feast of manna; others of a pebble that is cast in an election, or cast for acquittal by a court of judges; but this passage does not use the plural which might remind the reader of an assembly or of a court that is made up of a number of judges with each one voting. Some think of the victorious athletes in the Greek games who thus receive certification that admits them to a feast or entitles them to triumphal entrance into their home town. Others think that this stone is an amulet which was inscribed with a powerful, secret, magical name that enabled the bearer to pass through closed gates, to foil evil spirits, to enter the presence of deity.

Trench is right regarding this point, but not when he seconds a connection of this white stone and its inscription with the Old Testament Urim and Thummim and thinks of an inscription that contained the Tetragrammaton and that the new name on the white stone = the one mentioned in 3:12. This view introduces the supposition of the priesthood of believers in heaven. The Urim and the Thummim are just as unknown to us as is this white and inscribed stone in Revelation. On the former see Smith, *Bible Dictionary,* regarding what is really known and for a review of the theories. Hengstenberg, *Die Buecher Moses und Aegypten,* 154, etc., traces the Urim and Thummim back to Egypt although with the vital difference that the Egyptian priests operated with an abstraction of "truth" while the Jewish high priest had the guidance of God as long as the Urim and Thummim existed. This view is answered by Ed. Koenig, *Hebraeisches und Aramaeisches Woerterbuch,* 546, as *eine Sache von fraglichem Werte.* He also removes any connection with the Babylonian *Schicksalstafeln,* etc.

The simple fact is that, while the symbolism of "the hidden manna" is reasonably clear, that of the white inscribed stone, etc., is not. All we are able to gather with safety is that the whiteness points to holiness (as in 1:14) and that Isa. 62:2 promises, "Thou shalt be called by a new name, which the mouth of the Lord shall name"; see also 65:15, "Shall call his servants by another name." Rev. 3:12, "I will write upon him the name of my God and the name of the city of my God," etc. On no one's knowing this name save its bearer compare 19:12.

We may second Kretzmann: "There the believers shall also receive a fine, white precious stone, which is a testimony of the Holy Ghost to their faith." We venture to add that to the Lord's gift of sweet refreshment in the manna he will add the gift of highest honor in this holy white stone with the inscribed new name, the full blessedness of which he alone knows who receives this name. Jesus did some blessed renaming already here on earth: "Thou shalt be called Cephas," John 1:42.

One has well said that the scientific thing to do whenever we do not know is to say so. That applies to the interpretation of many Scripture passages but surely most often to passages in Revelation. Concerning heaven this confession of ignorance is the more in place, for all its realities are beyond our conception. When I receive my stone from the Lord I shall know all about its meaning.

Pergamum stands for the *churches into which the spirit of Balaam has made inroads,* the spirit which is out for worldly advantage and does not balk at idolatrous compromises and the doctrine that justifies such compromise. It is one of the churches that are inwardly *divided,* perhaps a martyr like Antipas and other true members being on the one side but tolerating members who have become Nicolaitans.

The Letter to Thyatira, verses 18-29

18) **And to the angel,** etc. See v. 1. **These things declares the Son of God, the One having his**

eyes as a flame of fire and his feet like gold-bronze. Thyatira was the home of Lydia, the seller (merchant) of purple in Philippi (see Acts 16:14). There is no reason to assume that she founded the church in Thyatira; we may rather take it that, like other churches in this territory, this one, too, was founded by some of Paul's assistants or by missionaries who came there somewhat later. Although the church addressed is found in a locality that was of smaller size than the other cities, this letter is the longest of the seven.

Here the Lord calls himself "the Son of God." "The Son of God" has no reference to "the similar terminology of the imperial cultus," for this cultus was far more prominent in Pergamum (see v. 13) than in Thyatira. "The Son of God" is here used in view of v. 26, 27 and its allusion to Ps. 2. The apposition, "the One having his eyes," etc., is repeated from 1:14, 15. None other has eyes (and also feet) like this One. While we accept the accusative reading φλόγα, the nominative variant φλόξ would be equally in order, just as καὶ οἱ πόδες, κτλ., is a nominative.

The flaming eyes penetrate into all the deceptions of the false prophetess of Thyatira, and the feet that are similar to gold-bronze (in 1:15, "as in a furnace, this having been fired") crush and burn to ashes all such opposition.

19) Once more the Lord says: Οἶδα (see v. 2). **I know thy works and thy love and thy faith and thy service and thy endurance and thy works, the last more than the first,** i. e., more in number as time goes on. The pronoun "thy" makes a division; first, "thy works," namely all the good evidence of deeds; next, "the love, the faith, the service, the endurance," a second "thy" with these four; finally, a third "thy" with the increase of the works.

The works denote the whole conduct. Love is placed next because all true works are the product and the evidence of the ἀγάπη, the love of true understanding coupled with corresponding purpose (see v. 4). This love is itself the product of faith. Hence this is placed next. The works as evidence of love are equally evidence of faith. Διακονία = service but that of a διάκονος, voluntary service for the benefit and the help of those needing it and freely rendered. At the wedding of Cana we find *diakonoi,* because they served freely. Mary who managed things found it necessary to tell them to do what Jesus would say lest they follow their own free ideas and think it foolish to do what this guest might say. *Douloi* are slaves whose sole business it is to obey. Διακονία is the service we render to our brethren; God needs no helpful service for himself. He accepts our obedience as his δοῦλοι who have no will save his will. Some think of eleemosynary work among the poor and needy, but we may include every kind of helpfulness. On "endurance" see 1:9 and 2:2; this means bravely to hold out under affliction that comes from adverse things.

Unlike Ephesus, Thyatira had not grown slack in love. Love had remained active and diligent so that the last works were not, indeed, better but more numerous than the first. The Lord here bestows high praise and full credit for all that he with his all-seeing eyes beheld in the church of Thyatira.

20) **Nevertheless, I have against thee that thou art letting the woman Jezebel go, the one claiming herself a prophetess; and she teaches and seduces my own slaves to commit fornication and to eat things offered to idols.** How can a church that has so much to its credit be guilty of what is here charged? One answer is that, while this church was active in works, it was not bound completely to the Word. It had many works; it is not praised for its faithfulness to the Word. In regard to this fault Thyatira has had many sisters. She is like Pergamum in this respect

but exceeds the latter; for Thyatira has permitted a vicious prophetess in her midst, while in Pergamum the Balaam-like Nicolaitan doctrine that came from without had affected a few members.

On the present indicative ἀφεῖς see R. 315: *dass du gewaehren laessest*, "that thou doest let the woman Jezebel have her way." We prefer the reading τὴν γυναῖκα, "the woman" without σου, which would make her "thy wife." The addition of "thy" which makes her the wife of the bishop of this church is poorly attested textually; it is also incredible that the bishop's own wife should have undermined his work in such a vicious way. Zahn thinks that the good man who was the bishop was not aware of his wife's doings. But this seems to be unlikely. The Lord is here not making a shocking revelation to a blind husband.

Another assumption is that this woman was the sibyl of the Chaldean sanctuary which stood outside of the walls of the city and is supposed to have existed already at this time. The woman of this letter cannot be such a sibyl, she is a pretending prophetess who operates right in the Christian Church as one of its members.

Some have assumed that her name was actually Jezebel. But this name is symbolical. What Jezebel, the wife of King Ahab, was for the northern kingdom of Israel that this woman was in the church at Thyatira.

The participial addition, "the one claiming herself a prophetess," is left in the nominative much as the apposition in v. 13 is a nominative, because this claim refers to what follows, namely her teaching, and not to what precedes. The ancient Jezebel did not claim to be a prophetess, she was a queen and used her power as a queen; this other woman operated as a pretending prophetess by teaching. This nominative is not a solecism; there is adequate reason for the case, the reason lying even on the surface. Nor should the word "prophetess" be understood in too high a sense. This woman was not more than a teacher. Even as a teacher she did not speak publicly in the church; she gathered a private following, a clique in her own house, and neither the elders nor the congregation took proper measures against her.

In v. 13 a relative clause follows the nominative; here a finite verb. With her false claim "she teaches and seduces my own slaves," δοῦλοι as in 1:1, and the possessive adjective is stronger than the pronoun "my"; "my own slaves" who as such ought to obey my voice alone and flee from such a false and lying voice, especially that of an evil woman. Her teaching was to the same effect as that of the adherents of the Nicolaitans mentioned in v. 14: that it was quite in order "to commit fornication and to eat meats sacrificed to idols" (see v. 14), but now the infinitives occur in reversed order, which is a minor matter as far as we are able to see. The gravity of the situation in Thyatira appears from this woman's leadership. She surrounded herself with the halo of a prophetess and secured much more of a following than the few persons who went wrong in Pergamum. We think of the success of Mrs. Mary Baker Eddy whose sect still persists.

21) The gravity is still more serious: **And I gave to her time to repent, and she does not want to repent from her fornication.** The ἵνα clause is used like an infinitive with an aorist to express actual repentance like the aorist in "does not want to repent." Many think that the Lord sent this woman some special warning which called her to repent, and they even figure out in what way he did this. But all that is said is that the Lord gave her time. The Word was preached in the congregation with its strong call to repent. But despite the Lord's patient extension of time this woman does not will to repent. We take the

phrase "from her fornication" in a comprehensive sense as including all her teaching and all the corresponding deeds.

22) The time of grace lasts for a long time, but when it ends, judgment follows. **Lo, I will throw her into a bed and those committing adultery together with her for great tribulation unless they repent from her works.** Even in judgment there is grace, but it is the last opportunity for repentance. Read the whole sentence as one thought. The sense is not that the woman shall be thrown into a bed, and that those who followed her shall be thrown into great tribulation, but that both she and they shall be thrown into a bed, and that this bed shall be a great tribulation for her and for them. The view that hers shall be a bed of sickness instead of a bed of sinful pleasure is not in harmony with the text. The view that sickness and the death of her children are punishments for licentiousness is not contained in these words. It is going too far to make "a bed" signify hell. Both the woman and her fellow adulterers shall be thrown "into a bed . . . for great tribulation," this preliminary judgment is the final call to repentance. "*Into* a bed . . . *for* great tribulation" is clear; while "*into* a bed" referring to the woman alone and "*into* great tribulation" referring to her following is not at all clear.

The texts vary between the aorist subjunctive and the future indicative after ἐάν; we may have either, R. 1010. "From *her* works" has better textual support than "from *their* works." Since she was the instigator, the works were hers. "From her works" with its plural only spreads out "from her fornication" (v. 21) with its singular. Between fornication and adultery, physical, spiritual, and, in this letter, both, there is only verbal difference.

23) **And her children I will kill in death.** Why death for her children? There is no answer if these

are taken to be the woman's physical children, whether they were born in wedlock or of her fornication. Whether she was married or single or had children is beside the question. Nor can "her children" refer to "those committing adultery with her," for the latter have already been dealt with in v. 22. These "children" are the second generation, the young "Jezebel brood" that may propagate her vileness after judgment has brought the older generation either to repentance or to its doom. A third generation shall not even begin in Thyatira. Whether these are children of heretics or not is immaterial — they are hers if they follow her works.

And all the churches shall realize that I am the One searching reins and hearts; and I will give to you, each one, according to your works. Γινώσκω and not merely οἶδα. What the Lord will do will go home to all the churches. They have heard from the Old Testament (Ps. 7:9; 26:2; Jer. 11:20; 17:10; and other passages) that the Lord tries, tests out reins and hearts. The verb is ἐρευνάω, "search," examine closely, as in John 5:39. "Reins (kidneys) and hearts," the reins by metonymy denoting the inmost stirrings (Ed. Koenig on the Hebrew *kilyah*) and the hearts indicating the seat of the thoughts and the will (the Hebrew and the Greek conception). Nothing that transpires in the soul is hidden from "the One having his eyes as a flame of fire" (v. 18). This fact must ever be a terror to all who are false. It is most necessary also for all the churches to realize from some plain example that they are under the eyes of the all-seeing Lord.

This is the same δώσω that is found in v. 26 and in the other letters to express the gracious gift and reward to the victors, but here it is general and includes the wicked as well and restates Ps. 62:12 as well as Matt. 16:27, and other New Testament utterances.

"To you" is personal, and the individualizing apposition "everyone" is even more so. All the judgments of the Lord accord with "your works" in the sense of public evidence as does also the last judgment, Matt. 25:34-46; but these works shall be seen and exposed according to their true inwardness and not as men may regard their superficial outward appearance.

24) **But to you I say, the rest in Thyatira as many as have not this doctrine, such as did not get to know the deep things of Satan as they call** (them): **I do not throw on you another burden. But what you have hold fast until I come!** "To you, the rest in Thyatira," are the faithful ones, "as many as have not this doctrine" taught by Jezebel, "such as (qualitative) have not known (aorist to express the simple past fact) or did not get to know (ingressive aorist) the deep things of Satan as they call them." The verb refers to experimental knowing; in this way one knows or realizes who practices a doctrine.

The debate centers on ὡς λέγουσιν. It is asked whether the heretics or the Christians are the subjects and speak of "the deep things (profundities) of Satan." Some think that the expression is ironical, that, while these Gnostic heretics called them "the deep things of *God*," the Lord here substitutes what these things really were, namely "the deep things *of Satan*." It is argued on the evidence of history that no Gnostic claim is found elsewhere that purports knowing "the deep things of Satan."

We take the words just as they read. The adherents of this woman spoke of "the deep things of Satan" and said that one must know them, realize what they are (γινώσκω) by experience and experiment. This justified their fornication, adultery, and eating at idol feasts. They looked down upon the innocent Christians who refused to experiment and refrained from these things. These superior heretics claimed that they killed the flesh by indulging the flesh, claimed to plunge into filth to prove that it could not harm them, that the innocent Christians were only weak and afraid when they refused to do the same.

This sort of teaching and experiment is advocated to this day. To know the world one must plunge into the world. To prove that one is immune one must make the test and subject oneself to infection. To probe the depths of Satan one must go down into these depths. What does one know about them if one does not do these things? Only in this way can one become strong and superior! The folly and the fallacy of such reasoning are obvious. To realize what fornication is I do not need to commit fornication; to know what murder is I do not need to kill a man. The same is true with regard to all "the depths of Satan."

Again, to touch pitch is to defile oneself, as the Germans say. To give even a finger to Satan means that he will take one's arm and may do far more. Even the shallows of Satan, to say nothing about the depths, are deadly. The parenthetic ὡς λέγουσιν plainly means, "as they call them," namely the heretics in Thyatira.

The Lord says to the faithful church members, "I do not throw on you another burden." What is the burden they already bear; and what would another burden be? Some think that this woman, etc., constitutes the former, and that Acts 15:28 indicates the latter. Or that the judgment which the Lord will execute on this woman and on her adherents is the burden to which the Lord will add nothing more. We take it that v. 25 explains.

25) The one burden resting upon all faithful Christians is to hold fast (the aorist imperative is effective) what they have and to do this until the Lord comes. To overcome Satan it is not necessary to sound the deep things of Satan. What we have is the Lord's Word and we hold it fast in true faith and obedience.

We need no further *gnosis*, either a Gnostic or another kind. What we have is mighty to save us. To hold it fast against all wrong doctrine and all dangerous practice is our sole burden. The word "burden" has no reference to Acts 15:28; the Lord uses it here because heretical opposition is always felt as a weight or burden that necessitates more strength in order to hold fast what we have. We do not regard λέγουσιν (R. 866) as gnomic, nor does ἔγνωσαν (also R. 866) have a present force. The addition of ἄν to ἄχρι οὗ makes the clause refer to an indefinite time; ἥξω is the future indicative and need not be made an aorist subjunctive, for even ὅταν may have the future (B.-D. 383, 2; R. 975).

26) Now follows the great promise as is done in the other letters. **And the one conquering and the one keeping my works until the end, I will give to him authority over the nations; and he shall shepherd them with an iron rod as the ceramic vessels are shattered as also I myself have received from my Father. And I will give to him the morning star.** Here the conqueror (see v. 7) is designated as being also the keeper of the Lord's works until the end. This reference to the "works" is added because of v. 23, "according to your works." The two articles indicate two distinct designations but refer to the same person as in 1:8, 18, and elsewhere. To hold fast what we have is both to conquer and to keep the Lord's works to the end. One keeps the Lord's works when he does the works which are his and not Satan's works. The victory lies in these works; and these works proclaim the victory.

The idea of the anacoluthon is extended too far by R. when he so terms this nominative. Grammatically it is perfectly in order. It is not as absolute a nominative as the one found in John 7:38. One ought to see the reason for this nominative: it stands alone and apart from the construction for the sake of emphasis on its contents. It is resumed by αὐτῷ, the same pronoun that is found in v. 7 and 17, although these two follow datives.

The first gift which the Lord will bestow is expressed in language that is appropriated from Ps. 2:8, 9. Yahweh's King, to whom the nations are given as his Messianic inheritance, will give the conqueror "authority over the nations." The interpretation is to be sought in 3:21 and 20:4. One by one, as we reach the end here on earth, we shall pass into heaven and there sit with Christ on his throne and together with him exercise kingly rule and authority over the nations until his Parousia. Certainly, only as a gift from him. Matt. 19:28, and I Cor. 6:3 express the same thought. This promise surpasses our earthly comprehension. We are not expected to comprehend now while we are achieving the victory; we are asked to believe and in the strength of this promise to be victorious until the end comes for each one of us.

27) Αὐτούς, masculine, after the neuter τῶν ἐθνῶν is construed *ad sensum.* The Hebrew of Ps. 2:9 means "break them." The LXX used the verb ποιμαίνω, "to shepherd." The Lord properly retains the verb found in the LXX (it appears also in 12:5 and 19:15). Like κρίνειν, "to shepherd" gets its force from its object: "to judge" the godly means to take their part and to give them their rightful due; but "to judge" the wicked means to send them rightfully to their doom. Likewise, "to shepherd" God's people is to lead them on green pastures; but "to shepherd" the heathen, the godless nations, is to do the reverse, C.-K. 958. For the latter "an iron rod" is needed, for what is done is "as the ceramic vessels are shattered" ("broken to shivers," our versions), κεραμικός is derived from the verb "to mix" clay for making pottery. How many heathen nations have already been smashed with the iron rod of omnipotence! We may punctuate, "with an

iron rod as the earthen vessels are shattered," or, "with an iron rod; as," etc.

Ἐγώ is emphatic, "as also *I myself* have received from my Father." The perfect implies that Jesus still has what he has thus received. This clause refers directly to Ps. 2 and the appointment of Jesus as absolute King over the nations. The following visions reveal how he uses this power over the nations, namely as shown already in Ps. 2:1-5.

28) This letter records a second gift for the victor: "and I shall give to him the morning star." Many authorities wrestle with this "star"; hope of an adequate interpretation has even been given up completely as in the case of the "white stone" inscribed with a new name (v. 17). This, indeed, is true, we cannot comprehend these mighty gifts that are given to the victor when he attains heavenly triumph in death. Especially as regards our coming heavenly glory we now see only as in a glass, darkly; also the Lord is able to speak of this glory only in veiled, figurative, symbolical language. The realities are too great for present human thought and language.

We have, to aid us here, Matt. 13:43. "The righteous shall shine forth *as the sun* in the kingdom of their Father." This at least is similar. Dan. 12:3 is also similar, "as the *brightness* of the firmament . . . as *the stars* forever and ever." Isa. 14:12 also affords some help, "How art thou fallen from heaven, O Lucifer, *son of the morning!*" This does not mean that Lucifer *is* "the morning star," and that he is given to us in some way; but that before his fall he was "a son of the morning." I Cor. 15:40, etc., affords far less, for Paul speaks of the *glory* of the resurrection *body* which is not attained until the last day; his language is not symbolic. So II Pet. 1:19, "until *day dawns* and a *lightbearer* (φωσφόρος) *arises* in your hearts," bears only a slight resemblance to the gift of the morning star. All that we may say about these passages is that they lie along the same general line of thought.

We obtain much more by noting 22:16: "I am the Shoot and the Offspring of David, the Star, the Brilliant One, the Morning One," ὁ ἀστὴρ ὁ λαμπρὸς ὁ πρωϊνός. We do not regard this passage as being different, for both its similarity and its difference help us. Jesus is descended from David's *royal* line, and thus "the Star" is the King himself (this is one of his great "I AM" statements). "The Morning One," added after "the Brilliant One" (each with a separate article) elucidate each other. It is the morning star that shines with greatest brilliance. To our mind the self-designation used in 22:16, resembles "the First-born of all creation" (Col. 1:15), "the First-born from the dead" (Col. 1:18), "the First-born among many brethren" (Rom. 8:29), these many brethren being "the general assembly and church of the first-born," Heb. 12:23.

Jesus himself is the royal Star; as such he *gives* to every victor "the star" of royalty, "the morning one" (τὸ ἀστέρα τὸν πρωϊνόν, the article being repeated as in 22:16); by this gift he makes us like himself: "we shall be like him" (I John 3:2), eventually even as to our bodies (Phil. 3:21) in the resurrection at the time of his Parousia. All this agrees with Ps. 2, with the royalty of Jesus as the King supreme, and with this King's first gift to us in v. 26, 27, authority over the nations.

The symbolism of the morning star is that of royal splendor. It is extending the expression unduly when the idea of the morning is pressed to the point of meaning the morning of the consummation, even to the paling of our splendor in the brilliance of Jesus as the Sun that rises when the full morning comes. The adjective "of the morning" suggests unfading, glorious brilliance both for Jesus in 22:16, and here for us. The Victor King Jesus *is* the brilliant Morning Star in royal splendor; and he *gives* to every faithful believer the gift to be like him in royal splendor. He and all these other victors shall shine together, all being as morning stars in brilliance, our brilliance being derived from him.

In 1:16 (2:1) Jesus has the seven stars in his right hand, and these seven are angels of the seven churches. This is a different use of the symbol of the star yet it also connects them with Jesus.

A wrong view is the result when one leaves Ps. 2 and searches in ethnic sources for what the Lord here promises. This iron rod is far different from "the well-known flail wielded by Horus, the Egyptian god." "The star" is more than a bit of "Semitic folklore" that is connected with the idea of "immortality."

29) **The one having an ear, etc.,** is explained in v. 7. In the last four letters this command is placed at the end and thus divides the letters into groups of three and four; but just why they are so divided we are unable to say.

We may designate Thyatira as an example of a *badly infected* church, one that has a virulent cancerous growth. Its very leadership was slipping into vicious hands. In III John 9 there is reference to usurpation by a man (Diotrephes), here it is exercised by a woman. Pergamum shows that heresy, etc., was making inroads from without, Thyatira has heresy and heathen life boldly raising their head among the membership itself. Pergamum is bad; Thyatira is worse; Sardis is the worst.

CHAPTER III

The Letter to Sardis, verses 1-6

1) **And to the angel, etc.** See 2:1. **These things declares the One having the seven spirits of God and the seven stars: I know, etc.** Sardis is a plural in the Greek. On its history see the Bible dictionaries. Already in 1850 it was reported that its site was wholly desolate and deserted. In the Lord's letter there is nothing that has a bearing on the city as such. The church in Sardis is selected to be the recipient of a letter only because of its own condition. Neither pagan opposition nor heretical and libertinistic excesses threatened this church; it suffered from spiritual dry rot and deadness.

The designations here used for himself by the Lord pertain not to the warning threat against Sardis but to the awakening of new life in her deadness. To state that, because they do not match the threat, these designations are general, is to start from a wrong premise. The seven spirits are the Holy Spirit in his mission as we have seen in 1:4; all spiritual life is created by him. The Lord sends us his Holy Spirit even as he poured out the Spirit on Pentecost; thus the Lord is "the One having the seven spirits." The Spirit works life and the activity of life only by means of the Word, and this Word is committed officially to the ministry which is symbolized by the seven stars (1:16, 20; 2:1); hence the seven stars are added to the seven spirits because spiritual life is to be revived.

Since no heresy is involved as was the case in Ephesus (2:6), no mention is made of the Lord's right hand as is done in 2:1, with reference to Ephesus. In

Ephesus the first love has declined to a marked degree; this love is a manifestation of life and needs the effective preaching of the Word by the seven stars of the ministry, which is the reason for referring to the ministry in 2:1. These letters to Ephesus and to Sardis are apt to be misunderstood when this difference is overlooked.

I know thy works that thou hast a name that thou art living and (yet) **thou art dead.** Zahn, *Introduction,* III, 425, restates Bengel's idea that here ὄνομα refers to the bishop's proper name as connected with the word "life," i. e., that his name was Ζώσιμος or Ζωτικός, Zōsimus or Zōtikus, and that in spite of having so noble a name which designated him as living, he is dead and ought to have a name that accords with this fact. This view merits no serious consideration. The plea that ὄνομα is never used in the sense of a designation that is devoid of the corresponding reality is untenable (C.-K. 798); "name" (nor is the article needed) may be used thus in any language. The plea that in v. 1 ὄνομα must be used as it is in v. 4 and 5 is answered by the fact that in these latter verses the word is plainly employed in a different sense.

Still more. Paul may have a play on the meaning of the personal name "Onesimus" in his letter to Philemon; these seven letters of the Lord are too great for such a play. "Thou hast a name that thou art living" refers to the *church* at Sardis and not only to its bishop and its elders. The church had the name *Christian* church, but its Christian life was dying inwardly: "thou art dead," thou as a church. To what extent this entire church is dead v. 4 indicates, namely not in its entire membership, for a few persons were still fully alive spiritually.

2) **Be thou awake and make firm the rest of the things which were about to die; for I have not found thy works as having been filled full in the**

sight of God! Γίνου γρηγορῶν is the present periphrastic imperative. Ἀρυπνεῖν is to be wakeful when one might be sleeping; γρηγορεῖν is to be awake when one is aroused. The latter word is used here. The Lord is right now arousing the church. The present imperative demands that it continue in this wakefulness. "Be thou watchful" in our versions presents a different idea and makes us think of enemies. "Aroused" and thus "awake" here means wide awake to see the deplorable condition of the dying church. Drowsy, sleepy, sleeping eyes would see nothing and would let the dying go on until it would be too late to interfere.

Aroused and awake, "make firm the rest of the things (τὰ λοιπά) which were about to die," the imperfect: on the verge of dying in the past and to the present moment. The aorist infinitive "to die" means definitely to lose the last spark of life. "The rest of the things" (neuter) are not the laymen as contrasted with the clergy but all else that is not included in the aroused wakefulness of clergy as well as of laity. Sardis is like a leaking, sinking ship, in which captain and crew are sunk in dull lethargy. They must wake up to the situation and thus must take measures to save the ship. The figure of νεκρός (v. 1) is continued in ἀποθανεῖν. Hitherto everything in Sardis was about to go into complete death (aorist). Instead of burning brightly, the spiritual life activities were like coals that are becoming dimmer and dimmer. Many things were already mere ashes and dead coals. Presently the whole fire would be dead. The aorist imperative στήριξον means to take strong, immediate, effective measures. "To make decisively firm" all that is ready to die completely conveys the idea of establishing it with new life and vitality so that it may be able to shake off this creeping death and to stand solidly against its inroads.

The reason for the command is the fact that the Lord "has found thy works not filled full in the sight of God." The predicative participle does not mean that there were not enough works. This expression offers no support for the Romish doctrine that, unless we have so many works, we are not justified, which leaves us in uncertainty whether we have enough works and are, indeed, justified. The works themselves were empty. The people went to church and did many other things, but the faith, the love, and the spiritual life that should have filled all their works had been growing less and less.

Note the perfect tenses: all along and to the present the Lord "has found" the works thus — "I know thy works" (v. 1). All along and to the present the works "have not been filled full," have become more and more formal, empty, hollow. Some of these works may have appeared "wonderful" enough to the Sardians themselves, but "in the sight of God" they were the reverse; compare those mentioned in Matt. 7:22, 23.

Throughout these letters, as in all Scripture, the works are regarded as open, undeniable evidence. "In the sight of God" is forensic: God is the Judge who judges the evidence and on the basis of this evidence pronounces not only a verdict that is just, but one that is undeniably, incontrovertibly just, a verdict to which the whole universe must agree.

Persecution is dangerous — some turn apostate; heresy is worse — often many are deceived; worst of all is the dry rot from within — the whole church dying from within. Its membership may be large, its works may be great in number and in size, but the life is dying out or is already dead.

3) The remedy: **Keep remembering, therefore, how thou hast been receiving** (perfect: all along) **and didst hear** (aorist: in the past) **and con-**

tinue to keep and repent! (aorist imperative: decisively). The tenses are instructive. Remembering is to continue all along (present imperative) and to it is to be joined complete repenting (aorist imperative), the two being used as in 2:5, where μετανοεῖς is explained. The second present imperative, "and continue to keep," adds this order to the remembering in order to bring out fully the thought that Sardis is not again to let go as it has once done so sadly. The perfect, "how thou hast been receiving," spreads this out in time while the aorist, "and didst hear" (constative), compresses all into one thought. Both of these might have been perfects or aorists; but this perfect is not "aoristic," nor is the aorist a perfect in force.

Prompt, true repentance is the one remedy for the death that has set in or has almost set in. This can be brought about only by means of the Word; it is the old Word and not something new. All that is needed is constant remembering and keeping. There is no necessity to refer to Heb. 6:4-8 and 10:26-29, the sin against the Holy Ghost; for the sin committed in Sardis was not even outwardly marked by blasphemy, it was a gradual dying by letting the power of the Word slip away. Spiritual life, even when it is fully lost in this way, may be restored.

If, therefore, thou dost not awake, I shall come as a thief, and thou shalt not realize at what hour I shall come upon thee. Οὖν is merely repeated even as both the gracious call to use the remedy and the warning threat rest upon the past and the present dying condition. The aorist is correct: "if thou dost not awake," for it signifies the prompt single act of rousing into wakefulness. To sleep on and to sink deeper into death will continue only for so long. Then the Lord will suddenly come in judgment as a thief comes to rob the sleeper who shall not even realize what hour it is, ποίαν ὥραν, an adverbial accusative (used without the idea of extent, though R. 470 wavers). How can sleepers or dead people know the kind of hour (ποῖος) it is when judgment strikes them? When judgment comes, everything is too late. We need not here think of the final coming of the Lord although it is never excluded; many preliminary judgments descend upon such men.

4) As in 2:5 something is said to the credit of Ephesus, so here: **Nevertheless, thou hast a few names in Sardis which did not befoul their robes, and they shall walk with me in white** (robes) **because they are worthy.** "A few names" = a few persons whose names were on the church register. Only a few! "Thou art dead" is thus correct just as exceptions prove the rule. The view that these few are to reform the rest is unsatisfactory; at least the Lord here addresses the church: "thou hast," and not these few to whom he refers in the third person. The idea is not that these few would not gladly assist in the restoration. There were a few persons of this kind at the time of Jesus' birth, Simeon, Anna, etc. Could they effect the reformation of the Sanhedrin? These few in Sardis were also most likely to be found among the poorer class who were largely ignored although they were the real jewels of the church.

Bengel stresses "thou hast" unduly, and his view has been passed on. He thinks that these few did not leave the dead church. How long to remain among the dead members, when to leave, where to go when things are bad in a congregation, are questions for the individual conscience in the individual situation and are not answered by this verb "thou hast."

Trench distinguishes between μολύνω, to smear or befoul, and μιαίνω, to color or to stain, the latter being capable of a good literal sense, and both alike being metaphorical. The ἱμάτιον is the long, loose outer robe. We find no symbolism in "their robes," for the whole expression is to be considered together: "they did not befoul their robes." To think of fornication is going too far. These were faithful Christians who had led true, clean Christian lives. Not so the rest of the members; one mark of their deadness was that they did not keep clean, they did not even note the smears in their conduct. One sign of spiritual life is to keep clean of befouling sin. Note John 13:10, 11. These few in Sardis were not sinless; they were like John (I John 1:8-10). We have no objection to referring to 7:14 or to our first cleansing in baptism as long as I John 1:8-10 is not forgotten.

The promise given to these few is also stated in the third person: "they shall walk with me (in company with me) in white (plural: robes), because they are worthy." The Lord says this to the whole church at Sardis so that all its members may be aroused and obtain this promise. These are heavenly white robes. They are mentioned frequently (4:4; 6:11; 7:9, 13; 19:8). We regard white (cf., 1:14) as the symbol of holiness and not of glory or of heavenliness or in 1:14 of age or of something else. Here the white robes = the perfect heavenly holiness. Those who hate the foulness and the smears of sin in their earthly life shall walk in perfect holiness, in purest white, with the Lord in heaven. White does not indicate priesthood. Walking with the Lord is not a priestly act.

"Because they are worthy" (also 16:6) states the Lord's estimate. To think that this worthiness is work-righteousness is to overlook what the Lord regularly reveals concerning works and conduct as being evidence of faith. This is not the first eschatological promise stated in Revelation, cf. 2:7, 17, 27, 28, and the eschatological titles and descriptions of the Lord. To be accounted worthy by the Lord means to be reckoned so by his grace, the grace which gave life, developed it, kept it sound and clean to the end. What the worthy ones did after receiving life was to use the grace by the power of grace so that they could say, "I live; yet not I, but Christ liveth in me," Gal. 2:20. And, "By the grace of God I am what I am; and his grace which was bestowed upon me was not in vain," I Cor. 15:10.

5) **The conquering one thus shall be enveloped in white robes; and in no wise will I erase his name out of the Book of the Life; and I will confess his name in the presence of my Father and in the presence of his angels.** As is the case in the rest of the seven letters, "the conquering one" also here receives the great promise that is made individually to him. "Thus" shall he be enveloped refers to v. 4 where the promise is stated in the plural, "they shall walk in company with me in white (robes)." The "white robes" are mentioned for the second time and again are symbolic of heavenly holiness. The verb means "to throw around," and the passive implies that the Lord will enfold or clothe them with perfect holiness. In this life all our holiness is still imperfect; in heaven it shall at last be perfect.

It has been asked what it is that these in Sardis conquer since neither persecution, heresy, nor fanaticism are mentioned in this letter. These are not the only foes. The great foes that threaten our spiritual life directly are carelessness, indifference, sleep and sloth, failure to remember, to keep, to continue in repentance, to avoid the world's foulness. Are not these enough for us to conquer? They creep in with stealth and are thus most dangerous. Unrecognized, they often do their damage unseen. Open, blatent hostility we easily see and brace ourselves against its assaults; but inner decay works when no defense is made. Those are heroes who fight the open foes; but no less are those heroes who conquer the insidious, intangible creeping death.

The idea of a book that records the names of God's people and thus of having one's name entered in this heavenly book and also of having a name erased, goes back to Exod. 32:32, where even the erasing is mentioned. Compare Ps. 69:28; Isa. 4:4; Dan. 12:1; Luke 10:20; Phil. 4:3; and Rev. 13:8; 17:8; 20:12; 21:27. In 20:12 we also have the books that contain a record of the deeds. The expression is figurative. The Lord's omniscience is like an infallible record: "The Lord knew (ἔγνω) those that are his," II Tim. 2:19; "Never did I know (ἔγνων) you, Matt. 7:23. The figure is a natural one; there is no need to trace it back to paganism as though Moses or Daniel adopted it from pagans. Whether it is based on genealogical or on governmental records of names makes little difference. To have one's name inscribed implies divine certification of a position and of corresponding rights with the Lord. To have one's name erased (ἐξαλείφω) is to lose both, and never to have it inscribed is never to have them. The figure lends itself to all these ideas.

"The Book of the Life" reads like the title of this book. One may dispute about the genitive; let us take it as a simple possessive. This book contains the names of all who have the true spiritual life. It is important to note that the statement is negative: "I shall not erase his name." This leads us to think of those whose names once appeared in this book but are now erased because they are dead (v. 1). Yet this negative is really a litotes regarding the living victor: his name shall ever remain in the book. It was written there when he was first begotten of the Spirit and the Word. Written thus, it assured him also of the eternal life in heaven. This is the same life (ἡ ζωή, definite, there is no other) that he has now (John 3:15, 16) by faith; but in our present state here on earth it may die out;

if it remains in us, temporal death only transfers it into glory.

A difficulty comes to our finite minds when the figure is applied to our foreordination. This, however, is due only to our inability to conceive eternity which is the opposite of time. God is not bound by time and its succession so that he at one time enters a name and then at another time erases it. This fits our ideas of time, but our minds are lost when we apply this to eternity. It is useless to make the attempt, since it usually leads into error, since we cannot even think in terms of timelessness. Here the thought remains in the domain of time as the future tense "I shall not erase" shows.

"Thus the entire Holy Trinity, God Father, Son, and Holy Ghost, directs all men to Christ, as to the Book of Life, in whom they should seek the eternal election of the Father. For this has been decided by the Father from eternity, that whom he would save he would save through Christ, as he himself (Christ) says, John 14:6; etc." *C. Tr.* 1085, 66. As regards wrestling vainly with eternity in this matter, "we should accustom ourselves not to speculate concerning the bare, secret, concealed, inscrutable foreknowledge of God, but how the counsel, purpose, and ordination of God in Christ Jesus, who is the true Book of Life, is revealed to us through the Word, etc.," 1067, 13, etc. This alone is safe.

Thirdly, "I will confess his name," etc., as promised already in Matt. 10:32 (where the Father is mentioned), and in Luke 12:8 (the angels of God), compare Mark 8:38. The three promises go together. We are unable to say why they are given in this order. For those who let their spiritual weapons and armor (Eph. 6:11, etc.) slip from them because of spiritual lifelessness there are no white robes, no names in the book of heaven, no confession of their names by the glorious Lord before his Father and his angels.

6) **The One having an ear, etc.,** is explained in 2:7; it is placed last in the last four letters.

Sardis is a church that is *dying and is already for a great part dead.* Unlike Laodicea, Sardis did not boast and imagine itself rich. It simply grew careless and indifferent. A blight was spreading over its life. Its life simply wilted and faded. The preaching went on, the attendance, the organization, and the work continued, but the preaching itself grew pallid. "Dead orthodoxy" is a fling at this church by those who think that life flourishes amid the stones of unorthodoxy. Sardis is *the secularized church.* Hence also heathenism did not resent its presence because it received no challenge from this church. It sank more and more into the lethargy of ordinary worldliness and let its garment become befouled. A pitiful type of church, indeed!

The Letter to Philadelphia, verses 7-13

7) The direction to write is the same as in 2:1. **These things declares the Holy One, the Genuine One, the One having the key of David, the One opening, and no one locks, and locking, and no one opens: I know thy works.** "These things declares," and "I know," are the same in all the letters, see 2:1, 2. The terminology used in this letter has been well called theocratic. It has a strong Jewish coloring which is due to the situation obtaining in Philadelphia where great success among the Jews awaited the congregation. The name "Philadelphia" was not given the city as denoting brotherly love but was taken from the founder, King Attalus Philadelphus. When, in his *Rise and Fall of the Roman Empire,* Gibbon makes a prominent point of the fact that "among the Greek churches of Asia Philadelphia is still erect, a column

in a scene of ruin, a pleasing example that the paths of honor and safety may sometimes be the same" (quoted in Bible dictionaries), we must correct his statement in accord with more recent occurrences in this territory.

All that we get from G. K. 87, etc., regarding ὁ ἅγιος is "designation of divinity." Thayer, too, is better than B.-P. despite the latter's rather misleading references to pagan citations and to the latest literature. C.-K. 34, etc., informs us that the adjective, which is rare in the older Greek, was filled with new meaning in the Scriptures especially in the New Testament. Used frequently in the Bible, the word "holy" was elevated from its secular use as applying only to *dem Hehren, Geweihten, Ehrwuerdigen,* to what is lofty and to be venerated and received a moral and a religious meaning. Even when eventually the Greeks called their gods "holy" and thereby ascribed to them all moral and ontological perfection, this ascription excluded love: the godhead does not exist in order to love but to be loved (Aristotle; see C.-K. 15 and 36) and included the envy of the gods: "In every good fortune, in every greatness, which comes to a man beyond what is ordinary, even without his arrogance, the godhead sees an infringement of its own privilege and guards the latter with jealousy" (Herodotus). The Greek mind never rose to that Biblical conception of holiness that, because God is holy, we, too, are to be holy.

This conception appears only in the religion of revelation and is not found in a synonym; it is found only in ἅγιος. In it are concentrated all the main principles and aims of the divine revelation to men who also are to be ἅγιοι. As God is ever "the Holy One," so our Lord is "the Holy One." This, indeed, declares Christ's deity, but in the sense here presented. Ὁ ὅσιος has a different sense although we also translate this "the Holy One." This word refers to one who reverences the everlasting sanctities and owns their obligation (Trench). A clear example is Joseph who, when tempted by Potiphar's wife, approved himself ὅσιος by reverencing the sanctities of the marriage bond which he could not violate without sinning against God.

Both designations thus fit Christ. Here ὁ ἅγιος is Messianic: Christ is "the Holy One," the fount of holiness for us ("the Holy One of God," John 6:69). The Jews rejected him as being accursed of God (Gal. 3:13) and found evidence for this in his suspension on wood; but he is "the Holy One," the Holy God himself (Second Person), who died for us to make us holy and to bring us into communion with the God of holiness.

"The Genuine One," ὁ ἀληθινός, is a second self-designation of Christ. This is to be distinguished from ἀληθής which designates one who is "true" in what he speaks and does. As "the Genuine One" Christ is not spurious, not a false Messiah as the Jews claimed by calling him "the hanged one." We must not fuse the two designations in the meaning "the genuinely Holy One." "The Genuine One" is an independent designation and includes all that our Lord is: in all that he is, he is genuine, in nothing is there mere empty claim or pretense.

Thus he is "the One having the key of David, the One opening, and no one locks (shuts), and locking, and no one opens." The fourth apposition elucidates the third. The order of the four cannot be changed. We recall Isa. 22:22: "And the key of the house of David will I lay upon his (Eliakim's) shoulder; so he shall open, and none shall shut, and he shall shut and none shall open." The Lord *has* the key; he may bestow it on others so that they may open and lock by his power and according to his Word. This amplifies

1:18: "I have the keys of the death and of the hades." Compare, Luke 1:32, "The throne of his father David." Our Lord alone has the power to admit to the Messianic house or kingdom, to grant us the right to participate in this kingdom and to shut out from such participation. Here one key is the symbolism of the double power, in 1:18 two keys are mentioned (Matt. 16:19; 18:18). Here the key "of David" makes us think of the Messianic kingdom, in 1:18 the two genitives refer to damnation, its opposite.

We should not restrict the use of this key to the judgment at the last day; it is used even now in the kingdom of grace. There is no irregularity in the finite verbs: "and no one locks — opens"; these might have been participles; but they are more weighty as finite verbs. There is an intentional contrast with the Jews. What they include or exclude is mere fiction; their admissions and their excommunications are nothing. "No one comes to the Father except through me," John 14:6.

8) "I know thy works" is enough. We accept the translation of A. V. and not the parenthesis of the R. V. which regards the following ὅτι as declarative: "*that* thou hast a small power." **Lo, I have given thee a door that has been opened, which no one is able to lock; because (ὅτι) thou hast a small power and didst keep my Word and didst not deny my name!** Here is a description of this church until this time: because it was faithful in keeping the Word and confessing Christ's name before men, he has hitherto and to the very present given it a door which still stands wide open (perfect participle) for its missionary work. Philadelphia is thus a true, faithful, successful church.

Some think that "door" refers to Christ through whom the church is to enter and to have salvation. When referring to John 10:7, 9, they overlook the fact that the Lord does not now say, "I *am* the open door," but, "I *have given* a door." The point of emphasis is not merely a "door" but "a door having been and thus remaining open." Use I Cor. 16:9; II Cor. 2:12; Col. 4:3, in all of which the door's being opened is mentioned; it has been opened to bring the gospel to others. In John 10 the sheep go in and also go out under the shepherd's care. In our passage there is no going out.

Here is the place to note that missionary work can be done only where the Lord opens the door. Acts 16:6, 7 furnishes an example: the provinces of Asia and of Bithynia were closed to Paul, but the door was opened to him in Macedonia (v. 9, etc.). The first missionaries that Louis Harms sent out in the Candace could not land where they had planned; the Lord opened a door for them in an altogether different place. Yet in due time Paul got to work in Asia, and I Pet. 1:1 shows that in due time Bithynia, too, was evangelized although not by Paul. We cannot take the gospel where we please but only where the Lord opens the door. He has the key.

There is nothing to indicate that the perfect "I have given" is prophetic and thus refers to the future. The Lord has enabled the church to do much missionary work in the past and to the very present. The relative clause, "which no one is able to lock" (αὐτήν is a pleonastic antecedent of ἥν that is drawn into the relative clause, R. 722), seems to hint that someone is trying to shut the door and to stop this missionary work but is not able to interfere with the Lord who still keeps the door open. We take it that hitherto successful work had been done among the Gentiles in Philadelphia, and neither Gentile nor Jewish opposition stopped it.

We see no indication that the opened door signifies that in the recent past the church was enabled to escape from persecution. There has been no persecution, nor does the symbolism of an opened door fit the idea of subsided persecution.

The three clauses which state the reason that the Lord has given such opportunity for success are in reality one reason: small power with nevertheless faithful adherence to the Word and confession of the name. "Thou hast small power" cannot refer to weak spiritual strength. The Lord does not open the door for work to those who are able only to limp through and able only to do little. Far better is the reference to numbers; nor need we fear to include the poverty of the members, lack of social prominence, etc. Bengel says that probably the bishop "cut no especial figure." Imagine a hitherto small church, a little flock, which might have kept quietly to itself and attempted very little. Then the Lord opened and kept open the door, and much was accomplished.

For at the same time this church which has small power "kept the Lord's Word" in its heart and in its preaching and teaching, none of the members losing it by carelessness, deadness, heresy, and lax living. On this keeping my Word and my words (plural) see John 14:23, 24 (τηρεῖν τὸν λόγον μου and τοὺς λόγους μου), also John 14:15; 15:10. Keeping Christ's Word is the essential thing. With it goes "didst not deny my name," namely by silence or openly before men. This is a litotes for, "didst confess my name." To keep inwardly and to confess outwardly makes us faithful; see Rom. 10:9,10. The ὄνομα is the revelation by which we know and apprehend and thus also confess Christ. Study ὄνομα in the New Testament.

A church such as this deserved the open door to make the power of the Word and the name successful by missionary work.

9) The Lord is opening the door still wider. If what he has done thus far deserves surprised attention

("lo" in v. 8), this new gift likewise deserves it (two more "lo"). **Lo, I am giving some of the synagogue of Satan, of those claiming themselves to be Jews and they are not but are lying; lo, I will make them that they shall come and shall do obeisance before thy feet and shall realize that I myself did love thee!** Until this time the open door for missionary work has concerned Gentiles; now the Lord is going to give the church also Jewish converts, right out of what he calls anew (2:9) "the synagogue of Satan."

Ἐκ is partitive, "some out of the synagogue." Διδῶ is the later form (R. 307); Revelation was written near the turn of the century. Τῶν λεγόντων is the genitive in apposition with "of the synagogue," and Ἰουδαίους is quite properly the accusative after the pronoun ἑαυτούς. Ἵνα introduces an object clause (R. 992) and may have the future indicative as well as the subjunctive. All these items are quite in order.

In 2:9 we saw that the Jews blasphemed. Those living in Philadelphia were no better for they, too, are called "the synagogue of Satan," claiming to be Jews when they were nothing of the kind but were lying. In Rom. 2:29 we see what a real Jew is. The Jews claimed to be God's real, beloved people; but the Christians alone were such people.

The second "lo," etc., repeats and explains the first. "I am giving" = "I shall make." The work of converting some of these Jews is the Lord's although it is done through the church. Ἵνα takes the place of infinitives, and we may translate: "I will make them come and prostrate themselves before thy feet and realize (acknowledge) that I myself (emphatic ἐγώ), i. e., I, the Holy One, the Genuine One, the One having the Key of David, etc., (v. 7), did love thee," i. e., as truly my own. These Jewish converts will join the church in order to be among those who are loved by the Messiah, whom they now acknowledge as such.

The prostration "before thy feet" is not an adoration of the church; these Jews, who have been hating all Christians, will come right into the Christian assembly and there at the very feet of the Christians and their elders will bow in true repentance, realizing and acknowledging the exalted Messiah's love for the church which they, too, beg to receive as members.

The wording is not at all figurative. But we must not imagine that the Christians sat on benches or on chairs in their services; they sat cross-legged on the floor in Oriental style. So also did the bishop or the speaker on the higher platform except when he stood up to read (Luke 4:16). To drop to the knees and to bow the head to the ground or the floor is still the Oriental attitude of worship. The fact that Jews, these vicious haters of Christ, would come to the humble church at Philadelphia, the members of this church would scarcely have believed. The Lord here promises this wonderful victory. It is his special gift to this faithful church.

Some commentators introduce the idea of persecution; we are unable to find an indication that the church had been persecuted either by Gentiles or by Jews.

10) To what the Lord has given and is now giving he adds a promise regarding the church itself. **Because thou didst keep the Word of my endurance, I, too, will keep thee out of the hour of the trial that is about to come upon the whole inhabited earth to try those dwelling on the earth.** The verbs match: "thou didst keep — I, too, will keep," both are used in the sense of *bewahren,* guard, hold, keep, preserve against loss, damage, etc. The aorist "didst keep" states the historical fact. This church held fully and completely to the Word as was stated in v. 8: "and didst keep my Word." No greater praise can be given to any church. Though we may do many works, they

are worthless unless we do the fundamental work, keep the Word; see John 14:23, 24. The Word is kept by the power which this Word itself supplies and by no other power. To how many preachers and churches can the Lord say what he here says?

In v. 8 we have simply "my Word," but now τὸν λόγον τῆς ὑπομονῆς μου, "the Word of my endurance." Why the addition of this genitive? We have ὑπομονή in 1:9; 2:2, 19, and have already defined it as being not merely "patience" but the brave perseverance, the remaining under oppressive things. It is never used with reference to God who is not affected by things although he is patient with men; to him μακροθυμία, "longsuffering," is ascribed. We regard the genitive as a genitive of content. The enclitic μου is not objective; thus C.-K. 725: *das von der mich erharrenden Geduld handelt,* "treating of the patience that hopes and waits *for me.*" To say the least, this would require ἐμοῦ. Nor can we translate, "my Word of the endurance," for then we should have had the same order of words that is found in v. 8: μου τὸν λόγον, κτλ., the enclitic being forward or at least directly after τὸν λόγον. Likewise, we cannot regard "the Word of the endurance" as one concept the whole of which is modified by "my"; for this is not a current concept but is found only here.

These interpretations regard "the endurance" as being *ours*: the Lord's Word about *our* endurance. Why not render, "the Word which deals with the Lord's endurance"? Is he not "the One having endured (ὑπομενηκότα, note this participle and our noun ὑπομονή) such great contradiction against himself by sinners," Heb. 12:3? Is he not the sign spoken against? Is he not the center of all Scripture as the suffering Messiah who came to endure? Is this letter not filled with expressions referring to Jews? He came to his own (the Jews), and his own did not receive him; he endured the rejection on the cross. This fits the context. Here is a church that clung faithfully to the Word that dealt with Christ, which was a *skandalon* (deathtrap) to the Jews and silliness to the pagans (I Cor. 1:23) because it spoke of this endurance of his. This is a church which, in his grace, the Lord will reward accordingly.

Though both Jews and pagans despised this Christ and would not accept the Word that told about him and his "endurance," this church in no way let go of this Word and in no way denied his name (v. 8). Some find a reference to persecution in this keeping of the Word; then the endurance is that of the church. But this is a reference to the endurance of Christ; and there is nothing in the latter that mentions persecution of the little flock in Philadelphia. When persecution or even martyrdom had taken place in any of the seven churches, the Lord does not fail to give it credit (2:2, 13, 19).

In the Greek κἀγώ σε are in effective juxtaposition: "also *I thee* will keep." What is meant by keeping this church "out of the hour of the trial that is about to come upon the whole inhabited earth (supply γῆς) to try those dwelling on the earth"? We note that ὥρα (originally, "season of the year") is at times used in its wider meaning as in Matt. 24:36, "of that day (date) and hour (time period) knoweth no one." While πειρασμός may mean "temptation," and the verb may mean "to tempt," here the two must mean "trial" and "to try," because all men on earth are involved, and since most of them are already in the devil's power, it would be pointless to speak of tempting them. The A. V.'s "of temptation," "to try," will not do. There is a debate as to whether τηρεῖν ἐκ means that this church will be kept untouched from the coming trial of the whole world of men, or only that it will be kept from going under during this trial; also whether ἐκ involves a difference from ἀπό. The ἐκ τοῦ πονηροῦ found in John

17:15 is then referred to. It is rather the context and less the preposition which makes us decide for the former: because this church has kept the Lord's Word, the Lord will keep it "out of" the hour of this impending trial.

Chiliasts think that this refers to the "Rapture" which shall occur after what they call the great "Tribulation." But such ideas can scarcely apply to the church in Philadelphia. This promise was dictated in the year 95 and was based on the faithful adherence of this church to the Word prior to 95. The promise here made is given to those who are members of this church in 95. Are we to imagine that these people are to see the millennium and at its start experience this "Rapture"? This impending trial is not the "great tribulation" that was foretold by Jesus in Matt. 24:21, for this occurred during the siege of Jerusalem in the year 70, twenty-five years before Revelation was written. Beside Matt. 24:21 chiliasts place Rev. 7:14, "the ones coming out of the tribulation, the great one," as though these two passages belong together, and as though their θλῖψις, "tribulation," equals the πειρασμός, "trial," of our passage. Even Rev. 13 is introduced in support of this "trial."

In the year 98 Trajan became emperor, and his policy against Christians was followed in the empire (ἡ οἰκουμένη ὅλη, sc. γῆ) for over a century. Some emperors increased the severity of persecution. See Meusel, *Kirchliches Handlexikon*, the article *"Christenverfolgungen."* Πειρασμός, "trial," "to try those dwelling on the earth," is the proper term; for not the Christians were on trial but the entire empire, its clash with Christianity showing what its nature really was. "The hour about to come" is this period which is here foretold before it actually began. The great promise given to the church in Philadelphia is that in this hour it shall be kept untouched and unharmed by the impending dangers. This promise is a mark of the Lord's signal favor toward this faithful church. The Lord has various forms of reward which he extends variously to individuals, to congregations, to church bodies. What he awards to this one church is not what he awards to all or to others. Yet every reward, whatever his favor may bestow, is to be appreciated by all of us as the gift of his grace and favor which is apportioned according to his wisdom.

11) **I am coming quickly! Be holding fast what thou hast in order that no one may take thy crown!** The fact that Christ is "the Coming One" he declares in 1:8. "I shall come as a thief" states how he will come (3:3). "I am coming quickly" announces that this second coming will occur without delay; this is repeated three times in 22:7, 12, 20. "Quickly" and the durative "I am coming" (not the punctiliar aorist) speak of the entire coming and not merely of its end. It includes all the advance judgments and not only the final one. Because 1800 years have passed and the world still stands, this promise and prophecy has been called false, unfulfilled. Some have tried to save its truth by making ταχύ mean "suddenly," thus giving it the same meaning and force as 3:3, "as a thief" who comes in a sudden, unexpected way. Yet the word means "quickly, soon," *bald, schleunigst.*

It is not necessary to understand "quickly" in a chronological sense as meaning "in a few days, months, or years," thus unduly restricting Matt. 24:36, "Concerning that day and hour no one knows," and Acts 1:7, "It is not yours to realize times or seasons, which the Father did place in his own authority." "Quickly" does not approximate the date of the arrival of Christ in his Parousia. Yet to say that it is to be taken "in an exalted religious sense" leaves us in a haze. "I am coming quickly," stated negatively, means, "I am making no delay." In the year 95 the Philadelphians, and in the present year we, are constantly to look for his coming. "Quickly" intends to keep *us* in constant expectation by shutting out any delay on the *Lord's* part. Already in Peter's time, more than thirty years before Revelation, mockers scoffed, "Where is the promise of his Parousia?" Everything remains just as it always has been since the creation. So these mockers laughed at the idea of a second coming. Peter answers them, "The Lord is not slack concerning his promise as some count slackness." A 1,000 years are in his sight as one day, and one day as a 1,000 years. In other words, leave the date and the "times and seasons" (Acts 1:7) to him and look to yourselves lest you be caught unprepared at the time of his coming.

The reason that the Lord's coming quickly is ever to be kept in mind is that we may hold fast what we have lest we lose our crown. Whether a great trial occurs in our time or not, whether such a trial strikes us, or whether the Lord shelters us so that it does not strike us, ever, because he is on the way, ever, because at an unknown time he will arrive in his Parousia, will descend as the Judge on the last day, we must hold fast what we have, what he has given us, his Word, the confession of his name (v. 8), all our spiritual treasures, blessings, attainments, that no one may take our crown. See 2:10 on "crown." To lose the crown is to lose "the life" (2:10), eternal salvation, our share in the kingdom. When Jesus warns that someone may take our crown, this, of course, does not mean that someone will rob us in order to place the crown on his own head. The devil, the world, and the flesh aim to deprive us of the crown of life by plunging us back into death where there is no crown.

We may lose our crown in many ways and not only by means of persecution. No persecution occurred in Sardis, yet because of mere carelessness, indifference, growing impenitence, many were losing their spiritual life, were dead and without the crown. The same must be said in regard to heresy. This may rob us of the crown but it is not the only robber. In fact, the admonition is here given especially to the faithful. They are the ones who may sink into false security and may thus lose what they have. The more we stand, the more we should take heed lest we fall. Observe that no less than our crown is at stake, and that this crown is not merely a degree of heavenly glory but the glory itself, our place and position in heaven as one of the Lord's victors.

12) **The conquering one, I will make him a pillar in the Sanctuary of my God, and he shall not go out outside again.** "The conquering one" appears in all seven letters, see 2:7. Here this expression is a pendant nominative as in 2:26, and thus is emphatic because of its independent case. Ναός is not "Temple" (ἱερόν, courts and buildings) but "Sanctuary," the central chamber where dwells the very presence of God. Here and elsewhere Christ calls the Father "my God" in reference to his human nature, cf., 3:2.

The debate as to whether this Sanctuary is the one on earth, the church militant, or the one in heaven, the church triumphant, is settled by the fact that in these letters all promises given to "the conquering one" refer to heaven. There is no conflict with 21:21, where the Lord God and the Lamb are called the Sanctuary in the city to come. We need not search for the *tertium comparationis* in the figure of "a pillar in the Sanctuary of my God," for it is given right here: "and he shall not go out outside." Put all the thought of beauty into the figure you may wish, the main thing is permanence: a pillar remains where it is. The addition of ἔξω to a verb compounded with ἐκ is common Greek usage. The victor's place in heaven is gloriously permanent; like a pillar in the heavenly Sanctuary he remains ever and ever in the presence of God.

And I will write upon him the name of my God and the name of the city of my God, of the New Jerusalem, the one coming down out of the heaven from my God, and my name, the new one. The inscription of these three names is an added figure to express permanence. These names seal the victor as forever belonging to God, the Holy City, and the Lord. We have no reason to think that ἐπ' αὐτόν means "upon the pillar." The intervening clause "he shall not go out" refers to the victor; this αὐτόν is the same as the first one and refers to the victor. This is not a reference to inscribed pillars or to pillars in the form of statues bearing inscriptions that are found in pagan temples. The Lord also does not say that he will write these names on the victor's forehead or on a breastplate. The writing of these names is itself symbolical; the idea that the angels and the saints are to read this writing is unacceptable, the more so because every saint has this written upon him. In connection with the white pebble inscribed with the new name (2:17) we saw that these heavenly realities, even when they are put into earthly symbols, are very much beyond our conception.

Just how these three great names will be written on each victor, in what language, with what ink, and how the writing will appear, we shall know in due time. Ps. 126:2. The names, written upon the victor, denote that he belongs to God forever, etc. Just what each name signifies we do not attempt to say. One might think that the first is "GOD," or rather the possessive "GOD'S" — but who knows anything about the language of heaven?

The same is true with regard to the second name which is described rather than named, "of the city of my God (Heb. 11:10), of the New Jerusalem, the one coming down out of the heaven from my God." It is so described also in 21:2. The apposition ἡ καταβαίνουσα is not in the oblique but in the assertive, independent nominative case, intentionally so and thus is not to be regarded as being irregular. Heaven and earth are still separated; in the consummation they shall be one as pictured in 21:3. In 21:9, etc., John sees the vision of this Holy City; the description is absolutely beyond all that human minds have ever conceived since all our images of earthly cities are less than child's play compared with this Eternal City. What, then, can we say in regard to its name and the writing of this name? What would prattling about it amount to?

The same is true with regard to our Lord's name, τὸ καινόν. No one knows it but he himself (19:12); we doubt that it is the one used in 19:13, 16. Even the victor's individual "new name" he alone will know (2:17).

13) **The one having an ear, etc.,** is explained in 2:7; it occurs at the end of the last four letters.

Philadelphia is the *faithful* church, faithful in adhering wholly and solely to the Word and in confessing the Lord's name. This faithful church receives a special promise of success (v. 8, 9) and a special promise of protection (v. 10). Both reveal how highly the Lord thinks of every faithful, confessing church. He will reward every church of this kind. The rewards will not always be the same; they will vary according to his wisdom and according to the individual circumstances of each faithful church but they will always be blessed.

The Letter to Laodicea, verses 14-22

14) **And to the angel, etc.,** is like the direction given in 2:1. This church is mentioned in Col. 4:16. In the year 361 a Council was held here which established the New Testament canon.

These things declares the Amen, the Witness, the Faithful and Genuine One, the Beginning of the

Creation of God: I know, etc. On "amen" see 1:7. Here "the Amen" is the Lord's self-designation, it is like "the truth" in John 14:6, save that "the Amen" is a Hebrew term while "the Truth" (ἡ ἀλήθεια) is Greek. Christ himself is absolute verity. The next name: "the Witness, the Faithful (as in 1:5) and Genuine (as in 3:7)," adds the truth that "the Amen" is the One who testifies, who bears witness (1:2, "the testimony of Jesus Christ"). As in 1:5, "the Witness" is a title that refers to the witness Christ bore here on earth. In I Tim. 6:13 Paul writes: "Christ Jesus, the One who witnessed before Pontius Pilate the noble confession." Some think that "the Witness" means that the Lord is witnessing to the Laodiceans in this letter, but this letter is not a piece of testimony that would lead the Lord to designate himself in so grand a way as "the Witness, the Faithful and Genuine One," John, too, taking up this title in 1:5.

Jesus is "the Amen" and "the Witness" quite apart from this letter as he is all else that is predicated of him (as in 1:5) and that he predicates of himself (as in 1:8; 2:1, 8, 13, 18; 3:1, 7). This, however, is true that he who is the Amen, the Witness, etc., here speaks to the Laodiceans and speaks as the One who is what he calls himself. The two adjectives are added with a second article, they are like an apposition and a climax (R. 776): "the Faithful and Genuine (Witness)," who in the testimony that he once bore here on earth is absolutely reliable and trustworthy and thus genuine and has no sham or pretense in him. Compare ὁ ἀληθινός in v. 7 and note the difference between this adjective and ἀληθής, "true." Who would dare to close his ears to anything this Person now says?

A third apposition follows, "the Beginning of the Creation of God," which recalls Col. 1:15-18, especially Ἀρχή, "Beginning," and "First-born of all Creation." This is not the most explicit reference to the Lord's pre-existence that is found in Revelation. Compare 1:8 and "the Son of God" in 2:18, to say no more. The fact that Christ is the *eternal* Lord is plain from everything that Revelation reveals. It is too philosophical and abstract to say that this designation makes him the *Weltprincip*, "the cosmic principle." "The *Archē*" resembles "the First" used in 1:17. By no means does this title mean that the Lord is the first creature created by God; he is the uncreated Son of God who is as eternal as the Father. "The Beginning of the Creation of God" has its exposition in John 1:3: "All things came into being through him, and apart from him not even one thing that has come into being"; plus v. 10, "the world came into being through him." Our Lord is the source of the creation of God, the beginning of it in an active sense. The two διά in John 1:3, 10, plus the χωρίς make him the absolute medium of the whole creation. Had it not been for him, there would have been no creation. All creation exists only with reference to him, otherwise it would not even exist.

All of this is contained in this title "the Beginning of the Creation of God." This is he who here speaks to the Laodiceans in order to bring them back into full, saving, blessed connection with him in whom the whole universe centers, apart from whom whatever we may be as creatures of God or may have of his creation is nothing.

15) **I know thy works** with infallible and complete knowledge, these works as evidence of what thou really art: **that thou art neither cold nor hot. Would that thou wert cold or hot! So, because thou art lukewarm and neither hot nor cold, I am about to spew thee out of my mouth.** As the works are always the open and the indisputable evidence, thus they are also in the final judgment (Matt. 25:35, etc.); they evidence the inward condition which the Lord alone sees and knows directly but which he reveals to us by means

of the evidential works. The Laodiceans, no doubt, imagined themselves to be fervent believers. They were like so many who are blind both to what they are and to what their works proclaim about them.

Laodicea is "neither cold nor hot." The latter word, ζεστός, from ζέω, to boil or seethe, R. 1097 regards as an active verbal "boiling," but we prefer the view of Liddell and Scott who regard it as the passive "boiled," heated hot. The Word heats us hot in faith and works. Cold does here not mean once hot and now grown cold. This is the meaning of νεκρός, "dead" (v. 2). Cold = never converted, never touched by the gospel fire; hot = really converted, actually heated by this blessed fire. The Lord wishes that this church were one or the other. Ὄφελον (unaugmented imperfect) has come to be nothing but a particle to express a wish. It is used with all three persons and with the imperfect expresses a wish regarding the present, with the aorist a wish regarding the past. Here it is the former. B.-P. 955 thinks it is a neuter participle with ἐστί to be supplied. We may translate, "O that thou wert!" Trench says well that the form is a wish but the fact expressed is deep regret.

16) This church is χλιαρός (χλίω, to become warm, liquefy, melt), "tepid, lukewarm," and thus nauseating. The observation is correct that this tepidness is not a rising from coldness toward the boiling point but the opposite. We must not let the figure rule the reality; the figure only serves the reality, and this reality is that of faith and life dying down until only intolerable tepidness remains. This condition is, indeed, worse than never having come into contact with the Word. For when the contact is finally made, the cold heart is often soon fired into true faith; but in cases where this fire once fired the heart and where the fervor has later sunk to mere tepidness, a worse state results. Here we

may consider passages such as Matt. 12:30; I John 2:15; James 4:4.

Yet even for this tepid church the day of grace has not ended. Why should this letter be addressed to it if that were not the case? Our versions translate, "I will spew thee out of my mouth," as though the verb used were θέλω. It is μέλλω, "I am about to," the act is pending, the Lord is still waiting. This letter is to cure the tepidness. The figurative language is appropriate. One can drink cold or hot water, but tepid water is nauseating. It causes only disgust. One spits out anything of this kind. Also the critics admire these verses and the telling language here employed even as the church has found it highly expressive. The state of being neither cold nor hot but lukewarm has occurred frequently and this language is an adequate description of the condition here referred to.

17) **Because thou claimest, Rich am I and I have become rich and I have need of nothing! and dost not know that thou on thy part art the one wretched and pitiable and beggarly and blind and naked: I counsel thee to buy from me gold refined by fire in order that thou mayest, indeed, be rich, and white robes in order that thou mayest, indeed, throw around thyself and that the shame of thy nakedness may, indeed, not be public, and eyesalve to anoint thy eyes in order that thou mayest, indeed, see.** Here we have the diagnosis of the disease and the prescription of the remedy. If the preceding figure is effective, these new ones are no less so.

There is an illusion and a false claim. This church judges itself and not only acquits itself, like the Pharisees in Luke 16:15 (which see), but also boasts pridefully. The opposite of this boast is true. "Rich am I and I have become or grown rich!" The simple fact is repeated by pointing to the process: all along "have

I grown rich," getting more and more, and thus I am today (this is the force of the perfect tense). And these riches are so great that "I have need of nothing" (οὐδενός), or, "I have need of not one thing" (οὐδέν), the texts varying between the genitive and the accusative. This is complete self-sufficiency which is based on wholly imaginary riches. It is utter self-delusion and blind pride.

To think of material riches or of material and also of imaginary spiritual riches, is to misunderstand the diagnosis. All these members were not wealthy. While monetary wealth often leads to pride, self-sufficiency, etc., an utterly false estimate of one's spiritual condition is brought about also by other causes. In the church today thousands are satisfied with their empty moralism, their arid rationalism, their pleasurable worldliness. This they have accumulated until they think, "I have need of nothing." They pity other churches. They have vastly improved the Christianity of their fathers. They have gone to the very top.

"And knowest not that thou, even thou (emphatic σύ), art the one wretched and pitiful and beggarly and blind and naked." But one article is used with these five terms and this article not only combines these five but also makes the long predicate interchangeable with the subject: "the actual one wretched, etc., thou art he" (R. 768). These five adjectives with the one article present five aspects of one and the same condition. Looking at it in one way, it is ταλαίπωρος (Rom. 7:24), "wretched," miserable, distressing. Looking at it again, it is ἐλεεινός, "pitiful," appealing to one's mercy. Another look shows it to be πτωχός, "beggarly," the word being derived from the verb to cringe as a beggar cringes. Next, τυφλός, "blind," and finally γυμνός, "naked." What a condition these five present! Worst of all, these people who are in this condition do not know their state but boast of being rich. The first three adjectives describe general states; "blind and naked" are specific. The successive καί heap up the deplorable features.

18) "Because" (ὅτι) of what is thus stated, "I counsel thee," etc. Does "I counsel thee" sound like irony? Does it imply aloofness, the fact that the Lord is no more intimate with this church? We do not accept these suppositions. In v. 17 the voice of the law disillusions this church and reveals its miserable sin; but now the voice of the gospel speaks. "I counsel" is friendly, it leads and draws. The Lord is not commanding. The gospel is never a stern command. Faith is indeed obedience, but it is the obedience of trust and confidence.

The figurative terms start with "I am *rich*" and are expanded by means of five adjectives that present the opposite state. In the counsel which the Lord offers three terms are sufficient, and these are the terms that offer concrete images: gold for real riches to remove the poverty, robes to remove the nakedness, eyesalve to remove the blindness. Here applies also what we said regarding the five adjectives used in v. 17, namely that the three terms also express only one condition in its three aspects.

The counsel is "to buy from me." The aorist is effective to indicate an actual purchase. Only he will buy who sees his need and stops saying, "I have need of nothing." Only he will come and buy "of me" who sees that the Lord alone has these treasures. To buy, and that of me, thus includes true contrition and true faith, a complete inner change. They are no longer to be lukewarm but now hot, indeed, fervent and glowing for Christ. The extended imagery of v. 17, 18 harmonizes in both a beautiful and an illuminating way with that of v. 15, 16. Yes, these things he declares who is the Amen, the Witness, the Beginning of the Creation. He alone has the words of life eternal (John 6:68).

But how shall these beggarly, blind, and naked ones "buy"? The answer is found in Isa. 55:1: "Ho, everyone that thirsteth, come ye to the waters, and he that hath no money! Come ye, buy, and eat! Yea, come, buy wine and milk without money and without price!" Buy *for nothing!* This is the strange, wonderful *gospel* buying. It must be thus. First, because these buyers have nothing with which to buy; secondly, because what they are to buy is priceless so that it would be a farce to offer anything as a price; thirdly, because in his infinite grace the Lord cannot allow this grace to be disparaged by any pretended merit of ours, as the Amen of absolute verity no such pretense and lie could possibly be allowed in this buying. "To buy" is "to find" (Matt. 13:44) the priceless treasure.

We buy without work-righteousness. To offer works is to purchase nothing. One interpretation pictures our "self-surrender," our contrition and our faith, our poverty, etc., as the money offered for this buying. This is untenable, however well it may be intended. "No money — without money and without price" (Isa. 55) alone is true. "In my hand no price I bring" (Toplady). "Buy" is not irony; it reveals the value of what we receive from the infinite Lord, it is not a value that indemnifies him. All that he bestows on us, priceless as it is, does not impoverish him. "Buy" is like "gold," etc., it is a human figure that agrees with these other human figurative terms, which only blindness improperly translates into the wrong reality. Here is no *meritum de congruo* as a price paid to obtain the *meritum de condigno,* the Roman theory, that the proper use of the grace first bestowed makes it fitting and congruous for God to pay us further grace for our merit.

Gold makes rich, white garments cover nakedness, eyesalve supplies sight. The three figures spread out the saving effects, which, however, are always inseparable. Salvation is gold in that it removes our poverty, white robes in that it covers our nakedness, eyesalve in that it gives us sight and knowledge.

Gold "having been fired (refined) out of fire" is gold without dross, absolutely pure gold, making its possessor truly rich. Our Lord offers us no inferior gold. This has been interpreted as being faith tried in the fires of persecution. The answer to this view is that this faith cannot be bought, even as faith, when not yet so tried, is only the hand into which the treasure is placed. We may think of the gold of Christ's righteousness imputed to us as believers. Then the white robes would be the robes of the same righteousness, recalling Isa. 61:10: "He hath clothed me with the garments of salvation; he hath covered me with the robe of righteousness, as a bridegroom decketh himself with ornaments, and as a bride adorneth herself with her jewels"; likewise, Matt. 22:11, all the guests at the King's Son's wedding clothed in the wedding garments provided by the King. "White" is the symbol of holiness as in 1:14; 2:17, so throughout, v. 7; 4:4; notably 6:11; 7:9, 13; 19:14; 20:11.

The view has been expressed that these Laodiceans were great businessmen who handled much money, and lived in fine state, because Laodicea is regarded as having been a wealthy city, for does not Tacitus report that after the earthquakes of 60 to 61 the city rebuilt itself without imperial aid? What happened thirty-five years before this time and pertained to secular conditions in no way influences the figurative language used by the Lord. Nor were all the members rich men either thirty-five years before this or now.

On the spelling of κολλούριον see R. 202. This is an elongated lump that was impregnated with medicines; thus it was used for "poultice" and for "eyesalve" as here. This figure is added, as is "blind" in v. 17, because of the sad condition diagnosed, "thou dost not know." Salvation is to see, to know. The eyesalve = the Word. Some think "eyesalve" = the Holy Spirit. To call the divine Person "eyesalve" violates the proprieties which the Scriptures always observe.

The effective aorists must be noted: "actually to buy — that thou mayest be actually rich — actually throw around thyself — may not actually be public (φανερόω often has this sense) — actually anoint — mayest actually see" and not in ignorance and self-delusion only think so. These are the true effects of actually having the Lord's salvation.

19) The Lord explains what he is doing and adds an admonition (οὖν). **I on my part** (emphatic ἐγώ), **as many as I have affection for I rebuke and discipline. Ever be zealous, therefore, and definitely repent!** This is what the Lord does with all whom he affectionately loves. Ὅσους ἐάν does not refer to the better part of the Laodicean church but to "as many as" he loves in all the churches. He is not treating this one church with exceptional severity. Any and all who need it he rebukes and disciplines. The present tenses match the indefinite "as many as."

Why does the Lord say φιλῶ when in 1:5, 3:9 (cf., Heb. 12:6) the verb used is ἀγαπᾶν? The one is the love of affection, the other the love of intelligence, understanding, and corresponding purpose. Certainly, the latter could be used here, nor does the former intend to bar out the latter. Often φιλῶ is less than ἀγαπῶ as the contexts show; but, here and notably in John 21:17 (where both verbs are used), φιλῶ conveys more. Jesus questioned not only the intelligent, purposeful love of Peter for Jesus, but even his personal affection and friendship, and this latter fact cut him most deeply. So also here (unlike Heb. 12:6) φιλῶ brings out the idea that beyond the love of intelligence and purpose the Lord has affection for those whom he rebukes and disciplines. The Laodiceans are to see not only love but actual affection in this disciplinary letter. As a Father deals with his sons whom he dearly loves, so the Lord does here.

Ἐλέγχω may mean "convict" or "rebuke," the latter being preferable here; παιδεύω may mean to educate, to chastise, and even to whip, to discipline. The comments vary. We need not be in doubt as to what these verbs mean: this letter contains the Lord's rebuke and discipline which is offered in the truest affection. The Lord is no soft Eli to his children.

The church should respond accordingly (οὖν). Note the change of tenses: the present imperative, durative, "be zealous," i. e., ever; "repent," aorist, punctiliar: do so at once, decisively. See the exposition on "repent" in 2:5 (2:16, 21; 3:3). Nor should these two verbs be reversed. "Ever be zealous" is to replace the condition of tepidness, and in this new zeal to mark its genuineness the very first thing should be the act of decisive repentance. The verbs do not mean that first there is to be a lot of zeal and then finally an act of repentance. Repentance assures pardon. While, as Luther says, our whole lives should be one continuous repentance, and while he who once truly repents will renew his repentance in the case of every future sin, all this is not the point, but the decisive repentance which will once for all end all lukewarmness in which no repentance could occur.

20) Immortalized in the loveliest paintings as in beautiful hymns, the promise of this letter is, indeed, incomparable in its imagery. **Lo, I am standing at the door and knocking! If one hears my voice and opens the door, I will go in unto him and will dine**

with him, and he with me. When we realize who this is that is dictating these words, that when he first saw him John fell at his feet as one dead (1:13-17), we marvel that he should stand knocking at any man's door and be waiting to be let in. Here we have all the sweetness of his heavenly grace, all the gentleness of the gospel which seeks to win our souls. This is his heavenly power to save. It is by winning that he saves.

"I am standing at the door" implies that it is *he* who comes, as here to the Laodiceans, so to all sinners; he is not far off waiting for *us* to come to him. He *sends* his gospel: "*Go* into all the world!" He does not ask the sinner to go to it. He stands at the door and keeps knocking as a Friend asking entrance. The thought is overwhelming that the everlasting King comes from his throne (v. 21) to ask a beggar (v. 17, πτωχός) to receive him. The perfect ἕστηκα is always used as a present, and thus both verbs are durative. These two tenses are not aoristic and do not refer to a momentary standing and just a knock or two and then indignant departure if the door is not at once opened. He comes and will even wait and knock again and again. It is the sinner's hour of grace when the King stands and knocks. Blessed hour, indeed! Who would not rush to open! He knows just when to come; he never chooses the wrong hour. Yet that hour does not continue indefinitely. It may pass, grace has its limits, the Lord may at last leave. Whether he will come again, who is able to say?

Ἐάν is the if of expectancy and contemplates that the King will be heard by the beggar and that the beggar will open the door. Therefore the aorists are now used, "actually hear my voice and actually open the door." The voice asking for entrance intensifies the knocking. The gospel in which the Lord comes calls and calls for the heart to open the door. This opening of the door is misunderstood by synergists who imagine that the sinner is able to open the door by an exercise of his will, by his own natural powers. They do not see that the will is bound and that, because it is thus bound, cannot possibly open the door. They imagine that opening and leaving barred and locked are on a par. They do not look closely and note what is here said (as elsewhere in Scripture) but take it for granted that the sinner opens or leaves closed as *he* determines *in and of himself*.

On the opposite side are the predestinarians with their irresistible grace, and this they limit to those elected in an absolute way from all eternity. The King knocks only at the door of these elect; he does so irresistibly, they are compelled to open. If he knocks at the door of the non-elect, this is not done in seriousness, for even if any of these open the door, it is only for a time. Christ did not atone for their sins, nor was their call serious on Christ's part, their doom was sealed in eternity by an act of absolute sovereignty.

The truth is that the King comes to the door, stands there, knocks, calls with his voice. In this lies the power that moves the will to open the door. The Lord's power of love and grace in and by his Word, which is the power of God to save (Rom. 1:16), reaches into the heart and moves it to open and to receive. This is the picture here presented. No one opens synergistically or Calvinistically. The genitive used with "hear his voice" always refers to the person.

"I will come in and will dine with him, and he with me" describes the fellowship that begins and continues; μετά is used twice in the sense of "in company with." The picture of dining together is also used elsewhere. Some find too much in the double expression; once the King is the host, and the sinner partakes of what the King provides, then the reverse is the case. This dining together is not postponed until we reach heaven, or until the Lord comes in his Parousia. This verse is not eschatological. Those who entertain this view think that every letter has a statement about the final coming of the King. When passages such as Matt. 25:1, etc.; Mark 13:29; Luke 12:36 are quoted, these are not parallel. The passages that belong here are those on the *unio mystica,* such as John 14:23; 15:5; I John 2:24; and many others that speak of Christ receiving us, we him, he and we being in union. As far as eternity is concerned, the feasting there is only the consummation of the dining together here on earth in blessed fellowship. We are now blessed with all spiritual blessings in connection with Christ Jesus (Eph. 1:3).

Neither does this dining refer to two kinds of food, one provided by Christ, the other by us. Even the knocking at the door is often misunderstood. This is the call which comes in and through the Word. We have even "my voice." There is no need to introduce *besondere Schickungen,* special providences. The efficacy lies in the Word alone. It is unnecessary to refer to a wedding feast and to quote passages that speak of a bridegroom. Nor does "I with him" refer to an eating that takes place here on earth, and "he with me" to one that will occur in heaven.

21) The eschatological feature is now stated in glorious fashion: **The conquering one** (see 2:7; for the nominative, 2:26; 3:12), **I will give to him to sit with me in my throne as I on my part did conquer and did sit with my Father in his throne.** The fellowship here below, pictured as dining together (μετά) in v. 20, shall be consummated in the royal fellowship on the throne in heaven. Once more δώσω, "I will give" as a pure gift of royal grace. The aorists, "as I on my part did conquer and did sit with my Father in his throne" are historical. Christ died as the Victor on the cross with the triumphant shout, "It is finished!" See further 5:5. He ascended to heaven and sat down at the

right hand of majesty and power. At the time of a victor's death he will make every victor sit down on the throne "in company with him" (another μετά). To sit down on this throne is to reign: "we shall reign as kings together with him," συμβασιλεύσομεν, II Tim. 2:12: "and they reigned as kings with Christ a 1,000 years," ἐβασίλευσαν, Rev. 20:4; "and they shall reign as kings for the eons of the eons," βασιλεύσουσιν, 22:5. This is the climax of what their being made a kingdom, βασιλεία, means (1:7).

"His throne" and "my throne" = the same throne and not two. There is no lack of room on this throne; there is no crowding. As regards the crown mentioned in 2:10 and in 3:11, whether this is that of a victor or of a king (Trench), we note that the victor sits on the Lord's throne as a king. No human tongue is able to describe this exaltation. It is promised to the most miserable beggar (v. 17) who repents and keeps the faith.

22) **The one having an ear, etc.**, see 2:7; it is placed last, see 3:6.

Laodicea is the *lukewarm church* that has grown tepid; the church that is *proud and self-satisfied;* all its wealth is an empty claim, an illusion. She has ever had many sisters. In this letter no threat of judgment is mentioned beyond, "I will spew thee out of my mouth," which is certainly ample. The gospel call and promise that would awaken intense fervor fills this letter.

CHAPTER IV

The Throne, chapter 4

1) One may, of course, consider chapters 4 and 5 together or even include the seals in the following chapters. This is done when an attempt is made to divide the whole book into formal parts. We have found no literary division that commends itself. This is not a book such as a writer would compose from certain material. It is a record. Chapter 4 is one vision in this record.

First, we have the mighty vision of Christ himself in 1:9-20. *He* dictates the seven letters. But this vision by no means reveals him with reference only to the seven letters or with reference only to the seven churches addressed in these letters. He is the supreme Figure in this entire revelation granted to John, and this does not include only his church. Because of his relation to the church he is Lord of all (Eph. 1:22, 23, and other direct statements to the same effect). When this second vision now reveals the throne, this advances the revelation to *the rule and the dominion* of God sitting upon this throne. A corresponding advance is made from the churches mentioned in chapters 2 and 3 to the "elders" in this vision, for these "elders" are the divinely appointed agents of the Word in and through whom God rules from his throne. Recall the seven stars in the right hand of Christ's omnipotence.

In 1:1, and thus in 1:9-20, the revelation is that of *Jesus Christ*; *he* reveals. Yet in 1:1, *God* gave the revelation to Christ in order that he might show it to us, and now in this vision God is revealed on his throne. We take the advance as it is made in its inner connection and do not try to cut up the book as a literary composition with literary parts by which too much is lost.

After these things I saw, and lo, a door opened in the heaven, and the voice, the first which I heard as of a trumpet speaking with me, saying, Come up here, and I will show to thee the things which must occur after these things! The view that the first phrase "after these things" may involve an interval of hours, even of days after the vision mentioned in 1:9, etc., is untenable. The idea that John was granted intervals for the purpose of writing, so that he would not have too much to record at any one time, is contradicted by 10:4: "I was about to write" when the seven thunders uttered their voices (see the introduction as regards John's writing). We who have never had a vision to write had better not apply to John our mechanical ideas in the recording of his revelation. "After these things," neither here nor elsewhere in similar connections, indicates such intervals for such a purpose but marks only the succession of what John saw.

We are unable to see that "after these things I saw" intends to mark divisions in the book, and that the simple "I saw" indicates minor parts or subdivisions. Examine the passages yourself.

"Lo," both here and in v. 2, is justified. After an interjection the nominative is the proper case. The perfect passive participle signifies a door that someone has opened and that John saw standing wide open and discloses the interior of heaven. At the same time the same voice spoke that John had heard in 1:10 and again it spoke to him, again it was "as of a trumpet speaking with me," ringing, penetrating, majestic, see 1:10. "The voice" has the article of previous reference; "the first which I heard," etc., identifies this voice. Surely, the speaker is the same as the one mentioned in 1:10, the Lord himself, no other voice or person is indicated in either place or connection. While "the voice" is feminine, λέγων is masculine simply because this befits the Person, "one saying." To speak of grammatical irregularity is rather pedantic.

"Come up (ἀνάβα, the suffix -θι being dropped in this aorist imperative, R. 328) here!" states that John is not merely to look in through the open door and to see what he may thus behold but is to enter and to see fully and at close range. "And I will show thee the things that must occur after these things" reverts to 1:1, "the things that must occur shortly." In 1:1 we also have the verb "to show." Jesus Christ is to show these things (1:1); he is now proceeding to do so. "Must be" is the same as in 1:1. Since Satan and the world are as they are, and the incarnate Son has come to destroy Satan's works and to erect his kingdom, certain things *must* occur (aorist infinitive; actually occur). Δεῖ expresses this inner necessity. What these things are God knows, and he has given the revelation of them to Jesus Christ to show it to John and through him to us (1:1). Some of these things appear in the promises and the warning threats in the seven letters; the full extent of them is now to be shown. The last μετὰ ταῦτα is the same as that found in 1:19: "after these things" that now are.

These things John is to be shown in the following visions. To human eyes and understanding they can be shown in no other way. Many symbols will be employed because they alone serve the divine purpose. They, indeed, *show* the realities and yet veil what is still altogether beyond being shown to us, which includes, for one thing, the times and the seasons (Acts 1:7) although many have set themselves to discover these more than all else. "Come up here" means that

John is to see these things from the vantage point of heaven itself where God's throne is found, the embodiment of his power and his dominion.

2) **Immediately I was in spirit** means so as to comply with this command. In 1:10 no more was necessary for John than to turn around when he was "in spirit" (the phrase is discussed there); here far more is required. We decline to speak of degrees of being "in spirit" so as to be able to see heavenly revelations. "I was in spirit" has the same force in 1:10 and here. This fact is properly repeated because of the command to come up to heaven. As for seeing the door opened in heaven and hearing the Lord's voice, already this required John's being in spirit (1:10); this seeing and this hearing he does right where he sits or stands. To come up to heaven through that distant open door is another matter, and thus we are told how John could obey this command, namely "in spirit."

Men will ask whether John's body remained on earth, whether his spirit, freed from its body, soared to heaven. They will speculate in one way or in another and yet will never know. Suffice it to say that Paul himself says that he does not know what took place in his case in this respect (II Cor. 12:2-4) when he went through the same experience. The Lord never has trouble on this score. In the power of his command, "Come up," John was there "in spirit." Supernatural things have a way of remaining so despite all human attempts to bring them down to natural conceptions.

And lo, a throne was standing in the heaven, and upon the throne One sitting, and the One sitting like in appearance to a diamond stone and a sard. "Lo," wondrous sight! This scene does not depict a palace or a temple; the imagery is not that of a great throne room. We often read and speak of God's throne (note 1:4, "before his throne"); we employ the language of the Scriptures when we speak of Christ's sitting at the right hand of the throne. When we speak thus we are quite right in not pressing the spatial terms and thinking of an elevated dais with a grand seat for a king, with space at its right and at its left and a great room in front of it. As in the other world time does not exist, so also space does not exist there. Yet we are unable to think in terms of timelessness and spacelessness. Revelation condescends and speaks as it does by employing imagery of space and time. There is a door; someone has opened it; John sees through the door; in spirit he is inside; there is a marvelous throne, also twenty-four other thrones, etc. Make all this as tremendous as you will when reading the words but do not stress our conceptions of space and time in order to draw deductions from them, for they would be picayunely, childishly false. The reality of heaven is inconceivable to us now; so is all that is in heaven, especially the One sitting on the throne. Symbols can alone "show" the ineffable realities to us to a degree that is possible for beings that are still of the earth.

All that is here described is presented in human form and language, is in condescension shown thus to John, is written thus for us. If we speak of symbolical terms, this, too, amounts to little, for the realities are beyond us, even what we may call the symbols transcend our poor powers of conception. *"A throne in the heaven"* designates *the infinite power, rule, and dominion* of the One sitting on this throne, *sitting* being his *infinite exercise* of this power and dominion over the universe. The One sitting on this throne is God; 5:7 shows that this One is distinguished from the Lamb. See also 3:21, the Lord sitting in his throne with his Father. The imperfect ἔκειτο is descriptive. Sitting is not rest but reigning as when a ruler is on his throne, with his power ruling his domain.

3) Καθήμενος, first, without the article = "One sitting"; next, with the article of previous reference, "the One thus sitting." He is now described as being "similar in appearance, ὁράσει, (dative of reference: as regards sight of him), to a diamond and sard stone," i. e., to the sight of John, who is seeing "in spirit." John is not speaking of ordinary physical sight. The comparison with these two jewels does not help us much in visualizing this Person, and we believe is not intended for such a purpose. The two precious stones, ἴασπις and σάρδιον, are not easily identified. The former cannot be our "jasper" which is opaque and colored and not a precious stone and thus does not fit 21:11, "like to a stone most precious, as to a jasper stone of crystal clear splendor or brilliance," which makes us think of nothing less than a diamond; see also 21:19. The sard (21:20) seems to be the blood-red carnelian. See the Bible dictionaries and also the English and the Greek dictionaries. Let us think of the flashing, white light of the diamond and of the brilliant, burning of the glowing carnelian, of *majesty joined to judgment*. This seems to be the best we are able to do.

And a rainbow round about the throne like in appearance to an emerald, translucent green in color. This recalls the vision granted Ezek. 1:26-28, the rainbow being mentioned in v. 28. The idea that, of the seven colors of the rainbow, the green only predominated is unwarranted; this bow has only the one color, emerald green which symbolizes grace. This bow is *about* the throne and hence is not added to the diamond and the sard color of the One on the throne. These jewels represent the divine attributes of the Person himself; the green bow indicates the effect of this Person's rule manifested in these attributes. It is his rule and his dominion as exercised that shine like a bow of grace. Green is also the color of hope, and the rainbow the symbol of peace ("grace to you and peace" in the epistles).

We may thus say that here are presented the holy, glorious majesty and the righteousness and the judgment over the universe of the One on the eternal throne, his dominion carrying grace and peace with all their blessings for all in his kingdom of which his throne is the center. This revelation of God pertains to all that follows until the consummation and is fundamental for all that must be (δεῖ in v. 1) both for the foes of this throne and for those who bow before its majesty, righteousness, and grace.

We shall thus not conceive this as a vision of the consummation when the storm of the ages is past, and when, *after* the storm, the bow of eternal peace shines. There is no mention of a storm that preceded; ἶρις is not the "*rainbow*" with seven colors, with green only predominating. Do not overload these statements. Only so much is true: this bow that is "similar in appearance to an emerald" refers to God's rule of peace *on the earth* ("on earth peace," Luke 2:14).

4) **And round about the throne thrones twenty-four and upon the thrones twenty-four elders sitting, enveloped in white robes, and upon their heads golden crowns.** First, the nominative: "thrones twenty-four"; next, the accusative: "twenty-four elders sitting." Both are construed *ad sensum*: there were thrones twenty-four; I saw twenty-four elders upon these thrones. There is no difficulty whatever especially when we note that the nominative merely indicates the presence of these thrones round about God's great throne and thus in relation to his throne; while the accusative states whom John saw sitting on these thrones.

Count how often "throne" ("thrones") is repeated in this chapter. This is the great *Throne Vision* which presents God's rule, power, dominion as these are symbolized to mortal vision.

What are we to see in these "presbyters" on thrones, enrobed in white garments, wearing crowns of gold? We reject all answers that refer to Jewish apocalyptics, Babylonian star deities, Persian Yazatas. In the better Christian answers we miss due reference to the word πρεσβύτεροι. These "elders" are not representatives of the church, of either the triumphant or the militant church, or of both. For in 3:21 every victor is given the right to sit together in *his* throne with Christ as Christ the Victor sat down in his Father's throne. The term "elders" points to the ministry of the Word. Examine the word as it is used in the New Testament and in 5:6, 8; 7:11, 13; 14:3.

While these twenty-four thrones are distinct, they are *around* God's throne as the bow of emerald is *around* (κυκλόθεν) and, like his throne, denote power, rule, dominion, the sitting of the elders indicating, as the sitting does in the case of God, the exercise of this power, etc. "Around God's throne" symbolizes derived power, etc. Here, too, the white robes symbolize the holiness of these elders and of their office. The golden crowns on their heads mark their royalty and the glory of their office which is in harmony with their thrones.

The Word that is committed to the holy ministry as God's own Word rules the whole world and thereby glorifies God. This Word lives and abides forever, I Pet. 1:23. Although it has been given into the hands of men, its holy, royal power is eternally supreme. To be sure, it governs in the church, but it judges also all who reject it (John 12:48) and penetrates all hearts (Heb. 4:12, 13).

The number "24" = 12 + 12, and is symbolic of the Old and the New Testaments combined, just as "144,000" (12 × 12 × 1,000) = the church of the two covenants combined. These two twelves appear in twelve patriarchs for Israel and in twelve apostles for the new Israel (compare the "twelve" in 21:12-14). Note that Israel's old patriarchs and the twelve apostles (John being one of them!) are here seen on thrones by John. Arguments to the effect that some of Israel's patriarchs were not the noble men they should have been are beside the mark. These thrones and their number and their occupants are symbolical. The main point lies in the word "presbyters." The number "twenty-four" has no connection with the twenty-four courses of the Jewish priesthood (I Chron. 23:4, etc.; compare Luke 1:5, Zacharias being of the course of Abia). This idea causes some to think of priestly service, which, however, does not agree with the word "presbyters." Others think of angels, non-fallen spirits who kept their principalities. Other mistaken opinions may be passed by.

John sees these thrones and these elders in heaven, white-robed and golden-crowned. This connects them with God's throne in heaven, from whom comes the power of the Word. This does not mean that the elders serve in heaven in a priestly service of God and that they are only representatives of the church, twenty-four notable ones, martyrs or outstanding church leaders who have finished their earthly course and are now in glory. The very word "presbyters," which denotes the office of the Word given to the church on earth, excludes such views. No personal names for these elders are mentioned so that we might think of twenty-four individual men or might say that God knows their names. The symbolism of the power and the dominion of the Word committed to the office of the Word by God calls for the mention of no names.

It is like the symbolism of the stars in the almighty right hand of the Lord (1:16; 2:1); these, too, are without names.

Another matter should not be overlooked, the connection with the emerald bow about the throne and the resemblance of God to a diamond and a sard (majesty, righteousness or judgment, and peace). From *him* comes the Word for men through *his* human instruments in the office *he* has created and given to the church. Luke 10:16. Always, in all ages, the Word spoken in God's holy office is as though it were spoken from heaven, whether in peace or in judgment; its majesty is divine. One reason that we meet so many strange interpretations of these elders is due to the fact that the ministry of the Word is not valued as highly as God values it.

5) **And out of the throne there go out lightnings and sounds and thunders.** "Out of the throne," the symbol of God's eternal power and dominion, proceed these tremendous manifestations. The twenty-four thrones symbolize delegated power, etc., that has been placed into hands that have been chosen by God, as we have stated, the power, etc., of the Word. These lightnings, etc., proceed directly from the throne itself which symbolizes the manifest rule of omnipotence as such. Since they are placed between lightnings and thunders, the φωναί are not "voices" that utter words but "sounds" that accompany the other two. Some separate and seek separate meanings for the three, but the three terms appear as a unit and are but one symbol, cf., 8:5; 11:19; 16:18.

The point to be observed is that lightnings, etc., are *above* the earth and the beings that dwell there; that these are manifestations which are utterly beyond human control. It seems to be enough to think of manifestations of omnipotent power going out from God. The earthly symbol of lightnings, etc., should not be restricted to manifestations in nature, for we are dealing with symbols regarding the throne. Psalm 29, the Thunder Psalm, contains the best commentary. In it note, "the God of glory thundereth." Deadly judgment and blasting wrath are not depicted. The symbol conveys no more than the *display* of omnipotent power. The Word tells about it, God also displays it.

And seven torches of fire burning before the throne, which are the seven spirits of God. The independent nominative without a copula or a verb effectively presents this symbol. Texts that have ἅ instead of αἵ merely attract the gender to that of the predicate. It is necessary to state that these "torches" are "the seven spirits of God"; otherwise we might think that these seven λαμπάδες, "torches of fire," are the same as the seven λυχνίαι mentioned in 1:13, 20, the lamp pedestals of gold, i. e., churches. Translate, "torches" and not "lamps," for the connotation of lamps is that they be placed on a lamp pedestal in order to remain there, even as each of the pedestals mentioned in 1:13 bears its lamp. These pedestals are to remain in their places but may be removed (2:5). Nor would one say, "lamps of fire." These are seven great torches of fire blazing before the throne, torches because they are to be carried afar from the throne.

These seven spirits before the throne of God denote the Holy Spirit; see the exposition of 1:4, where we also explain why the Spirit appears "*before* the throne," God sends him forth on his mission in the world (John 16:8-11). After his descent upon the 120 disciples at the time of Pentecost the symbol of fire and of blazing torches is not strange. Note Acts 2:17, "my Spirit upon all flesh."

6) **And before the throne, as it were, a sea transparent, similar to crystal.** Ἐνώπιον has the same force it had in v. 5b, "*before* the throne." To say that

what resembled a sea was also *under* the throne so that it formed the great floor (like that mentioned in Exod. 24:10), is unsatisfactory. Some seek to determine the relative position of all that John sees. They think of it as an earthly throne room or a temple that has places that are nearer and farther from the throne, this sea being the farthest away. Note again what we have said in regard to the conception of space in the other world. Κυκλόθεν, "around the throne" (v. 3, 4), ἐκ, "from," (v. 5); ἐνώπιον, "before," (v. 5, 6), ἐν μέσῳ, "amid," and κύκλῳ, "in a circle," (v. 6), are terms borrowed from the conception of space but denote only *relations to the throne* and no more. There is no space in heaven. Ἐνώπιον = in the presence or in the sight of the throne of God, in this relation to it.

Some of the newer commentators refer to "the upper heavenly ocean" found in Babylonian and in Persian writings and state that the Jews placed it into one or the other of their seven heavens. But this is of no assistance to us in arriving at an interpretation of this passage. Because "a river of life" is brilliant as crystal in 22:1, is not a reason for identifying it with what is here not "a sea" but only "*as* a sea transparent, similar to crystal." The statement that "the beauty of the Lord's glory" is here symbolized overlooks the expression "*before* the throne" and the fact that the One sitting on the throne has already been described as being similar to a diamond and a sard and not similar only to crystal.

Why should one think of the laver in the court of the priests in the Jewish Temple? How does that explain this symbol? The laver in the Temple furnished the water for the priests who butchered the animals and has not a remote connection with this crystal-clear sea. To see here the *coetus ecclesiae triumphantis,* the glorified church in serene peace while the world is a turbulant, tempestuous ocean, also leaves us unsatisfied. Some come nearer to what is acceptable when they speak of God's rule or of his judgments, yet they do not set forth the real significance of the terms and do so still less by what they add.

In the first place, we must add 15:2: "I saw as it were a sea, transparent, *mingled with fire,* and the conquering ones . . . *standing* on this sea, the transparent one." In the second place, we note the relation to the throne (the symbol of power, rule, dominion) and the sequence: first, the emerald bow of peace around the throne; next, the elders with his Word and revelation who are also around the throne; third, the omnipotence going forth in tremendous manifestations from the throne; and then, the Holy Spirit for his mission before the throne — all these in their respective relations to the throne, the power, rule, dominion symbolized by this throne. What properly is next in its relation to the throne? Shall we not say *the divine providence?* Is it not vast "as a sea," θάλασσα, which also means "ocean"? The very word suggests the deepest depths of earth-encircling extent. We automatically think of Rom. 11:33-36.

Not as we here on earth see what is "as a sea" did John see it, full of darkness and mysteries, unsearchable profundities, but as it is "before the throne of God" in heaven, "transparent, similar to crystal." All the wisdom of God — in heaven one can see clear to its bottom, it is so transparent, crystal-clear and yet so vast and deep. Can we now not understand 15:2 where it is stated that it is mingled with fire? Does divine providence not contain the fire of many a dire judgment? May we now not explain how the conquering ones stand upon what is as a transparent sea? Do they not stand upon God's providence as though what is "as a sea" is actually solid ground? The fire in it does not burn them. What seems to be liquid, solidly bears them up. Until this symbol receives a better interpretation we shall abide by this one.

Unclearness results when ὑαλίνη is translated "glassy," which leads some to think of smooth, unruffled waters and thus of heavenly peace, undisturbed serenity, and glorified saints. The word means "transparent"; here it is explained, "similar to crystal," i. e., in being clear, transparent. As for the ancient glass, it has been well noted that this was generally opaque and dull. Although we sing, "around the glassy sea," and our versions translate this adjective "of glass," it means "transparent," for which we ought not to substitute the idea of smoothness or of reflection from a glassy surface.

And in the midst of the throne and encircling the throne four living ones, studded with eyes before and behind. And the first living one similar to a lion; and the second living one similar to a young bull; and the third living one having his countenance as of a human being; and the fourth living one similar to a flying eagle. And the four living ones, each one of them having six wings, are studded with eyes around and within; and they have no pause by day and by night in saying: Holy, holy, holy, Lord God, the Almighty, the One who Was and the One who Is and the One who is Coming!

The ζῶα have been called the Sphinx of Revelation. One writer lists twenty-one efforts at solution. To this list may be added the view which refers to pagan conceptions and four great constellations of stars that uphold the throne of God.

The word ζῶον means "living thing" or "something living." "Living creature" (R. V.) may pass, but the word is derived, not from κτίζω, "to create" ("creature"), but from ζάω, "to be alive." All writers regret that the A. V. translates "beasts," which would be θηρία ("brute beasts"), Luther's *Tiere,* the Vulgate's *animalia — animantia* would have been preferable. The A. V. does better than Luther when translating Ezek. 1:5, by rendering *chayoth* "living creatures." We note that no derivative from ψυχή is used which restricts us to "life" as animating a physical body (σῶμα). A ζῶον has the life principle (ζωή) whether it is with or without a physical body. The neuter "living thing" is construed with the masculine participle ἔχων in v. 8, and when it occurs in the plural with the masculine λέγοντες because of the doxology which the living ones utter.

Do these "living ones" include the angels? This question is answered in 5:11, 14, where "the living ones" and "many angels" appear side by side and are thus different beings.

The claim that the four living ones are "throne angels" is answered by 5:11, apart from the fact that the Scriptures know nothing about such a group of angels. Thereby also the further claim is answered that the four living ones symbolize angels in general. Angels are not included among the four ζῶα.

This question regarding the ζῶα and the angels is acute because, in the first place, angels are certainly also employed by God as agents of his providence. Secondly, because of Ezek. 1:4-28; 10:1-22, where the *chayoth,* "the living ones," are called "cherubim" (note 10:15, 20), which involves all the passages in which cherubim are mentioned (see the Concordance) beginning with Gen. 3:24, and extending to Heb. 9:5, "the cherubim of glory." Thirdly, because of Isa. 6:2, etc., with its seraphim, which even utter a doxology that is similar to the one we have here in Rev. 4:8b.

It is easy to see why many commentators identify the four ζῶα of Revelation with the *chayoth* and the cherubim of Ezekiel and the seraphim of Isaiah and thus regard the ζῶα of Revelation as exalted angels (a special group) or as angels in general. We might ourselves do so if this were not excluded by 5:11. The ζῶα of Revelation are not angels. Angels are never symbolized in Revelation. In fact, *all* that Revelation borrows from the Old Testament is used in an independent way; we do not find even a single Old Testament quotation but only adaptations and nothing more. This is an important point which should be well noted. Thus Old Testament passages do not *govern* the interpretation of passages in Revelation. Whatever the cherubim and the seraphim of the Old Testament passages may signify, the four ζῶα of Revelation have their own significance, and this, according to 5:11, is different from angels.

This is the THRONE VISION. The word "throne" occurs nine times in v. 2-6, "thrones" twice, and "throne" three additional times in v. 9-11. Everything is in relation to the throne, the symbol of God's power, rule, and dominion. This is not a vision of heaven in general and of those dwelling there, nor a vision of heaven as it shall be at the time of the consummation. It is a vision of *God's rule and dominion* as it is *now* and includes all the agents and the agencies used by the throne. The four "living ones" are mentioned last. They symbolize the countless living, earthly agencies of God's providence and are thus fittingly introduced after the symbol of the transparent sea, the divine providence itself, which is vast, deep, crystal-clear to the very bottom. Among "the living ones" some would include also the inanimate agents of providence, but this is difficult to conceive since the symbol itself is taken from "life," "living ones."

The number "four" indicates the earth or the world where providence reigns until the end of time. We object to making a diagram of the throne and of the symbols connected with the throne as though the idea of space governed this symbol. Κυκλόθεν — ἐκ — ἐνώπιον —

and now ἐν μέσῳ and κύκλῳ (which has become an adverb that governs the genitive) are not *spatial* but express symbolical *relation* to God's rule and dominion. These interpretations have produced some strange ideas such as that the rear parts of these four living ones are under the throne, one living one being under the center of each side of the throne while the front part of each living one rises up before or above the throne. "Amid the throne" is not spatially in the middle of it but indicates that the four living ones are immediate agencies of the rule and the power that uses them. "Encircling the throne" indicates agencies that are used by this rule all around on every hand. In other words, God's providential rule and dominion radiates out from a *center* (ἐν μέσῳ) in an unbroken *circle* (κύκλῳ) of agencies.

"Full of" or "studded with eyes before and behind" symbolizes the ability to see in every direction, both backward to what the providence of God's rule on the throne wants executed and forward to where and in what its demands are to be executed in the whole world. There are so many eyes because providence and its rule is multitudinous in detail.

7) The four living ones are individualized. This is unlike Ezek. 1:4, 6, 10, 14, where the four have *one* likeness, *each* having four faces, that of a cherub, of a man, of a lion, of an eagle. Whatever may be said about Ezekiel, its significance is its own and does not govern that of Revelation. To say that John simplifies Ezekiel is to overlook the differences between what these two saw. Both men *saw;* they did not *compose.*

"The first living thing similar to a lion" does not say that only the face was similar to that of a lion; the same is true with regard to the second, "like to a young bull," μόσχος. Judging from the fourth, "similar to a flying eagle," the whole form is referred to by these three similarities. In Ezek. 1:5, 6 each figure has the likeness of a man, and each has four faces. In Revelation the third alone is described as "having his countenance (πρόσωπον) as of a human being (ἄνθρωπος and not ἀνήρ)." The countenance is enough, the entire figure is not described.

The order is significant: lion — young bull — face of a human being — flying eagle. The lion represents the wild places of earth; the young bull the cultivated parts; the human countenance the cities, towns, etc.; the flying eagle the whole expanse of air and sky. Lange's idea of the four forms of the divine government is one of the best of the many offered although it is too abstract. He becomes confused when he specifies by wrongly beginning with the ox in which he sees the spirit of sacrifice, then he regards the lion as the spirit of victorious courage, the human figure (πρόσωπον is not figure) as sympathy, and the eagle as ideality. We need not consider the many other opinions.

An early and widespread opinion considered these as symbols of the four evangelists: Matthew, the lion (royalty); Mark, the ox (patience); Luke, the man (brotherly sympathy); John, the eagle (soaring majesty). These symbolized the Gospels they wrote. This opinion led to the adoption of these symbols as we still see them in church decorations, paintings, drawings, etc. We need not say that the four Gospels or Gospel writers are not referred to in our verse and need not show that this symbolism is not appropriate.

8) Each one of the living things has six wings. In Ezek. 10:21, they have only four (1:8, "on their four sides"); but in Isa. 6:2, each of the seraphim has six wings. Wings symbolize swiftness for carrying out the will of God's providence. In Isaiah the six wings occur in pairs, and each pair has a separate function. Whether the number "six" is intended to portray the same three functions in Revelation we cannot say. The view that "six" = one less than "seven," so that six is to be taken in an evil sense (like

"666"), is untenable. We venture to say only that "six" is intended to be connected with the seraphim, whose doxology is here repeated. Ἓν καθ' ἓν αὐτῶν is distributive: "each one of them"; ἀνά (the German *je*) is distributive when it is used with numbers: *je sechs Fluegel.* This particle is not needed in the English rendition.

Once more we are told about the many eyes, which fact means to emphasize the seeing, but now, instead of "before and behind," we have κυκλόθεν καὶ ἔσωθεν, "around and within." "Within" does not mean underneath their wings. In v. 6, "before and behind" is used with reference to the throne: hundreds of eyes which see the throne they face and the will of providence in God's rule, and hundreds of eyes that see whither to go to carry out this will. In v. 8, "around and within" is to be regarded from the standpoint of the living things themselves whose wings speed them so swiftly in executing the providential will. When they go on their mission, their eyes see all that is around them so that nothing escapes them, and no omission or mistake occurs because of their failure to see all around; at the same time the eyes "within" or "from within" ever see all that is in the living ones themselves as serving God's providential will for all that is around them. This second reference thus properly belongs with the mention of the wings as designating swiftness in the execution of God's providences.

We correlate also the transparent, crystal-clear sea and all these eyes of God's agencies in his providence. Looked at with our dull eyes from below here on earth, the rule of God's providence is dark, utterly beyond us, but looked at from above in heaven and from the throne, all is crystal-clear to the very bottom in its absolute wisdom, purposes, results, etc. In accord with this heavenly transparency and this perfection are the agencies of the rule of providence, their eyes seeing the will, seeing the work to be done, their eyes missing nothing around them on which God's will is to be carried out and nothing within them by which they are to carry out that will.

At the same time these agencies for the wilds, the fields, the cities of earth, and the air and the sky above earth never pause "by day and by night" (genitive of time within) in declaring: "Holy, holy, holy, Lord God the Almighty, the One who Was and the One who Is and the One who is Coming!" This is the Trisagion, the Tersanctus. The agents of God's infinite rule of providence ceaselessly proclaim him "holy." Being his agents, in wondrous relation to the throne as instruments of his rule, they can never cease this glorifying. See the discussion on ἅγιος, "holy," in 3:7; on Κύριος ὁ ἅγιος, "Lord God," in 1:8; "the One who Was," etc., in 1:4, 8; "the Almighty," in 1:8. Whether "the One who Was" is placed first or second makes no difference.

The three "holy," like the entire name, refer to the Triune God. "The One who Is," etc., in 1:4 refers to the Father, in 1:8 equally to the Son. In 1:8 "the Almighty" is the Son, here he is the Triune God. To be sure, this doxology renews the one found in Isa. 6:3, but to say that John modifies it in a characteristic apocalyptic way is to deny that John heard even as Isaiah also heard. "The whole earth is full of his glory" is proper only in Isaiah where the seraphim cry their praise of God to each other. It does not belong here where the whole ascription directly concerns the Triune God. Those who are interested in Isa. 6:3, and in the threefold "holy" as signifying the Trinity, are referred to the author's *Old Testament Eisenach Selections,* 631, etc. Let us add that, while in Isaiah the symbol "seraphim" and their utterance to each other that the whole earth is full of God's glory restricts this symbol to the angels, here in Revelation τὰ ζῷα, as ministers of Gods throne and its world-wide providence, are restricted to all the other living beings by which God's rule in providence effects its perfect results. See 5:11, 14.

In regard to God's holiness let us add to all that is said under 3:7, that this is the attribute which separates God infinitely from all that is sin and sinful in a way such as no pagan ever conceived. This attribute is soteriological, it is holiness revealed and active from above to those beneath so as to make them holy by salvation or to cast them away forever in judgment. All God's providence in all his agents is directed to this end as all the following visions reveal, as these agents so mightily also declare. The One who Was in all time past, who Is now, who is Coming in the consummation at the last day, he is three times holy in all his providence.

9) **And whenever the living ones give glory and honor and thanksgiving to the One sitting upon the throne, to the One living for the eons of the eons, there will fall down the twenty-four elders before the One sitting upon the throne and will do obeisance to the One living for the eons of the eons and will throw their crowns before the throne, saying: Worthy art thou, our Lord and God, to receive the glory and the honor and the power because thou on thy part didst create all the things** (that exist), **and due to thy will they were and were created!**

The doxology of the living ones is always answered by that of the presbyters or elders. The praise of the agents of providence is always echoed in the praise of the agents of the Word. On the elders see v. 4. To have ὅταν with the indicative is quite in order (R. 972); B.-D. 382, 4). In the main clause the future has only modal value (R. 872), i. e., is due grammatically to the clause introduced by ὅταν.

What the doxology of v. 8 means is here explained as giving or ascribing to God "glory and honor and thanksgiving," acknowledging his δόξα, the sum of his divine attributes; bestowing upon him the τιμή or honor and reverence due to him; offering him the gratitude and the thanksgiving for all that he does. Regard the doxology of v. 8 as offering to God no less. To restrict this to God's grace and his works of grace is unwarranted; the same is true in regard to v. 10, 11.

Once more we have "the One sitting on the throne" (symbol of power, rule, dominion), but now the apposition, "the One living for the eons of the eons" (see 1:18 on the phrase). This is not merely "the Eternal One," nor is this the living ascribed to Christ who was dead and is living (1:17, 18; 2:8). "The One living forever" is not merely he who exists forever but who exists and acts and works. To be sure, this is an Old Testament designation, but to say no more than this means very little. These "living ones" speak as the agents of "the One living forever," who do his bidding and praise him in and for all that he as the Living One *does*. The Psalms are full of this praise. Read Ps. 103:19-22; 111:7-10; all of 145.

10) Those who think of "the elders" as symbolizing the church, the church in glory, the angels, etc., do so also at this place and arrive at incorrect results. The twenty-four elders are the agents of the Word. That such agents, especially when they are termed "elders," involve the existence of the church goes without saying. But so do the seven spirits before the throne, for certainly the Holy Spirit builds and preserves the church. Yet the church is not found in this vision. It has been noted that the elders and the living ones act together. Quite so. The seven spirits are the Holy Spirit in his mission, who cannot be placed on a par with the created agents; the thunders, etc., and the transparent sea are not personal and thus also are dis-

tinct. So these two, the elders as agents of the Word and the living ones as agents of God's providence, both related to the throne, act together in relation to the throne as here shown.

In response to the worship of the agents of providence comes the still greater response of the agents of the Word. The latter fall down before the One sitting on the throne who exercises all power, rule, and dominion (see v. 2), prostrate themselves in worship and adoration before the One living for the eons of the eons (this title being repeated from v. 9), and cast their crowns, the symbols of victorious royalty, before the throne. Their crowns, all the power, rule, victory, glory of the Word, are wholly derived from and ever dependent on the throne and on him who sits thereon. On the different cases with ἐπί see the judicious remarks of R. 601. He wears no crown, for no mission of victory, no act of victorious enthronement, no triumph pertains to him whose majesty as the Creator places him and his throne above and beyond anything of this kind.

11) This is the reason that in the praise of the agents of the Word his being the Creator is the subject. Those who would spiritualize and refer the words to redemption and spiritual creation do so because they think of the church and of its triumph and do not see the true significance of the throne and of this vision as the Throne Vision. It is the creatorship of τὰ πάντα, a concrete term, of all the things that exist (to be distinguished from the abstract πάντα) that evidences the absolute, eternal majesty and exaltation of the Triune God and of his throne. That, too, is why the four living ones and the transparent sea (providence) are essential in this vision, and why the praise of these ushers in the praise of the elders.

Ὁ Κύριος καὶ ὁ Θεὸς ἡμῶν, "our Lord and God" is vocative (R. 466). "Worthy to receive" (effective, constative aorist infinitive) means to be accorded the glory, etc., by all creation. In v. 9 and in 5:12 the nouns have no articles, properly not, for here in v. 11 "*the* glory and *the* honor and *the* power" are only articles of previous reference; they would be absent as they are in 5:12, if v. 9 had not preceded. In v. 9, "thanksgiving" is in place, for the four living ones are the agents of God's infinite rule of providence which ever calls for thanksgiving. In the doxology of the elders "the power" takes its place because here God is glorified in his original, absolute supremacy as the Creator. Thanksgiving looks forward to the results of the throne rule of infinite providence; power looks back to the source, the creatorship and the act of having created.

The doubling, "thou didst create all these things — they were created," emphasizes this ultimate act by means of two historical aorists, which in this final revelation and this last Biblical book repeat Genesis 1 and all else in Scripture which declares that God created all things. The passive, "they were created," calls for the same agent as the active, "thou didst create." Κτίζειν is the Hebrew *bara'*, to call into existence out of nothing or non-existence, an act that is incomprehensible to the finite mind.

"And due to, or because of thy will, they were" means "were" ever since the creative act called them into existence. This imperfect tense is exact. Τὸ θέλημα is a term that indicates result as its suffix -μα indicates and thus means not the will willing but the thing the will willed. What God's will willed is the ultimate cause of the things that were since creation, the ultimate cause of the act that created them. We have no further revelation and must stop with this θέλημα. Speculative minds seek to probe beyond this will into the nature of God, into necessity, etc., but only become confused, however profound their speculative deductions may sound. Some introduce the immmutability of God as though God's creating altered this into mutability or contingency whereas it did nothing of the kind.

John did not invent this vision. Even the mind of John could not do that. John saw this vision and set down what he saw for us so that we might apprehend it through his eyes. Beyond all question, this vision is fundamental for all that follows. The throne stands supreme, stands exalted and serene forever.

CHAPTER V

The Lamb and the Book, chapter 5

1) **And I saw upon the right** (hand) **of the One sitting on the throne a book written on the inside and outside, completely sealed with seven seals.**

The vision of chapter 4 centers on the throne and the One sitting on the throne, on the power, rule, and dominion of the Triune God. Everything is focused on the throne. To call it a vision of the heavenly *Ratsversammlung,* Council of Consultation, with chapter 5 forming a part of this Council, introduces a conception that is foreign to both chapters. "And I saw" marks an advance from chapter 4 to chapter 5. The throne (God's rule, power, dominion) stands forever, and he who sits on the throne and exercises this rule, etc., is acclaimed by all the agents of his rule. This vision (chapter 4) and its subject is complete in itself.

So is this new vision which has a new subject and a new significance. The throne and the One sitting thereon, the twenty-four elders and the four living ones remain in this new vision, and their significance remains unchanged; but now new symbols appear so that this vision, while it follows the other and is in connection with the other, stands out as distinct. As the first is *the Vision of the Throne,* so this second is *the Vision of the Lamb.* Both are world-wide in their scope; both are significant for all times until time shall be no more.

On ἐπί as used with different cases (two in this verse) see R. 601. He who sits on the throne in the exercise of all power, rule, and dominion (4:2, 3) is seen by John with a strange βιβλίον resting on the right hand of his majesty and power. The significance of the right hand has been stated in 1:16. Some conceive this book as being a codex with leaves, the writing being found on both sides of each leaf, each of the seven seals completely sealing so many leaves. Zahn argues that this is a flat book because it lies "*on* the hand" and says that the seven seals indicate that it is a testament. Yet such a book is grasped *in* the hand more often than it is held *on* the flat hand. To say that a roll would fall off the hand if it is not held *in* the hand is unconvincing. How a book in the form of a roll or scroll, one that is rolled upon a cylinder, can have seven seals puzzles many although they think that this was the form of this book. This difficulty is removed when we note that the book is not read, that only its seals are opened, and that upon the opening of each seal John sees a vision just as he reports.

This book is a symbol. "Having been written on the inside and on the outside" (perfect participle) with no space on either side of the parchment being left blank, helps to explain the symbol. So also does the added perfect participle, "completely sealed with seven seals" (κατά is perfective). This book = "the things that must occur after these things" (see 4:1 and its exposition, especially also the force of δεῖ, "must"). What has been written and thus forms a permanent record = all that is inevitable since God in his grace sent his Son into the world, since that Son came, since he and his kingdom invade the world, and since the evil powers in the world react as they are bound to do. For this reason there are seven seals, (three + four) the number of God acting on the world (four). See the seven trumpets and the seven bowls. Here is the full, complete record without a blank or a gap.

To call this a poor book because it has writing on both sides of the roll while any fine book would have the outer side of the parchment left blank, is to misunderstand the symbol, which has in mind a record so extensive, so complete that not even one more line could be added. The supposition that some writing was visible on the outside of the last turn of the roll, and that what was thus visible whetted curiosity as to what was hidden, is untenable. No writing was visible. The roll was enclosed in its case. The seals sealed the enclosure. The loosing (v. 2) or the opening (6:1) of each seal is not undertaken in order to release seven successive lengths of the roll, each length then to be read. Nothing whatever is read. When each seal is loosed or opened it releases the revealing symbolism of what the book contains. The whole record and all that it contains, all that "must occur," remain known to God alone. Only as much of it all as he wills is here revealed in further symbolism.

What the seals disclose is not merely what chapter 6 or chapters 6 to 8 state, but all that chapters 6 to 22 contain. The view that this book is a testament aims to place the fulfillment of what this book contains at the time of the Second Coming of Christ. This idea was suggested by the Jesuit Ribera in 1580 who, as Guinness says, "moved like Alcazar, to relieve the papacy from the terrible stigma cast upon it by the Protestant interpretation, tried to do so by referring these prophecies to the distant future instead of, like Alcazar, to the distant *past.*" This futuristic view presents two thoughts. Some place the happenings in the last seven years of the world just *before* what they call the rapture of the saints, others place them after the rapture. These "saints" are usually thought to be the Jewish believers. All this is generally heavily chiliastic; it includes the final conversion of the Jews and much else that is un-Biblical and fantastic. It is answered already in chapter 6, in the revelations that are connected with the seals.

2) **And I saw a strong angel heralding with a great voice, Who is worthy to open the book and to loose its seals? And no one was able in the heaven, or on the earth, or beneath the earth to open the book or to look therein. And I on my part began to sob much because no one worthy was found to open the book and to look therein.** All this is symbolic and in the strongest way brings out the truth that in the whole universe there exists no being save Christ who can take the book from the right hand of omnipotence in order to open it and to look therein (βλέπειν αὐτό), i. e., to read it.

"A strong angel" corresponds to "a great voice"; both terms are employed because the announcement is to reach every being everywhere. Although he himself is so strong, this angel does not pretend to open the book. "Who is worthy," etc., means, "Let him come forward and open the book!" Ἄξιος is similar to 4:11, "worthy" (literally, of proper weight) in the quality of his being, person, power, and attainment. To think only of ethical worthiness is too weak. "To open the book and to loose (unfasten) its seals" is not a hysteron-proteron, placing last what belongs first; the second infinitive is an appositional elucidation. To open = to do so by unfastening.

3) No one in the whole universe had the ability. No one in the heaven, not even among the greatest angels; no one on the earth among living men; no one beneath the earth among all who had died. The moment we get "beneath the earth" look out! At once we hear about the *Totenreich,* this fiction of a place between heaven and hell where all the dead go. See at length under "hades" in 1:18.

4) The imperfect, I on my part "started to sob greatly" is inchoative but intimates that something happened to stop John's sobbing. John sobbed "because no one worthy was found to open the book and

to look therein." Why should this cause him to sob? The answer is not littleness of faith; not disappointment because he was after all not to be shown the things that must occur (4:1); not, as has been supposed, preliminary knowledge on John's part of the dread things the book contained; not grief that all were so unworthy, himself included. But did not John know about Christ and that he would be the one who would be equal to this task? It is this question that causes the trouble. We must say that John, indeed, knew, but when no one was found, when it seemed as though the seals would not be opened, this prospect made John weep. This reaction on his part is intended to impress the more on him and on us the glorious worthiness of Christ.

All this becomes clearer when we hear the three following doxologies and learn that opening the book is not merely for the purpose of *seeing* what it contains and of *telling* John (and through him us) what it contains; opening it means *to execute* what is written in the book, not merely to tell the prophecies but *to make them come true* as real prophecies must come true in order to be real. To speak about divination in this connection is pagan; likewise, to call this "the Book of Doom" is to operate with a pagan idea. We have already seen that some find many pagan symbols and ideas in Revelation. It would be sad, indeed, if these prophecies should not be real, i. e., should not be carried out. That thought could occur only to a human being; hence it is John alone who is upset and sobs.

5) **And one of the elders says to me: Stop sobbing! Lo, there did conquer the Lion, the one out of the tribe of Judah, the Shoot of David, to open the book and the seven seals thereof** Fittingly it is one of the elders, one of the agents of the Word (see 4:4) and not an angel nor "a living one" who dries John's tears by pointing him to Christ. Λέγει is the

aoristic present in vivid narrative and is often used amid aorists. Negative present imperatives often mean to stop what one has started to do. "Lo" indicates the greatness of the announcement. The verb is placed first, the subject second, and this makes both emphatic, and the aorist ἐνίκησεν states the great historical past fact, "there did conquer," whereas we prefer the perfect, "there has conquered," compare 3:21, "as also I on my part did conquer."

Christ is the great Conqueror. His tremendous victory is that won on the cross. We regard the infinitive "to open the book," etc., as one denoting purpose or object; R. 1089, 1090 speaks of actual result, but here the book has not yet been opened. The victory has been achieved, it remains only to celebrate the triumph. That is what opening the book, i. e., revealing and bringing to pass all the mighty prophecies in it concerning the triumphant course and the glorious consummation of the kingdom, signifies. After Christ was Victor on the cross, this triumph "must occur" (δεῖ γενέσθαι, 4:1) despite all hostile powers and their most violent opposition. They were conquered already on the cross. Now all their opposition only serves to enhance and to display Christ's victory. "To open the book and the seven seals thereof" is again no hysteron-proteron, see v. 2.

Of greatest importance is the subject with its apposition: "the Lion, the one out of the tribe of Judah," which is a plain reference to Gen. 49:9, 10. The ἐκ indicates origin, the second ὁ is like an apposition (R. 776); "the Shoot of David" is a plain reference to Isa. 11:1, 10, as is Rom. 15:12. and Rev. 22:16. Christ's descent from Judah is utilized in a different way in Heb. 7:14. "The Lion" is a symbol of the Victor. For the victory we go back to Gen. 3:15. Ῥίζα is both root and shoot or sprout, here that of the royal line of David which had been cut down like a great tree but from the hidden root sent up this new royal Prince or Victor. One may think of David who was victor in many wars, while Solomon reigned in peace; but the title "son of David" is Messianic in the sense of denoting royalty, the victorious King of the eternal kingdom; compare Luke 1:32, 33. It is in keeping with the significance of the *elder* that he should thus go back into the Old Testament *Word* for these designations of the Victor.

It is debated as to whether these designations refer to the divine or to the human nature of Christ. How the latter can be brushed aside when Judah and David are mentioned we are unable to see. If anything is needed as regards the former, v. 6 is more than sufficient. Who but the Godman could have achieved the victory here referred to, have made possible the triumph that was foretold in the sealed book as accomplished?

6) **And I saw in the midst of the throne and of the four living ones and in the midst of the elders a Lamb standing as having been slain, having seven horns and seven eyes, who are the seven spirits of God having been commissioned into the whole earth.**

In this vision there appears what John saw just as was the case in the vision of the throne. That does not imply that all that he saw in the vision of the throne is now seen once more as some assume. In his vision of the Lamb and the book the thunders, etc., that go out from the throne and the transparent sea before the throne are not seen, for this vision has a different significance. Its center is the Lamb. Confusion results when this is not noted.

As in regard to the vision of the throne we refused to diagram positions, so we do also here. The two phrases "in the midst" are not spatial; they denote relation. They would denote this even if they were intended to be spatial. When the adverbs and the phrases of chapter 4 are added to these phrases and are understood in the spatial sense, the result is unimaginable. It is by such unclear means that the Lamb has been placed "on the glassy sea." But what such a position of the Lamb could signify is not clear.

As in 4:6, ἐν μέσῳ, used with reference to "the living ones" (but in connection with κύκλῳ), denotes *relation* to the throne as the symbol of power, rule, and dominion, so also it does here when it is now used with reference to "a Lamb" who is in the same relation to both the throne as the symbol of power, rule, and domination, plus the four living ones as the agents of infinite providence, and in relation to the elders as the agents of the Word. "In the midst" = as the center, as the director of this power and its two classes of agents the victorious Lamb is seen as the One who alone is able to open the book, i. e., in and by these agents to carry the contents of this book into perfect actual effect, to bring the kingdom, which from the foundation of the world (13:8) rests on his bloody sacrifice, to the eternal consummation at his Parousia.

Many ask why in Revelation ἀρνίον is used for "Lamb" instead ἀμνός as in John 1:29, 36, and elsewhere in the New Testament when Jesus is referred to. Only in John 21:15, ἀρνία μου, "my lambs," appears. The matter is quite simple. The oblique cases of ἀμνός are seldom used, those of ἀρνός being substituted, of which, in turn, the nominative was not used. Since in Revelation both the nominative and the oblique cases are required for "Lamb," neither ἀμνός nor ἀρνός were suitable but only ἀρνίον of which all cases were in use. See Liddell and Scott. This is the reason for the employment of ἀρνίον in Revelation, it is a merely linguistic matter in the Greek.

We are thus able to judge the wrong views that are advocated in regard to ἀρνίον. One is that the diminutive idea has disappeared from ἀρνίον as it has disappeared from θηρίον — which is not true. Even C.-K. 167 supports Spitta in regard to this wrong idea by claiming that here ἀρνίον = "a powerful ram," and by sustaining this view by the argument that the seven horns of the ἀρνίον require this idea, and that such a ram is often mentioned in current apocalyptic literature. We challenge all three assertions. The third is especially wrong because it assumes that *John* drew on Jewish apocalyptics whereas these visions were given to him by the Lord. The word ἀρνίον means "lamb," and all that is true is that the further diminution is lost, "little lamb," since "lamb" itself already contains a diminution. The idea of "a powerful ram" does not lie in the word. To quote from the *Book of Enoch,* or to refer to Egyptian mythology is of no assistance in arriving at the meaning and the use of the word ἀρνίον.

The first mention of ἀρνίον in Revelation occurs in the accusative. The fact that calling the conquering *Lion* from the tribe of Judah a *Lamb* is a strong paradox need scarcely be said; the paradox is solved by what follows. Whether we prefer the reading that has the neuter participle ἑστηκός or the one that has the masculine ἑστηκώς is of no import since the masculine ἔχων follows, and, in any case, this Lamb is a person whether the grammatical gender is followed or not. This perfect participle is always used in the present sense, "standing." While sitting on the throne (4:2, 3, 9) symbolizes the exercise of power and dominion on the part of God (and on the part of Christ when sitting at God's right hand), this does not apply when the Victor himself is symbolized as a Lamb. Stephen saw Jesus "standing" in the vision recorded in Acts 7:56, because he had risen to receive him. So here we take "standing" to mean readiness for action and not merely a natural attitude of this Lamb.

"Standing as having been slain" requires an "as" with the participle since ordinarily a slaughtered lamb does not stand but lies prostrate. Here is the paradox of 1:18: "And I was dead, and lo, living am I for the eons of the eons." The perfect participle conveys an abiding condition: once slain on the cross, Jesus ever remains the One thus slain. Paul uses ἐσταυρωμένος in the same way in I Cor. 2:2. It is too drastic to say that John saw a great, gaping gash in the throat of this Lamb. What it was that indicated the slaughter the Lamb had suffered is not indicated by a symbol and is not for us to supply.

The very next feature, "having seven horns and seven eyes," should warn us in this respect, i. e., not to operate with common physical notions. No lamb has seven horns and seven eyes. The horn is the symbol of might. The two "seven" are misunderstood when it is thought that they refer to "holy working" whereas the three indicate "holy being"; or when they are regarded as expressing "perfect might" and "perfect sight." 7 = 3 + 4, just as in 1:4, where we have the seven stars (1:13, 16, 20). Seven always refers to God and to men. The seven horns symbolize God's power as being directed to the world of men (Matt. 28:18).

The eyes symbolize sight, intelligence, wisdom, compare 4:6, 8. The number "seven" has the same meaning that it had in the case of the horns. Here, as in 4:5, this symbol is explained, "who are the seven spirits of God (1:4) having been commissioned into the whole earth." All the powers of the Holy Spirit belong to Christ. Here note I Cor. 2:10, 11, "the Spirit searcheth all things"; Rev. 2:23, "I am the One searching the reins and hearts." These horns and these eyes clearly belong together. It is debated as to whether the relative οἱ has only the eyes or both the eyes and the horns as its antecedent. The second alternative is removed when we recall why in 1: 4, the seven spirits are said to be "*before* the throne," and why in 4:5 they are symbolized as seven torches of fire burning *"before* the throne." Torches are borne afar. The Spirit carries the light and the revelation of God into all the world (Acts 2:17; John 16:8-11). In 1:4 and 4:5 "before the throne" indicates this relation, and now the literal statement "commissioned into the whole earth" states the matter directly and by mentioning "the whole earth" helps us to understand the number "seven" as we have explained it in 1:4. The fact that Christ has the seven spirits of God he himself has stated in 3:1.

Power and might, sight and revelation, as the two "seven" indicate, extend into and over the whole earth. Οἱ is to be construed only with ὀφθαλμούς. The seven eyes are interpreted for us so that we may not fail to understand. It is unfortunate that R. 414 remarks that the nominative masculine ἔχων is "wrong" in gender and in case, for every reader sees that the noun ἀρνίον is an accusative neuter. R. should have stated the reason for this nominative masculine participle, namely that this Lamb is a person, and that, therefore, a neuter participle with its mechanical grammatical gender would be out of place, and that the nominative case emphasizes the fact of "having." He who created language knows how to have his writer use it.

7) **And he came and has taken it out of the hand of the One sitting on the throne.** After the aorist "he came" the dramatic historical perfect "and has taken" visualizes the book as now being in possession of the Lamb, R. 897, 899. To ask how a lamb can take and have a book is to disregard the symbols. As regards "the One sitting on the throne" see 4:2; on ἐπί as used with different cases note R. 601. The slaughter of this Lamb made it the Victor forever, the Lion from the tribe of Judah, that is worthy to take the book and to carry into execution all that is sealed therein. The act of taking the book as here described is

shown to John only in this vision. We are not to date this act in the year 95 at the moment of the vision. Psalm 110 indicates the date, it was the moment when Christ sat down on the throne at God's right hand (3:21; Heb. 1:2-6, 8, 9; 2:9). Even then the actual date is not one of time as 13:8 reveals.

8) **And when he took the book, the four living ones and the twenty-four elders fell down before the Lamb, having each one a zither and golden bowls filled with incense odors which are the prayers of the saints. And they sing a new song: Worthy art thou to take the book and to open the seals thereof! Because thou wast slain and didst buy for God in connection with thy blood some of every tribe and tongue and people and nation and didst make them for our God a kingdom and priests, and they reign on the earth!**

What we said about the date applies also to the significance of this act. The taking of the book refers to the act of proceeding to convert its contents into reality in and through the kingdom despite all foes; and thus all the agents of Christ praise and glorify him. The vision does not intend to portray a great moment in the year 95 which John was permitted to witness. The idea of such a moment condescends only to our human conceptions, just as the whole vision and all its symbolism do. We also lose too much when we think of this scene as having taken place in heaven. The throne is the power, rule, dominion over the universe, and all the actors in the vision are seen *in relation* to this throne, which, of course, is pictured as being in the heaven (4:1, 2), the seat of God, yet all these agents of the Lamb in the execution of the Lamb's triumph do their work here on earth in their relation to the throne. That is the reason for all this symbolism. These inadequate remarks show how our minds strain even when they have these symbols as helps to grasp all that they intend to convey.

In 4:8-11 the four living ones and the twenty-four elders act together in their relation to the throne and to the One sitting thereon (exercising all rule, etc.), each group offering its praise. Now in their relation to the throne and to the Lamb and to all that the Lamb has done and will yet do the praise of the four living ones and of the twenty-four elders becomes one united acclaim. These four ζῶα are the agents of providence (see 4:6-8), and the twenty-four πρεσβύτεροι are the agents of the Word (4:4). They together "fell down before the Lamb" (as the elders do "before the One sitting on the throne" in 4:10) in worship and adoration symbolically expressed. Equal worship and equal honor are given to both in both visions; for the Lamb and the One sitting on the throne, as we have already been shown in the previous passages of Revelation, are one in deity.

The modifier, "having each one a zither and golden bowls filled with incense odors," we refer only to the elders, deeming it unnecessary to complicate the vision by including the living ones. The κιθάρα is the zither or lyre; some would retain the "harp" of English translations but they do so only because our versions have this translation here and in 14:2 and 15:2. So also φιάλη is a flat bowl here and elsewhere in Revelation, *Schale* in German, although the A. V. uses "vial," which is a vase with a narrow neck and not a bowl.

Here the symbol of the incense odors is interpreted. Whether we prefer the reading that has αἵ (the gender being attracted to that of the predicate αἱ προσευχαί) or the one that has ἅ (the gender of θυμιαμάτων) makes no difference. The debate as to whether the relative refers to the bowls or to the incense (we say incense odors in order to get a plural as is the case in the

Greek) is pointless because the bowls are employed in the symbol only for the sake of the incense, and not the bowls but the fragrant incense odors symbolize the prayers. The critical view that the relative clause is a late gloss is wrong. Revelation has too many clauses such as this when it interprets various symbols. Note those found in v. 6 and in 4:5 as examples.

It is trivial to ask and then to explain how the elders managed the zither and the incense bowl so as to play on the former. This is the same sort of practice as making spatial diagrams for these visions. Why not also ask what was done with the zither and the bowl when the elders fell down? Are not the odors coming from the bowls prayers? Symbols go beyond figures, and even figures are not intended as mechanical objects. "Each one a zither" is only the common individualization found with plurals, which might have been used also with reference to the bowls but is not necessary in the case of the second object. "Golden bowls," precious, is similar to the adjectives used in 1:13 and elsewhere. As to incense and prayers, we have Ps. 141:2: "Let my prayer be set forth before thee as incense." As regards 8:3-5, the imagery and the import are altogether different; nothing is gained by confusing the two.

"The prayers of the saints" is to be understood literally. The symbolical term "twenty-four elders" cannot, therefore, refer to the literal term "saints" (or "angels") as some interpret the twenty-four elders in connection with 4:4. Of course, when we consider the literal fact, the agents of the Word are also saints; but in their symbolical relation to the throne, to the One sitting thereon, to the Lamb in the midst of the throne, the very term "presbyters" shows that in this symbolical expression, not their literal standing as saints is referred to, but their office and agency regarding the Word and its relation to the throne. The ἅγιοι are

Christians. This term for them goes back to Acts 9:13 and to the Old Testament. The sense is passive, "saints," holy ones, whom God through Christ, the Spirit, and the gospel has separated unto himself. The blood of Christ and true faith so separate them. It is a mistaken view to stress only their holy living as making them saints, for this is only the result of being separated from the world for God. The directly passive form ἡγιασμένοι, "those having been sanctified," leaves no doubt as to the meaning. See the further exposition of ἅγιος in 3:7.

It is well said that glorified saints in heaven do not offer the incense of prayers, and that these are saints on earth. Προσευχαί are nowhere in Scripture attributed to the saints in heaven but only to those on earth. Προσευχαί are prayers in the widest sense, even in the broad sense of worship; so we do not restrict the term to petitions although these are not excluded. So also these elders represent the agents of the Word operating on earth and not in heaven. The fact that in this vision the elders have the golden incense bowls is thus most fitting, for the Word addressed to the saints by God always awakens in them the response of prayers, praises, etc., to God. This need not include the idea that the elders carry the prayers of the saints before the Lamb; when literal elders on earth voice the prayers of the churches they do so as themselves being praying saints.

9) After the aorist in v. 8 the present "they sing" is only the vivid present in narrative. The song is "new" because of its contents. The Lamb has been slain, the price of his blood has bought the saints, the promise of redemption has been fulfilled. The old song of the old covenant which awaited the Lamb thus becomes new.

We note that the doxology begins as did the one in 4:11, "Thou art worthy," and the one in v. 12, "Worthy is," etc., ἄξιος conveying the idea of weight, and the ὅτι clause (as in 4:11) justifying the ascription of worthiness. "To receive the book and to open the seals thereof" has been explained (v. 2): to execute all that is written in the book, to convert its prophecies into triumphant realities. We are told why the Lamb is worthy to do this, and we at once see that he and he alone has the wondrous ability: "because thou wast slain and didst buy for God in connection with thy blood some of every tribe, etc., and didst make them for our God a kingdom," etc. Here the historical aorist (second passive) is used, "thou wast slain," namely on Calvary, compare the perfect participle used in vs. 6 and 12. This is the blood theology so strongly antagonized by all rationalists and their followers, the modernists. Christ's sacrificial death makes him the Mighty One who brings the kingdom to its consummation of glory and triumph.

"And didst buy for God," etc., at once adds the full saving effect of this sacrificial slaying. Ἀγοράζω means "to buy"; it is the word used in I Cor. 6:20; 7:23; II Pet. 2:1; Rev. 14:4; the stronger ἐξαγοράζω occurs in Gal. 3:13; 4:5. Need we discuss the synonymous expressions? The ἐν phrase names the tremendous price: "didst buy in connection with thy blood." Here belong all those passages that speak of blood. It is "blood" even more than "death" that connotes sacrifice; for one may die without being slain and may be slain without being made a sacrifice. In the New Testament the Lamb's blood is called the "price," also the λύτρον or "ransom" price. The datives: "didst buy for God," and again in v. 10: "didst make them for our God a kingdom," repeat the dative that occurs in 1:6: "*for* his God and Father." God sent the Lamb to be slain in order with his blood to buy *for him.*

There is no textual warrant for inserting ἡμᾶς: "didst buy *us* out of every tribe," etc., and for substituting ἡμᾶς for αὐτούς in v. 10: "didst make *us*" etc., as the A. V. translates. This alteration of the text leads those who accept it to suppose that the elders are representatives of the whole church. It likewise raises the question as to whether the four ζῷα are to be included in the church when they sing this song together with the elders and also have been bought by Christ's blood. As to the latter we should at once see that the ἐκ phrase, "out of every tribe and tongue and people and nation" speaks about human beings alone. Whether the living ones sing together with the elders or not makes no difference; in view of 4:8 we may say that they do sing together. As far as the earthly creature world is concerned, Rom. 8:21 shows that it shall be emancipated from the slavery of the corruption to which it has been subjected unwillingly; yet the Scriptures do not say that Christ bought or ransomed the earthly creature world as he did the church. The effect of our purchase extends to this creature world as the effect of our fall did. That is all.

The correct reading removes these questions. The long ἐκ phrase does not need a pronoun, for it is partitive: the Lamb bought for God "some of every tribe," etc. But did he not buy also those who deny him and bring upon themselves swift destruction, II Pet. 2:1? Most certainly. The atonement is universal and not limited (Calvin). In many places the reference is made to those who actually appropriate this atonement, "the saints" of v. 8. Take Eph. 5:25-27 as a beautiful illustration: the church receives all that the atonement contains and does. In the praise here offered the whole *Una Sancta* on earth is included, it is world-wide and not limited to the church as it existed in the year 95 but also as it will exist in all future ages, when it shall draw its members from every tribe if one thinks of tribes, from every tongue if one thinks of languages, from every λαός if one thinks of multitudes which are combined and form a mass unit, from every ἔθνος if one thinks of nations, each having its own customs, etc. In tribe there is the idea of the same descent, in tongue that of the same language, in people that of the same interests, in nation that of the same political unity. None of these differences presents a barrier to the church, the communion of saints.

Also critical commentators have expressed admiration of the wonderful and grandiose contents of this vision. We have already explained that in these visions the elders appear and act in their relation to the throne and to the Lamb symbolically as agents of the Word, and that in a literal sense elders are a part of this great church on earth which is composed of the saints.

10) "And didst make them for our God a kingdom and priests" repeats 1:6 (see the interpretation). Here we have the addition, "and they reign on the earth." There is no substantial difference between the present tense "they reign" and the variant reading "they shall reign." Both tenses signify what is the result of the Lamb's making the saints a kingdom. Chiliasts point to the future tense and date this reigning in their future millennium. But here we read, "he *made* them a kingdom," not, "he *shall make* them." Does this kingdom have to wait until its reigning begins? Is it not reigning now? But does not the devil and the world reign now? We have answered this in 1:6 when explaining the *Basileia.*

11) **And I saw and heard a voice of many angels around the throne and the living ones and the elders, and their number was myriads of myriads and thousands of thousands, saying with a great voice: Worthy is the Lamb, the one having been slain, to receive the power and riches and wisdom and strength and honor and glory and blessing!**

"I saw and heard a voice" is a condensed way of stating the seeing the speakers, the angels, and at the same time hearing what they say (= the accusative φωνήν). "Angels" is to be understood literally. Revelation uses no symbolical term for God's good angels. John saw a vast host of angels "around" the throne and the living ones and the elders. This is the same κυκλόθεν that occurred in 4:3, and again it is not to be conceived as being spatial but as denoting relation to God's throne (power, rule, dominion) and to the living ones (the earthly agencies of God's providence) and to the elders (the agents of God's Word). "Around" expresses the relation of the great angel host to all three of these in the mighty operations of God regarding the earth.

This is the passage which clearly distinguishes the angels from the four ζῶα or "living ones." The angels are as distinct from the living ones as from the elders. All that we have said regarding the four living ones in 4:6 should be reviewed. The angels are *not* symbolized by the four ζῶα; they are not even included in this symbolical term.

"The angels" are here named, and this applies even to their vast number, "myriads of myriads and thousands of thousands." These are not partitive genitives, these are not myriads of *some* myriads and thousands of *some* thousands. The genitives are superlative, they are like the genitive in the expression "the eons of the eons" (1:6) and convey the idea of myriads multiplied by myriads (ten thousands multiplied by ten thousands), thus uncounted myriads, uncounted thousands, cf., Heb. 12:22, "an innumeral company of angels." In Dan. 1:10, we have the climax: first thousands and secondly myriads (ten thousands). Revelation does not adopt this Old Testament climax just as Revelation always uses Old Testament material in its own distinct and advanced way. Here we have an apparent anticlimax, first multiplied ten thousands and then multiplied thousands. But this really forms a climax that is greater than ever. The greatest number in current use among the ancients was the myriad. When this greatest number is multiplied by itself, even this does not exhaust the number of angels, there are still thousands of thousands. The thousands that are multiplied, like the myriads, are stated indefinitely.

12) There is no grammatical irregularity in λέγοντες. In the Greek the participle has number, gender, and case and thus expresses much more than our English participle. Here it is used *ad sensum;* a finite verb would also be used only *ad sensum* but would be less smooth. This doxology of the angels is phrased in the third person: "Worthy is the Lamb," etc., and is thus addressed to all who are in relation to the Lamb in order that all of them may assent and agree to this message of these messengers (ἄγγελοι).

"To receive" or "to take" is the same λαβεῖν that occurred in 4:11, where three objects were added, "glory, honor, and power"; this is now expanded into seven: three being the number of deity and seven (3 + 4) the number of deity plus humanity. If the Lamb, like our Lord God (4:11), is to receive power and riches, etc., this implies that the universe ascribes these seven to him as being truly his possession. Δύναμις is omnipotent power; ἰσχύς is strength as a possession whether it is put forth in action or not. These two are synonymous like honor, glory, and blessing. The first four: power, riches, wisdom, strength, are objective, the last three: honor, glory, and blessing, are subjective as being offered to the Lamb by others. Riches are all possessions. All seven pertain to the opening of the book and its seven seals, the infinitely glorious work of bringing the prophecies of the book to triumphant realization in the consummation of the kingdom. Yet we cannot distribute the seven ascriptions and assign one to each of the seven seals; all seven pertain alike to each of the seven seals.

13) **And every creature that is in the heaven and on the earth and beneath the earth and on the sea and the things in them all I heard saying: To the One sitting on the throne and to the Lamb the blessing and the honor and the glory and the might for the eons of the eons!** Like "the angels" "every creature," etc., is to be understood literally. Κτίσμα, as the suffix -μα indicates = created thing and thus reverts to 4:11, "thou didst create — they were created," so that the two doxologies at the end of each of these visions correspond. "Creature" emphasizes the connection with the Creator who by his act of creation called every one of them into existence. Yet the first doxology, 4:11, glorifies the Creator, the second lets the creatures glorify both "the One sitting on the throne and the Lamb" under whose feet as the Lamb (Redeemer) all things have been placed. Throughout this second vision and also in this doxology this second vision is an advance on the first.

John saw and heard the many angels (v. 11). How God enabled him to do so is beyond us although God never has difficulty in this respect. Now John uses only "I heard saying" because the entire stress is on what he heard. To say that John did not see the creatures when he heard their doxology is to risk an unwarranted conclusion although how he even heard such a universal acclaim passes our comprehension. The accusative plural λέγοντας is in natural order after "every creature"; so also the accusative after the accusative πᾶν κτίσμα; so also the masculine participle, for not only does "every creature" include persons, but speaking is a personal act in any case. When one hears *a person,* the genitive is in place; *what* one hears is stated in the accusative. Some grammarians think that the accusative may be used for both, and that this distinction does not hold. We think it does hold. Here where the speakers occur in the accusative as λέγοντας, the point is what these creatures say and not merely that they were heard saying something.

All the phrases, "in the heaven," etc., certainly cover the universe, for which reason there also seem to be four phrases. "And the things in them all" emphasizes the universality, "in them" meaning in the heaven, on the earth, beneath the earth, and on the sea. Shall we try to enumerate the creatures found in these four places? Who is able to do so? "Beneath the earth" has the same force it had in v. 3, and here again we refuse to accept the fable of the *Totenreich* (see v. 3). We also refuse to think of the devils. Compare Phil. 2:10.

In v. 12 εὐλογία appears last; now it is placed first and takes up and continues the doxology of the angels. Δύναμις occurs first in v. 12; its synonym κράτος occurs last in this doxology, "might" as exercised (ἰσχύς in v. 12 is "strength" as possessed). "Honor and glory" are alike in 4:11; 5:12; and here in v. 13 in this doxology of the creatures which consists of four items. In 4:11 the terms have articles: also here in 5:13. In v. 12 but one article is used which regards all seven as one great unit. When it is articulated, each term stands out by itself. In all three doxologies the repeated use of καί heaps up the ascriptions like a great tower of praise. See 1:6, for the phrase, "for the eons of the eons."

14) **And the four living ones kept saying, Amen!** The imperfect ἔλεγον is iterative. After each of the seven ascriptions in v. 12 and the four in v. 13, this great "Amen!" rang out, the seal of verity (see 1:7). In Handel's *Messiah* Isa. 9:6 is sung sweetly and serenely until a pause is reached; and then every voice and every instrument rings out with overwhelming united power: "WONDERFUL! — — COUN-

SELLOR! — — THE MIGHTY GOD! — — THE EVERLASTING FATHER! — — THE PRINCE OF PEACE!" There is a great silence between the names. So, I take it, John was permitted to hear these ascriptions of the vision although they were infinitely grander. After each ascription there was heard a pause, then the tremendous "Amen!" was heard as the seal. This is utterly beyond our poor imagination.

And the elders fell down and did obeisance. Compare 4:10, where both verbs are used, and 5:8 where one suffices. Thus this vision of the Lamb and the book is complete.

CHAPTER VI

The Six Seals, chapter 6

1) The commentators on Revelation are usually divided into five groups:

1. *The Spiritualizing Group* seeks to spiritualize everything into a poetic-prophetic description of the struggle that, since the fall of man, has been going on between righteousness and sin, Christ and Satan. This group opposes the prophetic-historical interpretation wherever this is possible, and we must understand this its motive and aim in order to be able to judge what it offers on crucial points where it proves itself inadequate by dissolving the historical prophecies into general spiritual ideas.

2. *The Preterite* and *the Futuristic Groups* may be taken together. These two may, in a minor way, be called historical. The first refers the prophecies to John's own time, to the Roman state and its emperors, to the Jews and the destruction of Jerusalem during the first century and generally dates Revelation early, in the year 68, and regards Nero as the beast (chapter 13) and accepts the fiction that Nero (either dead by his own hand or in hiding) was soon to reappear with a great army of Parthians to take Rome for himself and to be the great antichrist. The critical view assumes that Revelation is a fanciful human composition which utilized the historical material of the day and expressed it in Jewish apocalyptic imagery or in Babylonian, Persian, Egyptian and Grecian symbolism. This critical comment dates Revelation about the year 96 and may make Domitian the beast (13:1). Who-

ever wrote Revelation was mistaken on many points, especially regarding the Lord's return. The book has little value for us save for a few general spiritual ideas; it was "a tract for the writer's time."

The futurists place everything beginning with chapter 4 at the time of the Second Coming of Christ, in the last seven years, or in the period that ends with his Coming. The Jews are assigned a great role. Revelation has little direct value for the church prior to the last few years of its existence.

The preterist conception was first advocated by the Jesuit Alcazar in 1614, the futurist by the Jesuit Ribera in 1580. The one great object of both is to get rid of the terrible stigma which the Protestant interpretations placed on the papacy which it regarded as the great antichrist. This stigma is removed also by Protestant and by rationalistic writers who find no antichrist in popery, none even in II Thess. 2.

3. *The Chronological Group* seeks to fit the events of history in their chronological sequence into what Revelation reveals. They cite many dates of European history in due order, some writers figuring out also the dates yet to come including that of their millennium and of the Parousia. Many accept the idea that a day = an actual year. They name among other things, the decline of the Roman Empire, the persecutions of Diocletian (303), Constantine, the Gothic and the Saracen invasions, the Waldenses, the Reformation, the Inquisition, the French Revolution, and World War I and World War II. The world outside of Europe, save for the Turks, is disregarded in a narrow, provincial way.

Milligan's remarks suffice: "All the greatest incidents, and, it must be added, some of the most trivial details of the past or present (such as the red color of the stockings of the Romish cardinals) are to be seen in its prophetic page; and the pious mind derives its encouragement and comfort from the thought that these things were long ago foretold. But the whole school of historical interpreters has been irretrievably discredited, if not by the extravagance of paltriness of its explanations, at least by their hopeless divergence from, and contradictions of, one another. Besides this, it has been observed that to make the Apocalypse deal almost exclusively with these historical incidents belonging to the later history of the church, is to make a book that must have been useless for those for whom it was written. How could the early Christians discover in it the establishment of Christianity under Constantine, the rise of Mohammedanism, the Lutheran Reformation, or the French Revolution? Of what possible use would it have been to foretell to them events in which they could have no interest? Would they either be wiser or better if they had known them? Would they not have substituted a vain prying into the future for the study of those divine principles which, belonging to every age, bring the weight of universal history to enforce the lessons of our own time? Nothing has tended more to destroy the feeling that there is value in the Apocalypse than this continuous historical interpretation of the book. The day, however, for such interpretations has passed, probably never to return." Let us at least hope so.

4. *The Synchronous Group* also interprets historically. It claims that Revelation covers the history of Christianity in the world until the last day. It leaves out none of the vital data that affect the kingdom. It sees them tending toward the climax of the final judgment and the new heaven and the new earth. But not in a series of chapters in chronological succession as in a book of history. While certain new things set in in the times and seasons reserved for the Father's authority (Acts 1:7), what the visions reveal runs parallel to a great extent. This is the case with

regard to the first five seals, the sixth takes us to the end which may come at any moment. One vision may reach far back, another may concentrate on the end. Dates are not revealed, are not to be sought. No matter when one lives his earthly life, Revelation makes his own time intelligible in view of the end. The Throne Vision of chapter 4 dominates all time; so does the Vision of the Lamb and the Book. This has been termed the cyclic view but topical is better; synchronous is probably best.

And I saw when the Lamb opened the first of the seven seals and I heard one of the four living ones saying as with a voice of thunder: Be going! And I saw, and lo, a white horse! And the one sitting upon him having a bow. And there was given to him a crown. And he went out conquering and to conquer.

"I saw when," etc., properly fixes attention upon the moment of the first great act, the opening of the first seal; again in v. 12 on the moment of the opening of the sixth seal. The very wording of these two, "And I saw *when*," etc., distinguishes these two seals from the intervening four and their simpler phrasing, "And when he opened," etc. "Seven seals" to indicate what God does in and with the world. There are six in the present vision, which indicates that the revelation of the six is not complete; the seventh follows in 8:1, etc. The first four belong together. Just what connection there is between the four horsemen of this vision and the four mentioned in Zech. 1:8-10 we need not investigate; see Keil, *Die Zwoelf Kleinen Propheten,* 528, etc., on this subject.

The opening of each seal does not usher in the reading of a corresponding part of the book, in fact, although the book is full of writing (5:1), nothing is at any time read. Let us note also that what the opening of the six seals reveals is brief. Only two verses are devoted to each of the first four seals, three to the fifth, and a short paragraph to the sixth. The opening of the seventh seal in 8:1 is a different matter. It would seem that the six seals, together with the supplementary vision of chapter 7, are preliminary to the main revelation of the book. Many have felt this, but few have caught its full import.

Let us say that in the six seals we are shown the general lines, a broad, simple sketch, and nothing more. The idea that the release of each seal reveals a picture that is found in the book, as though this were a picture book, is unacceptable. In a different class belong the artists' attempts which have pictured scenes in Revelation, notably *Die Bamberger Apocalypse*; A. Duerer of the year 1498; P. Cornelius; J. Schnorr von Carolsfeld. See Zahn, *Offenbarung*, 122, etc. What John sees each time the Lamb opens a seal is not something that is recorded in the book. The call: Ἔρχου! does not mean that John is to draw near and to look into the book. We take it that the substance of each part of the contents of the book is revealed to John as its seal is released. All of the writing God and the Lamb alone know; it includes absolutely everything. To John and thus to us only as much is revealed as it is good for us to know.

On ἀρνίον see 5:6; on the ζῶα, 4:6. Let us say also this, that in chapter 4, then in chapter 5, and now in chapter 6, John saw what he says he saw and heard what he says he heard. Each time the scene includes so much and no more; we do not think that the three scenes should be fused into one. None of them can be diagrammed. So we also do not have the elders, the torches of fire, the transparent sea of 4:4, etc., nor the myriads of angels of 5:11, nor "every creature" heard by John in 5:13. The law of paucity is applied in the case of each vision. Μίαν = "first" (R. 671, etc.; B.-D. 247, 1) and not "one" (our versions). The two ἐκ are partitive. The genitive ἑνός fixes attention upon the speaker; what he says is quoted. The correct reading is: Ἔρχου without an addition. There is no need of complicating the grammar by accepting the reading that has the nominative φωνή instead of the dative φωνῇ which has been adopted by Westcott and Hort.

The fact that each of the four horsemen should be introduced by one of the four living ones appears fitting when these living ones signify the earthly agents of God's providence, for what the horsemen symbolize is certainly connected with God's providential work and its agents. The fact that the living ones do not act in connection with the opening of the other seals thus also appears proper. The souls of the slain martyrs are beyond the operations of providence and its earthly agents; so is the cataclysm of the end. To allocate the four living ones to the four seals in the order in which they are described in 4:7 provides nothing helpful. Why should the young bull usher in war, the flying eagle death and hell? It is not well to seek for too much.

"As with a voice of thunder" occurs only in connection with the first living one although each of the four says, "Be going!" Does the thunderous voice lift the first horseman above the other three? Or is it only because of brevity that the thunderous voice is not mentioned in connection with the three? Although the first horseman is regarded as being far above the others, it is not necessary to assume the former. "Be going!" is to be taken in the sense of, "Be on thy way!" This command is certainly not addressed to John, for the present imperative is durative. The command, "Come up here!" in 4:1 is properly an aorist. An appeal to John 1:46, "Be coming and see!" is pointless; for consider Rev. 22:17, 20: "Be coming! Be coming!" John was right at hand and certainly needed no voice such as thunder to tell him to be coming; nor did he run away each time and have to be called anew; and why was he not called for the opening of the last two of the six seals? These calls are directed to the horsemen and bid them to be on the way to their work. The addition, "and see" is introduced from John 1:46, because it is supposed that John is addressed with a voice of thunder. Compare verses 3, 5, 7 (A. V.).

By spiritualizing the command into a prayer and thinking of all creation as groaning and travailing and asking the Lord to come, what John heard is reversed; for ἔρχου starts the horsemen off and does not call them to come and to arrive. They are to *go* into the earth and not to *come* to the place where John is in spirit. Whether we are to translate ἔρχομαι "come," as in 22:17, 20, or "go," as in Matt. 28:19, depends on the situation or the context. Here, "Go!" is correct; for John saw the horsemen close at hand, he even describes them, and they were to proceed far over the earth and not to approach John and the living ones.

2) "And I saw, and lo, a horse" is for some reason the wording followed for introducing all save the second horse. Why the wording for the second is, "And there went out another horse, fiery," seems strange unless this "other" is peculiarly connected with the first horse.

Mauro reminds us of the classic passage found in Job (39:19-25) regarding the horse, and of other passages as being helpful for determining what these "Four Apocalyptic Horsemen" (as they have been called) signify. In the Orient the ass and the camel are the animals used for transportation. Horses are connected with war, conquest, triumph. Each of the four horses has "one sitting upon him," a rider who controls the horse, but only the fourth one is named.

Each rider is equipped for a mission, yet again the law of paucity is applied — we do not see the horsemen rushing away; ἐξῆλθεν (used only in v. 4) indicates movement so that we do not think that they were stationary when John saw them. Horse, rider, and what is said of him, are a composite symbol. This includes also the color of the horses.

It is plain that this white horse and his rider, crowned and conquering, is properly placed first. The other three are not his equal although they are introduced in the same language. Many think that the first rider represents Christ himself, and that 19:11-16 presents only a fuller picture; here Christ is shown as he starts on his victory, and in 19:11, etc., as he is about to complete it; futurists place also 6:2, etc., near the end. Yet Christ is undoubtedly the Lamb that opens all the seals; would *he*, then, be only one of these riders? Would one of the living ones order *him* to go as the other horsemen are ordered to go? Such considerations move some to think that Christianity is here personified as the other horsemen are personifications. The preterists think of a Roman emperor. Some point to the bow as the weapon of a Parthian victor. Thus we are directed to even an antichristian symbol, to a false Christ, or to human culture, or science personified. The white color is then intended to deceive. Yet the other three colors are true colors.

The other three horsemen are plainly personifications; it is, therefore, fair to conclude that the first also is. Those who think of Christ or Christianity are not far wrong. Those who refer to Matt. 24 are correct. Yet Matt. 24:5, 11 are not referred to; v. 6, 7 point to the three other horsemen, v. 9, 10 to the fifth seal and to the martyrs, v. 29 to the sixth seal and to the end. Matt. 24:14 fits this first horseman, yet not so much "the gospel of the kingdom" considered as the *saving* power; it is the gospel in the sense of the *whole* Word of God as Jesus speaks of it in John 12:48b.

The Word of God rides forth into all the world. Its carrier, the horse, is white, which is the color of holiness and of heaven. We retain this significance throughout. Perhaps the Roman victors always rode on white horses, but were there no exceptions? But this is not a rider such as those in a triumphal procession who ride through the streets of Rome with victorious legions, chained captives and loads of booty merely in celebration of a victory; this rider is alone and he rides forth to conquer by his own power. The Word of God conquers alone; its power lies wholly in itself. The color white is to denote victory, the horse, the bow, the crown, and the words, "conquering and to conquer" emphasize the victory. All the horses and all the riders conquer, all of them, although they are of different colors, cannot be withstood. It is the *holy* Word that comes first, must come first.

Why does this rider not carry a μάχαιρα, the Roman short sword (v. 4) to which the Word itself is likened in Eph. 6:17; or the ῥομφαία, the great sword (v. 8) which is associated with Christ in 1:16 and 2:13? To say that the bow of this rider plus the white horse mean nothing because arbitrary and even frivolous and ridiculous notions have been attached to them, does not satisfy. If white means nothing, why are these horses of different colors? The Roman sword and the Thracian great sword are in the hands of other riders. These come to close grips with their opponents, the bow is fitting for fighting at a distance; Ps. 45:5 is not ineptly quoted. No enemy, however far he may flee, escapes this bow.

"And there was given to him a crown," a στέφανος, on which see 2:20; 3:11. It may be argued as to whether this crown symbolizes only victory or also royalty; it is certain that the former is indicated. The Word does not need to win its victory in order to become a victor; it is a victor before an arrow is shot. God "gave" it a crown because it is his Word.

"And he went out conquering and to conquer." The ἔρχομαι in the compound verb means "to go" (A. V. "went") and not "to come" (R. V. "came"). John saw him go, not come. Call the aorist ingressive. The present participle "conquering" is descriptive; the ἵνα clause with its aorist (which is equal to an infinitive), "and to conquer," means to conquer completely, with finality. The use of two expressions emphasizes the conquering career; first, its course, next, its finality.

The power of the Word here described is directed against the enemies of the Lamb. So are the powers of the four horsemen. This is rather plain. But what about the believers? The question regarding these usually disturbs the commentators when they come to consider "hades" in v. 8. Some are also puzzled in regard to the work of the third horseman. What happens to believers is not included in the vision of the horsemen. Some will become martyrs; their souls, like Stephen's, are in heaven and not in the hades of a *Totenreich.* The first six seals are not exhaustive, they sketch certain fundamental outlines; all the rest follows in due order. There is no need to put into these preliminary revelations more than the simple great facts they intend to convey. Here only the tense of νικήσῃ reveals the finality of the victory of the Holy Word over all opposition in the world. That is enough.

3) **And when he opened the second seal, I heard the second living one saying, Be going!** Compare the remarks on v. 1. The genitives after ἤκουσα occur also in verses 5 and 7. These "when" do not occur in a temporal succession. John is given to see

and to hear everything in due order as his finite mind is able to receive the revelations.

4) **And there went out another horse, fiery. And to the one sitting on him, there was given to him to take the peace from the earth, and that they shall slay one another. And there was given to him a great short sword.**

All interpreters are agreed that *war* is here symbolized. Even when the significance of "white" is disputed, "red," πυρρός, the color of fire, "fire-red," is regarded as the symbol of war and bloodshed and the incendiarism of war.

Plain as this is because it so closely matches Jesus' own words: "You shall hear of wars and rumors of wars . . . For nation shall rise against nation, and kingdom against kingdom" (Matt. 24:6, 7) that no comment is needed, strange notions are added. Futurists think that these wars shall occur near the end and shall annul the promise of peace made by the deceiver on the first horse. Another view stresses "shall slay one another" and thinks that they denote civil wars and then dates them: after the great *Pax Romana* which continued for two centuries, from Julius Cæsar, B. C. 30, to Commodus, A. D. 192, the era of civil strife set in which continued for ninety-two years, in which thirty-two emperors and twenty-seven pretenders kept up the turmoil. This is a sample of provincialism. The venerable Bede and Calov think that the rider on the red horse is the devil. Some think of a war against Christians and place Nero or some emperor on the horse. Allied to these views is that of Mauro who makes this war spiritual, ignores Matt. 24:6, 7, and points to Matt. 10:34 and Luke 12:49-53, and then enumerates the persecutions of Paul and Barnabas recorded in Acts, traders following missionaries (the white horse) and starting hatred, the discovery of gold in the Rand of South Africa, the World War, the

Thirty Years' War, the breach of the *Pax Romana*, Catholics and Protestants, modernists and fundamentalists at war.

Ἐκ τῆς γῆς cannot be restricted to the Roman Empire. Slaying one another is not persecution of believers. In every war "they slay one another." Spiritualizing where there is no reason is always unfortunate; so is combining passages of Scripture that ought not to be combined. The white horse does not symbolize the saving gospel which then divides men so that they go to war. The μάχαιρα, the Roman short sword, is called "great," not because it was disproportionate to the horse and the rider, but because of the constant and the terrific slaughter it symbolizes.

The New Testament era is not different from that of the Old Testament as regards wars, famine, death. The wild passions of the wicked and the sin abroad in all nations constantly precipitate wars. In the midst of them and despite them the Lamb brings his kingdom to its triumphant consummation. Wars themselves, as signs of the ripening unto final judgment, are a continuous sign of the end, they are like great placard advertisements that are strung along the highway of the word's history. Scripture records this regarding the New Testament era, not merely as a prophetic fact but as a fact of judgment. As were all the riders, this one is also commanded, "Go!" to execute the Lamb's will.

Schemes and pacts to abolish war on earth, however well intended, are hopeless. As long as the world and the nations love sin and deal in unrighteousness, "Keep going!" must speed this rider of judgment on his fire-red way. Some thought they were waging World War I in order to end all war, and now, against their will, they learn that it was only pregnant with more wars and rumors of war.

5) **And when he opened the third seal, I heard the third living one saying, Be going!** Agents of providence speed also this rider on his way in the world.

And I saw, and lo, a black horse! And the one sitting on him having a balance in his hand. A ζυγός is the bar that either has scales at both ends of it or has a weight at one end and a pan suspended from the other. The nominatives simply flash the image on the screen, "lo" pointing to it in exclamation.

6) **And I heard as it were a voice amid the four living ones saying: A choinix of wheat at a denarius, and three choinix of barley at a denarius! And the oil and the wine do not damage!** In this symbol something resembling a voice speaks. To John it sounded ὡς φωνή, "as a voice." It was not that the third living one or one of the four spoke but like a voice "amid" all four. Here again, as in the case of all the phrases and adverbs occurring in 4:4-6, ἐν μέσῳ is not spatial but expresses relation. "Amid the four living ones" means that what spoke like a voice bore a certain relation to all four ζῶα, to all the agents of God's providence. The idea is not that they themselves spoke, nor that the Lamb or the throne spoke. The speaker is not the point of emphasis but the relation of what is said to all these symbolized agents and agencies of providence. All the agents of divine providence are involved in the judgment mission of this horseman.

To make this black horse a special opposite of the white one is misleading. All four symbolic colors have their own significance, each indicates the mission of its own horseman. Numerous references to wheat, barley, and then to oil and wine, on the plea of interpreting Scripture by Scripture, may prove confusing. What light can Luke 10:34, the good Samaritan's oil and wine, throw on this passage? Allegorizing is not interpreting. This horse is not the Roman army, the rider is not Titus at the time of the destruction of Jerusalem, the wheat and the barley are not Jews, and the oil and the wine are not Christians. This is a sample of such allegorizing.

The commonly accepted view thinks that this horseman symbolizes famine, and that "black" signifies hunger (Lam. 4:8, 9). Objection is raised to this view; Ellicott exclaims, "Did ever man hear of such a famine as this?" His own solution is also weak, for μὴ ἀδικήσῃ does not mean, "Do not deal unjustly in!" but, "Do not hurt or harm!" The idea of famine, the idea of justice and of injustice, only approach what is here symbolized. "Famine," real famine, appears in its place in v. 8. Mauro comes a bit nearer with his idea of industrialism, commercialism, international finance and commerce, which he blames onto the Jews and even finds prophesied in the Old Testament. He loses what cue he senses when he spiritualizes the oil and the wine and identifies them with God's Spirit and his joy and so ends by spiritualizing also "the bread by weight" by equating it with spiritual dearth. He thinks only the Christians will be left with the oil and the wine to comfort them. Those interpreters who regard this as a symbol of famine are more balanced when they think of the oil and the wine as being natural products like the wheat and the barley, that remain unhurt and thus reduce the severity of the famine.

The cry: "A choinix of wheat at a denarius, and three choinix of barely at a denarius!" is an offer made on the market. These are high prices but not, however, actual famine prices. A choinix (dry measure) = four cotylae or two sextarii (two xestes) = about two pints, a slave's scant ration of wheat for a day, three choinix of barley being equal in nourishment. A denarius is a day's wage. All that a man is able to earn in a day is his day's ration in wheat or in barley which barely keeps him alive. Nothing is left for his many other needs, for other food, and nothing for a family he may have. The idea of a famine has this much to support it: the ratio of price (the genitives denote price) to the quantity of grain. Yet famine is not the point to be stressed. Plenty of wheat and of barley is to be had at the indicated price, but the daily wage of the common man offers him scarcely enough to subsist because he is reduced to the grain ration alone. That is half of the picture. Those who think of justice feel the cue, but they should rather say injustice: a man is able to earn only a slave's ration of grain by a whole day's labor.

The other half of the picture is found in the command: "And the oil and the wine do not damage!" In negative aorist commands we have the subjunctive and not the imperative. Since they are unhurt, oil and wine also exist in plenty, but they are utterly beyond the reach of common workers. Need we say who enjoys them? Only the rich. Oil and wine are not even luxuries; they represent comfort, comfort that is denied the common worker. Olive oil is the fat of the Oriental world. That is why we read so much about olive trees and "oil" (olive oil) in the Bible. Wine is the common beverage. Hence so much is said about wine in the Scriptures. Mauro is on the right track when he speaks about commercialism, finance, etc., and even when he introduces the greedy Jew.

The judgment here symbolized is the calamity of dislocation, *the failure of just, equitable distribution of the products of the earth.* Even America learned all about it during the world depression that started in 1929, though it is an old, old story, that has many far blacker chapters than this recent one. The common workers live like slaves, they are half-starved if not worse; the few rich enjoy everything. Call it the wrong social system; blame it onto capitalism, name it commercialism, or use other terms. The balance is awry. What is measured out is not equal. Some commentators think they must combine the red and the black rider (war and famine); but this dependence is not correct. Revolutions (wars) often arise because of economic injustice. Men attempt to abolish war without abolishing the sin, wickedness, injustice that are in their hearts; so they determine to abolish social, industrial, commercial injustice, poverty and excessive wealth, without abolishing the moral cause back of them. The black horseman is ever riding in the whole world.

7) **And when he opened the fourth seal, I heard a voice of the fourth living one saying, Be going!** This order speeds this horseman of judgment on his way as the others had been commanded to go.

8) **And I saw, and lo, a livid horse, and the one sitting on him, name for him The Death. And the hades kept following after him. And there was given to him authority over the fourth part of the earth to kill in connection with a great sword and in connection with death and by the wild beasts of the earth.**

This symbol seems to be the plainest of all and seems to call for little exposition. It presents, not death in general, but *calamitous death* as a judgment. On the four deadly agencies compare Ezek. 14:21. Mauro allegorizes this passage and refers to Matt. 13:24, etc., and speaks of deadly spiritual forces, and lets the devil send out this horseman because *he* finds that new means must be employed, namely the killing lie. Preterists point to the period A. D. 248 to 296 when pestilence raged, when 5,000 died daily in Rome itself, and many towns that had escaped the ravages of the barbarians were entirely depopulated by the pestilence (Gibbon). But this is only one instance that occurred under only one of the four agencies.

This horse is χλωρός, livid, pallid, pale, which is surely a fitting color. "Was given authority," etc., means by the Lamb and not by the devil. The nominative ὄνομα αὐτῷ, is one of the several common ways employed in the Greek for introducing a name, here the rider's name, "The Death," who, like the other riders, is already personified by the substantivized participle "the one sitting upon the horse." So also ὁ ᾅδης is personified as it is in 20:14, the article being used in both instances for this reason. Hades "keeps following" the Death rider to gather in the souls of those whom he kills off, ἀποκτεῖναι, the effective aorist.

Here again we are told that hades is the *Totenreich*, the intermediate place into which all the souls of the dead go, and not hell, the place of the damned. The argument that seems to clinch this idea is the fact that calamitous death strikes also Christians, and that these surely do not go into hell, the place of the damned. Where, then, do they go save into the *Totenreich*? But where did the soul of Stephen go (Acts 7:59)? And what about Paul's desire to depart and to be with Christ (Phil. 1:23)? The departed saints of both Testaments at once entered heaven. Right here in v. 9 the souls of the slain martyrs are not in a *Totenreich* but beneath the heavenly altar. Compare 20:4. The vision of this fourth horseman does not deal with the godly.

These four are *riders of judgment*. In John 3:18 Jesus says, Ὁ πιστεύων εἰς αὐτὸν οὐ κρίνεται, the believer in Christ is not judged; John 5:24, εἰς κρίσιν οὐκ ἔρχεται, does not come into judgment. The judgments here symbolized sweep the ungodly into hades. The godly may die in war, suffer because of the injustice of wages and food, die during the calamitous deaths that again and again sweep the world, but these are afflictions (θλίψεις) for them, trials (πειρασμοί), chastisement as sons (παιδεία Κυρίου, Heb. 12:5), evidence of God's love and not judgment (κρίσις), not evidences of wrath. These symbols picture what comes upon the ungodly world and nothing more. So hell follows after this fourth horseman and swallows up the souls of his victims. To think of a *Totenreich* into which *all* men pass is pointless, for no man ever became immortal on earth since Adam fell. On the supposition of a *Totenreich* the Lamb would not need to send out his riders of judgment.

Many puzzle about "the authority over the fourth part of the earth," and some think of it geographically and refer it to the Roman empire, which they say was divided into West, East, Illyricum, and Central Italy. Jerome's Vulgate translates the singular τὸ τέταρτον as plural "four parts." "The fourth part of the earth" is quantitative like "the third part" mentioned in 8:7, and symbolizes the extent of the killing. On ῥομφαία, the terrible "great sword," which is a fitting instrument in the hands of men, see the notes on 1:16. Besides employing murderous men "The Death" uses "famine" and θάνατος, which, because of the rider's own name and because of the connection with "famine," means "pestilence." The Death kills ἐν, "in connection with" these three; the fourth are θηρία, "wild beasts," in the case of which ὑπό, "by," is the preposition preferred.

9) **And when he opened the fifth seal** (v. 12 the sixth; 8:1, the seventh) is in agreement with the statements about the first four seals. But the effect produced is entirely different in the case of the last three seals; each effect is wholly unique. No additional horsemen appear, no living ones shout, "Be going!" Regarding the fifth seal John writes: **I saw beneath the altar the souls of those that have been slain because of the Word of God and because of the testimony which they had, and they shouted with a great voice, saying: How long, Lord Absolute, the Holy**

and Genuine One, dost thou not judge and avenge our blood on those dwelling on the earth? And there was given to them, each one, a white flowing robe, and it was said to them that they shall wait yet a little time until there be filled full (in number) **also their fellow slaves and their brethren, those about to be killed off as also they themselves.**

Because an altar is now mentioned some think of a Temple scene and combine the throne scene of chapter 4 and the scene of the Lamb and the book with this altar and the whole arrangement of the Temple as it was found in Jerusalem, save that they locate everything in heaven. This view is found also in 4:6, where the "glassy" sea is regarded as the counterpart of the bronze laver that stood in the court of the priests. The horsemen are not brought into this view; they are placed on the earth although John is "in spirit" in heaven (4:1), and the living ones call forth each horseman in heaven.

Each vision is a separate entity and has its own meaning. This is also true with regard to the seven seals. The instant a seal is opened, John is permitted "in spirit" to see what that seal reveals. Each of these revelations is distinct. This fifth seal does not reveal a temple scene in heaven. Those who slew and who slay the martyrs do not function as priests about this altar; the bodies of the martyrs are not burnt on this altar. The slayers do not wash themselves and do not wash away the blood with water from the "glassy" sea beside this altar.

In line with such views is the further idea that John could not *see* these *souls* unless they had some sort of bodies. Commentators thus supply the bodies they deem necessary for John's seeing by either making the white robes of state the bodies or by inventing some sort of ethereal bodies as is done in connection with II

Cor. 5:1-4. Did the One sitting on the throne (4:2) also have a body so that John could *see* him? Did the myriads of angels (5:11) have bodies that John saw? This seeing was not done by means of John's natural eyes, for twice he has already told us that he was "in spirit." When does God ever have difficulty in letting men see what and whom he desires to have them see?

Some pause at the word ψυχαί and think that this refers to what once animated the bodies of the martyrs and is in contrast with πνεύματα; thus they introduce another perplexity. But such a contrast is not intended, and ψυχαί is merely the proper word with the genitive τῶν ἐσφαγμένων, "of those having been slain," the same participle being used with reference to the Lamb in 5:6, 12, and the finite verb in 5:9. The fact that no contrast is intended we see from the ψυχαί of 20:4, and by comparing these two passages and their ψυχαί with Acts 7:59, where Stephen prays, "Receive my spirit!" and Heb. 12:23, "spirits of righteous ones having been brought to the goal."

We furthermore cannot accept the idea of a *physical* altar of burnt offering and the *spatial* idea of these souls who have some sort of bodies lying in a mass "*under*" (A. V.), or "*underneath*" (R. V.) such an altar. Was there an open space under this altar of sufficient size to accommodate many martyrs? Why should the martyrs be assigned so peculiar a place in heaven? The souls of the martyrs who were slain for Christ's sake are connected with the altar of sacrifice because they were slain, because their blood was shed as holy blood, was poured out as a sacrifice to God and to Christ. "Beneath" = Lev. 4:7: the priest "shall pour all the blood of the bullock at the bottom of the altar of the burnt offering." The phrase is symbolical and lifts the blood of the slain martyrs into its true connection with God. Some stress this thought unduly when they find the ψυχή or life in the blood, the blood being the bearer of the physical life. They also speak of "animal souls." These ψυχαί have left their blood here on earth. The phrase introduced by "beneath," like the adverbs and the phrases occurring in 4:4, etc., is not to indicate space but relation. Rabbinical parallels have been adduced, but they are not parallels. The one speaks of Moses dwelling under the throne of God's glory; the other of the souls of the righteous being preserved under the throne of the glory. Neither speaks of martyrs or of the altar or of blood or of avenging this blood.

The martyrs have been slain "because of the Word of God and because of the testimony which they had." This is the Word whose speaker and source is God and the testimony which the great Witness or Testifier made (1:5; 3:4), which the martyrs had when, for the sake of both, they were slain on earth. We have the same Word and testimony in 1:9. The two διά only emphasize the two objects. The testimony is not an attestation of the faith and the faithfulness of the martyrs; those who slew them did not do so because Christ testified that the martyrs were true to him but because these martyrs refused to disown God's Word and Christ's testimony.

10) John heard these martyrs crying to God with a great voice: "How long, Lord Absolute, the Holy and Genuine One, dost thou not judge and avenge our blood on those dwelling on the earth?" God is addressed as ὁ Δεσπότης (from which we have "despot") because he is the Absolute Lord of the universe and because the slaying of those who submit to his Word and to his Son's testimony constitutes the most flagrant challenge to his absolute power and authority. There is no "O" in the Greek but only the nominative with its article used as a vocative. Ὁ ἅγιος καὶ ἀληθινός is an apposition and is explained in 3:7, where the designation is used with reference to Christ. As the slaying of the mar-

tyrs challenges the absolute authority of God, it thereby challenges him also as "the Holy One" who abominates all sin and as the One who is at the same time "Genuine" as though he were not what he is, namely the only real God but one who may be scorned with impunity. See the two ἀληθινός for God and for Christ in I John 5:20.

Some have found a difficulty in this cry for judgment and avenging in view of Luke 23:14, where Jesus prays for his murderers, and of Acts 7:60, Stephen's similar prayer. It is asked, pointedly, how can Stephen, the martyr, cry, "Lord, do not place this sin to their charge!" and his soul cry in heaven, "Avenge my blood!" Neither here nor in 19:2 ("hath avenged the blood") is the answer that this is the Old Testament spirit while Luke 23:14 and Acts 7:60 manifest the New Testament spirit. Is not the blood of all the Old Testament martyrs, from that of Abel to Zacharias, to come upon the New Testament persecutors of the witnesses whom Jesus will send (Matt. 23:35; Luke 11:51)? Is there a clash between the martyrs, those of the Old Testament crying one thing, those of the New another? The prayer for pardon is offered for those who still have the time of grace to repent; the cry for being avenged is uttered at the time when grace has come to an end and judgment alone is left. It is one and the same God who extends grace and then visits with judgment. These martyrs do not cry for vengeance upon the wicked who slew them; their cry involves something that is far greater.

They cry to have their blood avenged upon "those dwelling on the earth." They cry to God to send the final judgment. The question as to how many and who these martyrs are should thus answer itself: they are not all those of the Old Testament (Acts 7:52); not the martrys of what the futurists call the Great Tribulation; but the martyrs from the time of Stephen until the time of John's vision. Those of the Old Testament would cry for vengeance upon the Jews. Those yet to become martyrs appear in v. 11. "Those dwelling on the earth" are not men on earth in general but the ungodly who have no home but earth and want no other home. "The kings of the earth" is parallel and refers to the great and eminent among "those dwelling on the earth."

This brings us to the relation of the fifth seal to the other seals. The relation is not chronological so that the work of the four horsemen is completed before martyrs are slain and cry to God. The starting point of the seals is the Lamb even as *he* opens the seals. Nor is this opening to be dated in the year 95 when it was granted to John to see. This opening of the seals belongs to the exaltation of the Lamb who has himself been slain even as his having been slain enables him to open the seals. The fact that martyrs had already been slain and are revealed in this seal and that many more martyrs are to follow, is not a matter of dates as between the day of the Lamb's ascension in glory and the year and the day of this vision; it is wholly a matter of what was granted to John to see. Thus the sixth seal reveals the great signs of the end.

In what is said about the four horsemen there is no intimation regarding the church. These four horsemen bring something to the whole world, and their work continues to the end of time. Even in this fifth seal the church does not appear as such but only the early martrys and their future successors to the end of time. But there could be no martyrs without the church. Its existence and its continuation are implied. That, however, is enough. The martyrs slain and yet to be slain are the crown and the glory of the church, for their slaying reflects the slaying of the Lamb himself. *Martyrdom* is revealed in this seal as distinguishing the New Testament Era, *martyrdom for the sake of God's Word and Christ's testimony.* These slaughters are not due to the horsemen, to war or to death in general by which thousands are swept into hades. These martyrdoms lie on a higher plane, hence they are not symbolized by a new horseman. But this is true, like the four horsemen and even more than the last three of them, the martyrs point to the end, yea to the consummation at the end. The martyrs already slain cry, "How long!"

"And there was given to them, to each one, a white flowing robe," στολή, German *Talar*, a robe of state flowing to the feet. The aorist states only the past fact. John did not see the act of giving. When the gift was made to each of them need not be stated; we know when Stephen received his robe, namely when his spirit was received by Jesus. These are the same *stolai* that were mentioned in 7:9, 14. In 3:4, the ἱμάτια are the robes which the faithful wear in this life; but in 3:5, ἐν λευκοῖς refers to the heavenly white robes of the blessed in heaven. "White" symbolizes the beauty of holiness and not victory or priestliness. The robes do not refer to bodies or imply the existence of bodies; nor do these robes signify a special degree of glory. John did not die as a martyr, yet his degree of glory will be one of the highest. There is no need to refer to 3:4, where the twenty-four elders have white *himatia* and golden crowns, and to ask why the martyrs have no crowns. Why not also ask why the martyrs are not seated on thrones as were the elders when in 20:4 there are thrones for them and for others? The elders symbolize the Word in its relation to the throne (see 4:4) while here we have ψυχαί, actual persons. We have them depicted in only one condition, only with what serves that condition, which in no way prevents the picturing of other conditions in other connections and visions as in 20:4.

These robes of state are the martyrs' reward of grace. They also receive an answer to their cry. "And it was said to them that they shall wait yet a little time until there be filled full also their fellow slaves and their brethren, those about to be killed off as also they themselves." The passive aorist ἐρρέθη, "it was said to them," veils the speaker. 'Αναπαύω = to rest, here *abwarten* (B.-P. 92). Like the cry, "How long?" this reply is introduced by an aorist for the purpose of this vision and for what John is to know. This does not imply that these martyrs had kept silence until John appeared and *then* raised this cry and *then* received their robes and this reply. The correct reading is ἔτι χρόνον μικρόν; the three variants are textually quite inferior.

The reading that has the passive πληρωθῶσι does not yield the sense: until they be filled as far as number is concerned; and the reading that has the active πληρώσωσι does not signify: until they fulfill their course. Both may refer to either, and here the point is that of number: until the last martyr has been killed, has been added to fill the number. To be sure, all will complete their course, i. e., be steadfast until they are killed, but here the point to be made concerns their number. The moment that is full, the κρίσις and the ἐκδίκησις will follow. God wants so many martyrs in this wicked world "of those dwelling on the earth," so many that attain the high distinction of a bloody death. The cup of his wrath is not quickly spilled; it is filled slowly and then overflows at last. It was forty years after Christ's death before the Jewish nation was destroyed; Stephen's martyrdom was not enough. Throughout Revelation the term, "those dwelling on the earth," refers to men who are afar from God although the gospel was sent into all the earth. The immediate murderers of the martyrs are not the only guilty ones. Slaying martyrs is the climax of unbelief, the top of the mountain of guilt of the unbelieving earth-dwellers.

These other martyrs are called "the fellow slaves and the brethren" of those already slain. These are titles which apply to all of us as fellow believers, titles that were purposely chosen for this very reason. We note Christ's slaves in 1:1 and John himself as Christ's slave, and in 1:9, John as the brother of the others although he did not become a martyr. It is, indeed, a striking point and exceptional in every way, that God delays the final judgment until the world has killed off so many martyrs. There is certainly a reference to Matt. 24:9, but also an advance on that passage. Elsewhere we are told that the end will come when the full number of the Gentiles has come to faith, or when the gospel has been preached as a testimony to all nations, or when the antichrist has run his course. All these statements point to the same terminus.

12-14) **And I saw when he opened the sixth seal, and a great shaking occurred, and the sun became black as sackcloth of hair, and the whole moon became as blood, and the stars of the heaven fell to the earth as a fig tree casts her winter figs when shaken by a great wind. And the heaven was separated as a book roll being rolled up, and every mountain and island were moved out of their places.**
For those who will study Matt. 24:29 and II Pet. 3:10,
12 little comment will be needed. Here we have one picture of the end. The figures used are simply figures. Quaking, sun, whole moon (i. e., full moon), heaven, stars, mountains and islands are to be understood literally. The dispute as to whether this cataclysm is to be dated before or after what the futurists call the Great Tribulation and what they call the Rapture is unimportant. Here we get only one glimpse of the end of the world.

Mauro seeks to symbolize: the great shaking = social upheaval; the sun = supreme governmental authority that is blotted out as was the case at the time of the French Revolution; the mountains = conspicuous nationalities; the islands = lesser communities. But what about the moon and the heaven? What is here portrayed is not repeated upheaval in the course of history but, as all other pertinent Scripture shows, the cataclysm at the end of the world. A few others have sought to symbolize. Hengstenberg refers to *schwere und truebe Zeiten*, "grievous and somber times"; his interpretation of the sun is similar to Mauro's, but the stars are individual nobles and princes. Kliefoth thinks of eclipses of the sun and of the moon; with reference to the stars he speaks about comets and meteors; the heavens only "move back"; the mountains and the islands only shift their places. These phenomena are thus reduced to smaller proportions and occur again and again.

A most important point to be noted is that the sixth seal places us at the *end*. In succeeding visions we are again placed there. The visions are synchronous prophecy that reaches the end. But only in part. John is permitted to see some things more than once, but each time from a different perspective. Other things he is permitted to see but once. Some vistas are long, others are short. The five seals extend to the very end but do not name it. The fifth only mentions the end, "until," etc. The sixth presents only the end, really only certain phenomena occurring at the end. Because of the number six these six indicate that the revelation is *not yet complete;* much more is to follow. The seventh seal is still to be revealed.

A σεισμός is a quake or shaking and not merely an earthquake. Here it involves the dislocation of the universe. "The powers of the heavens shall be shaken," Matt. 24:29. On σάκκος compare Isa. 50:3; the adjective τρίχινος = made of hair. Such a black, ugly, rough sack was often used at a time of mourning and despair. "The sun became black," etc. = Matt. 24:29: "The sun shall be made dark," its light having been ended forever. This is not a passing eclipse. "The whole moon became as blood" = Matt. 24:29: "The moon shall not give her brightness." "The stars of the heaven fell to the earth" = Matt. 24:29: "The stars shall fall from the heaven." Ὄλυνθοι are figs "which grow during the winter under the leaves but ripen as seldom as the untimely figs of spring" (Liddell and Scott) and thus dry up and drop during a wind; compare Isa. 34:4. "The heaven was separated as a βίβλιον or book roll being rolled up" = Isa. 34:4. "The heavens shall be rolled together as a scroll" = II Pet. 3:10: "The heavens shall pass away with a great noise," v. 12, "being on fire shall be dissolved." Ἀποχωρίζω = to separate. What we call the heaven John saw separated from its place, shriveled and curled up like paper. On the mountains and the islands compare 16:20; they were moved so as to disappear.

15-17) **And the kings of the earth and the magnates and the chiliarchs and the rich and the strong and every slave and freeman hid themselves in the caves and in the cliffs of the mountains and say to the mountains and to the cliffs: Fall upon us and hide us from the countenance of the One sitting on the throne and from the wrath of the Lamb! Because there did come the day, the great one, of their wrath, and who is able to stand?** It has been said that men cannot do what is here stated when the cataclysm described in v. 12-14 occurs, but such a claim is unwarranted. So also is the comment that this is stereotyped apocalyptic language that is extravagant and not to be understood as it reads because it describes only a terrible earthquake, etc., and not the end of the world. The language that describes what these people do is to a degree taken from the Old Testament, Isa. 2:10, 19, 21; their cry from Hos. 10:8; but look also at Luke 23:30: "Then shall they begin to say to the mountains, 'Fall on us!' and to the hills, 'Cover us!'" For the whole read Matt. 24:30: "Then shall all the tribes of the earth mourn, and they shall see the Son of man coming in the clouds of heaven with power and great glory." John's vision contains nothing about the godly; Matt. 24:32 and Luke 21:29 do.

There are in reality not seven subjects, for after the five plurals we have "every slave and freeman" as the sixth. "Every" is followed by two singulars and regards the two as one. The number six fits the ungodly. Kings are the highest rulers on earth; μεγιστᾶνες are the high men at court, next to the supreme rulers in office; chiliarchs are the generals; the rich are the money-magnates; the strong are men who are distinguished by bodily strength or by strong influence on earth. "Every slave and freeman," an expression that is taken from the Roman world of John's time, takes in the entire lower class of men. The whole world had multitudes of slaves and thus also multitudes of slaves who were released freedmen.

This hiding in caves and in cliffs, this crying for the mountains and the cliffs to fall on them and to hide them from the wrath, is the graphic picture of terror and despair, cf., Luke 23:30. Note πέτρα which means a rocky mass, a cliff; πέτρος would be a boulder (Matt. 16:18, "Peter"). The tragedy of the Flood, of Sodom and Gomorrah, of the destruction of Jerusalem, prefigures this ultimate tragedy of terror and absolute despair. "The One sitting on the throne" is God (4:2), the throne symbolizing his absolute power and dominion, his sitting the exercise thereof. With him must be joined "the wrath of the Lamb"; for God *and* the Lamb are scorned by "those dwelling on the earth" (v. 10), their six classes, all the high and the low here named. The power of the Lamb is symbolized in 5:6. "Their wrath" combines God and the Lamb. The repetition of "wrath" is intentional; all of it now blazes forth. "Who can stand?" None of those who now cry in despair.

"There did come the day, the great one, of their wrath" recalls the many references to this "day" found in both Testaments. Mal. 4:1; Matt. 7:22; I Cor. 1:8; I Thess. 5:2; II Pet. 3:10; *et al.* Only this much is put into this vision; the rest follows in due course.

CHAPTER VII

The 144,000, chapter 7

1) This two-part vision is not an "intermezzo," an *"entre-acte,"* a sort of parenthesis. It is also not a part of, nor an appendix to, the sixth seal; nor an introduction to the seventh seal. The fact that the symbolism of this vision is not the opening of a seal, is not a reason for considering it parenthetical. Save for the martyrs mentioned in connection with the fifth seal nothing has been said about the *church;* a double vision is now accorded to the church. Its form accords with all six of the seals. Instead of being secondary, this vision is essential. John is to view it at this point, not as a matter of chronology, but as a matter of import. In connection with all that is opened and revealed in the six seals John must at this point see what is now revealed to him regarding *the church,* the supreme concern of the throne and of the Lamb. Chapter 7 is so vital in every way that, unless all this is understood, neither this chapter itself nor the rest of the visions will be properly apprehended.

After this I saw four angels standing upon the four corners of the earth, holding back the four winds of the earth in order that wind may not blow upon the earth nor upon the sea nor upon a tree. And I saw another angel coming up from sunrise having the seal of the Living God. And he cried to the four angels to whom it was given to hurt the earth and the sea saying: Do not hurt the earth nor the sea nor the trees until we seal the slaves of our God on their foreheads! And I

heard the number of those having been sealed, 144,000 having been sealed out of every tribe of Israel's sons.

Out of Judah's tribe 12,000 having been sealed.
Out of Reuben's tribe 12,000.
Out of Gad's tribe 12,000.
Out of Asher's tribe 12,000.
Out of Naphthali's tribe 12,000.
Out of Manasseh's tribe 12,000.
Out of Simeon's tribe 12,000.
Out of Levi's tribe 12,000.
Out of Issachar's tribe 12,000.
Out of Zebulun's tribe 12,000.
Out of Joseph's tribe 12,000.
Out of Benjamin's tribe 12,000 having been been sealed.

This is *the Church Militant* viewed in its completeness. It is still on earth and sealed as God's. The end of the world is postponed until all are duly sealed. In the second section of the vision, v. 9, etc., we have *the Church Triumphant* before the throne and the Lamb, singing in glory after all the marks of tribulation have been removed.

This is not a chronology, not a date *after* the cataclysm shown in the sixth seal or just before this cataclysm. The whole New Testament Era and its church are here compressed into one vision, and the glorified church into its complementary vision.

Μετὰ τοῦτο εἶδον simply states that after all that John saw in chapter 6 he saw what he now states. To begin with, "four angels on the four corners of the earth, holding back (or controlling) the four winds of the earth in order that wind may not blow upon the earth nor upon the sea nor upon a tree." These are God's angels and not devils. The unmodified word ἄγγελοι is never used to indicate devils. In Revelation God's angels are always called ἄγγελοι and are not symbolized. Here there are four angels for the four corners of the earth and the four winds. The three fours emphasize the number of the earth. Κρατοῦντας = to hold with κράτος or might, to control. The earth is not conceived as a flat square with four corners. We who know all about the globe still speak of north, south, east, west, and that makes exactly four and will continue to do so.

The winds held in control cannot signify judgments that sweep over the earth; for all kinds of judgments occur as time goes on. How would "a tree" be introduced into such a symbol? Still less fitting is "the complete judgment," complete because of the four winds from the four corners of the earth. This thought would require the aorist, yet we have πνέῃ, the present subjunctive, durative (or iterative), "may not be blowing, keep blowing." In the sixth seal the beginning of the complete and final judgment is couched in language that is far more tremendous than that of "a wind" which may blow upon "a tree." Some have thought of the winds as being human "opinions"; yet when did such opinions ever cease to blow about in the heads and the mouths of men? And what would "a tree" represent in connection with opinions?

It appears that the imagery of these three verses intends to convey one idea, the chief point of which is apparent in v. 3: it was given to these four angels *to hurt* the earth and the sea, and they are ordered *not to hurt* the earth and the sea or the trees. The verb ἀδικεῖν is used in this sense in 6:6, and repeatedly, both are effective aorists. The implication is that the causing of such hurt upon either the great areas of the earth or the sea or upon so little as a tree would interfere with the great work of sealing the slaves of our God. The thought thus conveyed is that nothing is ever to disturb even as much as an inanimate tree (the singular in v. 1) on earth so as to stop the essential work of sealing God's slaves. Thus there are no special symbols in these terms, "the four winds," "a wind," "the earth," "the sea," "a tree" (τι is only our indefinite article, R. 743), and "the trees" (v. 3). All of these naturally go together, the winds blowing over the earth and the sea and waving the trees and thus forming a composite symbol.

Ἄνεμος simply means "wind," and it may blow (πνέω) mildly or severely. Those who let "winds" symbolize "complete judgment" that is held back by the angels convert the word into "storms" or "tempests." May we not say that there is something mysterious and wonderful about the blowing of the four winds, whether this be gentle or severe? Man is not able in the least to control the winds: "The wind bloweth where it listeth, and thou hearest the sound thereof, but canst not tell whence it cometh and whither it goeth," John 3:8. God controls it. O yes, we say that natural forces and laws are back of it! But who operates these? Here we are shown God and four of his angels. The great thing John is given to see is the fact that all the winds are prevented from blowing at all; not so much as the trees are moved (v. 3) or even a single tree (v. 1) and that state continues for the whole time of the sealing (σφραγίσωμεν, "until we complete the sealing," aorist, v. 3). Let us translate thus: "God lets not even as much as a slight breeze of untoward influence here upon earth interfere with his supreme work of sealing as his own, his beloved slaves."

It seems as though this sealing should be revealed here where John is permitted to see the vision of the church; for he has seen those three awful horsemen going out into all the earth (6:3-8), war, injustice, death, and he has seen the martyrs, slain and yet to be slain, until their number is full (6:9-11). Well, God so controls matters that none of these forces and inflictions or any other down to the slightest wind or movement on earth, i. e., no influence whatever, shall prevent the sealing of the full number of his slaves.

2) "Another angel" places this one beside the four already mentioned and prevents us from considering this one to be Christ. The fact that he is only an angel we see also from what he says in v. 3, "until *we* seal the slaves of our God." John saw him coming up ἀπὸ ἀνατολῆς ἡλίου, "from sunrise." This is an expression that has never been successfully nor intelligently allegorized. Does not "another angel" place him in relation to the four that are standing in the east, west, north, south, so that his appearing is fittingly from the place of the sun's own rising with the light of day, seeing that he brings the heavenly seal for the sealing of God's slaves on earth? There is no more reason to allegorize or spiritualize here than in the items we have already discussed.

He comes and has with him the σφραγὶς Θεοῦ ζῶντος, "the seal of the Living God." The genitive makes "seal" definite so that we must not expect the article or think that this is only one of various seals. So also there is only one "living God"; hence there is no article with the genitive. This seal is the instrument for sealing God's slaves; and we may note that the noun "seal" is not used to refer to something that is to be affixed to the foreheads of God's slaves. Only the verb "to seal" and the participle "having been sealed" (perfect) appear. Anything like the use of a branding iron that leaves a brand and a scar on the forehead, is not indicated and is unjustified by the word δοῦλοι or "slaves." We have no conception as to what the angel's instrument for sealing could be. It is that of "the Living God." This is an Old and a New Testament title of God which presents him as the source also of life eternal for all who are his. This σφραγίς is his divine, heavenly means for sealing us as his own forever. The angel's "great voice" fits the four angels at the four corners of the earth; it rings out over earth and sea. The omission of "a tree" in the infinitive clause is only abbreviation.

3) The command is negative and thus has the aorist subjunctive and not the imperative. The aorist is peremptory and constative: not the least hurt is ever to be done anywhere. "Until we seal the slaves of our God" has the same constative and effective aorist: until this our work of sealing is completely done. Some think that this clause implies that after this terminus the angels are to let loose the winds so that they may do all the damage they can; but nothing of this sort appears in the vision. The imagery is not elaborated. After the sealing comes the end, and that is more than "winds" convey and any hurt they may cause.

The angel does not say, "*I* seal," but, "until *we* seal," and "we" is only the inflectional ending of the verb which is matched by "our God." The word "slaves" appears already in 1:1, where also John uses it with reference to himself (see 1:1 on its meaning). The supposition that only Jewish Christians are referred to because of v. 4-8, clashes with "the slaves of our God." In order to refer this to Jewish Christians the sealing is dated after the so-called Rapture. One opinion is that all the Gentile Christians will have perished in "the great tribulation" (v. 14) and that then the nation of the Jews will be converted, these converts then being sealed. But these are un-Biblical fancies. These slaves are the same as those mentioned in 1:1; this sealing extends through the entire New Testament Era. To say that these are already slaves of God and after being such slaves receive the sealing, is also unwarranted. How long must one be such a slave of God before this sealing is done to him? Are there two kinds, unsealed and sealed slaves of God? To be God's slave is to have the sealing.

What is this act of sealing and being sealed? Why does the angel say, "until we seal"? Why is the sealing ἐπὶ τῶν μετώπων, "on their foreheads," literally, on the space between the eyes (R. 609)? Sealing attests and certifies as in the case of documents that are stamped with a legal seal. Sealing protects against tampering. The tomb of Jesus was sealed in this way. Sealing hides from unauthorized eyes. Letters are sealed, the book was closed with seven seals (5:1). Sealing marks ownership; so, indeed, does a brand, but sealing for ownership is a higher, nobler mark. All these functions should not be combined, for that obscures the idea. Ownership is referred to: "Having *this seal*: The Lord knew them that are his," II Tim. 2:19. Some think that this sealing is to protect and to preserve in "the great tribulation"; but their ideas regarding this tribulation are unsatisfactory.

All we are able to say in regard to the angels' sealing of Christians is that God acts through agents and means. We are sealed with the Holy Spirit by the means of grace, Word and sacrament. The angels are not the direct agents; as in all that pertains to the church, they serve in appropriate ways and do not always need to use their hands directly.

All we are able to say in regard to the place of this sealing is that the forehead is the noblest part of man. The countenance identifies the person. In less figurative language the heart is sealed by his Spirit as being wholly God's. What the heart is, the face and the eyes reveal. Thus the divine stamp for all who are God's is fittingly impressed upon the forehead as being the mark of highest nobility. Some ask about the lettering of this seal and find it to be the Lamb's name and the Father's name (14:1) although this is not yet stated in the present vision.

4-8) John does not say how and from whom he heard that the number of those having been sealed is

"144,000 sealed out of every tribe of Israel's sons." The main thing is that he and we know this to be the number. It is here expressed by the Greek numeral letters for 144 that are prefixed to χιλιάδες: ρ′ = 100; μ′ = 40; δ′ = 4. In 14:1 this is written in words. Only people such as the Russellites take this 144,000 literally; they see in this actual number the sealed aristocrats of the millennium. The number is symbolical and is made up of 12 × 12 × 1,000. In 4:4 we have the same two twelves, but there they are added because the twenty-four elders refer to the Word (Old and New Testament) in its relation to the throne. Here we have multiplication, 12 × 12, and this is multiplied by the cube of 10, i. e., 10 × 10 × 10, which expresses completeness in the highest degree because now the perfectly complete number of God's people is symbolized. We have this perfection symbolized in the cube of the Holy City which is equal in length, in height, and in breadth, 144 cubits (22:16, 17). This is not to be visualized spatially. These two twelves, the one drawn from the number of the tribes of Israel, the other from the apostles, indicate the double fountain from which the *Una Sancta* has come in its completeness.

John does not say that in this part of the vision he saw the 144,000; he only heard their number. In 14:1, he says that he saw the Lamb and with him "144,000" and there tells us what was written on their foreheads. In our chapter John learns that nothing prevents the sealing of the complete number of the church; in chapter 14 he sees this complete number in company with the Lamb, all having the names on their foreheads. The 144,000 are the same in both chapters. The fact that at the time when John saw these visions and that even now so many centuries later many of the slaves of our God did not and do not yet exist, makes no difference, for God and in these visions their existence and their number are reality. So also in John 10:16.

Many introduce a pause as though this were needed for the operation of sealing. There is no pause between verses 3 and 4. The 144,000 cannot be placed somewhere in the course of history, after Constantine and at other times, nor do they face the Great Tribulation which is dated just before the end. Some go in the other direction and identify the sealing with God's eternal election. None of these views are presented in this passage.

More serious is the question as to whether the 144,000 are Jewish believers or all believers. Some speak only of Jewish Christians and Gentile Christians. Biederwolf tabulates thirteen arguments for the one view and twelve for the other and then, as far as he himself is concerned, says that the question is not of vital importance, especially not for Revelation. It is of such importance that a large number of wrong interpretations of the main visions of Revelation hinge on the wrong identification of the 144,000.

The 144,000 are *all of God's people.*

In the light of Scripture and of Revelation itself it is unwarranted to think that only some of God's slaves are sealed and not all.

"The sons of Israel" = those who as υἱοί (the word is not τέκνα) have the right and the standing of "sons." They are named from "Israel," the name that God himself gave to Jacob as the contender who prevailed, Gen. 32:26-28. The fact that "the sons of Israel" is the name for all believers is rather plain, hence the phrase "out of every tribe" and the twelve repetitions "out of the tribe of Judah," etc., are made issues on the assumption that these twelve tribes and the twelve names of the patriarchs point to Jewish believers only. This contention ignores the "12,000" which is predicated of each tribe ($\iota' = 10$; $\beta' = 2$). It assumes that the twelve names Judah, Reuben, etc., prove that these "sons" are Jewish.

Long ago, when the ten tribes of the northern kingdom had been deported into Assyria, these ten disappeared completely; they were absorbed by paganism. In addition, twenty-five years before John's writing the remaining two tribes, Judah and Benjamin, lost their national existence and never regained it. The one of the two twelves that are multiplied in the 144 which is taken from the apostles cannot well serve to indicate an ordered people; neither can the twelve sons of Jacob as mere *sons* of his. But the twelve *tribes* can. Thus we have, "out of every tribe of the sons of Israel," "out of the tribe of Judah," etc. But not *"some"* out of every tribe, more out of one than out of others, in *literal* numbers, in a *historical* census or inventory; but 12,000 out of each tribe. Why 12 × 12,000? This is symbolism. "The slaves of our God" are not a great mass of individuals, a loose or scattered aggregate; they are an ordered and organized people, God's great nation.

The symbolism for this divine nation could not be taken from the Jewish nation in its later days, after the deportation of the ten tribes or after the separation of the ten tribes from the two when two kingdoms were formed; but only from the twelve tribes as they once camped together on their desert journey, as they once received their inheritance in Canaan, as this one nation once was organized as one consisting of twelve parts or tribes. Even then they differed in the numbers that composed the tribes and in the relation of these tribes. Levi held a special position; Dan (which is not in this list at all) had its position. These numerical and other differences are here ignored. The symbolism of the divine, spiritual nation of God presents the picture of a perfect nation by means of twelve tribes, all consisting equally of 12,000 "out of each tribe" and thus totaling 144,000. Twelve is the number of God's people and of God's Word (the latter as seen in the twenty-four elders, review 4:4), and 10 × 10 × 10 is the number of fullest completeness.

This same symbolism is found in 14:1, and in 21:22, in the twelve gates and their twelve names "which are of the twelve tribes of the sons of Israel" ("sons," not "children" as our versions render inexactly). Mauro seeks to penetrate farther by delving into the significance of each of the names of the patriarchs because he notes that the list here given has several peculiarities; but this yields very little that is of value. Also the thought that the twelve names are arranged according to the degree of faithfulness is unsatisfactory. Benjamin is certainly not the least faithful of the twelve. Dan is omitted; Levi is listed as an ordinary tribe, and nothing is noted about its connection with the old priesthood; Ephraim is replaced by Joseph. A literal interpretation that refers this number to the Jews is unacceptable. The symbolical meaning which requires only the number twelve does not need to wrestle with these minor points.

Judah, the tribe from which Jesus descended (Heb. 7:14), is quite properly placed first. So Reuben is second, Levi is undistinguished. The suppositions that Dan is left out because the Danites were once idolatrous, or because the tribe had died out, or because the antichrist was to be a Danite, are fancies. In the table of names given in I Chron. 4, etc., Dan does not appear, and in Deut. 33, Simeon and Issachar are omitted. Let this suffice.

In the first part of the vision nothing whatever dares to interfere with the sealing of the "slaves of our God," and John hears of their significant symbolical number. In the second part of the vision he sees the whole multitude of the vast assembly before the throne of God and of the Lamb. The two parts together constitute *the revelation of the church. Sealed* —

Glorified! This is to be our picture and vision of *the church.* It is transcendent.

9) **After these things I saw, and lo, a great multitude which to number it no one was able, out of every nation and tribes and peoples and tongues, standing before the throne and the Lamb, clothed around with white flowing robes and palms in their hands. And they cry with a great voice, saying, The salvation to our God, the One sitting on the throne, and to the Lamb! And all the angels were standing around the throne and the elders and the four living ones. And they fell down before the throne upon their faces and did obeisance to God, saying: Amen! The blessing and the glory and the wisdom and the thanksgiving and the honor and the power and the strength to our God for the eons of the eons! Amen!**

Not until this point does John actually see the church. It is fitting that in the two parts of the vision that comprise this chapter he should see the church before the throne in eternal blessedness. Μετὰ ταῦτα merely marks the advance to what John now sees. It is a great multitude, which to number it (aorist: actually to do so) no one was able (descriptive imperfect; αὐτόν is the redundant antecedent drawn into the relative clause). The greatness of the multitude is brought out in the four-part phrase, "out of every nation and tribes and peoples and tongues" (5:9). The last three plurals are used *ad sensum* for greater effect. This multitude is gathered from over all the world (Matt. 28:19; Acts 1:8), every part of it with its host, no matter what sort of division is applied, that of nations bound by their customs and laws, that of tribes bound by blood ties, that of peoples as organized masses, that of tongues as the tie of language. This multitude is the sum total of the fruit of the gospel on earth, the net result of all mission work. A stupendous vision, indeed!

John sees this multitude "standing before the throne and before the Lamb"; ἑστῶτες is a plural because ὄχλος is a collective and because a singular participle would be out of place. Standing, they voice their acclaim (v. 10) as such who have the glorious right so to stand. The throne symbolizes the eternal power, rule, dominion of God (4:2) as John now sees it together with this multitude after this throne's work on earth has been brought to its final consummation. The Lamb (see 5:6) is the Savior, the sacrifice for the world's sin, and this multitude is the glorious fruit of his sacrifice.

Again we make no diagram, placing the throne and the Lamb here, the multitude there, the angels, elders, living ones elsewhere. Ἐνώπιον denotes the heavenly relation to the throne and the Lamb as we have noted various relations that were made visible to John in 4:3, etc. So also we do not join this vision to any of those that precede although John has been permitted to see the throne, the Lamb, the angels, the elders, and the living ones before this. Each vision is one distinct revelation in the series given to John.

Ὄχλος . . . ἑστῶτες is nominative because it follows the interjection ἰδού; but περιβεβλημένους is the accusative because it is governed by εἶδον: "I saw . . . clothed around with white flowing robes and palms in their hands." As in 6:11, στολή = *Talar*, state robe, long and flowing, festive. "White" = holiness throughout Revelation. "Palms" are best explained by a reference to John 12:13, where the idea is not that of victory or even of triumph but that of life and salvation. According to the Oriental conception the palm is a perfect tree which embodies everything that a tree should be and extends its life even to 200 years. Note the shout in v. 10, "Salvation!" The passive participle retains the accusative object of the active forms, R. 816; φοίνικες reverts to the deictic nominative.

This multitude is *the entire* church and not only a certain part of it, whatever the part supposed may be. Its identity is denied on three grounds: 1) this host no one was able to number while the 144,000 are numbered; 2) the 144,000 have been sealed while nothing is said about this host being sealed; 3) the 144,000 are on earth, the unnumbered host is in heaven. But certainly God knows their number, II Tim. 2:19b; John 10:14-16; and 144,000 is a symbolical number and is now interpreted as being so great that no man had the ability to make the count of the literal number that is symbolized by 144,000. The sealing has, indeed, been done on earth; that is why this host is now in heaven.

One reason that the 144,000 and the unnumbered host are supposed to be different is the misconception regarding "the great tribulation" (v. 14). When this is regarded as the last severe tribulation which has not yet come, then John did not see the *Una Sancta* but saw only a certain part of it. This offers the chiliasts and the futurists an opportunity to introduce their fancies. We are told by some that the identification of the 144,000 is not a matter of importance; but now we see that the interpretation of most of Revelation pivots on this very point which involves the host here described and thus this entire chapter and its relation to the rest of Revelation. For this chapter is *by no means* a mere intermezzo or minor scene.

10) The vast host of the blessed cry "with a great voice," and certainly the voice of such a host would be great, "The salvation to our God, the One sitting on the throne," exercising his power, rule, and dominion (see 4:3), "and to the Lamb!" The article in the expression ἡ σωτηρία means, not what may be called "salvation" in general, but "the actual salvation" which God and the Lamb have wrought. This is not salvation out

of tribulation or out of the final tribulation but the full and complete salvation from sin, death, and damnation. How can one think of limiting it in its saving power (the One sitting on the throne and the Lamb) or in the number saved or in that from which they are saved? Here all the saved ascribe their entire salvation to God and to the Lamb. Already here on earth the saints sing "salvation" (Ps. 3:8, and other passages), and God and the Lamb tell us about it when we begin to taste it; but our song is weak, our voices faint here below. What will the acclaim be when all the blessed join in one harmonious volume in the very presence of the throne and the Lamb!

The datives "to our God," etc., ascribe the absolutely complete salvation to God and to the Lamb. The pronoun "our" is a confession of God. There are no synergists or Pelagians in heaven.

Some connect this scene with the Jewish Feast of Tabernacles. The palms are then the festive spray or "lulab" that was carried by each celebrant, the fountains of waters of life (v. 17) correspond to Isa. 12:3 and John 7:37. Even the fact that "Tabernacles" is the name of the Jewish harvest festival is utilized. We cannot accept such a view.

11, 12) All the angels, whose myriads 5:11 mentions, together with the elders and the four living ones offer the doxological confirmation of the ascription of the salvation to God and to the Lamb. On the elders and the four ζῶα see 4:4, 6. Here again the ἄγγελοι, "the angels," are clearly distinguished from the ζῶα, "the four living ones," as was done in 5:11. The past perfect ἑστήκεσαν is always used as an imperfect, here it is descriptive as was ἑστῶτες in v. 9. Although they were at first standing like the vast host of the church, all these others fall down upon their faces before the throne and do obeisance to God as they utter their confirmation, "Amen!" etc. Fittingly they join in this, these heavenly messengers during all the ages of the world, the agents of his Word who conveyed the salvation (elders), plus the earthly agents of his providence in all the world (the four living ones).

On the two mighty "amen" see 1:7. The one before and the other after the doxology confess, confirm, and seal. Sevenfold is the ascription, each item has the article and is thus distinct as it was in 4:11. In 5:12 but one article is used with the seven. The variation from 5:12 and the order of the seven terms seem to be without special significance. "For the eons of the eons" is explained in 1:6. All the ascriptions refer to "the salvation" mentioned in v. 10. "To our God" in no way excludes the Lamb as we see in 5:12.

13) More follows. **And there answered one of the elders, saying to me: These, the ones clothed around with the flowing robes, the white ones, who are they? and whence came they?** It is fitting that one of the elders, an agent of the Word of salvation, should ask this question. Ἀπεκρίθη is regularly used when some situation calls for a remark; here it is the vision of this host. The purpose of the vision is not only that John may see this host and may hear the praise but that he and thus all of us may know who these are and whence they came. Note how the description of these is repeated and thus strongly emphasized: "clothed around," etc., for this is the wondrous thing, sinners appear in perfect holiness. The question asks not only who they are but at the same time whence they came so as now to be here in white before the throne and the Lamb.

14) **I said to him, My lord, thou knowest.** "My lord" is a form of reverent address; and "thou knowest" requests the elder to impart the answer instead of letting John make an attempt. For the point of the double question is not a general answer which John might venture to give, but an answer that will reveal

what this vision is intended to impart to John and to all for whom he is to write it. John does not intend to say, "Thou knowest, I do not"; or, "Thou knowest better than I." The answer John received is one concerning which we can be sure that he could not himself have given it. Εἴρηκα is the vivid, dramatic perfect (R. 902) in narrative (B.-D. 343, 1) which, like the present, may appear beside the matter-of-fact aorist.

And he said to me: These are the ones coming out of the tribulation, the great one, and did wash their flowing robes and made them white in the blood of the Lamb. Because of this they are before the throne of God and serve him by day and by night in his sanctuary. And the One sitting on the throne will spread his tabernacle over them. They shall not hunger any more, nor shall they thirst any more, nor shall the sun fall upon them, nor any heat; because the Lamb who is in the midst of the throne shall shepherd them and shall lead them to life's springs of water, and God shall wipe away every tear from their eyes.

The chief points of the vision of the unnumbered host are here interpreted for John. The substantivized present participle οἱ ἐρχόμενοι simply characterizes without reference to time, and it really makes little difference whether we translate, "they which come" (R. V.) or, "they which came" (A. V.) although the former is preferable. The futurists and the chiliasts and those who think that only a part of the number of the blessed are included, the part that will remain steadfast during the last woes, misunderstand the force of this participle. Thus Kliefoth: "The present ἐρχόμενοι speaks of what the multitude *does just now* before the seer's eyes." But the elder is describing the multitude which John has been looking at since v. 9 and which does not come while John is looking. Others interpret the participle as "implying that they *have just come.*" These have in mind "the frightful distress, immediately preceding the end, the very last time," and thus misunderstand the tense of this participle. Even to find iteration in the tense as I did in the *Eisenach Epistle Selections* II, 373, where I allowed myself to be misled, is wrong: one band after another coming up to the throne. The participle is only qualitative, as hundreds of present participles are both when they are substantivized and when they are modifiers of nouns. When they are substantivized they = nouns; as modifiers they = adjectives.

There is also a wrong interpretation of ἐκ τῆς θλίψεως, "out of the tribulation, the great (one)." The adjective is added by a second article and hence is emphatic, it is like an apposition and a climax, R. 776. Chiliasts and futurists usually spell this expression with capitals: "the Great Tribulation," in order the more to make this refer to the terrible time yet to come. They point to Dan. 12:1, as though this settles the matter, but especially to Matt. 24:21-28, which plainly refers to the destruction of Jerusalem, see the *Interpretation of St. Matthew's Gospel.* In "the tribulation, the great (one)" all the tribulations mentioned in all the passages that speak of tribulation are combined, and thus with reference to the church this tribulation of all the ages is rightly called "great." "Great" gathers up all of it. In Acts 14:22: "Through many tribulations (διὰ πολλῶν θλίψεων) we must enter into the kingdom of God," the word "many" spreads out the great multitude of tribulations. The tribulations of the last period are certainly included. Exceedingly severe tribulations appear from time to time; never is tribulation (*Bedraengnis*), pressure, entirely absent from the church while it exists in this wicked world. What we must bear individually varies, varies even on the different days of our own lives.

John sees the church which now has all tribulation behind it. It is in a place where no part of the long and great tribulation of the past will ever touch the blessed. Not even hunger, thirst, heat, nor a single tear shall be in evidence. We do not understand how anyone can refer this "great multitude" to the martyrs of the last days and can connect their martyrdom with the antichrist who is assigned only to the last days.

What preserved all the blessed while they were still in the great tribulation? The elder does not praise their fortitude nor any merit they achieved. This is what he adds: "and did wash their flowing robes and made them white in the blood of the Lamb." John sees these white robes as the blessed stand before the throne and the Lamb. It seems that already in this life we wear the robes in which we shall shine in heaven. The aorists express past facts: "they washed and whitened," which is one act, whitened by washing in the Lamb's blood, not two (Hengstenberg): washing being the forgiveness of sin and whitening being the living of a holy life. The washing in this blood removes all sin and all stain and thus renders clean, white, and holy. On this whiteness compare Isa. 1:18.

Blood is red, yet the Lamb's blood whitens. "To wash" occurs frequently in Scripture; "to whiten" is usually expressed by "to cleanse." The blessed wash and whiten themselves when the Lord cleanses them. To wash our robes means that we believe in the bloody expiation of the Lamb and appropriate this for ourselves. On the cleansing power of this blood note Heb. 9:14; I John 1:7-9 and the many other passages that refer to this blood. This blood and nothing else in the universe whitens us so that we may stand before God. The theology of this elder and of the unnumbered host of the blessed contradicts that of the moderns who want no mention of blood, of satisfaction, of expiation, of substitution, of sacrifice. Here on earth our robes still become stained (John 13:10) and need constant cleansing (I John 1:9); in heaven they will remain white in holiness forever.

Although the two statements about the blessed are connected only with *καί*, we regard them as bearing a relation to each other, the one that is naturally inherent in the two facts: those who wash their robes are those who come out of the tribulation to eternal glory. This applies to *all* "the slaves of our God" (v. 3), to the entire *Una Sancta.* John is permitted to see the whole church — no less. So God and the Lamb have ever seen it; so we must now ever see it through John's eyes.

15) This is the reason that John sees the *Una Sancta* "before the throne of God." The ἐνώπιον is not spatial but expresses relation. In 1:4 and 4:5 (the seven spirits) the "before" had the force of to execute the saving will of the One on the throne in all the earth, but, as the very next clause states, here the "before" implies to serve him in his sanctuary, ναός (not temple, ἱερόν). The verb λατρεύειν refers to service that is obligatory for all; public official service would be expressed by λειτουργεῖν. What this service is John has seen already in v. 10. The blessedness, the joy, and the glory of it are beyond mortal comprehension.

What the church does so imperfectly in its earthly sanctuaries shall there be done in supreme perfection. No weakness shall hinder, no fault shall mar, no disturbance shall interrupt it. That service will be our highest delight, and all who are privileged to join in it have begun to do so by joining their fellow slaves on earth ("fellow slaves" in 6:11). The word "sanctuary" is just as symbolical as the word "throne" and does not make this a temple scene. The word ναός is properly chosen, for in this service there are no priests, no Levites, no people, and no courts for these and for those, all are equally "before the throne," in direct relation to God. Concerning "by day and by night" the

Venerable Bede rightly says: *More nostro loquens aeternitatem significat.* There is no day and night in heaven, Rev. 22:5. This expression (genitives of time within) is used because here below changes of day and night affect us; there they shall no longer do so.

"And the One sitting on the throne will spread his tabernacle over them," σκηνώσει ἐπ' αὐτούς, "will tent upon them." What the Shekinah above the Mercy seat in the Tabernacle typified, what to a lesser degree the pillar of cloud by day and of fire by night in the desert journey of the Israelites illustrated, that shall be fully realized in heaven. Ezek. 37:27. Egypt is forever behind, God's people are forever with him in his sanctuary. We have another description in 21:3. God's presence shall ever be with his saints as though he dwelt in the same tent with them, yea, as though he spread his presence over them like a tent.

16) Much of the blessedness of heaven is necessarily stated in negative language. So here we have: "They shall not hunger any more, nor shall they thirst any more, nor shall the sun fall upon them nor any heat." The imagery here used recalls the hardships and the sufferings of the Israelites on their desert journey. This is a picture of the long, great tribulation. Hunger, thirst, sun, and heat symbolize all the hardships, trials, afflictions, pains, weariness, etc., of the faithful, godly life until the saints reach the Jordan of death and walk dry-shod into Canaan, the land where milk and honey flow, the country of verdant pastures and lovely flowers, full of solace and delight — our true home. The future tenses portray what ever awaits the blessed. The Scriptures condescend to the use of temporal terms because of the weakness of human language which cannot speak in terms of eternity (timelessness).

17) The negative description turns to an allied positive one. Why shall they not hunger, etc? "Be-

cause the Lamb who is in the midst of the throne (in this exalted relation to God's eternal dominion, 5:6) shall shepherd them and shall lead them to the water springs of life." This recalls Ps. 23:1. It is a striking statement that the *Lamb* shall *shepherd,* ποιμανεῖ, shall act the shepherd, but this is made possible by what this Lamb is and has done. Ἀνὰ μέσον (also written as one word) means no more than ἐν μέσῳ, and not "in the midst before," as the American Committee of the R. V. suggests, or "in the middle point in front of the throne," as some think.

The figure is expanded. The shepherd leads his flock to water. Trench calls expressions which combine figure and reality such as water of life, bread of life, Biblical allegory and says that they are self-interpreting. Here we have "life's springs of waters"; compare 22:1, "a river of water of life, clear as crystal." All that ζωή, "life," means, the very essence of life shall be ours in heavenly riches. This Lamb calls himself "the life" (John 14:6). Yet note that even in heaven all the blessed are dependent on the Lamb for life. Pure springs, flowing with waters, all life, shall eternally supply us. Heaven cannot be described to us in its realities, figures must serve while we are on earth.

Once more the negative returns in the statement that every tear shall be wiped away by God. Is the imagery that of a mother wiping away her child's tears so that it smiles and laughs again? Read Ps. 126, especially v. 1, 2, 5. Tears here, eternal joys there. It has been well said that he who does not want to weep here as a pilgrim cannot laugh there at home in glory. Now tears are bitter, but think of what follows forever! He who prefers to laugh with the world cannot expect to be among those whose faces shall feel the touch of the gentle heavenly hand that turns all tears into everlasting joy.

CHAPTER VIII

The Seventh Seal and the First Six Trumpets
Chapters 8 and 9

The Seventh Seal and Four Trumpets, chapter 8

1) **And when he opened the seventh seal, there occurred a silence in the heaven for about a half hour. And I saw the seven angels who stand before God, and there were given to them seven trumpets. And another angel came and stood at the altar, having a golden censer. And there was given to him much incense that he shall give it to the prayers of all the saints upon the altar, the golden** (one), **the** (one) **before the throne. And there went up the smoke of the incense for the prayers of the saints from the hand of the angel before God. And the angel has taken the censer, and he filled it from the fire of the altar, and he threw** (this fire) **into the earth; and there occurred thunders and sounds and lightnings and quaking. And the seven angels, those having the seven trumpets, prepared themselves to trumpet.**

Ὅταν is definite and is followed by the indicative, R. 958, 973, especially 1146. The opening of the seventh seal is recorded in practically the same words that were used in connection with the other six. The book of the prophecies and their certain fulfillment by the Lamb are now completely unsealed.

The silence that lasts for about one half hour is the hushed expectation of all as the removal of this last seal is now undertaken. The silence is in strongest constrast to the tremendous acclaim of the preceding vision, verses 7, 10, 12. No one even speaks as did the elder to John in 7:13-17. "About one half hour" is not a symbolical length of time but only an impressive length for John for whom all else in these visions is intended. The contents of the other seals is not ushered in with this impressiveness, for what this last seal uncovers is something that has not been revealed in earlier prophecies of Scripture as the contents of the first six seals have been.

Σιγή, "silence," is not σαββατισμός, "Sabbath" or Sabbath "rest" which occurs either after the end of the world in all eternity or during the millennium of which so many dream or at some point in the course of the world's history just before some terrible calamities. "Silence" ensues when no one speaks, when all are hushed, and a silence as long as this increases the tension of John to the utmost. What this silence ushers in is according, namely the seven trumpets of judgment and the seven bowls ("vials," A. V.) of the wrath of God and of the plagues. A few attempt to end the seventh seal with the half hour silence in heaven but fail to explain how this silence can be something that is so great as to complete the preceding great seals.

What the seventh seal uncovers cannot chronologically follow what the sixth seal reveals. The sixth seal portrays Matt. 24:29, the cataclysm which ushers in the Parousia at the end of the world. Those who let the seventh seal follow chronologically upon the sixth seal think that they secure the advantage of having all the judgments that are announced by the trumpets occur in the distant future, chronologically after 6:12-17, and thus they need not in any way be interpreted with respect to the present course of time. But whatever this advantage may amount to, it is bought at the price of misinterpreting the sixth seal (with certainly = Matt. 24:29) and, when so bought, really gains nothing. Already the four horsemen ride to the very end of time; the martys have their number completed at the end (fifth seal); also the sixth seal takes us to the threshold of the end.

2) Whether what John saw in v. 2-6 occurred during the one half hour of silence or at its conclusion is immaterial. The seven angels whom John now saw are the seven ordinary angels that were selected for the present task; they are not archangels, "throne angels," or evil angels (the unmodified word "angels" never means devils). The article is merely deictic, it is like "the seven thunders" in 10:3. "Who stand before God" does not make these seven a superior class; they stand in close relation to God as signaling the judgments that come from God. Draw no diagram. They had seven trumpets that were given to them for their present task.

"Seven" is the sacred number, three plus four. It is used here because God (3) will reckon with the world (4). In this revelation the judgments are revealed in seven sections. They might have been divided and revealed in an entirely different manner. Seals hide and must be opened in order to reveal; *trumpets* signal, announce, but not until they are blown. *Bowls* contain in order to empty their contents. The order of these could not be changed.

3) "Another angel" recalls "another angel" in 7:2. In connection with either passage we have no reason to think of anything except ordinary angels. John saw how this angel came and took his place (ἐστάνη) at (ἐπί, not "over") the altar, "having a golden censer, λιβανωτός." Without saying how or by whom this was done, John tells us that to this angel "there was given much incense (θυμάματα, substances for making smoke, the plural, it is derived from the verb θυμιάω) in order that he shall give (R. 984) it to the prayers of all the saints upon the altar, the golden (one), the one before the throne."

The discussion about this altar, and the question as to whether it is the same one that was mentioned in 6:9, or whether there are two, are uncalled for. This discussion arises from the view that we again have a scene of a temple that is furnished as was the old Jewish Temple, the throne signifying the mercy seat. What the throne is we have noted in connection with 4:2; the word occurs twelve times in that chapter and often after that. In 6:9, there is a reference to the altar of burnt sacrifice as the context shows; now we have a reference to the altar of incense. This alone was made of gold, and on it alone was incense burnt. But in each vision only what is mentioned appears, only what is symbolically necessary. We cannot start at 4:2, and picture *everything* that has been mentioned as taking place in heaven, and *all* who have been mentioned as being in heaven.

Here only the throne, the symbol of God's eternal power, rule, and dominion, is mentioned. This is found here because the seven angels and the judgments they announce with their trumpets are in necessary relation to God's throne of power and dominion, ἐνώπιον τοῦ Θεοῦ, "before God." These judgments come from him. Here there is only this golden altar. It is also ἐνώπιον τοῦ θρόνου, facing the throne. All the incense of prayer rises before God, is accepted by him. This angel is only the ministrant at the altar of incense. The censer he carries is not used for incense (see v. 5). He does not act the part of the high priest. This scene is not a high-priestly scene. The angel does not, like the ordinary priest, get live coals from the great altar of sacrifice to be placed on the golden altar of incense. Only the latter is mentioned here. From it the prayers of all the saints are already rising like incense smoke. What this angel does is to add much more incense (θυμιάματα, plural) to these prayers, to increase greatly the volume of the aromatic smoke.

In the Koine ἵνα may be followed by the future indicative.

4) The significance of all this is apparent. John says: "There went up the smoke of the incense material for the prayers of the saints from the angel's hand before God." We regard ταῖς προσευχαῖς as a dative of advantage. All this added incense material which goes up in a great volume of smoke represents the intercession of Christ for his church (*intercessio specialis*), which adds power and efficacy to the prayers of the church. The Lord increases the sweet savor of acceptable prayer. That is why he tells us to pray in his name, and why the hearing of our prayers is so certain. The angel does no praying, no interceding. He does nothing but to act as the Lord's "hand," and does that only in this vision which pictures the matter to John's eyes and thus uses the symbol of the golden altar and of incense material and its smoke. Therefore it is noted that the material "was given" to this angel. This passage does not teach the doctrine of the intercession of angels.

The word used is προσευχαί, the broadest term for "prayers," which should not be reduced to "petitions," to cries like those uttered by the martyrs in 6:10. All the prayers of all our worship, our praise and our thanksgiving as well as our petitions and our intercessions for each other, are supplemented and perfected by our Lord and result in the judgments of the trumpets which reach their climax in the final judgment (the seventh trumpet, 11:15-19). Think of the Lord's Prayer, which *he* taught us to pray, and that it comes to a climax in, "*Thine* is the kingdom," etc. We find no difficulty in the expression "all the saints." They are the saints on earth from the first to the last. All of them constantly offer the incense of prayer to God. The fact that some have passed into heaven, that some are not yet born, are mechanical considerations of time that should not be introduced into this vision so as to complicate what it reveals. For that matter, God is not bound to time, he is not compelled to wait until you kneel and pray.

5) Now the main symbolical act is presented for which the reception of our supplemented prayers forms the basis. The perfect tense εἴληφεν is only dramatical and entirely proper among aorists as we have seen this in the case of εἴρηκα in 7:14 (R. 899). John saw that the angel "has taken the censer," that "he filled it from the fire of the altar," and that "he threw (this fire) into the earth." The whole censer full of fiery coals this angel empties into the earth with a mighty throw. He threw a mass of the fire and not the incense material that sent up its sweet-smelling smoke to God. This hurling of the fire symbolizes the answer of God to the prayers of the saints that have been supplemented by Christ's own mighty intercession. God's judgments come upon the earth in order to destroy and thereby to warn until the climax of the final judgment is reached (11:15-19; v. 18: "to be judged, and to give the reward to thy slaves, to the prophet and to the saints and to those fearing thy name, the small and the great, and to destroy those destroying the earth").

The sixth seal (6:12-17) presents only the terrific phenomena that shall occur at the end; the seventh trumpet (11:15-19) presents an advance, the double reward. More details in regard to the final judgment are added in the subsequent visions. The point to be noted is that 6:12, etc., and 11:15, etc., take us to the end. This answers the interpretation which dates the trumpets in the world's history *after* the opening of the sixth seal.

Whereas there was "silence" before (v. 1), whereas the angels with the trumpets stood in silence, whereas the angel with the incense functioned in silence, whereas the cloud of incense was rising silently, the instant the fire is hurled out of the censer "there occurred thunders and sounds and lightnings and quaking," and the seven angels reach for their trumpets and are ready to trumpet in their turn. We must consider these thunders, etc., together. Review 4:15 (cf., 11:19; 16:18): "lightnings and sounds (not voices) and thunders" which are there said to proceed "out of the throne." Forget not Ps. 29. The Omnipotent on his throne is proceeding to act. John witnesses these tremendous manifestations; they are a part of this vision. Neither here nor in 4:15 does σεισμός mean "earthquake"; it does not mean "earthquake" even in 6:12. It means "shaking or quaking" and accompanies "thunder," etc. Only when the earth shakes may we render this Greek word "earthquake."

6) The seven angels with the seven trumpets now make ready to trumpet. This statement adds to the impressiveness. All that precedes in v. 1-5, i. e., all that is here symbolized and signified, forms the basis for the six trumpets of judgment which reach a climax in the seventh. John writes as though the trumpets hung on cords over the shoulders, each angel now taking his into his hand in order to blow it. On the trumpets see v. 2.

The First Four Trumpets, verses 7-12

7) These clearly belong together; v. 13 separates them from the last three which are also called "woes." The first four seals also belong together, for they bring the four horsemen.

We reject the following opinions. That of the preterist, that the seven trumpets depict the events which preceded the Jewish war and the destruction of Jerusalem. That of many English authorities: the four trumpets depict the ravages of the Goths and the overthrow of the Roman Empire. That of the futurist, that the seven trumpets depict the vengeance for which the martyrs in the sixth seal cry; or the events connected with the destruction of the antichrist; or the events connected with "the Great Tribulation" (but on this see v. 14). Old and new opinions: the trumpets only recapitulate and repeat the respective seals with different symbols.

Kretzmann allegorizes: the first trumpet is a hurricane of false doctrine which strikes the Church of God; second trumpet, heretical fanaticism which enters the Christian Church; third trumpet, great rationalists and other great teachers who poison the water of life for others; fourth trumpet, arbitrariness and speculations which darken God's light. So the fifth, the infernal spirits that like locusts swarm over the Church of Christ, evil hordes which vex Christendom. But the sixth he makes historical as Luther and others do: it is Mohammedanism. The trumpets, however, depict *world-wide judgments*, and the first six say nothing about the church.

We note the following as being helpful. The first seal is comprehensive: it is the great conqueror; but the other three, war, injustice, death are *non-miraculous* judgments. The six trumpets describe *miraculous* judgments; the miraculous that strike the wickedness of men are added to the non-miraculous that arise out of the wickedness of men themselves.

Again, the three seals, war, injustice, death, are *parallel* while the six trumpets eventuate in *a climax*. Take the first four: a miraculous *rain* — a flaming *mountain* hurled into the sea — a great flaming *star* falling *from the heaven* — the third of the *sun, moon, stars* blasted. Next hell vomits forth its *demons*. The climax is plain. In each of the six judgments a *miraculous and supernatural agency* is shown and then the devastating *effect*. The seventh trumpet takes us to heaven (11:15-19) and the end.

And the first trumpeted — the wording is the same in the case of the other six save for the addition of "angel" — **and there occurred hail and fire, having been mixed with blood, and were cast to the earth. And the third of the earth was burnt up, and the third of the trees was burnt up, and all green herbage was burnt up.** The two singulars χάλαζα and πῦρ are modified by the plural neuter perfect particle μεμιγμένα. Both hail and fire have been mixed with blood. Hail is ice, the opposite of fire. How hail and fire were mixed with blood we do not know, for the very combination of these three shows that natural hail, fire, and blood are not referred to.

They did not fall, they "were thrown" to the earth, ἐβλήθη, by an invisible hand, the hand of God's judgment. Some think that here γῆ must mean "land," because in v. 8 "sea" follows; yet for this superearthly rain, so horrible in its composition, such a distinction is needless. The effect is described as being terrible: "the third of the earth was burned up, and the third of the trees were burned up, and all green herbage was burned up" — burned up being repeated three times in solemn emphasis. That expression seems to refer to "fire," but what about the icy hail and the mixture with blood? This imagery is supernatural, miraculous, as is also the effect, that the rain caused this burning up. In 6:8 the death strikes the fourth of the earth; this judgment burned up the third of the earth, its effect reached farther.

Just as the admixture of blood with icy hail and blazing fire is utterly beyond nature, so is the effect that *the third* of the trees and *all* green herbage (χόρτος, not just "grass") was burned up. We should think it would be either one third of trees *and* herbage, or *all* trees and herbage. How can two thirds of the trees remain when all herbage is burned up? The whole description directs us toward the supernatural. This is the case also with regard to the next five trumpets. This judgment evidently intends to remind us of the one God sent upon Egypt, Exod. 9:18-26. That, too, was supernatural. It does not rain in Egypt, to say nothing of hailing. The mixture of hail and fire, the fire running along upon the ground — such a thing had never occurred in the land of Egypt since it had become a nation, i. e., since men knew the country. It was entirely miraculous, a manifestation of the hand of God. This first judgment which speaks of a mixture of blood and of one third of the trees and all the herbage being burned up is even more miraculous than the miracle that occurred in Egypt.

The cue that men are mentioned only incidentally in connection with the third trumpet, that in connection with the fifth men are tormented, and in connection with the sixth men are killed, is only a slight aid. *All these judgments* strike men. The solution that men are robbed of a third and more of their earthly subsistence by this first judgment, and of a third of their trade and commerce by the second, proves unsatisfactory when it comes to the third and the fourth trumpets, for these four belong together and form a climax of supernatural judgments. Allegorizing is always unreliable. To say that trees commonly picture notable men and grass ordinary people, is not correct. What would "the earth" be? What would the three verbs "burned up" mean in an allegory? In what way would the great men and the common run of men be burned up? Would two thirds of the great men be left, and *all* common people be destroyed? How is the hail to be allegorized, the fire, the blood, the mingling with blood?

To regard this as a vision of the destruction of Jerusalem (an event that is alread past), or of the invasion of the Goths, or of the fall of the western third of the Roman Empire, is equally unsatisfactory. The Goths, by the way, are also referred to in connection with the next two trumpets. The futurists say that the six trumpets describe the ἀρχὴ ὠδίνων, "the beginning of travail," the coming Great Tribulation, the destruction of the monster antichrist who is yet to come. According to this interpretation nobody can know what these six trumpets mean until the time of their fulfillment; all that *we* can do at this time is to read and to marvel.

It is, indeed, easier to point out the error of these attempts than to offer the right interpretation that will receive general acceptance. We venture to say this. The six trumpets describe supernatural judgments that descend with increasing terribleness. The devastation grows. The world is an Egypt in its wicked and growing opposition to God, in its increasing obduracy against his will. It is worse than Egypt and Pharaoh. Only some of the Egyptian plagues have partial counterparts in these visions, the other plagues go far beyond anything that occurred in Egypt.

The horror that is expressed in connection with each of the six trumpet blasts is, we think, to be viewed as a whole. Each is a composite unified piece of symbolism and is not to be plucked to pieces so that each piece (noun, adjective, verb, clause) is made a separate symbol with a special meaning. We cannot say the hail = this, the fire = that, the blood = something else; the earth = this, the trees = that, the herbage = something else. The meaning of each of the six horrors centers in *the effect.* The supernatural features presented in each horror serve only to heighten the effect to be produced. The more terrible the effect to be wrought, the more terrible is the supernatural cause. We shall say more when we come to the fifth trumpet.

We do not think that the first four judgments are to be dated, one in an early century, the second in a later century, and the next two still later. The four effects are a gradation: bad, worse, still worse, and worst of all. Where and when these effects set in, and how soon the climax of the four is reached in any place or at any time cannot be definitely stated. Judgments always depend on wickedness and on God's longsuffering. The description pertains to *the whole world.* Yet we do not think that these judgments strike the whole world with one blow but that they strike where and when judgment is due.

These are not physical or natural disasters. The physical features are presented in order to make everything *visible* to John's eyes; but they are such as plainly cannot be physical in the literal sense. Thus there are no little lumps of common hail, no blood of actual veins, etc., in this first judgment. Mauro senses what is meant when he speaks of the "political" or "politico-religious" sphere; likewise Kretzmann when he speaks of heresies, fanaticism, heretical leaders although he thinks too much of the effects on the church. The four trumpet blasts are *destructive religious delusions in the whole world,* "deceit of unrighteousness," sent down on those who reject the truth. "For this cause God sends them *deceit's working,* so that they believe *the lie,* in order that there may be judged all that did not believe the truth, but were well pleased with *the unrighteousness,*" II Thess. 2:10-12. Since religious delusions strike the very center of human life, *these delusions affect every part of human life and beget delusions in finance, government, commerce, education, in short, everywhere.* The true church is not included but only the apostate churches.

We regard this symbolism as a set of parables, although only to the extent of presenting visibly the invisible cause and its effect. Who sees what religious delusions really are and what untold damage they cause? Men love the deadly lie, the damnable unrighteousness. Therefore, when God's longsuffering reaches its limit, the lie is sent down upon men in all its destructiveness. Yet not as one judgment but in four gradations. Even judgment is restrained as much as is possible. The worse and the worst come only when and where they must come.

Take the first. Does the lie, some delusion, look so attractive? It is like a rain of hail and fire mixed with blood that strikes the earth. Hail and fire, mixed with blood, is wholly unnatural. No tempest such as this ever swept over the earth. *In even its mildest delusions the lie is wholly unnatural.* It is a monstrous terror. What is the wreckage that it causes when it is sent down on the lovers of the lie like a hurricane? Here it is made visible to the eye. It is as though the third of the earth was burned up and utterly blasted, as though the third of the trees was burned up (think of the terrible forest fires and what they leave), as though the green herbage which is far less resistant was burned up. "Burned up — burned up — burned up!" Three second aorist passives κατεκάη (κατακαίω, "to burn down," we say "up"). What a horror! Yet this is a true visible picture of what this delusion does in only its first stage of judgment. How many times has this first stage already done its burning up?

8, 9) **And the second angel trumpeted, and as it were a great mountain burning with fire was thrown into the sea; and the third of the sea became blood, and the third of the creatures in the sea, those having life, died, and the third of the ships was destroyed.** Exod. 7:14-25 is only a miniature of this. Note that we are not to stress the resemblance of these judgments to the plagues that befell Egypt, for the first trumpet reminds us of the seventh plague, the second trumpet of the first plague. Here is a judgment that is more stupendous than the Nile and all the water in Egypt turned to blood.

This judgment is not worse because the sea is struck but because the sea is added. Does the lie and its delusion call down such terror? Here the judgment is painted in visible colors. No earthly mountain ever blazed with fire and was hurled into the earthly ocean and turned the third of it into blood, etc. If such a thing had occurred, it would truly picture what the second degree of judgment is.

This is not a volcano hurling lava into the sea but a mountain that is all ablaze with fire, that is hurled into the ocean by an invisible hand, a mountain that is so great as to cause the effect described. In connection with the first trumpet the delusion seems to be composite, hail, fire, mixed with blood; in connection with the second it is unified, a great mountain. "A great mountain" is still a terrestrial image. "The sea" is now added to "the earth" that was mentioned in connection with the first trumpet. Corresponding to the trees and the herbage we have "the creatures in the sea, that have life" and "the ships." But the horrible effect now has "blood," the sea is turned to blood. "The third" continues.

Here the second stage of destructive religious delusion in all the world is made visible to John's eyes. How the world of men and the press would shriek if such monstrous destruction were wrought in nature! The past centuries have actually witnessed nothing less horrible in the religious domain; from this it has spread into all other domains. This is not the old paganism that still persists in the world but the terror of a new delusion which will not accept the gospel.

10, 11) **And the third angel trumpeted, and there fell out of the heaven a great star burning as a torch, and it fell on a third of the rivers and upon the springs of the waters. And the name of the star is called Absinthe. And the third of the waters became absinthe, and many of the people died from the waters because they were made bitter.**

As the great mountain burning with fire exceeds hail and fire mixed with blood, so the great star out of heaven burning as a torch exceeds the burning mountain. Little is gained by making this star a comet, save that some comet may look like a torch. For again the point is the frightful damage done, and here the damage is strange, indeed, for it is caused by a star falling to earth, which strikes "the third of the rivers" and "the springs of the waters." This is just as unimaginable as the phenomena mentioned in connection with the first and the second judgments. In all its stages delusion is utterly unnatural, unreasonable, and is rightly symbolized only by monstrous, unnatural imagery. The fresh-water rivers and springs alone are left, and now these are struck; but again only "the third" despite the greatness of this "great star out of the heaven."

Stranger still, this star bears the name Ἄψινθος (masculine because of ἀστήρ), "Absinthe," i. e., Wormwood. This is not the name of a star that is known among men; the name is a part of the symbolism, which must be left as a unit and not picked to pieces. The destructive effect of this astounding symbolism is that now the third of these sweet waters became "absinthe" (neuter because of τὸ τρίτον), "wormwood," or bitter as wormwood; εἰς with the accusative = the predicate nominative, R. 458. Compare Jer. 9:15; 23:15. The further effect was that "many of the human beings (ἄνθρωποι) died due to (ἐκ) the waters because they were made bitter." The remark that wormwood is not a poison is beside the mark, because the word "poison" is not used. Having nothing but wormwood water to drink, wicked men do not remain in health. "Many" corresponds to "the third of the waters." Many people are here introduced in order to complete the picture and not because people have not been destroyed by the two other judgments.

The reference to Iranian and Mandæan eschatology, where only a falling star is mentioned, or to springs which pagans thought bubbled up from an abyss of demons, is not helpful. Mauro and others allegorize: the star = a person, a man or an angel; Mauro's choice is the devil, Lucifer. Others find a reference to Attila the Hun, "the scourge of God," or to Pelagius, or to Origen (Luther's opinion), to Arius or to Gregory the Great. The futurists think of their antichrist.

The third trumpet makes visible the advance of religious delusion in the word which scorns the gospel. Here, too, the imagery is a unit and is unnatural as delusion always is both as to its cause and as to its effect. What leaders may be at the head of the intensified lie is immaterial. One may try to trace these successive judgments in past history and then raise dispute; we do not care to enter them. The difficulty will always be to distinguish between the great and the little heretics and the popular delusions among men generally in all departments of life. It would seem that our task is ever to keep clear of all of them, however we and others may rate their destructiveness. We prefer to think less of the names of leaders than of the force and the destructiveness of the judgments themselves. It is where the gospel should reign in all departments of life and yet is rejected that such judgments descend. The horror is to have nothing but wormwood even in life generally where men could and should have the gospel that is sweeter than honey and the honeycomb in all that pertains to life.

12) **And the fourth angel trumpeted, and there was smitten the third of the sun and the third of the moon and the third of the stars so that there was made dark the third of them, and so that the day did not shine for the third of it, and the night likewise.**

In this symbolism the heavenly bodies are smitten; hence we have no visible agent like the hail, the mountain, the star Absinthe whose damage strikes on earth. It is rather distressing to read the comment: "The writer forgets or ignores that he has already cleared the heaven of stars (6:13)." It is asked how darkening the third of the heavenly lightbearers made the day and the night fail to shine for a third. But there is no difference whether one third of the light giving surface was struck into blackness, or one third of the light as such ceased. Four times τὸ τρίτον is repeated as though now more than ever to emphasize this fraction which has already occurred seven times.

The climax of the lie and the delusion is that its judgment removes the light of truth itself. See this judgment in its complete form in Amos 8:11, 12; and in its preliminary form in Matt. 13:13-15, where Jesus also quotes Isaiah — he hides the light in parables. Terrible is the judgment when the light of the Word is taken away to any degree. For ourselves we think of the darkening that has taken place in the Greek and in the Roman Catholic churches, in rationalism, in modernism, and in many sects, plus all the skeptic, cynic, silly religious and non-religious, worldy folly and delusion spread among men in general. There is no need to point to specific dates, nor have any of these four judgments already run their course.

The resemblance to the fourth plague that befell Egypt, Exod. 10:21-23, is very slight. It is hard to understand how the preterists can refer to the dissolution of the Jewish nation in 70 A. D. Others regard the heavenly bodies as secular governmental systems, the partial darkening as political disorders. Others think of the Goths or the Mohammedans.

Introductory to the Fifth and the Sixth Trumpet, 8:13

13) All the judgments announced by the trumpets are introduced by the scene in heaven, v. 1-6; the last three also by a phenomenon occurring in heaven.

And I saw and heard an eagle flying in midheaven, saying with a great voice: Woe, woe, woe those dwelling on the earth due to the remaining blasts of the trumpet of the three angels about to trumpet! The correct reading is "an eagle"; very inferior textually is "an angel," and wholly unworthy of consideration "an angel as an eagle." The genitive follows ἤκουσα — John heard the eagle speak; ἑνός does not mean "one," but = our indefinite article, R. 674; "an eagle." Οὐαί may be followed by the dative or the accusative; it is like the Latin *vae mihi* or *me.* The three "woes" are spoken with reference to the following three trumpets. The eagle flies in midheaven because his woes pertain to all the dwellers on the earth. In Revelation "those dwelling on the earth" is regularly used as a designation for all those who reject the gospel and love the earth instead. The eagle does not speak to these "dwellers," his words are spoken so that John and we may take them to heart.

Once more we have a unit in the symbol, the intent of which is simply to announce to John and through him to us the coming trumpets which are more terrible than the first ones were. These last three are actual "woes." We see this in 9:12: "The first woe is past; behold, there come yet two woes hereafter!" and in

11:14: "The second woe is past; behold, the third woe comes quickly!" All three and then the second and the third separately are specially announced.

There is no reason for making the eagle the antithesis of the dove of peace or a bird of carrion (Matt. 24:28) or of ill omen or a symbol of vengeance. There is no need to allegorize: the eagle of the Roman legions — some expected prophet at the end of the world — Gregory the Great — Christ himself. Weidner rightly says: "Is it any wonder that men regard the Apocalypse as an enigma with such interpretations as guides!"

CHAPTER IX

The Fifth Trumpet and the First Woe, 9:1-11

1) If the first four trumpets have been variously interpreted, the confusion in regard to the fifth and the sixth is still greater. In fact, this confusion is so great that the few sober voices which in a measure touch the truth of the more elaborate symbolism of these two judgments are scarcely heard. One might, in the face of it all, simply give up in despair, close the book, and say nothing whatever. A number of interpretations are guesswork, mere fancies, if not worse. Some regard the Apocalypse as the product of a morbid imagination. These writers attempt no interpretation but seek to discover the pagan and the older apocalyptic sources for the imagery of the text.

The three horsemen, war, injustice, death (6:3-8) bring judgments that are the direct fruits of the human wickedness that is found in the world. The trumpets blow the signals for judgments which follow as *direct, supernatural inflictions* and are of an entirely different and more terrible type. Six are *horrible delusions;* they are followed by the seventh, the final judgment itself (11:14-18). They are progressive in their terror. This progressiveness is only in part one of time; it is one chiefly of degree. Where the truth of God is positively rejected the deadliness of the delusion must strike with increasing intensity. The areas affected vary, the succession of judgments is the same. In one area the succession proceeds rapidly, in another more slowly. All this takes place as God decides. All the judgments announced by the trumpets are *super-*

natural and thus unlike the second, third, and fourth horseman.

The fifth and the sixth judgments of delusion belong together as being *hellish;* hence the elaborate symbolism is *unimaginably monstrous.* It must be in order to present a true picture. All hellish delusions transcend all natural symbols. Because of their very nature they are entirely unnatural, unreasonable, monstrous, and a true, visible presentation must so depict them. The judgments of delusion here described exceed all that the Scriptures otherwise record. Revelation is the last and thus the fullest prophecy.

The fifth judgment shows the hellish delusion only in its *tormenting* effect; the sixth judgment adds the *killing* effect. Thus also these two belong together. There is no question that, as the final judgment approaches, delusion shall become more and more terrible. Yet we do not place the first trumpet in one century, the second in another, and so onward. The six are, to our mind, six pictures of six degrees of delusion with their awful effects. Their root is religious, but the effect extends into all departments of life. Out of the basic delusion come multitudes of others that spread woe, damage, terror, torment, and death among the ungodly dwellers on the earth. Some find references to wars, revolution, pestilence, political upheavals, and other dislocations. Some regard Arius as the fifth trumpet, Mohammed as the sixth, or the two stages of Mohammedanism as these two trumpets. In our time it is not popular to think of the papacy as the antichrist although the papacy is one of the worst religious delusions. Yet what about the hosts of rationalists, the swarms of evolutionists — to mention only these? *Let us not include too little!* The New Testament Era has been devastated by all manner of religious and unnumbered secular delusions. They ever go together. Where gospel sanity is rejected, sanity in all other departments of life is absent. We are living among a multitude of these delusions. These visions are to show us what they really are in order that we may be kept sane by means of the Word.

And the fifth angel trumpeted, and I saw a star having fallen out of the heaven to the earth; and there was given to him the key of the shaft of the abyss. And he opened the shaft of the abyss, and there came up a smoke out of the shaft as smoke of a great furnace, and darkened was the sun and the air due to the smoke of the shaft. And out of the smoke came out grasshoppers on the earth, and there was given to them power as the scorpions of the earth have power. And it was said to them, that they hurt not the herbage of the earth, nor anything green, nor any tree, only the human beings, such as have not the seal of God on their foreheads. And it was given to them not that they kill them, but that they be tormented for five months. And their torment (was) **as a scorpion's torment when he strikes a human being. And in those days human beings will seek death and shall in no way find it, and will desire to die, and death flees from them. And the likenesses of the grasshoppers like to horses having been prepared for battle; and upon their heads as crowns like to gold, and their faces as faces of human beings. And they had hair as hair of women, and their teeth were as of lions. And they had breastplates as iron breastplates; and the sound of their wings as sound of chariots of many horses running to battle. And they have tails like to scorpions and stings; and in their tails their power to harm human beings for five months. They have over them as king the angel of the abyss — name for him in Hebrew Abaddon, and in the Greek he has as name Apollyon.**

This star is not Satan despite Luke 10:18; for Satan, indeed, fell like lightning but not "out of heaven to the earth," and Satan, who himself fell into the abyss, has no key to open the abyss. When it is said that this star opened the shaft of the abyss, we have personification and plainly are not to think of a physical star. Thus "having fallen or dropped" simply places the star where it is able to use the key, the tense of the participle expressing perfected state (R. 1123). The wording of the four preceding judgments should certainly teach us that imagination is here to be abandoned, yet so many try, generally in a curious fashion, to imagine all that is said in this frightful symbolism. The point of the personification of this star is simply that *the whole judgment comes from God* and is sent upon men as *a curse*. In 8:10 God uses a star in one unimaginable way, here in another that is equally unimaginable. He still uses a star as his agent; in the sixth judgment he employs four angels and thereby marks an advance.

Some are of the opinion that "the abyss" is *not* hades or hell but some other place, and G. K. 9 states that the word denotes at least two other places, 1) the prison of the disobedient spirits, and 2) the *Totenreich* (realm of the dead), and that the inmates are to be set free from the prison. "The abyss" is one of several designations for hell. The Catholic interpreters think of three non-existing places: purgatory, the *limbus patrum*, and the *limbus infantum*. The Scriptures speak of two places in the other world, only two, heaven and hell. As there is only one blessed place, so there is only one accursed place and not two or three or more of these, and not one or more intermediate places, the inmates of which are to be released as. Catholics have theirs released from purgatory and from the *limbus patrum*.

2) The κλείς or "key" and the φρέαρ or "shaft," which is locked and, when unlocked, belches out infer-

nal volumes of black smoke over the earth that darkens the sun and the air, are only graphic imagery. Christ has "the keys of the death and of hades" (1:18), the power to lock into hell and, as is now added, to let hell belch forth its infernal punitive powers of delusion over the earth. "*As* smoke of a great furnace" plainly points to imagery in this graphic description and certainly fits all else that Scripture reveals about hell. This is also true with regard to the resulting darkening that is due to (causal ἐκ) what is "*as* smoke of a great furnace" and affects the sun and the air. In 8:12 the third of the sun, moon, and the stars is struck. Now the sun, the one true light of truth for men's souls and lives, is completely blotted out by hell's smoke. Men are totally deprived of the Word. This is not a reference to paganism where the divine sun never shone but to a place after it has shone for a time. The very air men breathe in connection with their education, thinking, philosophizing, managing, governing, etc., is black murk. Hell spreads its pall over them. The heavenly light of saving truth shines, but men live in this hellish atmosphere. It comes upon them as God's curse.

3) The frightful thing John saw is worse. "Out of the smoke came out grasshoppers on the earth," ἀκρίδες. Our versions render this Greek word "locusts," which is liable to lead us to think of the cicada, of which species we are especially acquainted with the seventeen-year locust. Locusts of this type do not devour everything that is green and do not come in great clouds upon the wind (see Exod. 10:12-15); these are the locusts that we commonly call grasshoppers. To say that only the smoke and not the grasshoppers came out of the abyss seems purposeless. Are they not described as hellish monsters? In Amos 7:1 this word means "green worms"; but in Judges 6:5; Jer. 46:23; Joel 1:4, as in Exod. 10:12, etc., the count-

less swarms and the voraciousness are the point of the plague, and this thought plays in here. But these are *hellish* grasshoppers and transcend all imagination as it was transcended already in the other four judgments.

These have, not by their own nature, but as having been given to them, an ἐξουσία like that of "the scorpions of the earth," a scorpion's power and a right to use that power. In v. 5 we have, "*as* a scorpion's torment"; in v. 10, "tails *like* to scorpions and stings," which doubly emphasizes this imagery and likeness. An erroneous opinion is entertained when it is supposed that the ancients considered the sting of the scorpion fatal. Here only "torment" is mentioned, and v. 5 excludes killing. Because scorpions only hurt terribly their likeness is here used. Who ever saw scorpion grasshoppers? All hell's vomit is monstrous, wholly beyond normal imagery. To enter among hellish things is like entering into an insane region. All that is here presented is only one hellish curse let loose on the earth.

4) As the three passives ἐδόθη, "there was given," in v. 1, 3, 6, so the passive ἐρρέθη, "it was said," intends to veil the agent. These passives convey the idea that hell is able to do nothing of itself and is used in judgment only as and how God determines and limits it in his absolute justice. The ἵνα clause is the object of "it was said." The texts vary between the subjunctive and the future indicative. Both are used in the Koine. Here we have abnormality although the power of scorpions already prepares us for it. Grasshoppers devour foliage and in ordinary imagery are made to do so; but these do not do so, they are *not* to hurt (ἀδικήσωσι as in 2:11; 6:6; 7:2, 3) the herbage, nor any tree, nor anything green, (οὐδέ . . . οὐδέ simply negatives single items and has nothing to do with ἵνα, contra R. 1159) but only (εἰ μή) the human beings, such as (οἵτινες, qualitative and causal: because they are such

as) have not the seal of God on their foreheads. Review the exposition of 7:2-4, and note that a wrong exposition of 7:2-4 will also be reflected here. This judgment comes upon those who are not sealed; those who are sealed unto God, the true believers, are exempt. It is plain that this positive restriction bars out any persecution, terrors of war, famine, and the like, which may affect also the godly. The hellish delusion that strikes the despisers of the Word through millions of hellish agencies leaves the lovers of the Word who are sealed as God's own by that Word, spiritually unharmed.

5) Since they have hellish power, we might think that these monsters would kill with their poison since it is much worse than that of earthly scorpions. But no, these monsters are not to kill; their victims are only to be tormented, the future passive after ἵνα. The infliction is worse than a rapid death (v. 6), it is like the burning torment that follows when a scorpion strikes a human being. For this torment shall come from these millions and millions of inescapable monsters who strike each victim with countless stings.

"For five months" is made doubly significant by its repetition in v. 10. The idea that a plague of ordinary grasshoppers in countries that suffer from them is confined to the five summer months is unsatisfactory; for, to say only this, no cloud of grasshoppers ever ravaged a territory "*for* five months," accusative of extent of time. The number five is symbolical; it is the half of ten. Egypt was struck by ten plagues, ten indicates the complete number. So these five are the half, the other half is to follow, and it does in the second woe (v. 12, etc.). We have five "months" because the symbolism is based on the year. Hengstenberg's "a long time but not the longest" is not sufficiently to the point; nor is Kuebel's "a measured time that dare not complete itself." Bengel says that a month = 15 $^{55}/_{63}$ years; 5

months = $79\frac{1}{8}$ years. Others speak of 5 × 150 mystical days which signify common years. Bengel refers to the years of Jewish suffering in Persia in the sixth century. This is not a reference to Gen. 7:24, nor to the Mohammedan victories (Mauro). The very fact that these monsters are not to kill indicates that this torment is only the half of what is to occur. The length of years cannot be figured from these symbolical "five months."

6) The language becomes Hebrew poetry in v. 6 to 9:

"And in those days the people will seek death,
And they shall in no way find it;
And will desire to die,
And death flees from them."

To think it singular that suicide is not committed by everybody and to reply that suicide was not Jewish, is to miss the point. To remark that the flight of death intensifies the torture is to evade the point. These monsters are forbidden to kill those that are not sealed (v. 5), they are permitted only to torment them. This type and this stage of hellish delusion produce only torment and woe that feel like thousands of scorpion stings. The idea that the unsealed, ungodly, deluded might kill themselves is foreign to the picture. It is a well-known fact that despite all their wishing to be dead, when the most painful curse of their delusion strikes them like scorpion stings, the ungodly never have the courage to commit mass suicide. The sealed, the true believers, are *not* struck by this frightful delusion; they ever possess the light of the Word, the peace of God in a cursed world.

Most commentators prefer to leave this verse uninterpreted.

7) The unearthly hellishness of these grasshoppers is fully elaborated:

"And the likeness of the grasshoppers like to
horses prepared for battle;
And upon their heads as crowns like to gold;
And their faces as faces of human beings,
And they had hair as hair of women.
And their teeth were as of lions.
And they had breastplates as iron breastplates.
And the sound of their wings as sound of chariots
of horses running to battle."

Dropping the poetical form, the description continues: "And they have tails like to scorpions; and in their tails their power to harm human beings for five months."

These are their ὁμοιώματα, "points of resemblance" in a number of respects; hence the repeated ὡς, "as" and ὅμοιος, "like." The seven καί pile up the resemblances in their monstrous unnaturalness. This is what the fifth stage of damnable delusion actually looks like. We are to see it on the basis of this revelation. The unsealed do not see it for they are blind, but they are compelled to feel the full effect of it.

See the valuable article "Locust" in Smith, *Bible Dictionary* II, 1669, etc., especially also the illustrations of *Œdipoda migratoria* and of *Acridium peregrinum.* "With the burning south winds (of Syria) there come from the interior of Arabia and from the most southern parts of Persia clouds of locusts (*Acridium peregrinum*), whose ravages to these countries are as grievous and nearly as sudden as those of the heaviest hail in Europe. We witnessed them twice. It is difficult to express the effect produced on us by the sight of the whole atmosphere filled on all sides and to a great height by an innumerable quantity of these insects, whose flight was slow and uniform, and whose noise resembled that of rain: the sky was darkened, and the light of the sun considerably weakened. In a moment the terraces of the houses, the streets, and all the fields were covered by these insects, and in two days they had nearly devoured all the leaves of the plants."

We quote another: "The destructive locust (the *Acridium peregrinum,* probably) comes suddenly . . . in clouds that obscure the air, moving with a slow and steady flight, and with a sound like that of heavy rain; settling in myriads on the fields, the gardens, the trees, the terraces of the houses, and even the streets, which they sometimes completely cover. Where they fall, vegetation presently disappears, the leaves and even the stems of the plants are devoured; the labors of the husbandman through many a weary month perish in a day; and the curse of famine is brought upon the land which but now enjoyed the prospect of an abundant harvest." See also *Standard Dictionary* on "grasshopper" and on "locust."

It is untenable when writers find the resemblances here sketched in actual grasshoppers. Look at the illustrations in Smith. Do you see anything like a horse prepared for battle, anything like crowns resembling gold, like human faces, like woman's hair, like lion's teeth, like iron breastplates? A good deal of imagination is necessary in order to hear in the flight of these insects the roar of an army of horses dashing into battle — the R. V. "war" is a faulty translation. This insect has two short antennae. Do these suggest woman's hair?

These resemblances are sometimes referred to as Mohammedan warriors on their horses, their long hair *flying* behind and not out in front of them. Their law forbids them to cut down trees, their turbans resemble crowns, they are as ferocious as lions, their fury is demoniacal. But these insects afflict human beings and are not human beings. Where are the Mohammedan scimitars and lances that are so distinctive of them? When did their horses wear iron breastplates? What about the "tails like to scorpions" and the power of stings in their tails to torment human beings?

The whole imagery is contrary to nature because it pictures devilishness. The delusion is like a multitudinous swarm of grasshoppers in its spread, and every part of it is like a monstrosity of hell with its effect according. The imagery is not that of insects that are a few inches long but that of powerful, terrifying creatures, millions of whom come upon defenseless human beings with a roar. This pictures what the fifth stage of the curse of delusion really is.

No natural grasshopper looks like a horse, but these hellish ones have that unnatural resemblance. And they do not resemble wild horses but horses that are fitted out for battle with armor plate, the very sight of them being terrifying. Something like crowns (see 2:10, here not indicating royalty but victory) and these like gold are on their heads. They are creatures whom it is impossible to withstand or to defeat, they are crushingly terrifying when they are truly seen. This swarming delusion is an inescapable curse of judgment.

"As faces of human beings" is not equivalent to faces of "men" (ἄνδρες, whereas John writes ἄνθρωποι, "human beings") who have beards and are riders on grasshopper horses. "As faces of human beings" = not with blind animal or insect instinct but with what resembles human intelligence, for these are hell's spawn and not products of earth and nature or even of human wickedness.

8) "As hair (in the Greek this is an idiomatic plural) of women" is a part of the list of likenesses: "As crowns — *as* faces of human beings — *as* hair of women — teeth *as* of lions — *as* iron breastplates — *as* sound of chariots." Natural grasshoppers have no hair, these hellish monsters have. It streams out from

under their crowns "as hair of women." Shall we say that they are like furies? "Women's hair" seems to be in place because "as faces of human beings" precedes; hence manes of horses or of lions are out of the question. This is as near as we can come.

Some do not attempt to interpret this feature, others offer: 1) barbarians who let their hair grow long; 2) the hair is thought to be on the grasshoppers' legs; 3) their antennae resemble the hair of girls — but look at the two short antennae projecting forward; 4) hair of women — effeminate; 5) = seductive; 6) = sabarytic indulgence; 7) to let the hair grow = to leave the passions without restraint; men who cut their hair, women who today cut theirs are no better than others who let it grow. We see no point in these ideas.

"Their teeth as of lions" descends from the crowns and the hair to the mouth that has these horrible teeth. Yet with such teeth they do not rend and devour. Nor are they like the mandibles of grasshoppers. These monsters have their power in their scorpion tails, their stings, and they do not kill even with these.

So we must say that all these ὁμοιώματα or "likenesses" reveal to spiritual eyes the composite monstrous *appearance* of this multitudinous fifth curse of delusion. Although it is intangible and invisible it is here made concrete and visible in its unnatural nature. We are to see it as John did so that we may never step out from the safe shelter of the Word.

9) From crown, hair, and teeth we come to thorax and wings. The latter two are found in actual grasshoppers. "As iron thoraxes or breastplates" makes us think of the armature of war horses who have iron plates over the chest. These are a sign of invincibility. The next picture is in line with this, namely, the sound of the wings "as sound of chariots of many horses (A. V. better than R. V.) running into battle." It is a roar of uncounted chariots that are

racing headlong into the fray and overwhelming everything that is in their path. "The sound . . . as sound," combined with the mention of "their wings," is fearfully suggestive of the manner in which this damnable type of delusion carries everything before it.

10) "Scorpions — to hurt the human beings for five months" reverts to v. 5, but now adds "tails" and "stings" and the fact that the entire power of these monstrosities is in their tails with which they strike their victims with the torment that is thrice impressively mentioned in v. 5. There is no killing in this delusion but only a sort of hell on earth. See how βασανίζω is used by the demons in Matt. 8:29; Mark 5:7; Luke 8:28, and βάσανοι in Luke 16:23, 28. "For five months" is to be understood as it was in v. 5; it is repeated for the sake of emphasis.

11) In nature clouds of grasshoppers are leaderless; not so these hordes of hell. They have over them as their king "the angel of the abyss," whose name "in Hebrew" (adverb) is "Abaddon," and "in the Greek" (supply γλώσσῃ) is "Apollyon." Both names are as symbolical as the name of the star in 8:11, "Absinthe." As this = Wormwood and intends to explain the cause of the bitterness and the hurtfulness of the affected waters, so these two names = "Perdition" and intend to explain the effect of these grasshoppers. In both "Absinthe" and "Apollyon" the essence of the two types of delusion is symbolized. The name is properly made masculine Ἀπολλύων and not the abstract feminine ἀπώλεια, "perdition," the opposite of σωτηρία, "salvation." There is no need to think of a connection with Apollo, one of the twelve greater gods, the god of the sun, of divination, pestilence, archery, medicine, music, and poetry, because the grasshopper is his mark as is done in G. K. 396 and 4.

This is not the star of v. 1 opening the abyss; not Satan; not some demon appointed over the abyss or over these hellish grasshoppers by Satan. This "angel of the abyss" and this "king" exist only in the vision as do the grasshoppers over which he is king, and his two names help to make concrete this fifth type of delusion which leads to perdition, the state obtaining in the abyss.

The Sixth Trumpet and the Second Woe, 9:12-21

12) **The first woe went; lo, there come yet two woes after this!** The aorist "went," ἀπῆλθεν, means that the vision of the first woe has passed from John's sight. The fact that these judgments are "woes" in a most significant sense is repeated from 8:13 and emphasized by "woe the first" and "two woes." These preambles (8:13; 9:12; 11:14) distinguish the woes from the first four trumpets.

13) **And the sixth angel trumpeted. And I heard a voice from out the horns of the altar, the golden, the one before God, saying to the sixth angel, the one having the trumpet: Loose the four angels, those that have been bound at the river, the great one, Euphrates! And there were loosed the four angels, the ones that have been prepared for the hour and day and month and year to kill the third of the human beings. And the number of the armies of the cavalry two myriads of myriads — I heard their number. And thus I saw the horses in the vision and those sitting upon them, having breastplates, fiery and hyacinthine and brimstony. And the heads of the horses as heads of lions; and out of their mouths proceed fire and smoke and brimstone. From these three inflictions there were killed the third of the human beings, as a result of the fire and of the smoke and of the brimstone proceeding out of their mouths. For the power of the horses is in their mouths and in their tails, for their tails are like unto snakes, having heads, and in connec-**

tion with them they hurt. And the rest of the human beings who were not killed in these inflictions did not repent from the works of their hands so as not to worship the demons and the idols, the golden and the silver and the bronze and the stone and the wooden, which are able neither to see nor to hear nor to walk; and they did not repent from their murders, nor from their sorceries, nor from their fornications, nor from their thefts.

Let us at once say that this sixth judgment, like the fifth, is a curse, a delusion sent as a curse, the worst, the most frightful of all. Like the others, it comes from God. Like the others, John sees it in concrete, visible symbolism as what it is and does; unbelieving men are struck only by its hellishness. This sixth curse is companion to and completement of the fifth, hence both are called woes. The six are pictured so that four present increasing extent, and two increasing severity, the sixth is the climax beyond which lies the final judgment. The six take place in the New Testament Era. We regard it as a mistake to seek dates in past history, a date for number one, another date for number two, and so forth. The spread and the severity may be swift or may be slow; the duration may last a longer or a shorter length of time. All this is determined by him who alone is the Judge and sends the curse. The times and the seasons remain completely in his ἐξουσία (Acts 1:7) and are not revealed. These are the main and outstanding realities although we may be unable to interpret some of the details of the symbolism. Their horror of unnaturalness forms one of the great marks and runs through all the details.

In the light of these six curses we who are sealed as God's own are to understand the delusions in the world around us in their actual origin, nature, purpose, and effect.

Ellicott, Barnes, and others, and lately Mauro are impressed by what seems to them to be a fully convincing correspondence between detailed features in the fifth and the sixth judgments and the two great invasions of Mohammedans that extended to the fall of Constantinople on May 29, 1453. Theirs is the one view which, in our estimation, alone deserves special attention because it is widely held and has been worked out with great detail. We are pointed to the *infidel* historian Gibbon as being completely convincing and Barnes states: "If Mr. Gibbon had *designed* to describe the conquests of the Turks as a fulfillment of the prediction, could he have done it in a style more clear and graphic than that which he has employed? If this had occurred in a *Christian* writer, would it not have been charged on him that he had shaped the facts to meet his notions of the meaning of the prophecy?" Some of the objections made to this view by Alford are recognized as valid by Craven, the editor of the Lange commentary, who, admitting their force, tries to remove their force and save the case.

Fifteen points are enumerated. Let us note number eleven, the terrible cannon used by the Turks, regarding which Craven quotes Gibbon at length as showing the fulfillment of the fire and the brimstone. Add number five to number seven which points to cavalry and the fact that the Turks count theirs by "myriads" and not by thousands. But all this together with a number of other points is simply war, i. e., the second horseman of 6:3, 4. We add number fourteen, which figures out that "the hour and day and month and year" = 391 years and 30 days, in the Julian calendar 396 years and 118 days = January 18, 1057 to May 16, 1453, when the fall of Constantinople was certain, although it actually fell on May 29. But we regard such an interpretation as too strange and farfetched to be acceptable.

In 6:3, 4 not one but *all* wars are presented. Wars are a *natural* phenomenon in a sinful world, and trumpets five and six are a thousand times worse than any and all wars; every detail in these curses is *supernatural* beyond all dating; they are *hellish* delusions of human minds and souls with a supernatural, unimaginable viciousness. For our part we think of passages such as Eph. 6:12.

Μίαν is merely an indefinite article: "a voice" (cf., "an eagle" in 8:13). The accusative φωνὴν λέγοντα speaks of what (not of whom) John heard. John heard "a voice from out the four horns of the altar, the golden, the one before God," giving an order to the sixth angel, which indicates that this curse comes by direct divine judgment. This is also true with regard to the five previous curses as well as 8:3-5, the preamble to them all. This is again the golden altar of incense (8:3), and its horns are not "bedewed with blood." This is the altar of the incense of the prayer of *all* the saints and is not to be restricted to the martyrs already slain and to their cry (6:10) which is not connected with the altar of incense. "From out the horns" means from the center of the altar table where the incense burned. The prayers of God's saints voice his will: "Thy will be done on earth as it is in heaven!" This applies also to God's judgment will. "Holy, holy, holy, Lord God Almighty!" (4:8) is not the acclaim of only the agents of divine providence and does not refer only to the holiness that makes holy and saves but also to the holiness that damns those who do not repent (v. 20, 21).

14) The nominative apposition ὁ ἔχων after the dative is deictic, as so often in Revelation. The order is that the sixth trumpet angel shall set free the four angels, "those bound at the river, the great one, Euphrates." "The four angels," etc., has the article because of the modifiers. There is no reason, because

of the article or otherwise, to identify these four with the four mentioned in 7:1. To think of them as being only symbols because their number is four, this number being symbolical, clashes with "the sixth angel" just mentioned; nor are these four angels evil because they carry out judgment, for this is the function of all the trumpet angels, even as God constantly sends judgment by the hand of his angels. "Having been bound" we regard as meaning having been restrained hitherto, so that the command now to loose them means to let them bring on the judgment. We get the impression that because of God's longsuffering this judgment, too, has been waiting until the hour when that longsuffering is exhausted and judgment *must* descend (δεῖ, 1:1).

"At the river, the great one, Euphrates" is not geographic so that we must think of hosts of pagan Parthian cavalry starting from this river as a base or of Saracenic hosts. Those are right who go back to the significance of the Euphrates in the Old Testament, yet not to its general significance as denoting the east whence death and destruction came, or whence punitive plagues arose for Israel, but as the place where the great world powers of Old Testament times: Assyria, Babylon, Persia, arose and spread their devastating dominion over the world (16:12). Here we have "the river" and "the great one" and not the city Babylon. In this sense the Euphrates is the world river, it is of greater significance than the Nile, which is the life only of Egypt. "At the river, the great one, Euphrates" does not place us at a geographical river or place but at the fountain of world dominance.

15) The four angels were loosed, they who had long before been made ready by God "for the hour and day and month and year" that John saw as having arrived, had been made ready "to kill the third of human beings," the same great fraction that was stated

in the first four judgments which is now advanced to human beings (in 6:8, "power over the fourth of the earth"). The four terms expressing time have but one article and thus cannot be added together so as to make so many hundred years and days (see the sample above: 396 years and 118 days). Hour, day, month, year is the way in which we still date, save that only in the case of very important events we specify also the hour. Here we have the most important judgment prior to that at the end of the world. Hence the reference to its date, which, however, is known and determined only by God (Acts 1:7).

16) "And the number of the armies of the cavalry two myriads of myriads," was made known to John, as he carefully states. Suddenly John saw these armies and heard their number. They roared out before his eyes. He does not say four armies with the four angels as their generals; we should not add this thought. On "myriads of myriads" compare the number of the angels in 5:11. Some say that 200,000,000 means no more than a vast number. In order to approach this literal number in the case of the Saracenes Bengel adds up all their armies during a period of two centuries. We have shown above that "myriads" is regarded as a Turkish way of counting; the Romans had their legions, each, when full, having about 6,000 men. But are the angels of heaven mentioned in 5:11 counted in Turkish fashion? This army is made up entirely of cavalry, τοῦ ἱππικοῦ, yet Constantinople fell by means of artillery. Gibbon, to whom appeal is made, describes how a deserter showed the Turks how to cast monster cannon that would hurl a 600-pound stone a mile to bury itself six feet in the earth where it fell. Gibbon also tells about galleys. This does not agree with this host of cavalry. "Myriads of myriads" seems less significant here than the fact that they are

doubled into "two" as though here there are twice the number needed to do this killing.

17) John says that "thus" he saw the horses "in the vision," thus as we are now told in detail. Just this one time does John add "in the vision" to "I saw." He apparently does this because thus far he has twice said, "I heard." John first notes the riders who have "breastplates, fiery and hyacinthine and brimstony," namely having these colors, all of which are hellish; ὑακίνθινος is a dark-red. Some place the breastplates on the horses, some on both horses and riders, the text only on the riders. The horses are frightful: their heads are "as heads of lions," they are not actual lions' heads but as frightful; their mouths spout "fire and smoke and brimstone," terrors of hell, these correspond to the colors of the breastplates of their riders. See 14:10, 11; 19:20; 20:10 for the significance of fire and brimstone.

18) They were "to kill the third of the human beings," and John reports that "there were killed (the plural *ad sensum*) the third of the human beings," this very proportion. He says ἀπό, "from these three inflictions," and then names them anew with the ἐκ of source, "as a result of the fire and of the smoke and of the brimstone," and repeats that these came out of the horses' mouths. Πληγή is a lash or blow. The fifth curse pictures only the intolerable torment and expressly excludes killing; the killing is depicted here and the fact that it was accomplished by the same agencies that make hell a place of horror and of death.

19) The pointed explanation (γάρ) that the power (ἐξουσία, as in v. 3 and 10) of the horses is "in their mouths" is added. For the third time attention is drawn to the horses' *mouths*. The *mouths* do the killing. There are riders, but none have weapons of offense. We are told by those who think of cavalrymen, especially of wild Turkish riders, that the flaming col-

ors of their cuirasses mark them as warriors; but where are sabers, scimitars, and lances? There are none. Nor do these riders kill, their horses do that. The riders show only that these are not wild, riderless horses. These horses are "armies," στρατεύματα, and not vast roving herds. The colors of the riders match only the fire, smoke, and brimstone coming out of the *mouths* of these millions of horses. They are supernatural like the swarms of grasshoppers. They belong together even as in this chapter they are paired, the one in order to torment, the other in order to kill.

Supernatural and equally monstrous is the power "in their tails." Here, too, we have an explanation (γάρ), their tails are like unto snakes having heads, like the hair of Medusa, one of the three Gorgons. The power of the grasshoppers is in their tails; these, however, have scorpion stings. Yet in this respect the grasshoppers' tails with scorpion stings and the horses' tails with snakeheads are alike. While they do not kill, they do hurt. The same verb is used in connection with both: ἀδικέω (v. 10, also 4). This hurting is the minor curse brought by the hellish horses.

Here there are millions of these horses who have such monstrous tails. What does Ellicott make of them? Horsetails borne by the Turkish Shahs as symbols of authority. Alford is right: "I venture to say that a more self-condemnatory explanation was never broached than this of the horsetails of the Shahs." He might have said more. Bengel's view is no better: the Turkish cavalry suddenly turning tail to hurt their pursuers. Another substitutes the kicks of the horses for their tails. Kretzmann throws a shield over these interpreters: "This picture is so definite that few believing commentators hesitate about identifying the movement with that of Mohammedanism at the beginning of the seventh century." Then he quotes Luther. Believing men often make exegetical mistakes. I venture to say that *few* believing men will accept this mistake. Consider these tails. They are not hoofs that strike to earth and trample to death but *tails* like *snakes* with *heads* doing *hurt!*

Horses that kill by belching forth fire, smoke, and brimstone, that hurt with tails like snakes having heads — mates to grasshoppers with scorpion tails and stings that cause torment: this symbolism, in our estimation, points to *the world curse in its ultimate stage, delusions of hell overrunning what should be Christian nations.* They have brought this killing curse upon themselves. In the fifth curse the abyss of hell sends out the swarms; in the sixth there are not merely swarming hordes but "armies," στρατεύματα, with ranks and files in "myriad" organization. While these are just as hellish with their fire, smoke, brimstone, tails of snakes with heads, they come from "the river, the great one, Euphrates," i. e., from the symbolic seat of great empires (Assyria, Babylon, Persia); for these ultimate, killing delusions arise in the greatest world nations and spread like organized military forces that hurt and kill everywhere.

Have these grasshoppers and these armies already been let loose in the world? One may dispute regarding that. John saw each vision complete, each in one picture, each one a frightful "woe." Yet, surely, these two delusions continue a long time, even to the final day of judgment. The question is, "Have they started?" For myself, I believe that they have. Wave after wave of delusion sweeps out from great nations that should be Christian, total irreligion, atheism, any number of false philosophies, religious secretism, atheistic science and its subversion of morality, every part of life feels the ἀδικεῖν, the βασανίζειν, the ἀποκτείνειν. The killing which John saw is not merely physical. "Perdition," Apollyon, rides high. God knows how much is yet to follow. But if these two woes have not yet started, if the blasts that sweep through the world are not yet these hellish ones at least in their incipiency, my mind staggers at what is yet to come.

20) Now at last, here at the end of the sixth curse, John was permitted to see the hardness and the impenitence which, in spite of this extreme severity of the last judgment, persisted. Those who were not swept away by the πληγαί, lashings or blows, "did not repent — did not repent," note the fearful repetition. On μετανοεῖν compare 2:5. There was no change of heart. "From the works of their hands" includes all the works indicated, those done against the first and those done against the second table of God's law. The "works" are mentioned because they are always the public and the undeniable evidence of what is in the heart, on which, therefore, all God's verdicts rest also in the final judgment at the last day, Matt. 25:34-46; Rev. 20:12,14.

Keep firmly in mind that this is a vision which was seen timelessly, supernaturally. John saw the whole curse and its result together as in a flash, "the third of human beings" killed or swept away, and with it "the rest (οἱ λοιποί, plural in the Greek) of the human beings who were not killed in these inflictions," all of them impenitent and not to be brought to repentance by anything God can do. In these visions John saw nothing whatever in regard to the Christians. These visions reveal only so much and no more. To insert more and so to bring in the true Christians causes confusion.

Ἵνα μή is consecutive and states result (R. 998), although B.-D. 391, 5, due to the older grammatical inhibition, still shrinks from finding actual result here. Translate, "So as not to worship (do obeisance to) the demons and to the idols, the golden and the silver and the bronze and the stone and the wooden." Then there is added what the Old Testament so often says of idols, "which are able neither to see, nor to hear, nor to walk." Ἵνα thus also is followed by the future indicative, which is quite in order. The result "not to worship" was not attained by repentance. "The works of their hands" means the ungodly deeds committed against both tables and does not mean that men made these idols, for note that "the demons" come first. Demons and idols belong together as I Cor. 10:20 shows, yet this does not mean that pagan divinities are devils but that the whole hellish kingdom is here said to revert to image worship, to setting up figures that are manufactured out of gold, silver, etc., as was done by the old Greeks and Romans, the East Indians, etc.

We are told by some interpreters that high cultural advance will not prevent this grossest reversion to idolatry. But this is vision and not literalism. The picture *is* that of grossest paganism, but a *picture* of what the *delusion* of men shall be. We think of what it already is despite the fact that the gospel has been preached for centuries. The picture is drawn negatively: *not* repent, "so as *not* to worship." All mental fictions in regard to God, all repudiations of the Triune God, all godlessness and conceptions of man as being an animal are here made equal to demon and idol worship even as they are nothing else. The god of the pagan, of the Jew, of the Mohammedan, of the irreligious scientist, of the intellectualist, etc., is a demon exactly as here portrayed. When, despite the gospel, the world is filled with this violation of the First Commandment, the seventh trumpet blast is not far off.

21) What was said in regard to the first table is also true in regard to the second table: "and they did not repent from their murders," etc. These are the gross vices; call them pagan if you will. Some puzzle about φάρμακα since witchcraft is usually listed in the first table as a crime against God and here seems to appear in the second. "Witchcrafts" are here listed beside "murders" as being used against men, which is rather

obvious. The translation *Giftmischerei*, "compounding poisons," and thus "poisonings," if taken literally, is of no aid, for it would imply a literal poisoning mania in the whole world. "Witchcrafts" is here listed on the basis of the Old Testament just like "the idols" and their Old Testament description and exactly like the other three crimes, as a mark of devil paganism. As murders include far more than actual bloodshed; fornication far more than this gross sin, and thefts far more than actual stealing, so we regard "witchcrafts" as implying far more than evil charms or poisonings; we refer it to all devilish spells cast upon men.

The sixth trumpet blast reveals to John the *world in its final impenitence*. What is then left? The answer is found in connection with the seventh trumpet (11:4-19).

CHAPTER X

The Rainbow Angel and the Two Witnesses, 10:1-11:13

The Rainbow Angel, chapter 10

1) Between the sixth and the seventh seals in chapter 7 John saw the vision of the church, which was so vital at that point for a proper understanding of the preceding six seals. Between the sixth and the seventh trumpets John now saw this further vision of the church which is combined with the witness of the Word. These two visions of the church are not mere interludes or intermezzos. The six seals and the six trumpets should not be dated in history to be followed by what these visions regarding the church show. These visions of the church have been placed where they are found because of their import in relation to the preceding visions. The vision of chapter 7 is essential in its place as shedding light on the whole of chapter 6 with its six seals. See the opening remarks on 7:1. The other, 10:1-11:13, is equally essential for chapters 8 and 9 and the six trumpets. So little are these two visions of the church of minor import that, without them and in the very sequence in which John saw them, neither the six seals nor the six trumpets can be rightly understood.

Many ask in regard to the six trumpets, especially in regard to the fifth and the sixth: "What about the church during the gradation of the judgments of delusion here depicted?" They then insert their own ideas into the six trumpets, at least into the fifth and the sixth, as regards the church. But the six trumpet scenes say nothing whatever about the church; all that pertains to the church as regards the six trumpets is embodied in the separate vision of 10:1-11:13. The same is true with regard to chapter 7 in relation to chapter 6 and the six seals. Chapter 7 does not follow chronologically upon the sixth seal, the cataclysm of the end. And the vision of the church and the Word (10:1-11:13) is not a part of the sixth trumpet of judgment, nor does this vision follow chronologically after the sixth trumpet.

This new vision of the church extends through the entire time of the six trumpets, it continues during the whole era of the frightful delusions which are sent upon the nations that ought to be Christian but are evil and spread over the whole world of men. These visions cannot be limited to Europe but deal with the whole world.

And I saw another angel, a strong one, coming down out of heaven, having thrown around him a cloud; and the rainbow upon his head, and his face as the sun, and his feet as pillars of fire, and having in his hand a little book having been opened. "Another angel" is too much like "another angel" in 8:3 to permit us to think that here Christ himself appears in the form of an angel. "Another" places this one among the various other angels of whom we have heard. His face and his feet may lead us to think of Christ as he is presented in 1:15, 16, yet the words used are not the same, and everything else in that vision of Christ transcends the description of this angel. "An angel, a strong one" is exactly like 5:2; ἰσχυρός, "strong," is added because of the whole appearance and the action of this angel.

When John writes that he saw him "coming down out of the heaven," we need only to remember that each of these visions presents all that is necessary for its purpose, and that thus there is no need to ask how John, while in spirit, could see this great angel coming down and taking his stand on sea and on earth. "Having thrown around him" (as a garment) is a passive with the accusative, which is often used with this verb, although it occurs with ἐν in 4:4. This perfect participle, like the other in v. 2, has its present connotation. The cloud thrown around him lends a heavenly majesty to the angel. The ἶρις, "rainbow" or "bow" like a great halo recalls the bow mentioned in 4:3, although this latter was greater, for it encircled the throne while here it rested only "upon the angel's head." Yet its significance is the same, it is a symbol of peace also for the church. His face like the sun describes his glory. His feet like pillars of fire describe his power over the enemies of the church. Other angels are not described in these visions; this one appears to John in such glorious symbolism because the revelation of which he is a part concerns the church.

2) Once more we have a nominative participle although it modifies the accusative ἄγγελον, which construction the grammarians call a "solecism" or labor to explain as does R. 892. Having case, number, and gender, it merely throws on the screen the fact that this strong and glorious angel has in his hand a "little book" that is not shut, not sealed, but "having been opened" and thus still being open in his hand. The diminutive "little book" indicates that it is entirely different from the book that was sealed with seven seals, which was mentioned in 5:1. The fact of its being open which was mentioned so that any eye may read it signifies that it contains revelation that is in no way to be hid or that requires special effort to become known. It is "little" enough so that John can take it and eat it.

This great and glorious angel with only this βιβλαρίδιον in his hand comes down and does a strange thing:

And he placed his foot, the right one, on the sea and the left one on the earth, and he gave a shout with a great voice as a lion roars. And when he gave the shout, the seven thunders uttered their own voices. Why this position, this tremendous shout, this answer of the reverberating thunders? We do not conceive the angel as being like a man in size so that his feet spread only as far as a man's feet may spread but think of a figure of vast height that is great enough to be clothed with a cloud. Thus one of his feet can be as a pillar of fire touching the ocean far out from the land, the other foot, a companion pillar, touching the earth far in from the ocean. Some note no connection with the little book and refer to this book again in connection with v. 8. But this little book is the main feature of this vision; everything else occurs because of it. The spread of the angel's feet is so wide because this little book pertains to "many peoples and nations and tongues and kings" (v. 11); his shout is so tremendous for the same reason, as are the voices of the seven answering thunders, God's power going forth. Perhaps there is no significance in stating that the right foot stood on the sea, the left on the earth when "one foot" and "the other" would suffice. Perhaps the right is here on the sea in order to indicate that the left that is on the earth is to step across the sea to the earth on the far side. It is certain that the whole world is involved.

3) No wonder that, when this strong angel ἔκραξε (used twice), uttered his shout, it was "with a great voice." The addition "as a lion roars" shows the greatness of the voice and recalls 5:5, "the Lion of the tribe of Judah," and other passages that mention lions, cf., Hos. 11:10; Amos 3:8; perhaps also Joel 3:16, although in the present vision the voice is only that of an angel, a representative of the Lord. Like an answer came the utterance of the seven thunders

with their own voices (ἑαυτῶν). The article is merely deictic like "the rainbow" (v. 1). We recall the "thunders" of 4:5, which proceeded out of the throne, and note the "thunders" of 8:5. We think that they must be referred to God who seconds and confirms the shout of this mighty angel. These manifestations are awe-inspiring to John and relate to the contents and the significance of the "little book."

4) **And when the seven thunders made utterance, I was about to write; and I heard a voice out of heaven saying, Seal what things the seven thunders uttered and do not write them!** Here we see that these thunders not only made a reverberating noise but also spoke something that John was about to write down. It may be possible that they spoke the same words in unison, or, as we deem less likely, that the seven spoke in succession. Biederwolf lists nine opinions as to what these thunders uttered. The fact that John was ordered *not* to write but to seal and to leave unwritten what these thunders uttered has not deterred some commentators from expressing their opinions. What was uttered by the thunders, and we may add what the angel first cried with a great voice, was not a part of the revelation that was intended for the slaves of God (1:1). This is not a literary device of John's for intimating to his readers that he knows more than he writes. When it is asked why it was given to John to know what he is ordered not to write and to make known, the answer is that this, too, is not for us to know. There is revealed what we *are* to know, namely that the thunders spoke and made no more reverberation.

The fact that there were seven thunders does not denote completeness, for that idea would be indicated by the number ten. This is the same seven that is found elsewhere, the sacred seven that involves God and the world. We need not speculate in regard to the voice out of heaven that gave John his orders and to ask whether it was God's or Christ's voice. Is it not enough to say that John knew that the voice conveyed the divine will to him? Why conclude that its coming out of heaven places John on the earth during this vision? This shifting of John from heaven to earth and back again is rather pointless. John was "in spirit" as he has twice stated. "A voice out of heaven" intends to connect this voice with God while John sees the angel standing on the sea and on the earth.

Those who note ἔμελλον γράφειν, "I was about to write," do not always note its import and sometimes directly deny this import, namely that John did his writing *during* the visions, immediately after seeing and hearing them. As soon as he heard what the thunders uttered he says, "I was about to be writing." That is plain, especially in view of 1:11, 19. To speak about a later standpoint *after* the visions had been completed is to disregard the words written by John; to say that the words merely belong to the vision is unsatisfactory. The imperfect, "I was about or on the point of writing," already implies that this intent was not carried out. R. 853 makes the command μὴ γράψῃς ingressive, "Do not begin to write!" But this aorist is peremptory, decisive. We may wonder how John could write "when" he received the visions but we take John's word for what he said he did. When Zahn thinks that hours, perhaps days and weeks intervened between the visions so that John had plenty of time to write, and that he was so old and so unused to writing that he had repeatedly to be ordered to write, this is unwarranted. We note that γράφειν is in the present durative tense, "to be writing," "I was about to engage in writing."

5) **And the angel whom I saw standing on the sea and on the earth lifted his right hand to the**

heaven and swore by the One Living for the eons of the eons, who created the heaven and the things therein and the earth and the things therein and the sea and the things therein, that time no longer shall be; but in the days of the blast of the seventh angel, whenever he is about to trumpet, there was brought also to its end the mystery of God as he gave the good news to his own slaves, the prophets.

The position of the angel "standing on the sea and on the earth" is once more mentioned because his great oath applies to sea and to earth. This is the reason that he took this position in the first place. The raising of his right hand to heaven is the appropriate gesture for making oath by God and is used thus to this day. Some say that he raised his right hand because he had the little book in his left; but what is to hinder us from thinking that he raised his right hand and not his left because his right hand held the little book? Does not his oath pertain to this little book? This little book is of vital importance for this vision.

6) Ὄμνυμι with ἐν is common, "to swear in connection with," in our idiom, "to swear by," and is, in our opinion, not Hebraic. The form of the oath agrees with the position of the angel, and both agree with what is here sworn. He swore "by the One Living for the eons of the eons" (see 1:6 for the phrase and compare 1:18), by the Eternal God, who is the Creator of heaven, earth, and sea, and of all that is in the three. "Who created" = Gen. 1:1, etc.: "In the beginning God created," etc. All revelation proclaims that God *created*, called into being what had no being. The first and the last book of the Bible agree. A Creator is a rational answer to the existences we see; the denial of him is irrational.

The angel swears by the Eternal, by the Creator, "that time no longer shall be," χρόνος οὐκέτι ἔσται. The χρόνος is "time," time as it ever moves on irrespective of anything to distinguish its movement. We have no modifier of any kind. The tick of the clock that ticked with the first stroke "in the beginning" of Gen. 1:1, when the Eternal One created heaven and earth shall tick for the last time. This most wonderful thing called "time," itself an astounding creation of God, ever moving, never faster, never slower, shall at last also cease. Do not say that then eternity shall begin. Eternity cannot begin, is *not* time, but its opposite. Our entire thinking is chained to time and succession in time, and therefore eternity is beyond all comprehension. The dogmaticians call it a *simul tota,* an absolute altogether, an absolute νῦν or now; but these are helpless attempts at a characterization.

Some of the German commentators have a different idea and claim that χρόνος must here mean *Frist,* "delay," or respite, and B.-P. 1415, adopting their views, puts this into his dictionary and cites two examples that have the expression to give χρόνος. But to *give* a man "time" still means "time," namely a certain amount of it; so also "time no longer shall be" means one thing and only one, namely what we call "time" shall be at an end.

Those who regard χρόνος as equivalent to "delay" then raise the questions about the *terminus a quo* and the *terminus ad quem* of this delay. These are answered chronologically: there shall be no *Frist,* delay or respite, between the sixth and the seventh trumpets of judgment. But this answer is of little help, for the climax of the curse of delusion (sixth trumpet) continues to the great day of the final judgment. In other words, between these two there is no stretch of time (χρόνος) free of this curse, and none of these commentators attempts to say why this fact should be announced with an oath. What *is* announced is that time itself shall cease to exist, the clock of time shall stop. One may compare Dan. 12:7, but must note the differences.

7) Therefore the angel adds that in the days of the blast of the seventh angel, whenever he is about to trumpet (to sound that blast), "there was brought also to its end the mystery of God," the blessed mystery, the good news which God gave to the prophets. One may view the last judgment and the end of the world in a punctiliar way but also as being spread out. Here the expression, "in the days of the blast (φωνή) of the seventh angel," does the latter. These seven angels and their seven blasts belong to the visions, and it is improper to speak of this last blast as sounding continuously during those days. The ὅταν is indefinite; and μέλλῃ σαλπίζειν, too, fixes our attention upon the time "whenever" this seventh angel "shall be about to trumpet," about to raise his trumpet to his lips and to blow it. The meaning is not that in that very instant time shall cease, for these statements appear in a separate clause; time shall be no more, "on the contrary" (ἀλλά), this angel's blast shall usher in the completion when the clock of time shall finally stand still.

Καί is "also," and the aorist passive ἐτελέσθη is the prophetic aorist; it is much like the epistolary aorist and places us at a point when the mystery of God "was brought also to its end." In English we should use the perfect, "has been brought to its end." Others call this expression a Hebraism: καὶ ἐτελέσθη = *vav consecutivum* with the Hebrew perfect; but in the illustrations which they cite, Exod. 16:6; 17:4, the LXX has καί with the future and not the aorist. The A. V.'s "should be finished" disregards the tense; the R. V.'s "then is finished" in a manner keeps the sense but not the tense. This is the prophetic aorist. It places us at a point where time is ended, where, upon looking back, we must say, "The mystery of God was brought to its end," in our idiom, "has been brought to its end." The passive implies that God brought it to its end.

"The mystery of God" has been called "God's scheme of redemption"; "the eschatological mystery of the world's history"; "the glorious completion of the divine kingdom"; "the glorious consummation of God's kingdom"; "anticipatory of 11:15-18." Since all these mean practically the same thing, we may accept all of them. "Mystery" is used because the world does not see and know what God is really doing during the course of the ages. "Mystery" implies that we ourselves do not know except by a revelation which God has supplied. The church has this revelation and walks in its light.

This becomes apparent in the added clause: "as he gave the good news to his own slaves, the prophets," literally, "gospeled his slaves," εὐαγγέλισε (active aorist, R. 1215) with the accusative of the persons, R. 474. John regards himself as one of these slaves (1:1). As slaves of God their will is wholly the will of God. The apposition "the prophets" is added because "his own slaves" would refer to all believers. These latter receive the good news mediately through the prophets (the Word) while here the immediate revelation is referred to which was granted to those slaves of God who are prophets. Some assert that "the prophets" excludes the Old Testament prophets, in fact, refers only to certain men in the New Testament who are called "prophets" and excludes even the apostles. Prophets undoubtedly includes all men of both Testaments who received God's direct revelation of the gospel mystery in order to convey it to others and most certainly includes also the apostles.

The great object of the whole of Revelation is concentrated in this sworn statement of this powerful and glorious angel that the gospel mystery shall be brought to its blessed consummation by God. Then time shall cease, the purpose for which God made it having been attained. Its supreme purpose is that the gospel may finish its course and not that men may spend a few years in spiritual darkness here on earth and then go into eternal darkness.

8) **And the voice which I heard out of heaven** (I heard) **again speaking with me and saying: Go, take the little book, the one that has been opened, in the hand of the angel, the one standing on the sea and on the land! And I went to the angel, saying to him, to give to me the little book. And he says to me: Take it and eat it up! And it shall make bitter thy belly, but in thy mouth it shall be sweet as honey. And I took the little book from the hand of the angel and I ate it up, and in my mouth it was sweet as honey, and when I did eat it, my belly was made bitter. And they say to me, It is necessary that thou again prophesy to many peoples and nations and tongues and kings.**

This is the same voice that forbade John to write what the seven thunders uttered (v. 4) and now again gives him directions. Ὕπαγε is exclamatory (R. 855) and is often used with other imperatives (R. 449) for the purpose of intensification just as we say, "go do this or that." John is to go and to take the booklet that is in the angel's hand. Once more it is noted that this booklet is open. It has never been closed. It has ever been God's revelation to men, his Word, the gospel of salvation. Once more it is noted that the angel bearing this booklet stands on the sea and on the earth. These are the two main things in the vision; so mighty an angel with so little a book, his fiery feet on sea and on earth. All men are under the divine judgment, but this little book is for their salvation. It contains the gospel mystery that is open and revealed "as God gospeled his own slaves, the prophets" (v. 7). The symbolism here revealed makes use of John as one of God's prophets just as it makes use of this strong angel. The latter pictures how the gospel Word comes directly from God for sea and for earth; the matter regarding John shows how it is transmitted to men, not by an angel or by angels, but by God's own slaves, the prophets, John being one of them.

9) We see that John did as he was bidden and asked the angel "to give him the booklet." It was not necessary for John to move from heaven to earth, between the sea and the earth, in order to get this book.

With the aoristic vivid narrative present tense John says that the angel told him to take and to eat up the booklet (the Greek κατάφαγε, "eat it down") and adds that it will make his belly bitter when it gets down into it but will be sweet as honey in his mouth.

10) This proves true. When John put the book into his mouth, it was honey-sweet, and when he ate it, his belly was made bitter. When the thought is repeated, ἔφαγον without κατά is enough, for when compound verbs are repeated, the simplex is sufficient. The fact that the sweetness is now mentioned before the bitterness is due only to the fact that in eating the mouth comes first. Κοιλία is the abdominal cavity with its various organs: "belly," and, when eating is referred to, the belly as containing the stomach. It is not John who uses this symbolism as though John borrows from Ezek. 2:8-3:3; it is the strong angel who borrows from Ezekiel. Yet in the case of Ezekiel there was no bitterness in the belly. Here, as elsewhere, the Old Testament features are exceeded, and

it is unwarranted to say that *John* used literary sources as though Revelation is a composition that was devised by John's own mind.

11) The indefinite plural λέγουσι, "they say to me," hides the speakers just as the passive does in many cases, and just as John's statement does: "I heard a voice saying" (v. 4 and 8). Here these unnamed ones explain to John what his eating the booklet means, namely that he must again prophesy to many peoples and nations and tongues and kings (note these four terms in 5:9 and 7:9, where "tribes" occurs instead of "kings"). The A. V. is correct in rendering ἐπί "before" many peoples, etc., not the R. V. nor its margin, "over" or "concerning"; for here the phrase is equal to the dative as R. 605 rightly explains despite the commentators who think of predictions that John is to utter *about* the many people, etc., an idea that results from their misconception of this vision. 'Επί is here used for the simple indirect object, or it has the juridical use which is illustrated in Acts 25:10: John is to prophesy *to* the whole world of men or *before* them, even also as this strong angel holding the little book has one mighty foot on the ocean, the other on the earth.

We hold that this entire vision or scene is *a unit* with every item being an integral part of the unit. The main point is the booklet, the open Word or gospel, which was given as good news already to all of God's prophets and which tells how God will complete his mystery of salvation through Christ when time reaches its end. This is to be made known to all the world. That is why the booklet has been opened and is open still. "Prophets" and "to prophesy" is to be taken in the regular sense of telling men God's saving will. John himself and what he is told to do are made an integral part of the symbolism. When he received this vision he was near the end of his life. He is used in this vision not for his own sake but as the representative of all the Old and the New Testament inspired prophets and apostles whose prophesying must reach many peoples, nations, tongues, kings (and thus their kingdoms) until the seventh trumpet sounds and the end arrives. "The gospel of the kingdom shall be preached in all the world for a witness unto all nations, and then shall the end come," Matt. 24:14. The voice of this prophesying and preaching is now sounding in the wide world.

This gospel comes from God as this is symbolized by this great and glorious angel. It is received immediately by God's slaves, the prophets, so that they may deliver it to all people and nations, etc., to the end of time. John is the last of this chosen number, a fit representative of them all. This world-wide prophesying is inaugurated by Christ in Matt. 28:19, 20. The means is the whole Bible. What the Old Testament contains is to sound forth together with the New. It is represented as a *βιβλαρίδιον*, "a booklet," for the gospel looks like a little thing; it is a "booklet" because its content is fixed in written form by God. Yet a mighty angel holds it, for it is the power of God unto salvation (Rom. 1:16). As a towering figure he plants his right foot on the ocean, his left on the earth. The prophesying is to reach many peoples, etc., the whole world, it is to be carried even far beyond the sea.

The eating of the little book is well interpreted as a taking the gospel into the heart on the part of John, the last of God's prophets, the representative of them all. This symbolic feature is taken from Ezekiel to show that John, the last prophet, is one of God's prophets. Πάλιν in v. 11, "thou must *again* prophesy" connects the remainder of this last prophet's work with all that precedes.

The gospel is certainly sweet as honey, for "he that believeth and is baptized shall be saved." To proclaim that is sweet beyond compare. Then, however, follows the bitterness: "he that believeth not shall be damned." "To the one the savor of death unto death; and to the other the savor of life unto life," II Cor. 2:16, and "savor" means taste. The fact that the sweet taste is placed in the mouth and the bitter taste in the stomach, merely separates the two; both are effects of the booklet. Some seek to find more as regards the mouth and the belly but end in unacceptable fancies.

One of the strangest interpretations of this chapter that we read states that this angel "came with great spiritual show, as one that personified Christ himself, as one that represented Christ's work, Christ's truth, Christ's kingdom. His threatening voice demanded acknowledgment of his person and of his doctrine, of his decrees, as they were contained in the booklet." "Thus this angel under the guise of the highest sanctity, represents the power of hell, which appeared with great show and under the name and the mask of Christ, but whose intention was through doctrines of men, which pleased the perverted flesh, to destroy both faith and conscience. This description . . . fits the pope of Rome as the true antichrist." John's mouth is taken to be the flesh, his stomach the heart and the conscience. This interpretation is prefaced with the statement: "The force of the entire picture seems to point to a preparation for the last woe, and in this sense it was understood by most Lutheran commentators." The fact is that Lutherans cannot claim this since the fact that the climax is found in the seventh trumpet is stated by the great angel himself in v. 7, as also a number of non-Lutherans note. The impression is, however, made that "most Lutherans" also support the interpretation that "this angel, under the guise of the highest sanctity, represents the power of hell" and "fits the pope in Rome." This assertion is not in accord with the facts of the case.

Some think that the little book is so little because its contents consists of only 11:1-13; some regard all of chapters 11 to 22 as its contents. It is also generally asked what the relation of the little open book is to the great book with seven seals (5:1). The wrong approach of these views is the effort to find dates for these visions. Whereas the vision recorded in chapter 10 includes the gospel preaching from the time of John until the seventh trumpet and the end, these views think that the little book contains something that occurs chronologically between the sixth and the seventh trumpets. The delusions portrayed by the trumpet reach to the seventh.

CHAPTER XI

The Witnesses, 11:1-13

1) The vision of chapter 10 continues. John does not start anew with "I saw" but proceeds with a narration of his own participation in a further symbolical act. Prophesying extends and maintains the church. Thus in chapter 10 we have the little book (the gospel), John's eating it and prophesying to many people, nations, tongues, kings; and now we see him measuring the result, the Sanctuary, the altar, the worshippers, i. e., the church, marking the boundary line between the church and all those who are without. This church will ever have its witness for the world, which is symbolized in its great power and its shameful treatment by the world.

Thus chapter 10 and this part of chapter 11 belong together as a great unit of Revelation. This vital connection with the six trumpets is apparent; we have sketched it at the beginning of chapter 10.

And there was given to me a reed like to a rod, (the giver) **saying: Up and measure the Sanctuary of God and the altar and those worshipping in connection with it! And the court, the one outside of the Sanctuary, reject and do not measure it because it was given to the heathen, and the city, the holy one, they shall tread it down for forty-two months.**

When discussing the six trumpets, many ask, "What is the fate of the church in these six judgments?" Here we have the answer. The revelation concerning the church is not inserted into the revelation relative to the ever-increasing curse of the delusions sent on the obdurate world in judgment. A clear division is made. The church, the *Una Sancta* of God, is, indeed, in the world but it is wholly separate from the world. Here it is thus shown, and the complete separation is brought out. God sends the gospel (the little book), God orders the prophesying of its blessed contents to many peoples, nations, tongues, and kings (chapter 10). The result is the church. But so many reject the gospel, remain outside of the church. Therefore as a judgment delusion with its terrible results is sent upon them (the six trumpets). These six increasing delusions are now fully understood. "For this cause God shall send them strong (and ever stronger) delusion, that they should believe a lie, that they all might be damned who believe not the truth (the little book), but had pleasure in unrighteousness," II Thess. 2:11, 12.

The passive again hides the agent who gave the reed to John and told him to do this measuring. Because we read in v. 3: "*I* will give to *my* two witnesses," many conclude that Christ must be the giver of the reed; but John in chapter 10 receives the booklet from the hand of a strong and glorious angel. God and Christ are the ultimate givers. There is no question in regard to this. The passive, "there was given to me," asks us to disregard the agent through whom the reed came into John's hands. The reed is "like a rod," it is not limber but stiff and is thus serviceable for measuring. With it John is to measure the church. This reed must then symbolize the Word or gospel in its function of determining who is in the church and who is outside of its bounds. In chapter 10 the Word or gospel is an open booklet that is to be prophesied in all the world. The two symbols are quite transparent.

The nominative participle λέγων is construed *ad sensum;* for the passive means that someone gave the reed to John, at the same time "saying" to him what to do. The addition of ἔγειραι, "rise," is merely *vox animum existantis* like our, "Up and measure," and implies neither that John has been sitting nor that he has been kneeling. All this is vision and symbolism; hence we reject those views which move John or his spirit about as though he were now in heaven, then on earth, and then again in heaven. Measuring with a rod, a line, a plummet is done for various purposes in the Old Testament and again in Rev. 21:15, etc. Each instance must be interpreted independently. Here the measuring fixes the boundary, the line of demarkation between what is inside of and belongs to the Sanctuary of God and what is outside of it and is profane. It draws the line of separation between the *Una Sancta* and the world. Need we say that the only rod which does this is the gospel?

John is to measure for all time "the Sanctuary of God and the altar and those worshipping in connection with it." Let us at once say that the three terms are a unit and denote the church, the *Una Sancta,* as being holy unto God, separate from "the court, the one outside," which is not to be measured as though it or any part of it is to be bounded and marked off as being holy to God. In our estimation it is apparent that *one* thing is to be measured and set off by itself and not *three* things. For how is the altar to be measured by itself? Or how are the worshippers to be measured? These two are added to "The Sanctuary of God" in an expository manner so that we may understand what is referred to.

The word is not ἱερόν, "the Temple" (our versions), for this includes all the courts; but ναός, "the Sanctuary," the one building that contained the Holy and the Holy of Holies where God is present. Only this word is used in the symbolism describing the church. The courts of the priests, of the men, of the women are very likely included in the term "the Sanctuary of God," thus leaving "the outside court," the court of the Gentiles, to symbolize all who are open to the world.

This fits the purpose of the symbolism very well; for these courts were separated from the outer court by a wall on which an inscription was found that forbade every Gentile, on pain of death, from passing within.

The symbolism is restricted to the hour when the incense was offered on the golden altar in the Holy Place while all the worshippers bowed in prayer in the courts of the priests, the men, and the women. It is a repetition of the scene described in Luke 1:8-10 and 21, 22. The altar referred to is the golden altar (8:3, 4), and thus the worshippers are mentioned in connection with it. The great stone altar of burnt offerings is not referred to; nor is there an uncertainty as to whether ἐν αὐτῷ refers to the altar or to the Sanctuary. The distinction that the worshippers cannot be "*in* the altar" and thus must be "*in* the Sanctuary" is pointless. The worshippers were never in the Sanctuary. It was too small, to say no more. Ἐν αὐτῷ means "in connection with it" (the altar). All the worshippers bowed in prayer when the incense was burned on the golden altar, in connection with it they worshipped in prayer. The idea that these worshippers are priests "in" the Sanctuary (1:6) is due to a misunderstanding of ἐν; "those worshipping" are not conceived as priests. Only two priests functioned at the altar in the Holy Place.

It is not necessary to introduce anything further regarding the Temple arrangements or the Temple rituals. The symbolism utilizes so much and no more. What it thus uses most certainly pictures the church in its separation from all who belong to the world, and it does so in a way that is both expressive and beautiful.

In chapter 7 we see the church as the sealed, the 144,000, the great multitude which no one could number, in its earthly relation to God, and in its consummation in heaven. This vision of the church properly precedes the vision given in this section. All the other visions are to be viewed in the light of this glorious and blessed consummation of the church. In chapter 11 we see the church in its relation to the world, first, as being separate, then, however, also as serving God's purpose in the world.

2) The outer court, that of the Gentiles in the Jewish Temple, symbolizes all that is unholy, that belongs to the world! It is ἔξωθεν, "outside," John is to "throw it out," to reject it as profane, is not to measure it, to draw no boundary to mark any part of it as belonging to the *Una Sancta.* "It was given to the heathen," τοῖς ἔθνεσι, to whom it belongs, who also freely enter this outside court. The A. V. translates "to the Gentiles," the R. V. "to the nations" (the word is used in this sense in 10:11, and repeatedly). Here neither of these renderings is proper, for a large number of Gentiles "out of every nation" (7:9) are found among the worshippers in connection with the altar and belong to the church that is separated from the world. Here we must render "to the heathen," to all those outside of the church who cannot be accepted as worshippers at God's and Christ's altar.

The symbolism of "the court outside" is expanded: "the city, the holy one, they shall tread down for forty-two months." What "the court outside" symbolizes is now symbolized anew by "the city, the holy one," Jerusalem. When we still speak of "the Holy City" we do so only because it once was holy and belonged to God. It is now rejected by God, its Sanctuary has disappeared; it is a Mohammedan city, the holy site of its Sanctuary is profaned by the Dome of the Rock, the Mosque of Omar, which occupies the place where the Sanctuary once stood. The symbolism of the words, "the holy city they shall tread down," is taken from the prophecy of Jesus recorded in Luke 21:24: "Jerusalem shall be trodden down of the Gentiles until the times of the Gentiles be fulfilled." The very verb here used, πατεῖν, is the same that Jesus employed, "to tread down, to trample," which here implies to desecrate. This trampled-down Jerusalem symbolizes the false Christianity which the profane world has invaded.

We see how precisely the line of demarkation is drawn by John's gospel measuring rod. Many may crowd into the court outside, but the getting outwardly near to the Sanctuary still leaves them barred from it. They may fill Jerusalem around the Sanctuary and its worshippers, but they are only in the city that was rejected by God and given over to heathen profanation. They are as little in the Church of God as are the fanatic Moslems who now fill and dominate Jerusalem.

The symbolic use which the heavenly voice here makes of the prophecy of Jesus recorded in Luke 21:24 is striking, indeed. Not only the rank pagan world which is far from the church is outside and scarcely needs to be marked off from it as being outside, but also all false Christianity which surrounds the church is the court outside, is the trampled, violated holy city, wide open to profane heathenism.

Of a piece with this symbolic language is the designation of time, "for forty-two months," accusative to indicate extent of time, which construction is used once more in 13:5. We take it that the actual time intended is that which is indicated by Jesus in Luke 21:24: "until the times (*καιροί*, seasons, periods) of the Gentiles shall be fulfilled." This word of Jesus has been misunderstood to imply that after the periods during which multitudes of Gentiles have flocked into the church, there shall come a time when the whole nation of the Jews will be converted. See the refutation of this view in the exposition of Rom. 11:25, 26. "The seasons of the Gentiles," the "forty-two months," are not followed by a millennium, a national conversion of the Jews, but by the seventh trumpet, the last woe (v. 14-19), the consummation.

Why the time is first designated in "months," and why the symbolic number of them is "forty-two," we are unable to say. The use of "five months" in 9:5, 10 is not so difficult. What adds to the difficulty of interpretation is the fact that in v. 3 the expression "1,260 days" is used, and again also in 12:6, these days amount to about "forty-two" months. Why is this second figure expressed in "days"? In addition to this we have in 12:14, as though reminiscent of Dan. 7:25 and 12:7, "a sesason and seasons and a half season," which is generally taken to mean: 1 plus 2 plus ½, i. e., 3½ seasons, the broken 7, which some term 3½ "years" and make 7 the number of completeness whereas completeness is expressed by 10 with 5 being used to indicate incompleteness, while the sacred 7 is used to show God in his relation to and dealings with men.

Why the time is first designated in "months," secondly in "days," thirdly in "seasons," I do not know. Their number seems to express the same duration of time. The important point is the terminus of this period of which we can be certain since this is the last woe and trumpet ushering in the end.

It would take many pages to review the multitude of opinions in regard to these three designations of time. We take note only of the following. Many speak of 1,260 *years* and count a symbolical "day" as a literal year. These years are then given definite dates in history: Joachin starts them at A. D. 1; Mede at 455; Cunninghame at 533; Bengel at 576; Fleming at 606; Ellicott at 608; Melanchthon at 660; Guiness at 672; Fysh at 727; etc. No two agree, and all end in confusion. Some bring in the Reformation.

Kuebel assigns forty-two months to the Gentiles, then an additional forty-two to the period when the Jewish nation is converted, each forty-two months = 3½ world years, the 84 months making seven years as the world week. Since the Sanctuary, the altar, the court outside, and Jerusalem, appear in the symbolism, many insert the national conversion of the Jews. Futurists such as Todd, Fausset, Godet, think that the physical Temple will be rebuilt in Jerusalem and the Jews will be at the head of Christianity, will resist the antichrist.

3) After the boundary of the *Una Sancta* has been exactly and truly fixed by the gospel rod and measure, the voice continues: **And I will give to my two witnesses, and they shall prophesy for a thousand two hundred and sixty days, having sackcloth thrown around them. These are the two olive trees and the two lamp pedestals standing before the Lord of the earth. And if anyone wants to hurt them, fire proceeds out of their mouth and devours their enemies; and if anyone actually wants to hurt them, in this way must he be killed. These have the power to lock up the heaven so that rain may not wet for the days of the prophecy; and they have power over the waters to turn them into blood and to smite the earth with every smiting as often as they may want.**

The *Una Sancta* is measured and *separated* and as such *testifies in the world.* Compare the exposition of 10:11: "Thou must prophesy to peoples and nations and tongues and kings," and note 11:9, "of the peoples and tribes and tongues and nations," which names those who heard the testimony. The church is ever separate from all those outside of it, yet she has a function to perform with regard to all of them.

This is a vision, and it pictures only so much of this function; we only confuse the issue when we try to find more. The missionary, converting, saving effect of the testimony of the church is not here symbolized. All those who are won for the church by the prophesying (10:11) and the testimony (11:7) until the very time when this is completed are not here pictured as being thus won but in v. 1, 2 as having already been won. The function of gospel testimony here portrayed is that of the church as it is separate from all those outside who are not won. They shall perish, not because testimony and witnesses have not appeared, but because these did appear, were rejected, were allowed to be killed and silenced to the great joy of all who spurned them. So much only appears in this part of the vision. That is why the whole of it (10:1-11:13) belongs here before the last woe and trumpet. It is not to be dated as following chronologically *after* the sixth trumpet but as being parallel to all six of the trumpets, all six being increasing waves of delusion, all six extending to the seventh trumpet, the end.

It is the speaker of v. 1 (λέγων) who continues in v. 3, but now quotes the Lord's words: "And I will give to my two witnesses, and they shall prophesy," etc. This explains "I" and "my." The definite article and "my" take it for granted that the Lord has his witnesses. How can he be without them? Have we not seen the great angel with the open booklet in chapter 10, heard his mighty oath, heard what John is told that he, John, *must* do, namely prophesy to the whole world, in 10:11? "You shall be *my witnesses* both in Jerusalem and in all Judea and in Samaria and unto the uttermost part of the earth," Acts 1:8.

"My *two* witnesses" does not denote two actual men as some suppose, who then picture them as being two mighty personalities like Enoch and Elijah or like Moses and Elijah. "Two" denotes competent legal testimony. From Deut. 17:6, 15, 19, where the principle is laid down that one witness is legally nil, that there must be at least two, throughout Scripture, ever and ever, no less than two witnesses are demanded. In all his contests with the Jews, Jesus ever pointed to *more than one* witness and in John 5:31 declared that his own lone witness could not be accepted as being sufficient. Revelation itself ends with *two* witnesses who establish the genuineness of its entire contents (22:6, etc.). There must be two. In this sense Christ is here quoted as saying "my *two witnesses*."

In 10:11 we have seen in what sense John is told that he must prophesy. Review the exposition. Now the word "prophesy" is again taken up: "and they shall prophesy" (note, too, "the prophets" in 10:7, and that in chapter 10 the little book or gospel accompanies this prophesying). The sense is not, "I will give them *that* they shall prophesy," i. e., enable them; but, "I will give or supply two witnesses." They shall be two so that their testimony cannot be legally set aside, so that all who do set it aside thereby legally condemn themselves. Their testimony, moreover, shall be that of prophets and not that of common, earthly witnesses but of divinely commissioned prophet-witnesses who testify to my own Word (the booklet). They shall prophesy, "having sackcloth (6:12) thrown around them," the symbol of repentance. Neither Elijah nor the Baptist wore "sackcloth," their apparel was only a cheap, coarse garment. "Sackcloth" is the direct symbol of repentance. The testimony of this prophesying is here not the regular preaching of the gospel in the church for the benefit of its own members but is like the preaching of Jonah in Nineveh, a call and a testimony to all those who are outside to repent.

This is to continue for 1,260 days. The time is here expressed in "days" rather than in "months" or in "seasons" because the testimony is to be ceaseless, sounding forth every day until it is at last silenced just before the end. These days have been placed *before* the forty-two months despite the fact that in Matt. 28:19, 20, Jesus plainly promises that he will be with his preachers "to the end of the world," and in Mark 16:15 orders the preaching "to every creature." It is inconceivable that here the *last* half of the time, the forty-two months, should be placed first, and the *first* half, the 1,260 days, last. The months and the days signify the *same* length of time.

The testimony and prophesying which is *rejected* by those who tread down the holy city is here symbolized. The six trumpets have already revealed the increasing delusions in the world which cause men to prefer the lie to the truth. Here there is revealed the *guilt* of the wicked which brings on the final judgment. Here we see the bitterness, the savor of death unto death, connected with the gospel as shown in 10:9, 10.

4) The speaker now continues in his own words and calls these witnesses "the two olive trees and the two lamp pedestals," appropriating the symbolism of Zech. 4:3, 11, 14, yet here using two lamp pedestals instead of one. In Zechariah the olive trees supply the lamps with oil, and in v. 14 we learn that the Old Testament symbolism pictures "the two sons of oil (anointed ones) that stand by the Lord of the whole earth." The Lord's prophet-witnesses are filled with the Holy Spirit who is the divine *source* of their prophecy and testimony; they are true prophets of the Lord. As "lamp pedestals" they bear the light of the Lord's Word just as in 1:13 the churches are such "lamp pedestals." So this symbolic designation states the *effect*. The olive trees and the lamp pedestals appear as coordinate predicates; in Zechariah their relation is stated: the trees constantly supply the oil for the lamps. Note also that the addition, "the ones standing before the Lord of the earth," repeats Zech. 4:14, "that stand by the Lord of the whole earth." These, the Lord says, are "my witnesses"; as he is the Lord of the earth, their prophet-witness is for the whole earth, for "peoples and nations," etc. (10:11; 11:9).

5) The Lord endows his witnesses with tremendous power. In the first place, with fire proceeding out of their mouth which devours their enemies who want

to hurt them (in this sense ἀδικεῖν was already used several times). "Out of their mouth" indicates the Word; its fire of judgment devours the enemies. The symbolism of the devouring fire is taken from Jer. 5:14: "Because ye (the false nation) speak this word (belied the Lord), behold, I will make my words in thy (Jeremiah's) mouth fire, and this people wood, and it shall devour them." Those who think of Elijah as he is presented in II Kings 1:10, etc., should remember that in his case only detachments of soldiers were consumed by fire.

The statement is repeated for the sake of emphasis; yet in the first instance we have εἴ τις θέλει, present tense: "if anyone engages in willing," in the second instance εἴ τις θελήσῃ, aorist subjunctive (R. 1017 is better than B.-D. 372, 3): "if anyone actually wills," i. e., with a positive volition. The distinction lies in the tenses. Οὕτω, "thus," must he be killed, namely by this fire. The Word in the mouth of the Lord's prophet-witnesses may be scorned but it is not an empty sound. Its judgments are fire that devours its enemies.

6) These witnesses have power to lock up the very heaven so that (ἵνα, result) rain may not wet for the days of this prophecy. This symbolism is taken from Elijah as he is presented in I Kings 17:1 (James 5:16). They likewise have power from the Lord to turn the waters to blood and to smite the earth with all kinds of smiting, "as often as they will" to do so. This symbolism is drawn from Moses as he is presented in Exod. 7:19, and from the ten Egyptian plagues. Πατάσσω is allied to πλήσσω and its noun πληγή, a blow, a smiting or a plague. "As often as they may will" does not indicate arbitrariness. Neither Moses nor Elijah acted arbitrarily; their will, when calling down judgments, was the Lord's will for they are called "God's own slaves" (10:7). Their prophet-testimony is his Word.

Many of the ancients and some of later times have thought that Enoch and Elijah are the witnesses here referred to and that they will return to earth as the two witnesses and will repeat these miracles of judgment. The reason that Enoch is preferred to Moses is because Enoch, like Elijah, did not die while Moses did. In v. 7 the two witnesses are killed, which would make Moses die twice. But this view that two great Old Testament personages will at some time reappear on earth regards as literal what is symbolical and far greater than the literal. The symbolism is plainly drawn from no less than *three* great Old Testament prophets: Jeremiah, Elijah, Moses. The reason is evident. Jeremiah dealt with the southern kingdom of Judah when its hardness of heart brought it into the Babylonian captivity; Elijah dealt with the northern kingdom of Israel under the hardened Ahab, Jezebel, and the priests of Baal; Moses dealt with hardened Pharaoh and the Egyptians, all of whom symbolize, as we have already noted, those who belong to "the court outside" and who "tread down the holy city" as the enemies of God, the full measure of whose guilt is here revealed as bringing on the last woe, the seventh trumpet, the final judgment.

The fact that the symbolism is drawn from three sources and not merely from two is already sufficient to dispose of the idea that two Old Testament witnesses are to reappear on earth in person, testify anew, and again die. We have explained the significance of "two." To think of two notable individuals who shall appear in the power of Moses and of Elijah (Jeremiah is left out) is but little better; for this leaves us at sea in regard to the 1,260 days, to say no more. The witnesses who shall prophesy during this time are, as John himself in 10:11, bidden to prophesy to the whole world, to "peoples and nations and tongues and kings" (11:9). *The true church, as being separate from all those outside* (11:1), *shall witness and prophesy by means of the little book* (the inspired gospel) *in its public ministry to the whole obdurate and hostile world in order to reveal its full guilt.* "This gospel of the kingdom shall be preached in all the world for *a witness* unto all nations; and then shall the end come," Matt. 24:14.

The power of this Word and witness shall not be less than it was in the days of Jeremiah, Elijah, and Moses who faced equal obduracy. The six trumpets mentioned in chapters 8 and 9 have already revealed the curses that are to be visited on the obdurate, among them being fire, blood, other plagues, and death. Now these powers of judgment are connected with the witnesses who wield the Word. The divine threats which its prophecies contain are no more empty than were the judgments executed by Jeremiah, Elijah, and Moses in their smaller spheres.

As for the symbolism of fire "proceeding out of the mouth" of the prophesying witnesses, devouring their enemies and thus killing them, shutting up the heaven not to rain "for the days of their prophecy," turning the waters into blood and striking the earth with all kinds of plagues, the words we place in quotation marks, to our mind, indicate that a *literal* repetition of the Old Testament plagues is out of the question. This view does not spiritualize these statements as though withholding rain here signifies only withholding the blessings of the gospel. Fire, blood, and other plagues have not been similarly spiritualized because this was found to be too difficult.

These Old Testament allusions point to fearful New Testament counterparts. It ever was, is, and will be a fearful thing for those who are enemies of the Word and the witnesses to fall into the hands of the living God, Heb. 10:31. What man is equal to the task of selecting those New Testament centuries whose judgments may come under the head of fire coming out of the mouth of the witnesses, the rainless heaven, the bloody water, etc.? Note well that these witnesses with the mighty Word are called "*my* witnesses," "standing before *the Lord of the earth,*" and also the phrase, "out of their mouth," which refers to the Word. It is the Word of this Lord of the earth that thus strikes down its enemies.

7) **And when they finish their testimony, the wild beast, the one coming up out of the abyss, shall do battle with them and shall conquer them and shall kill them. And their fallen corpse on the avenue of the city, the great one, which is called spiritually Sodom and Egypt, where also their Lord was crucified. And of the peoples and tribes and tongues and nations they look upon their fallen corpse for three and a half days, and their fallen corpses they do not allow to be placed into a tomb. And those dwelling on the earth rejoice over them and make merry, and they will send presents to one another because these two prophets tormented those dwelling on the earth. And after the three days and a half life's breath from God entered into them, and they stood upon their feet, and great fear fell upon those beholding them. And they heard a great voice out of the heaven saying to them, Come up hither! And they went up into the heaven in the cloud; and their enemies beheld them. And in that hour there occurred a great earthquake, and the tenth of the city fell; and there were killed in the earthquake seven thousand persons, and the rest became terrified and gave glory to the God of the heaven.**

The great facts here presented by the voice speaking to John (λέγων in v. 1) are obvious, whether one succeeds in explaining all the symbolical language in which these facts are couched or not. 1) The gospel testimony to the obdurate world which reveals its guilt is to be *finished;* nothing shall prevent that. 2) Not until that time has come, can the power of hell permanently silence this tormenting testimony. 3) This silencing will mightily rejoice the obdurate world. 4) God will set his seal of approval upon this testimony so that the obdurate world itself shall realize that the judgment pronounced upon it by this testimony will be fulfilled.

We regard this entire section as having been spoken to John by the voice mentioned in v. 1 after John had measured the bounds of the *Una Sancta;* the words of this speaker begin in v. 1. The tenses used in v. 7-13 can be explained without difficulty if this section is regarded as the narration of this voice. When it is read in any other way, clarity is lost.

Ὅταν has the aorist subjunctive τελέσωσι and means: whenever the time comes that the two witnesses actually complete their witness or testimony. This testimony shall, indeed, be fully completed. Nothing shall stop it before that completion is reached. All efforts to silence the witnesses before their task is done are nullified, as v. 5, 6 state, by the judgments which this testimony itself brings upon the enemies of the witnesses whom the Lord himself provides for the *Una Sancta.* In v. 3 we have explained the significance of "my two witnesses." Matt. 24:14 informs us what the completion of the testimony means: the preaching of the gospel of the kingdom in the whole inhabited world for a testimony to all the nations after which the end shall come. It is understood that this gospel testimony continues to save souls and to add them to the *Una Sancta* as long as it resounds; here, however, its other function is the point to be presented, namely that it is "a testimony to the nations" (ἔθνη) that reveals the guilt of their unbelief and obduracy by rejecting this testimony.

Even with all their obduracy men shall not be able to silence the testimony which damns them; this frightful deed "the wild beast, the one coming out of the abyss," will accomplish. This is the same ἄβυσσος that was mentioned in 9: 1, 2, 11, namely hell (compare, 17:8). We should not misunderstand the attributive present participle: ἀναβαῖνον; it characterizes the beast. Its home and origin is hell, and this word does not state *when* it rises from the abyss of hell. The article τὸ θηρίον has exactly the force of that used with τοῖς δυσὶ μάρτυσι, "the two witnesses," and is similar to a number of other articles that are deictic. This definite wild beast, definite, too, as having its home in hell, "shall do battle (πόλεμος as in 9:7, 9) with the witnesses," and we are impressively told, "and shall conquer them and shall kill them." The point of importance is that the damning "testimony" shall thus be silenced at last. This shall not be done until the testimony is actually finished as the Lord has determined. Then the Lord will bring about the end, will finish the mystery of God as he gave good news to his own slaves, the prophets (10:7).

The fact that all the obdurate enemies of the gospel will be the tools of the wild beast need not be stated. Who this hellish monster that thus silences this testimony is, the term θηρίον, "untamed, wild beast," sufficiently indicates. When we glance at 13:1, 11, and 17:8, it seems best to consider "the wild beast" of our passage as a preliminary and broad symbolical designation of *the whole antichristian power in the world.* Philippi (*Glaubenslehre* VI, 162) says "the pagan world power"; Kretzmann (*Popular Commentary* II, 623) "the Roman antichrist, personified in the pope of the Roman Church"; Mauro (*Patmos Visions,* 344) "governmental authority fully in the hands of Satan." All these views are too narrow. We think of the entire antichristian power that dominates the nations. See further chapter 13, where much more is said about the "wild beast."

While many of the interpretations given in Daechsel's *Bibelwerk* are untenable, we feel impressed by his comment on this passage to the effect that already now we see the beast at work, more and more conquering and silencing the testimony. He itemizes many observations to which we can add still more. The modern world and society are dominated by naturalism, which is far worse than the old paganism which never had the gospel, for the present growing paganism has deliberately scorned the gospel. The common press — think of the magazines — rings with hostile voices and is closed to all the essential truth of the Word. The schools for the children of the nation exclude the Word; colleges and universities make mock of the divine testimony. The religion taught in the vast networks of secretism is worldly or pagan moralism. The pulpits that voice nothing better are multiplying. The Roman antichrist spreads his blight far and wide. Millions living in so-called Christian lands live and die without religion or have mere scraps of the religion of the street. The voice of the true witnesses is heard ever less. The silencing succeeds more and more. Is not the time rapidly approaching when the holy voice of the gospel of God will be rendered silent forever?

8) Πτῶμα is a fallen dead body so that we translate, "their fallen corpse." The singular is like that used in the expressions, "their heart," "their head," etc.; in v. 9 we have the plural. This term accords with the killing of the witnesses. The imagery is expanded: the fallen corpse lies on the avenue of the great city, the πλατεῖα or broad street, the city's "Broadway," where large numbers see the corpse, and they will not allow the corpses (now plural) to be placed into a tomb, they want to feast their eyes on them. The fact that this description of the final silencing of the divine testi-

mony cannot be literally understood we consider obvious. Just as the scene presented in 10:1-10 is a unit, so here again this description of the corpses lying on the Broadway of Jerusalem, of everybody's gloating over them, jubilating and celebrating and sending presents to one another, is a unit, a sort of compound symbol in which each touch of color is not independent but only contributory to the picture. Why should one, for instance, think of two internationally known preachers who were clubbed to death and left lying on a street in Jerusalem or in Rome, etc.?

When we see in what sense the city is called "holy" in v. 2, we shall not expect this adjective a second time, where "great" is even naturally in place. Since in 14:8; 17:1, 5; 18:10 this word "great" is applied to Babylon, some would here think of Rome, and some cancel the clause, "where also their Lord was crucified," with its plain historical aorist. Some also talk of a difficulty since Jerusalem would now seem to be rebuilt, as though this symbolism would then deal with the comparatively small physical city of Jerusalem. In 1925 I rode completely around its outer walls on an ass in just one hour's time. Here Jerusalem is to be taken ideally, as the headquarters of all anti-Christianity. The actual city became such a symbol when it crucified Christ and never repented and was then razed to the ground. Whatever the city amounts to now, its past obduracy and judgment make it the symbol of the "great" center of the wild beast until the end of time. None of its streets is physically "wide" as we in America are acquainted with wide avenues. But this center of the beast and of its power has the widest avenue in all the world on which to display the final complete silencing of the divine witnesses.

Hence this city with its unholy greatness "is called Sodom and Egypt," namely πνευματικῶς, "spiritually," i. e., in expressive spiritual language, which calls it by names that in reality state what it is in God's eyes. The significant thing is that the name of another city, "Sodom," is not enough, the name of an entire country is added, "and Egypt." Both represent the extreme abomination. That is sufficient in this connection, and there is no need of seeking the extreme of idolatry or of something else in "Egypt." What is done in this great city, the center of the world of obduracy and abomination, is done for the whole world by the hellish beastly power.

No verb is needed. There the corpses lie! So also Christ was crucified where the most damnable obduracy reigned. This touch is significantly added. There is silence at last in the whole world, awful, ominous silence! So the Jews silenced the voice of the witness and prophet Jesus, stifled it in his blood on the cross. When the public voice of the gospel is finally stifled and smothered in the blood of the witnesses, "then shall come the end," Matt. 24:14. It *must* come then. The gospel testimony has been completed.

9) The subject of βλέπουσι is the partitive ἐκ phrase used as a noun: "Of the peoples, etc., they look upon the fallen corpse," etc. This great city is conceived as a metropolis, indeed, with its "peoples and tribes and tongues and nations," all with one article, all belonging together as one obdurate mass, making this a Sodom and an Egypt (compare such lists of four items in 5:9; 7:9; 10:11). The corpses are not allowed to be placed decently into tombs. All these followers of the beast want to feast their eyes on them; they are delighted now at last to see that the testimony of the Word to the nations (Matt. 24:14) will never be heard again. This letting the corpses lie on the main street for days, in the dirt, covered with flies, if not also attacked by Oriental dogs, and gloating with joy at their sight, is a picture of hellish beastliness in the treatment of the Word.

The point to be noted in the not placing the two silenced corpses into a tomb, out of sight, but letting them lie in the filthy street to be seen by all men, is that even after the two witnesses are silenced, the wicked world cannot let them alone and simply pass on in its obduracy. Even when it is finally and utterly silenced, the obdurate world cannot dismiss the divine testimony. It must talk about it, bring everybody to look at the voiceless lips. Though dead, these lips still speak (Heb. 11:4). The haters of the Word and testimony add still more to the mountain of their guilt. Those who spurn the Word *never* get rid of it. Their very rejoicing over its silencing keeps them busy with the Word. Strange, indeed, but absolutely true.

The length of "days three and a half" is not determined by the beast and his followers, as v. 11 indicates, but by the Lord. Their triumph is brief. This may be a resemblance to the days during which the crucified Lord lay in the tomb although that was not three and one half days, and his body was laid in a tomb. Here three and one half is the broken seven, the half of God's dealing with his slain witnesses, the other half of which is now to follow. As for the present tenses used here, they are vivid like the tenses used in v. 4-6, and need no further explanation; on ἀφίουσι see R. 315.

10) A world-wide rejoicing and celebration took place when the gospel was finally silenced in the world. Οἱ κατοικοῦντες ἐπὶ τῆς γῆς, "those dwelling on the earth," is a constantly recurring expression; follow it through 3:10; 6:10; 8:13; 13:8, 14; 17:8, and note that it designates those whose sole home is "the earth" and not heaven. Will there be believers left to mourn the witnesses? I Thess. 4:15 says that there will be such; but Luke 18:8 leads us to expect that there will be very few. Their voice of public testimony has finished its task (τελέσωσι, v. 7). The passive εὐφραίνονται is to be taken in the middle sense, "they make merry" (so in

Luke 15:23, when the prodigal returned), they stage a great jubilee. Giving one another presents recalls Esther 9:22, when all the Jews celebrated their deliverance after Haman had been hung on the high gallows. The ὅτι clause states what kind of celebration this is: "because these two prophets tormented those dwelling on the earth" by means of the Word and its judgments as noted in v. 5, 6. But note well that now they are called "prophets" instead of witnesses, "they shall prophesy," v. 3. Return to 10:11: John must prophesy to the whole world; and to 10:7, God's own slaves, the prophets. Hell fills the whole world with jubilation when the Word of the prophets at last lies forever silent in the street.

11) Now comes the complement indicated by the three and one half days of v. 9. After the three and one half days "life's breath from God" entered into the dead prophets, they once more stood on their feet, fully alive. Even hell and its beast and the whole world of men cannot conquer the Word. Here is a resurrection, followed by an ascension, that are somewhat, though only somewhat, like those of the Lord. The symbolism pictures it in the case of these two prophets who are called "prophets" in order the more to identify them with the Lord's Word. As far as men are concerned, the Word always has as its mouthpieces, witnesses or prophets. That is why in this sketch the Word stands before us in the person of these prophets. What happened to the Word when men threw it onto the street and celebrated its death, and that Word arose again to the terror of men, is made plastic and concrete by these two prophets of the Word. Here there is symbolized I Pet. 1:23: "The Word of the Lord endureth forever," Peter adding: "And this is the Word which by the gospel is being preached unto you."

12) The final task of the Word (witnesses, prophets) has been completed (τελέσωσι τὴν μαρτυρίαν αὐτῶν, v. 7), namely the revelation of the guilt of hellish, murderous obduracy against the Word; hence the Word is not bidden to do anything more in regard to this Sodom and Egypt where the beast murdered it to the joy of the whole world. The Word has been withdrawn forever! This is symbolized by the ascension of its two prophets which in a manner, but only in a manner, reminds us of the Lord's own ascension. The Lord himself ascended; these prophets who symbolize the Word, are bidden to ascend. We prefer the reading that has ἤκουσαν to that which has ἤκουσα, because we regard it as being textually assured and because it agrees with the contents, which are a narration of the voice λέγων in v. 1. Thus the two prophets "heard" a great voice out of the heaven saying to them, "Come up hither!" We have the genitive φωνῆς λεγούσης after ἀκούω because here the speaker is in the mind of the writer.

The imagery conveys the thought that as the Lord furnishes (δώσω in v. 3) the witnesses, these prophets, so he finally withdraws them. But these prophets are only the Lord's mouthpieces for his Word, so that throughout this symbolism and now also in its last part it is the Lord's Word that is kept in mind. He sends the Word and, when its task is done in the wicked world, he withdraws the Word. So we do not think of two notable prophets, say another Enoch and Moses, or another Elijah and Moses, who were killed physically, raised physically, and ascended physically to heaven, who appear immediately before the last woe and trumpet come to wind up the existence of the world. Thus we note, too, that in the command and in its compliance the verb used is ἀναβαίνω, *hinaufsteigen*, compare Acts 2:34; Rom. 10:6; John 3:13; 6:62, "walk on up" as one directs his servant or lets a servant direct other servants. Here, too, the identity of the one using this "great voice" remains veiled (as in v. 1). The voice is "great" because of the mighty command it utters.

Going up into heaven "in the cloud" (deictic article) accords with the statement, "and their enemies beheld them" (the same verb as that used in Acts 1:11), ἐθεώρησαν, which is identical with θεωροῦντας αὐτούς in v. 11. The Word is not removed from its enemies invisibly so that none of them knows that the Lord has finally taken it back to himself forever. They behold, they know. Already now when some *will* not have the Word they *shall* not have it. The day is rapidly approaching when its final removal is to take place.

Another feature is symbolized by the return of "life's breath," by this command from heaven, and by this going up "in the cloud'" as the chariot of the Lord: the beast and its followers have only murder and the vilest treatment for the Word (in its prophets), the Lord *glorifies* his Word (in its prophets). This is the Lord's answer to the obdurate enemies of his Word, his final answer with the final judgment as pronounced by the Word to follow. The world's silencing of the Word does not now proceed unconsciously and will not unconsciously be brought to its fatal climax; so also the Lord's glorification of his Word while it still resounds among his enemies in Sodom and Egypt is in many painful ways consciously brought home to its enemies, as indicated in v. 5, 6, and will certainly reach its climax in fear and in terror when the Word is finally completely removed.

13) "In that hour" of the removal of the Word in its prophets there occurred a great earthquake, one-tenth of the unholy city fell, 7,000 persons were killed in the earthquake; ὀνόματα ἀνθρώπων = persons reckoned by name (Thayer, 448). We regard this as the last part of the picture drawn for us in this chapter. The

aorists used since v. 11 are prophetic and thus accord with both the preceding vivid presents (v. 9, 10) and the futures (v. 7); for everything, beginning with ἔγειραι in v. 1, is spoken to John by the one referred to by the λέγων.

The removal of the Word is a catastrophe such as is caused when a terrific earthquake rocks the very foundations of the world, as when the central pillar that upholds the earth is removed. When the task of the Word, of its witnesses and prophets, is completed, God is through with the world. "Then will come the end," Matt. 24:14. The earth stands, not that men may crawl on its surface for the short term of their lives, but that the Word of the Lord through the church (v. 1) and the witnesses and prophets the Lord furnishes through her may accomplish its work. The catastrophe properly first strikes "the city" (v. 2, 8), the headquarters of the beastly opposition. When this totters, the rest will not stand for long.

Many puzzle about the fraction "one-tenth of the city" and about the "7,000 persons" killed. We take these figures to be symbolical. Not, however, in a good sense as though nine-tenths means 3×3, the holy three of God that is still operative for salvation; but in an evil sense. Since ten denotes completeness, one-tenth (not one fourth, or one third, as in 6:8 and in 8:7, 9, 10) appears to be a minor completeness of destruction and wreck. The first complete (one-tenth) stone falls out of the arch so that the complete arch (ten-tenths) must cave in. The added figure, "7,000" is to be regarded in a similar way. Three (denoting God) and four (denoting men), thus seven denoting God's dealings with men, multiplied by 1,000 (the greatest completeness, $10 \times 10 \times 10$): God is utterly through with men. "My spirit shall not always strive with man," Gen. 6:3. Hence the complete and final removal of the Word. What this removal means is written by this figure of "7,000" killed in this Sodom and Egypt. To figure that one-tenth of the city had 7,000 people, and that hence the entire population was ten-tenths or 70,000, and then to say that 7,000 are comparatively few, or, as others would have it, comparatively many, we consider wasted effort. To regard these as literal figures while the rest of the description is considered symbolical, we deem self-contradictory. Until we discover a better solution we abide by the one indicated.

"And the rest became terrified and gave glory to the God of the heaven" cannot mean that now at last all who were not slain repented. Repentance is impossible without the Word. When judgment descends, it is too late for repentance. "Because I have called, and ye refused; I have stretched out my hand, and no man regarded; but ye have set at nought all my counsel, and would none of my reproof; I also will laugh at your calamity; I will mock when your fear cometh; when your fear cometh as desolation, and your destruction as a whirlwind; when distress and anguish cometh upon you. Then shall they call upon me, and I will not answer; then shall they seek me, but they shall not find me," etc. Prov. 1:24-28. These words have already been partially fulfilled on different occasions, but they shall be completely fulfilled when the final judgment is due.

"The God of the heaven" is used also in Ezra 1:2; Neh. 1:4; Dan. 2:18. Because of the phraseology used in 16:9 and in Jer. 13:16 some think of a final grand repentance; but this view conflicts with the context and with passages such as Prov. 1:24, etc. When under the power of the beast of the abyss the enemies of God are struck with terror as the first blow of judgment descends and then acknowledge that there is a God of heaven, they have not thereby shown repentance. "Neither repented they" in 9:21 is still the fact.

The Seventh Trumpet and Last Woe, 11:14-19

14) **The second woe went past. Lo, the third woe comes quickly!** The third is especially announced as was the second in 9:12. It follows hard upon the other (ταχύ).

15) We might expect the seventh trumpet to reveal *the act* of the final judgment or some part of *the scene* of this judgment. It does something greater, it pictures a scene in heaven *after* the judgment and lets us hear what the judgment signifies for God and his Christ, for the obdurate world, and for Christ's prophets and saints. This is the climax of the preceding six trumpets together with the visions of chapters 10 and 11.

It has been well observed that there is a certain similarity in the seventh seal, the seventh trumpet, and the seventh bowl (16:17, etc.); all three of these sevens begin in a most majestic way with voices in heaven; all three place us most plainly at the end. Those are undoubtedly right who perceive that these three series of sevens are not consecutive, are not twenty-one successive chapters in the history of the world or of the church on earth, but that each group of seven takes us over the same ground and shows us three groups of parallel scenes, each group in its seventh member taking us to the end.

And the seventh angel trumpeted. And there occurred great voices in the heaven, saying: The kingship of the world became our Lord's and his Christ's, and he shall reign for the eons of the eons! John saw this vision as he had seen the others "in spirit" (1:10; 4:2). We see no necessity for moving John about and placing him in heaven, then on earth, and then again in heaven as though these were not visions, or as though visions require such shifting. The same is true with regard to the remarks which tell us that what John here records is "proleptic," what "occurred" here has not yet occurred, etc. Of course, the world has not yet come to an end, the dead have not yet risen. This is a vision. The correct word to characterize it is "prophetic." This word applies likewise to previous visions. Whether, as far as time is concerned, anything in them is past, present, or future, makes no difference in regard to what is revealed in these visions.

Once more let us note that here again the law of restraint, or let us call it the law of paucity and simplicity, governs. So much is revealed and not a bit more. So much is flashed on the screen; only what is necessary and no more. This vision is a glimpse of eternity when time is no more (10:6). It is curiously strange to be told that the great voices here heard by John are those of Luther, Zwingli, Calvin, and the preachers of the Reformation. Because the voices (feminine in the Greek) are those of persons, λέγοντες is properly masculine.

Why forbid us the question: "Whose great voices are here referred to?" They certainly are the voices of all the saints and all the angels in heaven after the day of judgment has brought the world and time to an end. This entire vision is wonderful in majesty and in beauty and is beyond all human and earthly conceptions. Our stammering comment must not dim any of its glory. "Great voices in the heaven" resound in one unspeakably "great" chorus, angels and saints being united. They declare *the fact* in two poetical lines:

"The kingship of the world became our Lord's and
his Christ's;
And he shall reign for the eons of the eons!"

While it does not have the form of praise or a doxology, the declaration of the fact is doxological in sense.

The Greek is satisfied with its simple aorist of the fact ἐγένετο (rendered "is become" in the R. V.) for which we should use the perfect, "has become." The translation of the A. V. is based on the wrong reading: "the kingdoms of the world are become" (plural). Even the correct singular is at times misunderstood as though all men in the world now acknowledge God as their King in the millennium here on earth. Ἡ βασιλεία τοῦ κόσμου is "the kingship, the royal reign, over the world." This has now come to belong completely, exclusively (aorist) to "our Lord" (i. e., God, the Lord of all these voices) and to "his Christ" (i. e., his Messiah). The usurpation of the devil, the rebellion of the wild beast (θηρίον, v. 7), which for so long a time disputed this divine kingship and gave battle (v. 7)to the Word and the witnesses or prophets, are forever ended. There is no longer an "outside court" (v. 2), no longer a city "called Sodom and Egypt" (v. 8), where Satan rules as the prince of this world. G. K. 581. All things are made new; heaven and earth are now one; the new Jerusalem, the Holy City, has come down; the Tabernacle of God is with men (note v. 19). Rev. 21:1-5. The mystery of God is completed with this seventh trumpet as God gave good news to his own slaves, the prophets, in all the Old and New Testament (see 10:7). The Final Consummation has come. "For the eons," etc., see 1:6.

In Acts 4:20 note "his Christ"; in Ps. 2:6, "my King"; in Ps. 10:16: "The Lord is King forever and ever"; in Dan. 7:14 the great passage in regard to the kingdom, to which add Luke 1:33, Gabriel's word; in Obadiah 21: "the kingdom shall be the Lord's"; in Rev. 12:10: "Now there came (has come) the salvation and the power and the kingdom of our God, and the authority of his Christ," plus 19:6: "Hallelujah, for the Lord our God, the Almighty, did come to reign!" What the prophets foretold has come to pass.

16) This brief statement of the tremendous fact is now expounded by the twenty-four elders. **And the twenty-four elders who sit before God on their**

thrones fell down upon their faces and worshipped God, saying: We thank thee, Lord God, the Almighty, the One who Is and the One who Was, because thou hast taken thy power, the great one, and didst reign! And the heathen were wroth, and there came thy wrath and the season of the dead to be judged and to give the reward to thy slaves, the prophets, and to the saints and to those fearing thy name, the small and the great, and to destroy those destroying the earth. Here John and we learn all that is involved in the kingdom's having become the Lord's.

It is most fitting that this should be told with thanksgiving by the twenty-four elders who are symbolical representatives of the Word in heaven; see the full explanation in connection with the first grand scene in heaven in 4:4. Here again their sitting before God on their thrones expresses their relation to God and their derived power (the Word) from God's own throne. They fell down and worshipped in deepest adoration, compare 4:10; 5:8, 14; "on their faces" as in 7:11.

17) The lines are poetical:

"We thank thee, Lord God the Almighty, the One
who Is and the One who Was,
Because thou hast taken thy power, the great one,
and didst reign!"

The elders voice the thanksgiving and the gratitude of the entire church, for these are "elders." On Κύριε ὁ Θεός, ὁ παντοκράτωρ see 1:8, and compare 16:7; 19:16 (18:8), and on "the One who Is," etc., see 1:4. "The One Coming" is omitted because the great coming is accomplished. All these titles properly indicate what is now said of God. "He shall reign." This statement of fact made in v. 15 is restated and amplified: "Thou hast taken thy power, the great one, and didst reign." His omnipotence he "has taken" (perfect, punctiliar-durative, R. 901) in order now to exercise it without restraint forever. The aorist "didst reign" is thus ingressive, "didst begin to reign." God allowed Satan and his enemies on earth to raise their heads against him for a long time! God restrained his power (δύναμις). Now this state of affairs is forever ended.

18) How an end was made of all opposition is described:

"And the heathen were wroth,
And there came thy wrath,
And the season of the dead to be judged,
And to give the reward to thy slaves, the prophets,
And to the saints and to those fearing thy name,
the small and the great,
And to destroy those destroying the earth."

"Were wroth" and "there came thy wrath" = Ps. 2:1-5, the raging of the heathen, kings and rulers blazing with wrath against Jehovah and his Anointed (Ps. 46:6; Acts 4:25, 26); God's wrath and displeasure. Note the paranomasia in ὠργίσθησαν and ὁ ὀργή σου: they were *wroth* — God's *wrath;* their wrath was inspired by the beast out of the abyss (v. 7), God's wrath is the answer of his holiness. God's wrath dropped its restraint on the day of final judgment which is here termed "the season (καιρός) of the dead to be judged," to be called from their graves so that the Christ might pronounce judgment (aorist, with finality) and in this judgment "to give the reward" of grace to all that are Christ's own.

Two classes are named: "to his slaves, the prophets," as in 10:7, whose will was God's will alone and whom he called to proclaim his will. The Old Testament prophets are to be included in view of 10:7. Next, "to the saints," whom he by his grace sanctified and set apart as his own from "the court outside" (v. 1, 2) as the *Una Sancta.* Καί with "those fearing his name" is epexegetical and defines these saints in accord with the response they made to his grace. To think of "the saints" as being Jewish believers and of "those fearing," etc., as being Gentile believers or proselytes, thus making three classes, draws in a distinction that had died out decades before and usually occurs only to the minds of commentators who think of a future national conversion of the Jews. The "name," of course, refers to God, but as he is revealed to us in his Word.

For some unaccountable reason the final apposition appears in the accusative in some important texts: τοὺς μικροὺς καὶ τοὺς μεγάλους. R. 414 makes no attempt at a solution. We prefer the reading that has the dative, "to the small and to the great," as in 13:16 and 20:12 in the sense of "to everyone" and not in the sense of children and adults or of weak and strong believers. "Those fearing the Lord, small and great" appears in Ps. 115:13, and here and in 19:5 seems to allude to this psalm.

While all the godly receive their reward, the last infinitive which is still dependent on ὁ καιρός states the fate of the ungodly: "and to destroy those destroying the earth," the timeless present participle characterizing these, and the aorist infinitive indicating their final destruction. "To destroy those destroying" (the destroyers) is exact justice. To destroy the earth refers to the work of their wickedness in raging against God in unbelief. The last judgment brings their final due.

19) As if in confirmation of the declaration of fact in v. 15 and in answer to the thanksgiving in v. 17, 18 John reports: **And there was opened the Sanctuary of God in the heaven, and there was seen the Ark of the Covenant in his Sanctuary, and there occurred lightnings and voices and quaking and great hail.** There is a division of opinion as to whether this verse concludes the seventh trumpet or begins a new vision; also, whether the record of the

seventh trumpet is here closed or extends onward until the seven bowls radiate from the seventh trumpet, i. e., through chapter 18. We regard this verse as belonging to what precedes. To say that no woe appears here is to ignore the fact that the destruction of the destroyers in the final judgment is a woe that is greater than any other. To think that the "lightnings," etc., denote further earthly penalties is to disregard the finality expressed in this paragraph (v. 15-19) and in particular the opening of the Sanctuary and the exposure of the Ark. Beyond this nothing that is in heaven can be shown us. When it is stated that these "lightnings," etc., *come out* of the Sanctuary, and that not what is seen *in the* Sanctuary is the main idea, this inserts something into the text which has no "coming out of" but only "there occurred" lightnings and does have "there was seen" the Ark.

We must again decline to bring in more than is here mentioned, namely the two altars and all else that belongs to the old Jewish Temple. Only what is named is used in the symbolism of this vision and nothing more. The idea that the Ark here "seen" is the one that was built by Moses and was carried off to Babylon but was ever since preserved in heaven, is untenable. Exod. 25:40; 26:30; 27:8; Acts 7:44 make this clear. On the ναός see v. 1. Let us not think that heaven is fitted out with a Sanctuary and an Ark; this is a *vision.* John sees in heaven what he here reports. God uses this Sanctuary in heaven and this holy ark as symbols. The fact of importance is that the Sanctuary "was opened," that the Ark "was seen." There was no veil. It is "the Ark of the Covenant," of the διαθήκη God made with Abraham and renewed with Israel which was symbolized in the Tabernacle with its Sanctuary and the holy Ark.

The R. V. wavers between "covenant" and "testament." We discuss this subject at length in connection with Heb. 7:22, which see. Here "covenant" is perfectly in order but it is to be understood in the sense of being a one-sided promise. This is not a mutual covenant or agreement between equals. It is *God's gift* to Abraham and to Israel which they only can receive. In it God solemnly assured them that he would send his Son as the Messiah to expiate the world's sin and to rule as the Savior-King forever.

In the expression "the Ark of the Covenant" the genitive is possessive: the Ark belongs to the Covenant. In the Tabernacle Sanctuary it was placed behind a veil to symbolize to Israel that this Messiah was yet to come. The veil in Herod's Temple was rent in twain when Christ died on the cross. It had served its purpose, the Expiator had come. Now there is even more: John sees the whole Sanctuary *open* so that the holy Ark *was seen;* for the whole Covenant is now fulfilled, the final consummation of the everlasting kingdom has arrived, time is no more, the mystery of God (his whole plan of salvation) has been completed and executed (10:7), the kingdom of the world has become our Lord's and his Christ's (11:15), the last judgment has been held (11:18). All this is summarized so that John may see it in the opened Sanctuary and the visible Ark.

We translate φωναί as we did in 4:5; 8:5; not "voices" but "sounds," for amid the lightnings and the thunders no voices are speaking. There are other tremendous sounds besides the thunders. So also σεισμός is "earthquake" only when it is used with reference to an occurrence on the earth and is only "quaking" when it is used with reference to a phenomenon that occurs in heaven.

Why was John permitted to see the phenomena of this vision in connection with the open Sanctuary and the visible Ark? These thunders, etc., are the symbols of omnipotent power in action. This was the case already in connection with the first mention of them in 4:5, where they proceed "out of the throne." All the *grace* of the Covenant that was symbolized in the Sanctuary and the Ark for all the blessed named in v. 18 has been carried to its glorious consummation as described in v. 15, etc., in connection with these terrible manifestations of *omnipotent power* against the enemies of this grace who rage in wrath against God's Anointed, against these destroyers of the earth (v. 18), this omnipotence being symbolized in "lightnings and sounds and thunders and quaking and great hail." These phenomena of omnipotence have to be added here just as in v. 18 we have to have both the godly and the ungodly. As we see it, there is no difficulty of interpretation.

Thus we also take it that in v. 15-19 we have the entire seventh trumpet. It here reveals the glory and the blessedness that shall prevail after time has ceased, after the final judgment. The last woe is here revealed in the final destruction of the destroyers, but in the past tense as its καιρός "came" (ἦλθεν) and not as it is yet to come (future) or as it is now in progress (present tense). Yet by placing us at the final consummation, this seventh trumpet and third woe involves all that follows in further visions. But not in such a way that these visions follow in a temporal succession — all time has ended — but so that John and we see anew and with greater fulness all that the final consummation involves. Thus far all the visions have thrown on the screen no more than brief, individual symbolical scenes. More is to be revealed in visions that are longer, fuller, richer in their grand features. Of course, they cover the same ground — what other ground is there to cover? These further visions start with the Incarnation itself and take us anew to the end of the world and the judgment but bring much new and fuller light. This is how we on our part regard what now follows.

CHAPTER XII

The Woman and the Dragon, chapter 12

1) The connection between this and the following visions is shown in the last paragraph of chapter 11. The seventh trumpet places us at the final, glorious consummation. The preceding visions have thrown on the screen only individual revelations that pointed to this consummation. We are now to learn still more. In chapter 12 we traverse the same ground once more. Beginning with the Incarnation, chapter 12 shows us the efforts of Satan to destroy Christ while he was on earth and, failing in this, to destroy the church as such and, failing also in this, to battle against many of the saints. Further visions, in chapter 13, etc., reveal the agencies of Satan: the beast, the lamb-beast, the great whore, all of which were used by Satan in his efforts against the church and her work.

As already pictured toward the end of chapter 12, this work of Satan extends through the New Testament era to its very close; but chapter 12 stops short of the goal, for several special visions will reveal the actual end, the final judgment: beast, lamb-beast, whore, and Satan himself cast into hell. Understanding this, we see how far the revelation of chapter 12 extends. Here there is pictured *the effort of Satan against Jesus and then against his church during the New Testament era until the end.* This vision stops just before the end and reserves the description of this for other visions.

And a great sign was seen in the heaven, a woman, the sun having been thrown around her,

and the moon beneath her feet, and on her head a crown of twelve stars, and she being pregnant. And she cried, being in travail and being in torment to give birth.

What is here seen is symbolism and is indicated as such by being called *"a sign"*; in v. 3 "another *sign.*" Both signs are of such a nature as to be *seen.* So we dismiss the question as to how this woman and this dragon could be "in the heaven." Such questioning is the more unnecessary since John here uses the exceptional wording "was seen," i. e., not only by John, and not his usual verb, "I saw."

This is a vision of "a woman" most glorious, the very sun being her magnificent robe (the perfect passive participle with its usual accusative as in 11:3 and elsewhere), the lovely moon being good enough only for her feet, and on her head "twelve stars." To have the sun as a robe, the moon as a footstool, and stars as a crown means to appear in heavenly splendor. As regards the sun, we note the appearance of Jesus in 1:16 and at the Transfiguration: "and his face did shine as the sun" (Matt. 17:2). In 10:1 the face of the angel is as the sun. We note that the description refers to the woman's entire raiment, also to her feet and to her head. Thus the beauty of the moon is utilized, for which we have the analogous expression, "fair as the moon," used with reference to the Messiah's Bride in Solomon's song 6:10. Only in the number of the stars we have an added symbol, "twelve" being the number of the church, the number of the patriarchs and of the apostles, both of whom are combined in "twenty-four" (see 4:4).

To seek the meaning in the appointment of sun, moon, and stars to *rule* the day and the night, is to obtain something that is incongruous. John sees the church in her real glory, for which reason also she is here seen in heaven and not on earth where her splendor is hidden by her lowliness as was the majesty of Jesus when he walked on earth in his humiliation.

The image of a woman is used because the birth of the Savior is to be pictured. Jesus uses a woman to represent the church in two of his parables, Luke 15:8; Matt. 13:33. The Old Testament makes the church Yahweh's Betrothed and uses the imagery of a woman in many striking and often lovely ways. "The King's daughter is all glorious within: her clothing is of wrought gold," etc., Ps. 45:13. The debate regarding the Jewish and the Christian church is unnecessary, as is also the discussion about the condition of Judaism in the days of Jesus or in the days to come. In Revelation the church is *one,* the *Una Sancta.* The fact that the Savior was a Son of David according to the flesh is understood and calls for no symbolism in Revelation.

2) Ἐν γαστρὶ ἔχουσα is idiomatic for "being pregnant or with child." The woman, so glorious in her reality, is here represented as about to give birth: "she cried being in travail or birthpains (ὠδίνουσα) and being in torment (βασανιζομένη, the word used in 9:5 and 11:10) or in pain to give birth." Compare passages such as Isa. 26:17; Micah 5:2; John 16:21. The cry of travail fills the whole Old Testament. "Oh, that thou wouldest rend the heavens, that thou wouldest come down!" Isa. 64:1. It is the constant longing and "waiting for the Consolation of Israel" (Luke 2:25), which is here represented as about to be fulfilled. This great travail is now about to end in the most blessed giving birth (τίκτειν). Roman Catholic interpretation finds Mary in this symbolism, at least an allusion to her. What is there is Gen. 3:15, "the Seed of the woman," the Incarnation of the Son of God, of Abraham's and David's son and heir.

3) **And there was seen another sign in the heaven, and lo, a dragon, fiery red, great, having seven heads and ten horns, and upon his heads seven**

diadems. Of this sign it is not said, as was said of the other, that it is "great"; instead of this John uses the interjection "lo," because this sign, or part of the vision, is astounding and horrible. The term "dragon" is wholly symbolical because no such monster exists among the beasts of the earth. The identity of this dragon is placed beyond question by v. 9 and by 20:2, where he is called "the devil and Satan." The word "dragon" expresses the extreme ferocious, murderous, beastly, cruel power with the connotation of horror for men. That the bestiality of the serpent and of the swine is combined in "dragon" is open to doubt. Gigantic strength, craft, malignity, and venom are combined in "dragon." That this "other sign" was also seen "in the heaven" needs no further explanation than that which is given for the phrase in v. 1. This is a vision and is thus "seen in heaven" where in the heavenly light the dragon appears as he really is. Πυρρός, "fiery red," is the color of hell and of blood (6:4); "great" indicates monstrous size and power.

The seven heads, the ten horns, and the seven diadems on the ten horns are plainly symbolical. The very intent of these figures is that we are *not* to draw a picture of this dragon; we could not if we tried, our imaginative powers are intentionally ruled out, our task is to find the meaning behind these symbols. We think we may safely say that when the holy number "seven" appears in connection with the devil, it indicates the arrogant assumption of a relation to men which belongs to God alone (three to designate God, plus four to designate men in the world).

"Heads" are not figures of mere intelligence as here also there are "on the heads seven diadems," διαδήματα, symbols of royalty. Royal heads denote royal majesty and dominion especially when they are bearing royal diadems. In his monstrous hellish power and malignity the devil usurps and arrogates to himself the dominion which is God's alone. The "horn" is the regular symbol of power, and "ten" is the number of completeness. Thus the ten horns of the dragon = the complete power arrogated by Satan in this usurped dominion over men. This *dragon,* the devil, would be God so that all men might bow before him.

On the difference between στέφανος and διάδημα see 2:10, the one being a victor's wreath, the other a fillet or ribbon bound about the head (sometimes several for several kingdoms) as a mark of royalty; the *stephanos,* however, is used also with reference to the king as a victor. We note that Jesus received a *stephanos* of thorns and then was mocked as *King* of the Jews. Here the woman has the twelve stars as her *stephanos,* her symbol of victory. "The victory ours remaineth" (Luther), and thus as victor the *Una Sancta* shall reign with Christ forever. The dragon has no *stephanos,* not even a usurped wreath of victory, but only "diadems," royal fillets of pretended kingship, symbols of arrogated dominion.

4) **And his tail drags the third of the stars, and he threw them to the earth.** This recalls the monstrous grasshoppers that rose in the smoke out of the abyss: "in their *tails* is their power" (9:10). The one third recalls this same fraction in the first four visions of the trumpets (8:7-12). The combination of the present tense σύρει and the aorist ἔβαλεν causes no difficulty, for in narrative the vivid present is aoristic and is readily combined with historical aorists. The fact that we here have a description of what his monstrous power has already actually done, seems plain. The purpose, too, is evident: we are to understand that, confronted by the monster who had done this to a third of the stars, the pregnant woman and her child about to be born are certainly in mortal danger. May we stop with this and see here only a figurative general statement of the dragon's power that is fearsome as the

very idea of this infernal dragon is fearsome? Or is there more here, a specific past deed of this dragon, Satan?

Some interpreters are content with the general figure: supernatural power exhibited even in the supernatural world. Some futurists speak of this power as yet to be exhibited, in fact some place also the birth and all else into the future and at the time of the judgment. The similarity of our passage to Dan. 8:10, 24 can hardly be brushed aside. The arrogance of the little horn, Antiochus Epiphanes, waxed so great that he cast some of the host of heaven and of the stars to the ground and stamped upon them; v. 24, he shall destroy the mighty and the holy people (holy ones), i. e., some of God's saints. Keil, *Commentar* on Daniel, 247, etc., interprets that as being the host of heaven, the hosts of Yahweh, which sometimes mean the stars and the angel hosts as also the hosts of his people (Exod. 12:41; 7:4; Gen. 15:5; Jer. 33:22). This may help us. The wording is analogous: the monster Antiochus, a man, threw down some of God's stars or saints; this dragon monster, Satan, threw down a third of God's stars, the angels, Jude 6: "the angels which kept not their first estate but left their own habitation."

That Satan drew other angels with him, he being the chief rebel, is the accepted fact. The fact that they lost their heavenly places is expressed by saying that Satan threw them on the earth. When stars fall, this is said to occur "to the earth." As for the tail, not only is the dragon always conceived as having a tremendous tail, here one that is so mighty as to sweep so many stars from the sky, but the hellish tail is the instrument of lying power (9:10; compare Isa. 9:15, "the prophet that teacheth lies, he is the tail"). Thus we here have a description of Satan's power manifested in the most terrible thing he has done.

For ourself we consider this interpretation better than the other which regards this as a general figure for supernatural power, a poetic wording for eagerness for combat, for magnitude of fury, and the like; better, too, than to let the tail refer to heresy, and the stars to bishops and rulers in ecclesiastical affairs, or the tail to some Roman emperor who was persecuting Christians over a third of the empire.

And the dragon was standing before the woman, the one about to give birth, in order that, when she gave birth, he might devour her child. Ἕστηκεν is the imperfect from στήκω, "was standing," waiting for the birth; τεκεῖν and τέκῃ are aorists from τίκτειν. As glorious as is the woman (v. 1), so fearful is the danger threatening her child about to be born. This child = Christ, the Seed of the Woman, born of a woman (Gal. 4:4), here presented as about to be born into the world. Here we have the Incarnation in Revelation. The pregnant woman is the church which is pregnant with the promise of the Messiah beginning with Gen. 3:15. Satan's one aim was "to devour" or destroy this Messiah. Confusion results when the child is made "Christ plus all his Christians" or the Christians alone.

5) **And she gave birth to a son, a male, who is about to shepherd all the heathen with an iron rod. And snatched away was the child unto God and unto his throne.** A long array of commentators regards this as a reference to the birth of Christ, and we must join them. Yet we must remember that this is a vision and thus we must not think merely of Bethlehem but in this birth must include the entire presence of Christ on earth as the Messiah. So also we have no difficulty with the intent of Satan regarding the child, for Satan certainly manifested it all along, beginning with the murderous scheme of Herod, in the temptations of Christ, and extending to his crucifixion. We may note

passages such as Matt. 2:16-20; Luke 13:31; Acts 4:25-27. Satan's intent is not one that is merely assumed; the reality of it was fully manifested.

The neuter ἄρσεν is an apposition to the masculine υἱόν: "a son, a male," and the difference in gender is wholly immaterial, for appositions do not require an agreement in gender. The point of interpretation to be noted is the question, why, when υἱόν already declares the child to be a son, ἄρσεν should be added. This repetition is an allusion to Isa. 66:7, and emphasizes the sex because of the great relative clause, "who is about to shepherd the heathen with an iron rod," which is taken from Ps. 2:9, and was used already in 2:27 and is to be used again in 19:15. In Ps. 2:9 the LXX uses "to shepherd," which, therefore, is retained in the quotations (see the exposition of this clause in 2:27, where two lines are quoted from this psalm).

We should not translate τὰ ἔθνη "the nations" (our versions) but, as is done in the psalm, "the heathen," even as "the heathen" rage against Jehovah and his Messiah. Therefore also they are treated to the "iron rod." Many see that the mighty Son with the iron rod, described also in psalm 2, undoubtedly is Christ. Yet some somehow let this Son signify Christ plus the Christians or even the Christians alone.

Even when Christ is found here, the futurists regard the quoted clause eschatologically as sketching the application of the iron rod in "the events that pertain to the time of the second advent." This view misunderstands psalm 2. Delitzsch is an example. He interprets psalm 2 correctly with reference to Christ's rule over the heathen during the entire New Testament era, and yet, when in his notes on Isa. 66:7 he refers to Rev. 12:5, he contradicts his own exposition of the line of the psalm and refers it only to the end.

Some assert that none of the apostles thought that 2,000 years would elaspse before the second advent and that, therefore, the iron rod must refer to the final judgment or to the end. The fact is that all the apostles left "the times and the seasons in the Father's authority," where Jesus rested them in Acts 1:7; but, with David in psalm 2, the apostles made Christ the King who is the King who rules with the iron rod over the raging heathen and their kings or leaders during the whole New Testament period whatever its length of "times and seasons," from the day of his exaltation onward to the end, may be.

The child was snatched away unto God and unto his throne. This is the glorification, ascension, and enthronement of the incarnate Son. "Whom the heavens must receive, until," etc., Acts 3:21. "Unto God" is insufficient, for this might refer only to safety in heaven. "Unto his throne" (see the notes on the "throne" in 4:3) signifies the enthronement of Christ, "the Lamb in the midst of the throne" (5:6), he thus wielding the iron rod of omnipotent power. The dragon had thought that he might "devour" him. The vision reveals the infinite exaltation of the incarnate Son. In the passive ἡρπάσθη God is the agent, compare Phil. 2:9; Heb. 1:4-14; 2:8, 9.

How Ellicott and the historical school can regard this as a reference to the elevation of Constantine to the throne of the Roman empire and quote Gibbon: "Christianity was seated on the throne of the Roman world," we fail to comprehend even when they include other emperors such as Theodosius who finally put an end to all toleration of paganism. As for the futurists, they would let the iron rod remain idle in the hands of the exalted Christ until the period of the second advent.

6) **And the woman fled into the wilderness, where she has there a place prepared of God, that there they may nourish her for a thousand two hundred sixty days.** This brief statement regarding the woman is elaborated in v. 13-17. It is inserted in ad-

vance at this point because one might wonder why the woman was not snatched with her Son "unto God and his throne," i. e., into the same place of power and safety. It is Christ who rules the heathen with a rod of iron from the throne of omnipotence and not the church. She must remain on earth in order to fulfill her mission there. Why she fled into the wilderness, how she fled, etc., is related in v. 13, etc. Let us say at this point that the woman and her giving birth to her Son are *not* placed in heaven; the phrases used in v. 1 and 3 produce confusion when they are so interpreted.

Glorious as the woman is (v. 1) and the mother of such a Son, she yet has to flee "into the wilderness" because of the fury of the dragon (v. 13). But God himself has there prepared a place for her where she is to be nourished until the days of her exile shall reach their end. With ὅπου, "where," ἐκεῖ, "there," is pleonastic as far as the grammar is concerned; but the two ἐκεῖ intend to emphasize the place where God prepared refuge for the church for these 1,260 days, the whole time until the end of the world (on the 1,260 days see 11:3). "Into the wilderness" is repeated in v. 14, and is thereby likewise emphasized. Until the Parousia the church, though it is so glorious, does not sit on a throne in a capital of earth like the pope in Rome, does not rule over nations in a world empire. The Lord has prepared a place for her "in the wilderness," away from all earthly grandeur, in lowliness and much want. It is not the entire wilderness to which the woman flees but a "place there, having been prepared from God," so prepared that she may remain there.

The old Jewish dream of a grand Jewish dominion over all the nations of the world, a dream that is constantly being revived to this day in the minds of all those who work to make the kingdom of God an outward world power and dominion, is just about the opposite of what John is here given to see in regard to the church. Ever, here on earth, she is not on the throne but in a place in the wilderness, a little flock under the cross. But the day of her final ἀπολύτρωσις, "ransoming," "redemption" (Luke 23:18; Rom. 8:23; Eph. 1:14), is fast drawing nigh.

Will the church starve and die in the wilderness? Indeed not! No more than Israel starved in the desert but was fed with manna; no more than Elijah starved whom the ravens fed. "That there they may nourish her for 1,260 days" (v. 14 repeating, "where she is nourished") is the Lord's provision. We are not told who "they" are that will nourish the woman. In the case of τρέφεται in v. 14 one might assume God as the agent but not in the case of τρέφωσιν which is plural. May we, perhaps, say that God will nourish the church in the wilderness through the prophets and the apostles and their written Word? Certainly, the food that sustains her in the world is the Word.

7) **And there occurred battle in the heaven: Michael and his angels to battle with the dragon. And the dragon battled and his angels and was not strong enough, nor was their place found any more in the heaven. And he was thrown, the dragon, the great, the serpent, the ancient, the one called (the) devil and Satan, the one deceiving the whole inhabited earth; thrown was he to the earth, and his angels with him were thrown.**

And I heard a great voice in the heaven saying:

Now there came to be the salvation and the power
And the kingdom of our God and the authority of his Christ!
Because thrown was the accuser of our brethren,
The one accusing them before our God by day and by night.

And they themselves conquered him because
of the blood of the Lamb
And because of the Word of their testimony,
And did not love their life up to death.
Because of this make merry, heavens, and
those tenting in them!
Woe to the earth and the sea!
Because the devil went down to you,
Having great fury,
Knowing that he has (only) **a little season.**

Here *the effect and result of the Savior's incarnation and his enthronement* are portrayed symbolically. At the same time this double section (v. 7-9; 10-12) leads over to v. 13-17, the dragon's persecution of the woman after the birth, etc., of her child.

The picture of the *battle* is illumined by the voice and its song of *triumph.* Unless it is read in the light of this song, the battle will not be understood; it will either remain an enigma or be interpreted in fanciful ways. The three statements that Satan "was thrown" in the battle are made clear by the statement in the song, "there was thrown the accuser of our brethren, the one accusing them before our God by day and by night." Note the identical verb ἐβλήθη in the identical sense. Note this verb in 19:20; 20:3, 10, 14, 15. In the battle scene he is so significantly called διάβολος, "slanderer," and Σατανᾶς, "Adversary," and in the song "the accuser, the one accusing by day and by night." By his utter defeat he lost this power of accusing "our brethren before God." Gone is "their place in the heaven" to bring accusation against the brethren before God; the Accuser "was thrown to the earth" as the song states it: "he came down to you," to the earth and the sea, there now to vent his fury since he is able now to reach no farther and to do no more. Let this suffice to show how the triumphal song helps to explain the battle and how together they depict the effect of Christ's incarnation and his enthronement.

In connection with the inability of the devil to accuse us we recall Rom. 8:1: "There is no adverse verdict (κατάκριμα) for those in connection with Jesus"; and 8:33: "Who shall bring a charge (or accusation) against God's elect?" We add Luke 10:18. On the occasion when Jesus told the apostles to rejoice because their names are written in heaven he prefaced this by saying, "I beheld Satan as lightning fall from heaven," his power to prevent our names from being written among the blessed being forever gone. Likewise John 12:31: "Now shall the prince of this world be thrown out." We have the very verb βάλλω, "to throw or throw out," which is used four times in Revelation.

Remembering the main import, let us see what we may do with the details. In the battle scene the symbolism appears in the verbs, in the action. "Michael and his angels" is to be understood literally; so also is "the dragon and his angels" except that the term "the dragon" is retained from v. 2, etc. Yet since he has "angels" (Matt. 25:41) as his army he, too, must be an angel. The past tenses, historic aorists, are like the preceding aorists. John's vision concerns mighty things that are past and done. When Satan and his angels were attacked by Michael and his angels they went down in utter defeat.

Πολεμός is "battle" as in 9:7, 9; 11:7 and not "war," πολεμεῖν, "to battle," and is construed with μετά and is not a Hebraism (Moulton, *Einleitung,* 172, 346). Many puzzle about the nominative "Michael and his angels" with τοῦ πολεμῆσαι and even alter the text; but this infinitive with τοῦ is only an explanatory apposition of πολεμός, it is like the English: "There will be a cricket match — the champions to play the rest" (R. 1066), which R. 1093 calls an independent parenthesis. Many infinitives have the article τοῦ. The infinitive conveys the thought that Michael and his angels attacked the dragon. The idea that the dragon tried to attack the Son on the throne should be dismissed. We meet Michael in Dan. 10:13, 21; 12:1, he is called "the archangel" in Jude 9. It would be hazardous to say that he is the only archangel because he alone is called so in Scripture; for we know that there are angels of different rank, Eph. 1:21; Col. 1:16; 2:15: one rank with one principality and the corresponding power, might, dominion and name or title, and other ranks each with its principality and its corresponding power, etc. See my exposition of these passages, where also the mistaken view of the ranks is discussed. As Satan was the general of the wicked angels in this battle, so Michael was the general of the holy angels. When it was attacked, this wicked host οὐκ ἴσχυσαν, "was not strong enough," suffered utter defeat, the aorist expresses the fact.

Because John writes: There occurred battle "in the heaven," the impossible did not take place, the eternal bliss and peace of heaven was not turned into tumult of battle. John also writes that the great sign, the woman, was seen "in the heaven," and that the other sign, the great fiery dragon, was seen "in the heaven" although the woman gave birth to her Son, and the dragon stood ready to devour her Son here on earth. These figures and events are visions and thus "were seen" and "occurred" in the heaven. The wicked angels had lost their ἀρχή (Jude 6) among the good angels in heaven, nor did they try to storm heaven after the Savior's Enthronement. This scene is presented as a supermundane battle, it is akin to Paul's phrase in Eph. 6:12, where he says that the demons, against whom we have to stand in the whole panoply of God, are ἐν τοῖς ἐπουρανίοις, "in the heavenlies."

It is an abstract, rationalizing deduction that Christ alone is able to conquer Satan, and that, therefore, "Michael" must here signify Christ. Did Christ have to take "his angels" along with him in order to win this battle? One is not rid of the angels by making Michael = Christ. How can the woman's child who is snatched to the throne in v. 5 now suddenly appear as Michael? The Russellites ("Jehovah's Witnesses") convert Christ into the created angel Michael and thus rob Christ of his deity. This is not a picture of the battle of the Savior which he fought against Satan here on earth and that ended with his enthronement at God's right hand but a picture of *the effect* of Christ's exaltation: no longer is the accuser able to accuse us before God; this world is judged, and the prince of this world is rendered helpless, John 12:31.

The question is asked as to why this effect of Christ's enthronement is here pictured as a mighty victory of *God's angels* over the hellish host. We are able to say this much: Christ employs human beings to bring the fruits of his enthronement to men and thus used angels to strike down the accuser who constantly would raise his head to accuse us before God. All the angels of God are most deeply concerned in the Son's work. We see them at the incarnation and the birth; twelve legions would have come to annihilate the army in Gethsemane; they appear at the resurrection, at the ascension, and heaven rang with their shouts at the enthronization. Then there is Heb. 1:14, and in Revelation all the visions of angels, among them the one of this battle of the angels, another of "the armies, those in the heaven," in 19:14. Here there is pictured only the *one* effect of Christ's complete victory; to attain this effect he who has all power in heaven and on earth (Matt. 28:18) used his angel army. We are unable to say more.

8) "Nor was their place found any more in the heaven" = v. 9: the accuser and deceiver "was thrown to the earth, and his angels with him were thrown down" = again v. 10: "thrown was the accuser of our brethren, the one accusing them before God by day and by night." Let him rave with his furious accusations, he is able to bring not one of them before God either by day or by night. Rom. 8:1, 33, 34. Every accusation against us is smothered in "the blood of the Lamb."

9) Ἐβλήθη — ἐβλήθη — ἐβλήθησαν. "He was thrown — he was thrown — they were thrown." Then once more in v. 10: ἐβλήθη, "because there was thrown the accuser." This fourth "was thrown" with its significant subject "the accuser of our brethren," which is emphasized by the apposition, "the one accusing them before God by day and by night," reveals what the emphatic repetitions of "was thrown," in fact, what this battle and this defeat really signify. The terrible accuser "was thrown," was flung afar. In John 12:31, Jesus said shortly before the defeat occurred: ἐκβληθήσεται ἔξω, "he shall be thrown out outside." Now we learn that this was, indeed, done. Perhaps it will help us to understand a little why Michael and the angels are employed in this act when we glance at Matt. 22:13, where the King does not soil his hands by throwing the fellow out but orders his *diakonoi*, his "ministers," to do so. The angels are ever the Lord's *diakonoi*, he can make them "a flame of fire" (Heb. 1:7).

Of equal importance with the four verbs is the fourfold subject: "the dragon, the great — the serpent, the ancient — the one called 'devil' and 'Satan' — the one deceiving the whole inhabited world." The interpretation given in v. 10 adds two more designations: "the accuser," etc., thereby supplying the necessary light. "The dragon" is explained in v. 3, where also "great" is added. "The serpent, the ancient" reverts to Gen. 3:1, etc., where Satan deceived Eve and gives to the term "serpent" the connotation of devilish cunning and deception. Note that in both instances the adjective is added with a second article which makes the adjectives emphatic, it is like an apposition or a climax (R. 776).

Ὁ καλούμενος means that he is known by the common name διάβολος, "devil," which means "slanderous one, false accuser." To this appellative there is added as a proper noun ὁ Σατανᾶς, a Grecized transliteration of the Aramaic *Satana,* which originally meant "one lying in ambush for" (M.-M. 570). Both names are here used in their fullest significance. Finally, ὁ πλανῶν, "the one deceiving the whole *oikoumene,* inhabited earth," the timeless present participle being substantivized and equal to the deceiver beyond compare. Each of the four items sheds its lurid light on the others, the four together tell us fully what the foe is.

It is *he* who *was thrown.* Subject and verb are transposed and thus emphasis is given to both. "*Thrown* was he," John repeats and then adds that also "his angels with him were *thrown.*" The defeat was absolutely complete. The agent implied in the passives is Michael and his holy angels. But now the clause is added, "Thrown was he to the earth." This does not imply that Satan had a place in God's heaven or had managed to invade the home of eternal blessedness. "To the earth" means that Satan was hurled so far, was brought so low. The ὅτι clause used in v. 10 explains. "To the earth" is added also because of v. 12: "There went down the devil to you, having great fury," etc., and because of what follows in v. 13, etc.

10) Now comes the song of triumph. "I heard a great voice in the heaven saying" (like the great voices in the heaven in 11:15). The accusative φωνήν is used because the substance is the main thing and not the unnamed speaker's person. In Isaiah "a voice" thus speaks repeatedly without need of saying whose voice

it is. All that the voice said interprets and explains the battle and the defeat of Satan. We may arrange the lines in the form of Hebrew poetry.

First of all, what does the defeat mean regarding *God and his Christ;* next, regarding *us* (v. 11); finally, for *those in heaven* and for *those on earth* (v. 12)?

This battle and this defeat mean that "now there did come" (in the English idiom: there has come), actually, fully, completely come (aorist), "the salvation and the power and the kingdom of our God and the authority of his Christ." How so? "Because thrown was the accuser of our brethren, the one accusing them before our God by day and by night." The σωτηρία is the full *salvation,* the great act of rescue and the resulting safety for all believers. Ἐγένετο, "it got to be," it has come to be fully and completely evident. So also has the δύναμις, the divine *power* that wrought this mighty salvation, that sent the Son of the woman in the incarnation, that exalted him to the throne despite the dragon, that sent the dragon to his complete defeat. In other words, there has come to be the βασιλεία of our God, his *kingdom,* i. e., his rule of grace and salvation by his blessed power in its full and complete sway to save men all over the world despite all the efforts of Satan. And with this kingdom and its rule there has come the *authority* of God's Christ, "his Christ" or Anointed, as in 11:15. This is the authority (πᾶσα ἐξουσία, "all authority") referred to in Matt. 28:18, the right and the power of Christ's Kingship in his human as well as in his divine nature.

Ὅτι states the evidence. This is *the main effect* (as we have already stated) of the incarnation and the enthronement: "Because thrown was (placed forward for the sake of emphasis) the accuser of our brethren, the one accusing them before our God by day and by night." The timeless substantivized participle ὁ κατηγορῶν characterizes Satan; this apposition strongly emphasizes the main point of this vision: the mouth of the great accuser is forever stopped. The names used in v. 9 point to these two designations: "the accuser, the one accusing," who makes it his terrible business to accuse. As the serpent he deceives, as the devil he slanders, as Satan he lies in ambush; yea, he is "the one deceiving the whole inhabited earth." Those whom he thus deceives and drags into sin he then accuses, holds up their sin and guilt, and calls on the justice of God to condemn them. "Thrown was he" never again to raise his voice in accusation. This is the mighty effect of God's deeds through the Son. Salvation is, indeed, complete.

Note that the voice calls the believers "our brethren." John heard this voice, but it addresses all those who are tenting or tabernacling in the heavens (v. 13) and makes all believers their brethren.

11) The voice adds: "And they themselves (αὐτοί, these our brethren) did conquer him (the accuser) because of the blood of the Lamb and because of the Word of their testimony." The picture presented by this conquering is that of the brethren standing before God's judgment seat in order to receive sentence from the Judge. When their case comes up, they win, have won. They have sinned, indeed, but their fearful accuser has disappeared, he has been "thrown" in utter defeat. Read Rom. 8:33, 34, 37; 16:20. The sins of all these brethren have disappeared "because of the blood of the Lamb" that was shed in expiation for them. They washed and made white their robes "in the blood of the Lamb" (7:14). How can anyone accuse them?

A second reason is added: "because of the Word of their testimony." This is "the Word of God and the testimony of Jesus Christ" (1:9) of which 6:9 says, "which they held." The blood is the expiatory cause, the Word and testimony the mediatory cause (διά with the accusative, both times to express cause). It is "their" testimony as received and "held" (6:9) by faith. Christ made it, they held it.

How they held it is added: "and did not love their life up to death" (John 12:25). They would rather suffer martyrdom than deny that blood and the Word and their testimony. We have an example in Paul, Acts 20:24. The extreme "up to death" is mentioned, but, as so often, only in order to include this and thus all lesser evidence of faithfulness; for the Lord needs only a few in order to fill up the number of bloody martyrs, (6:11), for others it is enough to be faithful in affliction.

It is rationalizing to say that, if the blood is so efficacious, the accuser might be allowed to appear since he would have no case; or, the other way around, if the accuser is thrown out to begin with, we should be acquitted only because the accuser is prevented from appearing against us. Even allowing this rationalizing — to be doubly safe is a good thing. But here by one and the same act the very Christ removes sin *and* accuser, guilt *and* accusation; nor could the one be done without in and by it doing the other.

12) The voice calls on the heavens (this plural is found only here in Revelation) and on "those tenting in them" to make merry, i. e., to celebrate (this verb is found in Luke 15:32; Rev. 11:10; 18:20) διὰ τοῦτο, because of this grand effect of Christ's enthronement. The dramatic vocatives, "heavens and those tenting in them," name the place and the inhabitants as is often done in dramatic language. Οἱ σκηνοῦντες leads us to think of ἡ σκηνὴ τοῦ Θεοῦ in 21:3, the heavens being the Tent or Tabernacle of God's heavenly presence. If one saved sinner causes joy among the angels in heaven (Luke 15:7, 10), how great must this joy be because of all the saved and God's whole salvation! Yet "those tabernacling in the heavens" applies to men and not to

angels although they join in the celebration; the "Tabernacle," which was copied by Moses, is intended for Israel and the godly, and in 18:20 those tabernacling are "the saints and the apostles and the prophets."

In sharp contrast with this call to be glad and to celebrate is the cry of the voice: "Woe to the earth and the sea, because the devil went down to you (earth and sea), having great fury (θυμός), knowing that he has (only) a little καιρός or period." As in the case of "heavens" so in the case of "the earth and the sea" the place is again mentioned; the reading τοῖς κατοικοῦσι τὴν γῆν κτλ.: "Woe to those dwelling on the earth," etc., (A. V.) is textually unsound although it is correct in sense, for these earth dwellers are referred to and that in the sense of 8:13 and 11:10, whose only home is the earth and the sea. This woe is intended for the ungodly. To them the devil "went down" with his "great fury" to lash them, too, into fury against the church on earth. He went down because "thrown was he to the earth" (v. 9). After his defeat this was all there was left for him to do, namely to persecute the church on earth (v. 13, etc.). What made it worse for the devil is that he had but a short period for this persecution, for the final judgment impends. In 8:13 and here the interjection οὐαί is followed by the accusative as the direct object of this "woe" (R. 1193); usually the dative of the indirect object is used.

13) The vision continues with historical tenses. **And when the dragon saw that he was thrown to the earth he pursued the woman who gave birth to the male. And there were given to the woman the two wings of the eagle, the great, so that she flew to the wilderness to her place, where she is nourished there for a season and seasons and half of a season away from the face of the serpent. And the serpent threw out of his mouth after the woman water as a river in order to cause her to be carried away by**

the river. And the earth helped the woman, and the earth opened its mouth and drank down the river which the dragon threw out of his mouth. And wroth was the dragon at the woman and went away to do battle with the remaining ones of her seed, those keeping the commandments of God and having the testimony of Jesus.

Verse 6 has already told us that the woman fled into the wilderness where God had prepared a place for her, where she was nourished for 1,260 days. We now learn more about this feature. When the dragon saw that he was thrown to the earth (significantly repeated from v. 9), was utterly defeated, and debarred from accusing the believers before God, he did the only thing left to him, he pursued the woman, not, indeed, just for her sake, but, as ἥτις (qualitative and causal) indicates, because she was the one who gave birth to the male (the neuter ἄρσεν occurred in v. 5 to designate the newly born male, now the masculine τὸν ἄρσενα is used because this male was taken to the throne). The monster pursued the church in order to destroy her.

14) We now learn that she escaped from him by means of flight. There were given her "the two wings of the eagle, the great," by which she flew to her place in the desert. The articles are generic: "*the two* wings," etc. The imagery of the eagle's wings is taken from Exod. 19:4 and Isa. 40:13, where God is mentioned as carrying Israel to safety on eagle's wings, and has nothing to do with 8:13. Ἵνα is consecutive even as the woman did fly to safety. Already in v. 6 we are told that she did not fly into the wilderness in general, where she would be lost and starve to death, but to a place in the wilderness that had been prepared as a refuge for her by God, where she could be properly nourished day by day. So John now writes that she flew on eagle's wings "to the wilderness to her place," where also she continues to be nourished there (ἐκεῖ

is pleonastic as it is twice in v. 6) in safety, "away from the face of the serpent."

This is transparent language. Here on earth the *Una Sancta* does not sit on an earthly throne. Her glory is spiritual (v. 1). She is a little flock. Here and there providential powers have fitted a place of refuge for her in the wilderness or in lowly places of the world. There God supplies her with the manna of the Word, the Bread of life, as he once nourished Israel in the desert for so many years. The *Una Sancta* is thus hidden "away from the face of the serpent." She is the church invisible, and is not to be confused with visible church organizations, so many of which aim at world prominence and world dominion and hold "world conventions" for the purpose of world movements. The serpent is not at all disturbed by these.

In v. 6 we have discussed the period of the woman's stay in her wilderness refuge, "1,260 days." By calling them "days" they are spread out. Now this period is called, "a period and periods and half a period," meaning one plus two plus one half, thus three and one half, the broken seven. On what we are able to say about the 1,260 days, the forty-two months, and the three and one-half periods see 11:2. We regard them as referring to the same extent of time, all three reaching to a point near the end. Whatever may be said of the use of three and one-half in Dan. 7:25; 12:7, in Revelation the halved seven = the time of God's protection of his church from the time of Christ's enthronement (v. 5) until the judgment. The half of the sacred seven may mean that the Old Testament Era is the first half, the New Testament Era the second half. The three and one-half may also indicate a graciously shortened time. The word καιρός may also be used because the three and one-half of them may denote that each is a "season" that is marked in some providential way.

The main consideration is that all three numbers (42 — 1,260 — 3½) be referred to the New Testament time.

15, 16) The dragon tried to destroy the woman by spewing out a great river of water in order to engulf and to drown her. But the earth drank up this river of water. The woman rose on mighty wings, reached her place in the wilderness, and was nourished in safety for the three and one-half periods. This river is not some war or other, some barbarian invasion, or the antichrist, or just the devil's hate and general persecution. As far as the imagery is concerned, we may think of Ps. 32:6: "Surely, in the floods of great waters they shall not come nigh unto him." Perhaps also of Ps. 74:15, although this refers to the crossing of the Red Sea and of the Jordan.

We note that στόμα, "mouth," is made prominent by being mentioned three times. Twice it is said that the dragon threw the river "out of his *mouth,*" and then that the earth *opened its mouth* and thus drank down this river and thereby *helped* the woman. It will not do to think only of what comes out of the devil's mouth; we must think also of what the earth eagerly drinks down with its mouth. Some think of a flood of heresies. The trouble with this view is the fact that heresies arise *in* the church, and the earth or men generally do not open their mouth to drink down such heresies and thereby to help the church.

We think of *all manner of delusions.* The devil throws them "out of his mouth." They are "waters as a river" that are intended to engulf the church or *Una Sancta.* The compound ποταμοφόρητον (M.-M. 530, a word that is found already 110 B. C. and again 262 A. D.), means "carried away by a river," inundated and thus washed away. These religious, philosophical, scientific, political, economic, educational, etc., delusions fail to engulf the *Una Sancta.* For the woman flies away on great eagle's pinions; and this river of delusion is so welcome to the earth, to the ungodly mass of men on earth, that the earth opens its mouth and drinks down the whole river, absorbs the waters. The symbolism is compact. The flight of the woman, the river thrown out "behind" her, drunk down by the earth, picture not just one phenomenon that is to be dated in some one historical year but the whole phenomenon, the whole river of delusion with all its waters.

We think of one of these delusions, the pseudo-scientific folly of evolution which is eagerly swallowed especially in America and is taught even to children in kindergarten. It is intended to engulf the *Una Sancta* and to sweep it away from the Word, but it fails. This may serve as a sample.

In chapters 8 and 9 we see delusions that are sent as a curse by God upon those who love the lie. Here the other side appears, delusion that is poured out of the devil's mouth, is drunk down by the earth's mouth. In chapters 8 and 9 the course of delusion is pictured in degrees; here "water as a river" is summary. Here, too, the escape of the *Una Sancta* is symbolized; in the six trumpets only the terrible effects produced on the world itself are pictured.

17) No wonder that "wroth was the dragon" because of his failure to flood the woman out of existence. He failed in the case of the child (v. 5), he failed again in the case of the woman. He was pitifully reduced "and went away to do battle with the remaining ones of her seed," the apposition with the characterizing timeless present participles describing them: with "those keeping the commandments of God and having the testimony of Jesus." Now he is again called "the dragon" because now, as in v. 7, the imagery is that of "doing battle" (the same expression that occurred in 11:7). In v. 15 "the serpent" is inserted which points to the cunning and the deceit of the river

of delusion. To do battle with "the remaining ones of the woman's seed" is intended to sound incongruous as though it took no less than a great battle to destroy these few. There is no need to tell about the outcome of this last disproportionate effort; it, too, proves to be a failure.

The reading, "of the woman and of some of her seed," should not be regarded as so difficult. The Old Testament speaks in the same way: Zion and the Daughter of Zion are terms for the church as such and for her children as being some of the members of the church. Satan's first great effort was directed toward drowning the whole *Una Sancta;* failing in this, he assails some of the members of the church. See Isa. 54:1-3, the barren woman who is to have many children, her "seed." The church is certainly every believer's mother. She precedes us and brings us forth as her "seed."

Οἱ λοιποί are the true believers to whom Satan brings the battle; against the church as such the gates of hell cannot prevail (Matt. 16:18). In this battle these believers have a difficult time; but the apposition shows that they hold out. For they are called "the ones keeping the commandments of God and having the testimony of Jesus." On keeping the commandments see John 14:15, 21, 23; 15:10; I John 2, 3, 4; and note Rev. 14:2. One keeps what is valuable and to be treasured which he will let no one take away, damage, or violate. These are not the commandments of Moses over against the gospel. Jesus calls them "my commandments" and "my words." They are the gospel commandments, chief of which is the call to believe and to confess; with this goes the call to follow him, to love, to live in true obedience. John's First Epistle develops this keeping of God's commandments.

"Having the testimony of Jesus" means all the testimony Jesus (this is his earthly name) bore while he was here on earth, the entire gospel. In I Cor. 2:1, it is called "the testimony of God"; compare I John 5:9-11. Then review Rev. 1:9; 6:9; 20:4. "Having" this testimony of Jesus (subjective genitive) means having it in the heart by faith. Because of this keeping and this having the dragon fights these believers. Mere outward members of visible church organizations do not count; this vision is not concerned with them. The faithful, persevering believers here and there, now and again suffer Satan's attacks but are armed and stand against them as victors (Eph. 6:11-17).

CHAPTER XIII

The Two Beasts, chapter 13

1) Note the remarks introducing chapter 12. In chapter 12 the vision shows the efforts of Satan to destroy Jesus while he was on earth and then to destroy his church, with both efforts failing. In chapter 13 Satan's efforts against the church are revealed anew in far greater detail. Chapter 13 is an elaboration of 12:13-17, of Satan's efforts to destroy the church. Satan, the dragon, employs two wild beasts which symbolize *the whole antichristian power* with its terrible sway and spread over the world of men, full of blasphemy, battling against the saints. In chapter 12 *Satan* alone is revealed; in chapter 13 also *his great agencies* which act like wild beasts. This marks the progress in the contents of the revelation. Chapter 13 covers the same ground as 12:13-17, but it brings much new light.

We cannot agree with the futurists who project all that is here revealed into the distant future and think that it will occur just before the end. The two wild beasts are operating now, have operated for a long time, ever since Christ's exaltation. Their *whole* operation with all that is yet to come is compressed in the symbolism. How far their frightful work has already progressed we, of course, do not know; Acts 1:7 still applies. As far as the compression is concerned, this is quite ordinary. Prophecy continually does this. Take the case of the Baptist. In Matt. 3:11, 12 he combines Pentecost and the final judgment. Since chapter 13 unfolds more of what lies in 12:13-17, and since chapter 12 does not introduce the end, chapter 13 likewise does not do so. We again reach the end in 14:14-29. Thus we may say that 13:1 to 14:13; yes, 12:1 to 14:13, belong together.

We think that those interpreters hold too narrow a view who see in the second wild beast (v. 11, etc.) no more than the papal antichrist of II Thess. 2. In 12:13-17 Satan's entire enmity against the New Testament *Una Sancta* is portrayed. Correspondingly, chapter 13 portrays the whole antichristian power which is marshalled against the *Una Sancta* by the dragon Satan. The second wild beast includes the papacy (II Thess. 2) but does not portray it separately as the papacy but combined with all forces of a similar nature in the whole world. In chapter 13 Satan marshals *the world* under his banner.

We disagree with those who find only a small part of ancient European history in chapter 13, certain Roman emperors who are indicated by the wild beast's ten horns or his seven heads, in particular the monster Caligula with his reign of three years, ten months, and seven days, or Nero and the legend of his return. Some write about this *world* vision as though it referred only to a bit of ancient Roman history. But these are *worldwide visions,* and not glimpses of past or future events in Europe alone.

The First Beast, 13:1-10

And he stood on the sand of the sea, ἐστάθη the dragon, not ἐστάθην, "I stood." The latter reading is inferior textually. For some reason the R. V. attaches this sentence to the last paragraph of chapter 12. Where John "stood" or whether he "stood" at all is wholly immaterial; where the dragon stood is material, for the two beasts that now appear in the vision are his great agents for operating in the world. Since one of his beasts comes up out of the sea and the other out of the earth, the dragon stood where sea and the earth meet. Hence also "the sand" is not a special symbol.

And I saw out of the sea a wild beast coming up, having ten horns and seven heads, and on his horns ten diadems, and on his heads names of blasphemy. "Out of the sea" is put forward for the sake of emphasis, not so "out of the earth" in v. 11. Some conclude that "the waters" mentioned in 17:15 interpret "the sea," so that it here means "peoples and multitudes and nations and tongues"; but they find no corresponding explanation for the other beast's coming up "out of the earth" save to say that the sea symbolizes "the confused disorder of the nations" and the earth "the ordered institutions of the nations." Those who think of the sea as surrounding the earth or the land come nearer to the truth. "The sea" and "the earth" are expressions that are equivalent to the whole world. The terms are so used in previous visions. The dragon thus stood where sea and earth meet. No further symbolism is to be sought in "the sea" and in "the earth." But the two ἐκ are important as denoting *source*.

Both of these wild beasts, as also the term θηρίον, "a brute," indicates, are *from beneath.* Not a thing about them is from above. Both are described as ἀναβαῖνον, "coming up" out of their mundane, low source. Both come up while the dragon, Satan (12:9), is standing on the seashore. These brutes do not arise on their own initiative, they are Satan's powerful agents. We may thus say that they are Satan's products; if it were not for Satan, they would not exist. The power found in these brutes is that of Satan himself. We might combine the dragon and the two brutes into one even as in 12:13-17 the dragon is found in everything; but this further vision differentiates so that we now see the terrible agencies employed by Satan. We accept all the connotations that θηρίον conveys, such as that of a cruel, destructive, frightful, ravenous, etc., monster. There is no reason for omitting cruelty, for instance.

The first brute is described as "having ten horns and seven heads." The horns have ten diadems, and the heads have names of blasphemy. In 12:3, the dragon (Satan) himself has seven heads and ten horns, although his seven heads and not his ten horns are crowned with diadems. One thing is certain, that this brute is described as being thoroughly satanic. The difference between the dragon with his seven heads bearing seven diadems and the brute with ten horns bearing ten diadems centers in the symbolical numbers "seven" and "ten"; for in both passages both numbers are beyond question symbolical. It has been well said that we should not introduce 17:10-18; for this vision has not as yet appeared. Like the dragon, the brute arrogates to himself the sacred "seven," the number of *God's* dealing with men. Dragon and brute have appropriated the "seven" for their *heads* as though all their *plans and designs* for men were holy and sacred as God's are. Yet the dragon's *heads* are crowned with the diadems as though his plans and purposes for men were *royal,* as those of Christ the real King are, and as though he uses his ten horns, the sum of his whole power, for man's true interest. The wild beast carries the diadems on his ten *horns* as though he operates with Christ's *royal* powers, to which powers, therefore, men should bow as to the superior authority.

This distinction is significant. The seven heads of the brute have no diadems because all that the brute executes is the pseudo-royal plan and design of the dragon's heads. The brute has the diadems on his horns, which are symbols of power, with which he dominates as though his deeds were royal. On "diadems" see 12:3. "Seven" is not the number of completeness; this is what "ten" denotes. But the seven heads of the brute bear "names of blasphemies" which reveal what is in these heads, namely, blasphemy against God. How many names are to be found on each head, etc., remains unsaid. The blasphemous name on each head is an arrogant title that is insulting to God.

2) **And the wild beast which I saw was similar to a leopard, and his feet as of a bear, and his mouth as a lion's mouth; and the dragon gave to him his power and his throne and great authority.** We may understand this as it is written. It presents a monster of indescribable horror who unites in himself so much that is terrifying: the leopard's great body that springs with cunning on his prey, the bear's great feet that embrace and crush, the lion's terrible mouth that roars and terrifies. But it becomes more impressive and illuminating when we turn to Dan. 7 and see that there four great beasts came out of the sea, the first being like a lion, the second like a bear, the third like a leopard, the fourth beyond any likeness to a beast on earth. These appeared successively. They were four terrible world powers to destroy Israel but who were crushed in succession. All that was so frightful about three of Daniel's beasts is combined in this one wild beast of Revelation. Daniel's fourth beast is not mentioned because it is unlike any earthly beast. The order found in Daniel: leopard, bear, lion, is reversed in order to indicate that only a combination is made in order to picture this one beast, that it is not a repetition of Daniel's vision and prophecy.

It is wasted effort to try to draw a picture of this brute. We have noted in connection with previous visions that drawing diagrams or pictures of them is not the purpose for which they were given but that the significance conveyed by the indepictable images is the whole intent. In all of nature there was never a dragon like this (12:3), nor such a brute-beast on land or in the sea.

To this brute "the dragon (Satan) gave his power and his throne and great authority." This does not imply that the dragon now retires and disappears. Quite the contrary, this brute is to use all the satanic power, is to exercise all the rule and dominion of the satanic throne (note what God's "throne" in 4:2 and elsewhere means), is to use "great authority" from Satan for Satan as Satan's fearful agent here on earth. Why Satan himself does not proceed we shall see in connection with 20:1-3.

3) We are told still more. **And one of his heads as having been slain unto death. And the stroke of his death was healed, and the whole earth gaped in wonder behind the wild beast and did obeisance to the dragon because he gave the authority to the wild beast, and they did obeisance to the wild beast, saying, Who** (is) **like to the wild beast? and who is able to do battle with him?** The importance of this feature that the wild beast had one of his heads "slain to death" and that the beast recovered from the death stroke appears from the second reference to this death in v. 14, and from the further reference in 17:8. We note also that ἐσφαγμένην is the same word that is used with reference to the Lamb in v. 8, and twice in 5:6, 12. Whether an actual resemblance of the wild beast to the Lamb in thus "having been slain" is intended, may be debated: both were slain, and yet both lived.

The fact that only "one" of the seven heads of the beast suffered the death stroke must not mislead us. One terrible blow was delivered, that was enough; it struck one of the heads, and that was enough. Thereby the beast himself was slain. This is a vision. The heads and the horns are viewed together. The imagery compresses the totality of the arrogant usurpation of divine power and rule ("seven" heads) and of the completeness of this lordly sway ("ten" horns) into small compass; yet the stroke that smote the one head slew the whole beast. Who delivered that death stroke? When did the beast receive it? This involves the other question, "What is symbolized by this θηρίον?"

Some critical commentators point to Nero (who, by the way, stabbed himself) and to the myth that he would return to Rome because he had *not* killed himself but had secretly fled to the Parthians who would furnish him with an army for retaking Rome and, when this failed to materialize as the years went on, that Nero would come back from the dead. But Nero has never returned and never will. Besides, it can scarcely be supposed that John or the Christians of his day believed this Nero-redivivus myth.

Others seek the fulfillment of this passage and of 17:8, etc., in the pages of history, among emperors, invasions of Rome, or in the papacy. Even to make the wild beast = "the ungodly governmental power of the world" is too narrow because of its "governmental" limitation; for the various antichristian governments are themselves only outgrowths or symptoms among many other symptoms and manifestations of something far deeper that is operating in the world. The wild beast = *the whole antichristian power* set in motion by Satan as the prince of this world. This antichristian power received its death stroke from Christ when he was glorified and enthroned. Christ has the keys of the death and the hades (1:18). Here belong all the passages which speak of Christ's victory, glorification, enthronement and 20:1-3.

The πληγὴ τοῦ θανάτου of the beast "was healed" so that the beast became alive again and continues his devastation. The final judgment did not at once follow upon Christ's enthronement. Satan was thrown to the earth (12:9) and allowed to manifest his antichristian power in the world. This was by divine sufferance. Centuries have passed; during all this time God gathers his saints despite all the antichristian power in the world. These saints conquer because of the blood of the Lamb (12:11). But the world of men ("the whole earth") ἐθαύμασεν ὀπίσω τοῦ θηρίου, "gaped in wonder behind the wild beast," some texts have the passive, "was made to wonder." The world admires the antichristian power and runs after it with admiration.

4) Ἡ γῆ is a collective; hence we now have the plural, "and they did obeisance to the dragon because he gave the authority to the wild beast." By stooping in admiration before the antichristian power men really stoop before the dragon himself whose agent the wild beast is. They are "the children of the devil" (I John 3:10). "Ye are of your father the devil, and the lusts of your father ye will do," John 8:44, in murder and in lies. They admire this father of theirs though, of course, *they* do not call him "the dragon" or "the devil." The fact that by doing obeisance to the wild beast they do obeisance to the dragon is shown by the addition: "and they did obeisance to the wild beast." The ἐξουσία of *both* is the same: "the authority" of the beast is the gift of the dragon. We now also hear the voice of wonder and admiration: "Who is like to the wild beast?" i. e., he is incomparable in his greatness. Hence: "Who is able to do battle with him?" i. e., he is invincible, he has the dragon's "power and throne." In the aorist πολεμῆσαι lies the thought of doing successful battle, of vanquishing the beast in battle. In Revelation the verb and also the noun = battle and not "war."

Indeed, at times even Christians imagine that the antichristian power in the world all about them is really invincible. Certainly, the voices heard in the whole earth triumphantly shout these two questions or their equivalents. Some Christians surrender; whole churches succumb. They keep the Christian name but yield to "the spirit of the age," to the new wisdom of "science," etc. "Great is Diana of the Ephesians!" This sweeps them away.

5) **And there was given to him a mouth to utter constantly great things and blasphemies. And there was given to him authority to operate for forty-two months. And he opened his mouth for blasphemies against God, to blaspheme his Name and his Tabernacle, them that tabernacle in the heaven. And there was given to him to do battle with the saints and to conquer them. And there was given to him authority over every tribe and people and tongue and nation. And they shall do obeisance to him, all those dwelling on the earth,** (each one) **whose name has not been written in the Book of the Life of the Lamb, the one who has been slain from** (the) **world's foundation.** No wonder the whole world runs after the beast, the antichristian world power.

Twice we have had the active ἔδωκε (v. 2 and 4) to express what the dragon "gave" to the beast; now, in marked contrast, we four times have the passive ἐδόθη (v. 5 and 7) to indicate what "was given" to the beast. God is the agent of these passives. The sense is not that of a good gift but of permission: a mouth — authority — to do battle were permitted the beast. These four statements are highly significant because they follow the challenging questions of the adorers of the beast: "Who is like to the beast? and who is able to battle with him?" All this blatant power of the beast, even the extent of time for its exercise, this battling with the saints and lording it over every tribe, etc., are due to God's permission who can at any time call a terrific halt by means of the final judgment. Let the dragon give to this his beast what he pleases, God is supreme over both.

Human logic so often objects to this divine *permissio.* It simmers down to the ultimate question:

"Why did God not annihilate Satan in the first place, stop his hellish work before it began?" One answer is that God knows what he is doing whether we comprehend or not. The arrogance of the human mind which dares to take God to task must ever be crushed as arrogance. That is enough. When reverent minds contemplate God's *permissio* in regard to Satan, antichristianity, and evil in the world, they soon perceive something of the ways of God such as God's triumph in winning so many saints for his Tabernacle in the heaven, in letting evil ripen fully for its judgment, and most of all in understanding to a certain degree that satanism and evil are not something that is simply at once to be crushed by omnipotence but to be brought to judgment as God does this through his Son. What goes beyond this *is* beyond us. The very origin of evil, the fact that a good angel could become Satan, is utter mystery to all human thinking, and, therefore, also God's permissions are a mystery.

"A mouth to keep uttering (durative present infinitive) great things," blatant, arrogant things, is defined by καί: "namely blasphemies" that are directed against God and all that pertains to God. The seven heads of the dragon bear "names of blasphemy." The heads are thus filled with blasphemy; and so is the mouth of the beast as the tool of the dragon. God lets the beast pour out great floods of blasphemy upon men, and the world of men drinks in all these blasphemies. The saints feast on the holy Word of God; the antichristian power fills men's souls with uncounted blasphemies, contradictions of God and of his Word. To think that these blasphemies are only those of certain vicious governments, lie only in the political field, is too limited a view. A thousand avenues pour out arrogant contradictions of God and of his Word.

In harmony with λαλοῦν, the durative infinitive, is the divine permission that the beast operate (constative aorist) "for forty-two months," the whole time until the end. On the "forty-two months" see 11:2. The point to be noted here is this blasphemy over the entire world and for all time until the very end.

6) In exposition and also in emphasis we hear that the beast "opened his mouth for blasphemies against God," πρὸς τὸν Θεόν, as though he were facing and challenging God. It is blasphemy to deny God, to reject the Trinity of God, to think of a "God" like that of the worldlings, to pervert any of God's and Christ's attributes, his justice, his grace in Christ, etc. Who can count all these blasphemies against God alone? It makes no difference whether the language is vicious or mild. So also there is no difference whether it is spoken in parliaments and in courts, in newspapers, in magazines, in books, over the radio, and on the public forum, in universities, in colleges, in homes, and on the street or in the shop.

Significantly the verb is added as an apposition: "to blaspheme (constative aorist) his Name," his ὄνομα, i. e., the revelation by which God makes himself known to men and by which they are to know him. To speak against this Name (revelation, Word) is blasphemy against God. That Name is to be blessedness, salvation, glory and praise for us; to turn it into myth, emptiness, folly for man's destruction is blasphemous, indeed. Καί states that this blaspheming attacks also "his Tabernacle, those tabernacling in the heaven." God's σκηνή or Tabernacle is his ναός or Sanctuary (11:1, 19) and is absolute holiness because it contains the Holy and the Holy of Holies. Yet not a locality is referred to, for the apposition is, "those tabernacling in the heaven," those in whom the holiness and the glory of God have attained their full goal in heaven. What this type of blasphemy is becomes obvious when we think of all that is involved before the saints can enter heaven: "the blood of the Lamb and the Word of their testimony" (12:11), their faith, confession, perseverance, and blessed death. To call all this a delusion and a folly, to tell men to live and to die without it, is certainly the most destructive blasphemy, no matter in what language it is expressed.

7) Thus we are also told that it was given to the beast "to do battle with the saints and to conquer them" (compare 12:17), for the saints here on earth oppose this endless blasphemy. The world hates and fights them (John 15:18, etc.). There is no contradiction when in 12:11 the saints conquer the dragon himself, and now the beast conquers the saints. The saints conquer by a blessed death because of the blood of the Lamb, but the beast conquers the saints here on earth by hurting and suppressing them with his arrogance and his blasphemies.

The next statement makes this clear, for to the beast "was given authority over every tribe and people and tongue and nation," world-wide success while the saints remain a small flock and are overridden in this world and the beast's banners fly high.

8) Because of the beast's authority over the world of men, "they shall do obeisance to him (this verb is construed with the accusative as well as with the dative, v. 4, R. 476), all they that dwell upon the earth," who care to dwell only there. In most willing submission they shall bow to the antichristian world power of the beast, the agency of the dragon. The future tense covers the time until the end. Note the recurrence of the expression "those dwelling on the earth," in 6:10; 8:13; 11:10; 13:14; 17:8. Here it is elucidated by the relative clause which has the distributive singular: "(each one) whose name has not been written in the Book of the Life of the Lamb slain from the foundation of the world," each one who as a person of this kind dwells on the earth. "The Book of the Life" is explained in 3:5; here and in 21:27 the genitive is

added, "of the Lamb." Here we are also once more told that this is the Lamb "having been slain," having shed his expiating blood with permanent effect.

Commentators debate as to whether they should construe, "having been slain from the foundation of the world," leaving together what the text places together, or, "has been written . . . . from the foundation of the world," placing the phrase across all that intervenes. Appeal is made to 17:8 where the phrase does modify "has been written." But when many, like the American Committee of the R. V., settle the matter in this manner, they overlook the fact that 17:8 has only "the Book of the Life" and not also the genitive, "of the Lamb, the one having been slain." Moreover, there is I Pet. 1:19, 20: the precious blood of the Lamb "who verily was foreordained before the foundation of the world"; compare John 17:24. To this add Eph. 1:4: God "elected us in connection with him (ἐν αὐτῷ, in Christ) before the foundation of the world." Stop and think a little. In other words:

9) **If anyone has an ear, let him hear!** The aorist means to hear effectively. How could there be the *Lamb's* Book of Life so that the name of any of the blessed might be written therein "from the foundation of the world," if the Lamb and his having been slain did not extend back before and "from the foundation of the world"? The old exegetes were right: the Lamb has been slain from the world's foundation. In eternity (timelessness), when God had the names of the blessed written into the Lamb's Book, his Son already then constituted that Book, his Son's sacrificial blood the ink for that writing (if we may venture to say so), the efficacy of his Son's death extended backward as also it extends forward from that day on Calvary. See how both γέγραπται and ἐσφαγμένου are perfect tenses, both alike reaching back. There is no more difficulty in understanding the phrase "from the found-

ation of the world" than there is in understanding the Lamb's slaughter which saved all the Old Testament saints. God has certain things done in time, but to God these things are done as completely before time as on the date in time; this slaying of the Lamb is one of them. God is timeless. To draw logical conclusions from our conceptions of time (time itself being a creation of God!) in regard to God who is timeless is to produce serious misunderstanding. As far as 17:8 is concerned, this is an abbreviation of what our passage states more fully as all latter statements may be briefer.

The reason that the names of these earth dwellers were never entered in the Book of Life is stated here: they ever bow in admiration and adoration before the antichristian world power (the beast). How could God, whose foreknowledge saw all from eternity, have their names entered in this blessed Book that is to be read at the last day (20:12)? Their eternal fate is that of the beast and of the dragon.

It is not John's admonition that whoever has an ear should hear. Seven times Jesus himself has already issued this call (2:7, and in each of the seven letters). Here this call is a part of the vision of the beast.

10) So also are the following words. We accept the reading: εἴ τις εἰς αἰχμαλωσίαν, εἰς αἰχμαλωσίαν ὑπάγει. This is a sententious statement as is also the next sentence. The reading has been disturbed by interpretative efforts which offer us only what the copyist thought, and not what John wrote. **If anyone (goes) into captivity, into captivity he goes!** We regard it as improper to insert or to assume a verb in the first clause that is *different* from that of the second clause. Hence we cannot accept the A. V., or the R. V. and its margin, neither of which conveys the sense. Some think that the sense of this statement is the same as that expressed by the next sentence: **If anyone shall kill with the sword, it is necessary that he with the**

sword be killed! This latter is the *jus talionis*, which does not make the former the same.

No: he who goes into captivity = he who shapes his course so that it corresponds with that of all these dwellers on the earth (v. 8), "into captivity he goes." How can he complain? This is the captivity of hell, the same αἰχμαλωσία that is referred to in Eph. 4:8, the only other place in the New Testament where this word is used. Thus to choose captivity and to go into it is this man's own will.

Now comes the *jus talionis*: if he shall kill with (ἐν, in connection with) the sword, with the sword he must be killed (Gen. 9:6; Matt. 26:52). But let us keep to the context. This is said with reference to one of the admirers of the beast who takes the earthly sword to help exterminate the saints ("to conquer the saints"); he must receive God's just retribution, must be killed with his divine sword.

This is not a warning to the saints to let the sword alone when defending themselves against antichristian persecutors. All they need is the ear that hears into what their enemies are going and how these enemies must end. Then the saints will be comforted. Let us note, too, that the word for "captivity" does not refer to an imprisonment of saints but to "war-captivity" for the warriors of the beast.

Therefore the last statement follows which is similar to that found in 14:12: **Here is the endurance and the faith of the saints!** i. e., right here in what has just been said. Ὑπομονή is more than patience, see 1:9 (2:2, 3:19; 3:10), namely the brave "remaining under" affliction which endures without weakening or complaint. This is joined with πίστις, the faith and confidence that relies on God wholly and without question. Endurance is the outcome and the proof of this confidence. Consider again the immensity of the antichristian power here depicted, take an inventory of its great features as they are present all over the world since the days of Christ; then these significant statements of v. 9, 10 will be quite clear.

The Second Beast, 13:11-18

11) **And I saw another wild beast coming up out of the earth. And he had two horns like to a lamb, and he kept speaking as a dragon.** Here, too, θηρίον has every connotation of a brute nature, of ferocity, etc.; thus this "beast" also comes up from below, its origin is mundane. We find no special symbolism in "the earth." The dragon stood on the sand of the sea, where the sea and the earth meet, and thus he has one beast on one side of him, the second on his other side. They are almost like two arms. Perhaps the first beast comes up out of the sea because the sea is conceived as being primary and the earth rises out of the vastness of the sea (II Pet. 3:6). See the note on v. 1.

The imperfect tenses εἶχε and ἐλάλει are descriptive. This wild beast has an innocent, harmless appearance. It has two little horny protuberances on its head and is like a young, playful male lamb that one might love and keep as a pet. It is not at all like the other wild beast which appears as a monstrosity with its many heads and many horns, with its leopard's body, bear's feet, and lion's mouth. But despite its lamblike little horns this second beast kept speaking "as a dragon," as the awful brute which gives Satan his name in chapter 12. "Like to *a* lamb" and "as *a* dragon" state the resemblances in a general though decidedly unmistakable way since we know that Christ is the Lamb of God and that Satan is the dragon out of the abyss of hell.

12) **And all the authority of the first beast he operates before him.** This is "the authority" which the dragon gave to the first beast (v. 2 and 4). It ema-

nates from the dragon, passes to the first beast from him, and thus also to the second. It is the same hellish ἐξουσία throughout. As the first beast is the agent of the dragon, so the second beast is the agent of the first beast. "*All* the authority" makes the second beast the complete agent of the first. The second beast operates the entire power of the first "before him," under his eye. We have the phrase with ἐνώπιον in 1:4 and in 4:5, 6 and there it expresses relation (see on the relations expressed in 4:3-5 by κυκλόθεν — ἐκ — ἐνώπιον, in regard to God's throne); we now have the hellish counterpart in the relation of the second beast to the first.

We must likewise note ποιεῖ, which recurs five times, although in English we cannot retain the same word. The first beast is distinguished by what is given to him (v. 2 and 4, ἔδωκεν; then in v. 5-7 ἐδόθη four times). The second beast is distinguished by his action or working: ποιεῖ, twice in v. 12, twice in v. 13, again in v. 16. He *speaks* as a dragon (ἐλάλει), and behold what he *works or effects* (ποεῖ)!

The first statement is comprehensive: this beast operates all the authority of the other. Now the specifications are stated: **And he affects the earth and those dwelling in it so that they shall do obeisance to the first beast whose death stroke was healed.** Here is the second ποεῖ: this beast's operation affects the earth and those dwelling in it; in regard to these dwellers see the note on v. 8, also v. 7: "every tribe and people and tongue and nation." These are all those whose one interest and one home is the earth. The ἵνα clause expresses result and is here construed with the future indicative (this construction as well as the meaning are frequent in the Koine): the operation of this beast has the constant result that the dwellers on the earth bow before the first beast. In v. 8 we learn only the fact: προσκυνήσουσιν αὐτόν, the earth dwellers "shall do obeisance to him"; now we have the explanation: the second beast ever keeps producing this result, ἵνα προσκυνήσουσιν τὸ θηρίον τὸ πρῶτον, "that they shall do obeisance to the first beast" (note the accusative as in v. 8), admire, adore, glorify this beast.

The relative clause: "whose death stroke was healed" (αὐτοῦ, redundant) does more than to identify; it recalls v. 3, and thereby becomes causal. The earth dwellers of all future times worship the beast because he recovered from his deathblow; the meaning is explained in v. 3.

13) A third ποιεῖ: **And he produces great signs so that even fire he makes come down out of the heaven to the earth before men** (generic article). Jesus says: "There shall rise false Christs and false prophets, and shall show great signs and wonders," Matt. 24:24. One of these signs is here singled out; fire descending before the very eyes of men, just as occurred in I Kings 18:38. The word "sign" means something which indicates something beyond itself; the word always has this ethical meaning. This fire sign differs from that of Elijah, for this fire does not devour anybody but appears only as a grand display, an exhibition of pyrotechnics and nothing more.

Some regard these "signs" as genuine miracles and not as sham displays. We are given the impression that the devil is about as omnipotent as God. This view is generally extended also to witchcraft and charms. Our people are to understand that charms produce supernatural results. Is it any wonder that even Christian people sometimes resort to these dark means? Others reduce this power of the devil and hold that only a certain, perhaps a small, percentage of these works is genuine. When we, therefore, here assert that Satan and his agents are unable to work genuine miracles and that their alleged miracles are nothing but sham, we expect emphatic contradiction. Yet we do not make this assertion hastily but after extensive investigation of the ramified subject of demonism and occultism.

We cannot be content with Matt. 24:24 and our passage; add II Thess. 2:9, Satan's working or operation ἐν πάσῃ δυνάμει καὶ σημείοις καὶ τέρασι ψεύδους, "in all power and signs and prodigies *of lie*," qualitative genitive: in *lying* power and *lying* signs and *lying* prodigies. The devil *imitates* the true miracles; he is unable to do more. His great weapon is *deceit.* More may be said.

14) **And he deceives those dwelling on the earth because of the signs which were given to him to perform before the beast, etc.** The whole performance intends *to deceive,* to lead astray, and that not merely "by means of the signs" (which would be διά with the genitive) but "because of the signs" (διά with the accusative), to support these signs lest men discover that they are faked. Enlightened Christians are not deceived; they see the difference. The genuine miracles of God and of Christ need nothing to support them and to prove their genuineness, while those of the beast require all manner of deceit to support them. For the devil and the beast want men to believe that their fake miracles are genuine. We only aid him when we believe this and on our part also induce people to accept these counterfeits as genuine coin.

It is ill-advised to tell us that God wants *to test* us through genuine satanic miracles. When two genuine gold coins are offered to me, what can I do but accept both as genuine? Does God ever offer a test which itself leaves me helpless? In II Thess. 2:9, the genitive ψεύδους does not imply that Satan's genuine miracles *confirm* the ψεῦδος, "the lie," mentioned in v. 11. The genitive is anarthrous and qualitative and marks Satan's power, signs, and prodigies as being "of lie," as being nothing but a lie; while "*the* lie" in v. 11 (articulated, definite) is the antichrist's doctrine which his dupes are to believe in place of "*the* truth" (also articulated, definite) which God offers in Christ. There is more to be said, but we pass on.

Lange sees in this fire which the beast causes to come down from the heaven to the earth in the sight of men "the fire of the Inquisition stakes"; Mauro, "the terrific papal anathemas which often carry with them the sentence of death by the sword or by flames." These views are due to the idea that the second beast symbolizes the Roman papacy. We need only to note that the fires of the Inquisition were lit by men in order to burn up victims; the fire of this beast comes out of heaven in order to astonish and to deceive dupes but not to burn anyone.

While we dismiss these opinions and think of fire that actually comes out of the skies before the astonished eyes of men, this "sign" does not necessarily consist of vast volumes of falling flames. To judge from the Scriptures, the devil never did much in the way of miracles. Look at what God wrought through Moses in Egypt and then see what a poor exhibition Jannes and Jambres put up in competition, and yet the Pharaoh believed the sorcerers but did not believe God. What did any of the many false prophets in Israel produce during centuries of time? Simon deceived many in Samaria, Elymas not many in Paphos (Acts 8:9-11; 13:8); they were only common charlatans. So we think that the beast will not need to bring down much fire in order to produce his great deception. The way in which this sign of fire is mentioned, it seems to form the climax of the beast's efforts which are reserved for the times near the end. At least, while history reports many antichristian signs and marvels, none have as yet been pyrotechnical exhibitions. It seems significant that the beast shall finally operate with "fire," especially in view of 19:20.

All these signs "were given" to the beast to be performed before the first beast. Here again ἐδόθη occurs, the passive we have met four times in v. 5-7 in the sense that God permits these beasts to have and to do certain things; see the notes on this verb in v. 5. These monsters operate only by divine sufferance without which they could do nothing. These five ἐδόθη are most important for us Christians; they furnish the light we need when we see the power and the operations of these beasts among the dwellers on the earth. These verbs steady us against all deceit. We see that God is ever supreme above the forces of hell here on earth.

We may call it another sign when we find the beast **saying to those dwelling on the earth to make an image for the wild beast who has the stroke of the sword and** (nevertheless) **lived. And it was given to him to give breath to the image of the wild beast so that the image of the wild beast both spoke and caused that as many as did not do obeisance to the image of the wild beast should be killed.** This is a repetition of Dan. 3, of Nebuchadnezzar's golden image which all his people were commanded to worship on pain of death; but this beast's image is given breath (πνεῦμα) and actually speaks.

The relative clause refers back to v. 3; see the interpretation of the death stroke and the recovery. When this fatal blow is now ascribed to "the sword," this feature brings out only the thought that the blow was mortal as when a sword splits a monster's head and kills with one stroke. The clause itself does more than to identify this as being the first beast, the whole antichristian world power that was struck down by Christ by his redemptive victory; it states the reason for having an image made of this beast, for, although it was slain, this beast ἔζησε, recovered, became alive (aorist). Note that it is the second beast's work to glorify the first beast, and the acme of this effort is reached by having this image made for the purpose of universal worship. Yet the lamblike beast does not himself construct this image, he orders his dupes, the earth dwellers (once more this significant designation), to make the image for themselves; they are to worship the work of their own hands as all idolaters do.

15) Once more ἐδόθη, "it was given," to the beast: God let the beast go so far as to give breath to the image so that it spoke and ordered all to be killed who refused it adoration. We prefer the reading ἐδόθη αὐτῷ, masculine, not αὐτῇ, feminine, one of the curious variants that occur in important texts and which no one is able to explain. Although θηρίον is grammatically a neuter, it is throughout regarded as a masculine and is personified. Only because to this beast "was given" was it able "to give" breath to the image it made men construct. Again this reminder must not escape our notice. Four times in succession we read "an image for the wild beast" and "the image of the wild beast" which impresses upon us the hideousness of this thing: human beings worshipping the effigy of a monster brute! The dative, "an image *for* the beast," means for his glory and his honor.

The first ἵνα clause may express result: "so that he both spoke . . . and caused," etc. The second ἵνα introduces an object clause: "he caused that as many be killed," and limits ὅσοι, "as many," by means of the ἐάν clause of expectancy: "if or in case they do not do obeisance." This is the monstrous tyranny of the lamblike beast,— death to all who refuse to surrender conscience and soul.

16) In how refined a manner this tyranny operates is indicated by another ποιεῖ. **And he causes all, the small and the great, and the rich and the beggarly, and the free and the slaves, that they give to them a mark on their right hand or on their forehead, and that one be not able to buy or to sell save the one**

having the mark, the name of the beast or the number of his name. Here is the wisdom! The one having a mind, let him count the number of the beast, for it is a human number. And his number 666.

The construction is: ποιεῖ . . . ἵνα . . . καὶ ἵνα μή, "he causes . . . that they give (δῶσιν with an indefinite subject, referring to the agents of the beast) to them . . . and that one be not able," etc. Ποιεῖ is followed by a number of accusatives: "he causes all, the small," etc.; we regard them as adverbial accusatives: "he causes in regard to all, the small and the great," etc., and αὐτοῖς gathers all of them again. "The small and the great" form a chiasm with the other two pairs in which the prominent persons are placed first.

The sieve is made so fine that the least of men may not slip through. Somebody is there to give to every person a χάραγμα, "a mark" like an engraved character either on the right hand, where everybody can at once see it, or on the forehead, where it is even more prominent. This marking is the devil's counterpart to the sealing of "the slaves of God," the 144,000, in 7:2-17, with the difference that God's slaves are sealed solely on their foreheads. Review this divine sealing, including 9:4. The beast apes God by also marking his dupes, and he wants to have all men marked as his own. We interpret this as we did the divine sealing. Yet note the difference: the former is a seal, the latter only a mark. The one is Christ's name, the other the name of the first beast (of the antichristian world power).

17) Those refusing to bow down before the image of the beast are to be killed (v. 15); one way in which to make sure that none will escape is to prevent them from even buying or selling. Those who are permitted to do so must bear as a mark "the name of the beast or the number of his name." This "or" is not to ex-

press an alternative but is explicative: to have "the name" as the mark means to have "the number of the name." It is the number that identifies.

18) It is a part of the vision when John records: "Here is the wisdom!" i. e., here is the place to apply Christian wisdom. This is also the force and the intention of the command plus the explanation: "The one having a mind, let him count the number of the beast!" i. e., let him use his mind. In the seven letters to the churches the one having ears is told to use them. The matter in regard to this number is not even difficult: "for it is a human number," ἀριθμὸς ἀνθρώπου. Our versions and almost all commentators translate: "for it is the number of *a* man," i. e., of some individual man, of some one human being. This cannot be correct, for John has just said that it is "the number of *the beast*." It is improbable, that here at the very end of the chapter John should inform us that the monster beast that is like a leopard with bear's feet and a lion's mouth, with seven heads and ten horns and diadems, is "a man," "some man" (indefinite, no article); yea, to inform us in regard to so vital a fact by the use of nothing more than a genitive, ἀνθρώπου, and not by a nominative predicate.

This genitive is adjectival; 666 is "a *human* number," and can thus easily be understood by one who has a *mind* and a fair measure of *wisdom* in his mind. In 21:17, we have the same type of a genitive, in fact, two of them: μέτρον ἀνθρώπου, ὅ ἐστιν ἀγγέλου, "a human measure which is (in this case also) angelic"; this is not some individual man's and some individual angel's measure. Why disregard 21:17 when interpreting 13:18? On ψηφισάτω, "let him count," compare the same verb in Luke 14:28.

Here, as in 7:4-8, John writes the number not in words but in Greek letters: χξϛʹ; χʹ = 600, ξʹ = 60, ϛʹ = 6, thus 666. This is the number 6, plus its multiple by 10, namely 60, again plus its multiple by 10 × 10 (intensified completeness), namely 600 — thus 666, three times falling short of the divine 7. In other words, *not* 777, but competing with 777, seeking to obliterate 777, but doing so abortively, its failure being as complete as was its expansion by puffing itself up from 6 to 666.

The wisdom needed is the spiritual sense which every Christian and not merely the erudite scholar should have to see this complete abortiveness, this futile effort to crowd out "7" and the multiples of "7," such as occur in "777," the number of God, Christ, grace, and salvation for men. The dwellers on the earth, those who bow to the beast and delight to wear the number "666" on hand and on forehead, i. e., in the deeds of the hand and in the thoughts of their minds, utterly lack this ordinary Christian wisdom; they glory in their shame (Phil. 3:19), which they wear with this "666," the number of the antichristian world power of which they are the enthusiastic slaves.

Those who are stamped with "666" are marked as being outside of God's and Christ's kingdom, as being the property of the monster beast, as being the slaves of the antichristian power that is symbolized by this monstrosity and is thus revealed as what it really is. The mark they bear, this "666," is that of *complete,* and not merely of partial, opposition to Christ; it marks them as being *at war* with Christ, yet at the same time as being doomed to the completest *defeat.* Although this fatal "6" should add to itself still more multiples of itself by "10" and make itself "666,666," it should not get beyond the abortive, the doomed six and sixes.

In this connection we recall 11:1, 2, where John measures the Sanctuary (the *Una Sancta*) and throws the court, the one outside the Sanctuary, outside and does *not* measure it because it was given to the heathen, and these shall trample the holy city for forty-two months. In 11:1, 2 God's people are marked off from all the ungodly; here, by means of the mark "666," the latter mark themselves off. The view that the distinction between those who are God's and those who are Satan's is veiled in mystery, is a deep secret, is hidden in an enigmatic χάραγμα, about which even the most learned must puzzle in helplessness, is untenable.

We must say more. The first beast which is presented to us as a blasphemous monster = *the whole antichristian power in the whole world and nothing less.* This power appears and works in all departments of human life. Therefore one should not think only of the ecclesiastical field and thus only of heresy, or only of the papacy, and, narrowing the concept still more, only of a final superpope whose actual name or whose title or whose something else shall = "666." These opinions are too restricted. The beast signifies much more. The second beast is the great agent and tool of the first, we may say his prophet (19:20), but a prophet in the widest sense, not merely an ecclesiastical prophet who works among church people but one who works upon *all the dwellers on the earth*; note v. 16 and the repeated ποιεῖ. This beast is "like to a *lamb*" (v. 11). "He deceives those dwelling on the earth." Therefore the first, horrible beast uses this second beast as his agent.

This second beast = *the whole antichristian propaganda in the whole world.* Both beasts are personifications, the one of *the ferocious power,* the other of *the deceptive activity or propaganda.* The latter operates like wolves in sheep's clothing (Matt. 7:15). He uses pulpits, cathedrals, the pope's *cathedra,* but far, far more; he speaks (ἐλάλει) like a dragon and in deceit (πλανᾷ) *through all mediums,* newspapers, magazines, books, schools, colleges, universities, parliaments, politicians, scientists, philosophers, merchants, mechanics, laborers, etc.; all the dwellers on the earth are to be dupes of the antichristian world power.

Hence they are told to make "an image of the beast" "for the beast," to bow before what they thus make as though it were an idol. This is far more than to offer worship to the statues of Roman emperors or to those of Romish saints; for this image is given breath and speaks and demands death for those who do not bow in adoration of it. This image is not formed like the panther with bear's feet and lion's mouth, many horns and heads (v. 1, 2), for then men would see what the beast really is and would flee from it. *Deceit* produces the image and certainly makes it look wonderfully attractive. Men themselves erect it. Where but in their own minds and hearts, where it breathes and speaks and persuades them to let no one live who does not likewise accept and honor this image.

The "image" conveys several thoughts. By means of this image everybody carries the beast in his heart. Christians make no image, they carry God in their hearts by means of his Word, whereby he truly speaks to them and tells them to save and not to kill others. Making and bowing down before an image is the worst idolatry. By bowing down before the antichristian world power all the dwellers on the earth make an idol of it and worship that idol; whoever rejects the true God and the Lamb does nothing less in his heart, no matter what he admits into his heart in place of the true God and the Lamb.

This may help us to understand the mark which is the name of the beast, the number of his name, a human number, as the text says, and thus easily understood, namely "666." To buy and to sell is not to be understood literally any more than the rest of this symbolism. Throughout history the boycott of hatred and opposition has again and again been used against Christians. The true confessors were barred out. Today many positions are closed to the man who is not a Mason, many academic honors are withheld from a known confessor of the Lamb, publication is denied the writings of one whose views do not accord with the number "666."

Thus "666" is not the number of some individual man, some man who will be the final antichrist who is all-powerful politically as well as ecclesiastically, say the final superpope. Nor should it be supposed that "666" is not a symbolical number but a numerical cryptogram that is arrived at by gematria, the scheme which takes the numerical value of the individual letters of a person's name, adds the figures together, and then writes their sum with the letters that form that sum. When the numerical value of all the letters in the beast's name are added together they are supposed to make a total of 666, which sum may be written out in words "six hundred and sixty-six," or, as John writes it, in the letter-numerals χξς', as shown above.

It is surprising to note how many men think that "666" is the product of gematria. Among these is Zahn, *Offenbarung,* in which he devotes fifty pages to the subject, and Ruehle in G. K. 463. Yet nowhere in Scripture, nowhere in Revelation do we meet with another case of gematria. Revelation employs symbolical numbers, but none are formed by gematria. In 7:4-8 we have numerical letters for "144" and for "12," for the "144,000" and the twelve "12,000," but these numbers are beyond question symbolical. A number that is produced by gematria would remain an insoluble conundrum; yet the very title of this book is "Revelation" (1:1)!

Take some name and set down the value of each of its letters, add these, write the sum. A hundred other names may produce the same sum. If we extend the idea to titles and to qualities or attributes we get additional hundreds that would give us this same sum. If, in addition, we are not certain whether the original name or title or titled name is given in Hebrew or in Greek letters, we are at sea worse than ever when we have before us only the sum total in letters, in the present case the sum total 666. Some argue for a Hebrew, others for a Greek name, the letters of which may be added up to make 666. So we get a veritable babel of names when 666 is regarded as a case of gematria.

But no amount of "wisdom" or of "mind" can tell what 666 means if it is the product of gematria. All guessing would be useless. It is the very purpose of gematria to *hide* the name from all who look at the number. Only a few initiates, who have both the name and its gematria numbers, are to know. Ruehle supposes that John was such an initiate and that he initiated a few close friends, and that John and these few knew the name that = 666. Ruehle supposes further that at the time of the end a few more initiates will appear. But John received this Revelation not for a few initiates but for all God's slaves (1:1). This "666" is not to remain a hopeless, enigmatic blank to all Christendom throughout all the centuries, one on which all are to use their wisdom and their mind in vain.

A new solution has been offered, the so-called triangle number. Take as an example the number, 10. It is the triangle number of 4, because 1, 2, 3, 4, when added = 10. Thus we are told that 666 is the triangle number of 36; and, in turn, 36 is the triangle number of 8, and this 8, so embedded in 666, is called the number of the beast, namely on the strength of "an eighth" in Rev. 17:11. But why should the beast be given the number 666 when this means 8? And when you have 8, what is the meaning of 8?

A few texts have "616" in place of "666" (note R. V., margin). This is not faulty transcription but a deliberate alteration that was made very early and against which the strongest protest was at once raised. The alteration was made so that by gematria the number would fit the emperor who is commonly known by his nickname Caligula (= little boot), whose name is Cajus Caesar (Γάϊος Καῖσαρ). When this name is reduced to numbers by gematria it is equal to 616, Gaius or Cajus being the *praenomen,* and Caesar not the title but the *cognomen* or family name. This was the man who made the effort to have his image erected in the Temple at Jerusalem, who reigned only three years, ten months, and one week (March 16, 37, to January 24, 41), which was taken to be the $3\frac{1}{2}$ years mentioned in Rev. 12:14. The idea that led to the selection of Caligula seems to have been that he typified the final personal antichrist in the minds of those who changed 666 into 616.

Little more need be said. In 616 we have a known alteration of the text; we have only another case of gematria; we have the claim that the gematria is solved and that 616 = Cajus Caesar. In other words, when the actual number 666 that was written by John could not be solved by gematria, a number was substituted which could be solved by gematria, and those who regarded this as a case of gematria were satisfied to change 666 to 616.

We have a very simple solution to offer in an effort to clear up this deplorable confusion. The beast = *the whole antichristian world power in the whole world of the New Testament Era* which operates through the second beast, the whole antichristian world propaganda during the New Testament Era. Hence the number of this beast is not a mere 6, not a mere 66, but the full 666, in opposition to 777. By means of common Christian wisdom *every Christian* is to understand the number for his own safety.

CHAPTER XIV

Zion — Babylon — the Sickles, chapter 14

1) Chapter 14 contains three visions that are plainly marked by καὶ εἶδον (v. 1, 6, 14). Those who count the angels and think that each appears in a separate vision have seven visions. The three visions complete the two visions of chapter 12. Despite all the antichristian power (13:1-10) and all the antichristian propaganda and tyranny (13:11-18), behold the Lamb with no less than 144,000 (v. 1-5). The two beasts secure a great following, but "Babylon, the great," as the angel proclaims, "fell, fell" (v. 6-13). All is clear in the light of the final judgment (v. 14-20). Just as the two pictures of the beasts are thrown on the screen, so are these three pictures of Zion, of Babylon, of the Sickles, and these five belong together. In fact, these five are to be considered together with chapter 12 and complete the two σημεῖα or "signs"; then in 15:1, etc., there follows another σημεῖον or "sign."

Observe how plainly the divisions are marked by the very wording: in 12:1, 2, "a great *sign* — and another *sign*," and in 15:1, "a *sign*, great and wonderful." Then in 14:1, 6, 14, three times εἶδον, "I saw." These plain marks should not be overlooked and chronology is not the decisive factor. To be sure, the woman and her son encounter the dragon and begin the New Testament Era; and the fall of Babylon and the thrusting in of the sickles of the final judgment are last and complete the New Testament Era. But that is all as far as chronology is concerned. All the rest lies between these two occurrences.

Mount Zion, 14:1-5

And I saw, and lo, the Lamb standing on Mount Zion, and with him a hundred and forty-four thousand, having his name and the name of his Father written on their foreheads! And I heard a sound out of the heaven as a sound of many waters and as a sound of great thunder; and the sound which I heard as zither players zither-playing on their zithers. And they sing, as it were, a new song before the throne and before the four living ones and the elders; and no one was able to learn the song save the hundred and forty-four thousand, those that have been bought from the earth.

"And I saw, and lo" (εἶδον καὶ ἰδού) emphasizes the greatness of the sight by means of the interjection. Once more the vision reveals "the Lamb standing" (5:6). There is no need again to say that he has been slain, yet we should remember all that is suggested by the designation "the Lamb." In this vision he is standing "on Mount Zion" (Σιών is an accusative apposition, or rather the term ὁ ὄρος Σιών). "Mount Zion" is here the opposite of "Babylon" which is mentioned in v. 8. It is a symbolical term that is derived from Zion, the highest elevation in Jerusalem, and used as a designation for heaven and not for a place on earth. A clear parallel to Mount Zion and those who are on it is Heb. 12:22-24.

In company with the Lamb (μετά) "a hundred and forty-four thousand" stand on this heavenly Mount Zion. Because the article is absent and John does not write "*the* 144,000," some think that these are not the 144,000 mentioned in chapter 7. The article would, however, change the sense: *the* fixed and complete sacred number already mentioned in chapter 7; while the absence of the article makes the number qualitative: so many, "144,000," as make up the complete sacred number with not a single one missing who would make this number incomplete. These are undoubtedly the same persons that were mentioned in chapter 7. Review what has been said in regard to them and their symbolic number in chapter 7; it applies here also. Here, however, so great a number, the complete *Una Sancta,* appears together with the Lamb on Mount Zion, in heaven; so many the Lamb delivered from the two beasts. John is permitted to see them after he has seen the two beasts and all "the dwellers on the earth" who bow before the beasts.

This solves the chronology regarding what John "saw" in v. 6-13, and then in v. 14-20. These divine visions can show the whole *Una Sancta* at any point and in any pertinent connection. Jesus knows all his sheep in all ages, can speak of them as he does in John 10:14-16, and can show them in their complete number. This also answers the question as to whether these 144,000 are Jewish believers or not; whether they are only a select number that is distinguished by a special degree of sanctity; whether this is a vision of the millennium with these 144,000 representing the converted Jewish nation in the millennium.

We see why these 144,000 stand on Mount Zion together with the Lamb: they have the name of the Lamb and the name of his Father permanently written (perfect participle) on their foreheads. Note "their foreheads" as in 7:3: the slaves of our God sealed on their foreheads. These two statements refer to the same thing. To be sealed on the forehead is to have the two names written on the forehead; both statements denote eternal ownership by the Lamb and by his Father. These two names are the seal because no man comes to the Father save by the Son (John 14:6). Thus the 144,000 are the opposite of all, the small and the great, the rich and the beggarly, the free and the slave, who have the mark of the beast on the right hand or on the forehead, which is the human number

666 (13:16-18). These the beast marked as his own, the 144,000 Christ has sealed as his own. Yes, they are so many, 144,000, not one is missing in the vision.

2) In chapter 7 John saw them as both *militant* and *triumphant*; here he sees them as *blessed.* He writes: "I heard a sound out of heaven, as a sound of many waters and as a sound of great thunder; and the sound which I heard, as zither players zither-playing on their zithers." On zither see 5:8 (15:2). Our versions translate "harp" and thus render smoothly: "harpers harping with their harps." Note the repetition of the word. In 15:2 we see that there are "zithers of God."

The φωνή which John heard is not "a voice" but "a sound," and its volume "as of many waters and as of thunder" is no surprise since we know that the 144,000 are in reality so many of all nations and tribes and peoples and tongues that no man could number them (7:9). There is no reason for supposing that this wondrous sound which rang forth "out of the heaven" came, not from the 144,000, but from some other source (from angels or from martyrs in heaven) and reached the 144,000 while these were still appearing on earth. It is a vast sound of heavenly music that came from the *Una Sancta* in heaven which not only filled heaven but reverberated far beyond this, "out of the heaven." To assign a locality to John on the basis of this phrase is unnecessary after he has twice told us that he was "in spirit."

3) The zithers accompany the singing: "And they sing, as it were (ὡς), a new song before the throne and before the four living ones and the elders." This song is new in the sense that no one was ever able to learn (and thus sing) this song save the 144,000. The apposition states the reason that these alone learned this song and why it is called "new," καινή, totally dif-

ferent from all old songs: "they that have been bought from the earth." They alone have had this experience, and only through this experience can one learn to sing the song that voices this experience. We hear the song, ᾠδή, sacred ode, in 15:3, 4. Compare also the new song mentioned in 5:9, etc., which is the prelude to this one. On "bought from the earth" compare I Cor. 6:20 and 7:23, where the same verb, ἀγοράζω, is used; the price is the Lamb's blood. "From the earth" = for heaven, away from "those dwelling on the earth" (13:8, 12, 14), who know no other home. This new song is like the new name (2:17), it is known only to its hearer. The old man with his old nature, all flesh cannot possibly learn the new song which requires the new man who is renewed in knowledge and has a new heart and a new life.

The throne before which the 144,000 sing is the same as the one mentioned in 4:2, and represents the power, rule, and dominion of God, and ἐνώπιον, as in 4:5, expresses relation. The four living ones and the elders are likewise those mentioned in 4:4, 6, and represent the earthly agents of providence as these are used by the throne and the earthly ministers of the Word; see the exposition in chapter 4. We thus understand why in this vision the 144,000 sing "before the throne and before the four living ones and the elders." Their salvation comes from the throne, and in its bestowal God's providence and the ministry of the Word were employed. Note how a second ἐνώπιον separates and yet combines the latter two.

4) In 7:13-17, the 144,000 are described as those who washed their robes in the blood of the Lamb and after affliction have their tears wiped away, a description that is pertinent to that vision. Now they are again described, but not again by an elder (the voice of the Word) since this symbolism need not be repeated, yet with the same two οὗτοι, *"these."* The de-

scription is again pertinent: these are the opposite of all the many followers of the beasts mentioned in chapter 13, even as they are in company with the Lamb and are sealed by his and the Father's name: **These are they who were not defiled with women; for virgins are they. These, the ones following the Lamb wherever he goes. These were bought away from men, first fruits for God and for the Lamb. And in their mouth there was not found** (what is) **lie; blemishless are they.**

We decline to make the 144,000 what they have been ironically called, "unmarried gentlemen" or bachelor gentlemen and unwed ladies. Since when are celibates, prominent among them monks and nuns, living in a superior holy state? Are Heb. 13:4 and the *divine* institution of marriage to be erased? This view regards the 114,000 as the elite, the supersaints of Christendom, whereas they are the entire *Una Sancta.* Nor are they the ones who have kept only from physical fornication, who have observed the Sixth Commandment in this regard or in all regards. Why are other commandments not mentioned, the fact that these did not steal (while other saints did), did not murder (while other saints did)?

This is symbolical language and is exactly like the last statement, "in their mouth there was found no lie," which is not a reference to the Eighth Commandment and to common lying. The main words are ἐμολύνθησαν, "were not defiled," and παρθένοι, "virgins," in the sense of II Cor. 11:2: "I have espoused you to one husband, that I may present you as a *chaste virgin* to Christ," compare 5:25-27, the *Una Sancta* as the pure Bride of Christ which is used by Paul as the model for Christian *marital* love! Note that this virgin condition is placed *first*; it agrees with 7:13, 14, with the white robes, but here the thought is constative (aorist), "were not defiled" and thus are now "virgins." They kept the purity they obtained through the Lamb's blood.

It is fruitless to cite Lev. 15:18 as proof that marital copulation is defiling; this passage presents a Jewish ceremonial regulation. It is equally bootless to cite Matt. 19:12 and I Cor. 7 as ascribing superior sanctity to celebates. That is a view we expect only from Romanists. The view that the 144,000 are the saints of the millennium or of the final tribulation and thus persons who will not think of marriage, disregards the symbolical number and puts a stain on marriage. Some are troubled about μετὰ γυναικῶν and yet answer their own question when they refer παρθένοι to *both* men and women. After the occurrences recorded in Gen. 6:4, physical defilement with pagan women came to be a symbol for defection from God and is such in an eminent way in this last New Testament book.

As virgin pure they are "these, the ones following the Lamb, wherever he goes." Hence we have had in 3:4, "who have not defiled their garments, and they shall walk with me in white." "The sheep follow him, for they know his voice," John 10:4. The substantivized present participle οἱ ἀκολουθοῦντες merely describes by naming a durative quality. Thus it is in place among the aorist finite verbs. All who belong to the *Una Sancta* have this characteristic of being followers of the Lamb in their earthly lives even as Jesus always calls, "Follow me!" As they keep from defilement in virgin purity, so they follow the Lamb. They ask no question, manifest no hesitation, but ever follow "wherever he goes," be the way easy or hard; ὅπου ἄν is indefinite although it is used with the indicative.

This following is not a reward as though the Lamb walks about in heaven and lets these follow him "wherever he goes" in heaven. This view makes the

144,000 a preferred bodyguard, a favored group of supersaints; others have to keep at a distance in heaven, these superelect walk with the Lamb. But following the Lamb is the opposite of following the two beasts.

How the 144,000 were brought to this purity and this association with the Lamb is plainly stated: "These were bought away from men (generic article), a first fruits for God and for the Lamb." In v. 3 we have, "those having been bought away from the earth"; now it is emphasized, "were bought away from men." All others are merely ἄνθρωποι who dwell on the earth (13:8, 12, 14), who want no other home; the 144,000 are purchased at a great price (I Cor. 6:20; 7:23) away from men, to be separate and to belong to God and to the Lamb. Ἀπαρχή is an apposition in the sense of "were bought as first fruits" (the English uses the plural). See James 1:18. The genitive to be supplied with ἀπαρχή is not τῶν ἠγορασμένων, "first fruits of those that haye been bought," for by this nominative apposition all who were bought are attached to the subject and are called "first fruits." The genitive is: "first fruits *of men.*"

The figure is that of the first fruits of the harvest which were holy to God. Those who are only "men," from whom the 144,000 were bought away, are the common harvest. So also we shall see a double reaping in v. 14-20, one of the godly, another of the ungodly. The view which makes the 144,000 the "first fruits" of all believers instead of all men is unacceptable; yet it is the view of some: "As a firstling's choice the 144,000 appear, both because of their special holiness (as virgins) and because of their special salvation (*they* alone walk in heaven with the Lamb)." There is neither such special holiness nor such special salvation; and thus no such firstlings. The passive verb permits the buyer to remain unexpressed.

5) The word ψεῦδος, "lie" (no article, qualitative), does not refer to common untruthfulness, just as παρθένοι refers to far more than common chastity. This is "lie" in the sense of I John 1:6-10; 2:22; 4:20, in the sense of the beast's deceit (13:14, "he deceives those dwelling on the earth"), "lie" that denies the Lamb. Not the least lie of this kind was found in the 144,000. Hence they are "blemishless" (Eph. 5:27).

Lange says well regarding Luthardt's view: "A reference to the *Israelitish* Church at the end belongs to a Judaizing chiliasm." Yet to say (Lange and others) that this vision has no reference to chapter 13 is unwarranted. Despite all the blasphemies of the first beast and all the deceits and the tyrannies of the second beast the Lamb has his 144,000, his great, complete, blessed *Una Sancta*.

Babylon, 14:6-13

6) This vision extends from the first εἶδον in v. 6 to the next in v. 14. We do not divide it into three visions, because all that the three angels proclaim belongs together. First, we see that, despite the dragon and the two wild beasts (chapters 12 and 13), there is the blessed *Una Sancta* on Mount Zion, singing her new song, separate and holy, in company with the Lamb (v. 1-5). In the second place, we see three angel messengers and hear their great announcement which causes the separation between Mount Zion and Babylon. This is nothing less than the gospel which is here presented as sealing the doom of Babylon and of all who do obeisance to the beast. Properly, we may say even logically, this second vision follows.

And I saw another angel flying in midheaven, having an eternal gospel to proclaim as gospel

upon those sitting on the earth and upon every nation and tribe and tongue and people, saying with a great voice: Fear God and give to him glory because there did come the hour of his judging and do obeisance to the One who made the heaven and the earth and the sea and fountains of waters!

When we translate ἄγγελος "angel" we are liable to think too much of a bodiless spirit (πνεῦμα) and too little of what the Greek ear hears in the word, namely "messenger." Yet here, as well as in the next two paragraphs, a messenger appears and delivers a great message. Each is a heavenly being, each proclaims a message directly from God. Some are puzzled about ἄλλον ἄγγελον; why he is called "another angel" when no angel is mentioned in v. 1-5 or in the two preceding chapters. Some think that angels and not the 144,000 sing the new song (v. 3), and that ἄλλον refers to these, which, however, is untenable; some go back to 10:1, where the last mention of an angel occurs. It has been proposed to cancel the word "other," which a few codices do. This first angel is called "another" in distinction from the next two: ἄλλος δεύτερος — ἄλλος τρίτος, "another, a second" — "another, a third." Each is "another" in this group of three.

The present participles "flying" and "having" are merely descriptive as is λέγων (v. 7). The beast and his antichristian deceit, propaganda, and tyranny come up "out of the earth" (13:11); this angel and the gospel appear "flying in midheaven." He and his message are from above, from heaven and from God. Neither the dragon nor the dragon's two heads can reach him "in midheaven" and stop his gospeling. All the antichristian power and its blasphemies (first beast, 13:1-10) and the antichristian deceitful, tyrannous propaganda among the dwellers on the earth (second beast, 13:11-18) are unable to reach this divine messenger "in midheaven" and to smother his "great voice."

He flies in midheaven so that he actually proclaims his gospel (εὐαγγελίσαι, effective aorist) "upon those sitting on the earth and (καί expository: namely) upon every nation," etc. "Sitting on the earth" is used in contrast to "flying in midheaven." "Those dwelling on the earth" (13:8, 12, 14) would not be proper, for this expression is always used in an evil sense to designate those who love only the earth and thus bow to the beasts. The gospel is for all men. "This gospel of the kingdom shall be preached in all the world for a witness to all nations" (Matt. 24:14) despite all that the devil can do.

The angel has an εὐαγγέλιον αἰώνιον εὐαγγελίσαι; the noun and the infinitive repeat and thus emphasize the gospel and the idea of good news. We need not ask what this gospel is, for its content is stated in v. 7. The older Protestants regarded this first angel flying in midheaven as a prophecy of Luther and his gospel, and to this day Rev. 14:6, 7 is the regular pericope for Reformation Day. Sometimes it was thought that Luther was prefigured by the third angel. The other two were thought to be Wycliff and Huss. When commentators reject this interpretation they do so without sufficient reason. The text for Reformation Day is well chosen, for the fathers of Reformation days selected it not because they identified the first angel *wholly* with Luther. The Reformer, too, preached only the old apostolic gospel. The angel with the eternal gospel is the messenger from heaven for the *whole* New Testament Era and thus most certainly includes a man like Luther who once more made the eternal gospel ring out in all its saving power and purity in the whole wide world despite all the devil's effort to hush his voice. Use the text as the fathers intended it to be used, and all is well. If any made the angel apply *only* to the Reformer, their only fault lay in the narrowness of their interpretation.

The appearance of the three angels cannot be restricted to the end with a reference to Matt. 24:31, and the opinion that this angel "has nothing to do with the preaching of the gospel during this present time." Even in 13:7 we see the saints, and in 13:17 those who do not accept the mark of the beast; these are the 144,000, who during the whole New Testament Era are the *Una Sancta* of the Lamb. They are the ones who accept the eternal gospel; without it they could not be "saints" (13:7) and belong to the sacred number of the blessed.

This is an "eternal" gospel, ever the same, from eternity to eternity, unchanging, not another or a different gospel though an angel from heaven preached it (Gal. 1:8, 9). The gospel is ever committed to the church to be preached to every nation, tribe, tongue, people (note the similar extent in 13:7, and elsewhere in Revelation, as in 10:11) by *human* preachers who are symbolized by the twenty-four elders (4:4) and by the two witnesses (11:3) and include John himself (10:11). The symbolism of these three angel messengers is not a contradiction; for as symbolism it conveys the idea that the threefold message comes from God.

7) The "great voice" is one that reaches "every nation," etc. As in prophecy (that of the Old Testament plus that of the Baptist), so in this angel vision the whole New Testament Era is compressed and the flying angel's great voice with his mighty call at once reaches every nation. The great gospel command is: "Fear God and give to him glory, because there did come (English idiom: has come) the hour of his judging, and do obeisance to the One who made the heaven," etc. In the first place, this is the eternal gospel as *the direct opposite* of the propaganda of the

second beast which makes "those dwelling on the earth" bow down before the image of the first beast. It is practically the word Jesus quotes from Deut. 6:13; 10:20 against Satan in Matt. 4:10: "Thou shalt do obeisance to the Lord thy God (*προσκυνέω*, the same verb that is found here), and him only shalt thou serve!"

In the second place, *ὥρα*, "the hour of his judging," is not to be understood in the narrow sense of the last day, for then the aorist *ἦλθεν* would be out of place. In Matt. 24:36, "the hour" is wider than "the day." Here it is still wider, for the hour of God's judging "came," actually came with the enthronement of the woman's son (12:5), with the exaltation of the incarnate Christ. Ever since that enthronement "the hour of *κρίσις* arrived," the hour of judging, (the word expressing an action). This is the sense of John 16:11: "The ruler of this world *κέκριται*, has been judged"; also of John 3:18, 19; "The one not believing has already been judged." Zahn is right when at one place he says that the judgment upon Jerusalem and that of the last day must, in the view of Scripture, be taken together and regarded as a unit. It is perfectly correct and even literally true: "the hour of his judging did come." Redemption is completed, judging is the work that is left to be done. It has begun, it is now in progress, it will reach its completion at the last day.

This "hour" is not only the last day. We are to think of the whole era of the enthronement that shall culminate when we shall see Christ on the great white throne at the last day. Therefore the call is now and ever continues to be, to fear God and give him glory and to do obeisance to him (effective, peremptory aorist), i. e., not to do obeisance to the beast and his image (13:8, 12, 14, where the same verb, *προσκυνέω*, occurs). This is the gospel call to every nation, tribe, tongue, people. This is the fear of holy reverence. To give glory to God is to acknowledge his δόξα, the sum of his divine attributes, including especially his love, his grace, his mercy in Christ, the Lamb. Only Unitarians (Arians, Mohammedans, Jews, modernists) leave out the incarnate Son and thereby insult the chief glory of God and render the obeisance of unbelief to the beast.

There is a reason for here calling God whom all men should worship "the One who made the heaven and the earth and the sea and the fountains of waters." It is the same reason that obtained for similarly describing God to the Athenians in Acts 17:24-31, where also his judging is mentioned; for describing him as the Creator to the Lystrians in Acts 14:15-17. To whom does the κρίσις belong save to the Creator who made all things and all men? This is doubly true, since he revealed the glory which all men should acknowledge in his Son, the Lamb, and his "judging" will be based on this. His designation as the Creator is taken from the Old Testament, Neh. 9:6; Ps. 33:5-9, and from Paul's description in Acts. Yet the addition of "springs of waters" to "the sea," namely all the sweet waters of the earth, is a new and an independent feature of this vision and is in line with the many similar features found throughout these visions. In Revelation the Old Testament language is ever only adopted and adapted; there is not a single quotation from the Old Testament.

To fear, glorify, and worship the true God is the one true religion, Matt. 4:10. To proclaim this fear is εὐαγγελίζεσθαι εὐαγγέλιον (v. 6). We decline to follow those who think only of a last and final effort to proclaim the gospel to every nation, tribe, etc.; this proclamation began with the Great Commission of the glorified Lamb. We decline to follow those who limit this "gospel" to a proclamation of the last judgment, leaving as the only gospel in it the fact that in that judgment the saints shall be vindicated over against their persecutors and accusers. We decline to allegorize "the sea" into the *Voelkerwelt,* and "water springs" into springs of salvation, leaving "the heaven" and "the earth" to be understood literally.

8) **And another, a second, angel followed, saying: There fell, there fell Babylon the Great, who from the wine of the passion of her whoring has been making all the nations to drink!** This announcement is made by a second angel and is thus distinct from the gospel call to every nation, tribe, etc. This second angel "followed" the first and thus likewise flew in midheaven; the same is true regarding the third angel (v. 9). "There fell, there fell Babylon the Great!" = 12:2, and employs the language of Isa. 21:9 (compare 51:7-10). We may render the two aorists, "is fallen, is fallen" (A. V.), or, "fallen, fallen is Babylon" (R. V.); the Greek aorist is used to indicate an event that has just happened (R. 843). Here the aorist is prophetic and speaks of a future event as of something that is already irrevocably in the past. The repetition of the verb produces tragic emphasis.

"Babylon" is not the *antichristian power,* for this, we have seen, is symbolized by the first wild beast (13:1-9). The second wild beast, the *antichristian propaganda,* helps the first in making "all the dwellers on the earth" (13:8, 12, 14) do obeisance to this beast and its image. All those who do this constitute Babylon, *the antichristian world city or empire,* which is named "Babylon the Great" after the Old Testament Babylon (called great by Nebuchadnezzar in Dan. 4:30), the great enemy of Israel, Jerusalem, Zion. Much more will be said about Babylon the Great and her fall in chapters 17 and 18. In the present connection only the great *fact* of her fall is stated.

The two beasts built up an *antichristian empire* — but behold Zion and the Lamb with the 144,000 in v. 1-5 — Babylon the Great fallen, fallen! The gospel did go out to every nation, tribe, etc., with its call to do obeisance to the true God (v. 6, 7), but in spite of it the beasts built this hostile Babylon which fell, yea, fell. We shall later hear what becomes of the two beasts themselves (19:20). We thus see why this second angel followed in this vision (v. 1-13). Perhaps we should print:

"Fallen, fallen is Babylon the Great!
She who from the wine of the passion of her whoring has been giving all the nations to drink!"

There is debate and uncertainty regarding the two genitives in the phrase: ἐκ τοῦ οἴνου τοῦ θυμοῦ τῆς πορνείας αὐτῆς. In v. 10; 16:1, and 19; 19:15, θυμός is God's "anger," and thus many conclude that θυμός signifies God's anger also here. But in the other passages "his" and "God's" are added while here the personal genitive is "hers," αὐτῆς. The solution that the construction is mixed is unsatisfactory: "the wine of the anger (*God's*) — the wine of *her* whoring," because there is only one personal genitive, namely "hers," and the two genitive nouns could not have two such opposite personal genitives. Both nouns in the genitive are "hers," even as αὐτῆς is placed last. B.-P. 569 translates, "the wine of her passionate fornication," making τοῦ θυμοῦ a qualitative genitive; yet he offers the mixed construction as a second choice, apparently because of the commentators.

The first meaning of θυμός is "strong feeling or passion" (Liddell and Scott); the derived meaning is "hot anger," and in this sense it is often combined with ὀργή: hot anger flaring up suddenly from the ὀργή of permanent wrath. Here "passion" fits perfectly.

But it is the second genitive τῆς πορνείας that is qualitative (although definite): "the wine of her whoring passion." Hers is not the passion of "whoring" in general (anarthrous) but of "the definite whoring" found only in her.

Ποτίζω is causative, *traenken,* and the perfect tense expresses the long continuance during the past. For a long time Babylon "has made all the nations (13:8, 16) drink" of the intoxicating wine of her whoring passion (17:2-5; 18:3, 9; 19:2). We render πορνεία "whoring" because of 17:1-5, which see.

What is meant by this heady wine of her passion (which is the passion that is marked by her whoring) chapter 13 had already shown. It is the worship of the blasphemous beast. The term "fornication" brings to mind all the Old Testament imagery which considers Israel's unfaithfulness to God adultery and fornication (a sample description is given in Isa. 57:3-12), imagery that continues into the New Testament and is thus also found in these visions; here it is only touched upon.

The preterists regard Babylon as a reference to pagan Rome alone; the historical interpreters as a reference to papal Rome; the futurists as a reference to the capital of the antichrist who is yet to come, either Rome or Jerusalem. Babylon, as the previous line of visions plainly shows, *is the entire antichristian* empire throughout the whole New Testament Era. Both pagan and also papal Rome would then be included.

9) **And another angel, a third, followed them, saying with a great voice: If anyone does obeisance to the beast and his image and receives a mark on his forehead or on his hand, he also shall drink from the wine of the anger of God, served unmixed in the cup of his wrath; and he shall be tormented in fire and brimstone before holy angels and before**

the Lamb. And the smoke of their torment goes up for the eons of the eons. And they have no respite by day or by night, those doing obeisance to the beast and to his image, and if anyone receives the mark of his name.

This is an exposition of Mark 16:16: "He that believeth not shall be damned." This is the negative side of the eternal gospel (v. 6). It is worded to match chapter 13 and is made a separate proclamation in order to bring out most plainly the truth that all who bow before the antichristian power do so, and can do so, only after having been fully and completely warned regarding the consequences.

This third angel "followed" the other two in the vision, which we take to mean that he, too, flew in midheaven and made all men hear. When it is asked why only the first and the third angel speak "with a great voice," the answer is not that the message of the second is intended only for the saints, and thus no great voice is needed. All three angels fly in midheaven, and the prophetic message about Babylon's fall is intended just as much for all men as the other two messages. Because the gospel call (v. 7) and the gospel warning re-enforcing this call (v. 9-11) are supreme, therefore these two are here proclaimed "with a great voice." The fact that Babylon should fall is self-evident.

"Do *you* fear God and do obeisance" to the Creator is put in the second person plural, in direct personal address, because men are jointly to do this and to be saved. The warning is given in the third person singular through the indefinite conditional clause, "if *anyone* does obeisance," etc. It is objective, individual, intended for any and everyone, whoever he may be. To do obeisance to the beast and his image is the directly opposite of doing obeisance to the Creator (v. 7) and reverts to 13:8, 15. The addition, "and receives a mark on his forehead or on his hand," adds the direct reference to 13:16-18, including the number 666 — see the exposition of this passage. On the construction of ἐπί, once with the genitive, and again with the accusative (reversed in 13:16) note R. 565; προσκυνέω, too, may be construed with either the dative or the accusative.

10) Καὶ αὐτός, "he also," means that anyone who worships the beast and receives his mark, who accepts *the cause,* thereby "also" accepts the *result,* the consequences. How can it be otherwise? Choose the beast, the antichristian power, and reject God and the Lamb, and you thereby "also" choose what the beast brings and alone can bring you, the cup of God's wrath, the torment of fire and brimstone. Look well at this καί. Men may shout ever so loudly that they do *not* choose these consequences, yea, that there is *no* such wrath, *no* hell of fire and brimstone, and they may laugh at the very idea, yet where do men ever see a cause that is without its result? The one inevitably produces the other.

The future of πίνω is πίομαι. To regard the two futures as futuristic (not as volitive) is highly effective; they state the inevitable future facts. Accept the wine of Babylon's fornication, and you shall drink "also," in consequence, "the wine of God's anger" (here θυμός = hot anger). Κεκερασμένου (the perfect participle of κεράννυμι) is here not used in the sense of "having been mixed," since ἀκράτου, "unmixed," follows, but in the sense of "having been (and thus being) *served*" unmixed. The ancients drank their wine mixed with water and spices; this wine of God's wrath is wholly unmixed and is served "in the cup (goblet, chalice) of his wrath," adding ὀργή to θυμός. It shall be unmitigated anger and wrath without one drop of added water (Luke 16:24). The two figures of "the wine" (v. 8 and 10) correspond, and the genitives "of her fornication," "of God's anger," "of his wrath" interpret what is meant.

First, the wrath of God; next, hell: to suffer the unmixed wrath is to be cast into hell: "he shall be tormented in fire and brimstone" (9:17, 18). In the Scriptures fire is regularly associated with hell, a fire that burns the bodiless devils, the souls of the damned (Luke 16:23, etc., see the comment) and finally also their bodies. The addition "brimstone," burning sulphur, brings out still more vividly the torment of hell. We need not speculate about this fire, its nature and its effects. Human expressions are used to represent what is really beyond our present powers of conception. This is also true with regard to heaven. The skepticism which offers the comment that "fire is the divine *cruelty* of the Semitic religions," that Revelation draws on the "grim popular *fancies*," may thus ease itself, but this does not abolish the unspeakable realities. If these are mere Jewish "fancies," then all that the Scriptures reveal about heaven is also nothing but such "fancies." Here the voice of one of God's angels speaks about hell — is he, too, a mere "popular fancy"? Are all the words of Jesus regarding heaven and hell empty fancies?

Especial exception is taken to the two phrases: "before holy angels and before the Lamb." Some texts omit the second phrase, but not enough of them to cause doubt as to the text. The phrase was apparently dropped because the Lamb is here mentioned *after* "holy angels" (qualitative, no article); but we often proceed from the less to the greater, and nobody raises an objection. Skepticism objects: "It is impossible for us to understand how such a sight could be compatible with heavenly happiness, but the psychological basis of the ghastly expectation can be verified in the cruder types of primitive and modern religion. This view evidently supposes that heaven and hell are so located spatially that angels and the Lamb ever have hell before their eyes. In 4:5 ἐνώπιον (like ἐκ and κυκλόθεν) are not spatial; in the other world there is no space (or time). To use such premises as a basis for objections is unwarranted. As far as Luke 16:23 is concerned, see the comment on that passage. The evident sense of ἐνώπιον is that angels (anarthrous, as being such) and the Lamb acquiesce in the perfect justice and the necessity of God's awful judgments; the two ἐνώπιον are juridical.

11) Some say that smoke is the indication of imperfect combustion. Is the brimstone imperfectly burnt or the bodies of the damned? "Smoke," like "fire and brimstone," is a mere human term and conveys what is implied by the conditions obtaining in hell. The smoke of their torment going up "for the eons of the eons" (see 1:6) indicates eternal torment (19:3). Hence the elucidation, "and they have no respite (no pause, ἀνάπαυσις) by day and by night" (genitives of time within). Then they are again designated: "those doing obeisance to the beast and to his image, and if anyone receives the mark of his name," and the "if anyone" of reality is repeated, cf., v. 9. Human language is compelled to use terms of time in an effort to present the timelessness of the other world where there is neither day nor night. Scripture condescends to our poor finite limitations of mind, for if the language of infinity were used, no human mind would understand.

12) **Here is the endurance of the saints, those keeping the commandments of God and the faith of Jesus.** Here, even more than in 13:18, this statement introduced with ὧδε is not an addition that was made by John but a statement that was made to John, which he is to record for his readers. As in 2:2 and elsewhere, ὑπομονή = the brave endurance which holds out under afflictions; it is thus a word that is never

used with reference to God. The thought of what awaits the adorers of the beast will furnish endurance for the saints when the beast conquers them (13:7), when the tyranny of the second beast strikes them (13:17). As "saints" who are set apart wholly for God they will think of the fate of all the worshippers of the beast and will bravely hold out.

The apposition οἱ τηροῦντες in the nominative is not irregular, for thus the apposition is made more deictic, the more so since the antichristians are designated in the same way in v. 11: οἱ προσκυνοῦντες κτλ.; both terms are substantivized, characterizing, present participles. The followers of the beast and the followers of God are direct opposites. The latter keep God's commandments, keep them as treasures, let no one tamper with them, these precious commandments which express his saving will in his Word, both gospel and law. "And the faith of Jesus" is explicative, for this faith and God's commandments are the same, the faith (singular) summarizing, the commandments (plural) spreading out in detail. See the expression in 12:17, "those keeping the commandments of God and having the testimony of Jesus." "The faith" is objective, *fides quae creditur*, and not subjective, *fides qua creditur*. The subjective idea lies in the participle "keeping." They treasure "the faith" in the sense of the doctrine which originates from Jesus. Revelation uses the simple name "Jesus" eleven times and refers to Jesus who lived and taught "the faith" here on earth.

"Babylon" is the whole antichristian empire; but v. 9, etc., speaks of the individuals in this empire. In the same way the *Una Sancta*, the church, and then also her children, the individual Christians, are spoken of. The view that Babylon is only the capital, and that these worshippers of the beast are others who are not in Babylon, does not commend itself.

13) The first εἶδον (v. 1) covers v. 1-5; the second εἶδον covers v. 6-13; then follows the third εἶδον which introduces v. 14-20. Thus v. 13 concludes the vision of v. 6-13. This beatitude is the conclusion of the eternal gospel as it is presented in v. 6, 7, and at the same time the complete opposite of the fate of Babylon and of "everyone" of her children (v. 8-11). Hence it is not a fourth angel who adds this beatitude but only "a voice out of the heaven." The beatitude is thereby kept distinct, yet not too much so; it is left in relation to the foregoing in the way we have indicated. It also follows naturally after the reminder to "the saints" in v. 12. All this, we think, deserves to be noted.

And I heard a voice out of the heaven, saying: Write: Blessed the dead, those dying in the Lord from now on! Yea, the Spirit declares that they rest from their toils; for their works follow with them. There is nothing to indicate whose voice this is as was the case in 10:4; nor are we to inquire. The fact that it speaks "out of the heaven" does not locate John outside of heaven and on the earth; for he receives all these visions "in spirit." In fact, from 4:1, 2 we conclude that whatever he saw or heard, no matter where, was seen and heard by him as from a point in heaven. This voice orders him to write. The order to write is at first general and applies to all the visions (1:11, 19), then specific, applying to each of the seven letters (chapters 2 and 3), then specific with reference to certain very important statements as here, in 19:9, and in 21:5. These orders, "Write!" do not mean, "after all the visions have been completed"; for in 10:4 John says, ἔμελλον γράφειν, "I was about to be writing," i. e., right then and there, but he was told *not* to write that portion (see 10:4). Here he is to write the whole statement that follows in this verse.

On μακάριοι, "blessed," the divine verdict, see the exposition of 1:3 and Matt. 5:3. Who are those that are here called "blessed"? The same people with reference to whom this divine verdict is pronounced in the other beatitudes where these people are only described in other words; consider 1:3 and Matt. 5:3-12 as samples. Here the blessedness is said to be theirs as being "the dead, those dying in the Lord from now on." We see them as those who have finished their earthly course; they are οἱ νεκροί; but οἱ ἐν Κυρίῳ ἀποθνήσκοντες, "the ones dying in the Lord," ἐν expressing living connection with him, the connection being indicated in v. 12, "the ones keeping the commandments of God and the faith of Jesus." See also I Cor. 15:18. Ἐν Κυρίῳ needs no article and is placed forward for the sake of emphasis. What happens to those dying *without* the Lord v. 10, 11 state; they are accursed, damned. The present participle, ἀποθνήσκοντες, is exactly like προσκυνοῦντες and τηροῦντες in v. 11, 12; all three are timeless and characterizing, and as such are substantivized by the article, are made nouns and placed in apposition.

In what their blessedness consists has been abundantly recorded in 2:7,11, 17, 26; 3:5,12, 21. It is summarized in the "crown" (3:11). These "dead," "the ones dying in the Lord," belong to the 144,000, the great *Una Sancta,* that was pictured in its blessedness in v. 1-5. By dying as true believers of the Lord their blessedness becomes inamissible; at death they receive the crown laid up for them (II Tim. 4:8). The debate carried on among the commentators as to whether to construe ἀπ' ἄρτι with ἀποθνήσκοντες, or with μακάριοι, or with the whole sentence is in our opinion pointless. For certainly "those dying from now on" have their blessedness from that same moment on. Nothing is gained by taking the expression out of its natural place and connecting it with a distant term or with no term at all.

This verse in all its detail has always been understood far better by the preachers, who have often used it as a text for funeral sermons, than by the commentators who create needless confusion through the questions which they introduce. Dying in the Lord from now on and blessed in dying thus refer to the whole period covered in these visions (v. 1-12), the whole period in which the eternal gospel is preached to every nation, tribe, tongue, and people (v. 6), the whole period during which the worshippers of the beast and of his image go into the fire, brimstone, and smoke of hell (v. 9-11), with Babylon already pronounced fallen, fallen. In no way does "the ones dying from now on" exclude the martyrs Stephen, James, Peter, Paul, who died before John received this vision. These visions deal with the New Testament Era, with the Lamb actually slain in fulfillment of the promise, and thus speak of those dying in the New Testament faith; what is to be said in regard to the blessedness of the saints of the Old Testament need not be added, for we easily supply this.

"From now on" does not mean from the beginning of the judgment on, in the far future, shortly before the end. Catholics say that those dying then will not have to stay in purgatory so long; some Protestants only modify this by leaving out purgatory: these blessed dead will not have to wait so long for their release from the *Totenreich,* for their resurrection. But "blessedness" cannot refer to brevity of time. He who dies in the Lord and enters heaven (there is neither a purgatory nor a *Totenreich*) goes from time into timelessness. How "blessedness" at death is described in Revelation we have stated. The ὑπομονή used in v. 12 does not make "from now on" refer to the last tribulation, for this would not be in keeping with the ὑπομονή mentioned in 1:9; 2:2, 3, 19; 13:10. These "dead who die in the Lord" are not only the martyrs; nor are they those who die at the very end of time and are in contrast with only the last followers of the beast. These views contradict this vision and the previous ones, in particular the descriptions of the blessedness of the dying saints at the end of each of the seven letters (chapters 2 and 3). These views, of course, make it impossible to use this text at the funeral of a faithful believer.

Ἀπ' ἄρτι cannot modify λέγει, a translation which our versions offer in the margin. It is the voice from the heaven that quotes what the Spirit says, and not the Spirit who now himself speaks to John. So Jesus himself refers to the Spirit as speaking to the churches (2:7, repeated in all seven letters). Ναί = "yea" and emphasizes the truth that this is, indeed, what the Spirit says, namely that those dying as just stated are blessed in "that they rest from their toils," etc. Ἵνα introduces an object clause as R. 992 states. Some, like our versions, still cling to the idea of purpose, "that they may rest," and thus they suppose that an ellipsis has occurred, which they then try to fill in to accord with the idea of purpose. Some regard ἵνα as being imperatival, an order: "Rest they from their toils!" But why such a command? The indicative after ἵνα is found in the Koine. Rest from labors and hard toil is the negative side of the blessedness of those who die in the Lord. So often the negative side is stressed (7:16, 17; 20:4; Isa. 25:8). On this rest compare 6:11; II Thess. 1:7; Heb. 4:9, 10. The future tense ἀναπαήσονται, from ἀναπαύω, is not inferior Greek (Thayer) but a second passive future (B.-P. 92; B.-D. 78) used as a middle, "rest themselves"; the tense is due solely to ἵνα, hence, "that they rest," not "shall rest," being relieved of all the κόποι, the wearing labor and strain in maintaining their faith and their faithfulness in this life.

Γάρ adds the explanation that their ἔργα or "works," not only such as they accomplished by toil but all of them that they in any manner wrought, follow with them, μετά go along in company with them. All their good works are referred to. The toil is left behind, they are out of it (ἐκ); not so their works, what they have accomplished in this life. These works go along with them as evidence and as testimony of their faith, which the Lord will use as such evidence in the final, public judgment which is described in Matt. 25:34-40: "Ye have done it *unto me!*"

The Two Sickles, 14:14-20

14) This vision is the complement to the preceding two (v. 1-5; 6:13). It reveals the twofold harvest of the final judgment. "But when the fruit is brought forth, immediately he putteth in the sickle, because the harvest is come," Mark 4:29. The godly are harvested first and then the ungodly, as in Matt. 3:12, the wheat, the chaff; Matt. 25:34-46. In Matt. 13:30 the cockle is only separated from the wheat, hence the cockle is mentioned first.

And I saw, and lo, a white cloud, and on the cloud One sitting like a Son of man, having on his head a golden crown and in his hand a sharp sickle. And another angel came out of the Sanctuary, crying in a loud voice to the One sitting on the cloud: Send thy sickle and reap! Because there did come the hour to reap, because dried out is the harvest of the earth. And the One sitting on the cloud threw his sickle on the earth, and reaped was the earth. The godly constitute this harvest.

After ἰδού we have the nominative νεφέλη; then, letting εἶδον govern, we have the accusative καθήμενον just as in 7:9 the accusative περιβεβλημένους κτλ. occurred after the nominative. The use of the nominative ἔχων after the accusative καθήεμνον is only deictic (this is a frequent construction in Revelation). The exceptional construction ὅμοιον υἱόν, this adjective with an accusative, is called a solecism by B.-P. 898 (see the same construction in the variant reading discussed in 1:13), but ὅμοιον is not a governing adjective; "like to a Son" (dative) but a modifying adjective: "Sonlike," so that υἱόν is in apposition with καθήμενον which is properly an accusative, and ὅμοιον is not to be construed with the participle but with "Son."

In view of 1:13 one cannot mistake this person — he is Jesus. John focuses attention upon the "white cloud," for this is used like a heavenly throne. We have found that *white* always symbolizes "holiness" cf., 20:11, "I saw a great *white* throne." Jesus judges in holiness. On υἱὸν ἀνθρώπου see the notes on 1:13. The article *"the* Son of man" is omitted in order to make a direct reference to Dan. 7:13, the source from which Jesus drew the designation he constantly used with reference to himself, on which see Matt. 8:20 or the parallels. In Dan. 7:13, note also the clouds. Here he appears with a golden *stephanos* on his head; the word stephanos is discussed in 2:10. Once his head wore the crown or *stephanos* of thorns, now it bears the crown of glory, of Heb. 2:7, "having crowned him with glory and honor," etc. In his hand is "a sharp sickle," the symbol of reaping. Note that *he* has the sickle in his own hand, for this first harvest is to be his own; an angel has the other sickle, for it cuts what shall be crushed by the great anger of God, the wicked. Both sickles are "sharp," they cut swiftly, completely.

15) If you care to, read "another angel" as you did in v. 6. Zahn cancels ἄλλον in v. 6 but retains the ἄλλος in v. 15 in order to make the One sitting on the cloud an angel, for strange reasons an angel in human form. He then adds that this One must be an angel otherwise he could not be given an order by this angel from the Sanctuary. But very few will be convinced by his argumentation; for at this very place the sig-

nificant term "the One sitting on the cloud" is repeated, and in the entire chapter wherever an angel is thought of he is called an ἄγγελος. "Another angel" is perfectly in order after the three that have already been mentioned in v. 6, 8, 9.

He somes "out of the Sanctuary." This is the place of God's holiness; for the order to proceed with the reaping is sent by God himself and is *in toto* the act of his holiness; see the same symbolism in v. 17, "out of the Sanctuary, the one in the heaven." On ναός see 7:15. The objection that an angel cannot give an order to Christ overlooks the fact that this is an angel from the very Sanctuary itself, the seat of God's holiness, and that to Christ as the Son of man, not indeed in his divine nature but in his human nature, all power and authority *were given* by the Father (Matt. 28:18), "And hath *given* him authority to execute judgment also, because he is the Son of man" (John 5:27), "hath committed all judgment unto the Son" (v. 22), compare Acts 10:42; 17:31. This is what is here symbolized; the angel only transmits the Father's order.

The symbolism includes more. "Send thy sickle and reap!" = Matt. 24:31: "And he shall send his angels . . . and they shall gather together his elect from the four winds, from one end of heaven to the other." These elect are the ἀπαρχή of God and the Lamb (v. 4), see the comment on this term. The reason for this order is: "Because there did come the hour to reap (aorist, reap with finality), because dried out (fully ripe) has become (aorist passive) the harvest of the earth." The θερισμός is the wheat that is to be gathered into the heavenly granary (Matt. 3:12). In v. 7 the ὥρα τῆς κρίσεως has come, which is not the same as the ὥρα θερίσαι; the hour of the judging includes much more, cf., Matt. 26:64, the judgment on Jerusalem and the Jewish nation, see this passage as well as Rev. 14:7.

16) Once more the Judge is called "the One sitting on the cloud." He does not step down and himself swing the sickle; "he threw his sickle on the earth, and reaped was the earth" (two effective aorists), the harvest was gathered with finality in accord with Matt. 24:31. Even human judges have their officers and attendants and only sit on the judgment seat and pronounce verdicts. So this Judge. The symbolism is transparent. It is, indeed, *his* sickle that gathers in the godly, but his angels bring them in from the four corners of the earth.

17) **And another angel came out of the Sanctuary, the one in the heaven, he, too, having a sharp sickle. And another angel came from the altar, the one having authority over the fire. And he called with a great voice to the one having the sickle, the sharp one: Send thy sickle, the sharp one, and gather in the grape clusters of the vine of the earth because its grapes have reached their prime! And the angel threw his sickle into the earth and gathered in the vine of the earth and threw it into the winepress, the great one, of the anger of God. And trodden was the winepress outside of the city, and there came out blood out of the winepress up to the bridles of the horses as far as a thousand six hundred stadia.**

The judgment of damnation is presented separately. It is *not* a parallel to the judgment of salvation but a secondary, inferior act. In the symbolism the two angels alone attend to it. One is another angel out of the Sanctuary in heaven, for this awful judgment is also an act of God's holiness. It is not the same δρέπανον that is used; it is one which only this angel brings. The word means any curved cutting instrument so that we translate "sickle" where grain is to be harvested but ought to translate "vineknife" where grapes are to be harvested. Both instruments are "sharp" for quick, complete work, yet in v. 18 τὸ δρέπανον τὸ ὀξύ twice emphasizes the sharpness of the knife in a marked way by the repetition of the article (R. 776).

18) Still another angel appears, this one from the altar; ἐκ = "from" and not "out of." We think of the angel, the altar, and the fire thrown on the earth mentioned in 8:3-5 (not of the altar mentioned in 6:9). Both angels come out of the Sanctuary and both are thus marked as bearers of God's holy judgment; yet, because the one comes particularly from the altar which symbolizes the prayers of the saints, we may see in his coming and his calling to the other angel to begin the judgment act the answer to the prayers of all the saints who asked God to end the wickedness of the world. His "authority over the fire" (definite: the fire of this altar) recalls 8:5. This is not the fire that symbolizes the fate of the wicked; it is the fire that is burning the incense on the altar and is causing the sweet-smelling smoke of the prayers of the saints to rise to God. We take it that the ἐξουσία over this fire signifies the authority that is given by God to declare when, according to God's will, the judgment is finally to come upon the wicked in answer to the prayers of the saints.

Therefore, like the angel in v. 15, this angel calls out with a great voice to begin also this second act of judgment: "Send the *drepanon!*" In Ps. 1:4 and in Matt. 3:12 the wicked are likened to chaff, in Matt. 3:12 they are to be burned with unquenchable fire. Here they are likened to grape clusters (βότρυες) on the vine of the earth, the berries (σταφυλαί) of which ἤκμασαν, have now reached their prime of ripeness so that they ought to be gathered (τρυγάω). The grain, too, is presented as being ripe, as being fully dried out on the stalk, ἐξηράνθη; both verbs are properly aorists. Both the grain and the grapes are ripe, and thus the two *drepana* are sent to cut them. Thus, we may say, God determines the time of the end. Still this vision is not complete. The symbolism says no more about the grain than that it "was harvested" (ἐθερίσθη), and about the grapes than that they were gathered and the winepress trodden; each vision presents only so much, the remainder is reserved for succeeding visions.

19) Also here the *drepanon* is simply thrown into the earth as though it did the work of cutting by itself and by its own power. But instead of the passive, ἐθερίσθη, used in v. 16 the active is now used, ἐτρύγησε; by throwing his knife into the earth the angel gathered the vine of the earth. It does not seem necessary to think that the whole vine was cut off, root and branch, and thrown into the winepress; in v. 18 the order is given that the clusters be gathered, so we take "he gathered the vine" to mean "he gathered the clusters from the entire vine" by stripping it bare. Likewise "he threw into the winepress" all the clusters of this vine.

In John 15:1, Jesus describes himself as the vine of which the Father is the husbandman. Does that imply that this vine of the earth is the opposite, the antichristian vine whose husbandman is the devil? In John 15 we read that the disciples are the branches that are to bring much fruit; here we hear only about the clusters and the berries, the fruit. But it is scarcely fitting to call the devil the vine; the wicked, its branches; their works, the fruit. Perhaps it is enough to say that the vine with all that is on it = Babylon (comprehensive, a unit), and the clusters and grapes = "anyone" (v. 9, 11: τὶς), see the discussion at the end of v. 12. Whether John 15 comes to mind or not, Isa. 63:1-6 certainly does, at least the awful treading of the winepress. In all such references to the Old Testament these visions use the Old Testament figures or symbols in an independent way.

The appositional genitive shows what the winepress is, namely "the anger of God" (θυμός, as in v. 10; see the note on v. 8). Great, indeed, is this winepress, hence τὴν μεγάλην is added to τὴν ληνόν with a separate article.

Textually more assured is the reading τὸν μέγαν, but this is not an anacoluthon (B.D. 49, 1), nor a solecism, but an apposition that uses the masculine gender of ληνός in order to make the apposition more pronounced. This is not a winepress such as is used today. It is cut out of a solid rock floor somewhat in the design of the figure 8, the one basin being round and receiving the grapes that are to be trodden out with the feet, the other basin being deeper so that the juice flows into it through the neck of the 8, into which a narrow channel is cut. The author saw such a press in the area about the Garden Tomb which is regarded as the place where Jesus was entombed. The Crusaders conducted water into it in order to water their horses. Robinson describes one in which the basin for the must is cut out of rock that is on a level which is two feet lower (Smith, *Bible Dictionary,* IV, 3545).

20) Since this vine spreads over the whole earth, and all its grapes are thrown into the winepress at the same time, the receiving vat is immense, and the treading out which is done at one time produces a torrent. "Trodden was the winepress," the aorist (from πατέω) to express the simple fact, no agent being mentioned with the passive. This was "outside of the city," 22:15 offers sufficient comment. Some commentators name the city: Rome — Babylon — Jerusalem — hell. Well, it is the city of Heb. 11:10; 12:2; Rev. 21:10, etc. We are not to think of any earthly city, for this is the final judgment.

The vision is striking: "and there came out blood out of the winepress," an ocean of blood from the victims of judgment, "up to the bridles of the horses as far as 1,600 stadia." One might think of must as being grape blood, which might serve in ordinary figures; in symbolism such a poetic conception does not apply. "Blood out of the winepress," this winepress which is the anger of God (θυμός, hot anger as it blazes forth in the final judgment), signifies the crushing death that will forever wipe out the wicked. For the devout reader there is no question whatever regarding "blood" flowing from this "winepress." Its depth, "up to the bridles of the horses" (generic articles), so that horses can almost swim in it, mentions horses that are bridled for riders only suggestively, since floods of blood are shed only in the greatest battles, and no earthly battle ever caused blood to flow in such a stream. To think of an actual army with its calvary in connection with this winepress is incongruous as is also a reference to "the battle of Armageddon."

A στάδιον = 600 Greek, 606¾ English, 625 Roman feet; 1,600 stadia = almost 165 of our miles. The "furlong" of our versions is approximately correct, although the distance, "1,600 stadia," is symbolical and uses the stadium as the general measure of distance (so also in 21:16), and the symbolical point of the number is by some regarded as $40 \times 40 \times 10$, with 40 expressing the number of punishment. But 40 is itself 4×10, and is elsewhere used with regard to time, 40 becoming significant since the 40 years in the wilderness. Hence $4 \times 4 \times 100$ seems preferable since distance is here measured, the number of the world multiplied by itself and by 100, i. e., 10×10 as emphasizing completeness.

Whether a stream of blood which is that long, or a lake of blood that spreads so far in all directions from the winepress is referred to, cannot be determined from the wording. The Greek uses ἀπό since he always measures from the far point toward the beholder and not, as we do, from the beholder to the far point; hence in our idiom "as far as." So great is the volume of the blood which symbolizes the judgment of all the wicked of all the earth.

Certain commentators who have difficulty with this chapter advance a documentary hypothesis and find sections that the author of Revelation pasted together. Verses 14-20 are regarded as such a section, which the author found somewhere and inserted at this point. Needless to say, we cannot consider such a view seriously.

We cannot think of a winepress that has been cut into a flat area of rock and produces a flood of blood that rises so far above the rock surface. Then the winepress itself would be engulfed. Symbolism is not a figure of speech but leaves figure and all visualization far behind and conveys its meaning in its own way. The fact that the symbolism of v. 17-20 describes the final judgment at the last day we consider beyond successful denial.

CHAPTER XV

The Seven Bowls, chapters 15 and 16

Seven Angels with Seven Bowls, chapter 15

1) The vision presented in this short chapter is preliminary to the pouring out of the seven bowls of wrath which is depicted in the next chapter. We must have the former in order to understand the latter.

In 14:8, the angel declares that Babylon the Great did fall, did fall. These are prophetic aorists; how she will fall we shall learn later. In 14:9-12 every member of the antichristian empire certainly receives the fullest warning that, if he continues as he is, hell is his fate. This is the warning of *the Word*. With it goes another warning in *deed*. The anger of God is not fully pent up until the last day in order then to burst forth upon the antichristian empire like an erupting volcano; fearful rumblings and explosions precede, these are advance warnings of the final explosion of the last judgment. These latter are symbolized by the seven bowls. They are the last warnings. The damned cannot say that in this life they had no taste of what the holy anger is; they defy and scorn also these warnings of judgment.

And I saw another sign in the heaven, great and wonderful; seven angels having seven plagues, the last, because in them there was brought to a finish the anger of God. This is a summary, advance statement. In 12:1, 3, two "signs" are presented; we now have the third, "another sign." All three are σημεῖα, "signs," that are full of supreme significance for the whole world of men, "signs" to be read in their significance by every one of us. The one is that of the woman and all that is revealed about her, the great

Una Sancta of God, his church. The next is the great fiery dragon and all that is revealed about him, the devil and his two beasts who constitute the antichristian power and its propaganda and raise up Babylon, the whole antichristian empire. Now follows the third sign. The other two do not merely stand in extreme opposition. God smites the antichristian empire with seven fearful πλῆγαι, "blows," we may call them plagues before he utterly crushes this empire in the last judgment. "Great and wonderful," through its greatness producing wonder and astonishment, is this third "sign."

Seven angels are God's ministrants and messengers to pour out these plagues. This is more than symbolical language, for God always employs his angels in this manner (Ps. 113:20). Their number, "seven," however, is symbolical as it is everywhere in Revelation, it refers to God's holy dealing with men, here his fearful punitive dealing by sending these blows, which, therefore, are not literally seven in number. But these are "the last" blows or plagues, the final preliminary judgments. This is emphasized: "because in them there was brought to a finish (to its goal or τέλος) the anger of God," θυμός (14:10, discussed in 14:8). The aorist ἐτελέσθη is prophetic as are the two used in 14:8, which speak of what shall be as already being past and done; in the passive verb form God is the agent who brings to the goal. The goal thus reached is the end or final judgment.

2) Before we are told more about these seven angels (cf., v. 5, etc.) who constitute so great and wonderful a sign, the vision again reveals the *Una Sancta* and connects it with God's translucent providence amid the praise of his holy and righteous works; for all these plagues are nothing less.

And I saw as it were a sea, transparent, having been mixed with fire, and those (coming) **victorious**

from the wild beast and from his image, and from the number of his name standing on this sea, the transparent one, having zithers of God. And they sing the song of Moses, the slave of God, and the song of the Lamb, saying:

Great and wonderful thy works,
Lord God, the Almighty!
Righteous and genuine thy ways,
King of the nations!
Who shall not fear, Lord, and glorify thy name?
Because alone sacred;
Because all the nations shall come and shall do obeisance before thee,
Because thy righteous verdicts were published!

This "sea" is undoubtedly the same one that was mentioned in 4:6, and again it is called ὡς θάλασσα, "as it were a sea." Some think that this is not the same sea because the article of previous reference is absent; but we have the same absence of the article in 14:1 in connection with "144,000," who also have been mentioned before. The article is properly absent because in 4:6 the sea is not described as it is here: "having been mixed with fire," nor does anyone stand on the sea in 4:6 as is the case here. We do not think of two seas and we also dismiss the many strange interpretations which assume that there are two.

This sea or ocean symbolizes the divine providence. See the fuller discussion in 4:6, also in regard to its being "transparent" (not "glassy"). The seven angels and the seven plagues that are now sent as the last belong in the domain of God's providence. Looked at from above, this sea is clear as crystal (4:6), utterly transparent to the very bottom; looked at from below, from earth, human eyes cannot penetrate its mysteries.

The perfect participle states that it has been and thus now is mixed with fire. This detail is not found in 4:6, for there the divine providence as such is referred to, here, the punitive providence, as this is symbolized by the seven angels who pour out the terrible contents of their bowls. We thus understand the further symbolism: the conquerors "standing on the sea, the transparent one" (emphasizing this point). This standing puzzles some, but all the saints of God are standing on God's providence, which is so clear and translucent, as though they were standing on solid ground, their feet being held up as on a rock. Although it is mixed with fire for the followers of the beast — shall we say in order to scorch them? — God's providence is our support and our safe ground. Being vast as an ocean, it covers every hair of our head. Nothing happens without divine providence. Review this chapter of Dogmatics.

Note how many times νικάω is used in Revelation. The present participle, τοὺς νικῶντας, is merely characterizing and equales the conquerors. When B.-D., 212, calls the construction with ἐκ *eigentuemlich* he really says very little, for we can see that without spéical effort; B.-P. says nothing about this construction; R. 598, like our versions, translates, "those conquering *over*." The three ἐκ are perfectly plain; they have the sense of "out of." The conquering ones have come as victors "out of" the battle with the wild beast, his image, and the number of his name, i. e., the number of the antichristian power "666" (see the entire previous chapter). They conquered the beast, conquered the tyranny that tried to force them to do obeisance to the beasts's image, to be marked on hand or on forehead with its number "666." As such conquerors they now have "zithers of God" (probably the genitive of the Giver) on which to play the music of the song of glory to God. Κιθάρας τοῦ Θεοῦ also has no article of previous reference although these heavenly instruments have been mentioned before as being held in the hands of the elders (5:8) and in the hands of the 144,000 (14:2), all of them being conquerors.

3) These conquering ones, standing on the transparent sea, "sing the sacred ode (5:9; 14:3) of Moses, the slave of God (whose will it was to do the will of God), and the sacred ode of the Lamb," i. e., the ode which was one as well as the other, the ode which is now quoted in full. Calling it the ode of Moses brings to mind Exodus 15, where Moses praises God for the deliverance from the drowned Egyptians. Some think of the song recorded in Deut. 31:30-32:47, and claim that the repetition τὴν 'ῳδήν indicates that the conquerors sang two different songs; but in v. 3, 4 we have only *one* song. The genitives "of Moses" and "of the Lamb" are objective: dealing with Moses, dealing with the Lamb. Yet this song deals with God himself. The sense, therefore, is: dealing with what God wrought through Moses who, therefore, is also called "the slave of God" who did God's will and not his own, and what God wrought through the Lamb. To both are ascribed deeds of deliverance, the one being a type of the other. In a certain sense they are two, and yet after all they are but one. Deliverance from the Egyptians foreshadows deliverance from the beast, his image, and his number. Heb. 3:5, 6 similarly combines Moses and Christ.

The ode magnifies God. "Great and wonderful thy works, Lord God, the Almighty!" (compare 1:8; 4:8; 11:17) great and wonderful in connection with the judgment upon the Egyptians in the Red Sea, great and wonderful in connection with the judgments of the seven bowls, so great as to fill us with wonder and astonishment.

"Righteous and genuine thy ways, King of the nations!" or "of the eons." Both readings are equally well attested textually; "of the saints" (A. V.) is textually not worth considering. The sense is, "King over the nations," ruling them in righteous ways; or, if we prefer, "King over the eons and all that transpires in them, ruling them righteously." This King's "ways" are the principles which his acts follow. They accord absolutely with the norm of right. No matter who judges these "ways" and God's works, their righteousness is bound to be acknowledged and triumphantly vindicated. Ἀληθιναί is not "true" in the sense of truthful as though this King kept his promises and his threats but "genuine," never is one of his ways sham, pretense, hollow. Look again at the ways of God's deeds performed through Moses and then at all his ways performed through the Lamb, including the judgments of the bowls.

4) On these great assertions rests the rhetorical question: "Who shall not fear, Lord, and glorify thy name?" Absolutely all must fear whether willingly or not. One verb is the aorist subjunctive, the other the future indicative; but the subjunctive also has future meaning; either form may be used, or, as here, both. The aorist, however, means, "come to fear," arrive at that point, a shade of meaning which "shall glorify" does not bring out. Here, as in so many connections, ὄνομα is not some individual name of God but the revelation by which men know and alone can know him. They all must glorify this "name." Compare the Son of God, Phil. 2:10.

The reason for this is: "Because (thou art) alone sacred," μόνος ὅσιος, masculine, referring to Κύριος. This is not ἅγιος, "holy," but ὅσιος, "sacred," *sanctus*, the opposite of *pollutus*, true to the everlasting sanctities, yea, embodying them. This word is not found often in the New Testament, note 16:5, and see Trench, *Synonyms*. The second ὅτι is evidential: "Because all the nations shall come to thee and do obeisance before thee," including all those who did obeisance to the beast (13:8, 15). Why shall they at last do this?

"Because thy righteous verdicts were published." These δικαιώματα are not the righteous demands but either the righteous acts or the righteous verdicts; the suffix -μα denotes result. The teaching of Scripture is that in the end the whole universe shall acknowledge the righteousness of all God's acts and verdicts.

5) **And after these things I saw, and there was opened the Sanctuary of the Tabernacle of the Testimony in the heaven. And there came out the seven angels, they having the seven plagues, out of the Sanctuary, having been clothed in pure, brilliant linen and girdled about the breasts with golden girdles. And one of the four living ones gave to the seven angels seven golden bowls full of the anger of God, the One living for the eons of the eons. And filled was the Sanctuary with smoke from the glory of God and from his power, and no one was able to enter into the Sanctuary until there were brought to a finish the seven plagues of the seven angels.**

Zahn's supposition that μετὰ ταῦτα covers an interval "of hours, days, or weeks," would lead us to think that these visions were spread out over a long period. Μετὰ ταῦτα cannot mean that much. The sense is that what v. 2-4 reports precedes the contents of v. 5, etc. Εἶδον simply resumes the summation of v. 1 which was placed before v. 2-4 in order to give v. 2-4 the right focus and bearing. The point of v. 2-4 is that the great ode refers to the *last* plagues, to the *finish* God's anger wrought, which thus is properly stated first.

John now tells how he saw the seven angels. The Sanctuary in heaven was opened, and the seven angels came out. This is again the ναός, not "the Temple" (our versions) but the Holy and the Holy of Holies, which symbolizes that these last plagues are sent from the very holiness of God; compare 14:15, 17. The symbol, however, is taken from the "Tabernacle" which was built by Moses and not from the stone structure that was erected by Solomon, even also as Moses has just mentioned. On "the Tabernacle of the Testimony" compare Acts 7:4. The Tabernacle testified to the holy presence of God among Israel in the wilderness and thus in symbolism becomes God's heavenly seat of presence for the heavenly worship of the saints. There is no need to introduce the Ark into this vision and by means of the Ark the two tables of the divine law. It is enough to note that the Sanctuary was opened and that the angels came out of it. They come out of the Sanctuary of the Tabernacle of the Testimony, from the presence of God's holiness which now, in the seven plagues, will attest itself for the last time.

6) These angels bear the seven plagues out of the Sanctuary. Two perfect participles with their present connotation describe them: "having been clothed in linen, pure, brilliant (or shining), and having been girdled about the breasts with golden girdles." The accusatives are common with passives and are retained from the active. The readings λίνον and λίθον are equally well attested. Because the latter is far more difficult, some accept it as the true reading by applying the canon that the more difficult reading is to be preferred since the easier reading may have been substituted. But this canon is itself doubtful as we have frequently found. Here λίθον, "cut stone," is regarded as a collective for jewels, and this is taken to refer to a garment that was beset with jewels. Yet καθαρόν, "clean and pure," seems out of place with λίθον; it is quite in place with "linen."

We take the pure, shining linen to equal white and to symbolize holiness in these agents of the holiness of God. The golden girdles recall 1:13. The girdle accompanies the robe, and, as in 1:13, "golden," indicates royalty. Already in 1:13, and so here, too, some think of this clothing as denoting priestliness, to which interpretation we should not be averse if the actions mentioned here and in 1:13 were those of priests but they are not priestly actions. Angels are bodiless spirits, and only when they appear to human beings on earth, or as here in these superearthly visions, are they clothed, etc. This in no way warrants the theosophic conclusion that they possess an ethereal body and, carrying this idea farther, that at death our souls also receive such a body, yea, that God himself possessess a body.

7) How the angels have the plagues when they emerge from the Sanctuary and yet are given the seven φιάλαι, "bowls" (R. V.), not "vials" (A. V.), although this latter is a choicer English term, we are unable to say. These "bowls" are "full of the anger of God, of the One living for the eons of the eons" (on this phrase see 1:6, and on "the One living for the eons," etc., 4:9; 10:6). As the One living forever he is not a dead idol but is ever active in his supreme life and being as the deity. Hence his "hot anger," θυμός, which is explained in 14:10, compare 14:8. This anger is now to be poured out, completely emptied upon the antichristian empire and all who belong thereto. Hence the seven bowls that are filled to the brim.

The seven seals are opened in order to *reveal*; the seven trumpets herald and *announce*; but the seven bowls do more than either, do more than to foretell: they forthwith and without further warning pour out and *execute* the long-restrained anger of the Living God. The bowls pour out the last plagues; their pouring out represents the finality. The seals strike the fourth part, the trumpets the third part; the bowls bring the very end. After all of them have been emptied, it has been well said, *dann ist's eben aus.* Yet they do not symbolize the final judgment itself and as such. They are seven *bowls*. The imagery goes only so far, it leaves something that is still to be shown in succeeding visions. We are at the end, but the supreme climax is still held in reserve.

On "the four living ones" see the exposition of 4:6-8. Why only one of them gave the seven bowls we are unable to say, nor can we determine which one did this. The fact that one of them should be employed for this act is most fitting. Since they represent the earthly agents of God's providence, this act turns over the execution of the last plagues (v. 1) to God's heavenly agents, the seven angels. The earthly agencies have done the work for which they were created; what remains they place into the hands of the heavenly agents. The Living God created all of them and uses them according to his design. Here it is once more plain that the four ζῶα are distinct from the angels and do not include them.

8) The act of transfer is completed. "And filled was the Sanctuary with smoke from the glory of God and from his power." So it happened in the vision of Isaiah (6:4) when this prophet was sent by God to bring judgment to Israel (6:9-12). See also Exod. 40:34, 35. Bengel calls the smoke, *tegmen majestatis divinae,* with which others agree; but as coming "out of the glory of God, and out of his power," the smoke brought it about that "no one was able to enter into the Sanctuary until there were brought to a finish (the same verb as in v. 1) the seven plagues of the seven angels." The smoke helps to symbolize the fact that all the work of grace of the Living God and of his Sanctuary has been completed, and that only the last plagues remain that are now swiftly to be finished. The entire δόξα, the sum of God's attributes, is concerned in these final acts. Καί specifies especially God's δύναμις, his almighty power.

CHAPTER XVI

The Seven Bowls Emptied, chapter 16

1) **And I heard a great voice out of the Sanctuary saying to the seven angels, Go and pour out the seven bowls of the anger of God into the earth!** Several times John hears "a great voice" which some commentators attempt to identify but which we, like John himself, leave unidentified. The one order is intended for the seven angels. They are forced to empty their bowls on the earth.

They do this in succession, but in rapid succession and cumulatively: one plague is piled upon another until the end is reached. This is evident in v. 11, where, during the fifth plague, the boils of the first are still active; likewise in v. 9, where the expression "these plagues" refers to all of them as they intensify each other. These plagues cannot be interpreted in a literal sense. Surely, the canon holds good: either literal throughout — which is frankly impossible — or symbolical throughout. Take as an example the frogs mentioned in v. 13, where the text itself says in literal language that they are "three unclean spirits"; the frogs are thus symbolical. Those who interpret literally are not consistent; they leave this method of interpretation rather soon and go over into symbolism. Moreover, if some of these plagues, as for instance the first four, are literal and affect nature, how does it come that, as v. 2 states, these plagues strike only "the human beings, the ones having the mark of the beast, and the ones doing obeisance to his image"? We see no way of avoiding the symbolical interpretation.

These plagues cannot be located in past history. The attempts to find them there furnish the best evidence. They precede the final judgment, bring us to the very door of it, but do not include this judgment. The final judgment is not a plague, is not to be paralleled with the seven plagues. Foreshadowings of some of these seven plagues there may have been or there may now be, but to what extent they have occurred we shall not attempt to say. For ourselves we say more, namely that these bowls deal with prophecy which is couched in symbolical language and that, while we attempt to remain entirely sober in our efforts at interpretation, we do not claim that we have succeeded in understanding all the symbols and have fully discovered the realities beneath them.

2) **And there went away the first and poured out his bowl into the earth, and there occurred ulcer, bad and wicked, upon the human beings, those having the mark of the wild beast and those doing obeisance to his image.** "There went away" is stated only in the case of the first angel and is understood with the rest. Ἐξέχεε is the second aorist; in v. 1 the reading varies between the present imperative ἐκχέετε (which Westcott and Hort regard as the second aorist) and ἐκχέατε, the second aorist imperative with the first aorist vowel α (see Thayer). When R. 342 claims that ἐκχέετε is "undoubtedly right" he claims rather much. The order given in v. 1 should be a peremptory aorist. The subject of ἐγένετο is ἕλκος, hence not, "it became," R. V., but, "there occurred." Ἕλκος = *ulcus* (from *ulcerare*), "ulcer," a suppurated, inflamed, running sore that refuses to be healed. The anarthrous subject is qualitative: "what is ulcer." It is described as κακόν, "bad," ugly, large and deep, a mean thing, and πονηρόν, "wicked," viciously inflamed and severely painful. Someone has called it smallpox; it was much worse.

It struck "those having the mark of the wild beast and those doing obeisance to his image," i. e., only these and not those who refused to accept that mark and to bow to that image (see 13:14-17), just as the Egyptian plagues did not touch the Israelites. While this fact is mentioned only in connection with the first plague, we take it that this was the case with all of them. We are, of course, reminded of Exod. 9:8-12; Deut. 28:27, 35, "the botch of Egypt," "the sore botch that cannot be healed, from the sole of thy foot unto the top of thy head." Yet, we have all along found that in Revelation these Old Testament reminders are only reminders. The imagery of Revelation is independent and stands by itself. Only the first of these seven plagues resembles one of the ten Egyptian plagues. Exod. 9:8-12 affords no light for interpreting this first plague.

We cannot think of a physical ulcer that afflicted the physical bodies of the millions of antichristians prior to the Parousia. We have already found that the adorers of the beast and of "Babylon" cannot be restricted to papists but signify all the antichristian multitudes of "every tribe and people and tongue and nation" (13:7) who are also called "all those dwelling on the earth" as being wholly earth-bound (13:8, 14), "all, the small and the great, and the rich and the beggarly, and the free and the slave" (13:16).

The interpreters that belong to the historical school see the fulfillment of this plague in the French Revolution, "that tremendous outbreak of social and moral evil, of democratic fury, atheism, and vice, which was speedily seen to characterize the French Revolution; that of which the ultimate source was in the long and deep-seated corruption and irreligion of the nation; its outward vent, expression, and organ in the Jacobin clubs and their seditious and atheistic publications; its result, the dissolution of all society, all morals, and all religions; with acts of atrocity and horror accompanying scarce paralleled in the history of man; and suffering and anguish of correspondent intensity throbbing throughout the whole social mass and corroding it." Read Carlyle, *The French Revolution.* Yet this lies in the past; it also affected principally only the French nation and not the whole antichristian world.

We remember that an "ulcer" often opens and discharges corruption that has accumulated in the body. This we take to be the antichristianity which, by the divine πληγή or blow, breaks out in virulent, painful, outward discharge. There is no such poison in the followers of the Lamb. In view of 13:17 we may, perhaps, think of virulent sores in the whole social, economic, educational, political world where the antichristian power rules. This is only the first plague, only one of the results, the lowest, let us say, the least of the outbreaks of inner rottenness and foulness. To call it only "moral" says too little. Our remark about social, economic, etc., ulcers we would have understood as involving a thousand aches and pains in all the departments of life. Note I Tim. 6:6-10 on the worshippers of mammon; add James 4:1-4; 5:1-6. So much for our reflections on this first plague. We see but dimly all that shall come like festering sores (Isa. 1:5, 6) out of the corruption of antichristianity when the severe hand of providence (note "one of the ζῶα" in 15:7) smites the followers of the beast. It may be much worse than we can imagine in advance.

3) **And the second poured out his bowl into the sea, and there occurred blood as of one dead, and every soul of life died, the things in the sea.** "Blood as of a dead person" is coagulated blood that soon decays and stinks. The sea is the ocean surrounding the land, and this entire sea turns into such vile blood that everything in it becomes dead and smelling to heaven. How far this advances beyond Exod. 7:17-21 is evident.

A literalistic interpretation of this plague offers almost insurmountable difficulties. To speak of "maritime power, commerce, and colonies" because "sea" is mentioned, or of international war by regarding "sea" as a symbol of the restless nations, is unsatisfactory. We see no point in stressing εἰς τὴν γῆν (v. 2) and εἰς τὴν θάλασσαν. They are, of course, opposites, but when the entire sea is stinking blood, what about all the land which the sea surrounds? In 13:1 the dragon stands on the seashore, and then one beast rises out of the sea, the other out of the earth; whether "the earth" and "the sea" are to be taken in the same sense in this passage are not apparent.

"The sea" is selected because it is water and, unlike "the earth," can be symbolized as being turned into "blood," here into "blood of one dead," putrid, stinking blood that fills the whole world with the smell of putridity and death. The inward rottenness of the followers of the beast breaks out in virulent ulcers; and in addition to this an ocean of putridity as of "blood of one dead" overwhelms them. All antichristianity is disease and erupts in boils and ulcers that will not be mollified or healed; secondly, it is death and envelops everything with the stench of rotting blood that is so terrible as though the whole ocean were rotting blood. Who does not smell death in the antichristian world of this day? What will it be when the whole antichristian beast power attains its height and this second bowl is poured out? Yet, even then, John 10:10b continues to apply to the followers of the Lamb. So much for our reflections on this symbolism in advance of its fulfillment.

4) **And the third poured out his bowl into the rivers and the springs of waters, and there occurred blood. And I heard the angel of the waters saying: Righteous art thou, the One who Is and the One who Was, the Sacred One, because these things thou didst judge; because blood of saints and of prophets they did pour out, and blood to them thou didst give to**

drink — worthy are they. And I heard the altar saying, Yea, Lord God, the Almighty, genuine and righteous thy judgings! We prefer the reading ἐγένετο (singular) αἷμα exactly as in v. 3 and understand it in the same sense; the plural, "they became blood," is evidently an alteration that was made by a scribe. The sense, of course, is the same. After v. 3 any reference to Exod. 7:17, etc., amounts to very little.

Nothing is gained by saying that rivers and springs nourish *vegetation* and by quoting Ps. 1:3; for the point is: "*blood* to them thou didst give *to drink*." Nor does this "blood" refer to wars as though blood always symbolizes wars. As for the sea and now the rivers and the springs, this third bowl is no mere appendix to the second by stating that the small amount of sweet water was now made blood as the vast ocean had been. The third bowl is *worse* than the second. Each stroke of judgment is more severe than the one preceding.

"The rivers and the springs of waters" are the sweet, drinkable water, and men must have water to drink. When this is turned into "blood," they have no place from which to obtain the water they must have. The fact that this is not to be understood literally but symbolically is evident; for if men died of thirst, what need is there of four more bowls, and what about the godly? Shall we not think of all the springs and the rivers of natural good sense, knowledge, and wisdom, from which all men must constantly draw for all departments of life? When these flow, when good sense, etc., is freely to be had, the natural life retains its natural soundness. Turn these rivers and their springs into blood, and you may imagine the result!

Yes, we see them muddied and contaminated now although they have not yet been made blood by the anger of God, which is still restrained. Political science is contaminated. See what that does to the nations. Good sense in marriage, in rearing children is muddied. Behold the results! Review all the different sides of the natural life and note what any contamination of good sense, etc., causes. When all these rivers and these springs turn into blood, who can fully imagine what the results must then be? Take this as the third blow of God's wrath in addition to the other two: corruption boiling out in boils, the odor of rotting death from the sea lying like a pall over the land, and now nothing but blood to drink!

5) But there is more in this symbol. "The angel of the waters" is this third angel who poured out his bowl into the rivers and the springs and not an angel of nature who is set over these waters as other angels are set over other elements of the earth, as some think who then quote the spurious passage, John 5:4 (which see). Besides silently executing his mission of anger, this third angel explains his act, for his act alone is not enough to make it fully understood. There is more to this "blood" than just blood.

God is righteous in that he judged ταῦτα, "these things," i. e., in issuing the verdict (κρίνειν) to turn the rivers and the springs into blood. On ὁ ὢν καί ὁ ἦν see 1:4; the third designation, ὁ ὅσιος, is explained in 15:4. It is eminently pertinent here (ὁ ἅγιος would not be) because he who is *Sanctus* and maintains all the sanctities here sends his judgment upon all those who trample and befoul these sanctities. It is also impossible that this One should ever judge unrighteously, unjustly.

The second ὅτι is in epexegetical apposition to the first. Here is absolute justice in regard to this blood: "*blood* of saints and of prophets they poured out," these followers of the beast and adorers of his image (v. 2), "and *blood* to them thou didst give to drink." Each time "blood" is placed forward for the sake of emphasis. They were avid for blood; they have now been given blood. Natural sense and decency of mind should have moved them to let the blood of saints and of prophets alone. The antichristian viciousness of the beast turned this sense into hate, murder, blood. It is pure justice that the springs and the rivers that were once sweet and palatable in natural fairness, right, and good sense, should be turned into "blood," the only drink they prefer. Because they drink blood, blood, blood, all their thoughts and their deeds will now be bloody, not only regarding the saints but regarding each other. "Blood" = murder; and as Matt. 5:21, etc., shows in regard to murder, and Matt. 5:27, etc., in regard to adultery, "blood" includes all the lesser viciousness that leads to actual bloodshed, all the lesser viciousness against saints and prophets and in this plague all the lesser crimes against each other with the constant climax being blood.

Cancel the "for" of the A. V. "Worthy are they," hence righteous is God for having this anger poured out in their behalf.

7) Two witnesses bear this testimony (compare the two mentioned in 11:3). The second is called "the altar," which is best referred to "the angel" who came "from the altar" (14:18) and not regarded as a personification of the altar itself, especially since we have this angel of the altar speaking also in 14:18. This second voice confirms the first: "Yea, Lord God, the Almighty!" ὁ παντοκράτωρ, 1:8; 11:17; 15:3, etc. "Genuine and righteous (transposed in 15:3) thy judgings!" κρίσις is a word expressing action, "acts of judging," and resembles the ὁδοί used in 15:3. "Genuine," without sham, pretense, hollowness; "righteous," in accord with the δίκη or norm of right, no matter by whom it be applied.

What about the followers of the Lamb? Read Ps. 46:4; 87:7: "All my springs are in thee"; Isa. 49:10; and forget not the "still waters" of Ps. 23:1-3.

8) **And the fourth poured out his bowl upon the sun, and there was given to it to burn the human beings with fire. And they were burned, the human beings, with a great burn, and they blasphemed the name of God, the One having the authority over these plagues, and they did not repent to give to him glory.** Strange, how little commentators venture to say in regard to this bowl. The literalists say no more than that "the sun" and the burning heat are physical, the majority of the rest say nothing at all about the sun and only a little about blasphemy and refusal to repent. One, however, lets the sun = Christianity: men turning the gospel or Christianity "in great part into a hot-blooded system of confession or negation, a thing of priesthood and of sects." Another has the sun = "supreme governmental authority" that has become tyrannical; but why men should blaspheme God for that instead of simply starting a rebellion, as men have always done, is not apparent.

After a threefold use of εἰς we now have four ἐπί ("upon the sun"), which seems to indicate that, as far as John is concerned, the seven plagues are to be divided into three and four and not, as some think, into four and three. It is pedantic when the R. V. and others seem to think that αὐτῷ may refer to the angel when every angel in this vision does no more than to empty his bowl.

The strangeness of the symbolism lies in the fact that instead of being darkened (8:12), the sun is made to burn or to scorch human beings by fire. The repetition emphasizes this as being the real point: "They were burned, the human beings, with a great burn"; καῦμα is a term that expresses result, R. 151, the usual accusative after passives is retained from the active, noun and verb are cognate, R. 478. Our reflections are these. The physical sun warms and cheers men physically with its normal heat; abnormal, excessive heat would be torture, a kind of hell. The rivers and the springs are the sources of drink; when they are turned into blood, they symbolize that the very drink of men will be bloody viciousness that manifests itself in all the passions that lead to "blood," to murder. This is what the followers of the beast absorb, "drink." The sweet water has been taken from them. Now comes something that is worse — the warming, grateful sun also is gone.

As men need physical water, so they need the physical sun; it sends its warmth from the skies, and that warmth envelopes them with comfort. What would happen if it turned into fire and scorching heat, πῦρ and καῦμα? What if all that makes life tolerable suddenly turned into utterly intolerable scorching and blistering burning, and this were ceaselessly poured out upon them from the very sky? Something like this, we venture to think, is meant by this symbolism. All drink has become blood; now, in addition, the whole sun and the sky have become scorching brass.

What about the followers of the Lamb? These ἄνθρωποι are, without question, those described in v. 2. Ps. 84:11: "The Lord God is a sun and shield: the Lord will give grace and glory; no good thing will he withhold from them that walk uprightly." Malachi 4:2: "But unto you that fear my name shall the Sun of Righteousness arise with healing in his wings." II Pet. 1:19, the sure Word of prophecy, "a light that shineth in a dark place, until the day dawn and the daystar arise in your hearts."

Those who are only ἄνθρωποι, "the dwellers on the earth" (3:10; 6:10; 8:13; 11:10; 13:8; 12:14; 17:10), who are wholly earth-bound by the beast shall have their sun at last scorch them to insane blasphemy. Those who are the Lamb's own shall ever have the sun of grace and glory with healing in his wings.

9) Not for one moment did these "human beings" think of repenting (see 2:5, 16, 21; especially 9:21) by confessing their worship of the beast in the dust and "to give to him glory" (infinitive of result: so as to give, so that they gave). They did the absolutely opposite, "they blasphemed the name (revelation) of God." The apposition adds the reason: "of the One having the authority over these plagues," four of which have already struck them, others of which are still pending. Righteous and just, indeed, are God's κρίσεις or "judgings" (v. 7).

10) **And the fifth poured out his bowl upon the throne of the wild beast, and his kingdom came to be as having been darkened. And they kept gnawing their tongues for pain, and they blasphemed the God of the heaven due to their pains and due to their ulcers and did not repent from their works.**

"Throne" is the seat of power, rule, and dominion. In 13:2 the dragon, Satan, gave his power and "his throne" and his great authority to the first wild beast, the antichristian power, and thereby made it the antichristian power that it is. The throne of the beast and the dragon are the same. This hellish throne is set up in opposition to the throne of God, 4:2; note all that is said in chapter 4 (also elsewhere) about this throne. "Shall *the throne* of iniquity have fellowship with thee, which frameth mischief as *a law?*" Ps. 94:20. The beast's seat of power, long untouched, is now struck by the anger of God which is poured out upon it from the fifth bowl.

The effect of this divine action is that suddenly the kingdom of the beast came to be (aorist) in a lasting condition of having been darkened (the predicate participle is the perfect tense). B.-D. 354 lists ἐγένετο . . . ἐσκοτωμένη as a periphrastic perfect tense; so does R.

375, although in 903 R. notes "a mixture of tenses" and in 902 states that "the perfect participle is, of course, predicate." We do not regard this as a periphrastic construction. A perfect tense would be out of place, for it would imply that the darkening set in *before* the bowl was poured out, which is not the case. None of the commentators translates this form as being a perfect tense; all translate, "was darkened," an aorist. When the anger struck the throne, the beast's kingdom at once became (ἐγένετο) darkened (predicate, the perfect participle has its present connotation), duratively darkened, never to be lighted up again.

The dark, awful pall of doom settled over the beast's kingdom, and that includes his throne; for we take it that the throne belongs to his kingdom. By means of his throne the beast built his kingdom, extended it to "all those dwelling on the earth" (13:7, 8, 16), ruled his vast antichristian following. "His kingdom" is the beast's following; for the next statement says that "they kept biting or gnawing their tongues for pain," they, the followers of the beast. The first three ἐκ phrases denote cause and may be translated "due to the pain— due to their pains and due to their ulcers." The last ἐκ denotes separation: "from their works."

The antichristian empire is itself darkness; in fact, τὸ σκότος, "the darkness," (with the article) is regularly used as a practical personification. Now this empire is struck with the darkness of God's anger, with beast-darkness blasted with judgment-darkness, the latter settling down to stay. Who will say what this dark pall signifies? To refer to Egypt or to some other darkening of the sun is of no aid. In this kingdom of the beast there was a sun, and the sun is a symbol of the opposite effect in the case of the fourth bowl. Only a "critic" would say that this darkness of God's anger cannot well cause such intense pain that men would bite their tongues, and that, therefore, the ulcers are added in v. 11 in order to save the situation. The imperfect ἐμασσῶντο, "they kept biting," is descriptive.

11) Once more two aorists of fact tell us about the blasphemy and the refusal to repent. The plan produces (ἐκ) only blasphemy against "the God of the heaven" on the part of the followers of the hellish beast. Lest we think only of the pain due to this last bowl of God's anger, a second ἐκ phrase is added which takes us back to the first bowl and thus surely includes also the other three. This is evident also in v. 9, where the term "these plagues" includes the first four and possibly also the rest. "The God of the heaven" (11:13) who sends his righteous anger on the kingdom of the beast only causes those who constitute this kingdom to rage in blasphemy against this heavenly power because it interferes with the powers of hell. When did the wicked ever cease to rage against heaven and God for bringing them to justice? Even now they did not repent from their works so as to turn from them and to give glory to God (v. 9; 11:13). Thus the final bowls must be poured out.

12) **And the sixth poured out his bowl upon the river, the great one, the (river) Euphrates. And there dried up its water so that ready was made the way of the kings, of those from the sunrising. And I saw out of the mouth of the dragon and out of the mouth of the wild beast and out of the mouth of the pseudo-prophet three unclean spirits, as it were, frogs. For they are spirits of demons, doing signs, who go out to the kings of the whole inhabited earth, to bring them together for the battle of the day, of the great one, of God the Almighty. Lo, I am coming as a thief! Blessed the one watching and keeping his robes lest he walk naked, and they see his shame! And they brought**

them together to the place called in Hebrew Har-Magedon.

Review what is said in regard to the Euphrates in the symbolism of 9:14, and note how it is used symbolically beyond anything connected with the Nile or the Tiber. It was the Euphrates where Assyria, Babylon, Persia assembled great hosts for tremendous conquests. Huge armies from beyond crossed this river which is even naturally "great." In this vision the name "Euphrates," its greatness, etc., are used symbolically and not physically or geographically. Here, in the symbolism, we may say, the throne of the beast must stand, which throne is itself a symbol of the beast's power, and the beast is a symbol of the antichristian power (13:1, etc.).

The sixth trumpet mentioned in 9:13, etc., signifies the sending of a curse of delusion. While it also comes from the Euphrates, the curse of 9:13, etc., is far different from what is now revealed in regard to the great preparation for the last battle of all the antichristian powers and their final absolute defeat; compare the exposition of 9:13, etc.

The anger of God which was poured out of the sixth bowl dried up the water of the great river and thus prepared the way so that the kings might cross with perfect ease and join with the powers of the throne at Babylon in order to march to the supreme battle. As the throne of the beast (v. 10) is symbolical, so are these kings from the sunrisings (plural: daily risings), in actual history the wild hordes of the Parthians. The point is not that uncivilized men join the civilized but the start of the great gathering of all the antichristian powers ("kings") for the final "battle," πολεμός (v. 14). In his anger, God himself prepares a road for them. Do not say that the crossing of the river could have been made by boats since there was no one to prevent this. That ignores the symbolism. All bars are let down as was done in Luke 22:53: "This is your hour and the power of darkness." The dried-up river is like an invitation — an invitation to doom. Ἵνα denotes result: "so that the way was actually made ready."

13) These "kings" do not, however, represent all the forces of the antichristian power. We are told how all the rest are assembled for the fatal expedition to the great battlefield. John saw "three unclean spirits" like "frogs," each one coming out of the mouth of the dragon (12:9), Satan himself; and out of the mouth of the wild beast (13:1, etc.), Satan's great agent, the antichristian power; and out of the mouth of the pseudo-prophet (13:11), the second wild beast. The three operate together in preparation for the final battle. "The mouth" is mentioned three times, for the spirits are to go out to speak. John himself interprets (γάρ) when he says, they are "spirits," namely, "demons." The Scripture always calls them ἀκάθαρτα, "unclean," vile, filthy, full of all vileness and wickedness.

It seems pointless to refer to the Egyptian plague of frogs, for here only three frogs are mentioned, and these are demons who are symbolized as frogs. How much shall we seek in the idea "frogs"? The morass, the mud, unclean, small, not powerful, expanding their throats and making a local, persistent noise? In the sixteenth century the Lutherans found the Jesuits in these three frogs. This view is apt in its way but is too restricted. Here there is far more than papal Rome. Lange calls them "the modern nightingales" who announce the new springtime of mankind.

One might wonder why this great dragon should send forth so small an agent as a frog; and also this monster beast and the second beast — three little frogs! But what do we know about the unspeakable things of hell? How inadequate would be the symbols we should design? Here the second wild beast is called the "pseudo-prophet," the false or lying prophet. This term expresses 13:14: "he deceives those dwelling on the earth because of the signs which were given him to do before the beast."

14) All three frog-demons are represented as "doing signs" (on which see 13:14), lying signs, that are impressive and convincing only to the followers of the beast. By the aid of such signs they go out to the kings of the whole inhabited earth (the οἰκουμένη) to gather all the antichristian forces together, to form one vast army "for the battle of the day, of the great one, of God the Almighty." This, too, is the day which the Lord hath made. The Almighty rules in the midst of his enemies. On their own initiative all the antichristian forces unite for supreme battle; the Almighty even smoothes their path. His "day, the great one," is due. This "day" is foretold throughout Scripture. The antichristian hosts imagine this to be *their* day in which they, with one united effort, will destroy the kingdom of the Lamb root and branch and will laugh in triumph forever. They mock at all that is foretold regarding this day (II Pet. 3:4); they boast of their own invincible might. On παντοκράτωρ see 1:8.

15) Some suppose that at this place John inserts a word to his readers; but evidently the speaker is Christ himself, whose voice speaks in this vision, and who needs no introduction because his words identify him. "Lo, I am coming as a thief!" is the voice we hear in 3:3; Matt. 24:43; compare I Thess. 5:2; II Pet. 3:10. Suddenly, unexpectedly, surprising even his own, Christ will come.

We must be ready as he has ever warned us. "Blessed the one watching (looking for Christ's coming) and keeping his robes lest he walk naked, and they see his shame!" This is an allusion to Rev. 3:18, and perhaps also to 7:14, to the white robes we buy from Christ, i. e., his righteousness, without which the shame of our nakedness (here expanded to "walk naked, and they see his shame"), our disgraceful sin, would be open to all eyes. Beatitude and warning are combined. Since it is united with the mighty promise, "Lo, I am coming!" this part of the vision is eminently effective and in place.

16) The narration closes: "And they brought them together." The froglike unclean spirits were completely successful. The vision concludes with this act. The battle is not described. All we see is the array of all the antichristian powers. It is significant that not a word is said about the Lord God's army. He needs no dry riverbed, no agents to call kings, for he is

THE ALMIGHTY.

The interpreters that belong to the historical school regard this as an indication of the devastation of Rome, and the chiliasts find in it "the day of Christ's appearing to establish his millennial kingdom." But we cannot understand their reasoning.

The place for the gathering of the marshalled host is named, "the place called in Hebrew (Aramaic, R. 104), Har-Magedon," more familiarly from the A. V.: "Armageddon." G. K. states: "The riddle of Ἅρ Μαγεδών still awaits solution" since such a Mount does not appear elsewhere in Scripture or in other ancient literature. Zahn devotes pages to a discussion of the word and yet does not advance the matter toward a solution beyond stating the acceptable reason why John did not translate the name as he does the one in 9:11 (compare the names found in John 1:42; 4:25; 9:7): to one who does not know Hebrew "har-Megiddo" (Zahn's spelling) would have no significant meaning in the Greek world language. The difficulty may be seen in part also in Thayer, not to mention many others. Valley of Megiddo is found but not "Mount or

Mountain," *har.* To say that "Mount" is here the opposite of "Mount Zion" in 14:1 is hazardous.

The fact that this army should be gathered on a height seems proper. The additional fact that the symbolical place of the vision would be located in the Holy Land, in the great plain of Esdraelon, would also seem proper. We might think of describing this army as attacking Jerusalem itself, which, however, would be unsatisfactory. To let the word mean "City of Slaughter" or "Hill of Slaughter" (Biederwolf and others) is unwarranted. Whether there is an allusion to Judges 5:19 and the destruction of the Canaanites is problematical; an allusion to II Kings 23:29, etc., is out of the question, for the victory goes to the wrong side. Although it is without a geographical location or even a satisfactory etymology, the name "Armageddon" has impressed itself upon the imagination as being the final battlefield against all evil powers to their utter defeat. This is about enough; we need to add only 19:11-21.

17) **And the seventh poured out his bowl** — note this terrible sevenfold refrain! — **upon the air. And there went out a great voice out of the Sanctuary from the throne, saying, It has occurred! And there occurred lightnings and sounds and thunders, and there occurred an earthquake, a great one, such a one as did not occur since human beings occurred on the earth, such an earthquake, so great. And the city, the great one, got to be in three parts, and the cities of the nations fell. And Babylon the Great was remembered before God to give to her the cup of the wine of the anger of his wrath. And every island fled, and mountains were not found. And great hail as of talent weight comes down out of the heaven upon the human beings; and the human beings blasphemed God due to the plague**

of the hail because great is the plague thereof exceedingly.

The seventh πληγή or blow is the fall of Babylon the Great. This was summarily announced in 14:8: "There fell, there fell, Babylon, the Great!" and now we see her fall. "Babylon" = *the entire antichristian empire* which was built up by the dragon, Satan, through the beast, the entire antichristian power (13:1-10), and by this power through the second beast, the entire antichristian propaganda (13:11-18), called the pseudo-prophet in 16:13. The kings from the sun-risings (v. 13) and the kings of the whole inhabited earth (v. 14) are viewed as her vassals, as powers that are parts of her empire, likewise the cities that fell (v. 19) plus the islands and the mountains (v. 20). Regarded as a great city, she has many vassals and thus constitutes the antichristian empire; viewed as "Babylon," she is still the antichristian empire. Whether she is only a unit (14:8) or is surrounded by many satellites, Babylon is no less than the whole antichristian empire. Papal Rome, Judaism, Mohammedanism, all paganism that rejects the gospel, all the secret, oath-bound, deistic organizations, all the anti-Trinitarian sects that deny the deity and the expiating blood of the Lamb, and all worldly indifferentists who also remain mere dwellers on the earth (3:10; 6:10; 8:13; 11:10; 13:8, 12, 14; 17:8) are parts of Babylon, constitute Babylon.

The seventh bowl is emptied on the air, not into it, for the angel empties the bowl from above, from the door of the Sanctuary in heaven. Why on the air? The answer is scarcely that lightnings, etc., may at once occur (v. 2). Revelation has already presented these as symbols of omnipotent power and of the throne. The answer is scarcely that the demons are supposed to infest the air, for we have read of only three demons, and these are represented as frogs who do not fly in the air; nor does this plague strike demons, it strikes Babylon. The sequence seems to be: the earth — the sea — the rivers and the springs — the sun — the exceptional bowls five and six — and now the all-enveloping air. Yet in the symbolism here used the anger poured upon the air does not poison the air so as to affect men's lungs. The effect produced is a convulsion that occurs in part in the air but chiefly in the earth itself. If we stop and think of the godly who remain unharmed amid all these plagues, also during this last one, if we also bear in mind that Babylon throughout has been described as consisting of "the dwellers on the earth," we shall see that here, too, as in the case of the other six bowls, the whole description is a unified symbol which applies only to Babylon and pictures the final fall of the whole antichristian empire. This is at least how we understand this terrible symbolism.

At once, at the time of the pouring out of the final measure of wrath, there rings out a great voice "out of the Sanctuary from the throne," out of the symbol of God's holiness, from the symbol of his power, rule, and dominion, which pronounces a single word, Γέγονε! The Germans can render it almost exactly: *Es ist geschehen!* "It is done!" in our versions is not exact, for the verb does not mean "to do." "It has become!" or, "It has occurred!" is more exact. The perfect is like that one word of Jesus on the cross: Τετέλεσται! "It has been finished!" The tense means that the climax has come to be and so remains now and evermore. Some call this tense proleptic because they regard the following verbs, ἐγένοντο — ἐγένετο — and the rest, as a reference to subsequent occurrences. We think that these verbs should be regarded as being included in the perfect γέγονε, which, by its very form, includes all of them. For the perfect means that what has been developing during a long time in the past has now occurred as in a final explosion. The sword of Damocles which has for so long a time been trembling on a thread now breaks the thread and, point down, plunges into Babylon.

18) Indeed, "it has occurred." For on the instant all that follows did occur. "There occurred lightnings and noises and thunders," symbols of omnipotence in action, see the exposition of 4:5a and note the relation to the throne in that passage, even as here, too, we have the throne. Φωναί, which is placed between lightnings and thunders, does not mean "voices" — whose voices would they be? These are "noises." Shall we say cyclonic roaring?

Yet these lightnings, etc., seem to be only adjuncts. A separate ἐγένετο adds the main thing that "occurred," namely, "an earthquake, a great one." Revelation has mentioned σεισμός before (6:12; 8:5; 11:13, 19). The one mentioned in connection with the sixth seal (6:12), and perhaps the one in connection with the seventh trumpet (11:19) symbolize the same thing that is here indicated, the effect of which is described as the final destruction of the antichristian empire. Hence it is described: "such a one as did not occur since human beings occurred (ἐγένοντο — note the repetition of this verb) on the earth," the apposition emphasizing: "so mighty an earthquake, thus great." Yet we repeat that all this is symbolism, that it applies to the antichristian world empire and should be understood accordingly.

19) Thus another ἐγένετο describes the instantaneous effect, the occurrence that the city, the great one, namely Babylon, "got to be (it is the best we can do in English) εἰς τρία μέρη." This is the εἰς used in the predicate which makes a phrase in place of the nominative (R. 458): "got to be three parts." The language is idiomatic; it does not mean that great rents in the

earth divided the city into three parts, but that the whole city and every structure in it fell in a heap in utter ruin. Every structure collapsed, one wall falling to the right, another to the left, the roof and the floors falling down between them. "Three parts" indicates this form of disintegration. So proudly Babylon stood when it was regarded as a great city, and so long. The beast had built it so strongly and lordly, and its strength seemed solid as though it could never fall. "It fell, it fell, Babylon the Great!" (14:8; Matt. 7:27: "and great was the fall of it").

How proudly the antichristian propaganda builds the Babylon of today! Godless science imagines that its structures cannot fall, they are granite, the Scriptures are only myths, childish stories. How can papal Rome, built on Peter, ever fall, seeing it overshadows the world? Reason simply must stand, and the "outworn categories of thought," the old, outmoded "thought patterns" of Scripture have long been crumbling into dust, the scientific religion of reason alone endures. View the massive towers of Babylon, the city, or the mighty empire Babylon and its unshakable strength! Fall? The very idea is preposterous! But already Ps. 1:4 reads: "like the chaff which the wind driveth away." Isa. 29:5: "The multitude of thy strangers shall be like small dust, and the multitude of the terrible ones as chaff that passeth away; yea, it shall be at an instant suddenly." But the Word stands as the Rock of Ages, and they who build on it fall not, for they are founded upon a rock, Matt. 7:25.

"And the cities of the nations fell," all the vassal cities of Babylon. Here the far-flung antichristian empire is viewed in its many parts. The comprehensive singular appears often in Scripture, and right beside it the expanding plural which spreads out the details. Thus "sin," and in the next breath "sins"; "work," and again "works." Similarly "the city, the great one," and now "the cities" in addition and in v. 12-14 the many "kings." Behold, they all "fell," the same word and the same tense that occur in 14:8.

We may regard καί as epexegetical, as stating why this utter destruction occurred: because "Babylon the Great was remembered before God (aorist, one great act of remembrance) to give to her the cup of the wine of the anger of his wrath," δοῦναι, also aorist, also one act. Of course, we note the series of genitives. There is an allusion to 14:10: "the wine of the anger of God, served unmixed (undiluted with water) in the cup of his wrath," compare 14:8: "the wine of the passion of her fornication." The cup "of the wine" is the genitive of contents. The anger "of his wrath" is the genitive of possession: the wrath (ὀργή), deep, strong, pent-up, now has a flaming outburst, anger (θυμός), with it. Our versions translate θυμός "fierceness," but "anger" seems preferable. The wine "of the anger of his wrath" has a double appositional genitive; the wine = the wrath that is hot with anger.

God restrains his wrath and hopes for and invites to repentance for a long time, note repentance in v. 9 and 11. He also lets the wicked fill up the measure of his wickedness and thus eliminates any charge that he is hasty and strikes too soon at men who might after all repent. Humanly speaking, this looks like forgetting. When judgment then strikes at last, this looks like sudden remembering. Scripture uses "remember" when referring to the blessing of the godly and to retribution upon the wicked.

20) "And every island fled, and mountains were not found." No city, even on the most remote island, no fortress of the antichristian empire on a single mountain height escaped the destructive final wrath. Insignificant island, formidable mountain, neither afforded refuge.

21) The utter destruction wrought is further pictured by the hail, which harmonizes with the air, lightnings, cyclonic roaring, thunders, and the unheard-of earthquake, the hail being the last symbolical item. All the destructive forces belong together and descend from heaven. They form a unit in the picture so that we think that the individual items, among them the hail, have no literal counterparts. Hail appears in 8:7; the hail mentioned in 11:19 may refer to the final hail. Such an earthquake never occurred, nor such hail, "great as of talent weight," ταλαντιαία, an adjective the English never formed. The talent varied in weight, 60 pounds is near the lower limit, 96 and above a 100 the higher limit. The present καταβαίνει is aoristic and is frequently used in narration along with simple aorists and lends a more graphic touch. We do not mix the tenses in this Greek fashion.

When we are once more told (v. 9 and 11) that the human beings blasphemed God, and did this in consequence (ἐκ) of the plague of the hail because great is the plague of it, σφόδρα, very much so, this means that absolutely nothing, not even this hail, produces anything but blasphemous rage in the people who bear the mark of the beast and do obeisance to his image (v. 2), for throughout the seven plagues these are called οἱ ἄνθρωποι, v. 2, a term which once for all describes them.

More is implied when this statement about the blasphemy is placed here at the end in connection with the hail. It does not imply that these human beings kept back their blaspheming until the hail came down out of the heaven (i. e., directly from God), for they blasphemed already during the fourth and the fifth plague. This vision only breaks off at this point; further visions will complete the picture. That explains why in this vision all these human beings are not killed but after the hail still stand shaking their fists at God and pouring out blasphemy. What these seven bowls portray is not physical action. These are the followers of the beast; they constitute the antichristian empire under the throne of the beast (v. 10). It is this empire upon which these last πληγαί or blows (15:1) fall. The picture presented in these seven last plagues is that of the cumulative destruction of the whole vast antichristian empire as such. Its power, rule, center, strongholds, fortifications at the last protect none of the followers of the beast; blow after blow leaves them exposed, able only to blaspheme. So the final blow crushes their empire utterly and forever. They are left standing in their rage of blasphemy. This intimates that further visions will show us what God will do with these human beings. Thus the vision stops short; thus we still see these ἄνθρωποι.

Here let us repeat the sentence with which we conclude the remarks on v. 1.

CHAPTER XVII

The Great Whore, 17:1-19:10

The History of the Great Whore, chapter 17

Chapter 17 presents the picture and the history of the great whore.

Chapter 18 presents her glory and the lament over her fall.

Chapter 19:1-10, the doxology to God for her judgment.

These three sections belong together. The great whore is Babylon, the antichristian empire pictured in its *seductiveness*.

1) **And there came one of the seven angels having the seven bowls and spoke with me, saying: Hither! I will show thee the judgment of the whore, the great one, the one sitting upon many waters, with whom there committed whoredom the kings of the earth, and there were made drunk those inhabiting the earth from the wine of her whoring. And he bore me away to a wilderness in spirit. And I saw a woman sitting upon a scarlet wild beast filled with names of blasphemy, having seven heads and ten horns. And the woman was clothed with purple and scarlet and goldened with gold and precious stone and pearls, having a golden cup in her hand full of abominations and** (having) **the unclean things of her whoring, and upon her forehead a name having been written:**

MYSTERY
BABYLON THE GREAT
THE MOTHER OF THE WHORES AND
OF THE ABOMINATIONS OF THE
EARTH

And I saw the woman being drunk from the blood of the saints and from the blood of the witnesses of Jesus. And I wondered, on seeing her, with great wonder.

John is granted the sight of this woman (v. 1-6), and then the angel explains (v. 7-18). The sight of her says much and is necessary for the understanding of the following explanation; but the sight also raises and intends to raise questions in John, which the angel then answers. In 7:13, etc., an elder explains quite similarly. But in 21:9, etc., we have the full counterpart to chapter 17. As one of the angels with a bowl here shows John the great whore, so in 21:9, etc., one of the angels with a bowl shows him the Lamb's Bride.

Is there the least gain in asking which of the seven angels with bowls this is and in arguing that it must be the seventh? Are we acquainted with each of them to be thus interested in which one is referred to?

The seven angels first came out of the Sanctuary (15:6); now one of them came to John and spoke with him. The μετά is used to express friendly association and is more than πρός which would mean simply facing John and delivering a message to him. This harmonizes with the angel's action in taking John with him to a place where he could see the great whore. John is asked to come along. Δεῦρο, "hither," an adverb, is prefixed to invitations or commands somewhat like our, "Come." The angel will show John the κρῖμα of the great whore, the judgment on her, not the κρίσις or action of judging but the result, the verdict upon her. It is a misunderstanding to say that the following contains no such *krima;* for v. 14-17 present the verdict as it shall be carried out, and all that precedes is the basis for it, without which the execution of this verdict could not be properly understood.

This is "the whore, the great one," ἡ πόρνη, with the verb πορνεύω and the noun πορνεία and also the plural τῶν πορνῶν following, all effectively repeating and impressing the idea of the *whore.* Thus all these expressions are to be translated similarly: *"the whore — to commit whoring — whoring — of the whores."* These words at once remind us of 14:8, where we have the first summary statement about Babylon the Great who makes all the nations drink of the wine of the passion "of *her whoring.*" All these terms that have the word "whore" bring to mind what the Old Testament has to say by means of this imagery of vile, filthy, abominable turning from God, which also runs through the New Testament until we here have its climax: "the whore, the great one" — "the mother of the whores." Note that in Revelation she is never called μοιχαλίς, "adulteress," for she was never bride or wife of the Lamb, never anything but a vile whore. Her sitting upon many waters = v. 15: "The waters which thou sawest, where the whore sits, are peoples and multitudes and nations and tongues." They are represented as "many waters" because of the countless waves that are always moving and surging and are seldom at rest. "Sitting" symbolizes established rule as we see from Christ's sitting at God's right hand and also from "the One sitting" on the throne (4:2).

2) This is, indeed, the supreme whore. The reason for calling her so is stated in the relative clause: "with whom there committed whoring (the verb is placed forward for the sake of emphasis) the kings of the earth." These, all these, are her paramours. It is not necessary to think that the next clause should also be a relative clause. It is not intended to be a parallel clause; it is purposely independent, for it interprets the greatness of this whore and what the whoring of all these kings of the earth with this monstrous whore means: "and there were made drunk those inhabiting the earth, from the wine of her whoring." This is plainly a repetition of 14:8: "the wine of the

passion of her whoring," which Babylon the Great gave "all the nations" to drink. Again the verb is emphatic: "drunk were they made." Note also the advance: "she gave to drink" (14:8), and now "they were made drunk" by receiving that wine of whoring. Note, likewise, that the abomination of whoring is intensified by the abomination of becoming drunk, the climax of filthiness in both expressions, yet both refer to the same thing.

So vast this whoring! Οἱ κατοικοῦντες τὴν γῆν repeats this significant expression from 3:10; 6:10; 8:13; 11:10; 13:8; 12:14; 17:8, but the accusative τὴν γῆν appears to be stronger than the phrase ἐπὶ τῆς γῆς. These are "the earth dwellers," whose whole heart and life are attached only to the earth, who have no love for heaven and the Lamb, for the cleansing of his blood, for holiness. In 13:8, "all those dwelling on the earth" are described as those whose names are not written in the Lamb's Book of Life, as those who do obeisance to the beast, the antichristian power. In 13:14-18 they are the ones deceived by the second beast, the antichristian propaganda (called "the pseudo-prophet" in 16:13), who carry the mark of the beast, namely his number "666." The multitude of them like "many waters" is recounted in 13:7: "every tribe and people and tongue and nation"; in 13:16: "all, the small and the great, and the rich and the beggarly, and the free and the slave"; and once more in 17:15: "peoples and multitudes and nations and tongues." The καί — καί — καί in all the lists heap up the terms, each one of which already signifies great numbers.

Need we be surprised to find that the true believers constitute so small a flock today and the antichristians so vast a host?

(1) The first wild beast (13:1-10) *is the antichristian power*.

(2) The second wild beast (13:11-18) is the *antichristian propaganda,* thus the pseudo-prophet of 16:13.

(3) Babylon the Great is *the antichristian empire,* either summarily the whole empire, as in 14:8, or the capital with many vassal kings and domains, as in 16:12-16.

(4) The great whore is again Babylon the Great; but now she is presented as being clothed with all *the antichristian seductiveness,* as luring the earth dwellers to commit whoredom and to be made drunk with the wine of her whoring.

(5) The kings of the earth (see them already in 16:12, 14) are not individual kings such as the various Roman emperors, or individual emperors and kings of later centuries, or individual rulers in dynasties. Nor are these kings political and national kingdoms such as England, Belgium, Italy, or the United States and France with its presidents, or others with their dictators. Even republican Rome hated the very idea of a king, the rule of one man in any form. These "kings of the earth" who keep whoring with the great whore, who assemble with Babylon at Armageddon for the last great battle, who in the end hate and burn the whore (17:16) and yet lament and bewail her judgment (18:9, 10) — all these statements are involved in the symbolical concept "the kings of the earth" ("of the whole inhabited earth," 16:14) — are *the various parts of the antichristian empire.* They are called "kings," and each naturally has his kingdom, because rule in the many and various domains of the earth is referred to. Itemize these as you please: government, politics, commerce, education, art, manufacture, labor, amusement, etc. As time has gone on, these domains grow larger and larger so that each can be subdivided again and again. In each domain prominent leaders continue to appear. These together

with the power they represent and with the masses they sway are "the kings of the earth."

Everywhere on the earth these "kings" are infatuated with the great whore. Her seduction carries all of them away. They are drunk with the wine of her whoring, impervious to the Lamb's Word and warning. The angel uses aorists as though everything were already past history. We do not consider them prophetic aorists; for in the preliminary announcement the angel may well speak of the history of the whore as having already been concluded.

(6) The earth dwellers are *the antichristian multitudes.*

In a sense Babylon, the whore, the kings, the earth dwellers, are one and the same. So, for instance, are Jerusalem and her children in Matt. 23:37. Nevertheless, each designation has its own significance so that all four can be placed side by side in these visions and can act together and upon each other as is here described.

3) John says that the angel bore him away in spirit to an ἔρημον, a wilderness, a desert or lonely place. We translate "in spirit" (not "in Spirit," i. e., the Holy Spirit, R. V.) just as we did in 1:10 and in 4:2. Whereas, in 15:1, 5, John's spirit saw the seven angels with the bowls as they came out of the Sanctuary in heaven, he is now to be shown the great whore on the earth and in spirit is thus borne away and placed where he can really see her. One may ask whether "the wilderness" mentioned in 12:14, where the church had her place of refuge, has some relation to "a wilderness" from which John saw the antithesis of the church, the whore of antichristian seduction. One may ask this the more since εἰς ἔρημον is without the article. We consider it best to think that John was not to see the whore by having his spirit stand in the brothel of her whoring. He was rather to view her

from "a desert," from a place that was clean and uncontaminated by the dwellers on the earth. There John's spirit stood with only the angel beside him.

And now in vision he saw the whore: "a woman sitting upon a scarlet wild beast filled with names of blasphemy, having seven heads and ten horns." We take this to be the beast mentioned in 13:1, which symbolizes the whole antichristian power. The woman, the whole antichristian *seduction*, is thus connected with the whole antichristian *power*. The connection, too, seems significant: she sits upon this beast; by her *seduction* to whoring she *exercises the power* of the beast. She is dependent on the beast; the beast carries her. The names of blasphemy on the beast are those mentioned in 13:1, as are also the seven heads and the ten horns. The fact that the beast is now described simply as "scarlet" harmonizes with the vision of the woman who is also clothed in purple and "scarlet." We regard "scarlet" as the color of sin, the opposite of white (see "scarlet" Isa. 1:18). The masculine γέμοντα intentionally makes the neuter "beast" a person, i. e., the masculine personifies. The point to be noted here is the whore's connection with the beast, her relation to him.

4) The woman is now described in her seductiveness. Perhaps we may note that nothing is said about personal beauty of face or of form. She is clothed (periphrastic past perfect: had been and thus still was) with purple and scarlet (the usual accusatives after a passive). "Purple" may be regarded as "royal." She was robed as a great queen in order to impress, to be desirable to the little kings. Yet "purple and scarlet" are like the sin-scarlet of the beast.

A second perfect participle extends the periphrastic tense: "and (was) goldened with gold and precious stone (representative singular, scarcely just one great jewel) and pearls." She was excessively bedizened with the richest ornaments, was indeed arrayed like the greatest and richest queen in order to impress and to allure. We try to reproduce the cognates: "goldened with gold."

We now hear what the wine of her whoring really is (14:8; 17:2): "having a golden cup in her hand full of abominations, and (having) the unclean things of her whoring." Γέμον is the adjective, its genitive βδελυγμάτων is anarthrous, hence general and qualitative; "full of everything of the nature of abomination to God." Καὶ (epexegetical) τὰ ἀκάθαρτα τῆς πορνείας αὐτῆς adds this articulated object of ἔχουσα and thus states that "cup full of abominations" means "the unclean things of her whoring," both accusative and genitive being specific.

A "golden cup" invites and entices to drink, for who would offer anything but the most precious drink in a golden cup? Indeed, in such a cup the antichristian seduction is served, and the earth dwellers drink to drunkenness. There is the gold of exquisite poetry and prose in the whore's literature; the chased gold of her seductive science; the exquisite cup of her philosophy; the brilliance of her music and entertainment. Extend the list yourself. Yet within "abominations," "the unclean things of the great whore's whoring." The earth dwellers cannot be sated. These are not merely what are commonly called immoralities; the worst are the religious abominations: the beast that carries the whore is full of "names of blasphemy."

5) "And on the forehead a name written (perfect with present connotation): "Mystery — Babylon the Great — The Mother of the Whores and of the Abominations of the Earth." John is permitted to see what this "woman" on the scarlet beast really is. Zahn thinks that she herself wrote this name. Another recalls that famous prostitutes of the Roman world published their names. We may picture the name as

having been written on a band and bound across the forehead; or as written directly on the forehead like the "666" of 13:16-18 on hand or forehead, and like the seal of the saints on their forehead (7:3; 9:4). We think the name is intended to reveal to John what this woman truly is. She bears her name on her forehead just as the scarlet beast bears all its "names of blasphemy" all over itself.

Some think that Μυστήριον is not a part of the name but an apposition to ὄνομα = "a mysterious name"; or a parenthetical note: "mystery," indicating that "Babylon," etc., is to be understood mystically and not literally. We cannot accept this view. "Babylon the Great" has occurred twice (14:8; 16:19) without a note of any kind; and the rest of the name: "the mother of the whores," etc., has been explained in v. 1-4. "Mystery" must be a part of the whore's name. Zahn is correct, as, in fact, the word itself also indicates, μυστήριον is not something that is to remain hidden, about which one can only speculate, but something that is intended to be revealed; and when it is something evil as here it is to be exposed. Left to himself, John can only wonder, but the angel, who showed him what causes his wonder, at once says, "I myself will tell thee τὸ μυστήριον, this Mystery of the woman," i. e., what this name of hers contains, namely all that the angel then unfolds. Yes, this woman is a strange phenomenon about which one may well wonder, but no longer is this true when she is placed in this clear light.

She is indeed "Babylon the Great" as already said in 14:8 and 16:19, a great empire, a capital with a large number of vassal kings (16:12-16), but also, and in the view here presented of her, "the Mother of the Whores and of the Abominations of the Earth," *the Supreme Antichristian Seductress,* all of whose daughters are whores, the mother of all the antichristian abominations of the earth. Τῶν πορνῶν is feminine:

"of the whores"; the reading is not πόρνων, masculine (R. 233). The whores of which she is the mother are in substance "the kings of the earth." The "abominations" she offers in her golden cup are her own product and are not obtained elsewhere.

6) All the earth dwellers, all of whom drink of her wine of whoring, are said to be made drunk. This woman herself does not remain sober; John says: "And I saw the woman being drunk (present participle: in this condition) from the blood of the saints and from the blood of the witnesses of Jesus" (18:24). Revelation often has the simple name "Jesus." The saints and the witnesses are the same persons. The repetition of the phrase intends to emphasize. Some connect scarlet (v. 4) with this blood, but improperly. In this connection we should think of the martyrs mentioned in 6:9-11. Yea, bloodthirsty is this whore.

"And I wondered, having seen her, with great wonder." The aorists express the simple fact, the accusative is the cognate accusative. John has been faulted for wondering, which faulting is unwarranted, for the vision was intended to make him wonder. John wondered, as he himself says, "on seeing her," i. e., at sight of her, the whole sight made him wonder. Why pry into this or that to solve his wonder? And why confuse this woman with the one mentioned in 12:1, etc.? Those who identify the degenerate church or the papacy with this whore and woman and then cannot understand why John wondered how the church could degenerate so have an unclear conception of these visions. The whole antichristianity and its seduction is more than the papacy which is but a part of it. In these visions there is no degenerate church, but only the *Una Sancta* ("saints — witnesses of Jesus") and the antichristian Babylon, the great whore, the mother of the whores. Once more, she is not an "adulteress" (μοιχαλίς), the church that is untrue to her Husband

(Christ), but a "whore" (πόρνη) who never had a husband of any kind.

7) First the angel lets John see, now he lets him hear and himself explains what John has seen. **And the angel said to me: Wherefore didst thou wonder? I myself will tell thee the mystery of the woman and of the wild beast, the one carrying her and having the seven heads and the ten horns.** Διατί asks the reason for John's wondering, and not as though faulting John in the sense that John has no business to be wondering, but as implying that there *is* a reason for John to wonder, that John has unanswered questions in his mind. Well, the angel is here to answer these: "I will tell thee the mystery of the woman and of the beast, the one carrying her." The two belong together: without the power of antichristianity the seduction of antichristianity would lose its world-wide effectiveness. Like a mighty beast the power carries the bedizened seduction. The sense of τὸ μυστήριον is explained in v. 5: something that is intended to be revealed. From this fact the whore gets her name "Mystery."

In v. 3 the beast is described as having seven heads and ten horns; this is now repeated by using the articles of previous reference because the angel will explain what these heads and these horns symbolize.

8) First, however, he speaks about the beast himself. **The wild beast which thou didst see was and is not and is about to come up out of the abyss and is going into perdition. And they shall wonder, those dwelling on the earth, whose names have not been written on the Book of the Life from** (the) **world's foundation, on seeing the beast, that it was and is not and shall be present.**

This is the strange thing about this beast which John has now seen twice, here and in 13:1, etc., that "it was and is not and is about to come up out of the abyss," which the angel repeats, "that it was and is not and shall be present." But in the first statement the history of the beast is completed by at once adding: "and is going to perdition," ἀπώλεια, the standing term for the perdition of hell. No more is here said about the end of the beast. The rest we learn in 19:20 and 20:10: perdition = the lake of fire and brimstone. This statement about the end of the beast is inserted here only incidentally so that John may at once know. The main point is the feature about the beast which caused all the earth dwellers (see v. 2 on this constantly repeated term) to wonder. We have heard about this wondering before, in 13:3, 4: "there did wonder the whole earth behind the wild beast," i. e., run after it, gaping in admiration and saying, "Who is like to the wild beast? and who is able to do battle with him?" In 13:3 "did wonder" presents the fact historically; "shall wonder" now presents it as happening in the time to come.

The wonder of admiration concerns the return of the beast. This return is restated from 13:3, 12, but more briefly and pointedly. In 13:3, 12 the beast received a deathblow in one of its seven heads and yet recovered and caused the whole world's admiration and exclamation because of the fact that no one could defeat the beast in battle. We saw in connection with 13:3, 4 that the exaltation of Christ delivered this deathblow to the beast, the antichristian power, and crushed it completely; yet the antichristian power was healed, recovered by the help of the dragon, Satan (12:9), who had given all his power, his throne, and authority, to the beast (13:2). This recovery made the blind earth dwellers imagine that the beast was invincible, that this recovery proved that nothing could ever conquer the antichristian power; hence they chose what they were certain was the winning side. We see it all about us today: the earth dwellers despise the

Una Sancta and Christ and glory in the invincibility of the power of antichristianity: "Who can do successful battle with it?"

It is this fact that is now restated. This beast which carries the woman and is identified as being the one mentioned in 13:1 by having seven heads and ten horns, "was and is not and is about to come up out of the abyss — was and is not and shall be present." "Is not" = when it received its death stroke through Christ's exaltation (13:3); "is about to come up" and "shall be present" = its recovery. Some date the tenses from the moment of the angel's speaking to John: "was" prior to this moment; "is not" at this moment; "about to come up" and "shall be present" some time after this moment. Those who think of the Roman emperors may date Revelation so early as to make the recovered beast and his return = Nero-redivivus.

These three tenses are past, present, future only in relation to each other: this beast "was," ἦν, for a long time in its own past; it did not continue thus, a death-blow struck it, οὐκ ἔστι, "is not," followed the "was"; then μέλλει ἀναβαίνειν and παρέσται succeeded "is not." He who knows about the exaltation of the Lamb and is guided by that is able to define the tenses correctly in their relation to each other.

In 13:1 the beast comes up "out of the sea" (see this passage); this is its *first* coming up to wield its terrible power over the earth dwellers. Now the angel says that the beast is about to come up "out of the abyss" and "shall be present." But this is its *second* coming up which follows "was" and "is not." Thus there is no conflict with 13:1. This phrase shows how terrible the death stroke was: it threw the beast into the abyss, and by means of its return it came up out of this abyss. Throughout these visions "the abyss" (articulated, definite) is hell; no one has ever shown that more than this one abyss exists. To speak of several abysses, none of which is hell, is unwarranted.

The fact that the names of the earth dwellers who admire the supposedly invincible beast have not been written in the Lamb's Book of the Life we have seen in 13:8, where also the phrase "from (the) world's foundation" is discussed. Instead of concluding that the antichristian world power, after once receiving a death stroke that causes its ἦν to become οὐκ ἔστι, is due for another stroke that will cause it "to go into perdition" (we read ὑπάγει and not the infinitive of the R. V., or the future of the A. V.), some interpreters conclude the opposite, namely that now nothing will ever destroy the beast. For this very reason the angel says, "it is going into perdition," is already on the way.

9) So much for the beast as a beast; now a bit of information in regard to its seven heads and its ten horns. **Here the mind, the one having wisdom!** This is a preamble like the one occurring in 13:18, the mind that has wisdom from the Word, let it apply its wisdom here, namely in regard to what the angel now says about the heads and the horns. Read the commentaries and see how many commentators have used such wisdom. It is a simple matter to see the many patent mistakes; this writer prays for wisdom that he may not likewise fall into mistakes, that he may at least harm no soul that reads his humble efforts. This has been his earnest prayer throughout; it is needed here especially.

The seven heads, the angel says, **seven mountains are, where the woman sits on them; and seven kings they are. The five fell** (our idiom: have fallen); **the one is; the other not yet did come** (our idiom: has not yet come); **and when he comes** (aorist: gets to come) **for a little he must remain. And the wild beast which was and is not also himself is an eighth and is out of the seven and goes into**

perdition. And the ten horns which thou didst see are ten kings, such as did not yet receive kingdom but receive authority as kings for one hour together with the wild beast.

The two numbers "seven" and "ten" cannot be understood literally; they must be symbolical, cf., 13:1. We cannot list seven actual kings, seven dynasties of kings with their kingdoms, or seven forms or types of secular government and then add ten kings who are represented by the horns, who, with their kingdoms, followed the first seven, thus making a list of seventeen secular kings.

Many commentators refer this statement of the angel to "Europe" as though these kings lived in the early ages or in the middle ages, as though the history of this beast transpires only in Europe, in the Roman Empire and its Cæsars, and then in the papacy and in ten further European governments (some say ten, but others have more, and some less) that arose out of the Roman or out of the Germanic empire *but all to be found in Europe* as though the beast were only the *European* antichristian power, as though all the rest of the world (save perhaps the foreign colonies of the European governments) is ignored.

With such an interpretation we class the view which makes the beast the antichristian *state* power. All that the angel says about "kings" is understood in this way. It is often stated outright, but sometimes it is only assumed. The pagan emperors of Rome seem to have led to this idea of having the antichristian state power represented by the beast, its heads and its horns. We regard this view as being too narrow. The papacy is often introduced, and the scarlet woman is regarded as a reference to it. This refers everything to religious and ecclesiastical matters only; and so we are told about Cæsaropapism which generally culminates in a tremendous personal antichrist who will at the end control all state and all ecclesiastical power and have his seat on the city of seven hills (hills, but v. 9 says ἑπτὰ ὄρη, "mountains"), Rome.

Most writers go back to 13:1 in order to find an interpretation for the seven heads and the ten horns, where they are found on the first beast to whom the dragon gave his power, his throne, and great authority. But the seven heads and the ten horns appear already on the dragon mentioned in 12:3. Heads and horns are not the same otherwise there would be seventeen of one or of the other. This would destroy the symbolism by the use of an unsymbolical number. Review the remarks made in connection with 13:1 as to why there are seven heads and ten horns and why in the case of the dragon the seven heads have seven diadems (12:3) but in the case of the beast the ten horns have these diadems. The gist is: seven proud *dragon heads* as though they are filled with *holy thoughts and designs,* and in the case of the dragon the seven *heads* crowned with seven diadems as though all the *designs in the heads* of the dragon were *royal.* So the beast, too, has seven heads like the dragon as though the antichristian power thinks the same holy thoughts as its hellish lord, the dragon. In the case of the beast the ten *horns* have the diadems, for these horns (powers) of the beast use only the designs conceived by the diademed dragon's heads.

The dragon has ten horns which are symbols of power, ten to indicate his power in its completeness. So also the beast has ten horns but in the case of the beast the ten horns wear ten diadems; its complete power is to be openly displayed as being royal; it is to reign, is to demand and to receive the servile obeisance of all the dwellers on the earth. Carefully, however, we are told (13:2) that *the dragon gave* his power, his throne (royal rule), his great authority to this first beast whom also the second beast serves.

All that is stated in 12:3 and 13:1, etc., we consider the basis for what the angel now tells John in regard to the significance of the seven heads and of the ten horns which he saw on the beast.

"The seven heads are seven mountains, where the woman sits on them," ἐπ' αὐτῶν is pleonastic. When v. 10 adds, "seven kings are they," we ought not to think that the symbol "seven mountains" is inadequate and thus turn our attention to "seven kings." The woman "sits" on these mountains, and since they are the seven heads of the beast upon which she "sits," we see more fully her relation to the beast, i. e., the relation of the antichristian seduction to the antichristian power. The heads of the beast are not his horns, nor is their symbolic number the same. These seven *mountain heads* of the beast appear to be *the high, proud, imposing thoughts, plans, designs of the antichristian power,* as "seven" they are pseudo-holy, they intend, as they tower into the sky, to replace and to usurp the holy, saving thoughts of God; men are to look only to these beast mountains. They carry the great whore, the antichristian seduction, and this attracts the earth dwellers. She "sits on them" and by her seduction exercises the sway of the thoughts and the designs in these mountain heads of the beasts. As "mountains" they appear vast, dominating, never to be overthrown as the earth dwellers also imagine although we cannot help but think of Jesus' word in Matt. 17:20.

10) "And seven kings are they," namely, the seven heads of the beasts. "Kings" views them from another angle. We do not think that "seven mountains" = seven empires, and that "seven kings" = seven rulers or ruling dynasties or types of government, one each for each empire. The seven heads and

head kings cannot signify the same thing as the ten horns and *horn kings*. Heads = dominating thoughts, plans, designs, seven of them to usurp the place of God's holy thoughts. Horns = powers which strike to overthrow, ten of them to indicate the sum of the beast's powers. Retain the symbolical numbers "seven" and "ten" and do not regard them as literal.

The five head kings "fell," the one head king "is" (exists), the other head king "did not yet come," and when he does come (aorist, actually come), he will have to (δεῖ) remain some little while (ὀλίγον, accusative to express extent of time). While this is said in regard to the head kings, one feels that it applies also to the head mountains. So the beast seems to have *one* design, one general dominating scheme *at a time* with which to enthrall the earth dwellers. There are at all times head kings, but not always do we find the same one. No less than five "fell," ἔπεσαν, the same verb used in the same sense as ἔπεσε in 14:8. Of the symbolic (not literal) seven only two are left, the one existing at the present time, and one yet to come to remain some little while. This is evidently not the will of the beast regarding his heads or head kings. *He* wanted none of his heads to fall in defeat. The present one will follow the other five; the last one, by the necessity (δεῖ) of God's will, is to remain for some little while but is then doomed like the others. So end the seven heads and head kings of the beast, the dominating thoughts, plans, designs with which, through the course of history, he sought to supplant the holy, saving plans of God and of the Lamb.

The numbers "five," "the one," "the other" are not symbolical but become so because of the symbolical "seven" of the "heads" and head kings. Since this "seven" is symbolical, we can in no way make a literal count of the mighty schemes with which the beast tried, tries, and is yet to try to supplant the holy plans of God. His last schemes and plans seem to culminate in the last battle presented in 16:12-16 and anew in 17:12-14 and in 19:11-21. The head and head king that "is" at present we regard as a reference to the plans of the beast that are in operation in John's time and still continue in our own time. So also we consider that these last two are to occupy our main attention. The "five" have already been demolished and lie in the past: All that they included we may gather from the old histories, when they are read with spiritual eyes, when by means of the beast Satan "deceived the nations" (20:3) during the time before Christ.

In 13:1 the beast appears as "having ten horns and seven heads" like the dragon in 12:3; so also in 17:3. No more is said in 13:1 and in 17:3. The beast is at once viewed with all his horns and all his heads; what a bearing his heads and also his horns have the further revelation contained in the angel's words states in these verses, 10-12, etc.

One more remark: "the kings of the earth" of v. 2 and the seven head kings and the ten horn kings (v. 10 and 12) are only similar symbols. In v. 2 "the kings" are mentioned only in general with the drunken earth dwellers; here in v. 10 we have them as a succession of head kings that are grouped under the pseudo-holy "seven."

11) Still more is said about the head kings. "And the beast which was and is not also himself is an eighth and is out of the seven and goes into perdition." "Which was and is not" repeats this fact regarding the beast from v. 8 and thereby again emphasizes what happened to the beast at the time of Christ's glorification as we have sought to explain in v. 8 (compare 13:3). In the repetition the abbreviated statement is enough; for what has already happened to the beast is

an indication of what will eventually happen as is also again stated by adding, "it goes into perdition" with all its heads and all its horns despite the might, arrogance, and defiance with which it lifts them on high and also despite the seduction employed through the woman, the great whore.

The statement that the beast "also himself is an eighth and is out of the seven" reads as though it has to make itself "an eighth" in order to help out when it comes to its last head king, its last schemes and plans of domination in its mighty efforts to supplant God's holy plans. So αὐτός, "he himself," appears as "an eighth." There is a difference of opinion as to how ἐκ τῶν ἑπτά is to be understood. The partitive view of ἐκ does not fit as though the beast is one of the seven head kings; perhaps ἐκ is resultant: "out of the seven" as the final resultant, their final concentration and consummation, the beast, this eighth himself, goes into perdition. This is repeated from v. 8 for the sake of emphasis.

12) This leaves the ten horns. Although they were seen in 13:1 and in 17:3, and although the horns, too, are "kings," they symbolize "such as did not yet receive kingdoms but receive authority as kings for one hour together with the beast." The number "ten" is symbolical. The ten Commandments = *all* of them; ten virgins, *all* of them; thus ten occurs repeatedly in the parables and elsewhere. Horns = power to strike. So we take the ten horn kings to be all the powers of the beast, the sum total of the antichristian power. Since they are presented separately as "ten horns" and are distinct from the "seven heads," we are to see in the ten horn kings the antichristian brute forces with a show of royalty, with dominance and rule. These have not yet received "kingdom," for they are to function toward the end μίαν ὥραν (accusative to express extent

like ὀλίγον in v. 10), for the space of an hour, and are given ἐξουσία, "authority" and power to wield accordingly; βασιλεία and ἐξουσία are substantially the same. Μετὰ τοῦ θηρίου = "in company with the beast," *all* his adjuncts aiding him when he rallies himself and *all* his forces for the last battle. We regard 16:12-15 as the exposition: "the kings from the sunrising — the kings of the whole inhabited earth" who come and are brought together at Armageddon for the final battle.

13) **These have one consent, and they give their power and authority to the wild beast.** Although they are so many, namely *all* the antichristian forces, these horn kings have one interest and one idea. They are absolutely unanimous in their antichristian intent. And thus they unanimously give all their power and authority to the beast so that the arch-antichristian monster power may use it for the last battle. This complete unanimity is produced by the three frog-like unclean spirits (16:13).

14) **These shall do battle with the Lamb, and the Lamb shall conquer them because he is Lord of lords and King of kings; and they together with him** (are) **called and elect and faithful.** This is "the battle of the day, the great one, of God the Almighty" mentioned in 16:14, which shall be fought against the Lamb, for which also by God's will the last head king (with royal *designs*) must (δεῖ) remain (v. 10), for which all of the ten kings (with royal, dominating *powers*) receive authority for one hour with the beast (v. 12). It is God's plan to have this "day" arrive when the beast and all his horn kings (powers) shall go into perdition.

On that "day" the Lamb shall conquer them in a final, absolute victory. See 19:11-21. How can this Lamb conquer such a monstrous wild beast — see the description in 13:1, 2 — who comes with the seventh head king (the beast's final royal plans) and with these ten horn kings (the totality of his arrogated royal powers) with the most terrifying might? Because the Lamb is

Lord of lords, King of kings

It seems strange that this grand double title, which is repeated in 19:16, receives but little attention on the part of the commentators. In particular, they do not seem to ask of what lords, of what kings the Lamb is Κύριος and βασιλεύς. In the previous verses "kings" are mentioned repeatedly. The Lamb is not the King of these. What kings are then left, of whom he can be King? Some think of secular kings such as King George of England, King Albert of Belgium, King so and so of this and of that country.

These "kings" and "lords" of which the Lamb is King and Lord are the Lamb's loyal vassals who are here called "they with him" (μετά, in his company) and are then described as κλητοί, ἐκλεκτοί, πιστοί: "called" by the gospel and that in the sense of effectively called (so throughout the epistles); "elect" from all eternity; "faithful," trustworthy — or shall we translate πιστοί, "believers"? The word "faithful" is used in the sense which it has in 1:5; 2:13; and most likely also in 3:14. How these can be called "kings" and "lords" (a synonym) appears from I Pet. 2:9 and Rev. 1:6. See the author's *Kings and Priests* on the subject of the royalty of believers. Will the saints, these kings and lords, be in "the armies" of 19:14? The R. V. lets also "those with the Lamb" conquer; but the A. V. is better. The Lamb is the Conqueror, the saints are with him only in order to share in his royal victory even as their royalty is bestowed upon them by him.

15) Reverting to v. 1, the angel explains: **And he says to me** — this preamble separates v. 15-18 from the preceding and makes it a unit by itself —:

The waters which thou didst see, where the whore sits, peoples and multitudes are they and nations and tongues. Note the similar lists of four in 13:7 and of four pairs in 13:16. Sufficient explanation is supplied in connection with v. 1.

16) Now an astonishing thing! The whore sits like a queen over all these peoples, etc., and makes them drunk with the wine of her whoring (v. 2), and yet what shall happen? **And the ten horns which thou didst see and the beast, these shall hate the whore, and desolated shall they make her and naked, and her flesh parts shall they devour, and her they shall burn up in fire. For God gave into their hearts to do his counsel and to make one consent and to give their kingdom to the beast until there shall be finished the words of God. And the woman whom thou didst see is the city, the great one, the one having kingship over the kings of the earth.**

At first the beast carries the whore (v. 3 and 7), and the ten horns (horn kings) on the beast harm the whore so little that they give their power and authority to the beast carrying the whore (v. 13) because they are delighted to see her ride. Now these same horn kings and the beast are said eventually to hate, strip, devour, and burn her up — four verbs. The commentators, for the most part, pass by the riddle as to how so violent a change occurs in the horn kings (powers) and even in the beast himself (the antichristian power). Of course, God brings it about (v. 17), but may we say no more? One has said more, namely that history commonly shows how provinces eventually destroy the central power. But we see what produces this silence in regard to the way in which the whore perishes: the commentators debate regarding what the whore represents and decide for pagan Rome or papal Rome or the apostate church of the future (see the convenient grouping in Biederwolf's *Millennium Bible,* together with the lists of arguments).

The whore is the tool of the beast, the delight of the kings, and so these latter coddle her. The antichristian seduction (the whore) wins the earth dwellers for the antichristian power (the beast) and delights the antichristian forces (the kings); as long as this continues, all is lovely for the whore. But then comes the battle (or perhaps it occurs during or immediately after this battle). The giddy drunkenness of the wine of the whore's whoring (v. 2) ceases to attract. The beast and the horn kings see that with her abominations she is bringing (or has brought) this awful battle upon them, and so like dogs and swine they turn and rend her.

Her end is that they shall hate her. "Desolated shall they make her and naked." This is the first act of hate. Ἠρημωμένην, the perfect passive participle with its present connotation is used as an adjective and is placed first. No one any longer courts the whore. "And naked" leaves her stripped of her gorgeous purple and scarlet robes and of her gold, jewels, and pearls (v. 4). The hate goes farther: "her flesh parts (σάρκας is plural; we should say simply: flesh) they shall eat" like beasts devouring a victim. Nothing shall be left of her who served abominations and the unclean things of her whoring (v. 4): "her (i. e., her herself) they shall burn up in fire." Just retribution for her! Also revelation of what the beastliness of this beast and his horns really are.

The fact that those who were infatuated with the whore are described as turning against the whore is not strange. The antichristian seduction that affords sin's delight is bound to disappoint and to disgust in the end. This is always true with regard to sin's delight. The statement that the lovers of the whore devour her like cannibals and burn her up is a picture of the reality. These acts are so unspeakably monstrous when they are placed in the divine light. We have seen how all the things of hell are monstrosities; so all the acts inspired by hell are monstrous. In v. 17 we learn that this destruction of the whore is accomplished by the will of God. He ever uses sin to devour and to punish sin, one antichristian force to bring just retribution on another. The reality governs this symbolism and its horribleness.

17) Thus we are now shown that behind this judgment on the whore (v. 1) — and it is surely a judgment that is fully merited — there appears the retributive will of God who at last brings on the battle that ruins the whore's success in seduction and thus "gave into their hearts to do his consent (γνώμη) and to make one consent (the same word: one consent with God) and to give their kingdom (βασιλεία, rule or *Koenigtum*) to the beast" when thus making away with their former tool and delight. Now all follow the beast blindly. They cannot go much farther "until there shall be finished the words of God," τελεσθήσονται (τελέω), shall be brought to their τέλος or goal, all the λόγοι, the prophetic statements God has made. Not one *logos* shall remain unfulfilled. Yes, the beast himself, the whole antichristian power in the world, shall agree with God in one consent (γνώμη) and bring on his (the beast's) own doom as he first brings on the whore's doom.

18) We have already, in v. 1 and throughout, stated fully what we understand by "the woman," and in what sense she is Babylon. According to one view Babylon is the great antichristian empire as an empire (summary), or the central city with many vassal domains (more detailed). According to another view Babylon is the whole antichristian seduction, "the mother of the whores" (specific character). Follow

what John wrote, and this becomes clear. R. 776 shows the force of the articles when they are repeated with the modifiers: "*the* city, *the* great," *the* one having kingship, βασιλείαν, *Koenigtum* over the kings of the earth (οἱ βασιλεῖς τῆς τῆς, in v. 2), namely by means of her seduction as this is brought out in the first part of the chapter.

Again the vision stops short. How the words of God shall be brought to their final goal remains for further visions.

Anticipating, let us add: in successive visions we are shown the dragon, the two beasts, the whore, and how they arise and dominate. These are Satan, the whole antichristian world power and the world propaganda, the whole antichristian world seduction. Their appearance is presented in separate visions, not because of a succession in time, but only because each is to receive full and separate attention in these revelations. In the same way, namely in separate visions, the doom of the three is revealed. But the order is reversed. First the doom of the whore or the antichristian seduction (Babylon), here in v. 16-18; next, the doom of the two beasts and their following (the whole antichristian power and propaganda) in 19:19-21; thirdly, the doom of the dragon, Satan, in 20:7-10. As the three do not appear successively but simultaneously in the reality, so the three disappear simultaneously in the reality. When this is perceived, much that is stated in this chapter becomes clear.

CHAPTER XVIII

The Magnificence of the Great Whore and the Lament over her, chapter 18

1) This vision adds new features to the previous one and reveals the tragedy of the great whore in all its details. It may be divided into three minor sections.

The First Part of the Vision, verses 1-3

After these things I saw another angel coming down out of the heaven, having great authority; and the earth was made light from his glory. And he cried in a strong voice, saying:

There fell, there fell Babylon the Great!
And did become a habitation of demons,
And a hold of every unclean spirit,
And a hold of every unclean and hated bird.
Because from the wine of the passion of her whoring there have been falling all the nations;
And the kings of the earth together with her did commit whoring;
And the merchants of the earth from the power of her wantonness grew rich.

The μετὰ ταῦτα does not denote an interval of hours, days, or weeks. It did not indicate such an interval in 15:5; it does not do so here. This angel adds to what the angel mentioned in 17:1, etc., shows and tells John about it. The one mentioned in 17:1 is one of the seven mighty angels with a bowl, and this one is equally great. He comes out of heaven, not to enter the wilderness of 17:3, but to appear above the earth where Babylon lies in final, absolute ruin. He has "great authority" to make his pronouncement so authoritative. Due to his glory and effulgence the earth was lighted up, yet not, we think, to show that "the light of the day of Christ is breaking for the earth after the night of judgment," but because of the pronouncement he now makes. In the light of his heavenly glory the ruin of Babylon on earth is fully revealed. Accompanying this angel's great authority and glory ἔκραξεν ἐν ἰσχυρᾷ φωνῇ, he shouts in a strong voice, the word "strong" is exceptional, "great" being the word usually employed. So tremendous is his voice, not in order that John may hear what he says, nor that all the earth may hear. Babylon is in ruins and does not need to be told, nor can she any longer hear; but because this angel proclaims a destruction that is so vast and terrible.

2) Some of the words recall those of the Old Testament: Isa. 13:21, 22; 34:13-15; yet we have throughout noted that in these visions there are only allusions to the Old Testament and nothing more. This is true with reference to the allusions to Daniel. "There fell, there fell Babylon the Great!" tragically repeats 14:8, see that passage. "And did become (in our idiom: has fallen — has become) a habitation of demons and a hold of unclean spirits and a hold of every unclean and hated bird," so foul a place, so desolate because of foulness and horror. Φυλακή may mean "prison" to which demons and unclean spirits are banished by God. Compare Isa. 34:13; 13:21, 22. It is a gruesome place that makes one's flesh creep, one's hair stand on end with horror.

3) This fate of Babylon is just: "Because from the wine of the passion of her whoring there have been

falling (perfect tense: for so long a time) the nations; and the kings of the earth together with her did commit whoring." This repeats 17:2, in particular "the wine of the passion of her whoring," "the kings of the earth," and "all the nations." We need not repeat the comment.

The last clause is new: "and the merchants (ἔμποροι) from the power of her wantonness (ἐκ to indicate source) grew rich." Στρῆνος = *Ueppigkeit*, luxurious, abandoned extravagance. Later we shall hear more about these "merchants" and also about "shipmasters." When we recall that Babylon = the whole antichristian seductiveness (see 17:2) in all the departments of human life for all the earth dwellers (see the lists in 13:7, 8, 16) we shall not regard these "merchants of the earth" as literal merchants but shall see that they are all those who pander to the antichristian seduction and themselves batten on this seduction.

The world is full of them today, many of them being great, multitudes of them being small. They set up their emporiums everywhere: thousands of them have big establishments in politics all over the world, hundreds of thousands have them in schools and education with seductive antichristian wares. Who will count them in books, magazines, the press! They import and export, ever doing a big selling business, finding delighted buyers everywhere, maintaining vast chain stores all over the world. Antichristian display wherever you turn. Babylon, "the Mother of the Whores" (17:5), is well served by her "merchants" who sell the seductive goods for her whoring. They "grow rich" through it, for it certainly pays. The verb agrees with "merchants," yet the whole statement is symbolical and should not be reduced to mere monetary riches but should be regarded in the light of what is regarded as profit in Babylon the Great.

The Second Part of the Vision, verses 4-19

4) **And I heard another voice out of the heaven saying:**

Go out, my people, from her
Lest you fellowship with her sins
And from her plagues lest you receive!
Because glued together were her sins up to the heaven,
And God did remember her unrighteous acts.

This is "another voice from the heaven" which speaks for God and thus says, "my people." The previous statements (v. 2, 3) are expressed by means of aorists: Babylon's fall is viewed as having occurred. This view properly precedes. This other voice addresses "my people" in imperatives, and we see that now Babylon is viewed as she was when she was still standing with all her seduction. God calls upon his people to separate themselves from Babylon lest they be involved in her awful judgment. This is the same call as those found in Jer. 50:8; 51:6, 45; Isa. 48:20; 52:11; II Cor. 6:17. God's people must definitely come out and separate from (aorist) all the antichristian seduction lest they have actual fellowship with the sins of this seduction. Their *κοινωνία,* fellowship, must be with God. Start with I John 1:3 and follow through what this epistle says on "fellowship" and then take up Paul, Eph. 5:11. The constant danger confronting God's people is to be taken in by the antichristian seduction which seeks to entice and to entangle them. What is said about Babylon and the whore does not occur at the very end. This call to "come out" had its application in John's time, it applies with equal force now. Even the least degree of fellowship with the antichristian seductiveness fellowships her sins and thus incurs the guilt which will receive "from her plagues," the seven *πληγαί* described in chapter 16.

5) The reason that God calls to his people to come out is now stated: "because (ὅτι) her sins were glued up to the heaven," meaning, have been glued together to form such a mass that it reaches even to heaven and demands punishment. In other words, "God remembered her ἀδικήματα," a term in -μα that expresses result, the unrighteous acts or results produced by Babylon, the antichristian seductiveness. This is the remembrance explained in 16:19, the cessation of God's long-suffering which precipitates the awful reckoning of judgment.

6) Hence the voice out of the heaven calls out:

Duly give to her as also she duly gave!
And double the double according to her works!
In the cup which she mixed mix to her double!
How many things glorified her and made (her) **wanton,**
So much torment give her and mourning!
Because in her heart she says: I sit as queen
And widow I am not and mourning I shall not see.

Who is to do this to Babylon? The plural imperatives sound exactly like the one used in v. 4, as though God's people are told to pay Babylon her due. The main reason for not accepting this view is that elsewhere Scripture does not agree with it. One may say that the executioners of this judgment are not named in the vision as they are not named in the parable in Matt. 22:13. Many think that the unnamed retaliators are the ones mentioned in 17:16, the more so since in 17:17, God puts his consent into their hearts. Perhaps this is correct.

'Από in ἀποδίδωμι = to give what is due, to give or pay in full. So here: "Duly give to her as also she duly gave!" Mete just as she did mete. God is just.

The seductress was generous, her reward shall be equally so. God does not hold back one penny from what is due anyone. That would be cheating, would be unjust. Babylon will have to sign a receipt in full.

"Double the double according to her works!" says the same thing. She was lavish, handed out her seductions διπλᾶ, "double." Do the same doubling for her, "according to her works." She dealt out "the double" in her works of seduction; it will not be just to give her "the single," only the half of what she earned, she would have the right to sue for the rest. Some think that these words mean that Babylon is to receive double the punishment that is actually due her, for which view they refer to Isa. 40:2. The fact that this would be injustice is ignored. The fact that Isa. 40:2 says the opposite is not understood even by Delitzsch who tries to excuse God; for there Israel receives double *grace and blessing* in place of penalties; see Isa. 61:7, etc.: "For your shame you shall have double (i. e., honor); and for confusion they shall rejoice in their portion: therefore in their land they shall have double: everlasting joy shall be upon them." See the author's *Eisenach Old Testament Selections*, 65, etc.

The passages to be quoted are Jer. 16:18; 17:18, and these as 50:15, 29 indicate: "As she hath done, do unto her — recompense her according to her work": thus in 16:18 and 17:18 "double" for her double sin. The scales of the balance of justice shall be even. Throughout Scripture there rings the expression: "according to the works," not in the sense of gaining merit for the godly but in the sense of public evidence in God's public judgment, evidence of faith in the godly, evidence of its absence in the ungodly (Matt. 25:31-46).

"In the cup which she mixed mix to her double!" The reference is to *her* cup with "the wine of the passion of her whoring" (17:3; 14:8), her "golden cup full of abominations"; and then to "the cup of the wrath of *God,*" "of the wine of the anger of *God*" (14:10). "Mix to her double" does not mean: double what she mixed, but: double as she mixed double whoring. Wine was mixed before it was drunk: so much wine and so much spicing was poured into water. As the whore Babylon mixed double portions of wine and spicing to make her dupes the more swiftly and completely drunk (17:2b), so a double quantity of God's wrath is to be mixed into her cup. This is again exact justice.

7) We regard ὅσα as the subject because τοσοῦτον βασανισμόν belong together as the object of the correlative clause, and because αὐτήν is not reflexive (as our versions make it): "How many things glorified her and made (her) wanton (note the corresponding noun στρῆνος in v. 3), so much torment give her and mourning!" just so much in precise justice. The amount will be excessive but not one particle beyond the excessive glory and wantonness (*Ueppigkeit*) with which she exalted herself. The measure of her exaltation is the measure of her abasement. "Torture" is the pain inflicted, "mourning" the reaction expressed.

He who is the Καρδιογνώστης, the Heartknower, adds the reason: "Because in her heart she says: 'I sit as a queen and widow I am not and mourning I shall not see'" (ἴδω, futuristic subjunctive). We should not pass lightly over "I sit" but notice "sitting" in 17:2, 3. The antichristian seduction "sits" established "as a queen," *exercises* her seductive power as she is upheld by the beast, the antichristian power. Her glorying in the fact that she is not a widow has no reference to a husband, for this is a whore; her boast refers to the multitude of her paramours, "the kings of the earth." No, we see that she is not a lonely, forsaken widow, but is ever surrounded by those who whore with her.

Never will she see (i. e., experience) mourning; πένθος is the very word found in the previous sentence.

8) Now God's voice speaks in future tenses. **Because of this, in one day there shall come her plagues, death and mourning and famine, and in fire shall they burn her up; because strong the Lord God, the One who judged her! And they shall sob and wail over her, the kings of the earth, the ones that committed whoring with her and wantoned when they see the smoke of her burning, standing from afar because of the fear of her torment, saying:**

Woe, woe! The city! The great one!
Babylon! The city! The strong one!
Because at one hour came thy judging!

The tenses are prophetic futures. "Because of this," Babylon's high boast and all that it involves, "in one day," i. e., suddenly, her plagues shall come and strike her down. The language recalls that of the Old Testament found in Ezek. 26, and 27, note 26:16. The images of the city and of the whore are interwoven even as cities and empires are commonly personified as females. The antichristian seduction shall collapse with its pride, arrogance, bloodiness. That collapse involves all who had part in it, who are here designated as "the kings of the earth," to whom "the merchants of the earth" are added in v. 3, and in v. 17, "every . shipmaster," etc. This makes the picture graphic. It is painted with unusual detail like many in the Old Testament because of the world-wide seduction which affects all the earth dwellers (3:10; 6:10; 8:13; 11:10; 13:8; 12:14; 17:8, the antichristian multitudes, 13:16), all of whom are involved in the fall of Babylon. The lament will be sounded from every quarter with a universal "Woe! Woe!" (v. 10, 16, 19).

Some offer little comment on v. 8-10, Zahn and Bousset but a single sentence. Yet one may ask why the order is "death, mourning, and famine," and then "in fire shall they burn her up," the latter repeating 17:16. Also, why all the lovers of the whore here lament over her while in 17:16 they hate her and themselves burn her up in fire. We may say that "death" is placed first, and then "mourning and famine" follow because the picture is that of a city which "death" invades but strikes down gradually, part after part, "mourning and famine" occurring in the parts before "death" reaches them in its progress. As for the hating and the burning of the whore, and yet all these "kings of the earth" lamenting, the solution is not that first these kings "cooled their vengeance" on the whore and then grieved that they had done so. Let the paradox remain. There *is* no reason in the unreason of antichristianity, least of all when its seduction works itself out to completion. The lover of a whore strangles her and then weeps like a fool.

Note the terrible repetitions of ὅτι, "because" (v. 5, 7, and now again): the sins that touch the heaven (*himmelschreiende Suenden*) — the proud whore — the just God. These causes bring about the doom. The ultimate cause is Κύριος ὁ Θεός (11:17), *he*, "the Lord God," is "the One that did judge her," *he* is ἰσχυρός, "strong." The aorist ὁ κρίνας is justified already because the act of judging always precedes its execution, no matter how long the interval between the two may be.

9) On "the kings of the earth" see 17:2, 12, 16; 18:3. These paramours of the whore symbolize the many antichristian powers and domains of the human life of the earth dwellers that are taken in by the whoredom of the antichristian seduction and swill the whore's wine of whoring, which is here brought out anew, "the ones that committed whoring with her and

wantoned." Once more they are personified in the symbolism of the vision, and we are told, "they shall sob (loud, unrestrained weeping) and wail (κόπτω, to beat the breast for one dead and thus to wail) over her." The images of the whore and the city are merged: "when they see (present, durative subjunctive) the smoke of her burning, standing (like terrified spectators) from afar because of the fear of the torment" (objective genitive). The imagery is that of a spreading conflagration. 'Απὸ μακρόθεν is the Greek idiom which always measures from the far point to the beholder; we do the opposite.

10) The lament is put dramatically into words: "Woe! Woe! The city! The great one!" We ought to consider each by itself, which makes it more poignant than to regard all as one combined wail. The same should be done with the next line: "Babylon! The city! The strong one!" Note how in each line, "the city" is placed in the middle, and how ἰσχυρά is purposely the same word as ἰσχυρός used in v. 8. The city is "strong" and vies with the Lord God, but *he* is "strong," he, "the One who judged her."

"Because at one hour (dative of time when) came thy judging" (κρίσις, the action of pronouncing a verdict, also the action, as here, of executing a verdict) puts the reality into the mouth of these wailing kings because the vision intends that this reality be noted. Hence once more ὅτι, "because." Yes, the delay has been long, but "in one hour came the great act of judging."

11) Now we see "the merchants," multitudes of them, all who make profit of any kind from the whore's antichristian seduction as sketched in v. 3. **And the merchants of the earth** (who do not trade in heavenly goods, who are "of the earth" like "the kings") **weep and mourn over her** (the dramatic present as though the scene is before our very eyes) **because**

their cargo no one buys any more, cargo of gold and of silver and of precious stone and of pearls and of byssus and of purple and of silk and of scarlet, and all thyine wood and every ivory utensil and every utensil from most precious wood and brass and iron and marble and cinnamon and amomum and incense and perfume and frankincense and wine and oil and fine flour and grain and cattle and sheep and (cargo) **of horses and of chariots and of bodies, even souls of human beings. And the flush season of the lust of thy life went away from thee; and all the fat things and the brilliant things perished from thee, and no longer them shall they find. The merchants of these things, the ones that became rich from her, shall stand from afar because of the fear of her torment, weeping and mourning, saying:**

> **Woe! Woe! The city! The great one!**
> **The one clothed with byssus and purple and scarlet**
> **And goldened in gold and precious stone and pearl!**
> **Because at one hour made desolate was so great riches!**

The whole business of pandering to the whore of antichristian seduction and of growing rich from the business has reached its end. This catalog is not to be understood in the literal sense, these merchants being the storekeepers on Main Street, their riches material dollars. On "the merchants" see v. 3. The godless politician and grafter of the government with his "cargo" of goods; the conscienceless lawyer in the court with his "cargo"; the skeptic editor, writer, professor with the "cargoes" they unload; the pulpiteer and ecclesiastic with the antichristian "cargoes" they unpack; and so forth in the whole antichristian world, in every corner of it, down to the peddlers and all that all salesmen of anything in the way of antichristian seduction and attraction offer, and all that in any way they make by it for their own satisfaction are here referred to. This picture is like a parable, for instance, that of the Rich Fool who was not rich toward God (Luke 12:16-21), but the imagery is on a supreme scale and covers every department of life and every cargo of antichristian seduction.

Note again the two significant ὅτι, "because," in v. 11 and 16 (note v. 8). Γόμος (from γέμω, to be full) = "cargo" and is repeated; each merchant has cargoes. "Precious stone" is singular (collective) while "pearls" is plural as in 17:4; while in v. 16 "pearl" is also a collective singular. "Byssus" = exquisite fine linen, in v. 16, βύσσινος, the adjective "made of fine linen," i. e., a garment. "Thyine wood" = the *citrus*, an odoriferous North African tree, the wood of which was used as incense or for inlaying. Ἐλεφάντινος, adjective, "from the elephant = ivory." Ἄμωμον, "amomum" = aromatic herbs of the ginger family, certain species of which yield the cardamoms and the grains of paradise of commerce. Θυμιάματα (plural) are all aromatic substances that are burnt as "incense"; λίβανος (singular) is the tree and also the white resin imported from Arabia (or from India?) and prepared from several varieties of a certain tree and very costly, the "frankincense" of Matt. 2:11. With the genitives ἵππων κτλ. supply γόμον, "cargo." The σωμάτων are *Leibeigene*, "slave bodies," and καὶ ψυχὰς ἀνθρώπων with its accusative drops back to the previous accusatives, explicative καί adding that these bodies, that are sold like animals, are "even souls of human beings." Σεμίδαλις is fine wheat flour; σῖτος, any kind of grain.

14) Ἡ ὀπώρα and its genitive is not "fruits" but the third of the seven seasons when there is abundance of everything, the flush season; hence here "the flush

season of the lust of thy life"; it is somewhat like "the heyday of thy youth" but in the evil sense; "the heyday of the lust of the life" of the whore, which has now passed away from her forever. This poetical expression is stunning. In rhythmic parallelism the elucidating thought is added: "and all the fat things and the brilliant things perished from thee, and no longer them shall they find," i. e., people, indefinite, no, not "them" but totally other things. In this verse the whore herself is dramatically addressed by God. The passing away of the heyday of her lust refers to her own person; the fat and the brilliant things to the adjuncts of her person. Read the similar devastating passage Isa. 3:16-24.

15) And now "the merchants of these things" who are interested in no other wares than those pertaining to the whore, the antichristian seductress, "they that became rich from her" (a similar apposition was added to the kings in v. 9), like the kings, "shall stand from afar because of the fear of her torment," like the kings "weeping and mourning" and in their way joining in the "Woe! Woe! The city! The great one!" In the two lines attributed to them in v. 9 the kings speak in kingly terms; in their three lines these merchants use mercantile language: the whore's clothing of byssus and purple and scarlet (which they supplied, v. 12): her being "goldened with gold and precious stone and pearl" (17:4; which these merchants also supplied, v. 12, to increase her seductiveness). What they regard as the cause of their grief and place into their ὅτι is that "at one hour (so in v. 10) so great riches" was made desolate, i. e., disappeared — *they* would think of "the riches."

17) Kings — merchants — and now the third group, sailors, even as many of the wares mentioned are imports from across the sea. **And every ship captain and everyone sailing for a place and sailor**

and as many as work the sea stood from afar and shouted on seeing the smoke of her burning, saying: Which (city is) **like to the city, the great one? And they threw dust on their heads and shouted weeping and mourning, saying:**

> **Woe! Woe! The city! the great one!**
> **She in connection with whom were made rich all those having the ships in the sea due to her expensiveness!**
> **Because at one hour she was made desolate!**

Κυβερνήτης = pilot, but is here to be taken in the sense of the captain who pilots his ship, whether he himself does the steering or not. Πᾶς ὁ ἐπὶ τόπον πλέων (there are variant readings) means "everyone sailing for a place," taking ship for doing business at seaports. Next ναῦται, sailormen in general; fourth, "as many as work the sea" by fishing, diving for pearls, building vessels, etc. All these, too, "stood from afar" and saw "the smoke of her burning" (so in v. 9). This question is not derived from "Which (city is) like," etc., in Ezek. 27:32 and does not mean: like in destruction. This question is the parallel to the one regarding the beast occurring in 13:4; as the beast, so the city is called incomparable in greatness and not in destruction. Both questions are a challenge and as such are so poignant with grief. Κόπτω in v. 9 is one form of expressing great grief; throwing dust on the head is another.

19) The "Woe! Woe!" is identical with that of v. 16; but the rest befits men of the sea, their profit from the city by way of ships ἐκ τῆς τιμιότητος (ἐκ indicating source) "due to her expensiveness," the expensive things in which she indulges.

Again a ὅτι and the dative "at one hour," but again a mere earthly one of earthly minds because the city "was made desolate" and all their seatrade is blasted.

The Third Part of the Vision, verses 20-24

20) The earth dwellers in general need not be considered separately in this part of the vision; we have seen and heard their chief representatives, kings, merchants, seamen, and that is enough. But these others belong in the vision: "heaven," the saints, etc., and the effect on them when they see the whore, the great city, the whole antichristian empire and seduction, ended. In supreme antithesis the voice out of the heaven (v. 4) calls to all these. **Celebrate over her, heaven, and the saints and the apostles and the prophets! Because judge did God the judgment regarding you from her!**

To say that this is "the call of the seer," and again to term this call an interruption of the sequence that betrays "an editor's hand," is a "critical" observation. To find fault with the apostrophe introduced here is to overlook the fact that a similar apostrophe is used in v. 14. In this terse call which is the absolute antithesis to the howlings of all these associates and these supporters of the whore that have been detailed at length, the climax is reached, and nothing less than the most dramatic apostrophe is in place. While Deut. 32:43 is analogous, Rev. 12:12a is the precedent even as to the wording.

Εὐφραίνου is the word used repeatedly in the parable of the Prodigal (Luke 15:23, etc.) and means "make merry" in the sense of, "Be celebrating, heaven!" The voice speaking for God orders celebration. We have the celebration described for us in 19:1-10; it is, indeed, high and holy. The mournings and the laments are at once introduced when the kings, the merchants, the seaworkers are introduced, not so the hallelujahs of the blessed. John heard these in a separate part of the vision. After a vocative (οὐρανέ) second members are always in the nominative: "and the saints and the apostles and the prophets." Each term has an article, the three are regarded as separate and distinct groups. Since they are plurals, and "heaven" is singular; moreover, since ὑμῶν, "of you," follows: we take it that "heaven" refers to these three groups, "the saints," etc. The voice does not call upon the angels to celebrate, for they have never been attacked by this antichristian seductiveness of the world whore. In 12:12, "those tabernacling in the heavens" are the ones now called, "the saints," etc. Certainly, the angels join them and aid them in the celebration, yet this is *their* celebration, in fact, would not take place save for them.

This is a vision. The celebration occurs in heaven. While the saints are on earth, their time of celebration has not yet come. What pertains to saints who may yet be on earth when Babylon falls is not a part of this vision. "The saints" are all believers who are separated and set apart from the world by God. "The apostles and the prophets" are such in the narrow sense, the Twelve plus Paul and the Old Testament prophets who were directly commissioned to oppose the antichristian seduction. "The prophets" certainly belong here even as in 17:10 the five head kings who have already fallen take us back into Old Testament times. We thus have the order in reverse: all the saints of the New and of the Old Testament: the apostles and, earlier than these, the prophets. One thinks of John who sees this vision. There is no difficulty at all; for what John sees takes place at the end when the holocaust of the antichristian seduction occurs; certainly, John, too, will then have joined his fellow apostles in heaven.

Now we have the last significant ὅτι (v. 7, 8, 10, 16, 19), the deepest of all: "Because *judge* did God the *judgment* regarding you due to her." The compact Greek is idiomatic. The verb is placed first for the sake of emphasis and is an effective aorist to indicate the final act of judgment. The cognate object is τὸ κρῖμα (a term ending in -μα that expresses result; in v. 10 we have κρίσις, a term with the suffix -σις that expresses action): God's final, decisive act of judging (ἔκρινεν) produced this κρῖμα, this judgment result, the burning up of Babylon, the whore, the antichristian seduction. In τὸ κρῖμα ὑμῶν the genitive cannot be subjective, for the saints, etc., did not produce this judgment result; it is the genitive of relation: this judgment result, produced by God's final act of judging, pertains to "you" because this whore did her utmost to seduce you. In 17:6 she is drunk from the blood of the saints and from the blood of the witnesses of Jesus (compare 18:24); in 18:5, God remembered her ἀδικήματα, all "the unrighteous things" she did against the saints. The just judgment result God has now meted out to her is thus ὑμῶν, "regarding you." Ἐξ αὐτῆς = "from her" (not "on her," our versions): this judgment result is justly exacted "from her" by God's final judging act.

This statement is misunderstood when it is taken to mean that the whore and the saints had a case in court before God, and that God decided the case in favor of you, the saints. She never appealed to God and came into his court to get God to pronounce a verdict in her favor; she rode the blasphemous beast (17:3). The antichristian seduction is the whore, and she never dared to appear in the holy court of God and of the Lamb. God's court is not like ours in which the criminal is permitted to bring a case in order to prove his innocence; the whore has no case. God does no more than to declare "the hour" (v. 10, 16, 19) of the execution of τὸ κρῖμα, the judgment result.

21) In a separate section of this vision this judgment result is presented anew. **And one strong angel took up a stone, as it were a great millstone, and threw it into the sea, saying: Thus with a swift rush**

shall be thrown Babylon, the great city, and shall not be found any longer! This is a symbolical act similar to those which the prophets were at times ordered to enact, similar to that of Agabus in the case of Paul in Acts 21:11. Jer. 51:63, 64 presents an act on a smaller scale. Εἷς is often no more than an indefinite article; our versions, "an angel." Yet here we regard it as the numeral: so great a stone it was, yet *one* angel picked it up and threw it into the sea, for he was "strong."

"Great millstone" = not one from a small handmill but one from a mill that is turned by an animal. Ὁρμήματι = "with a swift rush" in the sense of "with one great swing." We recall Matt. 18:6. The sea is mentioned and not some river or some lake, because of its depth from which the stone can never be raised.

The *tertium* is the swift, irrevocable plunge. To the symbol of fire and burning this of water is added.

22) In figurative language, but all of it negative, Babylon's doom is described. Note the five οὐ μὴ . . . ἔτι in fearful refrain.

And sound of zither players and musicians and
flute players and trumpeters
In no way shall be found in thee any longer!
And every craftsman of every craft
In now way shall be found in thee any longer!
And sound of millstone
In no way shall be heard in thee any longer!
And light of lamp
In no way shall shine any longer!
And voice of bridegroom and of bride
In no way shall be heard in thee any longer!

All of these are parallel statements, five of them, the half of ten. Five indicates incompleteness, the reader is to add the other five in order to make the list complete. Now two dreadful ὅτι are added to all the preceding ones:

Because thy merchants were grandees of the earth;
Because with thy sorcery there were deceived all the nations.

Finally, without symbolism or figure there follows the climax of monstrous guilt, but no longer in an apostrophe addressed to Babylon but pronounced like a verdict so the universe may hear:

And in her blood pools of prophets and of saints were found
And of all those slain upon the earth!

Once — but no longer! All is silent as the grave. The awfulness of the five negatives (all with futuristic subjunctives) should not be overlooked. All five are only figures. The "because" clauses add symbolism. The final "and" clause advances to reality.

The advance in the five figurative illustrations should be noted. First, no longer musical entertainments. But one might dispense with them. Second, no longer craftsmen of any craft, nothing of any kind longer made. That cuts far deeper. Third, no millstone longer grinds flour, no baking is done to sustain life. Who is left to eat it? Fourth, no lamp is lighted at night. Every night is dark. No eyes are left to see. Fifth, even in the dark no bridegroom and bride longer whisper to each other. There is not one couple, not one that might produce children and begin to introduce a start of life again. No longer — no longer! Add five more illustrations to these five if you wish.

23b) Why, — why? The reason for this silence of the grave has already been given. No need to mention "the kings of the earth" (v. 9, etc.) or the men connected with the sea (v. 17, etc.). Two short ὅτι are enough, the one taking us back to "the merchants of the earth" (v. 11-16), the other to the whore's cup (17:2) and to the wine in which she served her φαρμακεία — the word meant administering drugs and was used in an evil sense for "poisoning" and finally for baleful "sorcery."

The crime committed is the fact that "the merchants" (see v. 3) were "grandees *of the earth*" by their pandering to the antichristian seduction. So great they grew in their business of trading in these goods of seduction that involved all the earth. In the second ὅτι clause *deceiving* all the nations is the crime, the very work of the second beast (13:14) and of the dragon, the archdeceiver (12:9; John 8:44, liar). "All the nations" = 13:7, 16; 14:8; 18:3. The antichristian seduction = deception in the poisoning or sorcery of all the antichristian lies. Thus deceiving "all the nations" surely is the guilt that reaches "up to the heaven" (v. 5).

24) The last part of the guilt is set down in cold reality: blood pools of prophets and of saints (all nouns are anarthrous, qualitative) and of all those slain on the earth, the long line of martyrs (17:6). Dropping the word "apostles" (compare v. 20) is mere shortening in order to avoid four designations and to keep three as in v. 20. The participle must have the article because of its substantivization. The plural αἵματα we imitate by "blood pools."

CHAPTER XIX

The Doxology to God for His Judgment on the Whore, 19:1-10

1) The section from 17:1 to 19:10 constitutes a unit. It is one vision with distinct parts. 19:1-10 is the final piece. We do not subdivide this last section What is ordered by the voice of God in 18:20 is now carried out. In the same way 14:8 states the fall of Babylon summarily; after that the whole tragedy is presented at length. These features are quite obvious.

After these things (i. e., after the vision had presented the foregoing sections in chapters 17 and 18 this additional section was given without an interval) **I heard, as it were, a great voice of a numerous multitude in the heaven, saying:**

Hallelujah!

The salvation and the glory and the power of our God!
Because genuine and righteous his judgings;
Because he did judge the whore, the great one,
Who did corrupt the earth with her whoring;
And he did avenge the blood of his slaves from her hand!

And a second time they have said:

Hallelujah!

And her smoke is going up for the eons of the eons!

And there fell down the elders, the twenty-four, and the four living ones and did obeisance to God, the One sitting on the throne, saying:

Amen! Hallelujah!

And a voice went out from the throne, saying:
Be praising our God, all his slaves,
Those fearing him, the small and the great!

And I heard, as it were, a voice of a numerous multitude and, as it were, a voice of numerous waters and, as it were, a voice of strong thunders, saying:

Hallelujah!

Because reign did the Lord, God, the Almighty!
Let us rejoice and jubilate
And let us give the glory to him!
Because there did come the wedding of the Lamb,
And his wife did make herself ready!
And it was given to her that she be clothed in byssus, shining, pure;
For the byssus is the righteous acts of the saints.

In 17:1 to 19:10 the whole drama of the whore, Babylon, the antichristian seductress and her seduction, is presented in consecutive visions, and it closes with the hallelujah of the *Una Sancta* before the throne (on the throne see 4:2 and throughout chapter 4). Understanding this, we forego all efforts at time setting that mar so many commentaries, all the questions as to whether the Parousia has taken place at the point of time marked by 19:1-10, whether the resurrection has taken place, whether this or that has taken place or is yet to take place. Even the Hebrew word "hallelujah" is referred to the final national conversion of the Jews, and these "hallelujahs" are thought to usher in the 1,000 years of the millennium. As at other places of this book the fixing of date and time is either made a chief consideration or is quietly introduced as being legitimate. Yet all that this part of the vision presents is the celebration that was caused by the whore's fall, which, according to 18:20, takes place in heaven.

This appears to be the same "great multitude" as the one mentioned in 7:9, which also sang, "Salvation to our God!" The distinguishing feature of this vision is the recurring, "Hallelujah!" the Hebrew for, "Praise Yahweh!" It is found only here in the New Testament. Like "amen," is was adopted by the other languages without translation and stands as an exclamation. "Our God" signifies that this is the voice of the *Una Sancta,* which ascribes to him "the salvation and the glory and the power": "the salvation" he has bestowed on them, "the glory" or sum of his attributes manifested in that bestowal, and "the power" with which he brought Babylon to her fall. Note the definite articles which are improperly omitted in our versions. This is an exclamation, and thus no copula is needed. In v. 7, 9 we have the dative "to God," here the genitive "of God"; is of God = belongs to God. This is the praise of true acknowledgment.

Corresponding to the many ὅτι of chapter 18, we have two more here, and then two more in v. 6, 7. There is always a most adequate cause or reason. The two found here go together: first, the general statement: "genuine and righteous his judgings," the same one that is found in 16:7 and is explained there (compare 15:3); second, the specific case here celebrated: God's judgment on the great whore, whose foul guilt is added in the relative clause, "who did corrupt the earth with her whoring," this time saying "the earth" instead of "the nations." Ἔφθειρε is probably the first aorist, but it might be the imperfect, "kept corrupting" (R. 1220). To this is added the further specification, "and avenged the blood of his slaves out of her hand," cf., "his slaves" in 1:1. In 6:10 this blood cries for avenging; in 18:24 it is "is found in her." Ἐκ χειρὸς αὐτῆς is the same as ἐξ αὐτῆς: "did exact vengeance for the blood from or out of her hand," the hand which spilled that blood and was covered with it.

3) As the saints in heaven begin with "hallelujah," so a second time they shout a "hallelujah" and now in one line describe the climax of this vengeance on the whore: her smoke going up (14:11; 18:9) "for the eons of the eons" (see 1:6). The grammarians discuss the perfect tense εἴρηκαν, which some regard as "aoristic," but R. 902 explains it as a dramatic historical perfect; this is certainly a better explanation. Both the present tense and this perfect are entirely proper amid aorists.

4) Up to this point the vision reveals only this vast multitude in the heaven (v. 1); now we see that it includes also the twenty-four elders and the four living ones and the throne and the One sitting on the throne, all of them found in the great throne vision 4:2-4, 6, etc., where we have dealt with them at length. The twenty-four elders properly appear here with the whole *Una Sancta* in this exalted praise, for they symbolize the ministry of the Word committed to the church, the great means of "the salvation" of which the church now sings. Properly the four living ones appear together with the twenty-four elders, for they symbolize all the living earthly agencies of God's providence by which his power (δύναμις, v. 1) works on earth. As in chapter 4, elders and living ones appear in relation to the throne, the symbol of God's power, rule, and dominion. But in chapter 4 the vision has no *Una Sancta,* for it is the basic vision which reveals all that will work from the throne here on earth; now in this vision we see what has been wrought, not, in-

deed, all of it — this is shown part by part — but what appears in the celebrating multitude of the *Una Sancta* and in the vengeance on the great whore, the antichristian seduction that corrupted the earth (v. 1-3). This vision can be properly understood only in its relation to the one of chapter 4.

Yet we should not introduce into the present vision all that appears in chapter 4 or anything from any of the intervening visions (such as the Sanctuary, the angels, the altars, etc.). Each vision presents no more that John himself records, and to introduce more is to create confusion.

The throne is properly mentioned in this vision as a study of 4:2, etc., shows; also "the One sitting on the throne," sitting = exercising the power and dominion. As a climax to the hallelujah praise of the *Una Sancta* the representatives of the Word and of the agents of providence fall down and do obeisance in worship to God, the One exercising power and dominion on the throne, which is the symbol of both, the power and the dominion, and say, "Amen! Hallelujah!" the "amen" being the seal of verity (see 1:7), the "hallelujah" the triplication of that of the church.

All this is magnificent beyond adequate conception on our part. Let no one mar the wonderful significance by injecting curious questions — away with them! Absorb the vision in its grand import.

5) From the vast acclaim of the whole *Una Sancta* (v. 1-3) the vision moves to the acclaim of the elders and the living ones, then to the solo voice "from the throne" itself to which the whole *Una Sancta* then responds. More than this: the acclaim of v. 1-4 contains the negative side, the judgment on the great whore; the voice from the throne calls forth the corresponding far greater positive side, the praise of the Lamb and his marriage and his wife who made her-

self ready. The whore is judged; the Lamb's wife is exalted at the Lamb's side in heavenly array. This is the sequence and the inner content of the vision.

Just as hitherto in other visions, "a voice" speaks and remains anonymous. The fact that this is neither God's nor Christ's voice appears from its saying "*our* God." Some think that this is the Lamb's voice, but such a view is contrary to the analogy of Scripture. Christ never combines himself with us by saying "our God"; he does the opposite in John 20:17: "*my* Father, *your* Father — *my* God, *your* God." This distinction and difference is so marked in the Gospels that a valuable monograph has been written on these pronouns. This is a voice which can address the multitude of the *Una Sancta* and say "*our* God"; with that let us be content. It comes ἀπὸ τοῦ θρόνου. But "the throne" is not a throne chair for one occupant. The term is symbolical; one cannot draw an image of this "throne," for even we shall sit in company with (μετά) the Lord in this throne (3:21) and reign with him as kings (συμβασιλεύσομεν), II Tim. 2:12.

This voice calls from the throne, "Be giving praise to our God, all his slaves" (δοῦλοι, v. 2), and then the appositions describe them: "they that are fearing him, the small and the great." These designations are repeated from 11:18 (which see), "the great and the small"; they occur also in 20:12. This is the holy, blessed fear of God. The multitude of the blessed contains such great ones as the prophets and the apostles and the exalted list in Heb. 11 and such little ones as babes, the malefactor on the cross who came to fear God just before he died, and many lowly souls. There is no "hallelujah" in connection with this call because it is addressed to these slaves of God.

6) Forthwith the praise resounds, its volume is like that described in 14:2: "as it were, a voice of a

vast multitude" (repeated from v. 1), the appositional καί describing its inconceivable volume: "and, as it were, a voice of many waters (cataracts, ocean surf) and, as it were, a voice of strong thunders" (with tremendous reverberations). It begins with another, the fourth "Hallelujah!" which itself means, "Praise Jehovah!"

At once another ὅτι is added: "Because reign did the Lord God, the Almighty!" On this designation see 1:8; 11:17. The emphasis is on the verb: ἐβασίλευσε, "reign as king did he." We do not think that this aorist is equal to a present, "reigneth" (our versions), or that it is ingressive: *ist Koenig geworden; ist zur Koenigsherrschaft gelangt* (Zahn): is come to be King; has attained kingly rule. This aorist is historical and constative. It looks back over all past history and in all of it sees "the Lord God, the Almighty" and how ever and ever he reigned as King. Psalm 2 is the commentary; Psalm 110 is another.

7) Dramatically no "therefore" is added although this is the sense contained in the hortative subjunctives: "Let us be rejoicing (in our hearts) and be jubilating (or exulting in every outward demonstration. G. K. 18) and let us give (aorist: give with finality) the glory (δόξα, v. 1) to him!" This last is the supreme act of our exultation. Another positive ὅτι follows. The first is broad and general, this second is specific; so are the two ὅτι in v. 1, 2. "Because there did come the marriage of the Lamb," etc. The emphasis is on the verb: "it came!" The Greek uses the aorist to express what has occurred recently (R. 842, etc.) by just stating the fact, whereas we should employ the perfect, "has come" and note the relation to the present. "Is come" of our versions conveys the sense.

This tense is often misunderstood. Some writers forget that this is a vision, that it holds up to our eyes the heavenly host singing that the marriage of the Lamb has arrived, and that the Lamb's wife has made herself ready (the same aorist). This implies that the marriage or wedding feast has now begun. But with this implication the vision stops. It presents so much and no more. This has been true in the case of every previous vision, and will be so in the case of the others. It is so in the case of the parables. So much is flashed on the screen each time; the rest follows. The marriage celebration is not depicted in this scene.

The γάμος of the Lamb is the wedding celebration. The fact that it includes the δεῖπνον or feast is self-evident. To separate the two means to depart from the imagery of the ancient "wedding." This should not be confused with our present form of weddings, the essential of which is the legal marriage ceremony. The expression ἡ γυνὴ αὐτοῦ, "his *wife,*" should prevent confusion.

The old custom lends itself to what is here portrayed far better than our modern marriage customs. First came the betrothal which was made in public between the two families concerned. This made the two participants in the betrothal legally husband and wife; no priest or official was needed, the families and their heads sufficed. The betrothal was followed by an interval until the day when the groom led a festal procession to his bride's home, where she, too, had made herself ready, and brought her to his own home where festivities began and continued for a week, perhaps even longer. An exchange of marriage vows was not a part of these festivities.

It is this human imagery that is here used in part. The day for the wedding festivities has come, the betrothed bride, who is through that betrothal the wife, has made herself ready. Compare Matt. 25:1, etc., for a part of the imagery; also II Cor. 11:2 for the betrothal; Matt. 22:1, etc., for all the guests at the King's Son's wedding.

The Lamb's wedding starts with his Parousia; he comes to take his bride home for the heavenly feast and celebration. His betrothed, "his wife," his bride (21:2; 22:17), is the *Una Sancta,* the church. In Matt. 22 the bride (wife) cannot be introduced in addition to the wedding guests. The human imagery is not in all respects the exact counterpart of the divine reality; hence only so much as serves is used, in the parable it is the many wedding guests, for in reality the bride and the guests are identical. Millennialists regard the wedding celebration as the 1,000 years of the supposed millennium.

8) The wife of the Lamb has made herself ready. But not by doing anything of her own, as Pelagianists, Pharisees, rationalists, and even synergists imagine: "And it *was given* to her (given by the pure grace of God) that she be clothed in byssus (βύσσινον, the adjective: in what is made of byssus, finest linen), brilliant, pure." In 3:18 we see where this is bought.

Not the textual critics, all of whom find no textual question in the manuscripts, but some commentators question the γάρ clause and call it a late gloss, an explanation that was inserted by "the seer" (who is not John). They apparently overlook the fact that by these visions the Lord intends *to reveal,* and that for this reason interpreting expressions and clauses, which add the reality to the figure, are at times inserted so that John and we may understand. Hence here a clause is introduced which states that what is made of byssus, the βύσσινον (article of previous reference) is τὰ δικαιώματα τῶν ἁγίων, "the righteous acts of the saints." These were given to the Lamb's wife; for "the saints" *are* the Lamb's wife. With these righteous acts "she made herself ready." Δικαίωμα with its -μα suffix is a term that expresses result: a product of being or acting righteous as God regards righteousness. These are undoubtedly righteous works of which 14:13 says that they follow the blessed.

There is no difficulty between the imputed righteousness and the acquired, between the righteousness of Christ, the garment with which he clothes us, and this brilliant, pure garment of our own works of righteousness. When they are given the one, the saints are given the other; by having the second it is made evident that they have the first. In fact, that is the very evidence Christ will use in public at the last day, at his Parousia, in the final judgment (Matt. 25:34, etc.). For this very reason "the righteous acts" must be mentioned here. All the passages that speak of the judgment deal with works.

But are the works a βύσσινον, a robe of fine linen, and even λαμπρόν, brilliant like a lamp, καθαρόν, clean, pure, spotless? Is that not saying too much about them? Not according to Matt. 5:14 as far as brilliance is concerned; not according to Eph. 5:27 as far as cleanness and stainlessness are concerned. All the imperfections of our good works are made good by the perfect righteousness of Christ which is ours from the very start. So we "are clean every whit" (John 13:10).

9) **And he says to me: Write, Blessed they that have been called to the supper of the wedding of the Lamb!** Who says this? We do not go back to 17:1 for the answer. This must be the one whose voice speaks from the throne in v. 5, which also offers the best explanation for what John does in v. 10. He who called for the praise of the *Una Sancta* now commands John to write this great beatitude. On μακάριοι see 1:3,

the first beatitude of Revelation. The verdict certainly stands that they are blessed who finally sit down to the wedding supper of the Lamb. But this vision is intended for us who are still on earth, whose *dikaiōmata* are not yet completed. This beatitude is pronounced on *us*. Already now and not only at the Parousia we are blessed as "they who have been called to the supper." Note the perfect participle οἱ κεκλημένοι: we received the call some time in the past and ever since that time have that call and continue to have it. As throughout the epistles and elsewhere in Revelation the effective gospel call is referred to, the call which makes us believers and saints. The R. V. leaves that idea doubtful with its "are bidden," for this sounds as though only the invitation is referred to. Καλεῖν is so used in the Gospels, for instance in Matt. 22:3, 8, and κλητοί in 14; but never in the epistles. The invitation is not accepted by many, and although they received it, they are *not* blessed. The perfect participle here used could not designate them because of its present connotation.

What a blessed fact, that already in advance of the supper we are blessed. The glory of that supper casts its rays over us already in this antichristian world. John is properly told in regard to this word, "Write!" i. e., get it down in writing at once. Such commands to write specific things appear repeatedly in the visions.

And he says to me, These words are genuine ones of God! That is why John is especially told to write them. On the question as to when John wrote see 10:4. What is subject, what predicate? Plainly, the anarthrous ἀληθινοί with its genitive is the predicate; plainly, οὗτοι οἱ λόγοι belongs together and is the subject. Our versions and others who separate οὗτοι and make this alone the subject and then get a strange articulated predicate οἱ λόγοι and an awkwardly placed genitive τοῦ Θεοῦ, misunderstand the Greek. "These words" are the beatitude, but this beatitude as illumined by the whole vision which shows us the whole *Una Sancta* as the wedding is about to begin. Hence the plural "these words" is used. In v. 7 ὁ γάμος τοῦ ἀρνίου is enough; τὸ δεῖπνον is not added in order to add another detail regarding the wedding. To this *supper* of the wedding of the Lamb we are called, and this is included in the words that are "genuine ones of God." For as the Formula of Concord says, this call is no *Spiegelfechten,* sham fencing before a mirror. God's words are "genuine," solid gold, every syllable of them.

10) **And I fell prone before his feet to do obeisance to him. And he says to me: See to it, not! Thy fellow slave I am and of thy brethren, those having the testimony of Jesus. To God do obeisance! For the testimony of Jesus is the spirit of the prophecy.**

Several angels have spoken to John in previous visions and also an elder, yet in no case did John fall down to worship. There is, as far as we can see, only one explanation for his action here as well as in 22:8: he mistakes the speaker for the Lord himself. The speaker's voice comes "from the throne" (v. 5) and, like the Lord in previous visions, commands, "Write!" Note especially the seven letters to the seven churches. It is impossible to assume that John would ever knowingly worship any being save God and the Lamb or the Spirit.

Why did John include this incident in his record? He made the record, not as *he* deemed proper, but as *the Lord* had him make it; we have also seen that he made it at once even as γράψον means, "Write here and now!" Why does the Lord want this act of John's in the record? He wants it, that is enough. If we might venture to say more, it may be this: by the effect produced upon John to convey to us the grandeur of this vision with its voice from the very throne itself, which scarcely anything else could convey to us. Emphatically the voice forbids, Ὅρα μή, "See to it, not!" The present imperative is durative: "Ever see to it," and μή is elliptical.

The speaker calls himself John's σύνδουλος, nothing but John's fellow slave, "of thy brethren," one of their number, and adds the apposition, "those having the testimony of Jesus," the same designation as the one occurring in 12:17. The speaker is one who, like John and all the brethren, has a firm faith in the testimony which Jesus testified. Can this speaker be an angel? Is an angel ever designated in this way? The words sound as though the speaker is one of the Lamb's saints. Startling as this conclusion may sound, the more one considers it, the more it commends itself. Such a speaker may say "*our* God" (v. 5); may call on the *Una Sancta* to praise our God; and, most significant of all, may do this "from the throne," according to 3:21: "I will give to him to sit down with me in my throne as I sat down with my Father in his throne."

"To God do obeisance!" = Matt. 4:10, Jesus' own word. The sense is: to God alone. The fact that this includes the Lamb need not be stated to those who believe in the Lamb's deity. What the "testimony of Jesus" is, the speaker states: it is "the spirit of the prophecy," which may be explained: By holding firmly to the testimony which Jesus made and conveyed to us, thou and I and all the brethren hold the actual spirit of the prophecy, the inner content of the divine prophecy. "The prophecy" is definite like "the Word," "the salvation." Some restrict this to the prophecy contained in these visions of Revelation, but there is no need for such a restriction. Because we have and hold this testimony, which is no less than here stated, we worship no one but God while we are here on earth or, like this speaker, in heaven and on the throne.

The visions dealing with Babylon as the great whore, the antichristian seduction, are herewith concluded.

The Battle. The End of the Two Beasts, 19:11-21

11) The visions dealing with the whore are presented in an unbroken line. Not so those that deal with the two beasts. We have the beast and his ally in chapter 13 and glimpses of their end in the following visions. Now comes the great vision that fully reveals their frightful end, 19:11-21. This is likewise true with respect to the dragon. His story is related in chapter 12; his end is depicted in 20:7-10.

First, the dragon, Satan, *the source and head of all antichristianity* and his attempts, chapter 12. Then, his agents, the two beasts; the first beast, *the whole antichristian power,* and the second beast, *the whole antichristian propaganda;* he is also called the pseudoprophet, chapter 13. Third, Babylon, the great whore, *the whole antichristian seduction,* chapter 17, etc. The *Una Sancta* stands despite these.

The end of these three is shown in reverse order. First, that of the whore, 17:16 and chapter 18. Next, that of the beasts, 19:11, etc. Last, that of the dragon, 20:7, etc. Everything must occur in this order. The head of all antichristianity produces the whole *power* and the propaganda of antichristianity and in addition the whole *seduction* of antichristianity. All of these go down together even as they appeared together. The circumstance that each of the three is revealed in a separate vision should not lead us to think that there is an interval of centuries between their appearance. Where Satan is, there is the antichristian power (plus the propaganda) and the antichristian seduction. How could it be otherwise? The story begins with the incarnation and the exaltation of Christ (12:1-5). The fact that Satan, beasts, whore are thrown on the screen separately is intended only to focus all the light upon each in succession so that each may be seen completely.

The same method is followed in showing the end of the three. In reality all perish together. In order to end the seduction, the power must be ended; and in order to end the power, the author must be ended. How could it be otherwise? Yet each ends in a distinct way: the whore is desolated, stripped, devoured, burnt up (17:16) — so *the seduction* goes down; the beast and his ally are taken in battle and thrown into hell alive (19:20) — so the *power* perishes; the dragon and his multitudes are devoured by fire from heaven and are also thrown into hell (20:9, 10) — so is damned *the author, Satan.* Differentiated and shown as three, their end, as was their appearance, is represented separately. Each ends, and we see how. But in reality they end at the same time by the same hand and power, by the Parousia of the Lamb.

The rest of the visions that are interspersed throughout this complex which extends from chapter 12 to the end of chapter 20 have their significant position in the fundamental framework here outlined. Because this framework is not perceived, the interpretations of so many commentators become unclear. Biederwolf's *Millennium Bible* offers a jig-saw puzzle that neither he nor any other man can fit together because he lets 492 commentators furnish him with the pieces to which he adds a few of his own. What can one see through about 500 differently ground eyeglasses?

The imagery of the battle starts in 11:7; 12:7; 13:4, and heralds the last battle. Note well that the first vision which we have of this final battle is when we see all the kings gathered at Armageddon in 16:12-16. Already in that vision we see the Euphrates (implying Babylon), the beast, and his ally, the pseudoprophet (the second beast). But in this first vision the battle is not yet shown as being fought; the kings only gather. The second glimpse we catch of this final battle in 17:14-18. Again we see all the kings. The victory of the Lamb is only noted; but here the horrible end of the whore is revealed in detail. For the third time the battle is now shown (19:11-21): the King of kings rides forth, *he* attacks, the beast himself is attacked, and with him are all the kings. Now the whole defeat is shown. Finally there comes Satan himself with Gog and Magog and numbers as the sand of the sea (20:8-10). Although they propose to do battle, their effort is shown as not being a battle at all — fire out of heaven devours them (20:9).

These visions are not visions of *three* battles but of *one*. The whore goes down, the beast goes down, the dragon goes down as if to say, the cavalry, the infantry, the artillery, and the center, as if to say, the outworks, the walls, the citadel. By revealing the *one* final overthrow in *three* pictures the revelation is able to show in great detail the damnable character and the activity of the three, the dragon, the beast, the whore, and the damnation of judgment upon whore, beast, dragon. They arise together, they go down together. The archfiend does not wait to produce the antichristian power and seduction; nor does the Lord first destroy the latter and then the former. All this becomes plain when we note that only the dragon is an actual person, namely Satan, and that the two beasts and the whore are only symbolical personifications of Satan's power and his seduction. Let this suffice here; more will be stated when we consider 20:1.

And I saw the heaven having been opened (perfect with present connotation), **and, lo, a white horse**

and the One sitting on him called Faithful and Genuine, and in righteousness he judges and does battle. Moreover, his eyes a flame of fire, and on his head many diadems; having a name written which no one knows save he himself, and having thrown around him a robe having been sprinkled with blood. And his name has been called The Logos of God. And the armies, the ones in the heaven, were following him on white horses, clothed in byssus, white, pure. And out of his mouth proceeds a sharp great sword, that with it he smite the nations. And he, he shall shepherd them with a rod of iron; and he, he treads the winepress of the anger of the wrath of God, the Almighty. And he has on his robe and on his thigh a name written:

KING OF KINGS AND LORD OF LORDS

Here is Christ in his Parousia at the last day. Beyond all our powers of imagination is the image of Christ that is here revealed. All that the Scriptures reveal about his appearance at the time of his final coming exceeds imagination. Indeed, it must. The reason that Christ is here pictured as the King descending for battle is due to the fact that now all the previous imagery of battle is to be completed, and because this vision reveals the final defeat of the beast, the whole antichristian power. It is presented in the imagery of a battle at Armageddon (16:16), although now no place is named, for we have now advanced beyond 16:16. Some locate this coming of the King and the battle in past history; we regard that as untenable. Others place this battle at the beginning of the millennium and think that there shall be more than one Parousia. The Scriptures know of only one Parousia; and this is not followed by 1,000 years of glory for the church on earth.

In 4:1 a door was opened for John so that he might look in and see the throne in the great throne vision; here John sees the heaven itself opened wide so the King and his armies may ride forth for the last battle. In 15:5 the Sanctuary was opened so that the seven angels might go forth; here the heaven itself is opened to the Lord and to his armies. Again some commentators assign John a definite location as though he needs must be at some certain place in order to see this vision. We drop such views.

"Lo!" is justified. "Lo, a white horse (white is a symbol of holiness), and the One sitting upon him called (the participle is omitted in some texts) Faithful and Genuine." The white horse recalls the first of the four horsemen mentioned in 6:2. In that vision Christ goes forth for the preliminary victories, carries a bow to shoot from afar, and has a *stephanos,* the symbol of victory, about his brow. Here the armies of heaven follow him, he bears the great sword, wears many diadems, comes as the King of kings — this is the last battle. One writer has called attention to the contrast: Jesus rides an ass as the royal Son of David, as the King bringing salvation — now he is the King of kings on the great white charger who comes to do battle, to smite the beast, the whole antichristian power.

"Faithful and Genuine" are expounded in 3:14, where he calls himself by these names. Now, however, "Witness" is omitted, for here he is the warrior, and the two adjectives apply to him as the King. Hence the expository clause, "and in righteousness he judges and does battle." Therefore he is "Faithful," absolutely trustworthy, and "Genuine," with no sham about him. Differentiate ἀληθινός from ἀληθής, "truthful." The present tenses "he judges and does battle" are timeless and match the qualities "Faithful and Genuine." Thus both this double name and the two verbs apply also to this final judgment on the beast whom the Faithful and Genuine One comes to judge "in righteousness." "Do battle" is added because the beast is now to be judged and destroyed in battle. As hitherto, so now in this vision, we translate πολεμός and πολεμεῖν, not "war" and "to war," but "battle" and "do battle," as being more exact; "war" involves many battles, skirmishes, etc., while this imagery presents but one clash and one defeat.

Note well κρίνει (literal) and πολεμεῖ (symbolical). "He does battle" = "he judges." In 20:11-15 we shall see the complete vision of the final judgment and there note that this vision of the final judgment is the exposition of all that is shown in the three visions of battles. It is essential that this be understood. Both verbs are present tenses and as such descriptive of the last great act of Christ, the King. The literal κρίνει is made prominent in order to insure the correct interpretation of all that follows.

12) The description is devoted exclusively to this Supreme Warrior, because all power is in him, which the description also bears out. Δέ is not = καί, but = "moreover." "His eyes a flame of fire" repeats 1:14 and 3:18: eyes that are all-penetrating, strike through, burn and shrivel up the unrighteous, his enemies. "On his head many diadems," emblems of royalty, διαδήματα — see the discussion in 2:10. These diadems are not made of metal but are bands bound about the brow, hence "many" is not beyond imagination. The dragon and the beast also wear diadems, but theirs are emblems of usurped royalty, they are in opposition to this King, who wears his diadems in righteousness. These are "many" because all royalty truly belongs to him.

For the second time we hear about the King's "name": "having a name written (perfect participle with present connotation) which no one knows save he himself" one that is like that of the victor in 2:17. In this respect we shall be like Christ. It is fruitless to speculate about the letters of this name. When the marginal reference of the A. V. points to v. 16: "King of kings," etc., it is evidently in error. The fact that Christ should have a name that only he knows is less difficult to understand than the fact that every one of us, who are many, shall eventually be given a name which each of us alone will know, you not knowing mine, I not knowing yours. Is it, perhaps, a name that marks the most inward connection with God? In Christ the impenetrable connection, in each one of us a connection that is also impenetrable, peculiar and individual for each one? We do not know.

"Written" seems to point to so many written letters, which, although they are pronounced, convey a meaning only to the bearer. Neither in our case nor in Christ's is this anything like the seal mentioned in 7:2, etc. We do not think that in the case of Christ this name is intended to be the opposite of the names of blasphemy appearing on the beast (13:1; 17:3).

13) "Having thrown around him a robe having been sprinkled with blood" makes us think of the blood Christ shed in expiation: the Savior is the Judge, John 5:27. Many think of the blood of Christ's enemies and refer to Isa. 63:1-3; but the reference to this passage is found in v. 15b. Would there be two such references? The variants for the perfect passive participle ῥεραντισμένος (from ῥαντίζω, to sprinkle) have practically the same meaning. The prefixing of περί adds only the thought that the sprinkling occurred all around and not only on one side of the robe. Βεβαμμένον (from βάπτω) would mean "having been bathed with blood," which accords with the view of those who think of the blood of the enemy and of Isa. 63. The correct reading of the preceding participle is περιβεβλημένος.

"And his name has been called Ὁ Λόγος τοῦ Θεοῦ, The Word of God." This states another name. In v. 11 the participle καλούμενος means that "Faithful and Genuine" are currently applied to Christ; but this is not the case with regard to the finite verb κέκληται that is used with "The Logos of God." The sense is: In order to a certain extent to express the unique significance of Christ for the world "The Logos of God" has been made a name for him, not one that is commonly used for him in the church, but only whenever this special significance is to be made prominent, the fact that in his very Person he is the final saving revelation of God. See the exposition of ὁ Λόγος in John 1:1; John alone uses this name or title in John 1:1-3, 13, 14; I John 1:1, 2. John's use of this great term has no connection with Philo's impersonal *logos* and, as Zahn, *Offenbarung,* 587 adds, with the logos philosophy of Justinus, Valentinus, and his pupils Heracleon and Leucinus Charinus, which they in later times attempted to smuggle into the church. Zahn points out that before and also after the time of these men there were men who used the original correct idea of the Logos name for Jesus and quotes Ignatius and Hermas, two of these men.

We think that this *saving* name, "The Word," corresponds with the *saving* blood with which the Lord's robe has been sprinkled.

14) The armies that follow the Lord are mentioned only as being one of the items to be noted with regard to him. They are of a kind with the great sword, the reference to the iron rod and to the winepress, all are punitive and thus all belong together. These armies of heaven do not conquer the beast; they are like Christ's attributes, are a part of him. It is debated as to whether they are the angels or the glorified saints or both. The analogy of Scripture leads us to think of the angels (Matt. 24:31; 13:41; I Thess.

4:16; Mark 8:38: "when he cometh with the holy angels," also Luke 9:26). The white horses mark the riders as coming in holiness, and their βύσσινον (18:8), garment of fine linen, "white, pure" (or "pure white"), so marks their person. The holiness of heaven descends in order to abolish the beast of hell forever.

15) The sharp ῥομφαία proceeding out of the King's mouth recalls 1:16 (2:12), which see for the "great sword" mentioned here and in v. 21. The ἵνα clause is equal to an infinitive; it belongs here, for with this "great sword" he will now smite the nations in final judgment. "Out of his mouth" goes this "great sword" as explained in 1:16, which see.

"And he, he (emphatic αὐτός) shall shepherd them with an iron rod" repeats the reference to Ps. 2:9, which in 12:5 identifies the Son of the Woman as Christ, and is used already in 2:27 — see these passages where the verb "to shepherd" is also explained. The time to strike with the iron rod for complete destruction has now come in fulfillment of Ps. 2:9.

Another Old Testament reference to the same effect is added: "he, he (αὐτός) treads the winepress of the anger of the wrath of God, the Almighty." See 14:19, 20. Here we have the fulfillment of Isa. 63:1-3. One may construe the genitive differently: τὴν ληνὸν τοῦ οἴνου may be regarded as one concept, "the winepress," with τοῦ θυμοῦ κτλ. being the apposition; or τὴν ληνὸν, "the winepress," and τοῦ οἴνου, "of (for) the wine," with τοῦ θυμοῦ being the apposition to "the wine." On θυμός and ὀργή see 14:8-10, and note that these terms now are heaped up: "of the wine of the anger of the wrath of God." Wine or winepress = the anger (apposition) which, as the hot outburst, belongs to the wrath (possessive genitive), the deep steady indignation, which belongs to God (possessive genitive), who is the Almighty (apposition), παντοκράτωρ in 1:8. As grapes are crushed in a winepress, so the enemies are now to be crushed; 14:20 states to what depth their blood shall flow.

16) The fourth name, like the second, "having been written," is one that was used already in 17:14 in a similar connection: the Lamb shall conquer the kings who shall do battle "because he is Lord of lords and King of kings." The two titles are now transposed; this, however, is immaterial. "The ruler of the kings of the earth" which occurs in 1:5 is by no means the same, for in 1:5 they are the kings *of the earth* (see 6:15; 16:14; 17:2, 18; 18:3, 9), powers of earth allied with the beast and the whore. *We* are the kings of whom Christ is King, etc. See the exposition of 17:14. When it is said that this title was written on the King's mantle and on his thigh, our conception of this scene is that the title was written on a sign that hung over the mantle at the place of the thigh, and not on the cloth of the mantle at the place where the girdle looped it up in folds at the thigh — where it could scarcely be read — and not partly on the mantle and partly on the skin of the thigh — an unsatisfactory conjecture. The name was placed where all could see it without effort.

17) **And I saw one angel standing in the sun; and he cried with a great voice, saying to all the birds, those flying in midheaven: Hither, be gathered together for the supper, the great one, of God, that you may eat the flesh parts of kings and the flesh parts of chiliarchs and the flesh parts of strong ones and the flesh parts of horses and of those sitting on them and the flesh parts of all, of both free and slave and of small and of great!** Compare Deut. 28:26; Jer. 7:33; 16:4; especially Ezek. 39:17-20, yet Revelation always goes beyond what is appropriated from the Old Testament. Fittingly the angel stands in the sun because the heaven is opened so that the King and his angel army may ride to the

battle. Here we may translate ἕνα "one" angel, (all the rest are riding with the King) although the numeral is often only our indefinite article, "an angel." He summons all the wild birds to the immense slaughter and to the feast of carrion.

18) The imagery of a battle governs this vision. After a battle the vultures, eagles (they, too, eat carrion), crows, and every carrion eater rush to feast on the corpses. So the picture is here drawn but on a supreme scale. These verses correspond with v. 21. The Greek pluralizes σάρξ even when only one body is referred to (17:16, τὰς σάρκας αὐτῆς). The long list of "fleshes" is here used to show the immensity of the impending slaughter. The whole antichristian power with every least part of it is now to reach its just end. Some interpreters think of these kings, chiliarchs, etc., and even of these horses as being the men and the animals that are living at the time of the Parousia. As the beast represents the whole antichristian power, so these kings, etc., represent no king this and that, these chiliarchs no general this or that, these horses no cavalry or chariot steeds, but all the antichristian forces which the antichristian power has produced and armed in all departments of life, in man, woman, and child. We are dealing with the last judgment, with nothing less, with one snapshot of it as it appears in the symbolism of the last battle.

19) **And I saw the wild beast and the kings of the earth and their armies gathered together to do battle with the One sitting on the horse and with his army. And captured was the wild beast, and with him the pseudo-prophet, the one that wrought the signs before him in connection with which he deceived those that received the mark of the wild beast and those worshipping his image. Living were they thrown, the two, into the lake of the fire, the** (lake) **burning with brimstone. And the rest**

were killed with the great sword of the One sitting on the horse that came out of his mouth; and all the birds were gorged with the flesh parts of them.

The θηρίον has been fully described in 13:1-8; contrast this with the King (19:11-16). With the beast are "the kings of the earth" who in 16:12-16 were brought together for the battle of Armageddon. With the two beasts are "their armies gathered together." All these are "to do battle with the One sitting on the horse and with his army," ποιῆσαι is the effective aorist. The beast = the whole antichristian power; the kings of the earth = the antichristian forces in all the departments of life, these forces being royally pretentious and domineering; their armies = all the little antichristian forces that are built up and assembled by the major ones.

On the symbolism of "the kings" see 17:2, and also note "the dwellers on the earth," for these compose the armies of the beast and of the kings. The beast, the pseudo-prophet, and the whore are symbolical personifications. The dragon is Satan, a definite personal being. The kings (like the merchants and the men of the sea, 18:11, 17) are again abstractions or personifications; so also are these beast armies and still more so "the dwellers of the earth" (antichristian earthly-mindedness as it exists in persons); note also the remarks on v. 18.

20) As in a parable only so much of the figure is used in order to show only so much of the reality, so this is done also in symbolism and in the case of this battle. Jesus used many parables with all manner of imagery to reveal the kingdom of God; so here the imagery of the battle varies: 17:14-18; now 19:11-21; yet to follow, 20:7-10. We have much here, yet here, too, only so much. Only the outcome of the battle is shown.

Ἐπιάσθη, "taken, laid hold of, captured was the beast." This verb fits the action of battle; it also means arresting someone. Do not insist that the imagery tell us by whose hands this is done, etc. Now we hear that "the pseudo-prophet" was with the beast and was thus taken "in company with him." "Pseudo-prophet" refers to 16:13 and takes us back to 13:11-18, where we see his awful crimes and his guilt which are now restated by means of brief appositions: "the one that wrought the signs before him (13:14) in connection with which he deceived (13:14) those that received the mark of the wild beast (13:16-18) and those doing obeisance to his image (13:15)." We have already had the detailed exposition.

"*Living* were they thrown, these two, into the lake of the fire," etc. The emphasis is on "living," on being thrown into hell *alive* while all the rest were *killed* and their flesh devoured by the birds. Some commentators make an issue of ζῶντες. They state that this implies that these two must have physical bodies, not only in the symbolism, but also in reality; secondly, that these two must, therefore, represent two actual persons that are living at the Parousia (or at the time of this battle, wherever these commentators place its date), the beast being the personal antichrist, the second beast or pseudo-prophet being the personal tool of the antichrist. We are told that there will be *two human beings* who will lead the whole world to this battle, and that these will be thrown into hell bodily, while they are yet *bodily alive.* II Thess. 2 is introduced as proof that the antichrist will be one human being who is living at or near the end. See the writer's exposition of II Thess. 2. This prophecy in Thessalonians deals with the whole papacy, and not with only one final pope, or, if such a pope is discarded, with some other one human being.

Take Kliefoth as an example of one writer who is certain that the beast and the prophet are two human persons with bodies. He makes the statement, "Into hell, i. e., the second death, no one can go except *bodily.*" But what about the devils? Take Biederwolf who asks the question as to how ideal forms or emblems of mere powers can be cast *alive* into hell. But Philippi, one of the 492 writers whom he quotes on other matters, answers this question: "When, however, the beast and the false prophet are cast into the lake of fire, although they are not persons but only personifications of spiritual potencies, this imagery accords with Dan. 7:11. As applied to them, by this is expressed only their absolute and abiding abolition and destruction, whereas in the reality their adherents, who are not just abstractions but actual concrete persons, whose destruction is here presented in the symbolism of the slaughter, land in actuality in the lake of fire," *Glaubenslehre,* VI, 214.

This may be simplified. His antichristian power and propaganda are thrown into hell together with Satan, are thrown "alive" with all their might as it is; they do not need to be killed before this can be done. The imagery is equally exact in presenting the kings and the armies as being "killed," for these symbols denote the minor antichristian potencies as these are represented in actual human beings who may be killed although it is best to regard "were killed" as symbolical: all these minor potencies were completely wiped out and abolished.

As already stated, this vision presents only so much. The next, 20:15, presents the rest even in the plainest language. The symbolism keeps strictly to the realities. The beast and the prophet beast are the heads of this army, and when an army is completely overthrown, the fate of its leaders must be recorded. Did they, perhaps, escape to raise another army, were they killed in the battle or were they taken alive and, if so, what about their fate? Here there is an army that was utterly destroyed, and so we are told about the fate of the two leaders who led it to battle. The two are potencies that are very much "alive" and powerfully active. They are "alive," but that does not mean alive in *physical* bodies but alive as terrible potencies, to use Philippi's term. The bodily forms with which chapter 13 pictures them are symbolical, beastly, nonhuman; these hellish potencies could not be presented as being human, least of all as being clothed with *physical* human bodies. "Alive" is exactly the proper word, for both the symbolism and the reality. Cast into hell "alive" while the rest "were killed" takes care of another point: these two monsters, the heads and leaders, deserve the greater punishment. It can only be symbolized; but it *is* so symbolized.

Shall we ask how symbolized potencies can burn in hell? We state as an answer and let it apply also to 20:11, that, while all hellish potencies in the reality operate without a physical body and individual personality as we constantly experience their attacks here on earth, they are emanations of Satan who is, indeed, a spirit and a person, and as being fearfully "alive" they delude, enslave, and drag to hell human beings who are persons that have both bodies and souls. Thrown into hell implies that every power and potency which Satan was ever able to put forth for the delusion and destruction of men ends in hell (20:10), never, never again to appear outside of hell, never to come near the new heaven and the new earth (21:1, etc.).

Ἡ λίμνη τοῦ πυρὸς ἡ καιομένη ἐν θείῳ, "the lake of the fire, the one (the lake) burning with brimstone" = hell, and this designation for it occurs only in Revelation (here and in 20:10, 14, 15; 21:8). The texts have the genitive participle: τῆς καιομένης, on which R. 414 remarks that its gender agrees with "lake," its case with "fire." This reading appears to be a case of faulty transcription which was mechanically reproduced in succeeding texts. We note "in fire and brimstone" in 14:10. It is the description that marks this "lake" as hell. Some interpreters find a number of places in the other world, sometimes a new place for almost every designation that is used in the Scriptures, thus for the Gehenna — the hades — the abyss — the lake, etc. There are only two places, heaven and hell. Hell is variously designated, but so also is heaven: Paradise — Abraham's bosom — City of God — a city whose builder is God (Heb. 11:10) — Zion — the Sanctuary — the Tabernacle; yet these are not so many different places. A rose is sweet, give it any name; hell is hell, name it as you may. Human mentality is bound to spatial conception, hence we are able to use no other terms when speaking of hell or of heaven. On the relation between the hades and the lake of the fire see 20:14.

21) This vision does not present a general mêlée in which the combatants engage in hand to hand fighting until two leaders are captured. The reality itself forbids such a picture. The account reads as though the two leaders were at once taken, and as though in the same instantaneous act "the rest were killed," killed with the ῥομφαία, "the great sword," such as the Thracians used, which was so large that they did not carry it in their belt but in a sling that was suspended from the neck and the shoulder, killed, not by the many swords of the armies of the King of kings but by his one great sword, of which it is once more significantly said, "the one that came out of the mouth" and was not in his hand. In v. 15 ἐκπορεύεται and in 1:16 ἐκπορευομένη are present tenses because they give a general characterization of this sword; here the participle is the aorist and states the one act by which this sword killed all these antichristian armies. Paul makes the same

statement regarding the end of the papal antichrist, cf., II Thess. 2:8, whom we regard as one of "the kings of the earth" (v. 19) in the armies of the beast and the prophet: "the Lord Jesus shall make away with him by means of the spirit of his mouth." Even the imagery transcends imagination, which lets us feel how much the reality exceeds even the imagery by far.

"And all the birds were gorged with the flesh parts of them" completes the symbolism of v. 17, 18, which accords with that regarding the whore: "her flesh parts they devoured," namely the kings of the earth (17:16). Why is this added and even made so prominent by v. 17, 18? Because "the great sword" and "were killed" retains the symbols employed; and because the absolute abolition of even the last and least antichristian opposition is to be conveyed. But should these armies not also be cast into the lake of fire? You are right. They were: 20:15 says so. That statement is made in its proper place.

CHAPTER XX

The Thousand Years, chapter 20

What Happened at the Beginning of the 1,000 Years, 20:1-3

1) Review the remarks introducing 19:11. We now have the last vision of that battle in 20:7-10, that feature of it which centers about the dragon, about Satan himself (12:3, etc.); the light is now thrown on him. What the three battle scenes really signify is fully brought out in v. 11-15. This portrays the Final Judgment which is now described in its reality. Then there follows 21:1, etc.

Because v. 7-15 bring us to the end when time shall be no more (10:6), and because the vision now throws the light upon the author of all antichristianity and upon the manner of his end, therefore the two scenes in v. 7-10 and in v. 11-15 are preceded by the two scenes in v. 1-3 and in v. 4-6; and v. 7-15 is not made to follow immediately upon 19:11-21. Five times in v. 1-6 there occur the significant χίλια ἔτη, "1,000 years," and then again in v. 7: "when finished were the 1,000 years." In the "1,000 years" we have the cue to these two brief visions (v. 1-3 and 4-6) and to their relation to the visions in v. 7-15. The 1,000 years cover the whole period from 12:1 to 20:6, from the appearance of Satan as the dragon (12:3) to his final judgment (20:7-10). Note the full import of his *four* names in 12:7 and *the same four* names in 20:2. These 1,000 years thus extend from the incarnation and the enthronement of the Son (12:5) to Satan's final plunge into hell (20:10), which is the entire New Testament period. The first vision (v. 1-3) reveals in brief the state of the dragon during this New Testament period.

During this period the dragon operated by means of the beast (the antichristian power), his image, and his mark, the number "666" (see the whole of chapter 13), but the church remained, some of its members died as martyrs, others endured to the end (Matt. 24:13) and did not bow to the beast or receive his mark (Rev. 20:4). That is the least of their experience. Their souls entered heaven, sat on thrones of judgment, lived, reigned, judged with Christ in the power and the authority that from the very beginning meant eternal doom to the dragon, his agencies (the two beasts, the whore), and all his following, the doom now portrayed in the vision of the dragon in v. 7-10, and climaxed in the vision of the judgment itself, v. 11-15.

The preface, v. 1-6, is necessary for the last two visions of v. 7-15. Frightful as the dragon and all his agencies and all his following are — the various visions reveal it fully — his doom is sealed. Bound from the start, he is already judged by the very souls he hounded here on earth through his agencies; and what this judging means v. 7-15 reveal.

This is the relation of the four sections of this chapter to each other, and the relation of this chapter to all that precedes, especially from chapter 12 onward.

And I saw an angel coming down out of the heaven, having the key to the abyss and a great chain on his hand. And he seized the dragon, the serpent, the ancient one, who is (the) **devil and Satan, and bound him for a thousand years and threw him into the abyss and locked and sealed it over him that he should not still deceive the nations until there be finished the thousand years; after these it is necessary that he be loosed for a little time.**

Here is the explanation as to why we have the visions of the two beasts (chapter 13) without the dragon and the visions of the great whore (chapters 17 and 18) without the dragon, also the visions of the end of the whore and of the two beasts without the dragon, while in chapter 12 it is the dragon alone who is shown as seeking to kill the child of the woman and as then harassing the woman (the church). Satan, the dragon, is the archenemy, the ancient serpent who attacked Eve in Eden (12:9). All the opposition to Christ and to the church proceeds from him. Yet something has severely interfered with him and with his power. A part of it is shown in 12:7-12: the brethren could and did conquer him because of the blood of the Lamb and because of the word of their testimony although some suffered death (12:11), and the heavens and those tabernacling in them are called to celebrate (12:12). Chapters 13, 17, and 18 reveal that the dragon is compelled to work only through agencies, the two beasts, the great whore. It is he and yet not he. He has to resort to the two beasts, the antichristian power and the antichristian propaganda (chapter 13; note that when the lamblike beast speaks in propaganda he keeps speaking "as a dragon"). He has to resort to the antichristian seduction, the whore (Babylon, chapters 17 and 18).

This interference with the dragon enables *the brethren* to conquer him (12:11). It stops the dragon from direct invasion of the world, i. e., of *the nations.* He in his own person as the dragon cannot still deceive *the nations* (20:3); he is restricted to the use of the two beasts and the whore. Now in 20:1-3 we have revealed to us in completeness, beyond the revelation recorded in 12:7-12, what the incarnation and the enthronement of Jesus did to the dragon. Once, as in Eden, he himself went forth to deceive; by the incarnation and the enthronement of Jesus he was chained, thrown, and confined, compelled to resort to beasts and to a whore. Judgment thus already rests upon him: "Now shall the ruler of this world be thrown out outside," and included in this act of judging (κρίσις) is "this world," John 12:31. The brethren who have conquered him here on earth already sit on thrones in heaven with the great verdict (κρῖμα), 20:4, which comes to its execution by another and a final act of throwing (βάλλειν, in 12:9 twice; in 12:10, 13; in 20:3; and significantly again in 20:10; followed by two more "were thrown" and "was thrown," in 20:14, 15). Carefully combine all these statements that have the word βάλλειν.

"And I saw an angel coming out of the heaven, having the key of the abyss" is regarded by some as a reference to Christ himself. When explaining also some of the other visions these interpreters think that Christ appeared in the form of an angel. In his little volume *Saint John,* 170, the writer himself accepted their reasons, namely that in 1:18 Christ has the keys; that Christ is the Stronger who comes upon the strong one; that Christ may be called ἄγγελος, "messenger," as the one sent by the Father; and that coming out of heaven refers to Christ's incarnation and his saving mission. Yet such a view has its weakness. Although many angels appear throughout the book of Revelation, this would be the only place where Christ appears as "an angel." In 9:1 the key is given to an angel. The key remains Christ's possession although in 9:1 and again here it is used for Christ by an angel. So we correct our former view on this point and abide by the analogy of Revelation in which ἄγγελος is always an angel and never Christ himself. In 12:7 it is the angel Michael and not Christ himself who is referred to. Christ always acts through his angels.

In Revelation "the abyss" (in 9:2 with its smoke) is always hell. It is described thus in order to indicate its awful depth and darkness, whereas "lake of fire" (19:20) describes its length and its breadth with the connotation of depth. "Abyss" is not a deep ravine but, as "the pit" in the A. V. translation makes plain, a vast, deep hole provided with a shaft (9:1), with a mouth and a lid that can be locked and unlocked, and even sealed. The Scriptures speak of only one fearful place in the other world; other places are inventions of commentators (see 19:20). The key and the great chain are symbolical, the key to represent power to open and to close hell, the chain to represent power to render helpless. No literal, material chain can fetter a spirit; no key such as we know here on earth locks hell. The chain ἐπί the angel's hand pictures it as hanging down with its two ends. It is "great" because of Satan's might. Fancy has it wound round and round about Satan; but just how Satan is chained is beyond our human comprehension. So, too, we cannot understand how the angel ἐκράτησε, *packte*, overpowered Satan. Be content with what the symbolism conveys and insert nothing more. It is a very serious matter to resort to literalism. Keep to the realities that are pictured and pictured only symbolically.

2) The accusative χίλια ἔτη expresses extent of time: "for a thousand years." For so long a period was the dragon chained, locked up, and a seal placed on the lock over him, which fully pictures his confinement and restriction during all his time. We recall the seal affixed to Christ's tomb. Seals of this kind are attached to insure inviolability, to show upon inspection that no one has surreptitiously tampered with door or lock and released the captive. Complete and sure was the dragon's confinement for 1,000 years.

Most significant are the names: "the *dragon*, the *serpent*, the ancient one, who is (the) *devil* and *Satan*," because these four names certainly intend to take us back to the identical four terms found in 12:9: "the *dragon,* the great one, the *serpent,* the ancient one, the one called *devil* and *Satan,* the one deceiving the whole inhabited earth." On the terms themselves see 12:9. It is true, important terms are repeated also in Revelation when new, subsequent events are recorded. Many, especially the chiliasts, think that here the repetition is of this order. They place this binding of Satan subsequent to the battle mentioned in 19:11-21, and postulate another battle after the lapse of 1,000 years in 20:7-10. As they thus have two or three battles, so they debate whether to accept also two Parousias, one in 19:11, etc., another in 20:11, etc., one at the opening of their millennium and another at its close. Two (or three) battles — two Parousias (from which, however, some shrink) — and thus also two resurrections which nearly all adopt. Misconceptions at one point carry consequent misconception throughout.

The first misconception is found already in connection with the beast and the false prophet mentioned in 19:20 and in chapter 13. It regards them as two men, the one being the antichrist of the state, the other the antichrist of the church, although there is a great variety as to the details. After these two men and their following have been abolished (19:20, 21), Satan, too, — we are not told how soon after — is locked up, and a grand millennium sets in for 1,000 years; whore, beasts, dragon have disappeared, everything is lovely on earth, Christ himself is very likely visibly present on earth. The martyrs, perhaps all the dead saints, are raised up in a first physical resurrection and again walk on earth — these glorified persons are found among the unglorified who remain on earth. All the Jews will then be converted. This is usually made a prominent feature. We meet the opinion that even all the hardened Jews of all past ages will be raised up and converted. Many regard the Jews as constituting the aristocracy during the millennium, some even supposing that all of the Gentile Christians will have died and will not be among those resurrected. Yet, we are told, there will be found in the far four corners of the earth heathen nations who are usually termed barbarian who, at the end of the millennium, will be deceived by Satan when he is loosed for a little time, and will form the Gog and Magog under Satan when attacking the beloved City (v. 7-9).

The views of the chiliasts are so varied that each must really be treated separately. They range from the mild to the gross and clash with one another.

In the Augsburg Confession the fathers confessed that "they condemn also others, who are now spreading certain Jewish opinions, that before the resurrection of the dead the godly shall take possession of the kingdom of the world, the ungodly being everywhere suppressed" (*C. Tr.* 51, art. XVII). All present-day chiliastic views are only variations of the "Jewish opinions" condemned by our fathers as these were formulated in their time and as they are summarized in the great confession. Chiliastic subscribers to the Augustana naturally claim exemption, claim that *their* special kind of opinion is not at all Jewish but is purely Christian and Biblical doctrine and a great blessing to the church.

The old Jewish dream was that the Jews would eventually dominate and thus bless the whole world of nations. The Messiah for whom they looked was the one who would lift them to this height and usher in this era of Jewish supremacy. Jesus was the opposite of such a Messiah, and the Jews crucified him and have rejected him ever since. Jesus could not use the title "Messiah" during his ministry among the Jews because of this meaning which the Jews had attached to it; he used the term "the Son of man" to which no such national, political, earthly notions could be attached.

This "Jewish opinion" put on a Christian garb with a variety of Christian like ornamentations in the teaching of certain post-Apostolic fathers and their successors, to whom many present chiliasts still point as helping to prove the truth of their own chiliasm. No, not the wicked Jews but the believing church of Jesus is to dominate the world of nations in a final grand millennial period which will crown all the preceding periods of suffering and the cross. The Messiah will return in glory and usher in this millennial period of glory.

The old "Jewish opinions" were revamped, modified, given a Christian dress. Often the details were remarkable, like the immense grapevine of Papias which had the hugest clusters — Jerusalem rebuilt with the Temple in great grandeur — the whole Levitical service restored, etc. It was easy to add the 1,000 years from Rev. 20. Even when it is taken literally, 1,000 fits in attractively. Χίλια furnished the term "chiliasm," in the Latin "millennium." The elaborations varied and still vary greatly, for these depend on individual imagination, of which some have more, others less.*

---

*Zahn, *Offenbarung*, 622, quotes Irenaeus who claims to have received the following from Papias who, in turn, claimed that it came from Jesus: "There will come days in which grapevines will grow which will each have 10,000 main branches, and on each main branch 10,000 smaller branches, and on each smaller branch 10,000 twigs, and on each twig 10 clusters, and on every cluster 10,000 berries, and every berry, when pressed, will yield five measures of wine. And when one of the saints takes a berry, another berry will cry: 'I am a better berry, take me, and thank the Lord through me!' Similarly, the wheat kernel will produce 10,000 ears. And each ear will contain 10,000 kernels, and each kernel will furnish five double-pound measures of fine, pure bisquet flour, and all other tree fruits and seeds and herbs according to the measure suitable for them. And all the animals which use the food which the earth supplies will be peaceful and friendly in perfect obedience subject to man."

The basic idea underlying these views is the thought that it simply cannot be possible that the Christian Church must remain under the cross until the last day; it must reach a golden age on earth when it shines in triumph. The kingdom cannot remain in lowly humility until judgment day and not reach its triumphant consummation until that time. That would not be at all fitting. There *must* be a "millennium" before the end, a great time when the kingdom rules all the earth, either with the King himself being present here on earth, or at least with his glory being present in his church. Around this central conviction each chiliast builds the rest according to his ideas. The more conservative advocate the general idea of "a better time" for the church, a viewpoint which scarcely deserves the name chiliasm, although in Matt. 24 Jesus predicts worse and not better times as we approach the judgment day. Many labor and pray that "the kingdom" may come in this sense and cry out against us for robbing the church of this great "hope," i. e., the picture they individually make of it and of its fulfillment.

They thus seek to find as much Scripture proof as possible. In the case of some sects this seems to be their chief article of faith. The gold mine for proof is Revelation, in particular chapter 20 with its 1,000 years repeated six times. The prophets also yield a great deal. Then what is so ardently desired is found in a large number of other places in Scripture.

But ever it remains in essence "the old Jewish opinion." When the fathers of the Reformation saw it at their time they branded it "certain Jewish opinions." Chiliasts may hate this adjective and may seek to shake it off; nevertheless, the adjective "Jewish" is true.

$10 \times 10 \times 10 = 1{,}000$, namely 10 multiplied and raised to the third degree, that of highest completeness. Revelation is full, not only of symbolical numbers, but of symbols of all kinds. It would be strange, indeed, if "1,000 years" were here where it occurs in so marked a way, all of six times, to be understood in a literal sense. Here, however, we find more than the mere number: we are told what shall mark the entire length of the 1,000 years, and with what even they shall end. They begin with the binding and the imprisonment of Satan; during the entire 1,000 years he is not to deceive (πλανήσῃ, aorist) the nations as he once did; these years end when μικρὸν χρόνον, a little length of time, sets in, compare v. 7: "when the 1,000 years were finished."

No past history has a period of 1,000 years that even remotely corresponds with the state that is described in these verses. Read all the histories and see that this is true. Of course, search in the past for the 1,000 years could begin only after a sufficient number of years had already passed. But even now, although they have a period of 1,900 years within which to locate the 1,000, these millennialists have a sorry time of it, for if the 1,000 years are past, where is the "little time" following the 1,000, where is what v. 7-10 describes? And this is only "a little time," so that we may ask, "Where is what v. 11-15 describes, in other words, why do the earth and the world of men still continue as they are?"

The futuristic millennialists, commonly designated by the term "chiliasts," have a great advantage in the fact that they place the 1,000 years in the future, including, of course, the binding of Satan. They are free, too, to make the "1,000 years" symbolical if they wish. Since all lies in the future, what difference does it make to let 1,000 denote a fully complete cycle? We also note that "the year-day theory" has been applied, each day of 1,000 years duration denoting a literal year, thus 365,000 years of a future millennium. But most of the chiliasts are satisfied with a literal 1,000 years. Many count six millenniums of six workdays in a worldweek (6,000 years) and then one millennium like the Sabbath at the end of this worldweek — thus 7,000 literal years. These are harder to refute because they place everything into the distant future.

Most of the chiliasts disregard the Analogy of Scripture and the Analogy of Faith. Tell them that their doctrine is a *novum,* and you will find that this is the very feature that is so attractive to them. Did Jesus in John 5:28, 29 speak of the resurrection as being one? Well, that was like the Baptist's word in Matt. 3:11, 12 concerning Jesus. Rev. 20:5 adds to John 5 and informs us that the resurrection is to be divided into two parts with 1,000 years between the parts. The same is true with regard to everything else in this *novum* — what of it? In this last book of the Bible many entirely new revelations should be given! Yet the idea of a *novum,* after all, is not satisfactory to many chiliasts; they claim that they find the millennium taught in many other Bible passages, already in many notable ones in the Old Testament prophets, and then in many implications and hints scattered throughout the Scriptures, the main new feature of Rev. 20 being the "1,000 years."

3) Scripture speaks about only *one* binding of Satan that interfered most decisively with his deceiving the nations. Luke 11:21, 22: "When a strong man fully armed guardeth his own court, his goods are in peace: but when a stronger than he shall come upon him, and overcome him, he taketh from him his whole armor wherein he trusted, and divideth his spoils." Compare Isa. 53:12. Col. 2:15: "Having spoiled principalities and powers, he made a show of them openly, triumphing over them in it." I John 3:8: "For this purpose the Son of man was manifested, that he might destroy the works of the devil." John 16:11:

"The prince of this world is judged." Also Gen. 3:15. Heb. 2:14: "He also himself likewise took part of the same (flesh and blood), that through death he might destroy him that had the power of death, that is, the devil." This is the binding of Satan that is here symbolized. It is in part and for a different purpose (namely as regards the woman and the continuous existence of the church in spite of the devil) symbolized already in 12:7-17. It took place when Jesus cried triumphantly on the cross: "It has been finished!" and when he sat down at the right hand of God.

This binding of Satan as here symbolized is mentioned with reference to "the nations." This reference to "deceiving the nations" must be understood in connection with the symbolism of the two beasts and of the whore. Where is the dragon in those visions? We have the clear answer in 20:1-3. Who does the deceiving during the 1,000 years? The second beast, the pseudo-prophet serving the first beast. Not Satan himself. So states 13:14 and 19:20. The first beast = the whole antichristian power in the world; the second beast, the whole antichristian propaganda in the world. What about the whore, the whole antichristian seduction in the world? By her φαρμακεία, sorcery, drugs "were the nations deceived." So says 19:20. Satan is confined to these agents or agencies. Does this mean nothing in these visions when in addition in 14:6, etc., we see the angel flying in midheaven with "the eternal gospel to gospel it upon those sitting on the earth and to every nation and tribe and tongue and people," etc.? This is Matt. 24:14: "And there shall be heralded this gospel of the kingdom in the whole inhabited world for testimony to all the nations; and then shall come the end."

The binding of Satan means that he shall not prevent this heralding of the gospel to all the nations. Once the nations were without this heralding, all were under the deception of Satan. One nation alone had the Word. Then came Christ and his command: "Having gone into all the world, herald the gospel to every creature!" Mark 16:15; Matt. 28:19, 20. Where was Satan to stop it? The strong symbolism of being bound with a great chain and thrown into the abyss reveals how mighty was the foe who above all else intended to stop this heralding, and what was required to stop him, and how thoroughly he was stopped. Is the imagery too strong for you? Perhaps the Lord who uses it in this vision knows the dragon better than you do, seeing that he conquered him on the cross at the cost of his own death.

Only the antichristian propaganda in the face of the heralded everlasting gospel, only the antichristian seduction with its poisoning (19:20) still deceive the nations. That means: those who are deceived are deceived willingly by scorning the heralded eternal gospel. Willingly the kings listened to the frogs and gathered at Armageddon; willingly the kings and their armies gathered for the battle against the King of kings. All could have been under the King's banner. "How often would I, but ye would not" (Matt. 23:37).

So we see where *the Scriptures* have the 1,000 years begin. I will let the Scriptures tell me although 10,000 chiliasts insist that *they* must tell me! They may keep their *novum* which means "new thing," "novelty." So the 1,000 years are the complete New Testament era. John was in it; you and I are in it now. The two beasts and the whore are working now. This text is not concerned about the dim future so that chiliasts may embroider it at will. As it had validity for John, so it has for us.

Why "is it necessary" (δεῖ is used to express all types of necessity) that Satan is to be loosed again and that μικρὸν χρόνον? In regard to the "little time" we have Matt. 24:22, "except those days should be shortened," etc. In regard to the fact of the final work of Satan we have Rev. 20:7, 8, and Matt. 24:12, 21, 24, and especially Luke 18:8: "Nevertheless, when the Son of man cometh, shall he find faith on the earth?" In regard to this δεῖ or necessity we have only what we may be able to conclude from these Scripture passages, the substance of which we assume to be: that the work of the gospel on earth and among the nations is done. "Then shall come the end," Matt. 24:14, i. e., then it *must* come. That is the reason for the "1,000" years, the utter completeness of the years. There is a necessity in the nature of the situation which our eyes perceive; but as far as God is concerned, the necessities which he sees and on which he acts in his world plans, it is not wise for us to seek to investigate.

How long will this "little time" continue? Merely long enough to permit Satan to gather his host and to have the fire out of the heaven devour them. Some call this "little time" "The Great Tribulation" for the saints and introduce 7:14, where this expression occurs. Can you find a trace of it in v. 7-10? There *is* no trace. This is not a θλῖψις, a "tribulation," but the final judgment of Satan.

What Happens During the 1,000 Years, 20:4-6

4) See v. 1 for the relation of this part of the vision to the part preceding and to the part following. Although Satan is bound, there will be martyrs, in fact, 6:9-11 informs us that their number must be completed before the end comes. In the other visions we see the saints who did not love their lives unto death (12:11), whom Jesus calls to be faithful unto death that he may give them the crown of life (2:10), whom the beast conquered (13:7), who did not receive the beast's number "666" (13:17), who are included among those that are told to celebrate in 12:12 and in

18:20. Satan is bound; but the martyrs and the faithful confessors sit on royal thrones in heavenly glory, reign as kings with κρῖμα, the verdict of the judgment over Satan and all his following, given to them.

And I saw thrones, and they sat upon them, and judgment was given to them. And (I saw) **the souls of those having been beheaded because of the testimony of Jesus and because of the Word of God; and they such as did not do obeisance to the beast or to his image and did not receive the mark on their forehead and on their hand. And they did live and did reign in company with Christ for a thousand years. The rest of the dead did not live until there were finished the thousand years. This** (is) **the resurrection, the first one. Blessed and holy the one having part in the resurrection, the first one! On these the second death does not have authority; on the contrary, they shall be priests of God and of Christ and shall reign in company with him for a thousand years.**

Besides "the throne" (4:2 and often) we have seen "thrones" that were occupied by the twenty-four elders (4:4); especially notable is 3:21. There is also "the throne of Satan" (2:13) and "the throne of the beast" (16:10) which is "the dragon's throne" given to the beast by the dragon (13:2). "Throne" is the symbol of power, rule, and dominion, and "sitting on a throne" is exercising such rule. That is also the meaning of these thrones and of those who sat upon them. The aorist ἐκάθισαν is constative as are also the next three aorists: ἔζησαν, ἐβασίλευσαν, οὐκ ἔζησαν. Because of the term κρῖμα some think only of a judge's seat, but ἐβασίλευσαν, which is repeated in βασιλεύσουσι (v. 6), shows that royal thrones are referred to, and that we have the imagery of a king on his throne who exercises judgment and delivers verdicts as did King Solomon and all ancient kings. In v. 11 we have the same imagery:

"a great white throne and the One sitting upon it." "And they sat upon them" = all of the thrones which John saw occupied.

Before recording who occupied the thrones John states that the occupants did not sit merely in royal splendor; "judgment was given to them," κρῖμα (the word occurring in 17:1), a term in -μα expressing result, we may say "verdict," a sentence pronounced and to be executed. "Was given" (our idiom: had been given) is perfectly plain to us. These are thrones that are related to "the throne," we may say extensions of Christ's throne (in 3:21 it is one mighty throne). The decisions rendered from these thrones are identical with those rendered from the supreme throne, gifts of this throne, unspeakably great gifts, royal in power and authority. Such gifts, we may add, are the thrones themselves and the sitting upon them.

After thus fixing attention on the thrones and on their judgment of authority, every reader raises the question in his mind as to who the occupants of these thrones are. It is unwarranted to suppose that this question would not be answered. The very construction of the following supplies the answer, for we have another accusative that is dependent on εἶδον, "I saw." The occupants of the thrones were "the souls of those having been beheaded because of the testimony of Jesus and because of the Word of God; and they such as did not do obeisance to the beast," etc. There are two groups; for if οἵτινες referred to the beheaded ones, καί could not precede. There are not three groups: 1) judges; 2) martyrs; 3) saints generally. The text does not justify a division into three groups. Nor do the Scriptures support such a view. I Cor. 6:2, 3: "Do ye not know that the saints shall judge the world? . . . Know ye not that ye shall judge angels?" Compare Dan. 7:22: "Until the Ancient of days came, and judgment was given to the saints of the Most High; and the time came that the saints possessed the kingdom," i. e., possessed the royal rule in order to exercise it by participation as themselves being kings. Again, 2:26: "And the one conquering and keeping to the end my works, I will give to him authority over the nations." Add 3:21: "The one conquering, I will give to him to sit in company with me in my throne," etc. The Analogy of Scripture settles this matter.

John says he saw ψυχαί, "souls." This term applies also to καὶ οἵτινες. The martrys and the saints whom John saw were "souls." John could not say πνεύματα because this would not be exact since angels, too, are called "spirits" but have no "souls." In other connections "spirit" and "spirits" are in place (Acts 7:59; Heb. 12:23); here ψυχαί is clearly and completely *human.* So in 6:9 John writes: "I saw beneath the altar τὰς ψυχάς, the souls of those having been slain because of the Word of God and because of the testimony which they had." There we already met the argument about "souls" and the question as to how John could *see* "souls," and the proposition that they must have had some sort of a body in order to be seen (see 6:9). All the millennialists are certain that the "souls" mentioned in this verse have bodies, namely their own bodies by virtue of "the first resurrection" (v. 5). They misinterpret "the first resurrection" and thus "the souls" and the whole of v. 1-6, by placing it chronologically after 19:17-21, into their millennium with its two bodily resurrections. It is theosophy to claim that in the other world souls must at once have bodies.

The perfect participle τῶν πεπελεκισμένων = once beheaded, they ever after bear this character; so also ἐσφαγμένων in 6:9, and the singular ἐσφαγμένον used so often with reference to the Lamb. Πελεκίζω means to cut off with a πέλεκυς, an ax, hence literally, "those that have been axed" (this word is found only here in the

New Testament). One form of bloody execution is used as a representative of all forms. Instead of a general term a strikingly concrete individual term is used. Very few martyrs were actually beheaded, most of them died in other usually more painful and terrible ways. Among the apostles only Paul was beheaded; perhaps also James (Acts 12:2). There is no reason why beheaded martyrs should be made a separate, notable class. Peter was crucified; Stephen stoned; James, the brother of John, killed with the sword (Acts 12:2); James the Just was thrown from the Temple wall. As for the Romans, they loved to crucify, to cast before wild beasts in the arena, to strangle, and they used the ax or the sword only on Roman citizens as a less degrading mode of death. Note how "the Word of God and the testimony of Jesus" runs through Revelation: 1:2, 9; 6:9, of martyrs; 11:7, testimony; 12:11, 17; 19:10. The testimony of Jesus is the testimony he made and not that made by others about him.

The nominative καὶ οἵτινες with its finite verbs is not an "irregular" construction. By dropping the governance of εἶδον the οἵτινες clause becomes deictic and practically independent, the very thing intended. John saw many, many more souls than those of the martyrs, namely all the departed saints. They are described negatively with terminology used in 13:8, 12, 15, 16-18 (see the exposition in chapter 13). John does not supply the number of the thrones and of the martyrs and of the confessors. It serves no purpose to inquire whether he saw only those who had departed at the time when he received this vision or all those who during the entire 1,000 years came to take their royal places. The purpose of this vision is to reveal to John and to us the royal exaltation and the power of every martyr and of every faithful believer when his soul enters heaven. It serves the same purpose as that found in other visions, notably in the seven letters and in their great promises to every "conquering one," see in particular 2:27.

"And they did live and did reign (two constative aorists, R. 833) for a thousand years." Ἔζησαν = "they did live" and states the fact. "The rest did not live" states the opposite fact. The *souls* which John saw "lived": they had the ζωή, the true life, so often called the ζωὴ αἰώνιος. This "life" "the rest" did not have. The former obtained this life here on earth while they were still in the body. Their souls passed through bodily death and entered heaven with this ζωή, the divine life principle which makes alive (not βίος, course of life, etc.). The sole subject is ψυχαί, "souls," — not a word has been said about bodies. These "souls" lived, sat on thrones, received judgment, and reigned with Christ through the complete era, "1,000 years." The only inference is that their bodies slept in the grave on earth. Note well, the verb is *not* ἀναζάω, ἀνέζησαν, "lived *again*."

The plain and simple meaning of this verb is often misunderstood. It is thought to mean: "came to life *in the body* so as to be visible" — "they came out of death in a new, and that a *bodily* life" — "they are now restored to life, such life as implies the revivification of *the body*" — "the Greek word ἔζησαν is in the New Testament always applied to man in his complete condition of *body* and spirit united, and is never applied to the 'soul' as a disembodied entity." These are samples. The last contradicts John who here says: "I saw *the souls* . . . and they did live." Where does John place the bodily resurrection? As plain as day at the Parousia, v. 11-13: "I saw *the dead* standing — there were judged *the dead* — the sea gave up *the dead*." The bodily resurrection occurs at the Parousia at the end of the world where the Old and New Testament ever place it.

These souls "did reign in company with Christ (named without a symbol) for a 1,000 years." Why think of a special great throne for Christ that is surrounded by all these other little thrones? This statement defines the Giver in the passive ἐδόθη, who gave these souls "the judgment" and with ἐβασίλευσαν adds that "they kinged it," that "thrones" means kingly rule. When each martyr's and each confessor's soul enters heaven it joins Christ and all his kings in the kingly rule. This, too, is why he is called "King of kings and Lord of lords" (19:16; compare 17:14). All these enthroned souls are his "kings," his "lords," who reign μετά in company with him.

Perhaps a word should be added in regard to this reigning of the souls of the saints and in regard to the judgment given to them. The antichristian forces here on earth (beast, pseudo-prophet, whore, and all their following) imagine that they are supreme and that nothing is able to check their power and their plans. Well, they are mistaken. Let all true believers know it. The devil who is behind these forces and who embodies the real power that is in them has long ago been chained and, as one writer well states it, can reach out only to the length of his chain. These evil forces put on a great show and bluff of power; in reality they are already doomed. The real Ruler is Christ who rules even in the midst of his enemies; and he shares this rule of his with all his saints, for they are all one with him. This real rule extends over the whole world, over even the devils. This rule is exercised by means of the Word which is the complete expression of the divine will; its κρῖμα, Hebrew *mishpat*, its already fixed decision or verdict, is given to the saints. That means that every person, every power, and everything that is contrary to the Word is bound to be crushed, defeated, thrown down, thrown out (note the many βάλλειν); and that every person, every power, and everything in accord with the Word is bound to triumph in the end, to rise gloriously, to endure forever.

The souls of the saints in heaven thus rule in the whole heavenly fulness of their exaltation. They know in fulness what this rule means, and it is measureless joy to them. God's saints here on earth begin this rule because they have the Word which contains the divine will and all its verdicts. Every one of us who believes and confesses this Word, who preaches, teaches, supports, and lives this Word, by this Word now already judges the world and thus rules in royalty. The verdicts which Christ utters shall stand forever despite hell. Yet here our rule is more or less imperfect since it is exercised in our still imperfect state. But soon our souls shall rule in the perfection of glory.

5) As regards "the rest of the dead," all those who died in unbelief, John reports the opposite: "they did not live," using the same verb: οὐκ ἔζησαν, "they did not live" with the ζωή, the life everlasting. What is affirmed in regard to the souls named in v. 4 is denied in regard to "the rest of the dead." It is clear that "the souls" mentioned in v. 4 are those of martyrs and of saints who had died, who had left their dead bodies on earth like "the rest of the dead" whose souls also had left their bodies on earth, whose souls also had passed into the other world. These never obtained the ζωή, the true life, before their bodily death occurred, and thus, when they died bodily one by one, had no ζωή to live in the other world: οὐκ ἔζησαν, "not did they live" (again a constative aorist).

John writes that this was the case throughout the entire 1,000 years. In v. 5 we find the direct and complete opposite of v. 4. The godly die bodily one by one throughout the entire New Testament era, and then their souls enjoy the heavenly life; the ungodly likewise die bodily one by one during this era, but then their souls enjoy nothing of the kind. John does not need to add in regard to these that "they do not reign in company with Christ." He adds nothing. The vision is not concerned with the ungodly souls, to tell us where they are and what they do. The brief statement about them is merely by contrast to show what it means that the godly souls live and reign with Christ (Paul: "be with Christ," i. e., Paul's soul, Phil. 1:23).

"Until there were finished the 1,000 years," τελεσθῇ (compare v. 7), brought to a goal or terminus, τέλος, namely to the last day (the τέλος of Matt. 24:14), states how long this condition of *soul* will last. Until the end of the 1,000 years. What then? Why, then all souls, also those who never lived with the ζωή either before their bodily death or after, will receive their bodies (v. 12, 13) again: the souls of the godly will receive their bodies to partake of the life which these souls lived in heaven; the souls of the rest will receive their bodies but without the life these souls never had and never lived. This is the teaching of the Scriptures: in whatever state bodily death finds a man, with the ζωή or without the ζωή, in that state his soul remains until the last day, until God brings the τέλος or "end," and after that end his soul and his body, then reunited, remain in that state to all eternity.

The chiliasts disagree and say: "Until the 1,000 years were finished" means that, when the 1,000 years begin, those mentioned in v. 4 will receive their bodies in a first resurrection, while those spoken of in v. 5 will have to wait until the 1,000 years are finished! Chiliasts ask: "How can *souls* sit on thrones and be *seen* by John?" John speaks about *souls,* tells how long some will enjoy their eternal life in the other world, how long the rest will be without this eternal life, while both are *bodiless souls,* while both await the day of Christ's judgment and the resurrection of their bodies (v. 11-13). For this mighty fact these chiliasts substitute a delay in getting *bodies* back and say that some will have to wait 1,000 years for theirs. What of it? They ought to be most ready to wait, even 10,000 years, yea, do without their bodies forever; for getting them back certainly implies that, instead of being lifeless dust in the grave, their bodies will again be animated and will then suffer torment such as their souls suffered.

When John writes, "This (is) the resurrection, the first one" (the number being made emphatic by the second article), he plainly refers to what he wrote in v. 4. When the *souls* of martyrs and of saints pass to the thrones in heaven to live there in glory, "this is the first resurrection." John uses the term ἀνάστασις, "resurrection," *Auferstehung*, symbolically. Here on earth we poor mortals say that the godly *die* when their souls leave their broken bodies; John says that for their *souls* this is "the resurrection, the first one." For now these souls indeed live, in the fulness of the ζωή, in heaven, reigning on thrones as kings with Christ in glory. Certainly, there is no such resurrection for the souls of "the rest of the dead."

John does not speak of a second resurrection, but by saying "the first" he certainly implies a second, and again he uses the word in the symbolical sense. As the first transfers the soul to its throne in heaven, so the second transfers the soul's body. Neither of these two symbolical resurrections is for "the rest of the dead." Neither their souls nor their bodies are transferred on high to thrones, there to live in the ζωὴ αἰώνιος.

'Ανάστασις, always intransitive in the New Testament, the act of rising up, is commonly used with reference to the physical resurrection when the soul rejoins the body, reanimates it, so that after lying prone and lifeless or decomposed it rises up alive. The noun, it seems, is only once used figuratively in the New Testament, in Luke 2:34: "the falling and the rising up of many." The verb ἀνίστημι is commonly used to indicate the act of getting up, is used also with reference to bodily resurrection but, it seems, very seldom figuratively (in this respect resembling the noun): "Rise, sleeping one, and get up (ἀνάστα) from the dead, and Christ shall shine upon thee!" Eph. 5:14. When Paul speaks of baptism and its effects in mystical language he uses only "the likeness of his (Christ's) *anastasis*" (Rom. 6:5); when he speaks of our having been dead in transgressions and brought out of this condition by grace he uses "quickened together with Christ" and neither *anastasis* nor its verb. These are things worth noting.

For chiliasts confront us with the alternative: *anastasis* must mean either the physical, bodily resurrection or conversion and regeneration: ergo, since *tertium non datur,* and since here such a spiritual resurrection cannot be meant, the chiliast's point is proved: the first resurrection is physical, bodily. This is a twofold fallacy. 1) There is no such alternative. The New Testament does *not* use *anastasis* in the sense of a spiritual resurrection! And the New Testament is right in this. For when it is so generally used with reference to a physical resurrection, the sense is that the soul that was formerly in the body that is now dead returns to the body and makes it "rise up" alive. In regeneration and conversion such a thing does not take place. *To the person who was dead in sin nothing that he had before returns.* What occurs is entirely different. Paul has the right word: ὁ Θεὸς συνεζωοποίησε τῷ Χριστῷ καὶ συνήγειρε, God "quickened," "wrought life," and "raised up" (Eph. 2:5, 6). 2) The assumption, *tertium non datur,* is unwarranted. Confronting a person with such alternatives, only one of which he can choose, is a common way in all matters of life and thought for forcing that choice. But this type of argumentation often overlooks the fact that there *is* after all in the case at issue a third, perhaps even a fourth and a fifth to choose, one of which is by far the best and in matters of truth the only true choice to make. So it is here.

The *anastasis* which John terms the first applies, as John says, to the *souls*. He is not using the word in its literal sense but in a symbolical sense even as all these visions are full of both symbolical terms and symbolical aggregates. The implied second *anastasis* is necessarily the same, namely symbolical. No chiliastic logic and no argumentation can shake the connection of this *anastasis* with "the souls."

As regards the bodily resurrection of the dead all Scripture, from Dan. 12:2 onward to Rev. 20:12, 13, knows of only *one* that includes the ungodly as well as the godly. In John 5:28, 29 Jesus withheld nothing. The effort to divide this general resurrection into two sections and putting 1,000 years between them is exegetically unwarranted. To attempt this by means of a *sedes doctrinae* which is full of symbolical expressions is to reverse the sane exegetical principle that in the Scriptures figurative expressions must be interpreted as figurative and thus in harmony with plain literal statements. Whoever does the reverse follows a wrong exegetical, doctrinal, and even common sense principle.

6) So wonderful is this first resurrection that the vision adds the great beatitude which recalls the one occurring in 14:13, which pronounces eternal blessedness on those dying in the Lord from now on. This is what the first resurrection means: the dying person's soul is transferred to, literally "has part in, the rising up (*anastasis*), the first one." "Blessed" is he indeed! On μακάριος see 1:3. This verdict accords him the highest happiness. "Holy" is significantly added: the last trace of sin and of the flesh has been swept out of the soul at the moment of death. By its *anastasis*, its rising up, the soul passes into heaven to its royal

throne in a pure and stainless state. The body will follow in due time when the 1,000 years are ended, and the Lord calls it from the dust for its *anastasis*, its rising up to the same heavenly exaltation. "To have part in the first resurrection" = to be one soul that so rises up to heaven.

A negative and a positive statement offer the reason for this beatitude. "On these the second death does not have authority," it cannot ever even touch them. It is striking how the vision here speaks of "the *first* resurrection" and of "the *second* death," by that "first" implying a second, and then, reversed, by that "second" implying a first. He whose are the two resurrections (risings up to glory) suffers one death, the first only, the bodily; he who fails to attain the first resurrection suffers both deaths and, of course, fails to receive the second resurrection. The soul that passes to its throne in heaven left its body by physical death; that is for this soul and this body the only death, and the body shall follow the soul at the last day. The soul that leaves its body in physical death and does not rise up to heaven, that soul and its body are sundered, not only by physical death, but "the second death" has and retains ἐξουσία, authority and power, over them, sundering them both forever from the ζωή, from living the life eternal in heaven. Already here "the second death" is personified as a dread power with "authority." Verse 14 states what "the second death," thus personified, actually is. Death and hades being together thrown into the lake of fire = the second death. We usually speak of it as eternal death.

Now the positive is set over against the negative by ἀλλά, "on the contrary." "They shall be priests of God and of Christ and shall reign in company with him (Christ, v. 4) for a 1,000 years." This recalls 1:6 and 5:10; only these two passages, plus I Pet. 2:9, speak of what God has made us to be already in this life in preparation for the life we are to have in heaven. Our passage completes and crowns the others. As "priests" the blessed shall worship God and Christ in the perfection of holiness in heaven; and at the same time as kings "they shall reign" with Christ (explained in v. 4) for a 1,000 years, thus once more in a pointed way naming this symbolical number. Why does this vision not say, "shall be priests and reign *forever*"? The answer is given in the next clause: "when there shall be finished the thousand years." In v. 1-6 all is focused on the completion of the New Testament era, on what then occurs. The remainder of the answer is found in the visions of chapters 21 and 22 where we shall see abundantly what shall be forever and ever.

Much of v. 4-6 and all of v. 7-10 reads as though John did not see it; it reads like verbal prophecy. We consider it a mistake to think that John wrote these things independently, for instance, the beatitude. These visions, like parts of the preceding ones, are intended for us by the Lord and thus contain more than John saw. Divine revelation reveals and is not confined to reception by sight.

What Happens at the End of the 1,000 Years: the Battle, 20:7-10

7) **And when there shall be finished the thousand years, loosed shall Satan be out of his prison and shall go out to deceive the nations, those in the four corners of the earth, Gog and Magog, to gather them together for the battle, of whom their number as the sand of the sea. And they came up on the breadth of the earth and surrounded the camp of the saints and the city, the beloved one. And there came down fire out of the heaven and devoured them. And the devil, the one deceiving them, was thrown into the lake of the**

fire and brimstone where also the beast and the pseudo-prophet (were); **and they shall be tormented by day and by night for the eons of the eons.**

Review the remarks introductory to 19:11; they belong also here. We have here only another glimpse of the last battle, two visions of which we have already had. In this picture of it the light is focused on Satan. The imagery is dreadful accordingly. Why Satan is first confined and then loosed again we are told in v. 3, observe the note on why he *must* be loosed. For this climax with regard to Satan all the previous visions prepare, notably those from chapter 12 onward where he is shown as the dragon. As such he instigates all antichristianity, yet from chapter 13 on he is not pictured again. Verses 1-3 state the reason, his binding. But what he has instigated operates throughout the entire New Testament era, operates as the beast (13:1-10), *the antichristian power*, which in turn operates through the second beast (13:1-18) called also the pseudo-prophet, *the antichristian propaganda* of all antichristian deceit, all of which produces "Babylon," viewed as a great city and as an empire with many kings and thus also as the great whore with all her paramours, "the kings of the earth," the whore symbolizing *the antichristian seduction* which helps to carry men away. Then the end of all this antichristianity *must come*. The instigator of it *must* be loosed in order to precipitate the end.

It is at the same time the end of the instigator and of his agencies. When picturing this end of theirs the light is thrown upon each of them in turn: first, upon Babylon and the gathering kings (16:12-16) not forgetting the end of the whore (17:14-18); secondly, upon the beast and the pseudo-prophet in a glimpse of the final battle (19:11-21); and now the end of Satan himself with the battle imagery renewed. Yet all these are a composite picture of the end, each is a scene from the one battle at the end which is thrown on the screen separately. Down, down, down they go, Babylon, as empire and as whore, beast and lamb-beast or pseudo-prophet, and the dragon who is Satan himself, *all in one terrific fall*, the end.

This last view is dated: "when (ὅταν, whenever) there shall be finished the 1,000 years," when the New Testament era shall have been brought to its τέλος or goal, when the maximum completeness, symbolized by "1,000," has been attained. This dating, so significant, is necessary here although it applies also to all the other views of the end, because now we are to see what this completeness signifies: the work of the gospel among the nations must have been done completely (Matt. 24:14). All nations must have had the testimony; the last convert must have been gathered in. The rule of the saints with Christ means that this will be done despite all the agencies of the dragon (the two beasts, Babylon as city, empire, whore) : they rule with Christ for the 1,000 years (v. 4-6) ; the dragon was rendered helpless so that he might not prevent this gospel work among the nations (v. 1-3). God has his people, Christ's other sheep (John 10:16), among the nations; the complete period of time to bring their complete number to the fold must be rounded out. Satan is so bound and locked up that this time *is* rounded out.

"Then shall come the end" (Matt. 24:14). After the gospel work among the nations has been done, after the last soul that it can save has been saved, then the moment has arrived for the final settlement with all the monstrous antichristian opposition to God, the Lamb, the gospel, and the church; then Satan himself may step to its head: "loosed shall be Satan out of his prison and go forth shall he to deceive (aorist, effective) the nations, those in the four corners of the earth." Not as though they have not been deceived already; the lamb-beast is seen "deceiving (durative present) those dwelling on the earth" (13:14; 19:20, "the one that deceived"). This is the last deception: "to deceive to gather together" the nations from the four corners of the earth "for the battle." The second infinitive depends on the first (there is no καί). In 16:13-16 we have already seen a part of this deception, the three frogs persuading all the kings to gather together for the battle at Armageddon. The dragon is significantly shown there with the two beasts who emit these frogs. This last is the climax of deception.

Beyond this to gather together εἰς τὸν πόλεμον, "for the battle," nothing can go. It is the absolute limit of folly. "*The* battle" with its article refers to what has been said about it already in other visions. Throughout πόλεμος and also πολεμεῖν = "battle," "to battle," and not "war." The A. V.'s translation of this passage is correct. Absolute deception is required to plunge into this absolute insanity. The aorist infinitives imply success. Note well what this means: all the nations from the four corners of the earth now not only oppose and antagonize the Lamb and Christianity, they all "gather together," assemble, in satanic unanimity "for the battle," to wipe out forever from the earth the last saint and the last sound of the gospel. Yes, the gospel work for the nations is absolutely done. The end of the 1,000 years has plainly come. The final completeness is reached. Judgment is done (v. 11, etc.).

Did all these nations think that Christianity had so dwindled that faith had almost disappeared from the earth (Luke 18:8), that now with concerted effort they could annihilate it from the earth forever? Or had their hellish opposition reached the last degree of intensity, beyond which only the impotent rage of the damnation in hell lies?

How long did it take to effect this final deception? Verse 3 says, although in symbolism, μικρὸν χρόνον. What shall we say about those who even here figure out three and one-half or some other number of literal years? Since everything is ripe due to the long work of the beast and his prophet plus the whore, it would seem that, with the dragon himself loose again, the world would be ready to rage "to the battle" at once.

The four corners of the earth are not only the distant corners without the great center. Skeptics may sneer at the Bible because it makes the earth flat, square, with four literal, spatial corners. The four corners include the whole earth; for corners = the four directions, north, east, south, west, as we still speak of these four and ever will; compare 7:1. The four corners have been thought to denote distant, barbarous nations, and the apposition "Gog and Magog" to designate completely pagan nations. Kliefoth calls them "peripheral nations." But the relative clause says, "of whom the number of them (pleonastic antecedent added) as the sand of the sea." Will there be so many barbarous nations made up of so many people at the end? No, these are "all those dwelling on the earth," an expression that is so often used in Revelation.

"The nations, those in the four corners of the earth," are here called τὸν Γὼγ καὶ Μαγώγ, "Gog and Magog." Both names are taken from Ezek. 38 and 39; Gog is the prince and leader, Magog his land and his people. In Ezekiel this king assembles a great host and many allies and makes war on Israel which has returned from its exile and is pictured as being annihilated on the mountains of Israel by a rain of fire, hail, and brimstone. In Revelation the apposition is an allusion to Ezekiel both as regards "Gog and Magog" and as regards "fire out of the heaven" (v. 9). As dreadful as was "Gog, the chief prince of Meschech and Tubal," and the host of "the land Magog" (Ezek. 38:2) with their allies, so is this host, another "Gog and Magog."

Because the two names are an apposition to τὰ ἔθνη, they are even in G. K. supposed to be names of nations, and the deduction is made that, because Gog and Magog sound alike, they are names of nations, *ein unverstandener, mythischer Doppelname fuer das feindliche Voelkerheer.* The supposed "seer" is assumed to have appropriated these no longer understood names from late rabbinism. G. K.'s *Woerterbuch* has quantities of such "critical" views. The Apostle John received this vision with this apposition. If "Gog and Magog" are here used as is claimed in G. K., it is the divine Revelator who is using them in this mystifying fashion. While τόν, the article, might be construed with both nouns, the very names themselves preclude this idea. Τὸν Γώγ is a personal name just as it is in Ezek. 38:2, and Μαγώγ designates this leader's host. The idea that "Gog and Magog" are two nations is untenable. As an army has a commander, as Satan commands this army, so the apposition names the commander with his army and uses the article with his name as the Greek does with personal names in unnumbered connections and leaves the army's name without the article.

If G. K. and others are mistaken in their interpretation of Gog and Magog, what shall be said about the chiliasts Gray and Gaebelein and their periodicals and about others of that type with their unheard-of etymology and peculiar interpretations? For a thorough refutation read Theodore Graebner, *Prophecy and the War,* 46-73. These men read "the *chief* prince" of Ezek. 38:2, A. V. (margin, "prince *of the chief*") as, "the prince of *Rosh*" and thus, "the prince of Rosh, Meshech, and Tubal," and then claim that "all students of prophecy are agreed that Rosh is Russia," which is not true. Meshech and Tubal they claim "are reproduced in the modern Moscow and Tobolsk." "Russia, we may well conclude from this, will furnish the man who will head this confederacy of nations," namely in Rev. 20:8. And Gray claims: "Meshech and Tubal are the original forms of 'Moscow' and 'Tobolsk,' which were immemorially in possession of that nation. A reliable ancient map placed beside a reliable modern one will identify the territories." But the maps give this claim the lie just as all reliable etymologists will deny this derivation of the names. Graebner writes that "Moskva" first appears in 1156, and was not even then in possession of the Russian nation for the very good reason that the Russian nation did not yet exist. Tobolsk, in the far-off arctic corner of Siberia, was not "immemorially in Russia's possession." Not until 1577, about 2,000 years after Ezekiel, was it even visited by Russians; it became Russian by conquest only in 1639. Of a piece with this is the interpretation in which England is made "the Gog of prophecy." Ducks and drakes are likewise played with the other countries of Europe — but see Graebner; we are here concerned only with this apposition and not with the whole prophecy of Ezekiel. In order to understand the symbolical use of "Gog and Magog" in Revelation it is enough to know that in Ezekiel these were such great enemies of Israel that God himself wiped them out with fire, hail, and brimstone from heaven.

Here is sanity: "Whatever is in league today against the Christian Church — anti-Christian scientific speculation, higher criticism, the New Theology, New Thought, Mormonism, Eddyism, materialism, sensualism, secretism, birth-control, all the forces of Sin and Carnality which seek to corrupt the Church and to slay her inner life, are the 'Gog and Magog' of Ezekiel and John. But the great day of the Lord is even now approaching, which will witness their irrevocable doom." Graebner.

9) "And they came up on the breadth of the earth and surrounded the camp of the saints and the city, the beloved one," perfect participle: ever beloved in the past and continuing so now. "The breadth of the earth" is the whole expanse of the earth; hordes and hordes as far as one could see and farther still, and these encircling the saints with no avenue of retreat anywhere. This view of the battle goes far beyond the other two. In 16:16 we are shown only the gathering at Armageddon, still far from the saints. In 19:19, etc., we are shown only two armies in the open field, but there is no battle. Now the word "armies" (19:14, 19) is not used but "the sands of the sea," "the breadth of the earth," enemies to the encircling horizon, and only the παρεμβόλη, fortified camp, namely (καί) the πόλις the lone city for the saints. Is there no hope? Will the banner of this little camp or city fall, its defenders be wiped out? Look at ἡ ἠγαπημένη with its divine love of full comprehension and eternal purpose!

This is not the day of doom for the little camp and the city; it is the day of everlasting doom for this Gog and Magog, Satan and all these in numbers as the sand of the sea. "And there fell fire from the heaven and devoured them." That is all! It is the way of Scripture; an event so tremendous, and just one short sentence for the record. It is Ezek. 38:22 over again but multiplied a millionfold. Satan believed his own deceit although the truth was written in the Word; and the earth dwellers believed his deceit and scorned the Word. Now fire from heaven blasted the deceit, the deceiver, and all the deceived; reality, truth, the Word looked down from heaven and laughed (Ps. 2:4; Prov. 1:26).

10) "And the devil, the one deceiving them, was thrown into the lake of the fire and brimstone (one article with the two nouns) where also the beast and the pseudo-prophet were; and tormented were they by

day and by night for the eons of the eons," i. e., forever, see 1:6. As already set forth, it is the devil on whom this vision throws the light of final judgment; like the beast and the pseudo-prophet he is thrown "into the lake of the fire and brimstone" (see the lake in 19:20). When the apposition calls him "the one deceiving," it repeats the verb of v. 8 and once more makes plain what "the ancient serpent" of v. 2 (compare 12:8) means according to Gen. 3. The verb βάλλω runs through 12:9, 13; 14:19; 18:21; 19:20; 20:3, here, and v. 14 and 15: "thrown — thrown — thrown!" Compare 14:10: "shall be tormented in fire and brimstone . . . and the smoke of their torment goes up for eons of eons." On the genitives of time within, "by day and by night" (4:8), compare 14:8 — a use of expressions of time where there is timelessness.

Zahn states that eternal torment in hell is an *Aberglaube*, superstition. He writes somewhat like a Russellite. What purpose could God have in such eternal torment? As for men, a corpse has no sensation. Man is not immortal, nor is the devil. The blessed are made immortal by God. Fire burns until the objects thrown into it are consumed. A long time may be required to do the consuming, but this process does not continue forever. To be thrown into the lake of fire and brimstone means to be consigned to annihilation. The term "lake" is taken from the Dead Sea, and "lake of fire and brimstone" from the annihilation of Sodom and Gomorrah.

Zahn thinks that "for the eons of the eons" means only a long, long time. He refers us to a Hebrew lexicon, to *'olam* and *'olamim*. We wonder why he does not refer to Greek lexicons? Did John not write Greek: εἰς τοὺς αἰῶνας τῶν αἰώνων, and so a number of times beginning in 1:6? But look at the Hebrew lexicon. A most excellent one is Ed. Koenig's *Woerterbuch*: *'olam*, "often used in relation to God (Gen. 21:33, etc.), thus denoting *eternity* (Gen. 3:22, etc.)." We have discussed the Greek expression sufficiently in 1:6 where there is a reference to God and the word means "forever." We may add that in the Hebrew *'olam* often does mean only a long time, but in the Greek, everywhere in the New Testament, "for the eons of the eons" means only "forever," "to all eternity," and never "for just a long time." But for the great scholarship of Zahn we should have passed this by. The eternity of damnation in hell need not be treated here; this has been done so solidly that Zahn's rationalizings cause only regret.

Some seek to find the name of the beloved city, especially chiliasts for whom it is the millennial city Jerusalem that shall stand in such glory throughout the millennial 1,000 years. They are at a loss, however, to account for all these hordes that are in number like the sand of the sea and are brought against this glorious millennial city by Satan at so short a time before the end, after a 1,000 years of most glorious reign of Christ here on earth. They usually refer to the far distant four corners of the earth which will send out all these swarms like so many beehives.

This vision is still restricted. What about the beloved city after Satan is thrown into the lake? More visions follow, their story is not yet complete.

What Happens at the End of the 1,000 Years: the Judgment, 20:11-15

11) This vision presents the last judgment. Practically all symbolism is dropped. The dead stand before the throne, both the great and the small, and "judged were they, each one, according to their works" — language that is as literal as can be written. This vision completes the group presented in chapter 20. It

does more: it *interprets* the preceding vision of the battle and thus all three visions of battle, which we have found to be three views of one and the same battle, see the introductory paragraphs in 19:11. "For the πόλεμον of the day, the great one, of God the Almighty" in 16:14, is the same battle as ποιῆσαι τὸν πόλεμον, "to do the battle with the One sitting upon the horse and with his army" in 19:19, and the same as "to gather them together for the πόλεμον, the battle," in 20:8. Three times not "*a* πόλεμος" but "*the* πόλεμος," *the one,* not now one, now another, now a third.

Yet in the views we have in these visions, all marked so plainly by "*the* battle," there is never a trace of a battle mêlée, one warrior piercing another, many in the army of the King of kings going down before the victory is won. The prominent verb is συναγαγεῖν (συνήγαγεν) in 16:14, 16; συνηγμένα (participle) in 19:19; and again συναγαγεῖν in 20:8. The antichristian forces do this "assembling" on the grandest scale in 20:8. The King of kings, even in 19:14, has no need of assembling: his angel armies simply "follow" him. For with his angels he comes to *the final judgment* of all the antichristian hordes with their leader "the Gog" (20:8), their dominating power (the beast), and their propaganda (the second beast, the pseudo-prophet), their infatuating seduction (the whore, the seductress). The final judgment is still withheld in 16:16; we are shown only the assembling. But in 19:20, and in 20:9, 10 the final judgment is put into the symbolism by means of the significant ἐβλήθησαν — ἐβλήθη which are repeated in the vision of the actual final judgment in 20:14, 15: ἐβλήθησαν, ἐβλήθη, compare Matt. 25:46, "and these shall go away into punishment eternal."

All this means, as we see it, that these visions of battle symbolize *the final judgment,* Satan and all the antichristianity and the antichristian power, seduction, and following he has producecd are thrown — *thrown* — THROWN into the lake of the fire, hell. It is thus that the vision of 20:11-15 properly closes the series, closes it by now at the end furnishing the one thing yet needed, *the literal interpretation,* which is couched, as we have indicated, in literal language. The coherence is complete. The "Hallelujah" of 19:1, etc., is in its proper place.

In this light we translate: **And I saw a great white throne and the One sitting upon it, from whose face fled the earth and the heaven, and place was not found for them. And I saw the dead, the great and the small, standing before the throne. And books were opened; and another book was opened, which is of the life. And judged were the dead from the things having been written in the books according to their works. And the sea gave the dead, those in it; and the death and the hades gave the dead, those in them. And judged were they, each one, according to their works. And the death and the hades were thrown into the lake of the fire. This death is the second one, the lake of the fire. And if anyone was not found as having been written in the book of the life, thrown was he into the lake of the fire.**

"A throne" is here again the symbol of power, rule, and dominion, and thus the seat of the King. In this significance is included the power of judging even as in Scripture kings always act as judges, namely as the final and supreme court. In v. 4 those who sat on their thrones received the judgment as their royal right. Here now is the supreme throne for the final judgment of the universe. It is "great" indeed, fitting "the One sitting upon it," i. e., exercising the royal power of judging, and befitting the final, universal judgment that is now being held. Some think that this One is God and not Christ and point to 4:2, but overlook 3:21.

While this is a minor point, yet when Jesus describes the judgment in Matt. 25:31 (compare 24:30) and there, as well as in John 5:27, names himself, "the Son of man," as the judge, we interpret "the One sitting on the great white throne" accordingly. Why raise issues on every point? "White" is throughout the symbol of holiness. See this color in 19:11 and the names of the One sitting and the defining clause, "and in righteousness he judges," he who is "King of kings and Lord of lords" (19:16) and now judges on his "white" throne.

"From whose face fled the earth and the heaven, and place was not found for them," reveals his greatness but does far more. This is not an additional, preliminary judgment such as the earth has often seen before; this is the last, supreme judgment. It is not held on earth. Those who think that the throne will rest on this globe and then wonder about its globular shape, etc., should look anew at Matt. 24:29, 30. There will be no difficulty on this or on any other score, in particular as to how all will stand and find place before this throne and this Judge. It is hopeless with our poor mundane imagination to try in any way to picture the actual judgment scene which transcends all human conception. "The earth and the heaven" are mentioned together: the earth and the heaven as they have stood since creation, on which and under which men have lived since Adam, on which and under which Satan has built up sin and antichristianity.

Ἔφυγεν, "fled," is less strong than παρελεύσονται, "shall pass away," in II Pet. 3:10; Matt. 24:35; Mark 13:31, and ἀπολοῦνται, "shall perish," in Heb. 1:11. "Fled" is more like παλαιωθήσονται, "shall become old," in Heb. 1:11. This last verb matches Rev. 21:1, 5. "Fled from his face" does not mean "were annihilated," for many flee and still exist. The question as to what will become of our mundane heaven and earth, whether they shall be annihilated by fire or shall be made new and rejuvenated, cannot be decided on fractional evidence; one must consider all the passages together, including Rom. 8:22, etc., and Rev. 21:1-5, which plainly teach a rejuvenation, and not an annihilation. It is unfair to say of this finding that "it is dictated by the basic view which does not reckon with creative acts of the living God but would like to comprehend everything as being due to evolution" (Kliefoth). It is a plain question of what the Word says. "No place was found," none whatever, for the earth and the heaven, not even a place where Christ could now use them for the final judgment.

12) Since this section centers on the judgment, nothing more is said about what became of the earth and the heaven. John writes: "I saw the dead, the great and the small, standing before the throne." "The dead" means those who had died during the whole time that the old heaven and the earth stood, all the dead, from Adam on to the last one who gave up his soul in physical death, which is briefly expressed by the apposition: "the great and the small," even the tiny babes. "We must *all* appear before the judgment seat of Christ; that *everyone* may receive the things done in his body, according to that he hath done, whether it be good or bad," II Cor. 5:10. "We shall *all* stand before the judgment seat of Christ," Rom. 14:10. "And before him (who sits upon the throne of his glory) shall be gathered all nations; and he shall separate them one from another, as a shepherd divideth his sheep from the goats," Matt. 25:32. In all these passages as here in Revelation the resurrection of all of these, sheep as well as goats, is implied: "All that are in the graves shall hear his voice and shall come forth; they that have done good, unto the resurrection of life, and they that have done evil, unto the resurrection of damnation," John 5:28, 29.

Why do we add this proof for the simple Catechism truth which we teach our children, which the church has ever unitedly confessed: "From whence he shall come to judge the quick and the dead"? Because the chiliasts and the double resurrectionists deny this truth. They posit a bodily resurrection at the beginning of the 1,000 years of the millennium for the martyrs and the confessors mentioned in v. 4, which they call "the first resurrection" (v. 5), making this a bodily one. "The dead, the great and the small," standing before the throne they refer to the wicked dead who died before and also during the millennium; these are before the throne by virtue of what the chiliasts call the second bodily resurrection. In regard to the godly who die during the millennium we receive different answers. What "the first resurrection" means has been explained: it is *not* bodily and also *not* spiritual. The only bodily resurrection of which the Scriptures know is the one occurring at the last day when *all* the bodily dead, both the godly and the ungodly, shall rise at the voice of the Lord (John 5:28, 29). About all of them John speaks here.

But did not Jesus say in John 5:24 that the believer "comes not into κρίσις, judgment"? Yes, but why cite only this statement and not John 3:18: "The one believing in me is not judged; the one not believing *has already been judged"?* If, according to these two statements, the believer is not judged at the last day (as the double resurrectionists and the Chiliasts say), then, by the same token, also the unbeliever is not judged at the last day, for he has *already been judged,* long, long ago when he was in his unbelief, even before he died, Jesus himself says so apart from any vision. The Scripture speaks of two judgments; one that is secret and occurs now during the earthly life and at death, the other that is public and occurs at the last day before the universe. *Both* of these judgments apply to both the godly and the ungodly of all time. As to the latter judgment, Jesus himself describes it in detail in Matt. 25:31-46. Are the godly there? Is a verdict pronounced on them? Just as there is on the ungodly!

"Not to come into κρίσις" and "not to be judged" do not mean: not to stand among the dead at the last day. We have two verdicts that shall be pronounced at that day. They are exact opposites. Read them in Matt. 25. John says: "And judged were the dead from the things written in the books according to their works," which is precisely what Jesus says in Matthew, all are judged. To pronounce verdicts is to judge, to hear the verdict regarding oneself is to be judged. But to hear it as one among those at the right hand of the Judge is to hear the sweetest music, is not to come into judgment, not to be judged, but to have judging and judgment changed into the invitation: "Come, ye blessed of my Father, inherit the kingdom!" Matt. 25:34.

"And books were opened; and another book was opened which is of the life." Thus was the judgment held, "judged were the dead from the things written in the books according to their works." So Jesus says in Matt. 25 and names the works, those of both the godly and the ungodly. In Rev. 3:5 we have explained the book of the life at length and need not repeat. But other books are mentioned here. What they contain is stated: judged "from (ἐκ to indicate source) the things that have been written in the (these) books" (and are thus things of permanent record), judged thus "according to their works." These books contain the record of their works. It is the constant teaching of the Scriptures that at the final public judgment we shall be judged according to our works. This is repeated here in v. 14 with the addition of ἕκαστος: they, "everyone." The record and the judgment are not en masse but individual. As regards the book of life, this contains the names of the godly (3:5; 13:8).

All that is said in regard to the books and the book and their being opened is figurative and indicates the infallibility of the omniscient Judge on this great white (holy) throne and is Old Testament language (see 3:5). Thus also the number of the "books" and in addition to them this "book of the life of the Lamb slain from the foundation of the world" (as it is termed in 13:8; compare 21:27) is figurative, the plural expressing the many, many works of all the many, many who are to be judged. The idea is not that the one book is large enough to record the names of the godly because they are few in number; but that, many though they are, their names are precious and are all recorded in this one book. In this book Calvinism finds its decree of absolute election. The idea that the "books" contain only the works of the ungodly is as untenable as that the book contains the vouchers for what is in the books.

But if the books contain a record of the works of all the dead, will they not contain also the bad works which the godly have done as well as their good works? Not one bad work will they show. Peter's denial you will seek in vain. The blood of Jesus Christ, his Son, cleanses us from all sin, I John 1:7. Ours is the ἄφεσις, "the dismissal," remission, which blots out all our sins. Those "books" contain nothing but our good works and even these as made perfect by the righteousness of Christ, and these works as *the public evidence of our faith,* as such evidence demanding of the holy Judge the corresponding verdict, publicly justifying him in rendering it, demanding from the universe acknowledgment for the justice of the verdict and of the Judge. That is why the final judgment is public and why it includes and must include all men despite the chiliasts' contention to the contrary.

13) When John writes: "The sea gave the dead in it," this means that the natural sea gave the *bodies* of the dead for the last judgment. Nothing is said about the rivers and the lakes, and, more important still, nothing about the earth giving the bodies that were buried in graves or scattered in disintegrated dust. Fortunately, no one has thought that the sea held souls. Yet a few make "the sea" symbolical, like 17:15, "the waters peoples and multitudes are and nations and tongues"; but how "peoples, multitudes, nations, and tongues" can give the dead symbolically or in any other sense they do not explain to others. The sea alone is mentioned in regard to the bodies because the sea is so deep. A body sunk in its depth seems to be beyond all recovery (Matt. 18:6), yet if all the bodies in the *sea* come back to judgment, it does not need to be said that those on the *earth* will also return. To think that all the dead in the sea are wicked dead is obviously impossible.

The dead who stand before the throne are neither only bodies devoid of their souls, nor only souls devoid of their bodies, but the dead whose souls and whose bodies are united again, thus to be judged at the last day. Hence John writes, "and the death and the hades gave the dead in them." Separated from their bodies by death, the *souls, too,* are returned for the final judgment and are now again joined to their bodies. Whether one regards ὁ θάνατος and ὁ ᾅδης as personifications of two powers or leaves them unpersonified like "the sea," the Greek articles would be used, and although but one verb is used, it is the plural and, like the two articles, indicates a plural subject: "the death" is not identical with "the hades." "The death" is the power which separated the soul from the body in the godly as well as in the ungodly and removed the soul. Where the souls of the godly are taken by "the death" has been plainly told us in v. 4. Now "the death" gives these souls that were in it so that in their bodies they may "stand before the throne" on the day of final and public judgment.

"The hades" is thus properly added; for the souls of the ungodly, which at death were transferred to hades or hell (Luke 16:23), must also appear in their bodies "to stand before the throne" for the final public judgment. This is the reason for indicating this fact about the souls of the ungodly, which is done briefly by adding "and the hades." Hell, too, will "give." The forms ἔδωκεν and ἔδωκαν imply no compulsion but only ready and willing giving. All shall alike stand before the throne for the public judgment, the souls again being united with their bodies. The supposition that "the hades" leads us to think that all "the dead, both the great and the small, standing before the throne" (v. 12) are only the ungodly is untenable, for it disregards what is said about "the sea," disregards also all that is said about the last judgment in the rest of Scripture, notably in Matt. 25, as already indicated.

The double statement in v. 13 and the one in v. 11 about the flight of the earth and the heaven cause no difficulty for him who reads Matt. 24:29-31; v. 13 is added in order briefly to explain v. 12, where only the fact is stated that the dead stand before the throne. Yet once more, again with the verb placed emphatically forward, John writes: "And *judged were they*, each one (personally, each without exception), according to their work," i. e., according to the public evidence that is required in a public judgment. The fact that they were judged is the main thing in this vision, judged in this way as also all Scripture states. Twice it is stated in so many literal words. What has hitherto been put into picture form, in that of battle as far as the ungodly and antichristian are concerned, is now interpreted and put into literal language; wherefore also we now have the whole of it; this judgment will pronounce publicly also on the godly. The interpretation must necessarily include the latter otherwise it would be incomplete for Scripture readers and thus also misleading.

14) "And the death and the hades were thrown into the lake of the fire. This death is the second, the lake of the fire." The commentary on this figurative expression, "were thrown into the lake of the fire," is I Cor. 15:26: Ἔσχατος ἐχθρὸς καταργεῖται ὁ θάνατος, "as last enemy there is put out of effect (out of commission, abolished) the death" (here, too, the article), this dread power ὁ θάνατος, which, according to Rom. 5:12, "came into the world by means of the sin, and thus the death went on through to all men." Compare also 1 Cor. 15:54, 55. Here we see the end of this death which from Adam onward tore apart all men's souls and bodies. In the vision this end is stated symbolically, in I Cor. 15:26 it is stated literally.

In order to see why "the death and the hades" are made companions review the notes on 1:18 and on 6:8 where they ride out together. Here they end together. We need not say again that "the hades" is not *the Totenreich*. Zahn's argument that "to be thrown into the lake of fire for the eons of the eons" means annihilation for Satan, etc., thus also for "the beast and the pseudo-prophet," and now also for "the death and the hades," need not again be answered; he is interested in having Satan, the devils, the damned, and the lake of fire put out of existence, for him "the second death" thus = annihilation. Here, as in 6:8, "the death and the hades" are associated as companions very much like the "beast and the pseudo-prophet" (v.

10); both pairs are personifications and not actual persons. Thus in figurative or in symbolical language all of them, like the person Satan, are "thrown into the lake of fire," they end where Satan ends even as all four are due to Satan.

Some make "the beast and the false prophet" two human beings who are cast into the lake of fire. See, however, chapter 13. With "the death" nobody can do this, nor with "the hades." They are not two human beings. As regards "the death," the commentators seem well satisfied that it is here "thrown into the lake of fire." We, too, care nothing about elaborating the figurative expression by asking what becomes of "the death" in the lake. It is enough to know that it will never kill any more.

The same is true with regard to death's companion, "the hades." It will never receive another wicked human soul as it did when "the death" killed wicked men on earth. The only difficulty is that, when hades means hell, and the lake of fire also means hell, we may wonder how the one can "be thrown" into the other. We have the answer in the statement: "This death (οὗτος ὁ θάνατος, subject, not οὗτος alone as in our versions) is the second death, (namely) the lake of the fire" (apposition to ὁ δεύτερος). "This death" = the throwing of the two companions, death and hades, into the lake of fire. This is the second death, namely, to put it tersely: this death is the lake of fire. Here "the second (death)" is the term that corresponds to "the first resurrection" (v. 6). Both are alike symbolical expressions. The latter refers to the transfer of the souls of the blessed into heaven, the former to the transfer of death and hades and therefore also of all the wicked who were killed bodily by the death and whose souls were at first sent to the hades into the lake of eternal fire, i. e., the wicked, now with both body and soul, are after the final judgment in hell, the lake of the fire.

The difficulty regarding the hades being thrown into the lake of the fire thus solves itself. "The Gehenna" ("the Gehenna of the fire," Matt. 5:22), "the hades," "the abyss," "the lake of the fire," etc., all mean hell and not so many different terrible places despite what commentators and even dictionaries may say. Each of these terms has only its own connotation which is derived less from the etymology than from the use to which it is put. Thus ὁ ᾅδης, "the unseen place," (found ten times in the New Testament) = hell as the place into which *the souls* of the wicked go at the time of death until at the time of the resurrection the death and the hades give up these souls so that they may again be united with their bodies and thus stand before Christ's judgment throne and receive their verdict. "The lake of the fire," like the Jewish term "Gehenna" and "the Gehenna of the fire" = hell but as the place into which the wicked will be thrown with *body and soul* at the time of the final judgment.

Thus Jesus uses the right word in Luke 16:23: "In the hades having lifted up his eyes," in the hades because the reference is to the soul of Dives, his body being buried on earth as the parable itself states. Thus again Jesus uses the right word in Matt. 10:28: "Fear him who is able to destroy both soul and body in Gehenna," in Gehenna because soul and body, reunited on judgment day, are sent to hell as the place for both. As in Luke 16:23 Gehenna could not be substituted for the hades, so in Matt. 10:28 the hades could not be used in place of Gehenna. In Acts 2:27, "hades" is properly used with reference to "my soul" and is there a translation of the Hebrew *sheol.*

More becomes plain. Of the ten instances of the use of hades four appear in Revelation, and each of the four joins "the death" and "the hades." We see why. Because "the death" separates the body of the wicked from the soul and, while the body of the wicked lies in the grave (or the sea, v. 13) until judgment day, the wicked soul is kept in the hades until that day. It is thus that "the death" and "the hades" are companions in Rev. 1:18; 6:8; 20:13, 14. It is thus that the death and the hades are on the judgment day thrown into the lāke of the fire into which the bodies and the souls of the damned are thrown (v. 15). This means an end of hell's (hades') holding only wicked souls that were transferred to it by the killings of temporal death. Now, after the last judgment, there is only "the second death," "the lake of the fire," i. e., no more holding only of souls but only the everlasting burning for Satan (v. 10) and for all his antichristian powers (19:20) and for all his dupes, the latter with body and soul, in quenchless fire (20:10).

15) This is stated in so many words: "And if anyone (at the last judgment) was not found as having been written in the book of the life, *thrown was he* (forward for the sake of emphasis) into the lake of the fire," thrown body and soul. "These shall go away into everlasting punishment," Matt. 25:46. Compare Rev. 21:8; 22:15. What about the godly? The answer is given in chapters 21 and 22. In all the visions the law of paucity governs: so much and no more is told, the reader is kept in expectation to the very end of the last vision.

CHAPTER XXI

The New Heaven and the New Earth, 21:1-8

"Jerusalem the Golden!"

With the exception of the concluding verses of chapter 22 the rest of Revelation constitutes one large section, yet there are in it plain divisions, vision succeeding vision, and we shall consider them in order.

And I saw a new heaven and a new earth; for the first heaven and the first earth went away, and the sea is no longer. And the city, the holy one, New Jerusalem, I saw coming down out of the heaven from God, having been made ready as a bride having been adorned for her husband. And I heard a great voice out of the heaven saying:

Lo, the Tabernacle of God with the human beings!
And he shall tabernacle with them.
And they themselves shall be his people,
And he himself, God, shall be with them.
And he shall wipe off every tear from their eyes:
And the death shall be no longer;
Neither mourning nor outcry nor pain shall be any longer.
The first things went away.

And the One sitting on the throne said:

New do I make all things!

And he says:

Write! Because these words are faithful and genuine.

And he said to me:

They have occurred. I, the Alpha and the Omega, the Beginning and the End! I to the one thirsting will give out of the spring of the water of the life gratis. The one conquering shall inherit these things, and I will be to him God, and he shall be to me son. But for the cowards and unbelievers and such as have become abomination and murderers and whorers and sorcerers and idolaters and all the liars, their part in the lake, the one burning with fire and brimstone, which is the death, the second.

To take the place of the earth and the heaven that "fled" (20:11) John now sees οὐρανὸν καινὸν καὶ γῆν καινήν, "a new heaven and a new earth," καινός designating "new" with reference to the "old" (νέος would mean absolutely "new"). The explanation is added: "For the first heaven and the first earth went away." The heaven and the earth as we now see them in the universe, grand and wonderful, indeed, yet sadly disturbed by sin and evil, invaded by the dragon, the beast, the lamb-beast, the whore, full of the kings of the earth and the dwellers of the earth (all having but antichristian earth thoughts), "went away," disappeared; "for, behold, I create new heavens and a new earth, and the former shall not be remembered nor come into mind" (Isa. 65:17). "For the new heavens and the new earth, which I will make, shall remain before me" (Isa. 66:22). "Nevertheless we, according to his promise, look for new heavens and a new earth, wherein dwelleth righteousness" (II Pet. 3:13).

What the disappearance of the first heaven and the earth involves we see in Matt. 24:29; II Pet. 3:10, etc., and other passages. From Isa. 65:17 we gather that the new heaven and the new earth will involve a creative act of God. When some consider the flight, going away, passing away of the old an annihilation and the new a creation like that of Genesis 1, *ex nihilo*, they come into conflict with Rom. 8:20-23 and with our present passage. The newness of the heaven and of the earth shall be like our own. We shall be the same persons and have the same body and the same soul that we now have; but these made entirely new. Our newness begins with regeneration. Already this the Scriptures call a creation of God, Eph. 2:10; 4:24, so that we are καινὴ κτίσις, "a new creation," II Cor. 5:17; Gal. 6:15. After body and soul are glorified, we shall be new-created, indeed. The same will be true with regard to the new heaven and the new earth. This is more than an analogy, for man is the creature for whom the first heaven and the first earth were created, and if he is made new by creative acts without first having been annihilated, he the head of all this creation, shall God annihilate heaven and earth and create *ex nihilo* another heaven and earth? Combine what is here said with Rom. 8, and the answer is plain.

The first heaven and the first earth, so John saw, were gone, "and the sea is no longer," exists no longer. So "new" was the earth which John saw. Why no more sea? Is the answer too simple, that the function of the sea (ocean) will no longer be needed to supply evaporation, clouds, rain, rivers, and springs, so that men and animals and plants may have the water they need? Some say that John's words do not mean that there will be no sea; but such a statement sounds like a contradiction of John's words. We meet the symbolization of "sea." There will be no more turbulent, tossing nations on earth as there are now. But if "sea" is symbolical, then heaven and earth must also be figurative, which rather obviates this symbolizing of the sea. Moreover, it is not *the sea* of which 17:15 says that it is "peoples and multitudes and nations and tongues" but the "*many waters*" (17:1) — which is quite a different thing. Critics speak about the Egyptian tradition that the sea was not a part of nature but an alien element that was to be shunned as impure, unsocial, sterile; or they point to the Babylonian tradition according to which the sea was in bad association with the abyss as the abode of Tehom and Tiamat. Some refer to 13:1, the beast's coming up out of the sea. But such ideas have no appeal to the conservative Biblical interpreter.

2) The fact that the heaven and the earth are now entirely "new" is only a part of the whole truth. The old separation of the heaven of God, of angels, and of saints from our present heaven and earth where the dragon and all his antichristian powers have wrought their vicious effects, is forever ended. God's heaven and the new heaven and the new earth are joined together and made one. This is expressed in beautiful symbolical language full of significance: "And the city, the holy one, New Jerusalem, I saw coming down out of the heaven from God, having been (that has been) adorned for her husband." A great voice "out of the throne" itself states what this means: "Lo, the Tabernacle of God with human beings! And he shall tabernacle with them. And they themselves shall be his people, and he himself, God, shall be with them."

At one time God had only an earthly dwelling place here below among the nations of the earth in the midst of the one nation he selected to be the bearer of his promises made to Adam, to Abraham, and to his spiritual succession. We have it in the Tabernacle which Moses was ordered to construct at Sinai which became the Temple that Solomon was permitted to build. In both of these structures God manifested his presence, read Exod. 29:43-46; 40:34-38 in regard to the dedication of the Tabernacle, and I Kings 8:10, 11; II Chron. 5:13, 14; 7:2, 3 in regard to he dedication of Solomon's

Temple. Thus the Jerusalem of Israel became "the holy city."

But Jerusalem fell when God rejected this nation, when he destroyed it permanently as a nation, and with it the earthly Temple, a robber's den, such as the Jewish nation had allowed it to become. John 2:19; Matt. 21:13; 23:34-39; Luke 19:41-48; John 4:21. The statement of Jesus (John 4:21) extends over the New Testament time when God no longer has a local earthly place where he may tabernacle with men in a wicked world. Now Jerusalem is above, Gal. 4:26, "Mount Zion, the city of the living God, the heavenly Jerusalem," Heb. 12:22, the city with foundations, whose Builder and Maker is God, which already Abraham knew so well and looked for as a pilgrim on earth, Heb. 11:10 (Rev. 3:12). The once holy city, the old Jerusalem, is no longer holy. Like Abraham, we look for the heavenly, eternal city, whose holiness cannot disappear. John saw this city; he describes it as it was shown to him in v. 10, etc.

He saw it "coming down out of the heaven from God." Zahn regards καταβαίνουσαν as a timeless participle that is merely qualitative and thinks that John did not see the city descend. Present participles are used in this way, and Zahn could supply many examples; but few will believe that this participle indicates that John saw the city only *after* it had descended and that he did not view the descending itself. It descends "out of the heaven from God" where it has been hitherto. Ask not how a city can descend, and how John could see it descend. Such things are beyond mortal conception. The city itself is described in superearthly language. What John saw was the vision which God gave in such a manner that he could see it and that can be seen in no other way. Shall we think that now the heaven of God was empty because the

Holy City had left its place? Read on in v. 3. The imagery of "the Holy City, New Jerusalem," is only a part of what is here used. It was the Tabernacle and then Solomon's Temple that made the old Jerusalem the holy city.

The beauty of the New Jerusalem is described: "having been prepared as a bride having been adorned for her husband." The Psalmist sings of this beauty in Ps. 45:13, 14; 48:2-14. Jerusalem is like a heavenly bride who is decked in all her heavenly robes and jewels. Both perfect participles reach back into the past but center in the present: John saw the bride thus prepared and adorned. The imagery of the bride is continued in v. 9 and in 22:17. We do not think it necessary to separate New Jerusalem and the beauty of the bride in order to obtain the two thoughts: 1) God and his gifts to us and 2) we drawing nigh to God to receive them. The participle "having been made ready," does not separate, it joins. By means of the imagery of "the Holy City, New Jerusalem," of superearthly bridal beauty, Giver and recipients and their union are already pictured; for God's presence makes this city holy, and as a city it is filled with God's people; v. 3 makes this plain.

Rationalizing produces but unsatisfactory results. Were the new heaven and the new earth made after the judgment had been concluded? Did the blessed go from the judgment into God's heaven and then come down from there with the descending Holy City when the new heaven and the new earth were ready? How is I Thess. 4:17 to be introduced? Each vision shows so much and no more. To seek for more and thus to add more is not necessary. We cannot apply our poor, finite conceptions of time and succession in time and of space and distance in space to what is timelessness and spacelessness, for these latter are wholly inconceivable to us in our present state.

3) Whose was this voice "out of the throne"? Whenever an unnamed voice speaks in these visions, an effort is made to determine whose voice it is although John does not give this information. All we can say is that the great voice speaks about God and is thus not God's own voice but one that God employs although we admit that God may speak of himself in the third person as well as in the first.

What does this new heaven and new earth with the Holy City, New Jerusalem, descending as a beautiful bride, mean? The voice from God's own throne, the symbol of his eternal power and dominion which has wrought this consummation, tells John, "Lo, the Tabernacle of God with human beings!" μετὰ τῶν ἀνθρώπων has the generic article. This means, "He shall tabernacle with them." And this means, "They themselves shall be his people, and he himself, God (or God himself), shall be with them." The heaven of God and the new heaven and new earth created for men shall be joined, shall be the Holy City, New Jerusalem, God's Tabernacle with men, God tabernacling with them, they his people, he with them, their God. The final consummation of all God's plans in the creation of the world has been reached.

Put away all such thoughts as that the heaven of God shall be devoid of the Holy City, New Jerusalem, God's Tabernacle; that these shall occupy a local place on the new earth, and that much local space shall be unoccupied. When the voice from the throne itself exclaims "lo," know that finite mind cannot hope to understand all that it speaks. Lay hold on the simple μετά phrases: μετὰ τῶν ἀνθρώπων — μετὰ αὐτῶν — μετὰ αὐτῶν: God in company with men. This is the ultimate fulfillment of the name of Jesus: "Immanuel" = "God with us" (Matt. 1:23), and with us not only in grace but also in glory. Οἱ ἄνθρωποι = no more a separate people, no more an ἐκλογή scattered among "those dwelling on the earth" (see 3:10 for this designation). No more dead bodies of saints in the graves on the old earth, no more souls of saints in the Jerusalem above, no more souls on the old earth in mortal bodies. No more godless ones save in the lake burning with fire and brimstone (v. 8).

In this vision *the holiness* of God's union and communion with us is stressed. This is the Holy City descending out of holy heaven, the Tabernacle of God, the very term "Tabernacle" connoting holiness. All that are unholy are not here (v. 8). Yet "city," "Jerusalem," "Tabernacle," God "tabernacling," all = μετά God, "in company with" us, *the union and communion of God with us*. There is no μετὰ τοῦ Θεοῦ here, no mutuality, no reciprocity. It is all one-sided, *God* joined to us, *God* come to be eternally with us, the fact being emphasized by three phrases.

4) What this means is brought out negatively. So many descriptions of eternal blessedness are either figurative or couched in negation because the realities are inconceivable to us in our present state. Here especially the contrast between the old condition and the new is thought of. "He shall wipe off every tear from their eyes," which recalls all the tears shed on the old earth. What caused such tears? "The death." This shall be no longer, v. 14 records the end of "the death" (i. e., personifying it as the frightful death power); note also I Cor. 15:26. "Neither mourning nor outcry nor pain," these products of "the death" on the old earth and under the old heaven which pressed out so many, many tears. Summing it all up: "The first things went away" (our idiom: have gone away), all the *first* things of the *first* heaven and the *first* earth (v. 1). The simple aorist states the great fact.

5) Now speaks "the One sitting on the throne," i. e., exercising eternal power and dominion (4:2), Christ himself, as also his words and the names by

which he designates himself indicate. Those who think that God is referred to, or that εἶπεν — λέγει — εἶπε indicate different speakers (an angel for λέγει) seek to prove too much from the change of tense, for λέγει merely avoids three consecutive εἶπε. This aorist and this present are often used side by side in narration.

From the throne Christ said, "Lo, *new* do I make all things!" with the emphasis on "new," and the tense of ποιῶ is the present as is customary in general statements. This word is placed in an independent position because of the importance of the statement, because this importance is to sink into the reader's soul. By his grace Christ now makes us "new," καινός (see v. 1), a new creation, renewed in mind and soul, etc., the old man being put off, crucified, mortified, etc. But this present beginning of newness in us is to reach the consummation when "all things" are made new. John now sees them so.

This passage, v. 1-5, has ever been the hope, joy, and comfort of longing Christians and will ever remain so. It is easy to understand why in another separate statement Christ orders: "Write! Because these words are faithful (reliable, worthy of our faith) and genuine" (with no sham, no shortage as to meaning). Distinguish ἀληθινός from ἀληθής. The same statement is made in 22:6. Both adjectives are substantivized in 3:14; ἀληθινός occurs often (3:7; 6:10; 15:3; 16:7; 19:2, 9). The words ἀληθινός and ἀληθής do not mean the same thing; *echt* and *wahr*, "genuine" and "true," are not far apart in meaning and yet are not identical.

When John is to write we must determine from 10:4 (see the discussion). In addition to the original order to write (1:11, 19), reiterations of the order appear at important points, one of which is here. Does the order here imply that John should put down in writing only the words, "Lo, new do I make all things"?

Some think so. We include v. 3, 4, must do so because of the future tenses which are promises to be conveyed to us as being of utmost value. In fact, there is no reason for omitting the words of Christ that follow in v. 6-8.

6) These are given an independent position by means of the preamble, "And he said to me." Here is the proof that the *logoi* referred to are faithful and genuine: "Occurred have they." The perfect states that what these words say has just occurred and now is so. In this very vision John sees them as realities, as having come to pass. This shows how ποιῶ, "I make," is to be understood, namely not as referring to a making that is still incomplete.

All is done, all is made new; it is presented so that John may see it. Christ, as it were, signs his name to it all: "I, I (emphatic ἐγώ), the Alpha and the Omega (smoother English: Alpha and Omega), the Beginning and the End." Both titles, together with a third, "the First and the Last" (the three occur together in 22:13), receive full discussion in 1:8 and 1:17, which see. "The Alpha and the Omega" = God's *revelation* from the first to the last letter. "The First and the Last" = all *history* from start to finish. "The Beginning and the End" = all God's saving *work* from inception to consummation. The two titles here used eminently fit the statement: Γέγοναν! Indeed, the end of all God's revelation, the consummation of all God's work, both of which are summed up in Christ, are shown to John as having come to pass.

When John is told to write these faithful and genuine words, thus revealing their accomplishment in this vision under Christ's own double signature, this writing has us, the readers, in view and is intended to increase the longing of our hope by means of this strongest assurance and our courage and endurance by means of this divine certainty. Therefore Christ adds his double promise: "I, I (again emphatic) to the one thirsting will give out of the spring of the water of the life gratis. The one conquering shall inherit these things, and I will be to him God, and he shall be to me son." Note how ἐγώ and τῷ διψῶντι are effectively abutted.

"The spring of the water of the life" occurs only here. The passages usually quoted are John 4:10, 14, Jesus offering the water of life to the Samaritan woman; Isa. 55:1, the grand invitation to come and drink without money or price; John 7:37 (Isa. 12:3) which is also an invitation. These, however, deal with those who are yet without grace and call them to drink of the life water of grace. The passages to be quoted are 7:17: "he shall lead them to life's springs of waters"; 22:17; and, illuminating both, 22:1. For "the one thirsting" is one who has already drunk of grace and is now thirsty for the glory. His the great longing to be led by the Lamb to "life's springs of water" in the new earth, to walk beside "the river of life's water shining as crystal, going out from the throne of God and of the Lamb" (7:17 and 22:1). His thirst Christ promises to satisfy in the new earth and to do that δωρεάν, "gratis," by way of gift, for also this water is pure grace. The present context makes it impossible to think of the sinner's first reception of grace on the old earth. Little help is obtained from the thought: "Oriental thrones usually have a fountain of cool water springing up, and from this John doubtless draws his picture." It is not *John* who is here drawing a picture; it is *Jesus* who is making a promise.

7) What makes us thirst here on the old earth for the glory to come? The heat of affliction, especially of battle against so many antichristian foes and attacks. Fittingly the second promise follows to "the one conquering," ὁ νικῶν recalling "the conquering one" in

2:7, 11, 17, 26: 3:5, 12, 21, and the heavenly promises to him that assure his victory. Here it is beyond question a promise that shall be realized on the new earth: "he shall inherit these things," i. e., all the καινά, the new things on the new earth. "Inherit" is correct even as Christ adds, "he shall be to me a son." A son inherits. We are now in our minority; on that day we shall be of age and shall inherit. The heir must wait until the inheritance laid up for him may be duly his. All the passages regarding "children — heirs — inherit — inheritance" belong here.

Wondrous shall be this inheriting. It shall not be as here on the old earth where the testator must first die, which fact applied even to the testament mentioned in Heb. 9:16-20. On the new earth this, too, is new: "and I shall be to him God, and he shall be to me son." This shall be the inheritance even as Jesus says in the parable: "Son, thou art ever with me, and all that I have is thine," Luke 15:31. Yes, Christ here calls himself "God." Let the modernists note this.

8) Yet a plain warning is added for our sakes: "But for the cowards (those who give up in the fight and do not conquer, those who become frightened) and the unbelievers (who are not faithful) and such as have become abomination (perfect passive participle, anarthrous: any who have been made a stink, Thayer) and murderers and whorers and sorcerers (on φαρμακεία, see 18:23, also 9:21; these three designations apparently name some of the spiritual abominations which apply also to the great whore: the blood of the saints in 17:6; whoredom in her very name in 17:5; sorcery in 18:23) and idolaters and for all the liars (applies also to the second beast which made the image in 13:14, and is called the pseudo-prophet, the lying one, in 16:13; 19:20; 20:10) — their part in the lake,

the one burning with fire and brimstone (see 19:20), which is the death, the second one" (see 20:14). The neuter relative ὅ does not refer to μέρος alone but to the whole thought of having one's part in this lake. Compare the parallel passage 22:15.

All chiliasts try to make this section (v. 1-8) square with their ideas of the millennium. Men like von Hofmann and Luthardt labor with this Jerusalem "coming down out of the heaven," for according to their view it really comes down 1,000 years before John says that it does, namely at the beginning of these 1,000 years when, according to their view, Christ appears gloriously on earth, raises all the dead saints in the first bodily resurrection, and rules gloriously with them here on earth for the 1,000 years. They place the "new Jerusalem" here on earth 1,000 years too soon. The risen and glorified saints are already here, although on the four corners of the earth unglorified nations that are still hostile to Christ remain, and also others who are yet to be converted, many of whom will not be converted. Thus glorified and unglorified men live together at the same time here on earth, but that is an unscriptural idea. Chiliasts place the Parousia at the beginning of the 1,000 years; some of them have also a second Parousia at the end of the 1,000 years. At the end of these 1,000 years they place the supreme assault of Satan and his hordes on "the beloved city" (20:7-10) which is alrealy full of the risen and glorified saints. But what is left to come down out of the heaven at the end if the chiliastic millennium is already here for a 1,000 years?

Look at v. 4. Will there be tears to be wiped away, death, mourning, outcry and pain to be removed when for 1,000 years already the saints sit on thrones here on earth and rule with Christ during those 1,000 years? This is the error of chiliasm which claims that the following Old Testament passages are descriptions of the millennium: Isa. 2:4, swords beaten into plowshares, spears into pruninghooks, no more swords lifted up, no more wars (yet look at the very worst battle in 20:7-10); Isa. 65:25, the wolf and the lamb feeding together, the lion eating straw; other similar passages (see the author's *Eisenach Old Testament Selections,* 191, etc.; 715, etc., for the exegesis of these passages). These Old Testament passages describe the new earth in colors that are borrowed from the peace of Paradise. No dragon, Satan, can invade these conditions with the wild hordes of Gog and Magog (v. 7, etc.); nor will the saints be in a παρεμβολή, "fortified camp" (v. 9).

The Bride of the Lamb, the Holy City Jerusalem, 21:9 to 22:5

9) Much more is to be revealed about the "New Jerusalem" on the "new earth." **And there came one of the seven angels, of those having the seven bowls, of those laden with the seven plagues, the last ones; and he spoke with me, saying, Hither, I will show thee the Bride, the Wife of the Lamb!** This may be the same angel as the one mentioned in 17:1, for the words used to introduce him are the same: "And there came one of the seven angels, of those having the seven plagues," who uses the same words, "Hither, I will show thee!" In 17:1 he shows "the judgment of the whore, the great one"; now he has the delightful task of showing "the Bride, the Wife of the Lamb." Plainly, all that is vile and abominable is concentrated in "the great *whore,*" and all that is pure, lovely, beautiful, heavenly in "the *Bride and Wife* of the Lamb." So also the whore = Babylon; the Bride = "the city, the holy Jerusalem." The only difference we note is that the whore has been pictured as the seductress, the antichristian seduction, seducing the kings of the earth, the dwellers on the

earth; while the Bride is the whole *Una Sancta* which is composed of all the glorified saints. We see the whore increasing her following *before* the Parousia; the Bride is shown *after* the Parousia.

On Bride and Wife read the explanation of 19:7. The figure used in v. 2, "as a bride adorned for her husband," is now advanced to its reality and is again used in its reality in 22:17.

The reading τῶν γεμόντων (with the following genitive after a verb of filling) is fully assured and should not be changed. The verb γέμω is used with reference to ships that are filled with cargo. When Zahn and a few others are confused by this genitive and think it should be an accusative modifying φιάλας, this confusion is caused by their translation, "filled with," i. e., bowls, not angels, filled with the seven plagues. But filled ships are laden ships. Translate properly, like the R. V.: of the angels "who *were laden with*," literally, "of those *laden with*." Note that τῶν ἐχόντων has the apposition τῶν γεμόντων in perfect grammatical order. Why one of these angels is to show John the bride and not some other angel, is really not ours to inquire. May it be due to the fact that it is fitting that one commissioned to pour out one of the plagues now show John the full blessedness of the *Una Sancta* after the Parousia?

10) **And he bore me away in spirit to a great and high mountain, and he showed me the city, the holy one, Jerusalem, coming down out of the heaven from God, having the glory of God.** "He bore me away in spirit" repeats 17:3; "in spirit" is the same phrase that occurs in 1:10 and 4:2, and refers to John's spirit and not to the Holy Spirit as our versions indicate by capitalizing "Spirit." No high mountain was required to see the fate of the whore. To see "in spirit the Holy City, Jerusalem," descending out of heaven from God is a sight and a vision so

glorious that John is to see it from the height of a great mountain. This language is to convey also to us something of the unspeakable greatness and glory of what John saw not with natural but with spiritual eyes. This far transcends our imagination.

Καταβαίνουσαν out of the heaven from God" is the same expression that was used in v. 2, the participle having the same meaning and not expressing mere quality (see v. 2). The fact that John should a second time see and then be shown this coming down of the city should cause no difficulty; for this second vision of the city's coming down is to reveal to him much more than was given him to see at first. We might think that John is now shown the city after it had already come down; from the high mountain he views its glory as spread out beneath him. The great Revelator thought otherwise, he let John see this coming down twice, evidently in order that both he and we may perceive its full significance the more. Moreover, the angel now shows John much more than was given him to see in v. 1-8. As said repeatedly in regard to other visions, each one is limited to reveal so much and no more, enough for John and for us to take in at one time. Who would oppose his own little wisdom to this wisdom? The high mountain thus enables John to see this wondrous sight, the Holy City coming down. See v. 2 on the Holy City, on Jerusalem, and her coming down out of the heaven from God.

11) John is shown the city as "having the glory of God." It is this glory that is now to be revealed to him. In v. 1-8 it is *the blessedness* of God's union and communion with his people which is emphasized by the three μετά phrases in v. 3. Now it is *the glory* that is revealed. The glory of God fills the Holy City, the effulgence of his δόξα, all his divine attributes. For this he created heaven and earth and man; this purpose is now consummated.

We may once more pause to note how chiliasts labor to make all that is said about the Bride, the Holy City coming down out of heaven agree with their millennium in which practically all of this has come to the earth already 1,000 years earlier but with impossible incongruities such as divine and heavenly glory on an earth where unglorified men and conditions, yea, foes and enemies of the beloved city still exist and are finally gathered for a supreme battle (see at the end of v. 8).

Her luminary like a most precious stone, as a diamond stone, scintillating. She having a wall, great and high; she having twelve portals and at the portals twelve angels and names inscribed, which are those of the twelve tribes of Israel's sons. From the east three portals, and from the north three portals, and from the south three portals, and from the west three portals. And the wall of the city having twelve foundations, and on them twelve names of the twelve apostles of the Lamb.

Here is a part of the glory of the Holy City. The imagery taken from an earthly city is only a poor aid; it must be stretched into the humanly impossible. The inexpressible reality which is to be conveyed only in symbolism so as to leave *some* useful impression on our minds is plainly allowed to break through everything we have ever seen on this old earth. It cannot be otherwise. When Paul saw Paradise above without symbolism such as this of John's vision given him by God, Paul could not describe what he had seen and tells us so in II Cor. 12:1-4. To John was given what he tells us here. To attempt more than to convey the glorious impression here intended, for instance, to state how the twelve foundations were laid (v. 14), how the height of this city can be as great as its length and its breadth (v. 16), how this or that can be, is only to blur, perhaps ruin, what the Lord intends.

Ὁ φωστήρ is not "the light" but "the lightbearer" which makes the whole city shine with heavenly, wholly superearthly, radiance. Although John saw it in a symbolical vision, the only words given him to describe this source of light are weak human comparisons: "like to a most precious stone, as a diamond stone, scintillating," κρυσταλλίζοντι (this verb has as yet been found nowhere else). This is the description employed in the vision of the throne with reference to the One sitting on the throne (4:3). But in 4:3 two precious brilliant stones are mentioned, the ἴασπις, or diamond, and the sard: the one being brilliant white, apparently symbolizing the infinite majesty of the One sitting on the throne, the other brilliant red, apparently symbolizing his judgment and his justice (see 4:3). While John does not say that "the light-bearer" is God, v. 23 as well as 4:3 may induce us, if not to identify, at least to connect the two. Then, too, we see why the comparison with the sard is here omitted — the judgment is past.

12) The description continues in v. 12-14 with brief strokes by discarding the use of finite sentences. We, too, often write thus and thereby vividly point to this and to that great feature. The Greek participle is better suited to this purpose than ours because it has number, gender, and case. The two ἔχουσα are perfectly in order when standing alone. "Having a wall, great and high," ἡ πόλις is understood. The Mohammedan Jerusalem still has a massive wall; not so our American cities. Such walls protected ancient cities. Those entitled to enter were allowed to do so, others were kept out; the walls afforded a main defense in event of assault and siege. The great high wall of the Holy City on the new earth cannot have such a purpose. Nor can its twelve wonderful gates or portals with an angel for each, portals that are never closed (v. 25).

We have already indicated that the descent of the Holy City is not to be understood as leaving heaven empty; for the former separation of God's heaven from our earth is no more. Now we must add that the Holy City is not to be conceived as occupying a local space on the new earth with the rest of the space on the new earth being unoccupied. Let us tell ourselves that all our mundane ideas of time and of space do not apply to the new earth, and that all conclusions drawn from such ideas are unsatisfactory. How, then, shall we conceive the new earth and this city? This is beyond mortal conception in reality; even the symbolism of the vision already transcends conception. The symbolism only shadows forth what is far greater than itself.

Take as an example "the throne" in 4:2 and elsewhere: it is not a grand chair set on an elevation with space before it but the symbol of God's power, rule, and dominion in the universe. Likewise, "the Holy City, Jerusalem," is not many houses or palaces with streets, a surrounding wall with portals and angel guards, etc.; it is "Immanuel," "God with us," symbolizing ὁ Θεὸς μετὰ τῶν ἀνθρώπων — μετὰ αὐτῶν —μετὰ αὐτῶν (v. 3), "together and in company with" us forever.

Why the wall? Let us call it the symbol of *inclusion* for this our eternal union with God. Why the "portals" with their angels? Why just "twelve"? Why "names written" on the portals, and these the names of "the twelve tribes of Israel's sons"? The "portals" signify *entrance* into eternal and glorious union with God and in v. 26 bringing in, for the vision contains no going out and no taking anything out. The "names" on the "portals" are those of *God's chosen people*, for entrance and eternal union with God exist only for them. We know all about these names from chapter 7; they are used for the 144,000 sealed ones, for the whole *Una Sancta* that is now entered into glory, "a great multitude which no man can number" (7:9). They hunger and thirst no more (7:16 = 21:4); they are led to life's springs of waters (7:17 = 21:6b). This is the eternal union with God.

Portals = entrance for union. For we must all be brought in. Once we were outside, aliens, foreigners (Eph. 2:19), dead in sin, children of wrath, not one of us a native of the city (communion with God). Now there is no more going out. The idea is not that this union is compulsory; it seems that even this is indicated in v. 26, for the portals are never shut. Do you ask, why, then, portals at all? Because their symbolism tells so eloquently the part they play in this eternal union. Why an angel at these symbolical portals of this symbolical city? Forget not Gen. 3:24! Eternal union with God is not provided with doors into which anybody can run in any way that pleases him as so many imagine today. Eternal union with God has no doors into which "dogs" may enter (22:15). Liars (22:15) may claim fellowship with God (I John 1:6) but they never attain it. This presence of an angel at the portals adds its significant part.

Rightly does Lange ridicule the idea of Hengstenberg and of Kliefoth "that the angels are watchmen or guards for the city on the new earth against foes, of which the imagination, filled with the terrors resting upon the church militant, can conceive," as if, Lange says, the blessed inhabitants of heaven were timid children, or were threatened by empty terrors of the imagination! Bengel adds that the angels serve as ornaments. Into such vagaries men stray when they forget that all of this is symbolism which speaks to us here on this old earth so that we may know what our entrance into the eternal union (city) really means; read 22:14.

13) Yes, the three gates on each of the four sides of the wall denote catholicity, namely that of Matt. 8:11; 28:19; Mark 16:15, as also Rev. 21:24 states. On the new earth, however, the catholicity of the Communion of Saints is complete. The prophecies of Isa. 43:5, 6 and Matt. 8:11 are completely fulfilled.

14) Abraham longed for "the city having foundations, whose Builder and Constructor is God," Heb. 11:10. Paul knew "the foundation of the apostles and prophets" with Jesus Christ himself as the cornerstone. John saw the wall of the city "having twelve foundations, and on them twelve names of the apostles of the Lamb." Ἔχων, modifying τὸ τεῖχος, is used without declension, B.-D. 136, 4. Eternal union with God rests on the Word, with reference to which the Lamb himself said while here on earth: "Heaven and earth (the old) shall pass away, but my words shall not pass away." We now behold these foundations in the New Testament, the inspired writings of the apostles in which the Old Testament culminates. There is no union with God in eternity save for those who now rest their souls on the Word of the Lamb. For here, too, as in the case of the portals and the angels, the symbolism is intended to speak to us and is arranged with reference to our present state.

In 18:20 the apostles are among those addressed; here they are significantly called "the twelve apostles of the Lamb." On the symbolical significance of "twelve" which is repeated here, see chapter 7; on "the Lamb," 5:6. "Apostles" are they who belong to the Lamb slain for us on the cross; they are the ones that were commissioned by him to preach his Word to all nations during all ages, which they do through the New Testament which now speaks to all men, and he that hears them hears the Lamb. All of the apostles did not write, but those who were moved to write by the Holy Spirit wrote for all, wrote the Word and the doctrine which all taught. Their symbolical number is ever "twelve," and this number certainly includes Paul just as the symbolical number of the tribes of Israel is "twelve," although the names listed in chapter 7 do not contain Dan. It is not John who in 18:20 and now again speaks about "the apostles" of whom John himself is one; in this vision John is shown the "twelve foundations" by the angel who shows the city to him, and thus John sees the "twelve names." This answers the objection of impropriety on John's part in writing about the twelve names of the apostles when his own name is one of them, an objection which would have to include also Eph. 2:20.

Some commentators add something of their own to the various visions. They tell us how the twelve foundations were arranged and laid. Kliefoth divides each of the four walls into three sections, thus there are three apostles for each side, and thus there are four apostles as cornerstones. Lee thinks of twelve layers extending around the entire city.

15-17) **And the one speaking with me had a measure, a golden reed, in order to measure the city and her portals and her wall. And the city lies foursquare, and its length as great as its breadth. And he measured the city with the reed at twelve thousand stadia. The length and the breadth and the height of her are equal. And he measured her wall, a hundred and forty-four half-arm lengths, man's measure which is angel's.** In 11:1, 2 John is given a reed to measure the *Una Sancta* on the old earth; not so now. The city on the new earth the angel measures for John, for also this angel shows him the city, the *Una Sancta* in her eternal consummation. In chapter 11 John's measuring rod is not golden; the angel's is because of the glory of the city come down out of the heaven.

City, portals, and wall are measured, yet we hear nothing about the dimensions of the portals as we do about the dimensions of the city and of the wall. This seems to be due to the fact that the portals in the wall are a part of the city, and in the measuring from one corner to the next the portals were included.

16) The first result of the measuring noted is that the city lies foursquare, i. e., the surface covered is a perfect square as is already indicated to a degree in v. 13 by the three portals on the east, north, south, and west. The angel measured the city "ἐπὶ 12,000 stadia," "up to" so many. After saying that "the length of her (is) as great as (ὅσον, simple relative, R. 405) the breadth," and that "the city lies foursquare," some still think that the 12,000 stadia denote the whole circumference and not the length of each side wall; or they consider John's statement ambiguous. This reasoning is also applied to the height; those who reduce each wall to 3,000 stadia, also reduce the height. One reason for this is the fact that the great height of the city disturbs so many. How can a city be 12,000 stadia high? Some give ἴσα, which means "equal," the meaning "proportionate" but apply this meaning only to "the height," for they want this height reduced. A terraced mountain is suggested, only the peak of which would have the full height of 12,000 stadia. Many feel that at "144 half-arm lengths" the wall is proportionately too low, especially on the strength of the addition, "man's measure which is angel's." Both genitives are adjectival: "a *human* measure which (in this case) is (also) angelic." This same adjective genitive ἀνθρώπου appears in 13:18, where it is often understood as meaning "a man's (an individual man's) number." See 13:18.

This very addition intends to indicate that all of these measurements, being man's and angel's measure, are symbolical and are here used with reference to the Holy City which neither man nor angel designed or built, which came down from the heaven and was built by God himself (Heb. 11:10), this figure of a "city" thus itself only symbolizing what to us as yet can only be symbolized, namely the eternal, transcendent union with men which God designed and consummated through the Lamb. Therefore we should not read these measurements after our poor, human, spatial manner, such as men apply to human cities which are designed and built by them here on the old earth under the old heaven. These numbers do not signify spatial size and spatial proportion. A σπάδιον, 606$\frac{3}{4}$ English feet (see 14:20), and a πῆχυς, about one-half a yard, are not intended for us so that we may draw a design such as a man draws who maps out a city on paper. As far as such units of earthly measurement are concerned, others could have been used, but they would have to contain the symbolical number "twelve," this multiplied by itself, and for this city also the symbolical ten, multiplied $10 \times 10 \times 10$, or 1,000. All else is negligible.

This city is as high as it is long and as it is wide. It is a cube, a cube that has a twelve in it that is raised by 1,000, the symbolical twelve of the heavenly *Una Sancta* with the 1,000 of utmost completeness and perfection: God's union with the *Una Sancta* in eternal perfection. It is not "seven" in any form, for seven = three plus four, the symbol of grace for God's joining himself to men here on the old earth. It is used thus in 1:4; 4:5 with reference to the Holy Spirit regarding his mission for men on earth; used thus in 1:13-20 with regard to the churches on earth and with regard to their ministers on earth (also in chapters 2 and 3); used also in the seven seals, seven trumpets, seven bowls, all dealing with God in relation to men on earth; used even with regard to the dragon's heads (13:1), Satan's arrogation of God's right to deal with men on earth. But "twelve" is the symbolical number in 4:3, for the twenty-four elders, and "twelve" in chapter 7 for the 144,000, the number of those sealed for heaven, whom no one can number. It is thus that we now again have this "twelve" in the city and in its wall and could have no other number to express God's consummated eternal union with us.

This cube is foreshadowed by the Holy of Holies in the Tabernacle and in the Solomonic Temple, which was a room equal in length, breadth, and height, a perfect cube; the Holy Place had the same width and height but twice the length. The cube, having its three dimensions identical, symbolizes *perfection*. In the Holy of Holies, an earthly structure, the union of God with his own was a type and symbol of the perfect union on the new earth. In the case of the Tabernacle and the Temple the people could not enter the Holy of Holies. This was permitted only to the high priests as the type of the eternal High Priest. The eternal counterpart of the cubic Holy of Holies on the new earth is no longer a sanctuary with the people of God outside in the courts (v. 23) but a city, yea, "New Jerusalem" (v. 2), with all God's people in perfect, consummated, eternal union with God. Disregard the idea of a mountain with terraces extending to the summit; for this loses the great essential symbolized in the city that is and must be nothing less than a cube, one that is marked for us by the human measure which contains "twelve" and that multiplied and even raised by the "1,000" of final completion. No wonder no one goes out of this "city" even temporarily.

"The wall" of this city must also be marked by the same "twelve," both as to length and as to height. Being "foursquare," this applies also to the breadth and thus to the whole square of the area: 12,000 × 12,000 or 144,000,000 square stadia, although this figure is not stated in the description; yet see the number of the angels in 5:11, where myriads are found, namely ten thousands. This symbolical "wall" denotes that inclusion is inclusion marked in all directions (like the "city" itself) by the number of God's people, namely "twelve." Its length on each side, its height, its enclosed area are stated in "twelves," but so as by the multiples to indicate the inclusion that encloses the eternal final union of God with his own which is symbolized in the Eternal City.

18) **And the inlaying of her wall diamond. And the city pure gold, similar to pure glass. The foundations of the wall of the city adorned with every kind of precious stone. The first foundation, diamond; the second, sapphire; the third, chalcedony; the fourth, emerald; the fifth, sardonyx; the sixth, sard; the seventh, chrysolite; the eighth, beryl; the ninth, topas; the tenth, chrysoprase; the eleventh, jacinth; the twelfth, amethyst. And the twelve portals, twelve pearls; each and every one of the portals was of one pearl. And the avenue of the city pure gold, as transparent glass.**

The material of which the city is built is precious and beautiful beyond all imagination. All of it is pure gold and priceless jewels and pearls. Silver is ignored because it was regarded as being too tawdry and cheap. This is not gold as we see it in great government vaults, but everything is made of gold save where jewels and pearls are seen. These are not jewels and pearls as we know them, but are tremendous in size, vast foundation stones and doors that are each made of a single pearl. Stop imagining. Eye hath not seen what God has prepared for those that love him! All is intended to be humanly unimaginable. All of this language is human symbolism, which means that the

tion and lie — only those having been written in the book of the life of the Lamb.

We come to those who are in this city, in the eternal union with God and the Lamb. We are told what is not there and what is there for them. No Sanctuary did John see. On the old earth God had an earthly Sanctuary where Israel could draw near to him, where, however, a veil hung between him and them. When the use for this material Sanctuary was at an end, the Sanctuary and the Lamb were in God's heaven, altogether removed from the old earth. Now, after the earth is new and united to God's heaven, the eternal union, which the Sanctuary once represented, is effected. Now the Lord God, the Almighty, is this city's Sanctuary, he and the Lamb. The eternal union is immediate, absolutely complete. God and the Lamb are not a Sanctuary in the center of this city, to which those in the city must go in order to commune with them. The whole city is the Sanctuary, the whole city filled with the glorious Presence, God and the Lamb are the Sanctuary, we are in union with them, a union to which nothing can be added in all eternity.

23) So also no sun or moon is needed "to shine for her" (dative of advantage). God's glory has illumined (aorist for which the English prefers the perfect) the whole city, her lamp is the Lamb. The glory of God is God himself in all his radiant attributes; this glory fills the entire city with its uncreated light; so, too, it is with regard to the Lamb, the incarnate Son who died for us.

24) Those who dwell in this city "walk by this her light." All its fullness ever surrounds them in their eternal union with God and the Lamb. Διά is not local: walk "through" her light. Those who are in this city, in this eternal, exalted union, are called "the nations," and in the next clause we have "the

kings of the earth." The German interpreters call them *die Heiden,* pagan nations, and think of pagan kings who govern these nations. We are told that on the new earth these dwell outside of the city but are friendly; that the portals are ever open to them and allow them to come and to go. And men like Alford take the next step: "Besides the glorified church there shall be dwelling on the redeemed earth nations under kings and saved by means of influences of the heavenly city." It is also said that "nations" and "kings" are well organized nationalities because only in hades everything is disorganized. This is but the millennium over again. It is found not only in the "1,000 years" on the old earth but even in the new earth.

It is not sufficient to say that all that is here narrated about nations and kings is only decorative imagery that is modeled after the Old Testament, and that it satisfies the human idea that an imperial city ought to receive tribute from subject nations and kings.

"The nations" are the glorified saints, in 5:9, those "out of every tribe and tongue and people and nation," in 7:9, the "great multitude, which no one is able to number, out of every nation and tribes and peoples and tongues." But this does not imply that in the Eternal City they will appear as national groups, all the Englishmen as one nation, the Germans as another, the Chinese as a third. "The kings of the earth," hitherto repeatedly used in an antichristian sense (beginning at 6:15), does not refer to literal kings but is used symbolically. In the visions of the beast and the whore, 19:9, etc., these kings are the many minor earthly powers and their human representatives that were won for the beast and for the dragon by the lamb-beast and the whore. These meet their doom in 19:21. When the same term, "the kings of the earth," is used here in connection with the Eternal City, this is to convey the idea that not all these powers of the earth were won for Satan but that the Lamb, too, won many of their number for himself, great and powerful persons with their wide influence in all the various departments of life on the old earth.

These "bring their glory into the city." Again v. 26, "shall bring (οἴσουσι, the future of φέρω) the glory and honor of the nations into her." This is saying in symbolical language what is expressed literally in 14:13: "For their works follow with them (μετά)." The glory and the honor of the nations and of the kings are all that they wrought for the Lamb while they were here on the old earth, for which they receive reward in the Eternal City, namely the varying degrees of glory.

25, 26) On glancing through this vision we see that a part of the description is entirely verbless, a part of it is given in aorists, in v. 22, 23 two presents, in v. 24 a future and then a present, in v. 25 a subjunctive and a future, in v. 26 a future, in v. 27 another subjunctive. This variation in the presentation: "They shall walk" — "they bring" — "they shall not be shut" — "shall not be there" — "shall bring" — "shall not enter," is from the standpoint of the angel and of John, vivid presents and direct futures and futuristic subjunctives are used with reference to the timeless moment of v. 2 when the Holy City comes down to the new earth. *Then* this bringing takes place, *then* this not going in occurs. The idea that this difference is accomplished by shutting the portals so that some may go in and be brought in and some may not (κλεισθῶσιν is properly an aorist like εἰσέλθῃ; both are futuristic subjunctives and have their common negative οὐ μή). No, the portals are not shut.

Confused by the tenses and misunderstanding them from the standpoint of the continuance of the city throughout all eternity, some think of these nations and these kings as living *outside* of the city, on great areas not occupied by the city. Some regard them as friendly pagans who are unglorified and yet go in and out of the portals. Bengel has no night in the city but a change of day and night outside of it. Some think of converted pagans who are glorified but live outside of the city, who have the right to bring their glory and their honor in and, after going out and accumulating more for God, repeat their bringing in *in regem Verkehr,* in lively traffic, under the eyes of the angels at the portals who see to it that nothing κοινόν is brought in and that nobody who produces abomination and lie goes in. Having this picture, it is easy to take the next step: in the city itself only *Jewish* saints reside, but Gentile saints outside of the city have the right to bring in their glory and their honor. So, we are told, it will be to all eternity.

Then Paul was mistaken when he wrote that Christ broke down the wall of partition between Jews and Gentiles, that we are all one in Christ Jesus, that there are not two classes of Christians, a superior Jewish class and a second-rate Gentile class as once there were native Jews and proselytes from Gentilism. Then Jesus was mistaken when he said that they would come from the four corners of the earth and dine with Abraham, Isaac, and Jacob. In short, then the eternal bliss after the judgment will not be what the rest of Scripture leads us to believe. The chiliasts who claim that the entire Jewish nation will be converted at the beginning of the millennium and will become the aristocracy of Christianity find this prospect of Jewish superiority in the Eternal City to their liking and see it foretold in the Old Testament. We have already noted that they can scarcely separate their picture of the millennium from this of this Eternal City. But whether Jews are thus given special glory or not, the whole conception is unwarranted.

We repeat that in this vision of the new earth there is no unoccupied area. This city goes far beyond the Old Testament where the first and the second Jerusalem are viewed as one. The whole new heaven and new earth are the city. For this is the Eternal Union of God and the Lamb with all the saints. City, portals, foundations, etc., are symbols. When it is asked, "Why, then, does the city need portals?" if it is not for the purpose of this lively *Verkehr*, the symbolism is literalized from "entrance" for the saints into traffic between those outside and those inside. There is only one thing outside. Jesus calls it τὸ σκότος τὸ ἐξώτερον, "the darkness, the outer one," i. e., hell.

27) When the Lamb leads his own into this city, there shall not enter in πᾶν κοινόν, anything common, i. e., unholy (neuter), nothing of this even in a single saint, and not "one producing abomination and lie" (anarthrous, qualitative nouns), not one person of this kind. This repeats v. 8 in abbreviated form, v. 8 stating where all such and everything of this kind has its portion or place. No one shall enter when the great final entrance takes place "save (εἰ μή) those having been written in the book of the life of the Lamb," 20:12, 15; 3:5; see especially 13:8, where τοῦ ἀρνίου also appears. Are any of these left to camp outside, to enter now and then when they accumulate something to bring in, finally, as one states it, to buy a place inside? This question answers itself.

God grant me an entrance when the eternal day comes!

CHAPTER XXII

1) The description of the Holy City continues in 22:1-5, yet the repetition of καὶ ἔδειξέ μοι from 21:10 sets this last part off by itself. In 21:24-27 we see who dwells in the city, i. e., to whom entrance is given into the eternal union with God and the Lamb. Now John is shown something of the infinite blessedness of the life in the golden city.

And he showed me a river of life's water, bright as crystal, going out from the throne of God and the Lamb. Between her avenue and the river on this side and on that wood of life, bearing twelve fruits, according to each month duly giving the fruit of it. And the leaves of the wood for health of the nations. And nothing accursed shall be any longer. And the throne of God and of the Lamb shall be in her. And his slaves shall serve him and shall see his countenance. And his name upon their foreheads. And night shall not be any more; and they shall not have need of lamplight and of sunlight because the Lord God shall shed light upon them. And they shall reign (as kings) **for the eons of the eons.**

The description continues as in 21:10-27. It presents sketchy items, is largely verbless, and has a few futures and a present tense. It views matters from the standpoint of the angel and of John. The angel shows John what is in the city and what is done there, all, of course, in a vision. There is "a river of life's water." We regard ὕδωρ ζωῆς as one concept, "life's water," or "water of life." It is similar to the ὕδωρ ζῶν in John 4:10, "living water," but uses the genitive of the noun in place of the participle, yet this genitive is not qualitative but rather an apposition, it is not "water that has the quality of life," but "water that *is* life," ζωή, the very life or life essence. And there is a whole "river" of it, an inexhaustible abundance. In 7:17 the Lamb leads his own "to life's springs of waters," a figure that is slightly different; in 2:7 Christ "will give the victor from the wood (tree) of the life, which is in the Paradise of God."

It is a rather hasty conclusion to find the Holy Spirit in the symbolism of "a river of life's water" and to go still farther and to see the procession of the Spirit from the Father and the Son in the river's "going out from the throne of God and the Lamb." The Spirit's procession is an inner-trinitarian act that pertains to the Persons and not a procession ἐκ τοῦ θρόνου, "out of the throne," the symbol of eternal power and dominion. Neither the procession of the Spirit nor the *generation* of the Son are ever symbolized to the eye or the mind; they could not be. The claim that there is an association of the Spirit with water, say because of baptism, overlooks the strong Biblical connection of life with Christ who declares, "I am the life" (John 14:6;11:25); who is the Bread of life (John 6:26, etc., the entire discourse); who is called "the Prince of life" (Acts 3:15); of whom I John 5:20 says, "This is the genuine (ἀληθινός) God and life eternal," and in v. 12, "The one having the Son has the life; the one not having the Son of God does not have the life."

Yet the river does not symbolize Christ, for he is already symbolized as the Lamb. He does not flow out from "the throne." What is shown to John is the whole tide of eternal life going out from the throne or the eternal power of God and the Lamb. It is the life of glory for the blessed who are now in eternal, glorious *union* with God and the Lamb, a veritable "river," "brilliant as crystal," which recalls κρυσταλλίζων in 21:11, "crystal flashing," which is predicated of the diamond, the light-bearer who is God.

2) The R. V. mars the translation of the A. V. by drawing ἐν μέσῳ κτλ. to the preceding. Both of our versions mar the sense by construing τοῦ ποταμοῦ with the adverbs ἐντεῦθεν καὶ ἐκεῖθεν. According to their translations the river is "in the middle" of the avenue and the tree on the two sides of the river in the middle of the avenue. Ἐν μέσῳ, however, = "in between," "in the middle," with the avenue on the one side and the river on the other side, to which is added ἐντεῦθεν, "from here," and ἐκεῖθεν, "from there," which is the Greek idiom. If you are on the street and then look across to the river you see the ξύλον, and if you look at this middle area "from there" (from the river to the street) you see the same ξύλον; and, of course, also you are at the river. In other words, there is a beautiful park running throught the entire city which has the avenue on one side and the crystalline river on the other.

Quite a few see that ξύλον is a collective or at least an individualizing singular; some see that ἡ πλατεῖα in 21:21 is likewise such a singular as we have pointed out in 21:21 when noting the twelve great portals, eleven of which cannot be without avenues. But when this avenue is now mentioned the second time, many interpreters seem to forget that it it does not refer to only one. It is now strangely assumed to be only one and, oddly enough, with a tree-lined river running through its center. All these terms: "the avenue," "the river," "the wood," are comprehensive or collective. Look at any portal and you see its πλατεῖα (sc. ὁδός), its Broadway, and a river on one side (possibly a river on both sides) and the park area filled with "wood of life." Again ζωῆς is not merely a qualitative but an appositional genitive. The life in the eternal union with God (= in this city) is so abundant as to be symbolized in two ways: by these rivers and by these trees. It also appears as though the avenues running along these parks (the Greek word for them would be παράδεισος, paradise which is used in 7:7) at least hint at the constant access to this ξύλον and this ποταμός, as though one could at any point walk from the avenues into the parks and on to the rivers, "life" being found everywhere. This eternal union abounds with the life. Also, let me say for myself that ξύλον, the very word used so often with reference to the cross of Christ (Acts 5:30; 10:39; 13:29; Gal. 3:13; I Pet. 2:24), reminds me of the cross which is the wood or tree of life for all of us. It is never δένδρον, "tree."

Whatever allusion to passages of the Old Testament prophets such a Zech. 14:8 and Joel 3:18 may be found here is a minor matter. There is an allusion to Gen. 2:9 and 3:22, and yet it is only an allusion: "The tree of life in the midst of the garden" of Eden which after the fall was guarded by cherubim and a flaming sword. In Gen. 2:9 and 3:22 the LXX has ξύλον. Paradise lost is now Paradise regained. Being an allusion and nothing more, the imagery far exceeds the allusion to the Old Testament.

Ποιοῦν καρπούς, "making fruit," is the Greek idiom. "Twelve fruits" is again the symbolical number "twelve" referring to the *Una Sancta*: "according to each month duly giving (ἀπό in the participle = duly) the fruit of it." To speak of months in reference to this city is to use human terms of time for the eternity of timelessness for which we have no human language, and of which our little, finite minds are unable to form a true conception. Does the thought refer to ever-renewed quantity of one kind, or to many qualitative kinds? Why reduce it to one?

The symbolism is extended to the leaves: "and the leaves for healing — may we say: for health? — of the nations," the same "nations" mentioned in 21:26, who dwell in the city, in this eternal union with God. Here again many find outside nations referred to, people who come to gather these leaves in order to be cured of their paganism. How impossible this conception is we need not repeat. Here it would involve an eternal coming and thus an eternal existence of paganism, one that is never healed, τὰ ἔθνη being translated *die Heiden,* the heathen, in contrast with "the Jews," although this contrast is not always added by these commentators.

3) It sounds strange to read: "And nothing accursed shall be any longer." Then in an evident connection of thought: "And the throne of God and of the Lamb shall be in her" (i. e., in the city). We think this strangeness disappears, and the connection also becomes clear when we look at ξύλον ζωῆς in v. 2 and compare Gal. 3:13 with its ξύλον and its curse. To hang upon ξύλον or "wood" was to be accursed. So Christ hung on the cross as one accursed of God. This is the mark of the old Jerusalem. Christ bore the curse and removed it from us. Nothing of the kind shall be, i. e., exist, any longer, ἔτι, as it once existed in the case of the cross of Christ for our salvation. The foundation of the cross has attained its consummation, in the Eternal City the ξύλον is entirely a "wood of life." For here in this city, behold, "the throne of God and of the Lamb," symbol of the eternal rule and dominion in glory of God and the Lamb; "in her," in this consummation, in this eternal union of these two, God and the Lamb, with us.

The thought is far greater than that of 21:26b, even as κοινόν is far exceeded by πᾶν κατάθεμα; far greater also than that of 22:15 with its "dogs" (types of what is κοινόν, "common" or "unclean"). The context is to the same effect, for it connects us with living trees that are bearing fruit and leaves with inexhaustible life and the corresponding river. The ξύλον, the cross on which Christ bore the curse for us, was only a dead post. So we do not think of sin: that nothing accursed and sinful is found in this city. What the old rugged cross bought for us is now attained: Life, glorious and eternal in this city, in glorious, eternal union with God and the Lamb on their eternal, glorious throne.

4) Thus "his slaves shall serve him and shall see his countenance or face." Yea, "his name upon their foreheads." See how "his slaves" takes us back to 1:1, where also John calls himself one of these slaves. Review 1:1, and see that Christ's slaves are referred to. They see Christ's face on the throne; they bear his name, the symbol of his saving revelation, on their foreheads. This name on the forehead takes us back to 7:3, etc., where "the slaves of God" are sealed "on their foreheads" already in this life when they come to faith in the Lamb and accept his name or revelation.

This takes us back, by contrast, also to all the followers of the beast who receive the mark of the beast (i. e., of the antichristian power) on hand or on forehead, namely the number of the beast's name "666" (13:16-18). In the Eternal City the Lamb's slaves, bought by his blood to be his own forever (I Cor. 6:20; 7:23), whose will is wholly the will of him who bought them (this is the meaning of δοῦλοι, "slaves"), "serve him," λατρεύειν, with the service that is naturally due from all (λειτουργεῖν would mean official service rendered as representing others). So they served the Lamb on the old earth, but now they see the Lamb's own face, read the Lamb's will immediately and no longer only through the written Word.

Infinitely blessed and glorious shall that service be when all the Lamb's slaves can read the Lamb's will and his pleasure from the Lamb's own πρόσωπον. Those who misunderstood the slaves in 1:1, who see only Jewish Christians in 7:3, etc., misunderstand also the present passage. Many think that here the slaves are called God's, that the name, too, is God's (3:12), and that they see God's face (Matt. 5:8; other passages on the *visio Dei*). As for the name see 14:1. It might be God's or the Lamb's even as in substance there is no difference. The *visio Dei* is beyond question. It is "his slaves" and the context that decide what is here meant, and the context refers to Christ.

5) "And night shall be no more" after a fashion repeats 21:25; so also does, "and they shall not have need of lamplight and of sunlight because the Lord God shall light upon them" (21:23). While the substance of the thought is the same, the context advances from "walking" in this everlasting light to "serving" in this light. In 21:23 the light is also the Lamb's. So in 22:3 God and the Lamb are joined on the throne. When in v. 3 the face is the Lamb's, and now the light is the Lord God's, it is rather plain that the old expression of the dogmaticians applies, *the opera ad extra sunt communa sive indivisa,* God and the Lamb do not exclude one another.

It is serving the Lamb; yet, behold, the service! "And they shall reign (as kings) for the eons of the eons," or, to form a new verb, "they shall king it." Here belong all the references to the king among them 3:12; II Tim. 2:12; Rom. 5:17, as well as all the passages that speak of a crown. On the eon see 1:6 and its repeated use in Revelation.

Not being satisfied with what the text says, a few writers add the thought in regard to over whom this reigning will be exercised: over the damned in hell, is one opinion; over the ἔθνη (heathen) outside of the city is another. We do not need even Gen. 1:26. The kingship of God and of the Lamb shall be that of their slaves. The expressions οἱ δοῦλοι αὐτοῦ and βασιλεύσουσιν are intentionally used in the same context: his slaves — shall king it forever. The city = *the kingdom of glory.* In this kingdom where God is King, where the Lamb is King, we shall be kings with them, a kingdom unlike any that ever existed on the old earth (with only a king and subjects) but like the city, the like of which never existed on the old earth, a kingdom made up entirely of kings with "a King of *kings*" (see 19:16; also the author's little volume *Kings and Priests*).

The Visions and John's Record of Them Attested, verses 6-19

God's Attestation, verses 6-15
Jesus' Attestation, verses 16-19
John is dismissed, verse 20
John's farewell greeting, verse 21

God's Attestation

6) Unless it is perceived that in v. 6-19 we have two attestations, two witnesses for the revelations and for John's record of them, we shall be without a clear impression of what this section conveys. The two witnesses are: 1) "the angel of the Lord, the God of the spirits of the prophets," and 2) Jesus (v. 16). The testimony of at least two witnesses is required properly and legally to settle any matter. In regard to this requirement of two witnesses see the data compiled in 11:3. Here we have them.

If it be asked why these visions receive such an attestation at the end, their very character and their nature are the answer. Here is prophecy regarding the things that must occur couched in visions, many of them portrayed in strange symbolical actions and language. Are these human inventions? We meet commentators who think so and yet cannot discover the man who did the inventing. Many men smile at these visions and will scorn them as the vaporings of a diseased mind. The solemn, even legal attestation is needed for our sake so that we may be most completely assured.

And he said to me: These words — faithful and genuine! And the Lord, the God of the spirits of the prophets, commissioned his angel to show to his slaves the things that must occur shortly. And lo, I am coming quickly! Blessed the one keeping the words of the prophecy of this book!

Whether this is the angel mentioned in 19:9 or not, it is certain that he is the angel mentioned in 1:1, for in 1:1 we read, "having commissioned his angel," and, "to show to his slaves the things that must occur shortly," and in 1:3, "the words of the prophecy" and "the ones keeping" what they contain, expressions that are now repeated nearly verbatim. "Of this book" = "the things that have been written," cf., 1:3; a book contains writing. We now see that John derived the expressions he used in 1:1-3 from what the angel says here in 22:6, 7. As τοὺς λόγους τῆς προφητείας refer to the whole of Revelation, so also do οὗτοι οἱ λόγοι, which the angel attests as πιστοὶ καὶ ἀληθινοί, "faithful," trustworthy, "and genuine," with no fiction in any part of them. This is solemn attestation by the angel whom God himself employed to do the showing in the visions, certainly a most competent witness as to genuineness and trustworthiness, the more so since this angel speaks directly for God.

We have had this assurance before, in 19:9 and in 21:5; but in those two passages only in regard to what is there immediately involved. Here, in the context of v. 6, 7, we see that "these words" = "the words of the prophecy of this book," i. e., the contents of this entire book, its λόγοι as all its statements, and that as they are written by John: τὰ γεγραμμένα, "the written things." Note well that this angel speaks of *"this book,"* speaks of it to John himself in this vision. It is *not* a book which John is yet to write as some assume; it is one that has already been written as far as 22:5 at this very time when the angel speaks. John is also right here about to add the last few *logoi,* namely the twofold divine attestation. We saw this truth already in 10:4, in ἔμελλον γράφειν, "I was about to be writing" or, "I was on the point of writing." John was at that time forbidden to record a certain thing. These two passages settle the question as to *when* John wrote. It was *not* after all of the visions had been completed, his writing occurred as they came to him one by one, piece by piece. John's *written book* is here attested, the very manuscript itself.

An angel's testimony is of great weight for all true slaves of God and of the Lamb. But this angel's testimony is really much more. It is practically the testimony or attestation of God as he also most significantly adds, "And the Lord, the God of the spirits of the prophets, commissioned his angel to show to his slaves the things that must occur shortly." By divine commission the angel showed these impending things which also Christ ordered John to write (1:11, 19), which also John has done and is now finishing.

We cannot agree with those who aver that this sentence is a statement made by John; the angel is still speaking. He does not say, "God commissioned *me,* his angel"; for in these visions God used a number of angels to do the showing. Hence "his angel" is generic to designate whatever angel acted at any time in the visions. Τὸν ἄγγελον αὐτοῦ, like διὰ τοῦ ἀγγέλου αὐτοῦ, is what R. 408 calls a representative singular, here representative of the group employed. This means that the angel now speaking speaks for this group, which multiplies the weight of this testimony.

But its greatest weight is the fact that, by being commissioned by God, the angel's testimony is really God's own.

"The Lord, the God of the spirits of the prophets," is an entirely new designation but an eminently fitting one where "the prophecy of this book" is the subject of thought. The Lord is the God who uses the spirits of the prophets when communicating prophecy to his people. This is accomplished by the divine act of revelation to the prophet's spirit, and distinct from this act is the other act, namely inspiration for the prophet's *logoi* when he opens his mouth to speak and to tell the revelation, and when his hand takes the pen and writes the revelation as is the case here with John. To John, God's revelation was conveyed in visions. God has various ways of bestowing revelation; in these visions to John, God used "his angel," now one, now another. Several times John says that he himself was "in spirit." God used John's spirit as he had used the spirits of all the prophets. In John's case the revelation communicated "the things that must occur shortly," namely all the future things here revealed. Why they *"must* occur" is explained in 1:1.

We cannot agree with those who think that John is a prophet only because of these visions, and that the rest of the Twelve and Paul are to be considered only apostles and not prophets. All of them received immediate revelation, all of them also foretold future things. See what Paul foretold in his addresses in Acts, viz., to the Ephesian elders, and in many places in his epistles, notably in II Thess. 2. Peter did likewise, yea, John himself did so. The apostles were prophets in the same sense as the Old Testament prophets. Nor are "the spirits" of the prophets "the seven spirits" mentioned in 1:4 and 4:5, i. e., the Holy Spirit in his sevenfold activity. To be sure, all revelation and all inspiration are given by means of the Holy Spirit, but the genitive "the Holy Spirit of the prophets" does not occur; it would have to be the reverse, "the prophets of the Holy Spirit"; the Spirit uses their spirits, and not the reverse.

To show "to his slaves" repeats 1:1, and in neither place does δοῦλοι refer to anything save the Christians one and all, the whole Christian Church with all her members. That is why the slave John (1:1) was ordered to write, why right here the one "keeping the words of the prophecy of this book" (see 1:3) is pronounced blessed. This is you and I to this day whether we occupy some office in the church or not. See why we are called "slaves" in 1:1 and again in 22:4.

7) It is the angel who adds, "And lo, I am coming quickly!" He does it again in v. 12. On both occasions he adds a beatitude. Some think that Jesus himself speaks these words because they are spoken in the first person, "I am coming." This results in a medley of speakers that becomes so confusing that the "critics" think of redactors, of transpositions that should be made, etc. The opinion that from καὶ ὁ Κύριος onward not the angel is speaking but that John of his own accord is writing pertinent thoughts is likewise untenable as we shall see in v. 8, 9. That Jesus is coming quickly is, indeed, Jesus' own word as v. 20 shows. The angel quotes it twice, here and in v. 12. He does not need the preamble, "Jesus says," for the very words, "I am coming," show that Jesus is being quoted. "And lo" are the angel's words that would draw attention to this quotation from Jesus; for it is Jesus' own summing up of the main fact found in all the visions John has seen. Therefore, in 1:8 Jesus calls himself ὁ ἐρχόμενος, "the One coming," the same title that is applied to God in 1:4; 4:8.

"The One coming" is the Old Testament title for Jesus which speaks of his double coming, first in the incarnation and saving mission of the first advent or coming, next in his Parousia for the judgment in the second advent at the end of the world (Matt. 3:11, 12: "he that cometh" for *two* great acts; 11:3, the Baptist's question). How the coming and the Parousia of Jesus make also the Father "the One coming" we see in 1:4 and 4:8. In 2:5 Jesus tells the church at Ephesus, "But if not, I am coming for thee"; in 2:16, he tells the church at Pergamum, "But if not, I am coming for thee quickly." In ὁ ἐρχόμενος and in the verb ἔρχομαι we properly have the present tense, for this is a Coming One and a coming that fulfills *all* that is prophesied in these visions, beginning with those early churches, continuing in what the visions say "must occur shortly," thus culminating in the Parousia with Jesus on "the great white throne" (20:11-15). Hence also ἐν τάχει (v. 6; 1:1) is in place: *in Baelde,* "shortly," and is correct with reference to the things that must occur. They certainly will start "shortly" and without delay. Likewise the equivalent ταχύ, *bald,* "quickly," with "I am coming," I who will not let Satan proceed without interference. The phrase and the adverb do not designate the time of the Parousia as coming very soon after these visions, a view which already Acts 1:7 should prevent. It is likewise unwarranted to say that, since the Parousia has not yet come after all the centuries that have elapsed since ταχύ was spoken and then written by John, this word has proved itself false. The very opposite is true. Jesus' coming is attested by thousands of judgments which occurred during all these centuries, and its impending final judgment will prove the consummation.

It is the angel who adds the beatitude, "Blessed the one keeping the words of the prophecy of this book!" This reiterates the beatitude of 1:3. In 1:3 the reading and the hearing of the words are added to the keeping, which now does not need to be repeated, for only he who reads or who hears these words read to him will keep them. He may not keep them as all those do who allow themselves to be deceived by the pseudo-prophet and to be seduced by the great whore. All such are accursed. The verdict μακάριος (see 1:3) is pronounced on him who keeps, he is "blessed" for time and for eternity. Τηρεῖν is "to keep" as one keeps a priceless treasure, letting no one take it from him. That means to believe "the words of this book" as words that are faithful and genuine and, believing them, to live accordingly.

Here speaks the first witness of what this book contains, the angel commissioned by God. It is God's attestation delivered to you and to me by God's representative. At the same time here is the great purpose of this attestation so that you and I may, indeed, keep the words of this book. As at the beginning, in 1:3, so here, near the end, this purpose is clearly stated and impressed, both times in a benediction in order to urge us to the attainment of this purpose.

8) **And I, I John, the one hearing and seeing these things! And when I heard and saw I fell down to do obeisance before the feet of the angel, the one showing me these things. And he says to me: See to it, not! Thy fellow slave I am and of thy brethren, the prophets, and of those keeping the words of this book. To God do obeisance!**

Read the exposition of 19:10. Only one adequate explanation explains John's two acts: he twice mistook an angel for Christ himself. How could John do this a second time? The answer is found in the preamble: "And I, I John, the one hearing and seeing these things!" This is an exclamation which calls on the reader to regard John as one under the tremendous impression of the things he is seeing and hearing. The ἐγώ is properly added: "*I*, John, the one seeing and hearing!" Both of our versions translate this as a calm statement of fact and spoil what is exclamatory. In English the ὅτε clause means: "And when I had heard and seen" all these things recorded to v. 6, 7, "I sank down to do obeisance before the feet of the angel, the one showing me these things," the one who had just uttered v. 6, 7. John calls him an angel because that is what he discovers him to be. That John knew that this was an angel when he sank down to worship him is an unwarranted assumption. John had just heard this glorious being say, "And lo, I am coming quickly!" This together with all else that he had heard and seen, this as the climax of all else, made him feel sure that Jesus was now, indeed, before him. Mistaken in 19:10, John felt that he was now not mistaken. Nor is John so entirely wrong. In v. 16-19 it *is* Jesus who speaks to him. John's expectation that it would be Jesus himself who would thus attest "these words" is correct: Jesus does so. This is Ἀποκάλυψις Ἰησοῦ Χριστοῦ, "Jesus Christ's Revelation" (1:1), which he in his own person is thus sure to attest.

But in v. 6, 7 it is not yet Jesus, and John promptly discovers his mistake, the second he has made in this respect. Ὁ ἀκούων καὶ βλέπων are not timeless presents with ταῦτα referring to all of the visions. It makes little difference as to how far back ταῦτα extends. The participles "hearing and seeing these things" merely point backward, and thus the ὅτε clause with its two aorists, "when I had heard and seen," brings us to the present moment, to the act of John's prostration. In other words, after hearing and seeing all these things, now, at the climax, under the powerful impression of all that I had heard and seen including this last in v. 6, 7, now I sank down to worship, etc. To make the first ταῦτα refer to all the visions, and the second ταῦτα only to v. 6, 7 is untenable; both apply to

v. 6, 7 and both reach back equally far into the preceding visions.

9) John is stopped exactly as he was in 19:10. He is told that he is facing only an angel and that he must do obeisance to God. This angel, too, says that he is only John's "fellow slave and of John's brethren" (so in 19:10). Yet in 19:10 these brethren are called, "those having the testimony of Jesus," i. e., all Christians; now the brethren are divided into two groups: "the prophets and those keeping the words of this book" (v. 7). This does not imply that John is now to be exalted as a prophet; for also in 19:10 "prophecy" is exalted. "Prophets" reminds us of v. 6, "the God of the spirits of the prophets." John was exercising a prophet's function when he writes "the words of this book" so that all true Christians might keep them; and when he was serving as God's slave to aid John in this work, the angel, like all the other angels, was certainly John's fellow slave and brother, and thus they, the two, were "of the prophets," of their number.

It is claimed that John here presents *himself* as the second witness who attests the genuineness and the trustworthiness of the words of this book, Jesus being the third cf., v. 16. This view is not acceptable. It is John's book, John's record, that is to be attested. This is not due to the fact that *he* did the writing, for God could have chosen another, but because *"these words"* are trustworthy and genuine (v. 6). John cannot serve as a witness in addition to God's representative, the angel, and in addition to Jesus (v. 16, etc.). Moreover, what would his mere human mite add to the two mighty witnesses who speak here? Two witnesses are also wholly sufficient.

Why then this little addition regarding John's mistaken act? It is not *John* who pleases to make it, but the *Lord* who has him make it (just as in 19:10).

Again we say that this is enough. Again, if we venture to say more, it is so that you and I may understand something of the importance of the first testimony adduced in v. 6, 7 and still further in v. 10-15. When John heard this witness speak this testimony, after v. 7 he already fell down to worship him who made it, he already thought it the voice and the presence of Jesus himself. So great is this attestation.

10) The angel continues; καὶ λέγει μοι is inserted in order to separate what is said in v. 9 about John's mistake from what now follows. **And he says to me: Do not seal the words of the prophecy of this book! For the period is near. The one doing unrighteousness, let him do unrighteousness still; and the filthy one, let him be made filthy still; and the righteous one, let him do righteousness still; and the holy one, let him be made holy still. Lo, I am coming quickly, and my reward with me, duly to give to each one as his work is! I, I the Alpha and the Omega, the First and the Last, the Beginning and the End! Blessed those washing their flowing robes that theirs may be the right to the wood of the life and that by means of the portals they may enter into the city! Outside, the dogs and the sorcerers and the whorers and the murderers and the idolaters and everyone liking and doing** (what is) **lie!**

Through the angel God commands John not to seal "the words of the prophecy of this book" (so in v. 7; abbreviated in v. 9). To seal is to make inaccessible as 10:4 actually orders done with what the seven thunders uttered, which, however, when John is about to write even this writing, he is not to do. Not to seal is a litotes, expressing negatively what is intended positively: "Publish the words of the prophecy of this book!" Compare 1:11, "Write into a book and send to the seven churches!" All but a few sentences of this writing has now been written. The seven churches would be the first to receive the book, all other churches would receive it soon after them. "For the period is near" is the same statement found in 1:3, the period in which the things written in this book will occur. God's people must be ready, fortified by "the words in this book."

After the command of Jesus in 1:11 its repetition by God's angel might seem unnecessary. But this is far more than a repetition; this is God's own endorsement of the very *logoi* which John has written. By his angel he attests this entire book for us, all the "words" in it as now committed to writing, as being "trustworthy and genuine," so that all of us may keep them during this whole καιρός (v. 6, 7).

11) It is the angel who continues: "The one doing unrighteousness, let him do unrighteousness still," etc. This has been called ironical, but there is no irony. Nor is the sense: "The time is now too short to permit anyone to change," or, "Change while you yet can!" The four ἔτι: let him do so "still" — let him be made filthy "still" — let him be made righteous (or let him let himself be made righteous) "still" — finally: holy "still," are similar to Matt. 13:30, "Let both grow until the harvest!" If the unrighteous and the filthy will not be warned by the words of the prophecy of this book, the final revelation of God, there is nothing more to be done: let him go on, his μισθός is at hand. But the righteous and the holy, with the last words of God in this book ringing in his ears — let him go on, his μισθός is also sure and rapidly coming. Compare II Tim. 3:13, 14; Ezek. 3:27.

12) Because of the close connection in thought we cannot agree that Jesus now takes up the address; the angel is still speaking but is now quoting Jesus just as in v. 7. When Jesus does speak in v. 16, etc., we

shall see that it is he. So once more we hear: "Lo, I am coming quickly!" see v. 7. But now the addition: "and my reward with me, duly to give to each one as his work is." This is the Lord's μισθός so to give (ἀπό in the infinitive = duly). The singular τὸ ἔργον is collective: each man's life will in a sum be "his work," the public evidence of what is in his heart, either faith or unbelief. Compare 20:12, κατὰ ἔργα αὐτῶν, and Matt. 25:31-46.

13) This is signed by the Lord's own threefold signature: "I, I (ἐγώ emphatic) the Alpha and the Omego" = God's *revelation* from the first to the last written letter; "I, I the First and the Last" = all *history* from start to finish; "I, I the Beginning and the End" = all God's saving *work* from inception to consummation. Compare 1:8, 17; 2:6; 21:6.

14) A second benediction follows the one in v. 7: "Blessed those washing their flowing robes that theirs may be the right to the wood of the life, and that by means of the portals they may enter into the city!" This washing of the στολαί (flowing, festal, state robes, see 6:11; 7:9) recalls 7:14, where the unnumbered 144,000 are described. This washing "in the blood of the Lamb" (7:14) goes well with the keeping of the words of the prophecy of this book (v. 7). It assures the ἐξουσία (here "the right") to "the wood of the life" (see v. 2) and to entrance to the city (see 21:12), to the eternal union with God.

The A. V. has the less-attested reading: "they that do his commandments." In our opinion an early scribe made what he deemed an improvement by matching the doing of the commandments with "the work" mentioned in v. 12. There are other opinions, and some commentators choose the reading we deem inferior both textually and especially in substance in view of 7:14.

15) "Outside," namely outside of the city — 20:15 states where this is — "the dogs" (compare "the filthy one" in v. 11; also Phil. 3:2) — "the sorcerers" (compare φάρμακα in 9:21 and φαρμακεία in 18:23). On this and the other designations see 21:8, but "all the liars" is here made more graphic, "everyone liking (φιλῶν and not ἀγαπῶν) and doing ψεῦδος" (anarthrous: what has the quality of "lie").

This ends the first witness and endorsement of this book made by God through his angel. Verse 7 and v. 11-15 attach its great purpose to the great attestation. In v. 7 we have only the positive side; in v. 11 and 14, 15 the positive and the negative combined.

Jesus' Attestation

16) From Deuteronomy onward (17:6; 19:15), also throughout the New Testament legal testimony requires two or three witnesses, see, for instance, Matt. 16:16: 26:60; John 5:31-37; 8:17: II Cor. 13:1; Heb. 10:28; Rev. 11:3. Thus also this book and all its words are established as "faithful and genuine" (v. 6) by two witnesses and two attestations: one that of God by his angel, the other that of Jesus himself. The latter testifies in v. 16-19.

I, Jesus, sent my angel to testify to you these things in regard to the churches. I, I am the Shoot and the Offspring of David, the Star, the Brilliant, the Morning One. The two witnesses to this book agree verbatim in the cardinal point regarding the genuineness of "the words of this book" (v. 7, 9, 10): God *"commissioned his angel"* (v. 6); I, Jesus, *"sent my angel."* Ἀποστέλλω and πέμπω have the same force. The two witnesses also agree on the purpose of this sending: "to show to his slaves the things that must occur shortly" (v. 6); "to testify to you these things in regard to the churches." In v. 6 the third person is used, God's angel speaks to John and thus says, "to his (God's) slaves"; Jesus speaks to these slaves of God directly in the second person: to testify "to you." In v. 16 ταῦτα = ἃ δεῖ γενέσθαι ἐν τάχει occurring in v. 6. In fact, "these things in regard to the churches" = "the things that must occur shortly." All the things of all the visions are revealed in so far as they pertain to the churches, as these things affect them, as thus "you," the members of the churches, must know them. Ἐπί is neither "in" (A. V.) nor "for" (R. V.) but the German *ueber* (B.-P. 447), "in regard to," or, "on (what pertains to) the churches."

"My angel," like "his angel" in v. 6, refers to whatever angel God and Jesus employed in any particular vision. It was always the angel of God, of Jesus, their instrument and agent in showing, testifying, i. e., revealing. John, too, was only a receiving instrument. This book is written by John's pen and is to be published (v. 10). How will the members in all the churches know that its words are πιστοὶ καὶ ἀληθινοί (v. 6)? Through his angel God vouches for all that is in this book; Jesus, as a second witness, vouches for it. God and Jesus are the real authors.

In this book the simple form "Jesus" is used most frequently! We see why. This is the name he here uses to designate himself: "I, Jesus." Yet this is not a mere formal matter: "Jesus" is the name given him at the time of his incarnation and birth by God himself through the angel in Matt. 1:21; Luke 1:31. Now he is glorified and giving these revelatory visions as the *incarnate* Son of God, our Savior, who by these revelations is working to save us. That is why he adds this great "I AM" (ἐγώ εἰμι) to all the others found in the Scriptures, in particular to the significant titles used in v. 13. "I am the Shoot and Offspring of David"; ῥίζα is explained in 5:5, and is now defined by τὸ γένος. In the Greek "the Shoot" is feminine, and "the Offspring" is neuter, both terms thus stating what Jesus is in his human nature as David's descendant. The genealogy of Matt. 1 shows his legal relation to David (and to Abraham) by way of Joseph, his legal foster-father; the genealogy of Luke 3 shows his descent from David by way of the Virgin Mary. God's angel states what this means in Luke 1:32, 33: the eternal throne of David. This implies more than that David's line was "conserved" in Jesus, or that David's family was "concentrated in Jesus." We thus see how this "I am" fits the name "Jesus."

The following apposition, "the Star, the Brilliant, the Morning One," has been elucidated in connection with 2:28 (which see). This is the Star of Num. 24:17, which symbolizes the royalty of Jesus. Since they are added by two articles, each adjective is made an apposition, is emphasized separately, each is a climax to the noun (R. 776). In 2:28 we have noted that it is the sun and not a star that brings the day, and that it is not well to stress "the Morning One" in this direction.

Jesus, who is what he here says he is, places his seal and his signature on "the words of the prophecy of this book." Jesus stands beside the Lord, the God of the spirits of the prophets, in the sending of the divine representatives when producing this book. Their double divine testimony seals it for us and for the churches.

17) It is Jesus who adds: **And the Spirit and the Bride are saying, Be coming! And the one hearing, let him say, Be coming! And let the one thirsting be coming! Let the one willing take life's water gratis!** This is the Holy Spirit who dwells in the churches that are "the Bride"; yet not the Bride in heavenly glory as in 21:9, but the Bride as she is on the old earth; for in heaven and at the consummation

the Bride no longer says, "Be coming!" it is the Bride here on the old earth longing for the Parousia of Jesus. The Spirit dwells in her. This prayer "be coming" is not a double one, it is single. It is not as though the Spirit says, "Be coming!" and then also the Bride says so; but the Spirit moves her, and she is moved by him.

Note the tenses: λέγουσιν: ever this prayer of longing arises, ever the Bride yearns for the eternal union (symbolized by the city). Note also the present imperative, Ἔρχου: "Be coming!" i. e., proceed with thy work of coming. The aorist would refer to the one final act of coming; the present refers to all of the coming, even as Jesus is ὁ ἐρχόμενος, "the Coming One" (1:8) as is the Father (1:4) who comes in the coming of Jesus.

"The Bride" is a collective to designate the whole *Una Sancta* on earth. She does cry so in ardent prayer. Hence the singular ὁ ἀκούων: every member of the *Una Sancta* who hears this cry of the church is to echo it for his own person, is to unite his soul's prayer with that of the church. Hence we now have the hortative imperatives. He who can hear the voice of the church without raising his own is falling away from her. He who can hear the words of this book, this last revelation of Jesus, without the response, "Be coming!" is slipping into the company of those named in v. 15. The attestation here made to the words of this book has the great saving purpose that we may thus pray and keep these words and thus be blessed (v. 7, 14).

Thus the hortation follows: "And let the one thirsting be coming! Let the one willing take life's water gratis!" This invites to the promise made in 21:6: "I to the one thirsting will give from the spring of waters of the life gratis!" The one thirsting for life need not wait until the coming is completed, he is constantly himself to be coming (present, iterative imperative) to the Word, in particular also to this book, and his soul shall drink. Ὁ θέλων, "the one willing" to satisfy his thirst for the life, "let him take" (aorist to express actuality: actually take) life's water gratis, without money or price (see 21:6). No wonder the attestation of this book is so strong, seeing how blessed its purpose is!

18) Some critical commentators say that these words are but a Jewish formula of canonization which was very likely copied from other apocalyptic writings, "an unfortunate ending to a book whose value consists in the spirit that breathes in it, the bold faith and confident hope which it inspires, rather than in the literalness and finality of its disclosures." Not a few writers regard these words of Jesus a warning to copyists not to copy this book inexactly or to change the reading, to which the remark is added that the seer, whoever he was, failed in this purpose, for our present copies have a great many variant readings.

Whoever, like certain critics, eliminates John from this book, eliminates the faithfulness and the genuineness of "the words of this book" and the truth that John saw and heard these visions and that God and Jesus gave them to John as the words of this book say they did; whoever makes this book a composition of some unknown writer, a mixture of a variety of material, pagan, Jewish, mythological, superstitious, apocalyptic, etc., whoever makes the chief object of study the discovery of these Jewish, pagan, and other "sources": for him, it is to be feared, Jesus uttered this final μαρτυρῶ ἐγώ, "I myself testify." They would save "the spirit," "the bold faith and confident hope" in this book while they do not specify what is to be discarded. Anything that is dressed in fictional visions and in Jewish-pagan garb is to be discarded. True faith and hope cannot wear such garments. As for copying the text, the idea that Jesus here speaks of this does not call for an extended answer.

Testify do I myself to everyone hearing the words of the prophecy of the book: If anyone adds to them, God shall add to him the plagues, the ones that have been written (and are now on record) **in this book. And if anyone takes away from the words of the book of this prophecy, God shall take away his part from the wood of the Life and out of the city, the holy one,** (his part) **of the things that have been written in this book.**

It has been stated that the ἐγώ used here is not the ἐγώ of v. 16, but that of v. 8, i. e., not that of Jesus but that of John; but look at v. 20: the one testifying says, "I am coming quickly." So ὁ μαρτυρῶν = μαρτυρῶ ἐγώ, I, Jesus. The text says so; we need no further argument such as the majesty involved in v. 18, 19. Jesus says with an emphatic ἐγώ that he himself "testifies," which certainly means that we must accept his testimony or, that if we reject it, we do so at our peril. He testifies that God will add the very plagues that are written in this book to him who adds to the things (αὐτά) constituting this book. Likewise, that God will take away anyone's part in the life and in the Holy City, anyone's part in the blessed things written in this book (τῶν γεγραμμένων is dependent on τὸ μέρος αὐτοῦ), from anyone who takes away from the words of this book. The consequences following upon either act are the same. They are expressed in terms of exact justice: he who takes away — God shall take away; he who adds — God shall add. A just God cannot do otherwise. Note that ἀφελῶ is the future of ἀπαιρέω (R. 356); also that οἱ λόγοι does not mean mere vocables (*Woerter*) as found in a dictionary but "words" as thought-bearers (*Worte*), statements. He cannot keep the words of this book (v. 7, 9) who ruins them by injecting other things or casts some of the words aside.

The meaning of this testimony of Jesus' is altogether plain. We should not then say that this testimony applies to the entire New Testament. We do not intend to say that we are at liberty to add to or to substract from other Biblical books but not from this one. We hold them all equally inviolate. This word of Jesus' uttered by him in regard to this prophetic and last New Testament book will ever move us the more to do so with all the inspired books, in all of which the same truth, doctrine, gospel are given us to keep (τηρεῖν) inviolate. The main point, however, we must not overlook: Jesus here again attests *this* book, the trustworthiness and the genuineness of *all its* logoi.

The edge is sometimes taken off this testimony of Jesus by deflecting or by minimizing its meaning. We are told that it is John or whoever is assumed to be the author who employs "a solemn adjuration against mutilating or interpolating his book," a practice that is said to have been common in ancient times, so that other writers also tried to insure their effort against mutilation by appending similar solemn warnings. We are told that "here is a prophetic protest against spurious Revelations forged by false teachers in the name of the apostles." The statement is limited to a prohibition against false doctrine or against falsification of any main Christian doctrine, "against anything that affects the actual kernel of the book." But such views do not appeal to a conservative student of the Word.

Alford states the issue squarely: "This is at least an awful warning to those who add to it by irrelevant and trifling interpretations." Let me say for myself that I have kept the Lord's warning before my eyes so that I might not add or take away any of these *logoi* or any part of one of them. Here and now I fervently pray that, if in any *logos* I have gone amiss, he may pardon me, bring the correction to me, and prevent damage as a result of my error. I count every sentence in Scripture holy, to be touched only with sanctified heart and pen.

Jesus dismisses John

20) **There says to me the One testifying these things, Yea, I am coming quickly!** Ταῦτα, as ὁ μαρτυρῶν shows in connection with μαρτυρῶ ἐγώ in v. 18, refers only to v. 18, 19. By transposing verb and subject "the One testifying" is made emphatic. He testifies once more in this last promise: "Yes, I am coming quickly!" which we have already considered, which once more sums up all the revelations recorded in "the words of the prophecy of this book." The visions, the revelations, the "words" are at an end. This is the dismissal of the Lord's slave, John (1:1).

John understands and answers: **Amen: be coming, Lord Jesus!** This coming fills his heart, and this word of prayer, which echos the Lord's promise, rises to his lips. On "amen" see 1:7. John places it first as Jesus did while he was on earth.

John dismisses his readers

21) **The grace of the Lord Jesus with the saints! Amen.** In 1:4 "grace and peace" are the greeting to the seven churches; this same "grace" is referred to in this closing salutation. The readings vary: "The saints" — "all" — "all the saints." Yet they refer to the same people, namely to the saints of the seven churches. Some think that here the saints of the whole church are referred to; but the beginning

(1:4) and the end surely agree. The fact that this book is written for all the slaves of God and Christ while it is first of all to be sent to the seven churches, is stated in 1:1 and again in 22:6, so that we need not draw conclusions from the last phrase "with the saints" so as to include ourselves. We need not call "this book" a letter because of 1:4 and 22:21; it is, as we are so repeatedly told in this last chapter, a "book" but one that is intended for certain readers, which is entirely sufficient for the greeting and the salutation.

John adds no further words of his own. It is not in place for him to do so. All that each of the churches is to know the Lord himself has dictated in chapters 2 and 3.

The Lord Jesus grant us his grace as we read and ponder this his Ἀποκάλυψις.

Soli Deo Gloria